Fearless Critic

Praise for Robin Goldstein's restaurant guides

"Pulls no punches...even icons get goosed."

–Austin American-Statesman

"Deft, unblushing prose...good friends to the honest diner, they call it as they see it."

–T. Susan Chang,
Food & Travel Correspondent,
Boston Globe

"The authors...take pains t[illegible] out the esoteric culinary experi[illegible] foodies' hearts: back-alley [illegible]ving authentic Asian fare a[illegible]rmet eateries. Mos[illegible]tch real-life ex[illegible]

[illegible]rent

"Exceptiona[illegible]enced restaurantgoe[illegible].knowledgeable and enthusiastic about eating well."

–Yale Daily News

"In addition to being an informative guide...makes for a surprisingly good read and creates a vivid picture of the local dining scene."

–Austin Monthly

Fearless Critic

More praise for Robin Goldstein's restaurant guides

"Scathing and scintillating."

–*New Haven Register*

"Immensely useful, written with panache, as respectful of 'Roadfood' as of 'fine-dining'...one of the most compelling restaurant guides we've seen."

–Jane and Michael Stern,
Authors, *Roadfood;*
columnists, *Gourmet*

"Valiosos críticos culinarios."

–*El Mundo* Newspaper
Austin and San Antonio

"Not just a useful book—a pleasure to read. The only people who won't find it a pleasure are the owners of some of the really bad restaurants it warns us about."

–David Ball, Professor
Emeritus of Comparative
Literature, Smith College

Fearless Critic

WWW.FEARLESSCRITIC.COM

Fearless Critics and Undercover Chefs

Robin Goldstein is the founder and editor-in-chief of the *Fearless Critic* series. He has authored four books of restaurant reviews and has written for more than 30 *Fodor's* travel guides around the world, from Italy to Thailand, Argentina to Hong Kong. Robin is a graduate of Harvard University and Yale Law School, and has a certificate in cooking from the French Culinary Institute.

Alexis Herschkowitsch has written and edited for the *Fearless Critic Austin Restaurant Guide*, as well as *Fodor's* guides to Mexico, El Salvador, and Thailand. She is a graduate of the University of Texas at Austin, and has a WSET advanced wine and spirits certificate.

Justin Yu currently cooks at one of Houston's top restaurants. He grew up in Houston, and has cooked with James Beard Award winner Shawn McClain at Chicago's Spring. Justin is a graduate of the University of Houston and of the Culinary Institute of America in Hyde Park, New York.

Shaun Duffy is a private chef in Houston. He has been sous-chef at Houston's Quattro, and has also cooked at Picasso in Las Vegas' Bellagio hotel, and at Austin's Wink, Zoot, and Café at the Four Seasons. Shaun a graduate of the School of Culinary Arts at the Arts Institute of Houston.

Ryan Hackney has written for the *Let's Go* travel guides to Britain, Ireland, and Ecuador, and has authored two nonfiction books on Irish history and culture. He is a graduate of Harvard University, and lives in Houston.

Stew Navarre currently cooks at one of Houston's top restaurants. He is a graduate of the University of Houston's restaurant management program and of the Culinary Institute of America in Hyde Park, New York.

First edition, 2008

Printed in the United States of America

ISBN 978-0-9740143-4-0

Fearless Critic

WWW.FEARLESSCRITIC.COM

Contents

Acknowledgments

From Robin Goldstein and Fearless Critic Media: My deepest thanks and appreciation go first to Alexis, for her superhuman effort, spectacular writing and editing, talent for management, sublime company, and taste for buffalo wings. Many congratulations and thanks go out to Shaun, Justin, Ryan, and Stew, for their fearlessly brilliant food criticism, kaffir lime leaves, and deep devotion to the Fearless Critic cause. Delicious. I am eternally grateful, too, for the incredible work of our Associate Editors, Kacie Gonzalez, Taylor Calhoun, Ruby Madren-Britton, and Michael Sobolevsky. This book would not have been possible without you.

The unwavering support and boundless generosity of Susan Stubbs, Barry Goldstein, Lu and Hal Stubbs, and Rosie Goldstein has been as incredible as ever—I barely noticed that you were all a half a country away (or in Phoenix in the wee hours of the morning). And I would like to once again acknowledge the invaluable contributions of David Menschel.

I am extremely grateful to the many people in Houston that have also helped make this book possible and offered helpful advice, suggestions, and companionship at many meals: Margarita Barcenas, Tasneem Husain, David Kaplan, Tatiana Schnur, Chris Mrema, Padma Pavuluri, Brane Poledica, Hal Bayless, David Theis, Jeff Kaplan, Adam Brackman, Dina Kosma, Eirini Kaissaratou, Thomas Burke, David Kim, Leah Barton, and Carol and Andy Vickery.

Thanks to Austin writers Rebecca Markovits and Monika Powe Nelson, for their immeasurable contributions. Thanks also to Kent Wang, Morgan Friedman, Andrew Gajkowski, Steven Lauff, Kelly Stecker, Roy Ip, Claude Solliard, Charles Mayes, Brane Poledica, Matt Cohen, Bill Shinker, Erin McReynolds, Nat Davis, Claudio Guerrero, Bill Collins, Nancy Gonter, Chad Cain, Matt Lombardi, Heidi Johansen, Laura Kidder, Adam Taplin, and Josh Loving: each of you has generously supported Fearless Critic Media in a different way.

In Dallas, I salute Alex and Julie Herschkowitsch, Davis Michel, and Jeff and Janae Frank. In Austin, props also go out to Edward Mannix, Natalia Ramondo, John and Claire Champagne, Nancy and Tom Hudson, Lisa Simmons, Asher Price, Ashley Carker, Shay Fan, Kathryn Fondren, Jane Cohen and Larry Sager, Mark Strama, John Kelso, and everyone else who helped out with our first book. In DC, Nikia Bergan, Steven Hill, and Coco Krumme.

Heartfelt shoutouts, too, to the Fearless Critic Media Cabinet: Clare Murumba, Duncan Levin, Samantha Lazarus, Giuliano Stiglitz, Steve Maslow, Justin Nowell, Benjamin Lima, Michelle Gonzalez, Nate Baum-Snow, Daniel Horwitz, Andrea Armeni, Jake Katz, Leslie Silbert, Ben Rosenblum, Daniel Frommer, David Grewal, Nick, Cat, Hana, and Sanae Sandomirsky, Julian Faulkner, and Brian DiMarco.

From Alexis Herschkowitsch and Fearless Critic Media: Thanks to my parents, Alex and Julie, who've always been supportive of anything I put my mind to; Robin, for his efforts to teach me all there is to know about duck liver; Jenny Howe, with whom I'll share a bowl of solyanka and bottle of wine any time; and Alina Kamenetskaya, whose other-worldly knowledge of meat-curing processes is astounding.

We would also like to thank the people whose support of our local project has been invaluable: Steve Bercu, Sherry Brown, Frank Campbell, Mary Pat Helton, Tanis Jones, David Jabour, Crystal Kusey, Tim Kutach, Edmund LeStrange, Jason Lochner, Marisa Love, Charles Medlock, Melissa Mikol, Doug Mote, Chris Murray, Niki Nash, Kellie Nutt, Steve Ross, Laura Schneider, Abigail Scruggs, Erin Sibley, Gene Starner, Chad Stith, Lauren van der Meer, Jo Virgil, and Buzz Wilson.

From Justin Yu: First, thanks to Robin for giving me a medium to cheer on my favorite restaurants and to vent about the worst ones. To my Aunts Betty and Josephine for instilling a love for food in me, and to my family, mom, dad, Clinton, and Jennifer for nuturing it and dealing with my food experiments. To my girlfriend, Karen, for always giving me a herbivore's sense of humor, and to all my eating buddies, especially PAC, Thuy, and Christina, Duff, and Stew for taking home all the leftovers when I overorder. And to all the cooks and chefs who work the long days for bad pay and realize that food and see restaurants as an extension of culture, personality, and passion—and not the extension of a corporation—this one's for you. Keep on truckin'.

Preface

Eat around Houston for long, and you'll start hearing all sorts of impressive restaurant statistics. Sooner or later, someone will tell you that Houstonians eat a higher percentage of their meals at restaurants than anyone else. Someone else will mention that Houston has more restaurants, per capita, than any other. The data sources are always vague, of course, but in a business city like this one, people love to talk numbers, and certainly these are a testament to the dynamism of Houston's restaurant industry.

But the vibrancy of this food scene cannot be measured by the city's restaurant population, nor is it accurately represented by its out-of-home dining revenues. The soul of Houston dining, we think, is better approached by peering in at a few of the restaurants themselves. In our case, we've peered at more than 400, but there are two amongst these that—taken together—embody the spirit, the excitement, and the unresolved tension at the heart of culinary Houston.

The first is Da Marco, a chef-driven Italian kitchen that's so precise and authentic that it would do well not just in New York or LA, but probably even in Rome or Milan. What's so special about the elemental appeal of Da Marco's cuisine—of a whole roasted branzino flown in from Italy, for instance, the fish's sweet, delicate, white flesh effortlessly deboned and plated at the table to create one of the very simplest and most sublime of all Mediterranean taste experiences—is its tendency to pierce the barriers between the various categories of customers, between the food bloggers and the comfort-foodies, between the professional chefs and the microwavers, and maybe even between the adults and the kids.

Yet there is another, less talked about, element of Da Marco that's equally profound in its influence on Houston's dining scene: when the city's best pizza, by a fair margin—a buffalo-milk-and-tomato margherita cooked in a wood-burning brick oven that really would be taken seriously in southern Italy—is offered on the *dinner* menu at just $11, it opens Da Marco's doors, too, to a segment of people who wouldn't believe they could possibly afford to dine at the best restaurant in America's fourth-largest city. And yet they can. And that puts a positive pressure on the whole city to price food at accessible levels.

Houston's appreciation of Da Marco, as embodied in the restaurant's success, has also been emblematic of a move forward in the way the city thinks about food. Slowly but noticeably, there has been a recognition that a filet mignon with béarnaise sauce, served on a doilied tray by a tuxedoed waiter and serenaded by a piano player whose repertoire begins and ends with Andrew Lloyd Webber, is no longer the city's ideal of elegance; but neither, on its face, is the fussy modern fusion restaurant with stark, uncomfortable minimalist seating, track lights, and a menu full of needless adjectives.

Instead, there has been a creeping recognition that the freshness and provenance of ingredients can matter more than their prestige and price, and that the level of talent in the kitchen might not correlate so cleanly with the number of items of silverware at the place setting—or with the number of Google hits on a chef's name. As people get used to the unsettling fact that the new order isn't as neatly sorted as the old, some of the city's grande dames are starting to feel pressure to improve their value propositions. With oil at $92 a barrel, the status quo will probably continue. But come the next downturn, we could see a real shakedown of the new old guard—even amongst the names that still roll off people's tongues as "the best restaurants in Houston."

Some of the new restaurants that have come in over the past few years have experimented not just with menus that are more ingredient-driven and region-driven and less prestige-driven and fusion-driven, but also, most notably, with wine lists that take Houston's upmarket status quo, turn it upside down, and pour it out. Houston now has several restaurants that sell wine for as little as 1.6x wholesale—not much different from what you'd pay at a wine store. The same bottle of Volnay that would go for $90 at Mark's, Café Annie, or Pappas Bros. might now sell for $48 at Ibiza, Catalan, or Reef. Wine was made for food, and food for wine, and the opportunity to drink good bottles at accessible prices with dinner has been long overdue. Hopefully, this is just a beginning of a trend that will sweep the city, and America.

That said, several of these 21st-century restaurants have also failed, and while some of them have suffered from bad locations or microeconomic vagaries, others have tanked because, amidst all the fuss, they failed to deliver on their most basic of culinary charges: *to send out food that tastes good*. It's an all-too-common, often-fatal New American mistake to forget that no number of menu adjectives can correctly season a sauce or cook a meat to temperature, and that only a rigorous regime of proactive tasting can guarantee a kitchen's consistency.

Which brings us to our second restaurant that represents the soul of Houston—the other soul of Houston. Nowhere in the city is the simple charge to send out food that tastes good understood more intuitively, perhaps, than at Udipi Café, the yang to Da Marco's yin, a South Indian vegetarian restaurant on Hillcroft that embodies Houston's culinary essence every bit as much.

Udipi Café is but a grungy storefront, labeled with the humblest of all-caps sans-serif fonts, tucked into the humblest of highway strip malls—that cursed urban formation that defines so much of Houston's built environment, even in the face of efforts to create walkable mini-units in places like Midtown. Here, the restaurant meal takes on a real significance in the life of the community; it is a place where families gather, catch up on their neighbors' news, see their nieces and nephews and cousins and grandkids. The restaurant is also the community center, the Publick House.

It is at places such as Udipi that distant culinary traditions are honored most faithfully—in this case, it's the tradition of the Karnatka region of South India, home of the masala dosa, a place where vegetarianism is just part of the native cuisine. These are more than recipes; they're shared strands of a culinary identity that ties people together even in an urban landscape as alienating as Houston's can sometimes be.

The everyday alchemy happening in Udipi's kitchen is every bit as miraculous as it is in Da Marco's, and it's more mystical, in a way, in its conversion of the mundane to the extraordinary: the conversion of simple, inexpensive vegetables, legumes, and grains into delivery platforms for complex potions of spices from the East, creating spoonfuls of faraway flavor that can elicit an almost emotional longing in the unprepared. And it's sold for seven or eight dollars—all you can eat.

Of course, this is not just happening at Udipi Café. It's happening at Himalaya across the street, and at Middle Eastern places down the block, and at so many of the other humble immigrant establishments that have forged a legitimate restaurant row along Hillcroft. It's happening, simultaneously, at a parallel restaurant row out west along Bellaire Boulevard, at Vietnamese sandwich shops and phô houses and modest Chinese restaurants and grocery stores that are roasting ducks, chickens, and suckling pigs for their local communities. There, the shared culinary idiom is a central bond for the community; the supermarket is a place for shopping—and gossip, too. And it's happening, too, at tiny taquerías all over the city, a mere fraction of which are mentioned in this book (which is one of its chief shortcomings), where the deep, rich flavors of all the parts of the cow and pig you've never cooked with form the backbone of a sometimes challenging, always flavorful cuisine that is, like South India's, built around the most inexpensive of ingredients.

And with all due respect to Da Marco, other American cities have world-class Italian restaurants; but few, if any, have the unadulterated examples of South Indian, Middle Eastern, Southeast Asian, East Asian, and Latin American cuisines that Houston does. We have done our best, within these pages, to cover some of the best that we have tried, drawing, wherever possible, upon our contacts in the ethnic communities themselves. But the task was impossible, and for every worthwhile pupusería or noodle shop we've reviewed, there are surely several others that we have not. (And we heartily encourage you to tell us about them by writing to us at feedback@fearlesscritic.com.)

The challenge you face, as a restaurantgoer, is not how to choose where to go; there are myriad options at every price point, in every category; hopefully, we've given you a good starting point within these pages. Your real challenge, especially at lesser-known ethnic restaurants, is to break down the biggest barrier between chef and customer: the menu. This document tends to encourage narrowmindedness by allowing customers to make arbitrary decisions about kitchens they've never even seen, things they've never tasted.

So we encourage you to tell your chef that you don't want his menu—you want what *he or she* is eating, or at least what he or she is feeding the regulars. Accept your role as a foreign tourist in the chef's world, and accept all the vulnerability that role entails—but make it clear that you're up to the challenge, and that you want the real experience. Submit your mind and body to something unseen and unknown. Enter the chef's world. And let yourself be shown the way from here to somewhere else.

The Culinary District

The vast potential for historic downtown Houston to turn back into a real walking neighborhood has long been talked about, but it finally seems that the time is now, or at least is coming soon: the restored lofts are filling up, the light rail is in place, Discovery Green is on its way, and one of the main things the Historic District is really waiting for now is the restaurants that will provide a backbone for the evening life of downtown.

That's the idea behind the "Culinary District" initiative that's currently underway, under the leadership of Jeff Kaplan, Adam Brackman, and Monte Large, of Wulfe & Company. At press time, the Culinary District was still in the incubation phase, but the concept is to cluster restaurants, institutions, retailers, and culinary talent into one area, tied together with one overarching leasing strategy and incentives from the city and landlords. The group is putting together deals to install a host of new restaurants, gourmet shops, wine bars, and such in the Historic District. It's an effort that's long overdue, and its successful realization could yield dividends to the urban life of the city for decades to come.

Valet villains: enough is enough!

Valet parking is a valuable amenity in the crowded downtown area of a city. That is, it's helpful in an area where there's a real parking shortage, and where the valet is thus saving you the hassle of having to drive to a nearby garage, circle endlessly looking for a spot, or park illegally.

Where it's definitely *not* a valuable amenity is at a restaurant that has its own, perfectly sufficient parking lot that is needlessly controlled by a valet instead of being open to the restaurant's customers. The restaurant thus creates an artificial parking shortage. Often, the valet takes your keys and moves your car to a space only a few feet from where he's standing. Let us count some of the ways in which valet parking is not helpful in so many of the situations in which it's forced upon restaurantgoers in Houston:

It doesn't save you time. First, you have to remove your car key from your keychain (do you want to give your house key to a stranger with access to everything that happens to be in your car?). Then, you have to collect your valuables (GPS machines, mobile devices, iPods, and such) and take them into the restaurant with you, which can actually be quite awkward.

It costs money. $8 is the going rate in many places, but even when the valet parking is free, you're expected to tip a minimum of $2.

You are risking the well-being of your car. Plenty of valets in Houston have dented cars, crashed cars, crashed cars into other cars. Most valets don't have to submit to any practical driving test—they just interview, turn in their driving credentials, and start work.

Many valets in Houston have poor manual-transmission skills. Valets are grinding the gears on stick-shift cars all the time. You'll see stalling, and you'll hear lurching.

You're intimidated into valet parking even if there are free spaces nearby. Valets will often answer questions about the legality of nearby spaces dishonestly. On one occasion, we were actually *mugged* by Vin's valet; when we arrived at the restaurant, we had parked in a legal space on our own, but upon leaving, even though we had our own keys, we were blocked from returning to our car without paying the valet—who had provided no service of any kind to us—eight dollars, with the clear threat of intimidation if we did not pay.

The mandatory-valet system that has taken hold all over Houston is an abomination. The city's restaurant customers are becoming more and more irritated with the system, and restaurants should take action to end it wherever possible.

A space in the parking lot of a restaurant that you're about to patronize should not cost money, nor should it come with the obligation to surrender your keys. We ask readers to join us and express their displeasure with these valet systems to the restaurants that are sustaining them.

Italian-American "1.0" vs. "2.0"

Italian is the most misunderstood of all foreign cuisines that Americans think they know. That could be true in part because restaurants calling themselves Italian—like those calling themselves Mexican—are so ubiquitous around America. But while most people understand that Tex-Mex and so-called "Interior Mexican" are two different things, the perceived differences between Italian-American cuisine and authentic Italian cuisine are far fuzzier, because you almost never see the latter in America.

For instance, one bizarre yet rampant myth, spread even by many food writers, is that spaghetti and meatballs, fettucine alfredo, and lasagne are "Southern Italian," while, say, lobster ravioli with sun-dried-tomato-and-Marsala wine sauce, a fillet of salmon with gorgonzola atop angel-hair pasta, or a prosciutto-wrapped filet mignon would constitute "Northern Italian."

These characterizations could hardly be any further from the truth. None of the dishes mentioned above—neither the "Northern" ones nor the "Southern" ones—have ever been seen within the borders of Italy (with the exception of fettucine alfredo, which was theoretically invented in Rome but is served at only one restaurant in Italy, whose other three branches are in Disney World, New York's Rockefeller Center, and Las Vegas).

In reality, red sauces—like a basic reduced tomato sauce for spaghetti, referred to by Americans as "marinara," or by the Italians as "pomodoro" (tomato)—are found all over Italy. As for those dishes mislabeled as "northern Italian," they're really just straight-up American inventions.

Still, the distinction is one worth drawing. Below, we propose a new nomenclature for the two principal Italian-American culinary categories, which we then use throughout the book. Our categories are as follows:

Italian-American 1.0: This is the cuisine often referred to as "red-sauce Italian" and often mislabeled as "Southern Italian." This is a cuisine that was originally established by Italian immigrants in the early 1900s, many of which came from the region of Campania, around Naples (Caserta, Salerno, Benevento, Avellino, and so on). The hallmarks of the cuisine are the classic red-sauce dishes, including spaghetti and meatballs; chicken, veal, and eggplant parmesan (often served with a side of spaghetti); baked ziti; and baked lasagne. Fettucine alfredo, although a white-sauce dish, has become a standard part of this repertoire, too, as has garlic bread. Fried calamari and fried mozzarella are common appetizers. Another hallmark of Italian-American 1.0 is the squat, straw-covered bottle of Chianti. This cuisine dominated the Italian restaurants of small-town America in the 1950s through the 1980s, and still defines the menu of many Italian restaurants in Houston and across America.

Italian-American 2.0: This is the cuisine often mislabeled as "Northern Italian." In the late 1980s and early 1990s, a groundswell of Italian restaurants—some of them Italian-American 1.0 restaurants looking to upgrade, others of them new, and not all of them Italian-run—established a new vernacular of upmarket, more expensive "Italian" food, combining a host of nominally Italian-derived ingredients, but based less on tomato and cheese, and built more around proteins. The classic Italian-American 2.0 meal begins with a dish of olive oil in which you're meant to dip your bread (this is an American invention, not an Italian custom, but it's a good one). Classic 2.0 appetizers include fried calamari (a dish also seen in 1.0, although 2.0 usually serves it with a spicier sauce), prosciutto and melon, and bruschetta. Mains on the menu often include veal, chicken breast, shrimp, lobster, fillets of fish, and steaks, combined in various ways with prosciutto, Marsala, balsamic vinegar, goat cheese, gorgonzola, roasted red peppers, and sun-dried tomatoes. Amongst the most common combinations are a veal chop, chicken marsala, seafood over angel-hair pasta, and lobster ravioli. Osso buco often appears, too. The main protein is often placed on a bed of pasta, and topped with a sauce (again, a completely American innovation). Cheese shaved at the table from a rotary-hand-crank grater and pepper ground from a peppermill by a waiter at the table are also common elements. The wine list is often Tuscan-focused. Tiramisù is a 1.0-2.0 crossover dessert—Italian-American 1.5, if you will.

The Fearless Critic system

Welcome to a new kind of restaurant guide. We've written more than 400 full-page reviews rigorously rating more than 700 places to eat (including local minichains) in the greater Houston area. And as you might guess, the authors are very, very full.

The Fearless Critic's "brutally honest" philosophy can be summed up in one sentence: our duty is to the readers, not the restaurants. We do not accept advertising from dining establishments, chefs, or restaurateurs. We visit all restaurants incognito, and pay for our own meals. We visit most establishments several times, and most of our reviews are informed by years of repeat visits by our Undercover Chefs, local kitchen nerds who visit and evaluate each other's restaurants without identifying themselves.

In order to qualify for inclusion in this book, an establishment must serve food. Of course, we haven't included every restaurant in Houston; some people say there are more than 10,000 of them. We've focused on the restaurants that we thought it most important to review, whether for positive or negative reasons. This meant omitting most national-level "casual dining" chains, corner pizza joints, and generic fast-food-style purveyors with little to distinguish them. We've visited many more restaurants than we wrote up, and we've chosen to include only the places that we thought would be most relevant for readers given our space constraints.

Most reviews have one "lead author," whose initials appear at the end of the review; however, each review is edited several times and often modified based on other critics' opinions. In cases where there was not just one lead author, and the review was more of a joint effort, we've used the initials "FC" (Fearless Critic). Each critic's ratings are normalized, too, against other critics'. In spite of this, we haven't always achieved a perfect sense of balance in evaluation—each critic has his own quirks and unique preferences—but we've tried our best to minimize invididual bias. Still, the book is written by chefs, so you'll see some systematic preferences, particularly for pork fat and innards. Adjust your reading accordingly.

We're also sure, however, that we have also unwittingly omitted many true out-of-the-way gems, and for that we apologize in advance (and encourage you to let us know about them at feedback@fearlesscritic.com, so that they might be included in the next edition). But we hope that we'll also turn you on to a lot of little places with which you might not be familiar, and we hope we've done a generally good job covering a good portion of the eateries worth knowing about within the city of Houston. We have also included several restaurants in the suburbs that, by our judgment, are notable enough to be included.

As you'll see once you start reading, the Fearless Critic style is relentlessly opinionated—something you might not be used to when you read a restaurant review. We're happy to wax poetic if we love a place, but as First Amendment fans, we're also not afraid to tell you if a place is overpriced, rude, or just plain bad. (That said, whenever possible, we try to be entertaining while doing it.) Our goal is to evaluate the restaurants—good or bad—so you don't have to; we hope to help you decide where to eat, and also where *not* to eat.

Our book is ultimately a reference guide, so we focus more on evaluation of food and feel than we do on chefs' names and pedigrees. We're more restaurant inspectors than restaurant promoters, and we aim for a punchy evaluation of a restaurant's strengths and weaknesses that ends with a clear judgment and recommendation. We hope that the "Total Pleasure Grade," introduced for the first time with this book, will turn out to be an effective distillation of the whole evaluation. The grade appears in the upper right corner of every page.

Your hard-earned dollars matter a lot to us, and we hope that the money you've spent on this book will save you untold sums in the future by preventing you from wasting hundreds of dollars on potentially bad, boring meals. Therein, we believe, lies much of the usefulness of food criticism.

So, welcome to a new kind of restaurant review, and a new kind of restaurant guide to Houston. We hope you'll be a convert.

The rating scale

After the Fearless Critics and Undercover Chefs evaluate each establishment incognito, we all get together and assign one letter grade and two numerical ratings to each establishment. Ratings are bell curved, and there is no grade inflation.

Total Pleasure Grade (A to D-): If you just look at one thing on the page, look at the letter grade: it sums up how much we like the place, and it expresses how much pleasure we predict it will give you. Another word for the concept is "recommendability": how much, or little, we recommend the restaurant. Everything figures into this one final grade, from food and feel to price, value, creativity, and ambition. But the Total Pleasure Grade isn't just a sum of those numbers. Restaurants with good food and atmosphere, for instance, can still fall well into the Cs or Ds if they're exorbitantly overpriced, sleazy, or have a bad attitude—that's pretty much the opposite of pleasure for us. On the flip side, we award extra credit for many pleasure factors that don't really figure into Food and Feel ratings, such as the pleasure of a low-markup wine list—happily, a growing trend in Houston—or the pleasure of knowing that you're eating at a chef-owned restaurant whose ingredients come from a local farm. In some cases, as for Ibiza and T'afia, these factors are significant enough to elevate a restaurant's Total Pleasure Grade from a B to an A.

Food rating (1 to 10): This is strictly a measure of whether the food on offer is appetizing or objectionable, insipid or delicious. We close our eyes to reputation, price, and puffery when we taste, so don't be surprised to find a greasy spoon outscoring a historic, upscale, sit-down establishment, for one simple reason: the food just tastes better. Purveyors of sweets and specialty markets are ineligible for this rating, as they don't attempt to serve meals. Be forewarned that we use the whole 10-point scale, and this is the area where we're most severely critical, so if you're not as demanding as we are, please take the ratings with a grain of salt. We hope that fanatical foodies will appreciate our rigor and honesty. A food score above 8 is high praise and constitutes a solid recommendation; it's an honor bestowed on only 21% of Houston's restaurants. And just 21 establishments out of more than 400—only about 5% of rated resturants—were awarded a food score of 9 or above, with only one, Da Marco, scoring above 9.5.

Feel rating (1 to 10): Many guides rate the "service" and "décor" at a restaurant, but rather than counting the number of pieces of silverware on the table or the number of minutes and seconds before the food arrives, we ask ourselves a simple question: does being here make us happy? The most emphatic "yes" inspires the highest rating. We don't give out points for tablecloths or tuxedos. We reward warm lighting, comfortable accomodations, a finely realized theme, and a strong sense of place. If it's a place steeped in history, or just an eminently classic Houston joint (think Barbecue Inn), we give bonus points for that, because it's certainly part of the "feel." The dim glow of candles, dark wood, and old Texas paraphernalia at your local dive might just garner more accolades than the proliferation of accoutrements at a stuffy so-called "fine dining" restaurant.

Also figured into the "feel" rating is the question of whether you'll love or loathe the prospect of interacting with the people who stand between you and your meal. We don't expect the burger-flipper at a greasy spoon to start spouting off elaborate wine adjectives, but if a restaurant's staff is unusually helpful and caring, or extraordinarily enthusiastic and knowledgeable about what's coming out of the kitchen, then the "feel" rating will reflect that. On the flip side, if the staff is consistently indifferent or condescending—or seems to have gone on strike—then points will be deducted from the experience rating of the restaurant, which happens as often at high-priced places as it does at corner take-out joints. Consider this a nonviolent revolution in the food-review world. Viva.

The math: There's no grade inflation here. Let yourself get used to our system, and don't be scared off by a restaurant with a grade in the Cs. Only 23, or about 5.5% of the more than 400 rated restaurants, scored a straight A or above. About 14% were in the A range (A or A-), while about 38% received some form of B, and another 38% or so scored in the C range; about 9% got a D or a D-. We didn't give out any Fs: contrary to some popular belief, we do have a basic sense of mercy.

The other stuff on the page

Average dinner price: This dollar value is a guide to how much, on average, you should expect to spend per person on a full dinner at the restaurant, including one alcoholic beverage, tax, and a 20% tip (for table-service establishments; we encourage you to tip at coffeeshops and take-out joints too, but we don't figure it into the meal price). This is an imperfect science, but we go by what the average person tends to order at each place. At simple take-out places, this might be just a sandwich or the like; at more elaborate sit-down restaurants, we usually figure in the cost of shared appetizers (one for every two people) and desserts (one for every two people). For alcoholic drinks, too, we are guided by what people generally tend to order. At Armadillo Palace, it's a beer. At Lupe Tortilla, it's a margarita. At Chez Annie, it's a decent glass of wine. Keep in mind that at the higher-end restaurants, you will generally spend considerably less than the quoted price if you go for lunch, or if you order iced tea instead of wine. Only restaurants that serve meals are eligible for price estimates; this excludes dessert-and-coffee places, specialty grocery stores, and so on.

Cuisine category: Every establishment in *The Fearless Critic* is associated with one or more cuisine categories. Our "Lists" section includes a cross-referenced guide to all restaurants by cuisine. A few categories require a bit of explanation. We reserve the **Italian** designation for restaurants that resemble in some way the dishes that you might get in Italy; this relegates most, but certainly not all, of Houston's Italian restaurants into the **Italian-American** category. On the other hand, there's certainly no shame in being designated **Tex-Mex**—it's a culinary category of its own, and one that we can be quite proud of. But we reserve the true **Mexican** designation for the authentic, regional cuisine that some people like to call "Interior Mexican" (we don't). **American** covers bar food and traditional meat-and-potatoes fare, while **Light American** refers to places that focus on sandwiches, salads, and soups. **New American**, sometimes referred to as "construction cuisine," is a style of cooking pioneered on the West Coast that fuses elements from many world regions, often including Asia. The **Southern** category includes soul food, fried chicken, Cajun, and Louisiana Creole. And the **Latin American** category includes Central American, South American, and Caribbean food, along with so-called "Nuevo Latino" cuisine, but not Mexican food.

Establishment type: We have divided Houston's eating establishments into several categories. The largest category is **casual restaurant,** which means a place with waiter service at tables but a generally laid-back atmosphere without much fuss. An **upmarket restaurant** is a place with more elegant ambitions, marketed as a restaurant for a special occasion or an impressive date. The **counter service** category includes cafeterias, self-service places, and also establishments where you place an order at a counter but it is then brought out to your table (of which, in our opinion, Houston has far too many). We define **pub** as a place that's fundamentally a bar at heart, but also serves food, though the kitchen often closes before the doors. **Café** means a place whose primary business is the provision of coffee or tea, but they must also serve food to be included in the book. We've also included one food-serving **strip club** and one food-serving **movie theater**, as well as several notable **specialty groceries** in Houston, most of which also serve certain varieties of prepared foods that can be eaten straightaway. Houston's **wine bar** scene has taken off in the past couple of years, so we've seen it fit to add a special category for wine bars, although amongst them, we only include establishments that have some commitment to a real food program as well.

Address: We have included addresses and neighborhood designations for up to three locations, although, where feasible, we have indexed additional locations in the Lists section of the book. For chains with more than three locations, you should consult their web sites. For specific directions, we advise that you consult the wonderful Google Maps (maps.google.com), which now works well on PDAs and smartphones, or MapQuest (www.mapquest.com).

Special features: These appear in italics, following the address on the page. **Breakfast** and **brunch** generally mean that a restaurant has a special menu, or separate portion of the menu, geared toward those meals, not just that the place is open in the morning. By **date-friendly,** we mean establishments that we find particularly romantic in some way—and that doesn't necessarily mean tuxedoed waiters or high prices. We look for warm lighting, good vibes, and a sense of easy fun. **Delivery** can be limited to a certain geographical range or minimum order. **Kid-friendly** doesn't just mean a couple of high chairs in the corner; it means a place where the little ones will actually be happy, whether for culinary reasons or for the availability of special activities or play areas. The **live music** designation includes establishments that have it only on certain days or nights, so call ahead if it's atmospherically important to you. **Outdoor dining** can mean anything from a couple of sidewalk tables to a sprawling biergarten. **Wireless internet** has to be free to qualify—this is the 21st century, after all. We are particularly careful when choosing which establishments to flag as **vegetarian-friendly.** The designation is not limited to vegetarian-only places, but we look for menus where vegetarians will not just be accommodated—they'll actually have an ample selection.

Other practical information: We also list a telephone number, a website (if available); and whether, in our estimation, reservations are essential or advisable for dinner. As for the bar, "full" indicates that the establishment is licensed to serve hard liquor and, thus, mixed drinks and cocktails in addition to wine and beer. "Wine and beer" is another type of license; such places might serve just wine, or just beer, or both. There's also a handful of "BYO" restaurants, where you can bring your own wine or beer. We're fans of this concept—it can be a great opportunity to drink that nice bottle that's been sitting around the house, waiting for a good occasion.

Neighborhood explanations

We have divided the city of Houston into distinct neighborhoods to help sort out the restaurants geographically. Below, we've described the delineation of each neighborhood as it's used in the book. For your convenience, we've listed a neighborhood more than once if it overlaps more than one of the broad subdivisions below.

If a restaurant is located outside the city of Houston, its municipality is listed in lieu of a neighborhood designation. **All designations listed below are bounded by Houston city limits.**

North of the Loop

North Houston: north of Loop 610 and east of N. Shepherd Dr.

South of the Loop

South Houston: South of W. Bellfort Ave., south of Loop 610 but not including Meyerland, east of S. Post Oak Rd., and west of Rt. 288.

Southeast Houston: East of Rt. 288 and south of Loop 610.

West of the Loop

Northwest Houston: West of N. Shepherd Dr. and Durham Dr. and north of I-10, but not including Spring Branch.

Town & Country: North of Memorial Dr., south of I-10, east of Sam Houston Pkwy. North, and west of Gessner Rd.

Memorial: North of San Felipe St. and Forest Dr., south of I-10, east of Gessner Rd., west of and including Memorial Park.

Spring Branch: North of I-10, south of Hammerly Blvd., east of Beltway 8, and west of Loop 610 and I-290.

West Houston: North and west of Rt. 59 (Southwest Fwy.), south of I-10, but not including Chinatown, Westchase, Hillcroft, Galleria, Memorial, or Town & Country.

Westchase: North of Westpark Tollway, south of Briar Forest Dr. and San Felipe Dr., east of Wilcrest Dr., and west of (but not including) Hillcroft Ave. and Voss St.

Galleria: North of Rt. 59 (Southwest Fwy.), south of San Felipe St., east of (but not including) Hillcroft Ave. and Voss St., and west of Loop 610.

Hillcroft Area: Along Hillcroft Ave., north of Rt. 59 (Southwest Fwy.), and south of Westheimer.

Chinatown: North of Beechnut St., south of Westpark Tollway, east of Kirkwood Dr., west of Rt. 59 (Southwest Fwy.).

Bellaire: within Bellaire municipality; *or* north of Beechnut St., south and east of Rt. 59 (Southwest Fwy.), and west of West University Place.

Meyerland: north of W. Bellfort Ave., south of Holcombe Blvd., east of Chimney Rock Rd., southeast of the Bellaire municipality, and west of Buffalo Speedway.

Southwest Houston: south of Beechnut St., south and west of Meyerland, and west of S. Post Oak Rd.

Inside the Loop, north of I-10

Northwest Houston: West of N. Shepherd Dr. and Durham Dr., north of I-10, but not including the area delineated by Spring Branch.

Heights: North of I-10, south of Loop 610, east of N. Shepherd Dr., west of I-45

Northeast Houston: north of I-10 and east of I-45.

Inside the Loop, between I-10 and Route 59

River Oaks: North of I-59, south of Memorial Park and Memorial Dr., east of Loop 610, and west of Waugh Dr., but not including Greenway Plaza, Upper Kirby, or Montrose.

Greenway Plaza: north of Bissonet St., south of Westheimer Rd., east of and including Weslayan St., and west of and including Buffalo Speedway.

Upper Kirby: north of I-59, south of Inwood Dr., east of (but not including) Buffalo Speedway, and west of and including S. Shepherd Dr.

Washington: North of Memorial Dr., south of I-10, east of Memorial Park, and west of I-45.

Montrose: north of I-59, south of W. Gray St. and Inwood Dr., east of (but not including) S. Shepherd Dr., and west of and including Montrose Blvd.

Midtown: northwest of Rt. 59, southwest of I-45, and east of (but not including) Montrose.

Downtown: northeast of I-45, northwest of Rt. 59, and south of I-10.

East Houston: Inside Loop 610, east of Rt. 59, and east of Rt. 288.

Inside the Loop, south of Route 59

Bellaire: within Bellaire municipality; *or* north of Beechnut St., south and east of Rt. 59 (Southwest Fwy.), and west of West University Place.

Meyerland: north of W. Bellfort Ave., south of Holcombe Blvd., east of Chimney Rock Rd., southeast of the Bellaire municipality, and west of Buffalo Speedway.

West U: within the West University Place municipality; *or* north of Bellaire Blvd./Holcombe Blvd., south of but not including Westpark, and west of Kirby Dr.

Medical Center: north of Loop 610, south of W. Holcombe Blvd., east of Buffalo Speedway, west of Rt. 288 PLUS the triangle north of Holcombe, east of Main St., and south of MacGregor Dr.

Rice Area: North of the Medical Center, south of Rt. 59 (Southwest Fwy.), east of Buffalo Speedway, and west of Main St., Sunset Blvd., and Mandell St.

Hermann Park: North of MacGregor Dr., south of Rt. 59 (Southwest Fwy.), east of the Rice area, and west of Rt. 288 (South Fwy.).

East Houston: Inside Loop 610, east of Rt. 59, east of Rt. 288.

Brutally honest

As you might guess from the name of the book, *The Fearless Critic* is brutally honest. One of our Contributing Editors calls it "in-your-face" restaurant reviewing. One newspaper called it "scathing." And some people have suggested that this style of reviewing is rude to the restaurants. But we consider it rude for some restaurants to serve tasteless food at high prices, or to subject patrons to a disaffected attitude. And we're here to help you.

We think that too many food writers in America have not deigned to embrace the art of simple criticism, thus giving readers the ultimate raw deal. For how is one to choose between two places if both are portrayed in dizzying, worshipful prose? And how frustrating is it to find out that at least one of them was a waste of your time and money? If you're celebrating a special occasion, as one often does by dining out, the sting of disappointment after a bad meal is that much more acute. What's *definitely* rude—and costly—is for an unsuspecting patron to dine on the strength of a sugar-coated review, only to discover the truth the hard way, with friends or date in tow. In short, **our duty is to our readers, not to the restaurants.**

We do not accept advertising from restaurants, and we never identify ourselves when we dine. We also consult our Contributing Editors, combing their entire body of experiences to broaden our personal perspective on each restaurant, and assuring that our experiences were representative. Our goal is to save you the cost, disappointment, and possible discomfort of a bland, overpriced meal—and to point you preemptively in the direction of something better. Helping you choose, every time you eat out, is what makes this endeavor worthwhile for us. And so, within these pages, we tell you exactly what we'd tell a good friend if she called us up and asked what we *really* thought of a place.

This unapologetic approach may take a moment to get used to. But in the end, we believe opinionated commentary to be the highest possible compliment to the local dining scene. That is to say, the food here is definitely worth talking about. Houston is a serious culinary city, and it deserves a serious restaurant guide.

We don't expect you to agree with everything we say—sometimes, we don't even agree with each other—but we do hope you can appreciate our conviction that, in food writing, opinion is better expressed openly than buried between the lines. We believe that, over the course of a book full of more than 400 reviews, we will earn your trust. And whether you concur or dissent, we would love to hear from you; we'd like nothing better than to inspire more relentlessly opinionated diners in Houston. Visit us at **houston.fearlesscritic.com** to post your own opinions, or your thoughts on ours.

Fearless Critic quirks

Cooking times: as you might notice within these pages, we prefer most cuts of meat rare or medium-rare, and we prefer our fish and fowl moist and juicy rather than dry and more fully cooked. Specifically, our reviews often comment on whether or not establishments are willing to serve a dish as rare as we request it. Although we understand that there are many people who like their meat more cooked than we do, our complaint isn't with restaurants that serve meat medium or medium-well by default; it's with restaurants that refuse to serve meat rare *even upon emphatic request*. Still, people who like their meat cooked medium or more should take our comments with a grain of salt.

Seasoning: speaking of a grain of salt, we complain from time to time about undersalted dishes. Our position is that there is no such thing as salting "to taste" in the professional kitchen. As a matter of chemistry, a certain amount of salt is necessary to bring out the complexity in most savory flavors: meats, fishes, soups, sauces, and so on. If you don't believe us, try this experiment, suggested by Italian food guru Marcella Hazan: pour two half-glasses of red wine, dump some salt into one of them, swirl them both around, and smell both glasses. The salt really brings out the bouquet (you won't want to drink it, though...).

Undersalting is one of the most common ways that an otherwise well-executed dish can fall completely flat. This problem can usually be corrected with the salt shaker (unless the food is deep-fried, in which cases it's too late). But we think a dish should come to the table properly seasoned and ready to eat, not left in the final stages of preparation. If you want your meal with less salt than normal, you can ask for it, and the restaurant should honor the request. Otherwise, forcing the customer to finish that process is as absurd as plopping a salad down in front of a customer with a whole carrot and a peeler.

Most top chefs around the world would agree that proper seasoning is a matter of necessity, not opinion. At a recent seminar with famed chef Jacques Pepin, an audience member asked him whether or not the classic French recipe that he was preparing would "work" with less salt. Responded Pepin: "If you have dietary restrictions, then let me know, and I will underseason your food—at your own risk. But I'm your chef, not your doctor." Amen.

"Mains": you won't find the word "entrée" in *The Fearless Critic*. The word is inherently ambiguous, and particularly confusing to foreigners, as the French word "entrée" means "starter" or "appetizer." We're not sure how "entrée" came to mean a main course in the United States, but here we say "main course," or "main," if that's what we mean.

The *Fearless Critic* style guide: we don't italicize foreign words in this book, nor do we capitalize dish names unless they're invented by the restaurant. We're minimalists.

Fearless feedback

The heart and soul of this endeavor is our firm belief that the world of restaurant reviewing can only be improved by opening outspoken channels of communication between restaurants and their customers. We hope that the honest articulation of our opinions and dining experiences will encourage you to do the same—if you have a bad meal, or a great one, *tell the restaurant.* Tell them what was right and what was wrong. It can only help. And tell us; we've set up an interactive space at **www.fearlesscritic.com**, where readers can express agreement or dissent of any sort. The commentary found on the site is moderated only to keep out spammers, not to edit readers' opinions. It doesn't require registration, and you can even post anonymously. Please, read some reviews, go try some restaurants, and then log on and let us know what you think. Our critics will do their best to respond to posts from time to time. We look forward to hearing from you.

The fine print

This entire book is a work of opinion, and should be understood as such. Any and all judgments rendered upon restaurants within these pages, regardless of tense, are intended as statements of pure opinion. Facts have been thoroughly checked with the restaurants in person and via telephone; we have gone to the utmost lengths to ensure that every fact is correct, and that every ingredient in every dish is properly referenced. Any factual errors that nonetheless remain are purely unintentional. That said, menus and plates (not to mention hours of operation) change so frequently at restaurants that any printed book, however new, cannot help but be a bit behind the times. Check in at **houston.fearlesscritic.com** for the latest updates, restaurant news, discussion boards, and more.

About Fearless Critic Media

Fearless Critic Media is a lean, fiercely independent publishing house founded in 2006 and dedicated to providing useful information in an engaging format. Fearless Critic Media publishes relentlessly opinionated, irreverent, and comprehensive guides to dining in American cities. Look for other Fearless Critic restaurant guides, including *The Fearless Critic Austin Restaurant Guide*, which can be bought online at amazon.com and barnesandnoble.com as well as at bookstores, food and wine stores, and other retail stores in the Austin and Houston areas. For all of the latest information, please visit our publishing website at **www.fearlesscritic.com.**

Fearless Critic

Lists

Total pleasure Honor roll

Our **100 favorite** places to eat in Houston **overall.**

The Fearless Critic's **total pleasure grade** is a measure of **overall recommendability**, integrating food, feel, service, concept, and value. Here are the top 100 establishments for total pleasure, in rank order from top to bottom.

Rank		*Total pleasure grade*	*Cuisine*	*Location*	*Type*	*Price*
1	Da Marco	A+	Italian	Montrose	Upmarket	$77
2	Indika	A	Indian	Montrose	Upmarket	$65
3	Tony's	A	Italian	Greenway	Upmarket	$110
4	Dolce Vita	A	Italian, Pizza	Montrose	Casual	$38
5	Le Mistral	A	French	W. Houston	Upmarket	$74
6	17	A	New American	Downtown	Upmarket	$100
7	Vic & Anthony's	A	Steakhouse	Downtown	Upmarket	$94
8	Himalaya	A	Pakistani	Hillcroft Area	Casual	$14
9	Nippon	A	Japanese	Montrose	Casual	$42
10	Reef	A	New American	Midtown	Upmarket	$66
11	Udipi Café	A	Indian, Vegetarian	Hillcroft Area	Casual	$8
12	Gravitas	A	New American	Midtown	Upmarket	$72
13	Catalan	A	New American	Washington	Upmarket	$70
14	Pesce	A	Seafood	Upper Kirby	Upmarket	$85
15	Café Pita +	A	Bosnian	Westchase	Casual	$17
16	Rioja	A	Spanish	W. Houston	Upmarket	$62
17	TopWater Grill	A	Seafood, American	San Leon	Casual	$31
18	Ibiza	A	New American	Midtown	Upmarket	$72
19	Doneraki	A	Tex-Mex	Multiple	Casual	$30
20	Sasaki	A	Japanese	Galleria	Casual	$51
21	100% Taquito	A	Mexican	Greenway	Counter	$11
22	Peking Cusine	A	Chinese	W. Houston	Casual	$13
23	Phô Danh II	A	Vietnamese	Chinatown	Casual	$8
24	Café Rabelais	A-	French	Rice Area	Upmarket	$55
25	t'afia	A-	New American	Midtown	Upmarket	$65
26	Shade	A-	New American	Heights	Upmarket	$49
27	Shanghai Restaurant	A-	Chinese	Chinatown	Casual	$12
28	Taquería Del Sol	A-	Mexican	S. Houston	Casual	$18
29	QQ Cuisine	A-	Chinese	Chinatown	Casual	$10
30	Vieng Thai	A-	Thai	Spring Branch	Casual	$24
31	The Breakfast Klub	A-	American, Southern	Midtown	Counter	$11
32	Teppay	A-	Japanese	Galleria	Upmarket	$60
33	Gorditas Aguasctes.	A-	Mexican	Multiple	Casual	$9
34	Bice	A-	Italian	Galleria	Upmarket	$96
35	Sam's Deli Diner	A-	American	W. Houston	Counter	$9
36	Lupe Tortilla	A-	Tex-Mex	Multiple	Casual	$26
37	Bonga	A-	Korean	Spring Branch	Casual	$19
38	Fung's Kitchen	A-	Chinese, Seafood	Chinatown	Upmarket	$46
39	El Tiempo Cantina	A-	Tex-Mex	Multiple	Casual	$58
40	Luling City Market	A-	Barbecue	Galleria	Counter	$15
41	London Sizzler	A-	Indian	Hillcroft Area	Casual	$32
42	Frenchy's Chicken	A-	Southern	Multiple	Counter	$8
43	Guy's Meat Market	A-	Barbecue, Burgers	Medical	Counter	$8

44	Pollo Riko	A-	Latin American	Multiple	Fast food	$7
45	El Pupusodromo	A-	Salvadoran	Multiple	Casual	$12
46	Café Malay	A-	Malaysian	Westchase	Casual	$15
47	Asia Market	A-	Thai	Heights	Counter	$8
48	Sinh Sinh	A-	Chinese, Seafood	Chinatown	Casual	$36
49	The Tasting Room	A-	Pizza	Multiple	Wine bar	$33
50	Nam Gang	A-	Korean	Spring Branch	Casual	$23
51	Lynn's Steakhouse	A-	Steakhouse	W. Houston	Upmarket	$80
52	El Rey Taquería	A-	Mexican, Cuban	Multiple	Counter	$11
53	Phô Nga	A-	Vietnamese	Midtown	Casual	$9
54	Don Café	A-	Vietnamese	Chinatown	Counter	$5
55	Saffron	A-	Moroccan	Upper Kirby	Casual	$55
56	Backstreet Café	B+	New American	River Oaks	Upmarket	$71
57	Guadalajara	B+	Tex-Mex	Multiple	Casual	$34
58	Cyclone Anaya's	B+	Tex-Mex	Multiple	Casual	$35
59	Brasserie Max & Julie	B+	French	Montrose	Upmarket	$71
60	Sage 400	B+	Japanese	Galleria	Casual	$45
61	Hugo's	B+	Mexican	Montrose	Upmarket	$53
62	Red Lion Pub	B+	American, British	Upper Kirby	Bar	$25
63	1308 Cantina	B+	Tex-Mex	Montrose	Casual	$58
64	Mockingbird Bistro	B+	New American	River Oaks	Upmarket	$80
65	Lucky Pot	B+	Chinese	Chinatown	Casual	$15
66	13 Celsius	B+	Italian	Midtown	Wine bar	$32
67	Noé	B+	New American	Galleria	Upmarket	$100
68	Tookie's Hamburgers	B+	Burgers	Seabrook	Casual	$12
69	Chuy's	B+	Tex-Mex	River Oaks	Casual	$30
70	Pico's Mex-Mex	B+	Mexican, Tex-Mex	Bellaire	Casual	$19
71	Tony Mandola's	B+	Seafood	River Oaks	Upmarket	$63
72	Becks Prime	B+	American, Burgers	Multiple	Counter	$13
73	Pappasito's	B+	Tex-Mex	Multiple	Casual	$31
74	Field of Greens	B+	Light American	Upper Kirby	Counter	$11
75	Goode Co. Seafood	B+	Seafood	Multiple	Casual	$40
76	Harlon's Barbecue	B+	Barbecue	Multiple	Counter	$10
77	Jerusalem Halal Deli	B+	Middle Eastern	Hillcroft Area	Counter	$10
78	Pasha	B+	Turkish	Rice Area	Casual	$34
79	Istanbul Grill	B+	Turkish	Rice Area	Casual	$51
80	Thai Spice	B+	Thai	Multiple	Casual	$11
81	Ruth's Chris	B+	Steakhouse	Galleria	Upmarket	$86
82	La Michoacana	B+	Mexican	Multiple	Counter	$6
83	Kaneyama	B+	Japanese	Westchase	Casual	$33
84	Goode Co. Taquería	B+	Tex-Mex, Burgers	Multiple	Counter	$16
85	Chapultepec	B+	Tex-Mex	Montrose	Casual	$15
86	Garson	B+	Middle Eastern	Hillcroft Area	Casual	$29
87	Paradise Café	B+	Chinese	Chinatown	Casual	$12
88	Joyce's Ocean Grill	B+	Southern, Seafood	Multiple	Casual	$26
89	Hobbit Café	B+	American	Upper Kirby	Casual	$20
90	This Is it Soul Food	B+	Southern	Midtown	Counter	$11
91	Al's Quick Stop	B+	Middle Eastern	Montrose	Counter	$8
92	Bombay Sweets	B+	Indian, Vegetarian	Hillcroft Area	Counter	$9
93	Amy's Ice Cream	B+	Sweets	Upper Kirby	Counter	
94	Jungle Café	B+	Sweets	Chinatown	Counter	
95	Kenneally's Irish Pub	B	Pizza	Montrose	Bar	$16
96	Benjy's	B	Southwestern	Rice Area	Upmarket	$54
97	Thelma's Barbecue	B	Barbecue	Downtown	Counter	$10
98	Houston's	B	American	Multiple	Upmarket	$62
99	Laurier Café and Wine	B	New American	Greenway	Upmarket	$44
100	La Vista	B	New American	Multiple	Upmarket	$35

Good vibes

The Fearless Critic's "feel" rating measures the enjoyment we get from the atmosphere and people. Here are the **top 50.**

	Restaurant	*Feel rating*	*Cuisine*	*Location*	*Type*	*Price*
1	Café Rabelais	9.8	French	Rice Area	Upmarket	$55
2	t'afia	9.7	New American	Midtown	Upmarket	$65
3	Shade	9.7	New American	Heights	Upmarket	$49
4	Le Mistral	9.6	French	W. Houston	Upmarket	$74
5	Américas	9.6	Latin American	Multiple	Upmarket	$75
6	Rioja	9.5	Spanish	W. Houston	Upmarket	$62
7	Last Concert Café	9.5	Tex-Mex	Downtown	Casual	$16
8	Pesce	9.4	Seafood	Upper Kirby	Upmarket	$85
9	Backstreet Café	9.4	New American	River Oaks	Upmarket	$71
10	Benjy's	9.3	Southwestern	Rice Area	Upmarket	$54
11	Café Annie	9.3	Southwestern	Galleria	Upmarket	$106
12	Mark's	9.3	New American	Montrose	Upmarket	$112
13	Dolce Vita	9.2	Italian, Pizza	Montrose	Casual	$38
14	Hugo's	9.2	Mexican	Montrose	Upmarket	$53
15	Antica Osteria	9.2	Italian-American	West U	Upmarket	$67
16	Da Marco	9.1	Italian, Pizza	Montrose	Upmarket	$77
17	Catalan	9.1	New American	Washington	Upmarket	$70
18	Gravitas	9.1	New American	Midtown	Upmarket	$72
19	The Tasting Room	9.1	Pizza	Multiple	Wine bar	$33
20	Just Dinner	9.1	American	Montrose	Casual	$30
21	Treebeards	9.1	Southern	Downtown	Counter	$12
22	Indika	9.0	Indian	Montrose	Upmarket	$65
23	La Vista	9.0	New American	Multiple	Upmarket	$35
24	London Sizzler	9.0	Indian	Hillcroft Area	Casual	$32
25	Mockingbird Bistro	9.0	New American	River Oaks	Upmarket	$80
26	Brennan's of Houston	9.0	Southern	Midtown	Upmarket	$105
27	Armadillo Palace	9.0	American	Rice Area	Bar	$22
28	Vic & Anthony's	9.0	Steakhouse	Downtown	Upmarket	$94
29	TopWater Grill	9.0	Seafood	San Leon	Casual	$31
30	El Hidalguense	8.9	Mexican	Multiple	Casual	$37
31	Inversion Coffee House	8.9	Light American	Montrose	Café	$9
32	Brasserie Max & Julie	8.8	French	Montrose	Upmarket	$71
33	Sonoma Wine Bar	8.8	New American	Upper Kirby	Wine bar	$37
34	Chuy's	8.8	Tex-Mex	River Oaks	Casual	$30
35	Skyline Bar & Grill	8.8	New American	Downtown	Upmarket	$101
36	Lynn's Steakhouse	8.7	Steakhouse	W. Houston	Upmarket	$80
37	El Tiempo Cantina	8.7	Tex-Mex	Multiple	Casual	$58
38	Alamo Drafthouse	8.7	American	Multiple	Movie theater	$22
39	Ibiza	8.7	New American	Midtown	Upmarket	$72
40	Cyclone Anaya's	8.7	Tex-Mex	Multiple	Casual	$35
41	Saffron	8.7	Moroccan	Upper Kirby	Casual	$55
42	Tacos A Go-Go	8.7	Tex-Mex	Midtown	Counter	$10
43	Damian's	8.7	Italian-American	Midtown	Upmarket	$73
44	La Mexicana	8.7	Tex-Mex	Montrose	Casual	$27
45	El Pueblito	8.7	Tex-Mex	Montrose	Casual	$20
46	Dharma Café	8.7	New American	Washington	Casual	$38
47	Café Adobe	8.7	Tex-Mex	Multiple	Casual	$24
48	Quattro	8.7	Italian, Steakhouse	Downtown	Upmarket	$95
49	17	8.6	New American	Downtown	Upmarket	$100
50	SoVino	8.6	New American	Midtown	Wine bar	$44

The Most Delicious List

Houston's **top 100 kitchens** judged from a ***pure food*** perspective.

	Restaurant	*Food rating*	*Cuisine*	*Location*	*Type*	*Price*
1	Da Marco	9.7	Italian	Montrose	Upmarket	$77
2	Tony's	9.4	Italian	Greenway	Upmarket	$110
3	Vic & Anthony's	9.3	Steakhouse	Downtown	Upmarket	$94
4	17	9.3	New American	Downtown	Upmarket	$100
5	Himalaya	9.2	Pakistani	Hillcroft Area	Casual	$14
6	Nippon	9.2	Japanese	Montrose	Casual	$42
7	Udipi Café	9.2	Indian, Vegetarian	Hillcroft Area	Casual	$8
8	Indika	9.1	Indian	Montrose	Upmarket	$65
9	Le Mistral	9.1	French	W. Houston	Upmarket	$74
10	Reef	9.1	New American	Midtown	Upmarket	$66
11	Café Pita +	9.1	Bosnian	Westchase	Casual	$17
12	Bice	9.1	Italian	Galleria	Upmarket	$96
13	TopWater Grill	9.1	Seafood, American	San Leon	Casual	$31
14	Gravitas	9.0	New American	Midtown	Upmarket	$72
15	Peking Cusine	9.0	Chinese	W. Houston	Casual	$13
16	100% Taquito	9.0	Mexican	Greenway	Counter	$11
17	Doneraki	9.0	Tex-Mex	Multiple	Casual	$30
18	Phô Danh II	9.0	Vietnamese	Chinatown	Casual	$8
19	Dolce Vita	9.0	Italian, Pizza	Montrose	Casual	$38
20	Sam's Deli Diner	9.0	American	W. Houston	Counter	$9
21	Gorditas Aguasctes.	9.0	Mexican	Multiple	Casual	$9
22	Sasaki	8.9	Japanese	Galleria	Casual	$51
23	Shanghai Restaurant	8.9	Chinese	Chinatown	Casual	$12
24	Teppay	8.9	Japanese	Galleria	Upmarket	$60
25	Catalan	8.8	New American	Washington	Upmarket	$70
26	QQ Cuisine	8.8	Chinese	Chinatown	Casual	$10
27	Pesce	8.8	Seafood	Upper Kirby	Upmarket	$85
28	Taquería Del Sol	8.8	Mexican	S. Houston	Casual	$18
29	El Rey Taquería	8.8	Mexican, Cuban	Multiple	Counter	$11
30	Lupe Tortilla	8.7	Tex-Mex	Multiple	Casual	$26
31	Frenchy's Chicken	8.7	Southern	Multiple	Counter	$8
32	Bonga	8.7	Korean	Spring Branch	Casual	$19
33	Ruth's Chris	8.7	Steakhouse	Galleria	Upmarket	$86
34	Asia Market	8.7	Thai	Heights	Counter	$8
35	Morton's	8.7	Steakhouse	Multiple	Upmarket	$102
36	Fung's Kitchen	8.6	Chinese, Seafood	Chinatown	Upmarket	$46
37	El Tiempo Cantina	8.6	Tex-Mex	Multiple	Casual	$58
38	Luling City Market	8.6	Barbecue	Galleria	Counter	$15
39	Sinh Sinh	8.6	Chinese, Seafood	Chinatown	Casual	$36
40	Phô Nga	8.6	Vietnamese	Midtown	Casual	$9
41	Rioja	8.6	Spanish	W. Houston	Upmarket	$62
42	Don Café	8.6	Vietnamese	Chinatown	Counter	$5
43	Kaneyama	8.5	Japanese	Westchase	Casual	$33

44	Pollo Riko	8.5	Latin American	Multiple	Fast food	$7
45	Café Malay	8.5	Malaysian	Westchase	Casual	$15
46	Guadalajara	8.5	Tex-Mex	Multiple	Casual	$34
47	Becks Prime	8.5	American, Burgers	Multiple	Counter	$13
48	Guy's Meat Market	8.5	Barbecue, Burgers	Medical	Counter	$8
49	Lucky Pot	8.5	Chinese	Chinatown	Casual	$15
50	Ibiza	8.5	New American	Midtown	Upmarket	$72
51	El Pupusodromo	8.5	Salvadoran	Multiple	Casual	$12
52	Vieng Thai	8.5	Thai	Spring Branch	Casual	$24
53	Pappasito's	8.5	Tex-Mex	Multiple	Casual	$31
54	London Sizzler	8.4	Indian	Hillcroft Area	Casual	$32
55	Brenner's	8.4	Steakhouse	Memorial	Upmarket	$90
56	Saffron	8.4	Moroccan	Upper Kirby	Casual	$55
57	Sage 400	8.4	Japanese	Galleria	Casual	$45
58	1308 Cantina	8.4	Tex-Mex	Montrose	Casual	$58
59	Chuy's	8.4	Tex-Mex	River Oaks	Casual	$30
60	Goode Co. Seafood	8.3	Seafood	Multiple	Casual	$40
61	Bob's Steak & Chop	8.3	Steakhouse	Galleria	Upmarket	$101
62	Pasha	8.3	Turkish	Rice Area	Casual	$34
63	Sushi Jin	8.3	Japanese	W. Houston	Casual	$44
64	Mezzanine Lounge	8.3	American, Burgers	Upper Kirby	Bar	$16
65	Brasserie Max & Julie	8.2	French	Montrose	Upmarket	$71
66	The Breakfast Klub	8.2	American, Southern	Midtown	Counter	$11
67	The Tasting Room	8.2	Pizza	Multiple	Wine bar	$33
68	Goode Co. Taquería	8.2	Tex-Mex, Burgers	Multiple	Counter	$16
69	Houston's	8.2	New American	Multiple	Upmarket	$62
70	McCormick & Schmick	8.2	Seafood, American	Memorial	Upmarket	$61
71	Red Lion Pub	8.2	American, British	Upper Kirby	Bar	$25
72	Field of Greens	8.2	Light American	Upper Kirby	Counter	$11
73	Nam Gang	8.1	Korean	Spring Branch	Casual	$23
74	Lynn's Steakhouse	8.1	Steakhouse	W. Houston	Upmarket	$80
75	Tookie's Hamburgers	8.1	Burgers	Seabrook	Casual	$12
76	Thai Spice	8.1	Thai	Multiple	Casual	$11
77	Istanbul Grill	8.1	Turkish	Rice Area	Casual	$51
78	Turquoise Grill	8.1	Turkish	Upper Kirby	Casual	$22
79	Los Guanacos	8.1	Salvadoran	NW Houston	Casual	$10
80	Tony Mandola's	8.0	Seafood	River Oaks	Upmarket	$63
81	Backstreet Café	8.0	New American	River Oaks	Upmarket	$71
82	Mockingbird Bistro	8.0	New American	River Oaks	Upmarket	$80
83	La Michoacana	8.0	Mexican	Multiple	Counter	$6
84	Noé	8.0	New American	Galleria	Upmarket	$100
85	Finger Licking Bukateria	8.0	Nigerian	W. Houston	Casual	$14
86	Pappas Burgers	8.0	Burgers	Multiple	Counter	$16
87	Skyline Bar & Grill	8.0	New American	Downtown	Upmarket	$101
88	Alexander the Great	8.0	Greek	Galleria	Upmarket	$63
89	La Vista	7.9	New American	Multiple	Upmarket	$35
90	SoVino	7.9	New American	Midtown	Wine bar	$44
91	This Is it Soul Food	7.9	Southern	Midtown	Counter	$11
92	Pico's Mex-Mex	7.9	Mexican, Tex-Mex	Bellaire	Casual	$19
93	Phô Saigon	7.9	Vietnamese	Multiple	Casual	$14
94	Mom's Hand	7.9	Korean	Spring Branch	Counter	$9
95	Tan Tan	7.9	Chinese	Chinatown	Casual	$17
96	Onion Creek	7.9	American	Heights	Bar	$18
97	La Guadalupana	7.9	Mexican	Montrose	Casual	$11
98	Bombay Sweets	7.8	Indian, Vegetarian	Hillcroft Area	Counter	$9
99	Tacos A Go-Go	7.8	Tex-Mex	Midtown	Counter	$10
100	Abdullah's	7.8	Middle Eastern	Hillcroft Area	Casual	$14

By cuisine

Places to eat **listed by culinary concept, ranked by Total Pleasure Grade.** Unranked establishments (e.g. grocery stores) appear the bottom of the list if they're relevant.

	American	*Location*	*Type*	*Price*
A-	The Breakfast Klub	Midtown	Counter	$11
A-	Sam's Deli Diner	W. Houston	Counter	$9
B+	Becks Prime	Multiple	Counter	$13
B+	Red Lion Pub	Upper Kirby	Bar	$25
B+	Hobbit Café	Upper Kirby	Casual	$20
B	59 Diner	Multiple	Casual	$18
B	Houston's	Multiple	Upmarket	$62
B	Just Dinner	Montrose	Casual	$30
B	Kenneally's Irish Pub	Montrose	Bar	$17
B	Barnaby's Café	Multiple	Casual	$20
B	Avalon Drug Company	Upper Kirby	Casual	$16
B	Rudyard's British Pub	Montrose	Bar	$18
B-	Onion Creek	Heights	Bar	$18
B-	Baba Yega	Montrose	Casual	$14
B-	Red & White Wine Bistro	Downtown	Upmarket	$74
B-	Barbecue Inn	N. Houston	Counter	$18
B-	Daily Review Café	Montrose	Casual	$31
B-	Le Peep	Multiple	Casual	$14
B-	Mason Jar	Memorial	Casual	$24
B-	Armadillo Palace	Rice Area	Bar	$22
B-	Mezzanine Lounge	Upper Kirby	Bar	$16
B-	The Baker Street Pub	Multiple	Bar	$17
B-	Bistro Lancaster	Downtown	Upmarket	$70
C+	Mama's Café	Galleria	Casual	$15
C+	Little Hip's Diner	Washington	Casual	$10
C+	James Coney Island	Multiple	Fast food	$8
C+	Baby Barnaby's	Montrose	Casual	$10
C+	The Flying Saucer	Downtown	Bar	$18
C+	Dry Creek Café	Heights	Casual	$15
C+	Bistro Vino	Montrose	Upmarket	$60
C+	Bibas (One's a Meal)	Midtown	Casual	$16
C	Buffalo Wild Wings	Multiple	Bar	$22
C	Pappy's Café	Memorial	Casual	$16
C	Willy's Pub	Rice Area	Bar	$12
C	11th Street Café	Heights	Casual	$12
C	The Buffalo Grille	Multiple	Counter	$11
C-	Grand Lux Café	Galleria	Casual	$28
C-	Ziggy's Healthy Grill	Multiple	Counter	$16
C-	The Brownstone	Upper Kirby	Upmarket	$84
C-	Prince's Hamburgers	Multiple	Counter	$9
C-	House of Pies	Multiple	Casual	$11
D-	Kona Grill	Multiple	Casual	$54
D-	Aquarium	Downtown	Upmarket	$30
D-	Café Express	Multiple	Counter	$16

American (New): *see "New American"*

Barbecue

A-	Luling City Market	Galleria	Counter	$15
A-	Guy's Meat Market	Medical	Counter	$8
B+	Harlon's Barbecue	Multiple	Counter	$10
B	Thelma's Barbecue	Downtown	Counter	$10
B	Rudy's Country Store	Spring	Counter	$16
B-	Barbecue Inn	N. Houston	Counter	$18
B-	Armadillo Palace	Rice Area	Bar	$22
B-	Demeris Barbecue	Multiple	Casual	$10
C+	Smokey's Bar-B-Q	Multiple	Counter	$9
C+	Pizzitola's Bar-B-Que	Heights	Casual	$15
C	The County Line	N. Houston	Casual	$29
C-	Pappas Bar-B-Q	Multiple	Counter	$12
C-	Goode Co. Bar-B-Q	Rice Area	Counter	$14

Belgian

B-	Café Montrose	Montrose	Casual	$43

Bosnian

A	Café Pita +	Westchase	Casual	$17

Brazilian

C	Fogo de Chão	Westchase	Upmarket	$77
C	Nelore Churrascaria	Montrose	Upmarket	$58

British

B+	Red Lion Pub	Upper Kirby	Bar	$25
C-	Black Labrador Pub	Montrose	Bar	$26

Burgers

A-	Sam's Deli Diner	W. Houston	Counter	$9
A-	Guy's Meat Market	Medical	Counter	$8
B+	Becks Prime	Multiple	Counter	$13
B+	Tookie's Hamburgers	Seabrook	Casual	$12
B+	Goode Co. Taquería	Multiple	Counter	$16
B	Pappas Burgers	Multiple	Counter	$16
B	Adrian's Burger Bar	E. Houston	Counter	$9
B	Rudyard's British Pub	Montrose	Bar	$18
B-	Otto's BBQ & Burgers	Multiple	Counter	$11
B-	Christian's Tailgate	Multiple	Bar	$9
B	Mezzanine Lounge	Upper Kirby	Bar	$16
C+	Lankford Grocery	Midtown	Casual	$12
C+	Freeway Hamburgers	Memorial	Counter	$9
C+	Dry Creek Café	Heights	Casual	$15
C+	Whataburger	Multiple	Fast food	$8
C+	Tommy's Sandwiches	Medical	Counter	$9
C	Cliff's Hamburgers	Multiple	Casual	$8
C	Lucky Burger	Montrose	Counter	$6
C-	Prince's Hamburgers	Multiple	Counter	$9
C-	Charlie's Hamburger	Multiple	Counter	$9

Chinese

A	Peking Cusine	W. Houston	Casual	$13
A-	Shanghai Restaurant	Chinatown	Casual	$12
A-	QQ Cuisine	Chinatown	Casual	$10
A-	Fung's Kitchen	Chinatown	Upmarket	$46

Chinese *continued*

A-	Sinh Sinh	Chinatown	Casual	$36
B+	Lucky Pot	Chinatown	Casual	$15
B+	Paradise Café	Chinatown	Casual	$12
B	Tan Tan	Chinatown	Casual	$17
B	North China Restaurant	Memorial	Casual	$19
B-	San Dong	Chinatown	Counter	$9
B-	Tay Do Restaurant	Chinatown	Casual	$25
C+	FuFu Café	Chinatown	Casual	$10
C+	Kim Son	Multiple	Casual	$32
C+	Star Snow Ice	Chinatown	Counter	$7
C+	Big Bowl	Chinatown	Casual	$6
C	Hong Kong's Café	Chinatown	Casual	$7
C	Ocean Palace	Chinatown	Casual	$29
C-	YAO Restaurant & Bar	Westchase	Casual	$36
C-	PF Chang's	Multiple	Upmarket	$41
C-	Yum Yum Cha Café	Rice Area	Casual	$10
C-	Silver Palace	Bellaire	Casual	$11
C-	Lai Lai Dumpling House	Chinatown	Casual	$7
NR	Dynasty Supermarket	Chinatown	Grocery	
NR	Hong Kong Food Market	Multiple	Grocery	
NR	Welcome Food Center	Chinatown	Grocery	

Candies, cakes, and sweets

B+	Jungle Café	Chinatown	Counter	
B-	Thierry André Tellier	Multiple	Café	
C	The Dessert Gallery	Multiple	Counter	
C-	House of Pies	Multiple	Casual	
NR	The Chocolate Bar	Montrose	Grocery	
NR	Candylicious	Multiple	Grocery	

Caribbean *includes Cuban and Jamaican*

A-	El Rey Taquería	Multiple	Counter	$11
B	Latina Café	Montrose	Casual	$22
B	Stir-It-Up Coffee House	Midtown	Café	$13
B-	Café Piquet	Bellaire	Casual	$13
B-	El Mesón	Rice Area	Upmarket	$42

Ethiopian

B-	Blue Nile Ethiopian	Westchase	Casual	$25

French

A	Le Mistral	W. Houston	Upmarket	$74
A-	Café Rabelais	Rice Area	Upmarket	$55
B+	Brasserie Max & Julie	Montrose	Upmarket	$71
B-	Courses	Galleria	Upmarket	$51
B-	Chez Georges	Midtown	Upmarket	$75
C+	Hollywood Vietnamese	Montrose	Casual	$24
C+	Bistro Vino	Montrose	Upmarket	$60
C	Bistro Le Cep	W. Houston	Upmarket	$42
D-	Chez Nous	Humble	Upmarket	$94

German

B	Rudi Lechner's	SW Houston	Casual	$31

Greek

B-	Alexander the Great	Galleria	Upmarket	$63
C+	Bibas (One's a Meal)	Midtown	Casual	$16
C+	Yia Yia Mary's	Galleria	Counter	$20
D	Niko Niko's	Montrose	Counter	$20

Ice cream

B+	Amy's Ice Cream	Upper Kirby	Counter	
B-	Swirll Italian Yogurt	Rice Area	Counter	
C+	Paciugo Gelateria	Greenway	Counter	
NR	The Chocolate Bar	Montrose	Grocery	

Indian

A	Udipi Café	Hillcroft Area	Casual	$8
A	Indika	Montrose	Upmarket	$65
A-	London Sizzler	Hillcroft Area	Casual	$32
B+	Bombay Sweets	Hillcroft Area	Counter	$9
B	Mayuri	Galleria	Casual	$33
B	Pavani Indian Cuisine	SW Houston	Casual	$16
B-	Bombay Brasserie	Rice Area	Casual	$33
C+	Yatra Brasserie	Downtown	Casual	$42
C+	Shiva	Rice Area	Casual	$27
C+	Madras Pavilion	Upper Kirby	Casual	$20
C+	Khyber	Upper Kirby	Casual	$26
C	Kiran's	Galleria	Upmarket	$60
C	India's Restaurant	Galleria	Casual	$20

Italian *includes Italian-American*

A+	Da Marco	Montrose	Upmarket	$77
A	Tony's	Greenway	Upmarket	$110
A	Dolce Vita	Montrose	Casual	$38
A-	Bice	Galleria	Upmarket	$96
B-	Damian's	Midtown	Upmarket	$73
B-	Prego	Rice Area	Upmarket	$57
B-	Antica Osteria	West U	Upmarket	$67
B-	Arcodoro	Galleria	Upmarket	$75
C+	Quattro	Downtown	Upmarket	$95
C+	Buon Appetito	Medical	Casual	$34
C+	Barry's Pizza	Galleria	Casual	$15
C+	Carrabba's Italian Grill	Multiple	Casual	$52
C+	La Strada	Montrose	Upmarket	$59
C	Black Walnut Café	Multiple	Café	$12
C	Josephine's	Downtown	Counter	$17
C	Trevisio	Medical	Upmarket	$60
C	Nino's	Montrose	Upmarket	$57
C	Vincent's	Montrose	Upmarket	$45
C	Ponzo's	Midtown	Casual	$14
C-	Pronto Cucinino	Multiple	Counter	$15
C-	Grappino di Nino	River Oaks	Upmarket	$36
C-	Craiganale's Italian Deli	Downtown	Counter	$11
C-	La Griglia	River Oaks	Upmarket	$60
C-	Ciro's Italian Grill	Memorial	Casual	$35
C-	D'Amico's	Rice Area	Counter	$18
C-	Michelangelo's	Montrose	Casual	$52
D	Sorrento	Montrose	Upmarket	$64
D	The Grotto	Galleria	Upmarket	$55

Italian *continued*

D	Palazzo's	Multiple	Casual	$34
D	Collina's Italian Café	Multiple	Casual	$34
D-	Buca di Beppo	Upper Kirby	Casual	$30

Japanese

A	Nippon	Montrose	Casual	$42
A	Sasaki	Galleria	Casual	$51
A-	Teppay	Galleria	Upmarket	$60
B+	Kaneyama	Westchase	Casual	$33
B+	Sage 400	Galleria	Casual	$45
B	Sushi Jin	W. Houston	Casual	$44
B-	Osaka	Montrose	Casual	$42
B-	Kubo's	Rice Area	Casual	$44
B-	Azuma and Azumi	Multiple	Casual	$55
C+	Uptown Sushi	Galleria	Upmarket	$44
C	Sushi King	Upper Kirby	Casual	$39
C	The Fish	Midtown	Upmarket	$58
C-	RA Sushi	River Oaks	Upmarket	$43
C-	Miyako	Multiple	Upmarket	$38
C-	Zake Sushi Lounge	Upper Kirby	Casual	$43
C-	Tokyohana	Multiple	Casual	$40
D	Sake Lounge	Downtown	Casual	$40
F	Café Japon	Upper Kirby	Casual	$27

Jewish Deli

C+	Kenny & Ziggy's	Galleria	Casual	$20
C-	Kahn's Deli	Rice Area	Counter	$10
D	Katz's Deli	Montrose	Casual	$20

Korean

A-	Bonga	Spring Branch	Casual	$19
A-	Nam Gang	Spring Branch	Casual	$23
B	Tofu Village	Chinatown	Casual	$18
B	Mom's Hand	Spring Branch	Counter	$9
B	Korea Garden	Spring Branch	Casual	$32
C+	Seoul Garden	Spring Branch	Casual	$28
C-	Café 101	Chinatown	Casual	$14

Latin American *includes South American, Central American, Nuevo Latino*

A-	El Rey Taquería	Multiple	Counter	$11
A-	Pollo Riko	Multiple	Fast food	$7
B	Américas	Multiple	Upmarket	$75
B-	Churrascos	Multiple	Upmarket	$63
B-	Café Piquet	Bellaire	Casual	$13
B-	Pollo Campero	Multiple	Fast food	$9
C	Artista	Downtown	Upmarket	$69
C	Café Red Onion	Multiple	Casual	$37
C-	Amazón Grill	Multiple	Counter	$28

Light American *sandwiches, salads, soups*

A-	Sam's Deli Diner	W. Houston	Counter	$9
B+	Field of Greens	Upper Kirby	Counter	$11
B	Paulie's	Multiple	Counter	$15
B	Stir-It-Up Coffee House	Midtown	Café	$13
B-	Kraftsmen Bakery	Montrose	Casual	$12
B-	Inversion Coffee House	Montrose	Café	$9

Light American *continued*

B-	Taft St. Coffee House	Midtown	Café	$7
B-	Nielsen's Delicatessen	Galleria	Counter	$11
C+	Brown Bag Deli	Multiple	Counter	$7
C+	Empire Café	Montrose	Counter	$14
C+	Tommy's Sandwiches	Medical	Counter	$9
C	Black Walnut Café	Multiple	Café	$12
C	The Daily Grind	Washington	Café	$8
C-	Hungry's	Multiple	Casual	$18
C-	Craiganale's Italian Deli	Downtown	Counter	$11
D	Ruggles Café	Rice Area	Casual	$17
D-	Brasil	Montrose	Counter	$13
NR	Central Market	Upper Kirby	Grocery	
NR	Whole Foods	Multiple	Grocery	
NR	Spec's	Downtown	Grocery	

Malaysian

A-	Café Malay	Westchase	Casual	$15
B-	Malay Bistro	Chinatown	Casual	$10

Mexican (Regional)

A	100% Taquito	Greenway	Counter	$11
A-	Gorditas Aguasctes.	Multiple	Casual	$9
A-	Taquería Del Sol	S. Houston	Casual	$18
A-	El Rey Taquería	Multiple	Counter	$11
B+	La Michoacana	Multiple	Counter	$6
B+	Pico's Mex-Mex	Bellaire	Casual	$19
B+	Hugo's	Montrose	Upmarket	$53
B	Taquería Los Charros	Multiple	Casual	$8
B	La Guadalupana	Montrose	Casual	$11
B-	Teotihuacán	Heights	Casual	$11
B-	Taquería Arandas	Multiple	Casual	$9
B-	El Hidalguense	Multiple	Casual	$37
B-	Connie's Seafood Mkt.	Multiple	Counter	$24
C+	María Selma	Montrose	Casual	$32
C+	La Tapatía Taquería	Multiple	Casual	$12
C+	Tampico Seafood	Heights	Casual	$26
C+	The Tamale Couple	All of them	In your face	$5
C	Laredo Taquería	Washington	Counter	$8
C-	Chilos Seafood	Multiple	Casual	$21

Mexican (Tex-Mex): *see "Tex-Mex"*

Middle Eastern

B+	Jerusalem Halal Deli	Hillcroft Area	Counter	$10
B+	Garson	Hillcroft Area	Casual	$29
B+	Al's Quick Stop	Montrose	Counter	$8
B	Abdullah's	Hillcroft Area	Casual	$14
B	Café Caspian	W. Houston	Casual	$19
B	Café Lili	Galleria	Casual	$23
B-	Shawarma King	Galleria	Counter	$8
B-	Fadi's Mediterranean	Multiple	Counter	$15
C	DNR European Café	Montrose	Counter	$11
C	Aladdin Mediterranean	Montrose	Counter	$8
C-	La Fendée	Montrose	Casual	$30
D-	Yildizlar	Montrose	Counter	$11
NR	Phoenicia	W. Houston	Grocery	

Moroccan

A-	Saffron	Upper Kirby	Casual	$55

New American

A	17	Downtown	Upmarket	$100
A	Reef	Midtown	Upmarket	$66
A	Gravitas	Midtown	Upmarket	$72
A	Catalan	Washington	Upmarket	$70
A	Ibiza	Midtown	Upmarket	$72
A-	t'afia	Midtown	Upmarket	$65
A-	Shade	Heights	Upmarket	$49
B+	Backstreet Café	River Oaks	Upmarket	$71
B+	Noé	Galleria	Upmarket	$100
B+	Mockingbird Bistro	River Oaks	Upmarket	$80
B	Café Annie	Galleria	Upmarket	$106
B	La Vista	Multiple	Upmarket	$35
B	Laurier Café and Wine	Greenway	Upmarket	$44
B	SoVino	Midtown	Wine bar	$44
B-	Mark's	Montrose	Upmarket	$112
B-	Skyline Bar & Grill	Downtown	Upmarket	$101
B-	Masraff's	Memorial	Upmarket	$76
B-	Farrago	Midtown	Casual	$38
B-	Max's Wine Dive	Washington	Wine bar	$46
B-	Cova	Multiple	Wine bar	$47
B-	Courses	Galleria	Upmarket	$51
C+	Café Le Jadeite	River Oaks	Upmarket	$73
C+	La Strada	Montrose	Upmarket	$59
C+	Vin	Downtown	Upmarket	$86
C	Cava Bistro	Downtown	Upmarket	$54
C	Dharma Café	Washington	Casual	$38
C-	Truluck's	Galleria	Upmarket	$86
C-	Glass Wall	Heights	Upmarket	$78
C-	The Remington	Galleria	Upmarket	$101
C-	Julia's Bistro	Midtown	Upmarket	$60
C-	Sambuca	Downtown	Upmarket	$55
D	Monarch	Hermann Park	Upmarket	$93
D	Oceanaire	Galleria	Upmarket	$82
D	Zula	Downtown	Upmarket	$74
D	Ruggles Grill	Multiple	Upmarket	$61
D-	Bank	Downtown	Upmarket	$91

Nigerian

B	Finger Licking Bukateria	W. Houston	Casual	$14

Pakistani

A	Himalaya	Hillcroft Area	Casual	$14

Pan-Asian

B	Lemongrass Café	Bellaire	Casual	$25
B-	Jenni's Noodle House	Multiple	Casual	$14
B-	Bamboo House	Montrose	Casual	$23
C+	Café Le Jadeite	River Oaks	Upmarket	$73
C+	Blue Fish House	Upper Kirby	Upmarket	$19
C-	PF Chang's	Multiple	Upmarket	$41
C-	Mak Chin's	Washington	Casual	$25
D-	Kona Grill	Multiple	Casual	$54

Pizza

A+	Da Marco	Montrose	Upmarket	$77
A	Dolce Vita	Montrose	Casual	$38
A-	The Tasting Room	Multiple	Wine bar	$33
B	Kenneally's Irish Pub	Montrose	Bar	$17
C+	Frank's Pizza	Downtown	Counter	$15
C+	Barry's Pizza	Galleria	Casual	$15
C+	Carrabba's Italian Grill	Multiple	Casual	$52
C+	Star Pizza	Multiple	Casual	$14
C+	The Pizza Guy	All of them	In your face	$5
C+	Late Night Pie	Midtown	Counter	$20
C	Fuzzy's	Multiple	Counter	$12
C	Ponzo's	Midtown	Casual	$14
C-	Mr. Gatti's and Gattitown	Multiple	Casual	$12
C-	La Griglia	River Oaks	Upmarket	$60
D	The Grotto	Galleria	Upmarket	$55
D	Collina's Italian Café	Multiple	Casual	$34

Salvadoran

A-	El Pupusodromo	Multiple	Casual	$12
B	Los Guanacos	NW Houston	Casual	$10

Seafood

A	TopWater Grill	San Leon	Casual	$31
A	Pesce	Upper Kirby	Upmarket	$85
A-	Fung's Kitchen	Chinatown	Upmarket	$46
A-	Sinh Sinh	Chinatown	Casual	$36
B+	Goode Co. Seafood	Multiple	Casual	$40
B+	Tony Mandola's	River Oaks	Upmarket	$63
B+	Joyce's Ocean Grill	Multiple	Casual	$26
B	McCormick & Schmick	Memorial	Upmarket	$61
B	Mardi Gras Grill	Heights	Casual	$17
B	Pappadeaux	Multiple	Casual	$45
B-	The Cajun Greek	Galveston	Casual	$19
B-	Pappas Seafood	Multiple	Casual	$48
B-	Connie's Seafood Mkt.	Multiple	Counter	$24
B-	Massa's	Downtown	Casual	$42
B-	Sam's Boat	Multiple	Casual	$15
C+	Blue Fish House	Upper Kirby	Upmarket	$19
C+	Tampico Seafood	Heights	Casual	$26
C+	Smokey's Bar-B-Q	Multiple	Counter	$9
C	The Fish	Midtown	Upmarket	$58
C	Ocean Palace	Chinatown	Casual	$29
C-	Truluck's	Galleria	Upmarket	$86
C-	Chilos Seafood	Multiple	Casual	$21
D	Oceanaire	Galleria	Upmarket	$82
D	Willie G's	Galleria	Upmarket	$87
D	PK's Blue Water Grill	Memorial	Casual	$44
D-	Aquarium	Downtown	Upmarket	$30

Southern *includes fried chicken, soul food, Cajun, and Creole*

A-	Frenchy's Chicken	Multiple	Counter	$8
A-	The Breakfast Klub	Midtown	Counter	$11
B+	This Is it Soul Food	Midtown	Counter	$11
B+	Joyce's Ocean Grill	Multiple	Casual	$26
B	Mardi Gras Grill	Heights	Casual	$17
B	Pappadeaux	Multiple	Casual	$45

Southern *continued*

B	Adrian's Burger Bar	E. Houston	Counter	$9
B-	Brennan's of Houston	Midtown	Upmarket	$105
B-	The Cajun Greek	Galveston	Casual	$19
B-	Pollo Campero	Multiple	Fast food	$9
B-	Treebeards	Downtown	Counter	$12
C+	Crescent City Beignets	Greenway	Fast food	$12
C+	Ouisie's Table	River Oaks	Upmarket	$61
C+	Yo Mama's Soul Food	NW Houston	Casual	$22
D	PK's Blue Water Grill	Memorial	Casual	$44
D-	Cleburne Cafeteria	West U	Counter	$17

Southwestern

B	Café Annie	Galleria	Upmarket	$106
B	Benjy's	Rice Area	Upmarket	$54
C-	Julia's Bistro	Midtown	Upmarket	$60

Specialty groceries *in alphabetical order*

NR	Canino's	Heights	Light American
NR	Candylicious	Multiple	Sweets
NR	Central Market	Upper Kirby	Light American
NR	The Chocolate Bar	Montrose	Sweets
NR	Dynasty Supermarket	Chinatown	Chinese
NR	Hong Kong Food Market	Multiple	Chinese
NR	Phoenicia	W. Houston	Middle Eastern
NR	Spec's	Downtown	Light American
NR	Welcome Food Center	Chinatown	Chinese
NR	Whole Foods	Multiple	Light American

Spanish

A	Catalan	Washington	Upmarket	$70
A	Rioja	W. Houston	Upmarket	$62
B-	El Mesón	Rice Area	Upmarket	$42
D-	Mi Luna	Multiple	Upmarket	$63

Steakhouses

A	Vic & Anthony's	Downtown	Upmarket	$94
A-	Lynn's Steakhouse	W. Houston	Upmarket	$80
B+	Ruth's Chris	Galleria	Upmarket	$86
B	Morton's	Multiple	Upmarket	$102
B	Smith & Wollensky	River Oaks	Upmarket	$91
B-	Brenner's	Memorial	Upmarket	$90
B-	Bob's Steak & Chop House	Galleria	Upmarket	$101
B-	Churrascos	Multiple	Upmarket	$63
C+	Fleming's	Multiple	Upmarket	$88
C+	Pappas Bros. Steakhouse	Galleria	Upmarket	$105
C	Fogo de Chão	Westchase	Upmarket	$77
C	Taste of Texas	Memorial	Upmarket	$54
C	Capital Grille	Galleria	Upmarket	$92
C	Nelore Churrascaria	Montrose	Upmarket	$58
C-	Strip House	Downtown	Upmarket	$98
C-	Palm	Galleria	Upmarket	$95
D-	Spencer's Steak & Chop House	Downtown	Upmarket	$90

Tex-Mex

A	Doneraki	Multiple	Casual	$30
A-	Lupe Tortilla	Multiple	Casual	$26
A-	El Tiempo Cantina	Multiple	Casual	$58
B+	Guadalajara	Multiple	Casual	$34
B+	1308 Cantina	Montrose	Casual	$58
B+	Pico's Mex-Mex	Bellaire	Casual	$19
B+	Cyclone Anaya's	Multiple	Casual	$35
B+	Chuy's	River Oaks	Casual	$30
B+	Pappasito's	Multiple	Casual	$31
B+	Goode Co. Taquería	Multiple	Counter	$16
B+	Chapultepec	Montrose	Casual	$15
B	Tacos A Go-Go	Midtown	Counter	$10
B	Taco Milagro	Multiple	Counter	$19
B	Irma's	Downtown	Casual	$26
B	Taquería Cancún	Multiple	Casual	$10
B	Spanish Flowers	Heights	Casual	$18
B	Mission Burrito	Multiple	Counter	$9
B	Taquería Los Charros	Multiple	Casual	$8
B-	Armandos	River Oaks	Upmarket	$64
B-	Escalante's	Multiple	Upmarket	$44
B-	Teala's	Montrose	Casual	$33
B-	Sam's Boat	Multiple	Casual	$15
B-	Last Concert Café	Downtown	Casual	$16
B-	Chacho's	Galleria	Casual	$19
B-	La Mexicana	Montrose	Casual	$27
B-	Berryhill Baja Grill	Multiple	Counter	$12
B-	Houston Tamales Factory	Heights	Casual	$10
B-	El Mesón	Rice Area	Upmarket	$42
C+	María Selma	Montrose	Casual	$32
C+	La Tapatía Taquería	Multiple	Casual	$12
C+	Mama's Café	Galleria	Casual	$15
C+	Taco Cabana	Multiple	Fast food	$8
C+	El Pueblito	Montrose	Casual	$20
C	Cantina Laredo	W. Houston	Upmarket	$44
C	Freebirds World Burrito	Multiple	Fast food	$8
C	Sylvia's Enchilada Kitchen	W. Houston	Casual	$18
C	López	W. Houston	Casual	$19
C-	Otilia's	Spring Branch	Casual	$21
C-	Cadillac Bar	Heights	Casual	$28
C-	Las Alamedas	Spring Branch	Upmarket	$42
C-	Santos	Westchase	Casual	$38
C-	Mama Ninfa's	Downtown	Casual	$17
D	Molina's	Multiple	Casual	$30
D	Tila's	River Oaks	Upmarket	$50
D	Cabo's Mix-Mex Grille	Downtown	Casual	$25
D	Café Adobe	Multiple	Casual	$24
D	Ninfa's	Multiple	Casual	$21
D	Ruchi's Taquería	Multiple	Casual	$16
D	Felix	Montrose	Casual	$18

Thai

A-	Asia Market	Heights	Counter	$8
A-	Vieng Thai	Spring Branch	Casual	$24
B+	Thai Spice	Multiple	Casual	$11
B	Thai Racha	Spring Branch	Counter	$9
B	Nidda Thai Restaurant	Montrose	Casual	$17

Thai *continued*

B-	Tony Thai	Chinatown	Casual	$28
B-	Nit Noi Thai	Multiple	Casual	$33
C+	Kanomwan	E. Houston	Casual	$19
C+	The Golden Room	Montrose	Casual	$24
C+	Nit Noi Café	Multiple	Casual	$13
C	Mai Thai	Upper Kirby	Casual	$23
C-	Thai Pepper	Montrose	Casual	$26
C-	Thai Sticks	Montrose	Casual	$38

Turkish

B+	Pasha	Rice Area	Casual	$34
B+	Istanbul Grill	Rice Area	Casual	$51
B	Turquoise Grill	Upper Kirby	Casual	$22

Vegetarian-focused

A	Udipi Café	Hillcroft Area	Casual	$8
B+	Field of Greens	Upper Kirby	Counter	$11
B+	Bombay Sweets	Hillcroft Area	Counter	$9
B+	Hobbit Café	Upper Kirby	Casual	$20
C+	Madras Pavilion	Upper Kirby	Casual	$20
C-	Ziggy's Healthy Grill	Multiple	Counter	$16

Vietnamese

A	Phô Danh II	Chinatown	Casual	$8
A-	Phô Nga	Midtown	Casual	$9
A-	Don Café	Chinatown	Counter	$5
B	Tau Bay	Chinatown	Casual	$10
B	Phô Saigon	Multiple	Casual	$14
B	Cali Sandwich	Midtown	Counter	$5
B	Bodard Bistro	Chinatown	Casual	$9
B-	Tay Do Restaurant	Chinatown	Casual	$25
C+	Jasmine Asian Cuisine	Chinatown	Casual	$19
C+	Kim Son	Multiple	Casual	$32
C+	Hollywood Vietnamese	Montrose	Casual	$24
C+	Mai's	Midtown	Casual	$25
C	Van Loc	Midtown	Casual	$15
C-	Café 101	Chinatown	Casual	$14
C-	Lee's Sandwiches	Multiple	Fast food	$5
D-	Vietopia	Greenway	Upmarket	$40

Wine bars

A-	The Tasting Room	Multiple	Wine bar	$33
B+	13 Celsius	Midtown	Wine bar	$32
B	SoVino	Midtown	Wine bar	$44
B	Sonoma Wine Bar	Upper Kirby	Wine bar	$37
B-	Max's Wine Dive	Washington	Wine bar	$46
B-	Cova	Multiple	Wine bar	$47

By location

Places to eat **listed by neighborhood or suburb, ranked by Total Pleasure Grade.** For detailed definitions of all the neighborhoods, please refer to pages 14-16.

	Bellaire	*Location*	*Type*	*Price*
A-	Gorditas Aguasctes.	Mexican	Casual	$9
A-	Frenchy's Chicken	Southern	Counter	$8
B+	La Michoacana	Mexican	Counter	$6
B	Lemongrass Café	Pan-Asian	Casual	$25
B-	Café Piquet	Cuban, Latin American	Casual	$13
B-	Taquería Arandas	Mexican	Casual	$9
B+	Pico's Mex-Mex	Mexican, Tex-Mex	Casual	$19
B-	Pollo Campero	Latin American, Southern	Fast food	$9
B-	Pappas Seafood	Seafood	Casual	$48
B-	Demeris Barbecue	Barbecue	Casual	$10
C+	La Tapatía Taquería	Mexican, Tex-Mex	Casual	$12
C+	James Coney Island	American	Fast food	$8
C-	Silver Palace	Chinese	Casual	$11
D	Ninfa's	Tex-Mex	Casual	$21

	Chinatown (Bellaire)			
A	Phô Danh II	Vietnamese	Casual	$8
A-	Shanghai Restaurant	Chinese	Casual	$12
A-	QQ Cuisine	Chinese	Casual	$10
A-	Pollo Riko	Latin American	Fast food	$7
A-	Fung's Kitchen	Chinese, Seafood	Upmarket	$46
A-	Sinh Sinh	Chinese, Seafood	Casual	$36
A-	Don Café	Vietnamese	Counter	$5
B+	Lucky Pot	Chinese	Casual	$15
B+	Thai Spice	Thai	Casual	$11
B+	Paradise Café	Chinese	Casual	$12
B+	Jungle Café	Sweets	Counter	
B	Phô Saigon	Vietnamese	Casual	$14
B	Tan Tan	Chinese	Casual	$17
B	Taquería Cancún	Tex-Mex	Casual	$10
B	Tofu Village	Korean	Casual	$18
B	Tau Bay	Vietnamese	Casual	$10
B	Bodard Bistro	Vietnamese	Casual	$9
B-	Tony Thai	Thai	Casual	$28
B-	San Dong	Chinese	Counter	$9
B-	Tay Do Restaurant	Vietnamese, Chinese	Casual	$25
B-	Taquería Arandas	Mexican	Casual	$9
B-	Malay Bistro	Malaysian	Casual	$10
C+	Jasmine Asian Cuisine	Vietnamese	Casual	$19
C+	FuFu Café	Chinese	Casual	$10
C+	Kim Son	Vietnamese, Chinese	Casual	$32
C+	James Coney Island	American	Fast food	$8
C+	Star Snow Ice	Chinese	Counter	$7
C+	Big Bowl	Chinese	Casual	$6
C	Hong Kong's Café	Chinese	Casual	$7
C	Ocean Palace	Seafood, Chinese	Casual	$29
C-	Café 101	Vietnamese, Korean	Casual	$14

Chinatown (Bellaire) *continued*

C-	Lai Lai Dumpling House	Chinese	Casual	$7
C-	Lee's Sandwiches	Vietnamese	Fast food	$5
NR	Dynasty Supermarket	Chinese	Grocery	
NR	Hong Kong Food Market	Chinese	Grocery	
NR	Welcome Food Center	Chinese	Grocery	

Downtown

A	17	New American	Upmarket	$100
A	Vic & Anthony's	Steakhouse	Upmarket	$94
A-	Frenchy's Chicken	Southern	Counter	$8
A-	El Rey Taquería	Mexican, Cuban	Counter	$11
B+	Becks Prime	American, Burgers	Counter	$13
B	Morton's	Steakhouse	Upmarket	$102
B	Irma's	Tex-Mex	Casual	$26
B	Thelma's Barbecue	Barbecue	Counter	$10
B-	Skyline Bar & Grill	New American	Upmarket	$101
B-	Red & White Wine Bistro	American	Upmarket	$74
B-	Jenni's Noodle House	Pan-Asian	Casual	$14
B-	Otto's BBQ & Burgers	Burgers	Counter	$11
B-	Bistro Lancaster	American	Upmarket	$70
B-	Last Concert Café	Tex-Mex	Casual	$16
B-	Treebeards	Southern	Counter	$12
B-	Azuma and Azumi	Japanese	Casual	$55
B-	Massa's	Seafood	Casual	$42
C+	Yatra Brasserie	Indian	Casual	$42
C+	Kim Son	Vietnamese, Chinese	Casual	$32
C+	James Coney Island	American	Fast food	$8
C+	Nit Noi Café	Thai	Casual	$13
C+	The Flying Saucer	American	Bar	$18
C+	Whataburger	Burgers	Fast food	$8
C+	Quattro	Italian, Steakhouse	Upmarket	$95
C+	Vin	New American	Upmarket	$86
C+	Frank's Pizza	Pizza	Counter	$15
C	Josephine's	Italian	Counter	$17
C	Artista	Latin American	Upmarket	$69
C	Cava Bistro	New American	Upmarket	$54
C-	Strip House	Steakhouse	Upmarket	$98
C-	Craiganale's Italian Deli	Italian-American, Light American	Counter	$11
C-	Pappas Bar-B-Q	Barbecue	Counter	$12
C-	Sambuca	New American	Upmarket	$55
C-	Mama Ninfa's	Tex-Mex	Casual	$17
D	Zula	New American	Upmarket	$74
D	Cabo's Mix-Mex Grille	Tex-Mex	Casual	$25
D	Sake Lounge	Japanese	Casual	$40
D	Ninfa's	Tex-Mex	Casual	$21
D-	Bank	New American	Upmarket	$91
D-	Spencer's	Steakhouse	Upmarket	$90
D-	Aquarium	Seafood, American	Upmarket	$30
D-	Café Express	American	Counter	$16
NR	Spec's	Light American	Grocery	

East Houston

B+	Pappasito's	Tex-Mex	Casual	$31
B	Taquería Los Charros	Mexican, Tex-Mex	Casual	$8
B	Adrian's Burger Bar	Southern, Burgers	Counter	$9
B-	Taquería Arandas	Mexican	Casual	$9
B-	Pollo Campero	Latin American, Southern	Fast food	$9

East Houston *continued*

B-	Pappas Seafood	Seafood	Casual	$48
C+	Kanomwan	Thai	Casual	$19
C+	James Coney Island	American	Fast food	$8
C-	Mr. Gatti's and Gattitown	Pizza	Casual	$12
C-	Pappas Bar-B-Q	Barbecue	Counter	$12
D	Ninfa's	Tex-Mex	Casual	$21

Galleria Area

A	Doneraki	Tex-Mex	Casual	$30
A	Sasaki	Japanese	Casual	$51
A-	Teppay	Japanese	Upmarket	$60
A-	Bice	Italian	Upmarket	$96
A-	Luling City Market	Barbecue	Counter	$15
A-	The Tasting Room	Pizza	Wine bar	$33
B+	Sage 400	Japanese	Casual	$45
B+	Ruth's Chris	Steakhouse	Upmarket	$86
B+	Becks Prime	American, Burgers	Counter	$13
B+	Thai Spice	Thai	Casual	$11
B+	Noé	New American	Upmarket	$100
B+	Pappasito's	Tex-Mex	Casual	$31
B+	Harlon's Barbecue	Barbecue	Counter	$10
B+	Joyce's Ocean Grill	Southern, Seafood	Casual	$26
B	Café Annie	Southwestern	Upmarket	$106
B	La Vista	New American	Upmarket	$35
B	Morton's	Steakhouse	Upmarket	$102
B	Houston's	New American	Upmarket	$62
B	Pappas Burgers	Burgers	Counter	$16
B	Américas	Latin American	Upmarket	$75
B	Mayuri	Indian	Casual	$33
B	Pappadeaux	Seafood, Southern	Casual	$45
B	Café Lili	Middle Eastern	Casual	$23
B-	Bob's Steak & Chop	Steakhouse	Upmarket	$101
B-	Alexander the Great	Greek	Upmarket	$63
B-	Shawarma King	Middle Eastern	Counter	$8
B-	Courses	French, New American	Upmarket	$51
B-	Arcodoro	Italian	Upmarket	$75
B-	Sam's Boat	Tex-Mex, Seafood	Casual	$15
B-	Chacho's	Tex-Mex	Casual	$19
B-	Berryhill Baja Grill	Tex-Mex	Counter	$12
B-	Thierry André Tellier	French, Sweets	Café	$9
B-	Nielsen's Delicatessen	Light American	Counter	$11
C+	Pappas Bros. Steakhouse	Steakhouse	Upmarket	$105
C+	Yia Yia Mary's	Greek	Counter	$20
C+	La Tapatía Taquería	Mexican, Tex-Mex	Casual	$12
C+	Barry's Pizza	Italian-American, Pizza	Casual	$15
C+	Mama's Café	American, Tex-Mex	Casual	$15
C+	Carrabba's Italian Grill	Italian-American, Pizza	Casual	$52
C+	Uptown Sushi	Japanese	Upmarket	$44
C+	James Coney Island	American	Fast food	$8
C+	Kenny & Ziggy's	Jewish Deli	Casual	$20
C	Capital Grille	Steakhouse	Upmarket	$92
C	Cliff's Hamburgers	Burgers	Casual	$8
C	Kiran's	Indian	Upmarket	$60
C	India's Restaurant	Indian	Casual	$20
C	The Dessert Gallery	Sweets	Counter	
C-	Truluck's	Seafood, New American	Upmarket	$86
C-	Grand Lux Café	American	Casual	$28

Galleria Area *continued*

C-	Palm	Steakhouse	Upmarket	$95
C-	The Remington	New American	Upmarket	$101
C-	Miyako	Japanese	Upmarket	$38
C-	House of Pies	American, Sweets	Casual	$11
D	Oceanaire	Seafood, New American	Upmarket	$82
D	Willie G's	Seafood	Upmarket	$87
D	Ruggles Grill	New American	Upmarket	$61
D	The Grotto	Italian-American, Pizza	Upmarket	$55
D	Palazzo's	Italian-American	Casual	$34
D	Ninfa's	Tex-Mex	Casual	$21
D	Ruchi's Taquería	Tex-Mex	Casual	$16
D-	Kona Grill	American, Pan-Asian	Casual	$54
D-	Café Express	American	Counter	$16

Galveston

B-	The Cajun Greek	Seafood, Southern	Casual	$19

Greenway Plaza Area

A	Tony's	Italian	Upmarket	$110
A	100% Taquito	Mexican	Counter	$11
A-	Lupe Tortilla	Tex-Mex	Casual	$26
A-	El Tiempo Cantina	Tex-Mex	Casual	$58
B+	Guadalajara	Tex-Mex	Casual	$34
B+	Joyce's Ocean Grill	Southern, Seafood	Casual	$26
B	Laurier Café and Wine	New American	Upmarket	$44
B-	Le Peep	American	Casual	$14
B-	Berryhill Baja Grill	Tex-Mex	Counter	$12
C+	Crescent City Beignets	Southern	Fast food	$12
C+	Taco Cabana	Tex-Mex	Fast food	$8
C+	Paciugo Gelateria	Sweets	Counter	
C-	Tokyohana	Japanese	Casual	$40
C-	Prince's Hamburgers	American, Burgers	Counter	$9
D	Molina's	Tex-Mex	Casual	$30
D	Collina's Italian Café	Italian-American, Pizza	Casual	$34
D-	Vietopia	Vietnamese	Upmarket	$40

Heights

A	Doneraki	Tex-Mex	Casual	$30
A-	Gorditas Aguasctes.	Mexican	Casual	$9
A-	Asia Market	Thai	Counter	$8
A-	Shade	New American	Upmarket	$49
B+	Thai Spice	Thai	Casual	$11
B+	Cyclone Anaya's	Tex-Mex	Casual	$35
B	Spanish Flowers	Tex-Mex	Casual	$18
B	Mardi Gras Grill	Southern, Seafood	Casual	$17
B	Mission Burrito	Tex-Mex	Counter	$9
B-	Onion Creek	American	Bar	$18
B-	Teotihuacán	Mexican	Casual	$11
B-	Connie's Seafood Mkt.	Seafood, Mexican	Counter	$24
B-	Christian's Tailgate	Burgers	Bar	$9
B-	Berryhill Baja Grill	Tex-Mex	Counter	$12
B-	Houston Tamales Factory	Tex-Mex	Casual	$10
C+	Tampico Seafood	Seafood, Mexican	Casual	$26
C+	Pizzitola's Bar-B-Que	Barbecue	Casual	$15
C+	Dry Creek Café	American, Burgers	Casual	$15
C	11th Street Café	American	Casual	$12
C-	Glass Wall	New American	Upmarket	$78

Heights *continued*

C-	Cadillac Bar	Tex-Mex	Casual	$28
D	Collina's Italian Café	Italian-American, Pizza	Casual	$34

Hermann Park (Museum District)

D	Monarch	New American	Upmarket	$93
D-	Café Express	American	Counter	$16

Hillcroft Area

A	Udipi Café	Indian, Vegetarian	Casual	$8
A	Himalaya	Pakistani	Casual	$14
A-	El Pupusodromo	Salvadoran	Casual	$12
A-	London Sizzler	Indian	Casual	$32
B+	Bombay Sweets	Indian, Vegetarian	Counter	$9
B+	Jerusalem Halal Deli	Middle Eastern	Counter	$10
B+	Garson	Middle Eastern	Casual	$29
B	Abdullah's	Middle Eastern	Casual	$14
B-	El Hidalguense	Mexican	Casual	$37
C-	Pappas Bar-B-Q	Barbecue	Counter	$12

Hobby Airport *grades and prices reflect airport branches only*

B	Pappas Burgers	Burgers	Counter	$16
B-	Harlon's Barbecue	Barbecue	Counter	$12
B-	Barry's Pizza	Multiple	Casual	$8
C+	Pappasito's	Tex-Mex	Casual	$11

Humble

D-	Chez Nous	French	Upmarket	$94

Intercontinental Airport *grades and prices reflect airport branches only*

A	Pappadeaux	Multiple	Casual	$52
B-	Harlon's Barbecue	Barbecue	Counter	$12
C+	Pappasito's	Tex-Mex	Casual	$11
C-	Pappas Bar-B-Q	Barbecue	Counter	$12

Katy

B	Alamo Drafthouse	American	Movie theater	$22
C+	Carrabba's Italian Grill	Italian-American, Pizza	Casual	$52
C+	James Coney Island	American	Fast food	$8

Medical Center Area

A-	Frenchy's Chicken	Southern	Counter	$8
A-	Guy's Meat Market	Barbecue, Burgers	Counter	$8
B+	Pappasito's	Tex-Mex	Casual	$31
B	Pappadeaux	Seafood, Southern	Casual	$45
B	Reggae Hut	Jamaican	Counter	$13
B-	Taquería Arandas	Mexican	Casual	$9
C+	Buon Appetito	Italian-American	Casual	$34
C+	Smokey's Bar-B-Q	Barbecue, Seafood	Counter	$9
C+	Tommy's Sandwiches	American	Counter	$9
C	Trevisio	Italian-American	Upmarket	$60
C-	Pappas Bar-B-Q	Barbecue	Counter	$12

Memorial Area

B+	Guadalajara	Tex-Mex	Casual	$34
B+	Goode Co. Seafood	Seafood	Casual	$40

Memorial Area *continued*

B+	Cyclone Anaya's	Tex-Mex	Casual	$35
B	La Vista	New American	Upmarket	$35
B	McCormick & Schmick	Seafood, American	Upmarket	$61
B	North China Restaurant	Chinese	Casual	$19
B-	Brenner's	Steakhouse	Upmarket	$90
B-	Masraff's	New American	Upmarket	$76
B-	Escalante's	Tex-Mex	Upmarket	$44
B-	Nit Noi Thai	Thai	Casual	$33
B-	Le Peep	American	Casual	$14
B-	The Mason Jar	American	Casual	$24
B-	Thierry André Tellier	French, Sweets	Café	$9
C+	Freeway Hamburgers	Burgers	Counter	$9
C	Taste of Texas	Steakhouse	Upmarket	$54
C	Fuzzy's	Pizza	Counter	$12
C	Pappy's Café	American	Casual	$16
C	The Buffalo Grille	American	Counter	$11
C-	Ciro's Italian Grill	Italian-American	Casual	$35
D	Collina's Italian Café	Italian-American, Pizza	Casual	$34
D	PK's Blue Water Grill	Seafood, Southern	Casual	$44
D	Ninfa's	Tex-Mex	Casual	$21
D-	Café Express	American	Counter	$16
NR	Whole Foods	Light American	Grocery	

Meyerland

B-	Fadi's Mediterranean	Middle Eastern	Counter	$15
B-	Escalante's	Tex-Mex	Upmarket	$44
C+	James Coney Island	American	Fast food	$8
C-	Miyako	Japanese	Upmarket	$38
C-	Charlie's Hamburger	Burgers	Counter	$9
D	Ruchi's Taquería	Tex-Mex	Casual	$16
D-	Café Express	American	Counter	$16

Midtown

A	Reef	New American	Upmarket	$66
A	Gravitas	New American	Upmarket	$72
A	Ibiza	New American	Upmarket	$72
A-	t'afia	New American	Upmarket	$65
A-	Phô Nga	Vietnamese	Casual	$9
A-	The Breakfast Klub	American, Southern	Counter	$11
A-	The Tasting Room	Pizza	Wine bar	$33
B+	This Is it Soul Food	Southern	Counter	$11
B+	13 Celsius	Italian	Wine bar	$32
B+	Cyclone Anaya's	Tex-Mex	Casual	$35
B	Tacos A Go-Go	Tex-Mex	Counter	$10
B	SoVino	New American	Wine bar	$44
B	Phô Saigon	Vietnamese	Casual	$14
B	Cali Sandwich	Vietnamese	Counter	$5
B	Barnaby's Café	American	Casual	$20
B	Stir-It-Up Coffee House	Light American, Jamaican	Café	$13
B-	Damian's	Italian-American	Upmarket	$73
B-	Brennan's of Houston	Southern	Upmarket	$105
B-	Farrago	New American	Casual	$38
B-	Chez Georges	French	Upmarket	$75
B-	Taft St. Coffee House	Light American	Café	$7
B-	Christian's Tailgate	Burgers	Bar	$9
C+	Lankford Grocery	Burgers	Casual	$12
C+	Bibas (One's a Meal)	Greek, American	Casual	$16

Midtown *continued*

C+	La Tapatía Taquería	Mexican, Tex-Mex	Casual	$12
C+	Mai's	Vietnamese	Casual	$25
C+	Late Night Pie	Pizza	Counter	$20
C+	Whataburger	Burgers	Fast food	$8
C	The Fish	Seafood, Japanese	Upmarket	$58
C	Van Loc	Vietnamese	Casual	$15
C	Ponzo's	Italian-American, Pizza	Casual	$14
C-	Julia's Bistro	Southwestern	Upmarket	$60
C-	Ziggy's Healthy Grill	American	Counter	$16

Montrose

A+	Da Marco	Italian, Pizza	Upmarket	$77
A	Indika	Indian	Upmarket	$65
A	Dolce Vita	Italian, Pizza	Casual	$38
A	Nippon	Japanese	Casual	$42
B+	1308 Cantina	Tex-Mex	Casual	$58
B+	Brasserie Max & Julie	French	Upmarket	$71
B+	Chapultepec	Tex-Mex	Casual	$15
B+	Hugo's	Mexican	Upmarket	$53
B+	Al's Quick Stop	Middle Eastern	Counter	$8
B	Latina Café	Cuban	Casual	$22
B	Rudyard's British Pub	American, Burgers	Bar	$18
B	Nidda Thai Restaurant	Thai	Casual	$17
B	Just Dinner	American	Casual	$30
B	Paulie's	Light American	Counter	$15
B	Kenneally's Irish Pub	Pizza, American	Bar	$17
B	La Guadalupana	Mexican	Casual	$11
B-	Mark's	New American	Upmarket	$112
B-	Osaka	Japanese	Casual	$42
B-	Baba Yega	American	Casual	$14
B-	Kraftsmen Bakery	Light American	Casual	$12
B-	Jenni's Noodle House	Pan-Asian	Casual	$14
B-	Daily Review Café	American	Casual	$31
B-	Teala's	Tex-Mex	Casual	$33
B-	Café Montrose	Belgian	Casual	$43
B-	Demeris Barbecue	Barbecue	Casual	$10
B-	Inversion Coffee House	Light American	Café	$9
B-	La Mexicana	Tex-Mex	Casual	$27
B-	Berryhill Baja Grill	Tex-Mex	Counter	$12
B-	Bamboo House	Pan-Asian	Casual	$23
C+	María Selma	Mexican, Tex-Mex	Casual	$32
C+	Brown Bag Deli	Light American	Counter	$7
C+	La Strada	Italian-American, New American	Upmarket	$59
C+	Hollywood Vietnamese	Vietnamese, French	Casual	$24
C+	Baby Barnaby's	American	Casual	$10
C+	The Golden Room	Thai	Casual	$24
C+	Empire Café	Light American	Counter	$14
C+	Taco Cabana	Tex-Mex	Fast food	$8
C+	Bistro Vino	French, American	Upmarket	$60
C+	El Pueblito	Tex-Mex	Casual	$20
C	DNR European Café	Middle Eastern	Counter	$11
C	Nino's	Italian-American	Upmarket	$57
C	Vincent's	Italian-American	Upmarket	$45
C	Nelore Churrascaria	Steakhouse, Brazilian	Upmarket	$58
C	Lucky Burger	Burgers	Counter	$6
C	Aladdin Mediterranean	Middle Eastern	Counter	$8
C-	Pronto Cucinino	Italian-American	Counter	$15

Montrose *continued*

C-	La Fendée	Middle Eastern	Casual	$30
C-	Thai Pepper	Thai	Casual	$26
C-	Thai Sticks	Thai	Casual	$38
C-	Black Labrador Pub	British	Bar	$26
C-	Michelangelo's	Italian-American	Casual	$52
D	Sorrento	Italian-American	Upmarket	$64
D	Niko Niko's	Greek	Counter	$20
D	Ruggles Grill	New American	Upmarket	$61
D	Katz's Deli	Jewish Deli	Casual	$20
D	Ruchi's Taquería	Tex-Mex	Casual	$16
D	Felix	Tex-Mex	Casual	$18
D-	Yildizlar	Middle Eastern	Counter	$11
D-	Brasil	Light American	Counter	$13

North Houston

A	Doneraki	Tex-Mex	Casual	$30
A-	Pollo Riko	Latin American	Fast food	$7
A-	Lupe Tortilla	Tex-Mex	Casual	$26
A-	Frenchy's Chicken	Southern	Counter	$8
A-	El Rey Taquería	Mexican, Cuban	Counter	$11
A-	El Pupusodromo	Salvadoran	Casual	$12
B+	Thai Spice	Thai	Casual	$11
B+	Pappasito's	Tex-Mex	Casual	$31
B+	Harlon's Barbecue	Barbecue	Counter	$10
B	59 Diner	American	Casual	$18
B	Phô Saigon	Vietnamese	Casual	$14
B	Taco Milagro	Tex-Mex	Counter	$19
B	Pappadeaux	Seafood, Southern	Casual	$45
B-	Pollo Campero	Latin American, Southern	Fast food	$9
B-	Barbecue Inn	American, Barbecue	Counter	$18
B-	Nit Noi Thai	Thai	Casual	$33
B-	Pappas Seafood	Seafood	Casual	$48
B-	Sam's Boat	Tex-Mex, Seafood	Casual	$15
B-	Baker Street Pub & Grill	American	Bar	$17
C+	Carrabba's Italian Grill	Italian-American, Pizza	Casual	$52
C+	La Tapatía Taquería	Mexican, Tex-Mex	Casual	$12
C+	James Coney Island	American	Fast food	$8
C	Cliff's Hamburgers	Burgers	Casual	$8
C	Freebirds World Burrito	Tex-Mex	Fast food	$8
C	The County Line	Barbecue	Casual	$29
C	Buffalo Wild Wings	American	Bar	$22
C-	Chilos Seafood	Mexican, Seafood	Casual	$21
C-	PF Chang's	Pan-Asian, Chinese	Upmarket	$41
C-	Mr. Gatti's and Gattitown	Pizza	Casual	$12
C-	Pappas Bar-B-Q	Barbecue	Counter	$12
C-	Tokyohana	Japanese	Casual	$40
D-	Café Express	American	Counter	$16
NR	Hong Kong Food Market	Chinese	Grocery	

Northwest Houston

B	Los Guanacos	Salvadoran	Casual	$10
C+	Yo Mama's Soul Food	Southern	Casual	$22

Rice University Area

A-	Café Rabelais	French	Upmarket	$55
B+	Goode Co. Seafood	Seafood	Casual	$40
B+	Thai Spice	Thai	Casual	$11

Rice University Area *continued*

B+	Pasha	Turkish	Casual	$34
B+	Istanbul Grill	Turkish	Casual	$51
B+	Goode Co. Taquería	Tex-Mex, Burgers	Counter	$16
B	Benjy's	Southwestern	Upmarket	$54
B-	Kubo's	Japanese	Casual	$44
B-	Prego	Italian-American	Upmarket	$57
B-	Cova	New American	Wine bar	$47
B-	El Mesón	Spanish, Cuban, Tex-Mex	Upmarket	$42
B-	Le Peep	American	Casual	$14
B-	Armadillo Palace	American, Barbecue	Bar	$22
B-	Bombay Brasserie	Indian	Casual	$33
B-	Swirll Italian Yogurt	Sweets	Counter	
B-	Baker Street Pub & Grill	American	Bar	$17
B-	Azuma and Azumi	Japanese	Casual	$55
C+	Brown Bag Deli	Light American	Counter	$7
C+	Shiva	Indian	Casual	$27
C	Black Walnut Café	Italian-American, Light American	Café	$12
C	Buffalo Wild Wings	American	Bar	$22
C	Willy's Pub	American	Bar	$12
C-	Hungry's	Light American	Casual	$18
C-	Goode Co. Bar-B-Q	Barbecue	Counter	$14
C-	Yum Yum Cha Café	Chinese	Casual	$10
C-	Kahn's Deli	Jewish Deli	Counter	$10
C-	D'Amico's	Italian-American	Counter	$18
C-	Amazón Grill	Latin American	Counter	$28
D	Ruggles Café	Light American	Casual	$17
D-	Mi Luna	Spanish	Upmarket	$63

River Oaks

B+	Tony Mandola's	Seafood	Upmarket	$63
B+	Backstreet Café	New American	Upmarket	$71
B+	Mockingbird Bistro	New American	Upmarket	$80
B+	Chuy's	Tex-Mex	Casual	$30
B	Mission Burrito	Tex-Mex	Counter	$9
B	Smith & Wollensky	Steakhouse	Upmarket	$91
B-	Armandos	Tex-Mex	Upmarket	$64
B-	Escalante's	Tex-Mex	Upmarket	$44
B-	Thierry André Tellier	French, Sweets	Café	$9
B-	Berryhill Baja Grill	Tex-Mex	Counter	$12
C+	Fleming's	Steakhouse	Upmarket	$88
C+	Café Le Jadeite	Pan-Asian, New American	Upmarket	$73
C+	Ouisie's Table	Southern	Upmarket	$61
C+	Nit Noi Café	Thai	Casual	$13
C-	RA Sushi	Japanese	Upmarket	$43
C-	Grappino di Nino	Italian-American	Upmarket	$36
C-	PF Chang's	Pan-Asian, Chinese	Upmarket	$41
C-	La Griglia	Italian-American, Pizza	Upmarket	$60
C-	Charlie's Hamburger	Burgers	Counter	$9
D	Tila's	Tex-Mex	Upmarket	$50
D	Café Adobe	Tex-Mex	Casual	$24
D-	Café Express	American	Counter	$16

San Leon

A	TopWater Grill	Seafood, American	Casual	$31

Seabrook

B+	Tookie's Hamburgers	Burgers	Casual	$12

South Houston

A	Doneraki	Tex-Mex	Casual	$30
A-	Taquería Del Sol	Mexican	Casual	$18
B	Phô Saigon	Vietnamese	Casual	$14

Southeast Houston

B+	Harlon's Barbecue	Barbecue	Counter	$10
B	Pappas Burgers	Burgers	Counter	$16
B-	Connie's Seafood Mkt.	Seafood, Mexican	Counter	$24
C+	La Tapatía Taquería	Mexican, Tex-Mex	Casual	$12
C+	James Coney Island	American	Fast food	$8
C-	Chilos Seafood	Mexican, Seafood	Casual	$21
C-	Mr. Gatti's and Gattitown	Pizza	Casual	$12
C-	Pappas Bar-B-Q	Barbecue	Counter	$12
C-	Prince's Hamburgers	American, Burgers	Counter	$9

Southwest Houston

A-	Pollo Riko	Latin American	Fast food	$7
A-	Frenchy's Chicken	Southern	Counter	$8
A-	El Pupusodromo	Salvadoran	Casual	$12
B	Pavani Indian Cuisine	Indian	Casual	$16
B	Rudi Lechner's	German	Casual	$31
B-	Fadi's Mediterranean	Middle Eastern	Counter	$15
C-	Pappas Bar-B-Q	Barbecue	Counter	$12
D	Ninfa's	Tex-Mex	Casual	$21

Spring

B	Rudy's Country Store	Spring	Casual	$16

Spring Branch

A-	Bonga	Korean	Casual	$19
A-	Vieng Thai	Thai	Casual	$24
A-	Nam Gang	Korean	Casual	$23
B+	Becks Prime	American, Burgers	Counter	$13
B+	Goode Co. Taquería	Tex-Mex, Burgers	Counter	$16
B+	La Michoacana	Mexican	Counter	$6
B	Mom's Hand	Korean	Counter	$9
B	Thai Racha	Thai	Counter	$9
B	Taquería Cancún	Tex-Mex	Casual	$10
B	Korea Garden	Korean	Casual	$32
B-	Taquería Arandas	Mexican	Casual	$9
B-	Pollo Campero	Latin American, Southern	Fast food	$9
B-	El Hidalguense	Mexican	Casual	$37
B-	Demeris Barbecue	Barbecue	Casual	$10
C+	Brown Bag Deli	Light American	Counter	$7
C+	Smokey's Bar-B-Q	Barbecue, Seafood	Counter	$9
C+	Seoul Garden	Korean	Casual	$28
C-	Otilia's	Tex-Mex	Casual	$21
C-	Las Alamedas	Tex-Mex	Upmarket	$42
C-	Prince's Hamburgers	American, Burgers	Counter	$9
C-	Charlie's Hamburger	Burgers	Counter	$9
D	Café Adobe	Tex-Mex	Casual	$24

Sugar Land

A	Udipi Café	Indian, Vegetarian	Casual	$8
A-	Lupe Tortilla	Tex-Mex	Casual	$26

Sugar Land *continued*

B+	Becks Prime	American, Burgers	Counter	$13
B-	Baker Street Pub & Grill	American	Bar	$17
D	Café Adobe	Tex-Mex	Casual	$24
D-	Kona Grill	American, Pan-Asian	Casual	$54
D-	Mi Luna	Spanish	Upmarket	$63
D-	Café Express	American	Counter	$16

Town & Country Area

B+	Pappasito's	Tex-Mex	Casual	$31
B	59 Diner	American	Casual	$18
B	Pappadeaux	Seafood, Southern	Casual	$45
B-	Escalante's	Tex-Mex	Upmarket	$44
C+	James Coney Island	American	Fast food	$8
D-	Café Express	American	Counter	$16

Upper Kirby Area

A	Pesce	Seafood	Upmarket	$85
A-	Saffron	Moroccan	Casual	$55
A-	The Tasting Room	Pizza	Wine bar	$33
B+	Becks Prime	American, Burgers	Counter	$13
B+	Red Lion Pub	American, British	Bar	$25
B+	Pappasito's	Tex-Mex	Casual	$31
B+	Field of Greens	Light American	Counter	$11
B+	Hobbit Café	American	Casual	$20
B+	Amy's Ice Cream	Sweets	Counter	
B	59 Diner	American	Casual	$18
B	Houston's	New American	Upmarket	$62
B	Turquoise Grill	Turkish	Casual	$22
B	Taco Milagro	Tex-Mex	Counter	$19
B	Pappadeaux	Seafood, Southern	Casual	$45
B	Sonoma Wine Bar	New American, Italian	Wine bar	$37
B	Barnaby's Café	American	Casual	$20
B	Avalon Drug Company	American	Casual	$16
B-	Churrascos	Latin American, Steakhouse	Upmarket	$63
B-	Le Peep	American	Casual	$14
B-	Pappas Seafood	Seafood	Casual	$48
B-	Mezzanine Lounge	American, Burgers	Bar	$16
C+	Blue Fish House	Seafood, Pan-Asian	Upmarket	$19
C+	Carrabba's Italian Grill	Italian-American, Pizza	Casual	$52
C+	James Coney Island	American	Fast food	$8
C+	Madras Pavilion	Indian, Vegetarian	Casual	$20
C+	Star Pizza	Pizza	Casual	$14
C+	Khyber	Indian	Casual	$26
C+	Taco Cabana	Tex-Mex	Fast food	$8
C+	Whataburger	Burgers	Fast food	$8
C	Sushi King	Japanese	Casual	$39
C	Mai Thai	Thai	Casual	$23
C	Freebirds World Burrito	Tex-Mex	Fast food	$8
C	Café Red Onion	Latin American	Casual	$37
C	The Dessert Gallery	Sweets	Counter	
C-	Ziggy's Healthy Grill	American	Counter	$16
C-	Miyako	Japanese	Upmarket	$38
C-	Zake Sushi Lounge	Japanese	Casual	$43
C-	The Brownstone	American	Upmarket	$84
C-	House of Pies	American, Sweets	Casual	$11
D	Palazzo's	Italian-American	Casual	$34
D	Ninfa's	Tex-Mex	Casual	$21

Upper Kirby Area *continued*

D	Ruchi's Taquería	Tex-Mex	Casual	$16
D-	Buca di Beppo	Italian-American	Casual	$30
D-	Café Express	American	Counter	$16
F	Café Japon	Japanese	Casual	$27
NR	Central Market	Light American	Grocery	
NR	Whole Foods	Light American	Grocery	

Washington Area

A	Catalan	New American	Upmarket	$70
A-	El Rey Taquería	Mexican, Cuban	Counter	$11
A-	El Tiempo Cantina	Tex-Mex	Casual	$58
B	Taquería Los Charros	Mexican, Tex-Mex	Casual	$8
B-	Max's Wine Dive	New American	Wine bar	$46
B-	Cova	New American	Wine bar	$47
B-	Otto's BBQ & Burgers	Burgers	Counter	$11
C+	Little Hip's Diner	American	Casual	$10
C+	Star Pizza	Pizza	Casual	$14
C	Laredo Taquería	Mexican	Counter	$8
C	Dharma Café	New American	Casual	$38
C	The Daily Grind	Light American	Café	$8
C-	Mak Chin's	Pan-Asian	Casual	$25
D	Molina's	Tex-Mex	Casual	$30

Webster

A-	Lupe Tortilla	Tex-Mex	Casual	$26
C	Freebirds World Burrito	Tex-Mex	Fast food	$8

West Houston

A	Le Mistral	French	Upmarket	$74
A	Peking Cusine	Chinese	Casual	$13
A	Rioja	Spanish	Upmarket	$62
A-	Sam's Deli Diner	American	Counter	$9
A-	Pollo Riko	Latin American	Fast food	$7
A-	Lupe Tortilla	Tex-Mex	Casual	$26
A-	Frenchy's Chicken	Southern	Counter	$8
A-	El Pupusodromo	Salvadoran	Casual	$12
A-	Lynn's Steakhouse	Steakhouse	Upmarket	$80
B+	Becks Prime	American, Burgers	Counter	$13
B+	Pappasito's	Tex-Mex	Casual	$31
B	Sushi Jin	Japanese	Casual	$44
B	Los Guanacos	Salvadoran	Casual	$10
B	Finger Licking Bukateria	Nigerian	Casual	$14
B	Phô Saigon	Vietnamese	Casual	$14
B	Pavani Indian Cuisine	Indian	Casual	$16
B	Pappadeaux	Seafood, Southern	Casual	$45
B	Café Caspian	Middle Eastern	Casual	$19
B	Rudi Lechner's	German	Casual	$31
B	Alamo Drafthouse	American	Movie theater	$22
B-	Churrascos	Latin American, Steakhouse	Upmarket	$63
B-	Fadi's Mediterranean	Middle Eastern	Counter	$15
B-	Nit Noi Thai	Thai	Casual	$33
B-	Berryhill Baja Grill	Tex-Mex	Counter	$12
C+	Carrabba's Italian Grill	Italian-American, Pizza	Casual	$52
C+	La Tapatía Taquería	Mexican, Tex-Mex	Casual	$12
C+	James Coney Island	American	Fast food	$8
C+	Nit Noi Café	Thai	Casual	$13
C+	Yo Mama's Soul Food	Southern	Casual	$22

West Houston *continued*

C	Cantina Laredo	Tex-Mex	Upmarket	$44
C	Buffalo Wild Wings	American	Bar	$22
C	Café Red Onion	Latin American	Casual	$37
C	Bistro Le Cep	French	Upmarket	$42
C	Sylvia's Enchilada Kitchen	Tex-Mex	Casual	$18
C	López	Tex-Mex	Casual	$19
C-	Hungry's	Light American	Casual	$18
C-	PF Chang's	Pan-Asian, Chinese	Upmarket	$41
C-	Pappas Bar-B-Q	Barbecue	Counter	$12
C-	Lee's Sandwiches	Vietnamese	Fast food	$5
D	Palazzo's	Italian-American	Casual	$34
D	Collina's Italian Café	Italian-American, Pizza	Casual	$34
D	Ninfa's	Tex-Mex	Casual	$21

West U

B	Paulie's	Light American	Counter	$15
B-	Antica Osteria	Italian-American	Upmarket	$67
C	The Buffalo Grille	American	Counter	$11
C-	Pronto Cucinino	Italian-American	Counter	$15
D-	Cleburne Cafeteria	Southern	Counter	$17
NR	Whole Foods	Light American	Grocery	

Westchase

A	Café Pita +	Bosnian	Casual	$17
A	Doneraki	Tex-Mex	Casual	$30
A-	Café Malay	Malaysian	Casual	$15
B+	Becks Prime	American, Burgers	Counter	$13
B+	Kaneyama	Japanese	Casual	$33
B	Phô Saigon	Vietnamese	Casual	$14
B-	Blue Nile Ethiopian	Ethiopian	Casual	$25
B-	Le Peep	American	Casual	$14
C+	La Tapatía Taquería	Mexican, Tex-Mex	Casual	$12
C	Fogo de Chão	Steakhouse, Brazilian	Upmarket	$77
C	Fuzzy's	Pizza	Counter	$12
C-	YAO Restaurant & Bar	Chinese	Casual	$36
C-	Pappas Bar-B-Q	Barbecue	Counter	$12
C-	Santos	Tex-Mex	Casual	$38
C-	Amazón Grill	Latin American	Counter	$28
D	Molina's	Tex-Mex	Casual	$30
NR	Hong Kong Food Market	Chinese	Grocery	
NR	Whole Foods	Light American	Grocery	

The Woodlands

A-	Lupe Tortilla	Tex-Mex	Casual	$26
B+	Guadalajara	Tex-Mex	Casual	$34
B+	Becks Prime	American, Burgers	Counter	$13
B	Américas	Latin American	Upmarket	$75
B	Taco Milagro	Tex-Mex	Counter	$19
B-	Nit Noi Thai	Thai	Casual	$33
B-	Sam's Boat	Tex-Mex, Seafood	Casual	$15
B-	Baker Street Pub & Grill	American	Bar	$17
C+	Fleming's	Steakhouse	Upmarket	$88
C	Black Walnut Café	Italian-American, Light American	Café	$12
D	Café Adobe	Tex-Mex	Casual	$24
D-	Mi Luna	Spanish	Upmarket	$63
D-	Café Express	American	Counter	$16

By special feature

Ranked by **Total Pleasure Grade** unless otherwise noted.

	Breakfast	*Cuisine*	*Location*	*Type*
A-	Gorditas Aguasctes.	Mexican	Multiple	Casual
A-	Taquería Del Sol	Mexican	S. Houston	Casual
A-	The Breakfast Klub	American, Southern	Midtown	Counter
A-	El Tiempo Cantina	Tex-Mex	Multiple	Casual
A-	El Pupusodromo	Salvadoran	Multiple	Casual
A-	El Rey Taquería	Mexican, Cuban	Multiple	Counter
B+	La Michoacana	Mexican	Multiple	Counter
B+	This Is it Soul Food	Southern	Midtown	Counter
B	59 Diner	American	Multiple	Casual
B	Taquería Cancún	Tex-Mex	Multiple	Casual
B	Tacos A Go-Go	Tex-Mex	Midtown	Counter
B	Stir-It-Up Coffee House	Light American, Jamaican	Midtown	Café
B	Taquería Los Charros	Mexican, Tex-Mex	Multiple	Casual
B	Avalon Drug Company	American	Upper Kirby	Casual
B	La Guadalupana	Mexican	Montrose	Casual
B-	Onion Creek	American	Heights	Bar
B-	El Hidalguense	Mexican	Multiple	Casual
B-	Taquería Arandas	Mexican	Multiple	Casual
B-	Daily Review Café	American	Montrose	Casual
B-	Inversion Coffee House	Light American	Montrose	Café
B-	Le Peep	American	Multiple	Casual
B-	Thierry André Tellier	French, Sweets	Multiple	Café
B-	Chacho's	Tex-Mex	Galleria	Casual
B-	La Mexicana	Tex-Mex	Montrose	Casual
B-	Kraftsmen Bakery	Light American	Montrose	Casual
B-	Houston Tamales Factory	Mexican, Tex-Mex	Heights	Casual
C+	Mama's Café	American, Tex-Mex	Galleria	Casual
C+	Lankford Grocery	Burgers	Midtown	Casual
C+	Little Hip's Diner	American	Washington	Casual
C+	La Tapatía Taquería	Mexican, Tex-Mex	Multiple	Casual
C+	Bibas (One's a Meal)	Greek, American	Midtown	Casual
C+	Crescent City Beignets	Southern	Greenway	Fast food
C+	Empire Café	Light American	Montrose	Counter
C+	Baby Barnaby's	American	Montrose	Casual
C+	El Pueblito	Tex-Mex	Montrose	Casual
C+	Taco Cabana	Tex-Mex	Multiple	Fast food
C+	Dry Creek Café	American, Burgers	Heights	Casual
C+	Whataburger	Burgers	Multiple	Fast food
C+	Kenny & Ziggy's	Jewish Deli	Galleria	Casual
C+	Tommy's Sandwiches	American	Medical	Counter
C	Black Walnut Café	Light American	Multiple	Café
C	Cliff's Hamburgers	Burgers	Multiple	Casual
C	The Buffalo Grille	American	Multiple	Counter
C	11th Street Café	American	Heights	Casual
C	The Daily Grind	Light American	Washington	Café
C	Laredo Taquería	Mexican	Washington	Counter

Breakfast *continued*

C-	Ziggy's Healthy Grill	American	Multiple	Counter
C-	Craiganale's Italian Deli	Light American	Downtown	Counter
C-	House of Pies	American, Sweets	Multiple	Casual
D	Katz's Deli	Jewish Deli	Montrose	Casual
D	Ruchi's Taquería	Tex-Mex	Multiple	Casual
D	Ninfa's	Tex-Mex	Multiple	Casual
D-	Brasil	Light American	Montrose	Counter
NR	Whole Foods	Light American	Multiple	Grocery
NR	Central Market	Light American	Upper Kirby	Grocery

Brunch

A	Indika	Indian	Montrose	Upmarket
A	Catalan	New American	Washington	Upmarket
A	Le Mistral	French	W. Houston	Upmarket
A	17	New American	Downtown	Upmarket
A	Gravitas	New American	Midtown	Upmarket
A	Rioja	Spanish	W. Houston	Upmarket
A	Doneraki	Tex-Mex	Multiple	Casual
A-	Gorditas Aguasctes.	Mexican	Multiple	Casual
A-	Shade	New American	Heights	Upmarket
B+	Guadalajara	Tex-Mex	Multiple	Casual
B+	1308 Cantina	Tex-Mex	Montrose	Casual
B+	Backstreet Café	New American	River Oaks	Upmarket
B+	Hobbit Café	American	Upper Kirby	Casual
B+	Hugo's	Mexican	Montrose	Upmarket
B+	Cyclone Anaya's	Tex-Mex	Multiple	Casual
B	Turquoise Grill	Turkish	Upper Kirby	Casual
B	North China Restaurant	Chinese	Memorial	Casual
B	McCormick & Schmick	Seafood, American	Memorial	Upmarket
B	Benjy's	Southwestern	Rice Area	Upmarket
B-	Baba Yega	American	Montrose	Casual
B-	Brennan's of Houston	Southern	Midtown	Upmarket
B-	Churrascos	Latin American	Multiple	Upmarket
B-	Prego	Italian-American	Rice Area	Upmarket
B-	Max's Wine Dive	New American	Washington	Wine bar
B-	Daily Review Café	American	Montrose	Casual
B-	Escalante's	Tex-Mex	Multiple	Upmarket
B-	Le Peep	American	Multiple	Casual
B-	The Mason Jar	American	Memorial	Casual
B-	Masraff's	New American	Memorial	Upmarket
B-	Farrago	New American	Midtown	Casual
B-	Alexander the Great	Greek	Galleria	Upmarket
B-	Arcodoro	Italian	Galleria	Upmarket
B-	Bistro Lancaster	American	Downtown	Upmarket
C+	Quattro	Italian, Steakhouse	Downtown	Upmarket
C+	La Strada	New American	Montrose	Upmarket
C+	Ouisie's Table	Southern	River Oaks	Upmarket
C+	Empire Café	Light American	Montrose	Counter
C+	Kenny & Ziggy's	Jewish Deli	Galleria	Casual
C	Cantina Laredo	Tex-Mex	W. Houston	Upmarket
C	Ocean Palace	Seafood, Chinese	Chinatown	Casual
C	Nelore Churrascaria	Steakhouse, Brazilian	Montrose	Upmarket
C	Pappy's Café	American	Memorial	Casual
C	Bistro Le Cep	French	W. Houston	Upmarket
C	Dharma Café	New American	Washington	Casual

Brunch *continued*

C-	Grand Lux Café	American	Galleria	Casual
C-	Hungry's	Light American	Multiple	Casual
C-	Ziggy's Healthy Grill	American	Multiple	Counter
C-	Las Alamedas	Tex-Mex	Spring Branch	Upmarket
C-	Mak Chin's	Pan-Asian	Washington	Casual
C-	Michelangelo's	Italian-American	Montrose	Casual
D	Tila's	Tex-Mex	River Oaks	Upmarket
D	Monarch	New American	Hermann Park	Upmarket
D	Sorrento	Italian-American	Montrose	Upmarket
D	Ruggles Grill	New American	Multiple	Upmarket
D	Palazzo's	Italian-American	Multiple	Casual
D-	Mi Luna	Spanish	Multiple	Upmarket
D-	Brasil	Light American	Montrose	Counter

BYO

A	Café Pita +	Bosnian	Westchase	Casual	$17
A-	Vieng Thai	Thai	Spring Branch	Casual	$24
A-	Café Malay	Malaysian	Westchase	Casual	$15
B+	Istanbul Grill	Turkish	Rice Area	Casual	$51
B+	Garson	Middle Eastern	Hillcroft Area	Casual	$29
B+	Field of Greens	Light American	Upper Kirby	Counter	$11
B	La Vista	New American	Multiple	Upmarket	$35
B	Just Dinner	American	Montrose	Casual	$30
B	La Guadalupana	Mexican	Montrose	Casual	$11
B-	Jenni's Noodle House	Pan-Asian	Multiple	Casual	$14
C+	Kanomwan	Thai	E. Houston	Casual	$19
C+	Little Hip's Diner	American	Washington	Casual	$10
C+	Dry Creek Café	American, Burgers	Heights	Casual	$15
C	DNR European Café	Middle Eastern	Montrose	Counter	$11
C	Aladdin Mediterranean	Middle Eastern	Montrose	Counter	$8
D	Ruggles Café	Light American	Rice Area	Casual	$17
D	Collina's Italian Café	Italian-American, Pizza	Multiple	Casual	$34

Delivery

A	Doneraki	Tex-Mex	Multiple	Casual	$30
A-	El Tiempo Cantina	Tex-Mex	Multiple	Casual	$58
A-	Café Malay	Malaysian	Westchase	Casual	$15
B+	Guadalajara	Tex-Mex	Multiple	Casual	$34
B+	1308 Cantina	Tex-Mex	Montrose	Casual	$58
B+	Pappasito's	Tex-Mex	Multiple	Casual	$31
B	Irma's	Tex-Mex	Downtown	Casual	$26
B	Finger Licking Bukateria	Nigerian	W. Houston	Casual	$14
B	Café Caspian	Middle Eastern	W. Houston	Casual	$19
B	Latina Café	Cuban	Montrose	Casual	$22
B	Rudi Lechner's	German	SW Houston	Casual	$31
B-	Fadi's Mediterranean	Middle Eastern	Multiple	Counter	$15
B-	La Mexicana	Tex-Mex	Montrose	Casual	$27
B-	Demeris Barbecue	Barbecue	Multiple	Casual	$10
C+	Barry's Pizza	Italian-American, Pizza	Multiple	Casual	$15
C+	Shiva	Indian	Rice Area	Casual	$27
C+	Pizzitola's Bar-B-Que	Barbecue	Heights	Casual	$15
C+	James Coney Island	American	Multiple	Fast food	$8
C+	Star Pizza	Pizza	Multiple	Casual	$14
C+	Hollywood Vietnamese	Vietnamese, French	Montrose	Casual	$24
C+	Late Night Pie	Pizza	Midtown	Counter	$20
C+	Kenny & Ziggy's	Jewish Deli	Galleria	Casual	$20

Delivery *continued*

C+	Frank's Pizza	Pizza	Downtown	Counter	$15
C	Cliff's Hamburgers	Burgers	Multiple	Casual	$8
C	DNR European Café	Middle Eastern	Montrose	Counter	$11
C	Josephine's	Italian	Downtown	Counter	$17
C	Fuzzy's	Pizza	Multiple	Counter	$12
C	India's Restaurant	Indian	Galleria	Casual	$20
C	Lucky Burger	Burgers	Montrose	Counter	$6
C	11th Street Café	American	Heights	Casual	$12
C	Ponzo's	Italian-American, Pizza	Midtown	Casual	$14
C-	Hungry's	Light American	Multiple	Casual	$18
C-	Craiganale's Italian Deli	Light American	Downtown	Counter	$11
C-	Mr. Gatti's and Gattitown	Pizza	Multiple	Casual	$12
C-	Mama Ninfa's	Tex-Mex	Downtown	Casual	$17
C-	Prince's Hamburgers	American, Burgers	Multiple	Counter	$9
C-	Goode Co. Bar-B-Q	Barbecue	Rice Area	Counter	$14
D	Collina's Italian Café	Italian-American, Pizza	Multiple	Casual	$34
D	Palazzo's	Italian-American	Multiple	Casual	$34
D-	Yildizlar	Middle Eastern	Montrose	Counter	$11

Good date places

A+	Da Marco	Italian, Pizza	Montrose	Upmarket	$77
A	Indika	Indian	Montrose	Upmarket	$65
A	Dolce Vita	Italian, Pizza	Montrose	Casual	$38
A	Vic & Anthony's	Steakhouse	Downtown	Upmarket	$94
A	17	New American	Downtown	Upmarket	$100
A	TopWater Grill	Seafood, American	San Leon	Casual	$31
A	Reef	New American	Midtown	Upmarket	$66
A	Gravitas	New American	Midtown	Upmarket	$72
A	Pesce	Seafood	Upper Kirby	Upmarket	$85
A	Ibiza	New American	Midtown	Upmarket	$72
A	Rioja	Spanish	W. Houston	Upmarket	$62
A-	t'afia	New American	Midtown	Upmarket	$65
A-	Shade	New American	Heights	Upmarket	$49
A-	Café Rabelais	French	Rice Area	Upmarket	$55
A-	Fung's Kitchen	Chinese, Seafood	Chinatown	Upmarket	$46
A-	El Tiempo Cantina	Tex-Mex	Multiple	Casual	$58
A-	London Sizzler	Indian	Hillcroft Area	Casual	$32
A-	Frenchy's Chicken	Southern	Multiple	Counter	$8
A-	Café Malay	Malaysian	Westchase	Casual	$15
A-	The Tasting Room	Pizza	Multiple	Wine bar	$33
A-	Lynn's Steakhouse	Steakhouse	W. Houston	Upmarket	$80
A-	Saffron	Moroccan	Upper Kirby	Casual	$55
A-	Pappasito's	Tex-Mex	Multiple	Casual	$31
B+	Sage 400	Japanese	Galleria	Casual	$45
B+	1308 Cantina	Tex-Mex	Montrose	Casual	$58
B+	Red Lion Pub	American, British	Upper Kirby	Bar	$25
B+	Tony Mandola's	Seafood	River Oaks	Upmarket	$63
B+	Backstreet Café	New American	River Oaks	Upmarket	$71
B+	Brasserie Max & Julie	French	Montrose	Upmarket	$71
B+	Mockingbird Bistro	New American	River Oaks	Upmarket	$80
B+	Noé	New American	Galleria	Upmarket	$100
B+	Chuy's	Tex-Mex	River Oaks	Casual	$30
B+	Chapultepec	Tex-Mex	Montrose	Casual	$15
B+	13 Celsius	Italian	Midtown	Wine bar	$32
B+	Paradise Café	Chinese	Chinatown	Casual	$12
B+	Hobbit Café	American	Upper Kirby	Casual	$20
B+	Hugo's	Mexican	Montrose	Upmarket	$53

Good date places *continued*

B+	Cyclone Anaya's	Tex-Mex	Multiple	Casual	$35
B+	Amy's Ice Cream	Sweets	Upper Kirby	Counter	
B+	Jungle Café	Sweets	Chinatown	Counter	
B	Café Annie	Southwestern	Galleria	Upmarket	$106
B	Laurier Café and Wine	New American	Greenway	Upmarket	$44
B	SoVino	New American	Midtown	Wine bar	$44
B	Turquoise Grill	Turkish	Upper Kirby	Casual	$22
B	Rudyard's British Pub	American, Burgers	Montrose	Bar	$18
B	Sonoma Wine Bar	New American, Italian	Upper Kirby	Wine bar	$37
B	Just Dinner	American	Montrose	Casual	$30
B	Lemongrass Café	Pan-Asian	Bellaire	Casual	$25
B	Alamo Drafthouse	American	Multiple	Cinema	$22
B	Américas	Latin American	Multiple	Upmarket	$75
B	Benjy's	Southwestern	Rice Area	Upmarket	$54
B	Café Lili	Middle Eastern	Galleria	Casual	$23
B-	Antica Osteria	Italian-American	West U	Upmarket	$67
B-	Brennan's of Houston	Southern	Midtown	Upmarket	$105
B-	Mark's	New American	Montrose	Upmarket	$112
B-	Osaka	Japanese	Montrose	Casual	$42
B-	Prego	Italian-American	Rice Area	Upmarket	$57
B-	Farrago	New American	Midtown	Casual	$38
B-	Armandos	Tex-Mex	River Oaks	Upmarket	$64
B-	Cova	New American	Multiple	Wine bar	$47
B-	El Mesón	Spanish, Cuban, Tex-Mex	Rice Area	Upmarket	$42
B-	Blue Nile Ethiopian	Ethiopian	Westchase	Casual	$25
B-	Daily Review Café	American	Montrose	Casual	$31
B-	Escalante's	Tex-Mex	Multiple	Upmarket	$44
B-	Nit Noi Thai	Thai	Multiple	Casual	$33
B-	Café Montrose	Belgian	Montrose	Casual	$43
B-	Armadillo Palace	American, Barbecue	Rice Area	Bar	$22
B-	Chacho's	Tex-Mex	Galleria	Casual	$19
B-	Swirll Italian Yogurt	Sweets	Rice Area	Counter	
B-	Arcodoro	Italian	Galleria	Upmarket	$75
B-	Azuma and Azumi	Japanese	Multiple	Casual	$55
C+	Buon Appetito	Italian-American	Medical	Casual	$34
C+	Yatra Brasserie	Indian	Downtown	Casual	$42
C+	Uptown Sushi	Japanese	Galleria	Upmarket	$44
C+	Seoul Garden	Korean	Spring Branch	Casual	$28
C+	Khyber	Indian	Upper Kirby	Casual	$26
C+	The Golden Room	Thai	Montrose	Casual	$24
C+	Empire Café	Light American	Montrose	Counter	$14
C+	Nit Noi Café	Thai	Multiple	Casual	$13
C+	The Flying Saucer	American	Downtown	Bar	$18
C+	El Pueblito	Tex-Mex	Montrose	Casual	$20
C+	Paciugo Gelateria	Sweets	Greenway	Counter	
C+	Café Le Jadeite	Pan-Asian, New American	River Oaks	Upmarket	$73
C	Mai Thai	Thai	Upper Kirby	Casual	$23
C	Cava Bistro	New American	Downtown	Upmarket	$54
C	Bistro Le Cep	French	W. Houston	Upmarket	$42
C	The Dessert Gallery	Sweets	Multiple	Counter	
C-	RA Sushi	Japanese	River Oaks	Upmarket	$43
C-	Mak Chin's	Pan-Asian	Washington	Casual	$25
C-	Tokyohana	Japanese	Multiple	Casual	$40
C-	Black Labrador Pub	British	Montrose	Bar	$26
D	Tila's	Tex-Mex	River Oaks	Upmarket	$50

Kid-friendly

A	Udipi Café	Indian, Vegetarian	Hillcroft Area	Casual	$8
A	Himalaya	Pakistani	Hillcroft Area	Casual	$14
A	Doneraki	Tex-Mex	Multiple	Casual	$30
A	Rioja	Spanish	W. Houston	Upmarket	$62
A-	The Breakfast Klub	American, Southern	Midtown	Counter	$11
A-	Shanghai Restaurant	Chinese	Chinatown	Casual	$12
A-	Sam's Deli Diner	American	W. Houston	Counter	$9
A-	Lupe Tortilla	Tex-Mex	Multiple	Casual	$26
A-	Luling City Market	Barbecue	Galleria	Counter	$15
A-	Pollo Riko	Latin American	Multiple	Fast food	$7
A-	Café Malay	Malaysian	Westchase	Casual	$15
A-	Sinh Sinh	Chinese, Seafood	Chinatown	Casual	$36
A-	Don Café	Vietnamese	Chinatown	Counter	$5
B+	Guadalajara	Tex-Mex	Multiple	Casual	$34
B+	Tookie's Hamburgers	Burgers	Seabrook	Casual	$12
B+	Becks Prime	American, Burgers	Multiple	Counter	$13
B+	Chuy's	Tex-Mex	River Oaks	Casual	$30
B+	Pappasito's	Tex-Mex	Multiple	Casual	$31
B+	Field of Greens	Light American	Upper Kirby	Counter	$11
B+	Goode Co. Taquería	Tex-Mex, Burgers	Multiple	Counter	$16
B+	Paradise Café	Chinese	Chinatown	Casual	$12
B+	Hobbit Café	American	Upper Kirby	Casual	$20
B+	Amy's Ice Cream	Sweets	Upper Kirby	Counter	
B	59 Diner	American	Multiple	Casual	$18
B	Taco Milagro	Tex-Mex	Multiple	Counter	$19
B	Irma's	Tex-Mex	Downtown	Casual	$26
B	Tan Tan	Chinese	Chinatown	Casual	$17
B	Pappadeaux	Seafood, Southern	Multiple	Casual	$45
B	Barnaby's Café	American	Multiple	Casual	$20
B	Bodard Bistro	Vietnamese	Chinatown	Casual	$9
B	Mission Burrito	Tex-Mex	Multiple	Counter	$9
B	Alamo Drafthouse	American	Multiple	Cinema	$22
B	Pappas Burgers	Burgers	Multiple	Counter	$16
B	Café Lili	Middle Eastern	Galleria	Casual	$23
B-	Baba Yega	American	Montrose	Casual	$14
B-	Barbecue Inn	American, Barbecue	N. Houston	Counter	$18
B-	San Dong	Chinese	Chinatown	Counter	$9
B-	Red & White Wine Bistro	American	Downtown	Upmarket	$74
B-	Fadi's Mediterranean	Middle Eastern	Multiple	Counter	$15
B-	Otto's BBQ & Burgers	Burgers	Multiple	Counter	$11
B-	Connie's Seafood Mkt.	Seafood, Mexican	Multiple	Counter	$24
B-	The Mason Jar	American	Memorial	Casual	$24
B-	La Mexicana	Tex-Mex	Montrose	Casual	$27
B-	Treebeards	Southern	Downtown	Counter	$12
B-	Swirll Italian Yogurt	Sweets	Rice Area	Counter	
B-	Pollo Campero	Latin American, Southern	Multiple	Fast food	$9
B-	Alexander the Great	Greek	Galleria	Upmarket	$63
B-	Berryhill Baja Grill	Tex-Mex	Multiple	Counter	$12
C+	Brown Bag Deli	Light American	Multiple	Counter	$7
C+	Lankford Grocery	Burgers	Midtown	Casual	$12
C+	Carrabba's Italian Grill	Italian-American, Pizza	Multiple	Casual	$52
C+	FuFu Café	Chinese	Chinatown	Casual	$10
C+	Kim Son	Vietnamese, Chinese	Multiple	Casual	$32
C+	Crescent City Beignets	Southern	Greenway	Fast food	$12
C+	Freeway Hamburgers	Burgers	Memorial	Counter	$9

Kid-friendly *continued*

C+	Star Snow Ice	Chinese	Chinatown	Counter	$7
C+	James Coney Island	American	Multiple	Fast food	$8
C+	Star Pizza	Pizza	Multiple	Casual	$14
C+	Big Bowl	Chinese	Chinatown	Casual	$6
C+	Baby Barnaby's	American	Montrose	Casual	$10
C+	Dry Creek Café	American, Burgers	Heights	Casual	$15
C+	Whataburger	Burgers	Multiple	Fast food	$8
C+	Paciugo Gelateria	Sweets	Greenway	Counter	
C+	Yia Yia Mary's	Greek	Galleria	Counter	$20
C	Fogo de Chão	Steakhouse, Brazilian	W. Houston	Upmarket	$77
C	Cliff's Hamburgers	Burgers	Multiple	Casual	$8
C	DNR European Café	Middle Eastern	Montrose	Counter	$11
C	The County Line	Barbecue	N. Houston	Casual	$29
C	Josephine's	Italian	Downtown	Counter	$17
C	Freebirds World Burrito	Tex-Mex	Multiple	Fast food	$8
C	Nino's	Italian-American	Montrose	Upmarket	$57
C	Vincent's	Italian-American	Montrose	Upmarket	$45
C	Fuzzy's	Pizza	Multiple	Counter	$12
C	Taste of Texas	Steakhouse	Memorial	Upmarket	$54
C	Nelore Churrascaria	Steakhouse, Brazilian	Montrose	Upmarket	$58
C	Pappy's Café	American	Memorial	Casual	$16
C	The Buffalo Grille	American	Multiple	Counter	$11
C	López	Tex-Mex	W. Houston	Casual	$19
C	The Dessert Gallery	Sweets	Multiple	Counter	
C	Ponzo's	Italian-American, Pizza	Midtown	Casual	$14
C-	Grand Lux Café	American	Galleria	Casual	$28
C-	Pronto Cucinino	Italian-American	Multiple	Counter	$15
C-	Santos	Tex-Mex	Westchase	Casual	$38
C-	PF Chang's	Pan-Asian, Chinese	Multiple	Upmarket	$41
C-	Las Alamedas	Tex-Mex	Spring Branch	Upmarket	$42
C-	Cadillac Bar	Tex-Mex	Heights	Casual	$28
C-	Mr. Gatti's and Gattitown	Pizza	Multiple	Casual	$12
C-	Pappas Bar-B-Q	Barbecue	Multiple	Counter	$12
C-	Ciro's Italian Grill	Italian-American	Memorial	Casual	$35
C-	Tokyohana	Japanese	Multiple	Casual	$40
C-	Mama Ninfa's	Tex-Mex	Downtown	Casual	$17
C-	Prince's Hamburgers	American, Burgers	Multiple	Counter	$9
C-	Goode Co. Bar-B-Q	Barbecue	Rice Area	Counter	$14
C-	Lee's Sandwiches	Vietnamese	Multiple	Fast food	$5
C-	Charlie's Hamburger	Burgers	Multiple	Counter	$9
C-	House of Pies	American, Sweets	Multiple	Casual	$11
C-	Amazón Grill	Latin American	Multiple	Counter	$28
D	Molina's	Tex-Mex	Multiple	Casual	$30
D	Katz's Deli	Jewish Deli	Montrose	Casual	$20
D	PK's Blue Water Grill	Seafood, Southern	Memorial	Casual	$44
D	Ninfa's	Tex-Mex	Multiple	Casual	$21
D-	Aquarium	Seafood, American	Downtown	Upmarket	$30
D-	Buca di Beppo	Italian-American	Upper Kirby	Casual	$30
D-	Café Express	American	Multiple	Counter	$16
NR	Candylicious	Sweets	Multiple	Grocery	
NR	The Chocolate Bar	Sweets	Montrose	Grocery	
NR	Central Market	Light American	Upper Kirby	Grocery	
NR	Whole Foods	Light American	Multiple	Grocery	

Outdoor dining *continued*

B	Smith & Wollensky	Steakhouse	River Oaks	Upmarket	$91
B	La Guadalupana	Mexican	Montrose	Casual	$11
B-	Kubo's	Japanese	Rice Area	Casual	$44
B-	Brenner's	Steakhouse	Memorial	Upmarket	$90
B-	Onion Creek	American	Heights	Bar	$18
B-	Baba Yega	American	Montrose	Casual	$14
B-	Brennan's of Houston	Southern	Midtown	Upmarket	$105
B-	Tony Thai	Thai	Chinatown	Casual	$28
B-	Churrascos	Latin American	Multiple	Upmarket	$63
B-	Shawarma King	Middle Eastern	Galleria	Counter	$8
B-	Antica Osteria	Italian-American	West U	Upmarket	$67
B-	Max's Wine Dive	New American	Washington	Wine bar	$46
B-	Cova	New American	Multiple	Wine bar	$47
B-	Daily Review Café	American	Montrose	Casual	$31
B-	Teala's	Tex-Mex	Montrose	Casual	$33
B-	Escalante's	Tex-Mex	Multiple	Upmarket	$44
B-	Nit Noi Thai	Thai	Multiple	Casual	$33
B-	Last Concert Café	Tex-Mex	Downtown	Casual	$16
B-	Otto's BBQ & Burgers	Burgers	Multiple	Counter	$11
B-	Sam's Boat	Tex-Mex, Seafood	Multiple	Casual	$15
B-	Taft St. Coffee House	Light American	Midtown	Café	$7
B-	Le Peep	American	Multiple	Casual	$14
B-	Café Montrose	Belgian	Montrose	Casual	$43
B-	Christian's Tailgate	Burgers	Multiple	Bar	$9
B-	Armadillo Palace	American, Barbecue	Rice Area	Bar	$22
B-	Bombay Brasserie	Indian	Rice Area	Casual	$33
B-	Chacho's	Tex-Mex	Galleria	Casual	$19
B-	La Mexicana	Tex-Mex	Montrose	Casual	$27
B-	Treebeards	Southern	Downtown	Counter	$12
B-	Swirll Italian Yogurt	Sweets	Rice Area	Counter	
B-	Kraftsmen Bakery	Light American	Montrose	Casual	$12
B-	Masraff's	New American	Memorial	Upmarket	$76
B-	Alexander the Great	Greek	Galleria	Upmarket	$63
B-	Farrago	New American	Midtown	Casual	$38
B-	Arcodoro	Italian	Galleria	Upmarket	$75
B-	Berryhill Baja Grill	Tex-Mex	Multiple	Counter	$12
B-	Baker Street Pub & Grill	American	Multiple	Bar	$17
C+	Buon Appetito	Italian-American	Medical	Casual	$34
C+	Barry's Pizza	Italian-American, Pizza	Multiple	Casual	$15
C+	Brown Bag Deli	Light American	Multiple	Counter	$7
C+	Mama's Café	American, Tex-Mex	Galleria	Casual	$15
C+	Lankford Grocery	Burgers	Midtown	Casual	$12
C+	Bibas (One's a Meal)	Greek, American	Midtown	Casual	$16
C+	Crescent City Beignets	Southern	Greenway	Fast food	$12
C+	Smokey's Bar-B-Q	Barbecue, Seafood	Multiple	Counter	$9
C+	Shiva	Indian	Rice Area	Casual	$27
C+	La Strada	New American	Montrose	Upmarket	$59
C+	Star Pizza	Pizza	Multiple	Casual	$14
C+	Ouisie's Table	Southern	River Oaks	Upmarket	$61
C+	Tampico Seafood	Seafood, Mexican	Heights	Casual	$26
C+	Empire Café	Light American	Montrose	Counter	$14
C+	Hollywood Vietnamese	Vietnamese, French	Montrose	Casual	$24
C+	The Flying Saucer	American	Downtown	Bar	$18
C+	Bistro Vino	French, American	Montrose	Upmarket	$60
C+	El Pueblito	Tex-Mex	Montrose	Casual	$20
C+	Taco Cabana	Tex-Mex	Multiple	Fast food	$8
C+	Dry Creek Café	American, Burgers	Heights	Casual	$15

Outdoor dining *continued*

C+	Paciugo Gelateria	Sweets	Greenway	Counter	
C+	Fleming's	Steakhouse	Multiple	Upmarket	$88
C+	Yia Yia Mary's	Greek	Galleria	Counter	$20
C+	Vin	New American	Downtown	Upmarket	$86
C+	María Selma	Mexican, Tex-Mex	Montrose	Casual	$32
C	The Fish	Seafood, Japanese	Midtown	Upmarket	$58
C	Black Walnut Café	Light American	Multiple	Café	$12
C	Cliff's Hamburgers	Burgers	Multiple	Casual	$8
C	DNR European Café	Middle Eastern	Montrose	Counter	$11
C	The County Line	Barbecue	N. Houston	Casual	$29
C	Artista	Latin American	Downtown	Upmarket	$69
C	Nino's	Italian-American	Montrose	Upmarket	$57
C	Cava Bistro	New American	Downtown	Upmarket	$54
C	Fuzzy's	Pizza	Multiple	Counter	$12
C	Buffalo Wild Wings	American	Multiple	Bar	$22
C	Bistro Le Cep	French	W. Houston	Upmarket	$42
C	The Buffalo Grille	American	Multiple	Counter	$11
C	11th Street Café	American	Heights	Casual	$12
C	Dharma Café	New American	Washington	Casual	$38
C	The Daily Grind	Light American	Washington	Café	$8
C	Aladdin Mediterranean	Middle Eastern	Montrose	Counter	$8
C	The Dessert Gallery	Sweets	Multiple	Counter	
C	Ponzo's	Italian-American, Pizza	Midtown	Casual	$14
C-	Grand Lux Café	American	Galleria	Casual	$28
C-	Chilos Seafood	Mexican, Seafood	Multiple	Casual	$21
C-	Ziggy's Healthy Grill	American	Multiple	Counter	$16
C-	Glass Wall	New American	Heights	Upmarket	$78
C-	Miyako	Japanese	Multiple	Upmarket	$38
C-	Grappino di Nino	Italian-American	River Oaks	Upmarket	$36
C-	Zake Sushi Lounge	Japanese	Upper Kirby	Casual	$43
C-	La Griglia	Italian-American, Pizza	River Oaks	Upmarket	$60
C-	Craiganale's Italian Deli	Light American	Downtown	Counter	$11
C-	Sambuca	New American	Downtown	Upmarket	$55
C-	Mak Chin's	Pan-Asian	Washington	Casual	$25
C-	Ciro's Italian Grill	Italian-American	Memorial	Casual	$35
C-	Tokyohana	Japanese	Multiple	Casual	$40
C-	D'Amico's	Italian-American	Rice Area	Counter	$18
C-	Mama Ninfa's	Tex-Mex	Downtown	Casual	$17
C-	Black Labrador Pub	British	Montrose	Bar	$26
C-	Thai Sticks	Thai	Montrose	Casual	$38
C-	Goode Co. Bar-B-Q	Barbecue	Rice Area	Counter	$14
C-	Michelangelo's	Italian-American	Montrose	Casual	$52
C-	The Remington	New American	Galleria	Upmarket	$101
C-	Julia's Bistro	Southwestern	Midtown	Upmarket	$60
C-	La Fendée	Middle Eastern	Montrose	Casual	$30
C-	Amazón Grill	Latin American	Multiple	Counter	$28
D	Tila's	Tex-Mex	River Oaks	Upmarket	$50
D	Monarch	New American	Hermann Park	Upmarket	$93
D	Niko Niko's	Greek	Montrose	Counter	$20
D	Molina's	Tex-Mex	Multiple	Casual	$30
D	Katz's Deli	Jewish Deli	Montrose	Casual	$20
D	Ruggles Café	Light American	Rice Area	Casual	$17
D	Collina's Italian Café	Italian-American, Pizza	Multiple	Casual	$34
D	Cabo's Mix-Mex Grille	Tex-Mex	Downtown	Casual	$25
D	Ruchi's Taquería	Tex-Mex	Multiple	Casual	$16
D	Sake Lounge	Japanese	Downtown	Casual	$40
D	PK's Blue Water Grill	Seafood, Southern	Memorial	Casual	$44

Outdoor dining *continued*

D	Café Adobe	Tex-Mex	Multiple	Casual	$24
D-	Kona Grill	American, Pan-Asian	Multiple	Casual	$54
D-	Vietopia	Vietnamese	Greenway	Upmarket	$40
D-	Mi Luna	Spanish	Multiple	Upmarket	$63
D-	Café Express	American	Multiple	Counter	$16
D-	Brasil	Light American	Montrose	Counter	$13
D-	Café Japon	Japanese	Upper Kirby	Casual	$27

WiFi available *free wireless Internet access on premises*

A	17	New American	Downtown	Upmarket	$100
A	Peking Cusine	Chinese	W. Houston	Casual	$13
A-	Shade	New American	Heights	Upmarket	$49
A-	London Sizzler	Indian	Hillcroft Area	Casual	$32
A-	Sinh Sinh	Chinese, Seafood	Chinatown	Casual	$36
B+	1308 Cantina	Tex-Mex	Montrose	Casual	$58
B+	Red Lion Pub	American, British	Upper Kirby	Bar	$25
B+	Brasserie Max & Julie	French	Montrose	Upmarket	$71
B+	Thai Spice	Thai	Multiple	Casual	$11
B	59 Diner	American	Multiple	Casual	$18
B	La Vista	New American	Multiple	Upmarket	$35
B	Reggae Hut	Jamaican	Medical	Counter	$13
B	Rudyard's British Pub	American, Burgers	Montrose	Bar	$18
B	Rudy's Country Store	Barbecue	Spring	Counter	$16
B	Mayuri	Indian	Galleria	Casual	$33
B	Lemongrass Café	Pan-Asian	Bellaire	Casual	$25
B	Rudi Lechner's	German	SW Houston	Casual	$31
B	Stir-It-Up Coffee House	Light American, Jamaican	Midtown	Café	$13
B-	El Hidalguense	Mexican	Multiple	Casual	$37
B-	Prego	Italian-American	Rice Area	Upmarket	$57
B-	Max's Wine Dive	New American	Washington	Wine bar	$46
B-	Jenni's Noodle House	Pan-Asian	Multiple	Casual	$14
B-	Last Concert Café	Tex-Mex	Downtown	Casual	$16
B-	Inversion Coffee House	Light American	Montrose	Café	$9
B-	Taft St. Coffee House	Light American	Midtown	Café	$7
B-	Christian's Tailgate	Burgers	Multiple	Bar	$9
B-	Farrago	New American	Midtown	Casual	$38
B-	Bistro Lancaster	American	Downtown	Upmarket	$70
B-	Chacho's	Tex-Mex	Galleria	Casual	$19
B-	La Mexicana	Tex-Mex	Montrose	Casual	$27
B-	Swirll Italian Yogurt	Sweets	Rice Area	Counter	
B-	Kraftsmen Bakery	Light American	Montrose	Casual	$12
B-	Masraff's	New American	Memorial	Upmarket	$76
B-	Demeris Barbecue	Barbecue	Multiple	Casual	$10
B-	Berryhill Baja Grill	Tex-Mex	Multiple	Counter	$12
B-	Baker Street Pub & Grill	American	Multiple	Bar	$17
C+	Brown Bag Deli	Light American	Multiple	Counter	$7
C+	Yatra Brasserie	Indian	Downtown	Casual	$42
C+	Crescent City Beignets	Southern	Greenway	Fast food	$12
C+	Shiva	Indian	Rice Area	Casual	$27
C+	La Strada	New American	Montrose	Upmarket	$59
C+	The Flying Saucer	American	Downtown	Bar	$18
C+	Quattro	Italian, Steakhouse	Downtown	Upmarket	$95
C+	Frank's Pizza	Pizza	Downtown	Counter	$15
C	The Fish	Seafood, Japanese	Midtown	Upmarket	$58
C	Black Walnut Café	Light American	Multiple	Café	$12
C	DNR European Café	Middle Eastern	Montrose	Counter	$11
C	Artista	Latin American	Downtown	Upmarket	$69

WiFi available *continued*

C	Hong Kong's Café	Chinese	Chinatown	Casual	$7
C	Cava Bistro	New American	Downtown	Upmarket	$54
C	Buffalo Wild Wings	American	Multiple	Bar	$22
C	Willy's Pub	American	Rice Area	Bar	$12
C	The Daily Grind	Light American	Washington	Café	$8
C	The Dessert Gallery	Sweets	Multiple	Counter	
C-	Chilos Seafood	Mexican, Seafood	Multiple	Casual	$21
C-	Julia's Bistro	Southwestern	Midtown	Upmarket	$60
C-	Miyako	Japanese	Multiple	Upmarket	$38
C-	Zake Sushi Lounge	Japanese	Upper Kirby	Casual	$43
C-	La Griglia	Italian-American, Pizza	River Oaks	Upmarket	$60
C-	D'Amico's	Italian-American	Rice Area	Counter	$18
C-	Black Labrador Pub	British	Montrose	Bar	$26
C-	Thai Sticks	Thai	Montrose	Casual	$38
C-	Lee's Sandwiches	Vietnamese	Multiple	Fast food	$5
C-	Amazón Grill	Latin American	Multiple	Counter	$28
D	Monarch	New American	Hermann Park	Upmarket	$93
D	Collina's Italian Café	Italian-American, Pizza	Multiple	Casual	$34
D	Café Adobe	Tex-Mex	Multiple	Casual	$24
D-	Kona Grill	American, Pan-Asian	Multiple	Casual	$54
D-	Vietopia	Vietnamese	Greenway	Upmarket	$40

Wine-friendly restaurants *with good wine lists and low or reasonable markups. Ordered by quality and value of the wine, not of the restaurant overall.*

1	Catalan	New American	Washington	Upmarket	$70
2	Ibiza	New American	Midtown	Upmarket	$72
3	Lynn's Steakhouse	Steakhouse	W. Houston	Upmarket	$80
4	Reef	New American	Midtown	Upmarket	$66
5	Café Rabelais	French	Rice Area	Upmarket	$55
6	13 Celsius	Italian	Midtown	Wine bar	$32
7	Chez Georges	French	Midtown	Upmarket	$75
8	Sonoma Wine Bar	New American, Italian	Upper Kirby	Wine bar	$37
9	Le Mistral	French	W. Houston	Upmarket	$74
10	Rioja	Spanish	W. Houston	Upmarket	$62
11	Cova	New American	Multiple	Wine bar	$47
12	Dolce Vita	Italian, Pizza	Montrose	Casual	$38
13	Da Marco	Italian, Pizza	Montrose	Upmarket	$77
14	Brasserie Max & Julie	French	Montrose	Upmarket	$71
15	La Vista	New American	Multiple	Upmarket	$35
16	SoVino	New American	Midtown	Wine bar	$44
17	Laurier Café and Wine	New American	Greenway	Upmarket	$44
18	The Tasting Room	Pizza	Multiple	Wine bar	$33
19	Shade	New American	Heights	Upmarket	$49

Vegetarian-friendly guide

Rank-ordered lists of places to eat that are **unusually strong in vegetarian options.** This doesn't just mean that there are salads or veggie pastas available; it means that vegetarians will really be happy with the selection at these places.

All vegetarian-friendly establishments

A	Udipi Café	Indian, Vegetarian	Hillcroft Area	Casual	$8
A	Indika	Indian	Montrose	Upmarket	$65
A	Dolce Vita	Italian, Pizza	Montrose	Casual	$38
A	Himalaya	Pakistani	Hillcroft Area	Casual	$14
A	Gravitas	New American	Midtown	Upmarket	$72
A	Peking Cusine	Chinese	W. Houston	Casual	$13
A-	Vieng Thai	Thai	Spring Branch	Casual	$24
A-	Shanghai Restaurant	Chinese	Chinatown	Casual	$12
A-	Fung's Kitchen	Chinese, Seafood	Chinatown	Upmarket	$46
A-	London Sizzler	Indian	Hillcroft Area	Casual	$32
A-	Café Malay	Malaysian	Westchase	Casual	$15
A-	Nam Gang	Korean	Spring Branch	Casual	$23
A-	Saffron	Moroccan	Upper Kirby	Casual	$55
B+	Field of Greens	Light American	Upper Kirby	Counter	$11
B+	Jerusalem Halal Deli	Middle Eastern	Hillcroft Area	Counter	$10
B+	Lucky Pot	Chinese	Chinatown	Casual	$15
B+	Thai Spice	Thai	Multiple	Casual	$11
B+	Noé	New American	Galleria	Upmarket	$100
B+	Hobbit Café	American	Upper Kirby	Casual	$20
B+	Bombay Sweets	Indian, Vegetarian	Hillcroft Area	Counter	$9
B+	Amy's Ice Cream	Sweets	Upper Kirby	Counter	
B+	Jungle Café	Sweets	Chinatown	Counter	
B	Tacos A Go-Go	Tex-Mex	Midtown	Counter	$10
B	Pavani Indian Cuisine	Indian	SW Houston	Casual	$16
B	Cali Sandwich	Vietnamese	Midtown	Counter	$5
B	Abdullah's	Middle Eastern	Hillcroft Area	Casual	$14
B	Taco Milagro	Tex-Mex	Multiple	Counter	$19
B	Mayuri	Indian	Galleria	Casual	$33
B	Lemongrass Café	Pan-Asian	Bellaire	Casual	$25
B	Stir-It-Up Coffee House	Light American, Jamaican	Midtown	Café	$13
B	Tofu Village	Korean	Chinatown	Casual	$18
B	Korea Garden	Korean	Spring Branch	Casual	$32
B	Benjy's	Southwestern	Rice Area	Upmarket	$54
B	Café Lili	Middle Eastern	Galleria	Casual	$23
B-	Baba Yega	American	Montrose	Casual	$14
B-	Tony Thai	Thai	Chinatown	Casual	$28
B-	Prego	Italian-American	Rice Area	Upmarket	$57
B-	Shawarma King	Middle Eastern	Galleria	Counter	$8
B-	Jenni's Noodle House	Pan-Asian	Multiple	Casual	$14
B-	Fadi's Mediterranean	Middle Eastern	Multiple	Counter	$15
B-	Blue Nile Ethiopian	Ethiopian	Westchase	Casual	$25
B-	Daily Review Café	American	Montrose	Casual	$31
B-	Nit Noi Thai	Thai	Multiple	Casual	$33

All vegetarian-friendly establishments *continued*

B-	Last Concert Café	Tex-Mex	Downtown	Casual	$16
B-	Inversion Coffee House	Light American	Montrose	Café	$9
B-	Taft St. Coffee House	Light American	Midtown	Café	$7
B-	Bombay Brasserie	Indian	Rice Area	Casual	$33
B-	Thierry André Tellier	French, Sweets	Multiple	Café	$9
B-	Swirll Italian Yogurt	Sweets	Rice Area	Counter	
B-	Kraftsmen Bakery	Light American	Montrose	Casual	$12
B-	Arcodoro	Italian	Galleria	Upmarket	$75
B-	Bamboo House	Pan-Asian	Montrose	Casual	$23
C+	Yatra Brasserie	Indian	Downtown	Casual	$42
C+	FuFu Café	Chinese	Chinatown	Casual	$10
C+	Kim Son	Vietnamese, Chinese	Multiple	Casual	$32
C+	Shiva	Indian	Rice Area	Casual	$27
C+	Star Snow Ice	Chinese	Chinatown	Counter	$7
C+	Star Pizza	Pizza	Multiple	Casual	$14
C+	Khyber	Indian	Upper Kirby	Casual	$26
C+	Empire Café	Light American	Montrose	Counter	$14
C+	Big Bowl	Chinese	Chinatown	Casual	$6
C+	Madras Pavilion	Indian, Vegetarian	Upper Kirby	Casual	$20
C+	Paciugo Gelateria	Sweets	Greenway	Counter	
C	Mai Thai	Thai	Upper Kirby	Casual	$23
C	Kiran's	Indian	Galleria	Upmarket	$60
C	Freebirds World Burrito	Tex-Mex	Multiple	Fast food	$8
C	The Buffalo Grille	American	Multiple	Counter	$11
C	Dharma Café	New American	Washington	Casual	$38
C	The Daily Grind	Light American	Washington	Café	$8
C	India's Restaurant	Indian	Galleria	Casual	$20
C	Aladdin Mediterranean	Middle Eastern	Montrose	Counter	$8
C	The Dessert Gallery	Sweets	Multiple	Counter	
C-	Julia's Bistro	Southwestern	Midtown	Upmarket	$60
C-	Grand Lux Café	American	Galleria	Casual	$28
C-	Hungry's	Light American	Multiple	Casual	$18
C-	Ziggy's Healthy Grill	American	Multiple	Counter	$16
C-	Grappino di Nino	Italian-American	River Oaks	Upmarket	$36
C-	Mak Chin's	Pan-Asian	Washington	Casual	$25
D	Ruggles Café	Light American	Rice Area	Casual	$17
D-	Yildizlar	Middle Eastern	Montrose	Counter	$11
D-	Café Express	American	Multiple	Counter	$16
D-	Brasil	Light American	Montrose	Counter	$13
NR	Candylicious	Sweets	Multiple	Grocery	
NR	Canino's	Light American	Heights	Grocery	
NR	Central Market	Light American	Upper Kirby	Grocery	
NR	The Chocolate Bar	Sweets	Montrose	Grocery	
NR	Hong Kong Food Market	Chinese	Multiple	Grocery	
NR	Phoenicia	Middle Eastern	W. Houston	Grocery	
NR	Welcome Food Center	Chinese	Chinatown	Grocery	
NR	Whole Foods	Light American	Multiple	Grocery	

Vegetarian-friendly with top food ratings

9.2	Udipi Café	Indian, Vegetarian	Hillcroft Area	Casual	$8
9.2	Himalaya	Pakistani	Hillcroft Area	Casual	$14
9.1	Indika	Indian	Montrose	Upmarket	$65
9.0	Gravitas	New American	Midtown	Upmarket	$72
9.0	Peking Cusine	Chinese	W. Houston	Casual	$13
9.0	Dolce Vita	Italian, Pizza	Montrose	Casual	$38
8.9	Shanghai Restaurant	Chinese	Chinatown	Casual	$12
8.6	Fung's Kitchen	Chinese, Seafood	Chinatown	Upmarket	$46

Vegetarian-friendly with top food ratings *continued*

8.5	Vieng Thai	Thai	Spring Branch	Casual	$24
8.5	Café Malay	Malaysian	Westchase	Casual	$15
8.5	Lucky Pot	Chinese	Chinatown	Casual	$15
8.4	London Sizzler	Indian	Hillcroft Area	Casual	$32
8.4	Saffron	Moroccan	Upper Kirby	Casual	$55
8.2	Field of Greens	Light American	Upper Kirby	Counter	$11
8.1	Nam Gang	Korean	Spring Branch	Casual	$23
8.1	Thai Spice	Thai	Multiple	Casual	$11
8.0	Noé	New American	Galleria	Upmarket	$100
7.8	Bombay Sweets	Indian, Vegetarian	Hillcroft Area	Counter	$9
7.8	Tacos A Go-Go	Tex-Mex	Midtown	Counter	$10
7.8	Pavani Indian Cuisine	Indian	SW Houston	Casual	$16
7.8	Abdullah's	Middle Eastern	Hillcroft Area	Casual	$14
7.7	Cali Sandwich	Vietnamese	Midtown	Counter	$5
7.7	Baba Yega	American	Montrose	Casual	$14
7.6	Jerusalem Halal Deli	Middle Eastern	Hillcroft Area	Counter	$10
7.6	Taco Milagro	Tex-Mex	Multiple	Counter	$19
7.6	Mayuri	Indian	Galleria	Casual	$33
7.6	Tony Thai	Thai	Chinatown	Casual	$28
7.6	Prego	Italian-American	Rice Area	Upmarket	$57
7.5	Hobbit Café	American	Upper Kirby	Casual	$20
7.5	Shawarma King	Middle Eastern	Galleria	Counter	$8
7.5	Kraftsmen Bakery	Light American	Montrose	Casual	$12
7.3	Lemongrass Café	Pan-Asian	Bellaire	Casual	$25
7.3	Benjy's	Southwestern	Rice Area	Upmarket	$54
7.3	Fadi's Mediterranean	Middle Eastern	Multiple	Counter	$15
7.2	Tofu Village	Korean	Chinatown	Casual	$18
7.2	Jenni's Noodle House	Pan-Asian	Multiple	Casual	$14
7.2	Arcodoro	Italian	Galleria	Upmarket	$75
7.1	Blue Nile Ethiopian	Ethiopian	Westchase	Casual	$25
7.1	Daily Review Café	American	Montrose	Casual	$31
7.1	FuFu Café	Chinese	Chinatown	Casual	$10
7.0	Bamboo House	Pan-Asian	Montrose	Casual	$23
7.0	Stir-It-Up Coffee House	Light American, Jamaican	Midtown	Café	$13
7.0	Nit Noi Thai	Thai	Multiple	Casual	$33
7.0	Yatra Brasserie	Indian	Downtown	Casual	$42

Vegetarian-friendly with top feel ratings

9.5	Last Concert Café	Tex-Mex	Downtown	Casual	$16
9.3	Benjy's	Southwestern	Rice Area	Upmarket	$54
9.2	Dolce Vita	Italian, Pizza	Montrose	Casual	$38
9.1	Gravitas	New American	Midtown	Upmarket	$72
9.0	Indika	Indian	Montrose	Upmarket	$65
9.0	London Sizzler	Indian	Hillcroft Area	Casual	$32
8.9	Inversion Coffee House	Light American	Montrose	Café	$9
8.7	Saffron	Moroccan	Upper Kirby	Casual	$55
8.7	Tacos A Go-Go	Tex-Mex	Midtown	Counter	$10
8.7	Dharma Café	New American	Washington	Casual	$38
8.6	Nam Gang	Korean	Spring Branch	Casual	$23
8.6	Amy's Ice Cream	Sweets	Upper Kirby	Counter	
8.5	Bamboo House	Pan-Asian	Montrose	Casual	$23
8.5	Taft St. Coffee House	Light American	Midtown	Café	$7
8.4	Pavani Indian Cuisine	Indian	SW Houston	Casual	$16
8.4	Lemongrass Café	Pan-Asian	Bellaire	Casual	$25
8.3	Noé	New American	Galleria	Upmarket	$100
8.2	Udipi Café	Indian, Vegetarian	Hillcroft Area	Casual	$8
8.1	Stir-It-Up Coffee House	Light American, Jamaican	Midtown	Café	$13

Vegetarian-friendly with top feel ratings *continued*

8.0	Baba Yega	American	Montrose	Casual	$14
8.0	Arcodoro	Italian	Galleria	Upmarket	$75
8.0	Empire Café	Light American	Montrose	Counter	$14
7.9	Taco Milagro	Tex-Mex	Multiple	Counter	$19
7.9	Mak Chin's	Pan-Asian	Washington	Casual	$25
7.8	Fung's Kitchen	Chinese, Seafood	Chinatown	Upmarket	$46
7.8	Jungle Café	Sweets	Chinatown	Counter	
7.7	Korea Garden	Korean	Spring Branch	Casual	$32
7.7	Jenni's Noodle House	Pan-Asian	Multiple	Casual	$14
7.6	Cali Sandwich	Vietnamese	Midtown	Counter	$5
7.6	Prego	Italian-American	Rice Area	Upmarket	$57
7.6	Nit Noi Thai	Thai	Multiple	Casual	$33
7.5	Blue Nile Ethiopian	Ethiopian	Westchase	Casual	$25
7.5	Kraftsmen Bakery	Light American	Montrose	Casual	$12
7.5	Kiran's	Indian	Galleria	Upmarket	$60
7.4	Daily Review Café	American	Montrose	Casual	$31
7.4	Star Snow Ice	Chinese	Chinatown	Counter	$7
7.4	Grand Lux Café	American	Galleria	Casual	$28
7.3	Mayuri	Indian	Galleria	Casual	$33
7.1	Café Malay	Malaysian	Westchase	Casual	$15
7.0	Lucky Pot	Chinese	Chinatown	Casual	$15
7.0	Hobbit Café	American	Upper Kirby	Casual	$20
7.0	Thierry André Tellier	French, Sweets	Multiple	Café	$9
7.0	Kim Son	Vietnamese, Chinese	Multiple	Casual	$32
7.0	Star Pizza	Pizza	Multiple	Casual	$14
7.0	Khyber	Indian	Upper Kirby	Casual	$26
7.0	The Daily Grind	Light American	Washington	Café	$8

Vegetarian-friendly and date-friendly

A	Indika	Indian	Montrose	Upmarket	$65
A	Gravitas	New American	Midtown	Upmarket	$72
A-	Fung's Kitchen	Chinese, Seafood	Chinatown	Upmarket	$46
A-	London Sizzler	Indian	Hillcroft Area	Casual	$32
A-	Café Malay	Malaysian	Westchase	Casual	$15
A-	Saffron	Moroccan	Upper Kirby	Casual	$55
B+	Noé	New American	Galleria	Upmarket	$100
B+	Hobbit Café	American	Upper Kirby	Casual	$20
B+	Amy's Ice Cream	Sweets	Upper Kirby	Counter	
B+	Jungle Café	Sweets	Chinatown	Counter	
B	Lemongrass Café	Pan-Asian	Bellaire	Casual	$25
B	Benjy's	Southwestern	Rice Area	Upmarket	$54
B	Café Lili	Middle Eastern	Galleria	Casual	$23
B-	Prego	Italian-American	Rice Area	Upmarket	$57
B-	Blue Nile Ethiopian	Ethiopian	Westchase	Casual	$25
B-	Daily Review Café	American	Montrose	Casual	$31
B-	Nit Noi Thai	Thai	Multiple	Casual	$33
B-	Swirll Italian Yogurt	Sweets	Rice Area	Counter	
B-	Arcodoro	Italian	Galleria	Upmarket	$75
C+	Yatra Brasserie	Indian	Downtown	Casual	$42
C+	Khyber	Indian	Upper Kirby	Casual	$26
C+	Empire Café	Light American	Montrose	Counter	$14
C+	Paciugo Gelateria	Sweets	Greenway	Counter	
C	Mai Thai	Thai	Upper Kirby	Casual	$23
C	The Dessert Gallery	Sweets	Multiple	Counter	
C-	Mak Chin's	Pan-Asian	Washington	Casual	$25

Vegetarian-friendly and kid-friendly

A	Udipi Café	Indian, Vegetarian	Hillcroft Area	Casual	$8
A	Himalaya	Pakistani	Hillcroft Area	Casual	$14
A-	Shanghai Restaurant	Chinese	Chinatown	Casual	$12
A-	Café Malay	Malaysian	Westchase	Casual	$15
B+	Field of Greens	Light American	Upper Kirby	Counter	$11
B+	Hobbit Café	American	Upper Kirby	Casual	$20
B+	Amy's Ice Cream	Sweets	Upper Kirby	Counter	
B	Taco Milagro	Tex-Mex	Multiple	Counter	$19
B	Café Lili	Middle Eastern	Galleria	Casual	$23
B-	Baba Yega	American	Montrose	Casual	$14
B-	Fadi's Mediterranean	Middle Eastern	Multiple	Counter	$15
B-	Swirll Italian Yogurt	Sweets	Rice Area	Counter	
C+	FuFu Café	Chinese	Chinatown	Casual	$10
C+	Kim Son	Vietnamese, Chinese	Multiple	Casual	$32
C+	Star Snow Ice	Chinese	Chinatown	Counter	$7
C+	Star Pizza	Pizza	Multiple	Casual	$14
C+	Big Bowl	Chinese	Chinatown	Casual	$6
C+	Paciugo Gelateria	Sweets	Greenway	Counter	
C	Freebirds World Burrito	Tex-Mex	Multiple	Fast food	$8
C	The Buffalo Grille	American	Multiple	Counter	$11
C	The Dessert Gallery	Sweets	Multiple	Counter	
C-	Grand Lux Café	American	Galleria	Casual	$28
D-	Café Express	American	Multiple	Counter	$16

Vegetarian-friendly delivery

A-	Café Malay	Malaysian	Westchase	Casual	$15
B-	Fadi's Mediterranean	Middle Eastern	Multiple	Counter	$15
C+	Shiva	Indian	Rice Area	Casual	$27
C+	Star Pizza	Pizza	Multiple	Casual	$14
C	India's Restaurant	Indian	Galleria	Casual	$20
C-	Hungry's	Light American	Multiple	Casual	$18
D-	Yildizlar	Middle Eastern	Montrose	Counter	$11

What's still open?

This is our late-night guide to Houston food. These places claim to stay open as follows; still, we recommend calling first, as the hours sometimes aren't honored on slow nights.

Weekday food after 10pm

A	Himalaya	Pakistani	Hillcroft Area	Casual	$14
A	TopWater Grill	Seafood, American	San Leon	Casual	$31
A	Gravitas	New American	Midtown	Upmarket	$72
A	Nippon	Japanese	Montrose	Casual	$42
A	Doneraki	Tex-Mex	Multiple	Casual	$30
A	Sasaki	Japanese	Galleria	Casual	$51
A	Rioja	Spanish	W. Houston	Upmarket	$62
A-	Gorditas Aguasctes.	Mexican	Multiple	Casual	$9
A-	Taquería Del Sol	Mexican	S. Houston	Casual	$18
A-	QQ Cuisine	Chinese	Chinatown	Casual	$10
A-	Teppay	Japanese	Galleria	Upmarket	$60
A-	Shanghai Restaurant	Chinese	Chinatown	Casual	$12
A-	London Sizzler	Indian	Hillcroft Area	Casual	$32
A-	Frenchy's Chicken	Southern	Multiple	Counter	$8
A-	Bice	Italian	Galleria	Upmarket	$96
A-	Sinh Sinh	Chinese, Seafood	Chinatown	Casual	$36
A-	The Tasting Room	Pizza	Multiple	Wine bar	$33
A-	Nam Gang	Korean	Spring Branch	Casual	$23
B+	Red Lion Pub	American, British	Upper Kirby	Bar	$25
B+	Becks Prime	American, Burgers	Multiple	Counter	$13
B+	Kaneyama	Japanese	Westchase	Casual	$33
B+	Chuy's	Tex-Mex	River Oaks	Casual	$30
B+	Chapultepec	Tex-Mex	Montrose	Casual	$15
B+	13 Celsius	Italian	Midtown	Wine bar	$32
B+	Amy's Ice Cream	Sweets	Upper Kirby	Counter	
B	59 Diner	American	Multiple	Casual	$18
B	La Vista	New American	Multiple	Upmarket	$35
B	SoVino	New American	Midtown	Wine bar	$44
B	Taquería Cancún	Tex-Mex	Multiple	Casual	$10
B	Spanish Flowers	Tex-Mex	Heights	Casual	$18
B	Morton's	Steakhouse	Multiple	Upmarket	$102
B	Tan Tan	Chinese	Chinatown	Casual	$17
B	Finger Licking Bukateria	Nigerian	W. Houston	Casual	$14
B	Rudyard's British Pub	American, Burgers	Montrose	Bar	$18
B	Pappadeaux	Seafood, Southern	Multiple	Casual	$45
B	Kenneally's Irish Pub	Pizza, American	Montrose	Bar	$17
B	Smith & Wollensky	Steakhouse	River Oaks	Upmarket	$91
B	Sonoma Wine Bar	New American, Italian	Upper Kirby	Wine bar	$37
B	Bodard Bistro	Vietnamese	Chinatown	Casual	$9
B	Taquería Los Charros	Mexican, Tex-Mex	Multiple	Casual	$8
B	McCormick & Schmick	Seafood, American	Memorial	Upmarket	$61
B-	Onion Creek	American	Heights	Bar	$18
B-	Damian's	Italian-American	Midtown	Upmarket	$73
B-	Tony Thai	Thai	Chinatown	Casual	$28

Weekday food after 10pm *continued*

B-	Armandos	Tex-Mex	River Oaks	Upmarket	$64
B-	Antica Osteria	Italian-American	West U	Upmarket	$67
B-	Max's Wine Dive	New American	Washington	Wine bar	$46
B-	Mark's	New American	Montrose	Upmarket	$112
B-	Osaka	Japanese	Montrose	Casual	$42
B-	Cova	New American	Multiple	Wine bar	$47
B-	Taquería Arandas	Mexican	Multiple	Casual	$9
B-	Blue Nile Ethiopian	Ethiopian	Westchase	Casual	$25
B-	Last Concert Café	Tex-Mex	Downtown	Casual	$16
B-	Inversion Coffee House	Light American	Montrose	Café	$9
B-	Armadillo Palace	American, Barbecue	Rice Area	Bar	$22
B-	Thierry André Tellier	French, Sweets	Multiple	Café	$9
B-	Chacho's	Tex-Mex	Galleria	Casual	$19
B-	La Mexicana	Tex-Mex	Montrose	Casual	$27
B-	Arcodoro	Italian	Galleria	Upmarket	$75
B-	Berryhill Baja Grill	Tex-Mex	Multiple	Counter	$12
B-	Mezzanine Lounge	American, Burgers	Upper Kirby	Bar	$16
B-	Baker Street Pub & Grill	American	Multiple	Bar	$17
B-	Azuma and Azumi	Japanese	Multiple	Casual	$55
C+	Barry's Pizza	Italian-American, Pizza	Multiple	Casual	$15
C+	Yatra Brasserie	Indian	Downtown	Casual	$42
C+	Mama's Café	American, Tex-Mex	Galleria	Casual	$15
C+	FuFu Café	Chinese	Chinatown	Casual	$10
C+	Jasmine Asian Cuisine	Vietnamese	Chinatown	Casual	$19
C+	Uptown Sushi	Japanese	Galleria	Upmarket	$44
C+	Kim Son	Vietnamese, Chinese	Multiple	Casual	$32
C+	Bibas (One's a Meal)	Greek, American	Midtown	Casual	$16
C+	Crescent City Beignets	Southern	Greenway	Fast food	$12
C+	Seoul Garden	Korean	Spring Branch	Casual	$28
C+	La Tapatía Taquería	Mexican, Tex-Mex	Multiple	Casual	$12
C+	James Coney Island	American	Multiple	Fast food	$8
C+	Hollywood Vietnamese	Vietnamese, French	Montrose	Casual	$24
C+	The Flying Saucer	American	Downtown	Bar	$18
C+	Late Night Pie	Pizza	Midtown	Counter	$20
C+	Bistro Vino	French, American	Montrose	Upmarket	$60
C+	Taco Cabana	Tex-Mex	Multiple	Fast food	$8
C+	Whataburger	Burgers	Multiple	Fast food	$8
C+	Mai's	Vietnamese	Midtown	Casual	$25
C+	Vin	New American	Downtown	Upmarket	$86
C	The Fish	Seafood, Japanese	Midtown	Upmarket	$58
C	Van Loc	Vietnamese	Midtown	Casual	$15
C	Buffalo Wild Wings	American	Multiple	Bar	$22
C	Willy's Pub	American	Rice Area	Bar	$12
C	Sushi King	Japanese	Upper Kirby	Casual	$39
C-	Grand Lux Café	American	Galleria	Casual	$28
C-	Strip House	Steakhouse	Downtown	Upmarket	$98
C-	Chilos Seafood	Mexican, Seafood	Multiple	Casual	$21
C-	RA Sushi	Japanese	River Oaks	Upmarket	$43
C-	Miyako	Japanese	Multiple	Upmarket	$38
C-	Grappino di Nino	Italian-American	River Oaks	Upmarket	$36
C-	Zake Sushi Lounge	Japanese	Upper Kirby	Casual	$43
C-	PF Chang's	Pan-Asian, Chinese	Multiple	Upmarket	$41
C-	La Griglia	Italian-American, Pizza	River Oaks	Upmarket	$60
C-	Cadillac Bar	Tex-Mex	Heights	Casual	$28
C-	Silver Palace	Chinese	Bellaire	Casual	$11
C-	Sambuca	New American	Downtown	Upmarket	$55
C-	Café 101	Vietnamese, Korean	Chinatown	Casual	$14

Weekday food after 10pm *continued*

C-	Tokyohana	Japanese	Multiple	Casual	$40
C-	Black Labrador Pub	British	Montrose	Bar	$26
C-	Thai Pepper	Thai	Montrose	Casual	$26
C-	Thai Sticks	Thai	Montrose	Casual	$38
C-	Lee's Sandwiches	Vietnamese	Multiple	Fast food	$5
C-	House of Pies	American, Sweets	Multiple	Casual	$11
C-	The Remington	New American	Galleria	Upmarket	$101
D	Tila's	Tex-Mex	River Oaks	Upmarket	$50
D	Monarch	New American	Hermann Park	Upmarket	$93
D	Willie G's	Seafood	Galleria	Upmarket	$87
D	Sorrento	Italian-American	Montrose	Upmarket	$64
D	The Grotto	Italian-American, Pizza	Galleria	Upmarket	$55
D	Ruggles Grill	New American	Multiple	Upmarket	$61
D	Katz's Deli	Jewish Deli	Montrose	Casual	$20
D	Palazzo's	Italian-American	Multiple	Casual	$34
D	Cabo's Mix-Mex Grille	Tex-Mex	Downtown	Casual	$25
D	Ruchi's Taquería	Tex-Mex	Multiple	Casual	$16
D	Sake Lounge	Japanese	Downtown	Casual	$40
D-	Kona Grill	American, Pan-Asian	Multiple	Casual	$54
D-	Vietopia	Vietnamese	Greenway	Upmarket	$40
D-	Mi Luna	Spanish	Multiple	Upmarket	$63
D-	Café Express	American	Multiple	Counter	$16
D-	Brasil	Light American	Montrose	Counter	$13
D-	Café Japon	Japanese	Upper Kirby	Casual	$27

Weekday food after 11pm

A	Doneraki	Tex-Mex	Multiple	Casual	$30
A-	Gorditas Aguasctes.	Mexican	Multiple	Casual	$9
A-	Taquería Del Sol	Mexican	S. Houston	Casual	$18
A-	Shanghai Restaurant	Chinese	Chinatown	Casual	$12
A-	London Sizzler	Indian	Hillcroft Area	Casual	$32
A-	Frenchy's Chicken	Southern	Multiple	Counter	$8
A-	Sinh Sinh	Chinese, Seafood	Chinatown	Casual	$36
A-	The Tasting Room	Pizza	Multiple	Wine bar	$33
B+	Becks Prime	American, Burgers	Multiple	Counter	$13
B+	Chapultepec	Tex-Mex	Montrose	Casual	$15
B+	13 Celsius	Italian	Midtown	Wine bar	$32
B+	Amy's Ice Cream	Sweets	Upper Kirby	Counter	
B	59 Diner	American	Multiple	Casual	$18
B	SoVino	New American	Midtown	Wine bar	$44
B	Taquería Cancún	Tex-Mex	Multiple	Casual	$10
B	Spanish Flowers	Tex-Mex	Heights	Casual	$18
B	Tan Tan	Chinese	Chinatown	Casual	$17
B	Rudyard's British Pub	American, Burgers	Montrose	Bar	$18
B	Kenneally's Irish Pub	Pizza, American	Montrose	Bar	$17
B	Smith & Wollensky	Steakhouse	River Oaks	Upmarket	$91
B	Sonoma Wine Bar	New American, Italian	Upper Kirby	Wine bar	$37
B	Bodard Bistro	Vietnamese	Chinatown	Casual	$9
B-	Onion Creek	American	Heights	Bar	$18
B-	Max's Wine Dive	New American	Washington	Wine bar	$46
B-	Taquería Arandas	Mexican	Multiple	Casual	$9
B-	Armadillo Palace	American, Barbecue	Rice Area	Bar	$22
B-	Chacho's	Tex-Mex	Galleria	Casual	$19
B-	Mezzanine Lounge	American, Burgers	Upper Kirby	Bar	$16
B-	Baker Street Pub & Grill	American	Multiple	Bar	$17
C+	Mama's Café	American, Tex-Mex	Galleria	Casual	$15

Weekday food after 11pm *continued*

C+	La Tapatía Taquería	Mexican, Tex-Mex	Multiple	Casual	$12
C+	FuFu Café	Chinese	Chinatown	Casual	$10
C+	Hollywood Vietnamese	Vietnamese, French	Montrose	Casual	$24
C+	The Flying Saucer	American	Downtown	Bar	$18
C+	Bibas (One's a Meal)	Greek, American	Midtown	Casual	$16
C+	Late Night Pie	Pizza	Midtown	Counter	$20
C+	Bistro Vino	French, American	Montrose	Upmarket	$60
C+	Taco Cabana	Tex-Mex	Multiple	Fast food	$8
C+	Whataburger	Burgers	Multiple	Fast food	$8
C+	Mai's	Vietnamese	Midtown	Casual	$25
C	Buffalo Wild Wings	American	Multiple	Bar	$22
C	Willy's Pub	American	Rice Area	Bar	$12
C-	Chilos Seafood	Mexican, Seafood	Multiple	Casual	$21
C-	RA Sushi	Japanese	River Oaks	Upmarket	$43
C-	Café 101	Vietnamese, Korean	Chinatown	Casual	$14
C-	Lee's Sandwiches	Vietnamese	Multiple	Fast food	$5
C-	House of Pies	American, Sweets	Multiple	Casual	$11
D	Katz's Deli	Jewish Deli	Montrose	Casual	$20
D	Cabo's Mix-Mex Grille	Tex-Mex	Downtown	Casual	$25
D	Ruchi's Taquería	Tex-Mex	Multiple	Casual	$16
D-	Brasil	Light American	Montrose	Counter	$13
D-	Café Japon	Japanese	Upper Kirby	Casual	$27

Weekday food after midnight

A-	Gorditas Aguasctes.	Mexican	Multiple	Casual	$9
A-	Frenchy's Chicken	Southern	Multiple	Counter	$8
A-	Sinh Sinh	Chinese, Seafood	Chinatown	Casual	$36
B+	Becks Prime	American, Burgers	Multiple	Counter	$13
B+	Chapultepec	Tex-Mex	Montrose	Casual	$15
B	59 Diner	American	Multiple	Casual	$18
B	Spanish Flowers	Tex-Mex	Heights	Casual	$18
B	Kenneally's Irish Pub	Pizza, American	Montrose	Bar	$17
B	Smith & Wollensky	Steakhouse	River Oaks	Upmarket	$91
B-	Onion Creek	American	Heights	Bar	$18
B-	Taquería Arandas	Mexican	Multiple	Casual	$9
B-	Chacho's	Tex-Mex	Galleria	Casual	$19
B-	Mezzanine Lounge	American, Burgers	Upper Kirby	Bar	$16
B-	Baker Street Pub & Grill	American	Multiple	Bar	$17
C+	Mama's Café	American, Tex-Mex	Galleria	Casual	$15
C+	FuFu Café	Chinese	Chinatown	Casual	$10
C+	La Tapatía Taquería	Mexican, Tex-Mex	Multiple	Casual	$12
C+	Hollywood Vietnamese	Vietnamese, French	Montrose	Casual	$24
C+	The Flying Saucer	American	Downtown	Bar	$18
C+	Bibas (One's a Meal)	Greek, American	Midtown	Casual	$16
C+	Late Night Pie	Pizza	Midtown	Counter	$20
C+	Taco Cabana	Tex-Mex	Multiple	Fast food	$8
C+	Whataburger	Burgers	Multiple	Fast food	$8
C+	Mai's	Vietnamese	Midtown	Casual	$25
C	Willy's Pub	American	Rice Area	Bar	$12
C-	Café 101	Vietnamese, Korean	Chinatown	Casual	$14
C-	House of Pies	American, Sweets	Multiple	Casual	$11
D	Katz's Deli	Jewish Deli	Montrose	Casual	$20
D	Ruchi's Taquería	Tex-Mex	Multiple	Casual	$16

Weekday food after 1am

A-	Gorditas Aguasctes.	Mexican	Multiple	Casual	$9
A-	Sinh Sinh	Chinese, Seafood	Chinatown	Casual	$36
B+	Becks Prime	American, Burgers	Multiple	Counter	$13
B+	Chapultepec	Tex-Mex	Montrose	Casual	$15
B	59 Diner	American	Multiple	Casual	$18
B	Spanish Flowers	Tex-Mex	Heights	Casual	$18
B	Smith & Wollensky	Steakhouse	River Oaks	Upmarket	$91
B-	Onion Creek	American	Heights	Bar	$18
B-	Chacho's	Tex-Mex	Galleria	Casual	$19
B-	Mezzanine Lounge	American, Burgers	Upper Kirby	Bar	$16
B-	Baker Street Pub & Grill	American	Multiple	Bar	$17
C+	FuFu Café	Chinese	Chinatown	Casual	$10
C+	La Tapatía Taquería	Mexican, Tex-Mex	Multiple	Casual	$12
C+	Hollywood Vietnamese	Vietnamese, French	Montrose	Casual	$24
C+	Bibas (One's a Meal)	Greek, American	Midtown	Casual	$16
C+	Late Night Pie	Pizza	Midtown	Counter	$20
C+	Taco Cabana	Tex-Mex	Multiple	Fast food	$8
C+	Whataburger	Burgers	Multiple	Fast food	$8
C+	Mai's	Vietnamese	Midtown	Casual	$25
C	Willy's Pub	American	Rice Area	Bar	$12
C-	Café 101	Vietnamese, Korean	Chinatown	Casual	$14
C-	House of Pies	American, Sweets	Multiple	Casual	$11
D	Katz's Deli	Jewish Deli	Montrose	Casual	$20
D	Ruchi's Taquería	Tex-Mex	Multiple	Casual	$16

Weekday food after 2am

A-	Gorditas Aguasctes.	Mexican	Multiple	Casual	$9
B+	Becks Prime	American, Burgers	Multiple	Counter	$13
B+	Chapultepec	Tex-Mex	Montrose	Casual	$15
B	59 Diner	American	Multiple	Casual	$18
B	Spanish Flowers	Tex-Mex	Heights	Casual	$18
B-	Chacho's	Tex-Mex	Galleria	Casual	$19
C+	Bibas (One's a Meal)	Greek, American	Midtown	Casual	$16
C+	Late Night Pie	Pizza	Midtown	Counter	$20
C+	Taco Cabana	Tex-Mex	Multiple	Fast food	$8
C+	Whataburger	Burgers	Multiple	Fast food	$8
C+	Mai's	Vietnamese	Midtown	Casual	$25
C-	House of Pies	American, Sweets	Multiple	Casual	$11
D	Katz's Deli	Jewish Deli	Montrose	Casual	$20
D	Ruchi's Taquería	Tex-Mex	Multiple	Casual	$16

Weekend food after 10pm

A+	Da Marco	Italian, Pizza	Montrose	Upmarket	$77
A	Indika	Indian	Montrose	Upmarket	$65
A	Vic & Anthony's	Steakhouse	Downtown	Upmarket	$94
A	Le Mistral	French	W. Houston	Upmarket	$74
A	Gravitas	New American	Midtown	Upmarket	$72
A	17	New American	Downtown	Upmarket	$100
A	Reef	New American	Midtown	Upmarket	$66
A	TopWater Grill	Seafood, American	San Leon	Casual	$31
A	Pesce	Seafood	Upper Kirby	Upmarket	$85
A	Catalan	New American	Washington	Upmarket	$70
A	Himalaya	Pakistani	Hillcroft Area	Casual	$14
A	Ibiza	New American	Midtown	Upmarket	$72
A	Doneraki	Tex-Mex	Multiple	Casual	$30
A	Nippon	Japanese	Montrose	Casual	$42

Weekend food after 10pm *continued*

A	Sasaki	Japanese	Galleria	Casual	$51
A	Tony's	Italian	Greenway	Upmarket	$110
A	100% Taquito	Mexican	Greenway	Counter	$11
A	Rioja	Spanish	W. Houston	Upmarket	$62
A-	Gorditas Aguasctes.	Mexican	Multiple	Casual	$9
A-	t'afia	New American	Midtown	Upmarket	$65
A-	Shade	New American	Heights	Upmarket	$49
A-	Taquería Del Sol	Mexican	S. Houston	Casual	$18
A-	QQ Cuisine	Chinese	Chinatown	Casual	$10
A-	Teppay	Japanese	Galleria	Upmarket	$60
A-	Shanghai Restaurant	Chinese	Chinatown	Casual	$12
A-	Fung's Kitchen	Chinese, Seafood	Chinatown	Upmarket	$46
A-	El Tiempo Cantina	Tex-Mex	Multiple	Casual	$58
A-	London Sizzler	Indian	Hillcroft Area	Casual	$32
A-	Frenchy's Chicken	Southern	Multiple	Counter	$8
A-	Bice	Italian	Galleria	Upmarket	$96
A-	Sinh Sinh	Chinese, Seafood	Chinatown	Casual	$36
A-	The Tasting Room	Pizza	Multiple	Wine bar	$33
A-	Nam Gang	Korean	Spring Branch	Casual	$23
A-	El Rey Taquería	Mexican, Cuban	Multiple	Counter	$11
A-	Saffron	Moroccan	Upper Kirby	Casual	$55
B+	Sage 400	Japanese	Galleria	Casual	$45
B+	Guadalajara	Tex-Mex	Multiple	Casual	$34
B+	1308 Cantina	Tex-Mex	Montrose	Casual	$58
B+	Red Lion Pub	American, British	Upper Kirby	Bar	$25
B+	Tony Mandola's	Seafood	River Oaks	Upmarket	$63
B+	Goode Co. Seafood	Seafood	Multiple	Casual	$40
B+	Ruth's Chris	Steakhouse	Galleria	Upmarket	$86
B+	Backstreet Café	New American	River Oaks	Upmarket	$71
B+	Brasserie Max & Julie	French	Montrose	Upmarket	$71
B+	Istanbul Grill	Turkish	Rice Area	Casual	$51
B+	Kaneyama	Japanese	Westchase	Casual	$33
B+	Noé	New American	Galleria	Upmarket	$100
B+	Chapultepec	Tex-Mex	Montrose	Casual	$15
B+	13 Celsius	Italian	Midtown	Wine bar	$32
B+	Hobbit Café	American	Upper Kirby	Casual	$20
B+	Hugo's	Mexican	Montrose	Upmarket	$53
B+	Cyclone Anaya's	Tex-Mex	Multiple	Casual	$35
B+	Chuy's	Tex-Mex	River Oaks	Casual	$30
B+	Pappasito's	Tex-Mex	Multiple	Casual	$31
B+	Amy's Ice Cream	Sweets	Upper Kirby	Counter	
B+	Pico's Mex-Mex	Mexican, Tex-Mex	Bellaire	Casual	$19
B	59 Diner	American	Multiple	Casual	$18
B	Café Annie	Southwestern	Galleria	Upmarket	$106
B	Laurier Café and Wine	New American	Greenway	Upmarket	$44
B	La Vista	New American	Multiple	Upmarket	$35
B	SoVino	New American	Midtown	Wine bar	$44
B	Spanish Flowers	Tex-Mex	Heights	Casual	$18
B	Taquería Cancún	Tex-Mex	Multiple	Casual	$10
B	Morton's	Steakhouse	Multiple	Upmarket	$102
B	Houston's	New American	Multiple	Upmarket	$62
B	Mardi Gras Grill	Southern, Seafood	Heights	Casual	$17
B	Taco Milagro	Tex-Mex	Multiple	Counter	$19
B	Tan Tan	Chinese	Chinatown	Casual	$17
B	Finger Licking Bukateria	Nigerian	W. Houston	Casual	$14
B	Rudyard's British Pub	American, Burgers	Montrose	Bar	$18
B	Rudy's Country Store	Barbecue	Spring	Counter	$16

Weekend food after 10pm *continued*

B	Mayuri	Indian	Galleria	Casual	$33
B	Café Caspian	Middle Eastern	W. Houston	Casual	$19
B	Pappadeaux	Seafood, Southern	Multiple	Casual	$45
B	Barnaby's Café	American	Multiple	Casual	$20
B	Kenneally's Irish Pub	Pizza, American	Montrose	Bar	$17
B	Smith & Wollensky	Steakhouse	River Oaks	Upmarket	$91
B	Sonoma Wine Bar	New American, Italian	Upper Kirby	Wine bar	$37
B	Tacos A Go-Go	Tex-Mex	Midtown	Counter	$10
B	Bodard Bistro	Vietnamese	Chinatown	Casual	$9
B	Taquería Los Charros	Mexican, Tex-Mex	Multiple	Casual	$8
B	Pappas Burgers	Burgers	Multiple	Counter	$16
B	McCormick & Schmick	Seafood, American	Memorial	Upmarket	$61
B	Américas	Latin American	Multiple	Upmarket	$75
B	Benjy's	Southwestern	Rice Area	Upmarket	$54
B-	Kubo's	Japanese	Rice Area	Casual	$44
B-	Brenner's	Steakhouse	Memorial	Upmarket	$90
B-	Bob's Steak & Chop	Steakhouse	Galleria	Upmarket	$101
B-	Onion Creek	American	Heights	Bar	$18
B-	Baba Yega	American	Montrose	Casual	$14
B-	Damian's	Italian-American	Midtown	Upmarket	$73
B-	Tay Do Restaurant	Vietnamese, Chinese	Chinatown	Casual	$25
B-	Tony Thai	Thai	Chinatown	Casual	$28
B-	Churrascos	Latin American	Multiple	Upmarket	$63
B-	Prego	Italian-American	Rice Area	Upmarket	$57
B-	Shawarma King	Middle Eastern	Galleria	Counter	$8
B-	Armandos	Tex-Mex	River Oaks	Upmarket	$64
B-	Antica Osteria	Italian-American	West U	Upmarket	$67
B-	Max's Wine Dive	New American	Washington	Wine bar	$46
B-	Mark's	New American	Montrose	Upmarket	$112
B-	Cova	New American	Multiple	Wine bar	$47
B-	El Mesón	Spanish, Cuban, Tex-Mex	Rice Area	Upmarket	$42
B-	Taquería Arandas	Mexican	Multiple	Casual	$9
B-	Blue Nile Ethiopian	Ethiopian	Westchase	Casual	$25
B-	Malay Bistro	Malaysian	Chinatown	Casual	$10
B-	Daily Review Café	American	Montrose	Casual	$31
B-	Teala's	Tex-Mex	Montrose	Casual	$33
B-	Escalante's	Tex-Mex	Multiple	Upmarket	$44
B-	Last Concert Café	Tex-Mex	Downtown	Casual	$16
B-	Inversion Coffee House	Light American	Montrose	Café	$9
B-	Armadillo Palace	American, Barbecue	Rice Area	Bar	$22
B-	Bistro Lancaster	American	Downtown	Upmarket	$70
B-	Osaka	Japanese	Montrose	Casual	$42
B-	Bombay Brasserie	Indian	Rice Area	Casual	$33
B-	Connie's Seafood Mkt.	Seafood, Mexican	Multiple	Counter	$24
B-	Thierry André Tellier	French, Sweets	Multiple	Café	$9
B-	The Mason Jar	American	Memorial	Casual	$24
B-	Chacho's	Tex-Mex	Galleria	Casual	$19
B-	La Mexicana	Tex-Mex	Montrose	Casual	$27
B-	Swirll Italian Yogurt	Sweets	Rice Area	Counter	
B-	Masraff's	New American	Memorial	Upmarket	$76
B-	Alexander the Great	Greek	Galleria	Upmarket	$63
B-	Farrago	New American	Midtown	Casual	$38
B-	Arcodoro	Italian	Galleria	Upmarket	$75
B-	Pappas Seafood	Seafood	Multiple	Casual	$48
B-	Berryhill Baja Grill	Tex-Mex	Multiple	Counter	$12
B-	Mezzanine Lounge	American, Burgers	Upper Kirby	Bar	$16
B-	Baker Street Pub & Grill	American	Multiple	Bar	$17

Weekend food after 10pm *continued*

B-	Azuma and Azumi	Japanese	Multiple	Casual	$55
C+	Pappas Bros. Steakhouse	Steakhouse	Galleria	Upmarket	$105
C+	Blue Fish House	Seafood, Pan-Asian	Upper Kirby	Upmarket	$19
C+	Barry's Pizza	Italian-American, Pizza	Multiple	Casual	$15
C+	Yatra Brasserie	Indian	Downtown	Casual	$42
C+	Mama's Café	American, Tex-Mex	Galleria	Casual	$15
C+	Carrabba's Italian Grill	Italian-American, Pizza	Multiple	Casual	$52
C+	La Tapatía Taquería	Mexican, Tex-Mex	Multiple	Casual	$12
C+	FuFu Café	Chinese	Chinatown	Casual	$10
C+	Jasmine Asian Cuisine	Vietnamese	Chinatown	Casual	$19
C+	Uptown Sushi	Japanese	Galleria	Upmarket	$44
C+	Kim Son	Vietnamese, Chinese	Multiple	Casual	$32
C+	Crescent City Beignets	Southern	Greenway	Fast food	$12
C+	Shiva	Indian	Rice Area	Casual	$27
C+	Seoul Garden	Korean	Spring Branch	Casual	$28
C+	Star Snow Ice	Chinese	Chinatown	Counter	$7
C+	James Coney Island	American	Multiple	Fast food	$8
C+	La Strada	New American	Montrose	Upmarket	$59
C+	Star Pizza	Pizza	Multiple	Casual	$14
C+	Ouisie's Table	Southern	River Oaks	Upmarket	$61
C+	The Golden Room	Thai	Montrose	Casual	$24
C+	María Selma	Mexican, Tex-Mex	Montrose	Casual	$32
C+	Empire Café	Light American	Montrose	Counter	$14
C+	Hollywood Vietnamese	Vietnamese, French	Montrose	Casual	$24
C+	Nit Noi Café	Thai	Multiple	Casual	$13
C+	Big Bowl	Chinese	Chinatown	Casual	$6
C+	The Flying Saucer	American	Downtown	Bar	$18
C+	Bibas (One's a Meal)	Greek, American	Midtown	Casual	$16
C+	Late Night Pie	Pizza	Midtown	Counter	$20
C+	Bistro Vino	French, American	Montrose	Upmarket	$60
C+	El Pueblito	Tex-Mex	Montrose	Casual	$20
C+	Taco Cabana	Tex-Mex	Multiple	Fast food	$8
C+	Whataburger	Burgers	Multiple	Fast food	$8
C+	Paciugo Gelateria	Sweets	Greenway	Counter	
C+	Café Le Jadeite	Pan-Asian, New American	River Oaks	Upmarket	$73
C+	Fleming's	Steakhouse	Multiple	Upmarket	$88
C+	Yia Yia Mary's	Greek	Galleria	Counter	$20
C+	Mai's	Vietnamese	Midtown	Casual	$25
C+	Frank's Pizza	Pizza	Downtown	Counter	$15
C	Cantina Laredo	Tex-Mex	W. Houston	Upmarket	$44
C	The Fish	Seafood, Japanese	Midtown	Upmarket	$58
C	V n	New American	Downtown	Upmarket	$86
C	Fogo de Chão	Steakhouse, Brazilian	W. Houston	Upmarket	$77
C	Mai Thai	Thai	Upper Kirby	Casual	$23
C	Black Walnut Café	Light American	Multiple	Café	$12
C	Capital Grille	Steakhouse	Galleria	Upmarket	$92
C	Van Loc	Vietnamese	Midtown	Casual	$15
C	Artista	Latin American	Downtown	Upmarket	$69
C	Freebirds World Burrito	Tex-Mex	Multiple	Fast food	$8
C	Nino's	Italian-American	Montrose	Upmarket	$57
C	Cava Bistro	New American	Downtown	Upmarket	$54
C	Vincent's	Italian-American	Montrose	Upmarket	$45
C	Taste of Texas	Steakhouse	Memorial	Upmarket	$54
C	Fuzzy's	Pizza	Multiple	Counter	$12
C	Buffalo Wild Wings	American	Multiple	Bar	$22
C	Ocean Palace	Seafood, Chinese	Chinatown	Casual	$29
C	Nelore Churrascaria	Steakhouse, Brazilian	Montrose	Upmarket	$58

Weekend food after 10pm *continued*

C	Café Red Onion	Latin American	Multiple	Casual	$37
C	India's Restaurant	Indian	Galleria	Casual	$20
C	Bistro Le Cep	French	W. Houston	Upmarket	$42
C	Aladdin Mediterranean	Middle Eastern	Montrose	Counter	$8
C	The Dessert Gallery	Sweets	Multiple	Counter	
C	Sushi King	Japanese	Upper Kirby	Casual	$39
C	Ponzo's	Italian-American, Pizza	Midtown	Casual	$14
C-	Truluck's	Seafood, New American	Galleria	Upmarket	$86
C-	Grand Lux Café	American	Galleria	Casual	$28
C-	Hungry's	Light American	Multiple	Casual	$18
C-	Strip House	Steakhouse	Downtown	Upmarket	$98
C-	Chilos Seafood	Mexican, Seafood	Multiple	Casual	$21
C-	RA Sushi	Japanese	River Oaks	Upmarket	$43
C-	YAO Restaurant & Bar	Chinese	Westchase	Casual	$36
C-	Santos	Tex-Mex	Westchase	Casual	$38
C-	Miyako	Japanese	Multiple	Upmarket	$38
C-	Grappino di Nino	Italian-American	River Oaks	Upmarket	$36
C-	Zake Sushi Lounge	Japanese	Upper Kirby	Casual	$43
C-	PF Chang's	Pan-Asian, Chinese	Multiple	Upmarket	$41
C-	La Griglia	Italian-American, Pizza	River Oaks	Upmarket	$60
C-	Las Alamedas	Tex-Mex	Spring Branch	Upmarket	$42
C-	Cadillac Bar	Tex-Mex	Heights	Casual	$28
C-	Silver Palace	Chinese	Bellaire	Casual	$11
C-	Julia's Bistro	Southwestern	Midtown	Upmarket	$60
C-	Sambuca	New American	Downtown	Upmarket	$55
C-	Pappas Bar-B-Q	Barbecue	Multiple	Counter	$12
C-	Mak Chin's	Pan-Asian	Washington	Casual	$25
C-	Café 101	Vietnamese, Korean	Chinatown	Casual	$14
C-	Ciro's Italian Grill	Italian-American	Memorial	Casual	$35
C-	Tokyohana	Japanese	Multiple	Casual	$40
C-	D'Amico's	Italian-American	Rice Area	Counter	$18
C-	Black Labrador Pub	British	Montrose	Bar	$26
C-	Thai Pepper	Thai	Montrose	Casual	$26
C-	Thai Sticks	Thai	Montrose	Casual	$38
C-	Prince's Hamburgers	American, Burgers	Multiple	Counter	$9
C-	Lee's Sandwiches	Vietnamese	Multiple	Fast food	$5
C-	Michelangelo's	Italian-American	Montrose	Casual	$52
C-	House of Pies	American, Sweets	Multiple	Casual	$11
C-	Palm	Steakhouse	Galleria	Upmarket	$95
C-	The Remington	New American	Galleria	Upmarket	$101
C-	Yum Yum Cha Café	Chinese	Rice Area	Casual	$10
C-	La Fendée	Middle Eastern	Montrose	Casual	$30
C-	Amazón Grill	Latin American	Multiple	Counter	$28
D	Tila's	Tex-Mex	River Oaks	Upmarket	$50
D	Monarch	New American	Hermann Park	Upmarket	$93
D	Willie G's	Seafood	Galleria	Upmarket	$87
D	Sorrento	Italian-American	Montrose	Upmarket	$64
D	Niko Niko's	Greek	Montrose	Counter	$20
D	The Grotto	Italian-American, Pizza	Galleria	Upmarket	$55
D	Molina's	Tex-Mex	Multiple	Casual	$30
D	Ruggles Grill	New American	Multiple	Upmarket	$61
D	Zula	New American	Downtown	Upmarket	$74
D	Katz's Deli	Jewish Deli	Montrose	Casual	$20
D	Oceanaire	Seafood, New American	Galleria	Upmarket	$82
D	Ruggles Café	Light American	Rice Area	Casual	$17
D	Collina's Italian Café	Italian-American, Pizza	Multiple	Casual	$34
D	Palazzo's	Italian-American	Multiple	Casual	$34

Weekend food after 10pm *continued*

D	Cabo's Mix-Mex Grille	Tex-Mex	Downtown	Casual	$25
D	Ruchi's Taquería	Tex-Mex	Multiple	Casual	$16
D	Sake Lounge	Japanese	Downtown	Casual	$40
D	PK's Blue Water Grill	Seafood, Southern	Memorial	Casual	$44
D	Café Adobe	Tex-Mex	Multiple	Casual	$24
D-	Aquarium	Seafood, American	Downtown	Upmarket	$30
D-	Kona Grill	American, Pan-Asian	Multiple	Casual	$54
D-	Bank	New American	Downtown	Upmarket	$91
D-	Vietopia	Vietnamese	Greenway	Upmarket	$40
D-	Spencer's	Steakhouse	Downtown	Upmarket	$90
D-	Buca di Beppo	Italian-American	Upper Kirby	Casual	$30
D-	Mi Luna	Spanish	Multiple	Upmarket	$63
D-	Café Express	American	Multiple	Counter	$16
D-	Brasil	Light American	Montrose	Counter	$13
D-	Café Japon	Japanese	Upper Kirby	Casual	$27

Weekend food after 11pm

A	Himalaya	Pakistani	Hillcroft Area	Casual	$14
A	Gravitas	New American	Midtown	Upmarket	$72
A	Tony's	Italian	Greenway	Upmarket	$110
A	Doneraki	Tex-Mex	Multiple	Casual	$30
A	Rioja	Spanish	W. Houston	Upmarket	$62
A-	Gorditas Aguasctes.	Mexican	Multiple	Casual	$9
A-	Taquería Del Sol	Mexican	S. Houston	Casual	$18
A-	Shanghai Restaurant	Chinese	Chinatown	Casual	$12
A-	London Sizzler	Indian	Hillcroft Area	Casual	$32
A-	Frenchy's Chicken	Southern	Multiple	Counter	$8
A-	Sinh Sinh	Chinese, Seafood	Chinatown	Casual	$36
A-	The Tasting Room	Pizza	Multiple	Wine bar	$33
A-	El Rey Taquería	Mexican, Cuban	Multiple	Counter	$11
B+	Sage 400	Japanese	Galleria	Casual	$45
B+	Red Lion Pub	American, British	Upper Kirby	Bar	$25
B+	Chuy's	Tex-Mex	River Oaks	Casual	$30
B+	Chapultepec	Tex-Mex	Montrose	Casual	$15
B+	13 Celsius	Italian	Midtown	Wine bar	$32
B+	Amy's Ice Cream	Sweets	Upper Kirby	Counter	
B	59 Diner	American	Multiple	Casual	$18
B	SoVino	New American	Midtown	Wine bar	$44
B	Spanish Flowers	Tex-Mex	Heights	Casual	$18
B	Taquería Cancún	Tex-Mex	Multiple	Casual	$10
B	Taco Milagro	Tex-Mex	Multiple	Counter	$19
B	Tan Tan	Chinese	Chinatown	Casual	$17
B	Rudyard's British Pub	American, Burgers	Montrose	Bar	$18
B	Kenneally's Irish Pub	Pizza, American	Montrose	Bar	$17
B	Smith & Wollensky	Steakhouse	River Oaks	Upmarket	$91
B	Sonoma Wine Bar	New American, Italian	Upper Kirby	Wine bar	$37
B	Tacos A Go-Go	Tex-Mex	Midtown	Counter	$10
B	Bodard Bistro	Vietnamese	Chinatown	Casual	$9
B-	Kubo's	Japanese	Rice Area	Casual	$44
B-	Onion Creek	American	Heights	Bar	$18
B-	Damian's	Italian-American	Midtown	Upmarket	$73
B-	Tony Thai	Thai	Chinatown	Casual	$28
B-	Armandos	Tex-Mex	River Oaks	Upmarket	$64
B-	Max's Wine Dive	New American	Washington	Wine bar	$46
B-	Mark's	New American	Montrose	Upmarket	$112
B-	Cova	New American	Multiple	Wine bar	$47
B-	Taquería Arandas	Mexican	Multiple	Casual	$9

Weekend food after 11pm *continued*

B-	Last Concert Café	Tex-Mex	Downtown	Casual	$16
B-	Inversion Coffee House	Light American	Montrose	Café	$9
B-	Armadillo Palace	American, Barbecue	Rice Area	Bar	$22
B-	Connie's Seafood Mkt.	Seafood, Mexican	Multiple	Counter	$24
B-	Chacho's	Tex-Mex	Galleria	Casual	$19
B-	Arcodoro	Italian	Galleria	Upmarket	$75
B-	Berryhill Baja Grill	Tex-Mex	Multiple	Counter	$12
B-	Mezzanine Lounge	American, Burgers	Upper Kirby	Bar	$16
B-	Baker Street Pub & Grill	American	Multiple	Bar	$17
C+	Mama's Café	American, Tex-Mex	Galleria	Casual	$15
C+	La Tapatía Taquería	Mexican, Tex-Mex	Multiple	Casual	$12
C+	FuFu Café	Chinese	Chinatown	Casual	$10
C+	Uptown Sushi	Japanese	Galleria	Upmarket	$44
C+	Kim Son	Vietnamese, Chinese	Multiple	Casual	$32
C+	Crescent City Beignets	Southern	Greenway	Fast food	$12
C+	Pizza Guy vs. Tamale Couple	Pizza vs. Mexican	All of them	In your face	$5
C+	James Coney Island	American	Multiple	Fast food	$8
C+	La Strada	New American	Montrose	Upmarket	$59
C+	Hollywood Vietnamese	Vietnamese, French	Montrose	Casual	$24
C+	Big Bowl	Chinese	Chinatown	Casual	$6
C+	The Flying Saucer	American	Downtown	Bar	$18
C+	Bibas (One's a Meal)	Greek, American	Midtown	Casual	$16
C+	María Selma	Mexican, Tex-Mex	Montrose	Casual	$16
C+	Late Night Pie	Pizza	Midtown	Counter	$20
C+	Bistro Vino	French, American	Montrose	Upmarket	$60
C+	El Pueblito	Tex-Mex	Montrose	Casual	$20
C+	Taco Cabana	Tex-Mex	Multiple	Fast food	$8
C+	Whataburger	Burgers	Multiple	Fast food	$8
C+	Mai's	Vietnamese	Midtown	Casual	$25
C+	Vin	New American	Downtown	Upmarket	$86
C+	Frank's Pizza	Pizza	Downtown	Counter	$15
C	The Fish	Seafood, Japanese	Midtown	Upmarket	$58
C	Buffalo Wild Wings	American	Multiple	Bar	$22
C	The Dessert Gallery	Sweets	Multiple	Counter	
C	Sushi King	Japanese	Upper Kirby	Casual	$39
C-	Grand Lux Café	American	Galleria	Casual	$28
C-	Strip House	Steakhouse	Downtown	Upmarket	$98
C-	Chilos Seafood	Mexican, Seafood	Multiple	Casual	$21
C-	RA Sushi	Japanese	River Oaks	Upmarket	$43
C-	Miyako	Japanese	Multiple	Upmarket	$38
C-	Zake Sushi Lounge	Japanese	Upper Kirby	Casual	$43
C-	PF Chang's	Pan-Asian, Chinese	Multiple	Upmarket	$41
C-	La Griglia	Italian-American, Pizza	River Oaks	Upmarket	$60
C-	Cadillac Bar	Tex-Mex	Heights	Casual	$28
C-	Sambuca	New American	Downtown	Upmarket	$55
C-	Café 101	Vietnamese, Korean	Chinatown	Casual	$14
C-	Tokyohana	Japanese	Multiple	Casual	$40
C-	Black Labrador Pub	British	Montrose	Bar	$26
C-	Thai Sticks	Thai	Montrose	Casual	$38
C-	Lee's Sandwiches	Vietnamese	Multiple	Fast food	$5
C-	House of Pies	American, Sweets	Multiple	Casual	$11
D	Tila's	Tex-Mex	River Oaks	Upmarket	$50
D	The Grotto	Italian-American, Pizza	Galleria	Upmarket	$55
D	Molina's	Tex-Mex	Multiple	Casual	$30
D	Katz's Deli	Jewish Deli	Montrose	Casual	$20
D	Cabo's Mix-Mex Grille	Tex-Mex	Downtown	Casual	$25
D	Ruchi's Taquería	Tex-Mex	Multiple	Casual	$16

Weekend food after 11pm *continued*

D	Sake Lounge	Japanese	Downtown	Casual	$40
D-	Kona Grill	American, Pan-Asian	Multiple	Casual	$54
D-	Mi Luna	Spanish	Multiple	Upmarket	$63
D-	Brasil	Light American	Montrose	Counter	$13
D-	Café Japon	Japanese	Upper Kirby	Casual	$27

Weekend food after midnight

A	Doneraki	Tex-Mex	Multiple	Casual	$30
A-	Gorditas Aguasctes.	Mexican	Multiple	Casual	$9
A-	Taquería Del Sol	Mexican	S. Houston	Casual	$18
A-	Shanghai Restaurant	Chinese	Chinatown	Casual	$12
A-	Frenchy's Chicken	Southern	Multiple	Counter	$8
A-	Sinh Sinh	Chinese, Seafood	Chinatown	Casual	$36
A-	The Tasting Room	Pizza	Multiple	Wine bar	$33
A-	El Rey Taquería	Mexican, Cuban	Multiple	Counter	$11
B+	Chapultepec	Tex-Mex	Montrose	Casual	$15
B+	13 Celsius	Italian	Midtown	Wine bar	$32
B+	Amy's Ice Cream	Sweets	Upper Kirby	Counter	
B	59 Diner	American	Multiple	Casual	$18
B	SoVino	New American	Midtown	Wine bar	$44
B	Taquería Cancún	Tex-Mex	Multiple	Casual	$10
B	Spanish Flowers	Tex-Mex	Heights	Casual	$18
B	Tan Tan	Chinese	Chinatown	Casual	$17
B	Rudyard's British Pub	American, Burgers	Montrose	Bar	$18
B	Kenneally's Irish Pub	Pizza, American	Montrose	Bar	$17
B	Smith & Wollensky	Steakhouse	River Oaks	Upmarket	$91
B	Tacos A Go-Go	Tex-Mex	Midtown	Counter	$10
B	Sonoma Wine Bar	New American, Italian	Upper Kirby	Wine bar	$37
B-	Onion Creek	American	Heights	Bar	$18
B-	Max's Wine Dive	New American	Washington	Wine bar	$46
B-	Cova	New American	Multiple	Wine bar	$47
B-	Taquería Arandas	Mexican	Multiple	Casual	$9
B-	Armadillo Palace	American, Barbecue	Rice Area	Bar	$22
B-	Chacho's	Tex-Mex	Galleria	Casual	$19
B-	Mezzanine Lounge	American, Burgers	Upper Kirby	Bar	$16
B-	Baker Street Pub & Grill	American	Multiple	Bar	$17
C+	Mama's Café	American, Tex-Mex	Galleria	Casual	$15
C+	La Tapatía Taquería	Mexican, Tex-Mex	Multiple	Casual	$12
C+	FuFu Café	Chinese	Chinatown	Casual	$10
C+	Crescent City Beignets	Southern	Greenway	Fast food	$12
C+	Pizza Guy vs. Tamale Couple	Pizza vs. Mexican	All of them	In your face	$5
C+	La Strada	New American	Montrose	Upmarket	$59
C+	Hollywood Vietnamese	Vietnamese, French	Montrose	Casual	$24
C+	The Flying Saucer	American	Downtown	Bar	$18
C+	Bibas (One's a Meal)	Greek, American	Midtown	Casual	$16
C+	Late Night Pie	Pizza	Midtown	Counter	$20
C+	El Pueblito	Tex-Mex	Montrose	Casual	$20
C+	Taco Cabana	Tex-Mex	Multiple	Fast food	$8
C+	Whataburger	Burgers	Multiple	Fast food	$8
C+	Mai's	Vietnamese	Midtown	Casual	$25
C+	Frank's Pizza	Pizza	Downtown	Counter	$15
C	Buffalo Wild Wings	American	Multiple	Bar	$22
C-	Café 101	Vietnamese, Korean	Chinatown	Casual	$14
C-	Lee's Sandwiches	Vietnamese	Multiple	Fast food	$5
C-	House of Pies	American, Sweets	Multiple	Casual	$11
D	Katz's Deli	Jewish Deli	Montrose	Casual	$20
D	Cabo's Mix-Mex Grille	Tex-Mex	Downtown	Casual	$25

Weekend food after midnight *continued*

D	Ruchi's Taquería	Tex-Mex	Multiple	Casual	$16
D-	Mi Luna	Spanish	Multiple	Upmarket	$63
D-	Café Japon	Japanese	Upper Kirby	Casual	$27

Weekend food after 1am

A	Doneraki	Tex-Mex	Multiple	Casual	$30
A-	Gorditas Aguasctes.	Mexican	Multiple	Casual	$9
A-	Taquería Del Sol	Mexican	S. Houston	Casual	$18
A-	Frenchy's Chicken	Southern	Multiple	Counter	$8
A-	Sinh Sinh	Chinese, Seafood	Chinatown	Casual	$36
A-	El Rey Taquería	Mexican, Cuban	Multiple	Counter	$11
B+	Chapultepec	Tex-Mex	Montrose	Casual	$15
B	59 Diner	American	Multiple	Casual	$18
B	Taquería Cancún	Tex-Mex	Multiple	Casual	$10
B	Spanish Flowers	Tex-Mex	Heights	Casual	$18
B	Tan Tan	Chinese	Chinatown	Casual	$17
B	Smith & Wollensky	Steakhouse	River Oaks	Upmarket	$91
B	Tacos A Go-Go	Tex-Mex	Midtown	Counter	$10
B	Sonoma Wine Bar	New American, Italian	Upper Kirby	Wine bar	$37
B-	Onion Creek	American	Heights	Bar	$18
B-	Max's Wine Dive	New American	Washington	Wine bar	$46
B-	Taquería Arandas	Mexican	Multiple	Casual	$9
B-	Armadillo Palace	American, Barbecue	Rice Area	Bar	$22
B-	Chacho's	Tex-Mex	Galleria	Casual	$19
B-	Mezzanine Lounge	American, Burgers	Upper Kirby	Bar	$16
B-	Baker Street Pub & Grill	American	Multiple	Bar	$17
C+	Mama's Café	American, Tex-Mex	Galleria	Casual	$15
C+	La Tapatía Taquería	Mexican, Tex-Mex	Multiple	Casual	$12
C+	FuFu Café	Chinese	Chinatown	Casual	$10
C+	Pizza Guy vs. Tamale Couple	Pizza vs. Mexican	All of them	In your face	$5
C+	La Strada	New American	Montrose	Upmarket	$59
C+	Hollywood Vietnamese	Vietnamese, French	Montrose	Casual	$24
C+	The Flying Saucer	American	Downtown	Bar	$18
C+	Bibas (One's a Meal)	Greek, American	Midtown	Casual	$16
C+	Late Night Pie	Pizza	Midtown	Counter	$20
C+	Taco Cabana	Tex-Mex	Multiple	Fast food	$8
C+	Whataburger	Burgers	Multiple	Fast food	$8
C+	Mai's	Vietnamese	Midtown	Casual	$25
C+	Frank's Pizza	Pizza	Downtown	Counter	$15
C	Buffalo Wild Wings	American	Multiple	Bar	$22
C-	Café 101	Vietnamese, Korean	Chinatown	Casual	$14
C-	Lee's Sandwiches	Vietnamese	Multiple	Fast food	$5
C-	House of Pies	American, Sweets	Multiple	Casual	$11
D	Katz's Deli	Jewish Deli	Montrose	Casual	$20
D	Ruchi's Taquería	Tex-Mex	Multiple	Casual	$16
D-	Café Japon	Japanese	Upper Kirby	Casual	$27

Weekend food after 2am

A	Doneraki	Tex-Mex	Multiple	Casual	$30
A-	Gorditas Aguasctes.	Mexican	Multiple	Casual	$9
A-	Taquería Del Sol	Mexican	S. Houston	Casual	$18
A-	Frenchy's Chicken	Southern	Multiple	Counter	$8
A-	El Rey Taquería	Mexican, Cuban	Multiple	Counter	$11
B+	Chapultepec	Tex-Mex	Montrose	Casual	$15
B	59 Diner	American	Multiple	Casual	$18
B	Spanish Flowers	Tex-Mex	Heights	Casual	$18

Weekend food after 2am *continued*

B	Tan Tan	Chinese	Chinatown	Casual	$17
B-	Taquería Arandas	Mexican	Multiple	Casual	$9
B-	Bibas (One's a Meal)	Greek, American	Midtown	Casual	$16
B-	Chacho's	Tex-Mex	Galleria	Casual	$19
C+	Mama's Café	American, Tex-Mex	Galleria	Casual	$15
C+	Pizza Guy vs. Tamale Couple	Pizza vs. Mexican	All of them	In your face	$5
C+	La Strada	New American	Montrose	Upmarket	$59
C+	Hollywood Vietnamese	Vietnamese, French	Montrose	Casual	$24
C+	Late Night Pie	Pizza	Midtown	Counter	$20
C+	Taco Cabana	Tex-Mex	Multiple	Fast food	$8
C+	Whataburger	Burgers	Multiple	Fast food	$8
C+	Mai's	Vietnamese	Midtown	Casual	$25
C+	Frank's Pizza	Pizza	Downtown	Counter	$15
C-	Lee's Sandwiches	Vietnamese	Multiple	Fast food	$5
C-	House of Pies	American, Sweets	Multiple	Casual	$11
D	Katz's Deli	Jewish Deli	Montrose	Casual	$20
D	Ruchi's Taquería	Tex-Mex	Multiple	Casual	$16

Best bites of Houston

Bacon mushroom Swiss burger, Sam's Deli Diner
Banana pancakes, 59 Dinner
Bananas Foster, Brennan's
Barbecued duck, Dynasty Supermarket
BBQ Burger, Guy's Meat Market
Beef brisket, Luling City Market
Beef brisket, Thelma's
Beef fajitas, Pappasito's
Beef noodle soup, San Dong Noodle House
Beef shawarma wrap, Abdullah's
Bellini, La Strada
Berry cobbler, Café Annie
Black forest cake, Jungle Café
Boiled crawfish, Mardi Gras Grill
Buttermilk pierogi, Gravitas
Butterscotch malt with pineapple, Avalon Drug Company
Cabrito asado, El Hidalguense
California spot shrimp, Sinh Sinh
Cantalope juice, El Rey Taquería
Cevap sandwich, Café Pita +
Cheese enchiladas with chili gravy, López
Cheeseburger, Becks Prime
Chicken-fried steak, Barbecue Inn
Chile con queso, Chuy's
Churrasco, Américas
Cotoletta alla Milanese, Bice
Croque madame, Le Mistral
Crunchy French toast, Benjy's
Dim sum, Fung's Kitchen
Enchiladas Guadalajara, Guadalajara
Flour tortillas, Lupe Tortilla
Free food samples, Central Market
French fries, Barnaby's
French fries, Niko Niko's
Fried chicken, Frenchy's
Fried chicken and waffles, Breakfast Klub
Fried Gulf seafood combination, TopWater Grill
Fried oyster po' boy, Goode Co. Seafood
Fufu, Finger Licking Bukateria
Goat-brain masala on peshawari naan, Indika
Gorditas, Gorditas Aguascalientes
Grand Marnier soufflé, Tony's
Grilled fish with naan, Himalaya
Grilled mahi-mahi, Pesce

Grilled quail, Doneraki
Hamburger, Houston's
Hot dog, James Coney Island
Item #12, Mai's
Lamb kibbeh, Café Lili
Lemonade, Irma's
Lunch buffet, Udipi Café
Margarita, Armandos
Mezcal flight, Hugo's
Nasi lemak, Café Malay
Negitoro, Nippon
Nem nhonh nha trong, Bodard Bistro
New York strip, Brenner's
Old Bordeaux, Lynn's Steakhouse
Old Burgundy, Café Rabelais
Pad Thai, Asia Market
Paella, 17
Pan-fried green onion cakes, Lucky Pot
Panna cotta with saba, Da Marco
Parrillada, El Tiempo Cantina
Peking duck, Peking Cuisine
Phô, Phô Danh II
Phoenix chicken, Phô Nga
Piquillo peppers with smoked duck breast, Ibiza
Pizza, Kenneally's
Pork belly sandwich, QQ Cuisine
Pork belly with Steen's cane syrup, Catalan
Pork bun with juice (soup dumplings), Paradise Café
Porterhouse steak, Vic & Anthony's
Pupusas, El Pupusudromo
Quebexas, Max's Wine Dive
Ratafia, T'afia
Red Devil Roll, Azuma
Salade Landaise, Brasserie Max and Julie
Salt and pepper pork ribs, Shanghai Restaurant
Seafood Pancake, Bon Ga
Seven-course beef, Jasmine Asian Cuisine
Shawarma, Jerusalem Halal Deli
Shiner Bock and a movie, Alamo Drafthouse
Som tam, Vieng Thai
Soup dumplings, FuFu Café
Steamed mussels in white wine sauce, La Vista
The Piggyback, Tookie's Hamburgers and More
Torta de carne asada, 100% Taquito
Tres leches, Churrascos
Triple Bypass Burger, Dry Creek Café
Truffle egg toast, Dolce Vita
Vietnamese sandwich, Don Café
Village Burger, Field of Greens
Whole roasted branzino, Da Marco
Yellowtail belly nigiri sushi, Kaneyama

Fearless Critic

100% Taquito

Total pleasure grade

An unexpectedly authentic dose of Mexico City with showstopping asada-and-cheese tortas

9.0 *Food* **5.6** *Feel* **$11** *Price* **Mexican**

Counter service
Sun.-Thurs. 11am-10pm;
Fri.-Sat. 11am-11pm.
Outdoor dining.

Greenway Plaza
3245 Southwest Fwy.
(713) 665-2900
www.100taquito.com

Bar Wine and beer only
Credit Cards Visa, MC, AmEx
Reservations Not accepted

Residents of West U, Greenway Plaza, and Upper Kirby are all thankful for this particular and peculiar University of Houston student business plan: a disarmingly authentic chilango taquería in a part of Houston where genuine Mex-Mex food is hard to find. 100% Taquito covers all the bases with fair prices, manageable portion sizes, quick service, and excellent execution of mini-tacos in deliciously authentic corn tortillas.

The place is full of quirks, from its location in an otherwise homogenized strip along the I-59 service road, to the full-on Mexico City taxicab that sits in completely restored form inside the restaurant, to the faux-dingy Mexican storefronts painted on the walls. Unfortunately, bright lighting, high ceilings, and industrial-style tables quickly turn the atmosphere cafeteria-like.

But it is on the paper plate, or in the take-out bag, that 100% Taquito shines. An extensive but manageable menu showcases authentic versions of sopes, quesadillas, and tortilla soup, but the appropriately tiny, delightfully cheap tacos are the headliner. You'll see beefier guys walk toward the well-endowed salsa-cilantro-and-onion bar with five or six at a time. Amongst fillings, tinga (soft, gentle brisket) earns well-deserved praise, but our favorite filling is the carne asada, whose meaty, sensationally seasoned singe epitomizes the best of the genre. Surprisingly, it is in the torta—not the taquito—that the carne asada shows best. With apologies to the Philly fetishists, this is the best cheese-steak in the city. The meat's juices, opaque from a smear of mayonnaise, absorb into the fluffy cavities of fresh-baked bread. Add to this a slice of ripe avocado, shredded lettuce and tomato, the tang of chile, correctly melted cheese, and the optional acidity of spicy pickled carrots, and you have a sandwich that is an everyday miracle of balanced flavors and satisfying textures.

Mexicans tend to go to seafood places when they want seafood, and this isn't one, so skip the puny, underwhelming shrimp in any form. And we don't quite buy into the tres leches hype here. For something sweet, we prefer the aguas frescas (horchata and such), the unusually balanced frozen margaritas, and the underappreciated cucumbers, jicamas, and oranges with chile, lime, and salt—yet another welcome dose of unexpected authenticity. –RG

11th Street Café

A breakfast standby where it's never too early for chili and cheese with the hippies

C *Total pleasure grade*

4.8 *Food* **5.4** *Feel* **$12** *Price* **American**

Casual restaurant
Mon.-Fri. 7am-10pm;
Sat.-Sun. 8am-10pm.
Breakfast. Delivery. Outdoor dining.

Heights
748 E. 11th St.
(713) 862-2514

Bar None
Credit Cards Visa, MC, AmEx
Reservations Accepted

Hard up for places in town to get a good breakfast? Well at least you're not alone: breakfast is a well-documented Houston dilemma. 11th Street Café is one place that our morning-dazed Undercover Chefs turn for their groggy needs: the coffee's hot, the biscuits are fresh, and the service is just what you would expect deep, down in good ol' Texas. Sure, you probably could've cooked a better breakfast at home, but on certain mornings, you'd need the energy supplied by a chili-cheese omelet in order to *cook* a chili-cheese omelet, and 11th Street Café is there to solve this chicken-and-eggs problem.

The 11th Street Café is a humble shack of a restaurant in the Heights. You know what that means: hippies! Thankfully, this is not the ugly underbelly of hippie culture that stillbirthed such culinary disasters as curry-marinara tofu burgers and seitan-soy sauce Greek salads. Rather, we're talking about the kinder, gentler hippie influence, a vibe that eases the restaurant into a happy, relaxed pace, melting away every last bit of the ordering stress that tends to plague the ordinary diner. Slackers, neighborhood characters, and your average Heights citizens are amongst the congenial regular faces that bring about this hypnotic sense of calm.

Breakfast and pizza, in the end, are what this local dive is known for. Eggs your way, biscuits, pancakes, and potato chunks they call hash browns: this is a breakfast that will please your stomach (at least for the moment) and ease your state of mind. Do not skip out on the chili-cheese omelet. It does sound like a horrible mistake, and it probably is, but for 30 minutes of pure, childish pleasure, it's well worth it…and anyway, how many of us haven't, at some point in our lives, pursued thirty minutes of pure, childish pleasure without considering the future ramifications?

Lunch and dinner are more miss than hit; hot and cold sandwiches and meatloaf don't offer enough bliss to hand over hard-earned pennies, even if it won't take too many. If you must go beyond breakfast, try the pizza, whose pleasures are hard to deny, even if its crisp crust and bubbling toppings are easily beaten by the competition. Regardless, this is a neighborhood café worth supporting—even if it's not your neighborhood. –SD

13 Celsius

A hip new wine bar with showstopping charcuterie

B+ *Total pleasure grade*

7.6 *Food* **8.2** *Feel* **$32** *Price* **Italian**

Wine bar
Sun.-Fri. 4pm-midnight;
Sat. 4pm-1am.
Date-friendly. Outdoor dining. Wine-friendly.

Midtown
3000 Caroline St.
(713) 579-8466
www.13celsius.com

Bar Full
Credit Cards Visa, MC, AmEx
Reservations Accepted

This neighborhood wine bar and charcuterie shop might be the only of many in Houston that insists on storing and serving its reds at—you guessed it—13° Celsius. This is a refreshing change from the tepid "room temp" libations so many wannabe wine bars irresponsibly pour. 13's well-thought-out European cheese selection and paper-thin slices of cured meats like prosciutto, served up from an expensive professional meat slicer, are other reasons to visit.

The wine list is studded with quirky, unique, good-value wines that come from around the world, with an emphasis on Italy. We don't have any specific beef with California wines, but Houston restaurants have a bad habit of presenting predominantly Cal/New World lists that get incredibly old after a while—not to mention the stained teeth you'll be left with after downing a few glasses of super-concentrated, inky wines. Your palate and dentist will both appreciate 13's refreshing departure from the local norm.

Some restaurants use the modern, run-down-warehouse look as a cop-out for skimping on interior expenses. But here, it really works, and it's in the grand enoteca (Italian wine bar) tradition.

You're well advised to begin with a glass of German Riesling, and follow it with one of the charcuterie samplers. They're better than the cheeses; Brillat Savarin, for instance, is well aged, but could use some Dijon, or cornichons, or a little compote…its only accoutrements are a few wimpy almonds.

An open courtyard toward the rear of the space offers a unique pseudo-outdoor dining experience. Plush leather couches and a more-than-suitable bar make it a must-check-out for groups and single wine enthusiasts. Don't know anything about wine except the fact that it's made from grapes? No worries—talk with the bartender, and he'll set you up with something accessible. Other servers' wine knowledge varies, but attentive service is a constant. If you're in the mood for a shoulder-to-shoulder experience with the latest hip-hop pounding in your ear, this is not the place for you. If a relaxed atmosphere is in order, 13 Celsius is a great alternative to the monster-ville that Midtown can be on a Saturday night. –SN

1308 Cantina

Is $187.99 too much for Tex-Mex?

8.4 *Food* **8.2** *Feel* **$58** *Price* **Tex-Mex**

Casual restaurant
Sun.-Tues. 11am-9pm; Wed.-Thurs. 11am-10pm; Fri.-Sat. 11am-11pm.
Brunch. Date-friendly. Delivery. Outdoor dining. WiFi.

Montrose
1308 Montrose Blvd.
(713) 807-8996
www.1308cantina.com

Bar Full
Credit Cards Visa, MC, AmEx
Reservations Recommended

At what point do prices shatter the barrier of reason and get in the way of your enjoyment of flavor and execution? Certainly that breaking point can be lower when it's Tex-Mex you're talking about, but quality ingredients, great flavors, and consistency still manage to justify the sky-high asking prices at 1308 Cantina. Here, spruced-up traditional Mexican fare like carnitas and mole verde take a back seat to giant, sizzling parrilladas: high-grade proteins in the hands of people who know what they are doing. At this Tex-Mex temple, brother of the similar El Tiempo, nachos and quesadillas *start* above $10, six "amantes shrimp" command $30.49, and parrilladas for four are priced up to a brazen $187.99 Still, that feeds six Undercover Chefs, and the kitchen delivers a lot in return.

With a more upmarket vibe than El Tiempo, 1308 draws pretty people and fashion trendsters from all walks of life. Above all, they are rewarded by the delicious grilled quail. Houston is just about the only city that routinely quails up the Tex-Mex parrillada, and it pays dividends: with all due respect to the renowned chefs of Houston, we believe that the three best places for these little birds in the city are Mexican: 1308, El Tiempo, and Doneraki. Here, they're spicily rubbed, treated with eminent care, and cooked to a beautiful medium rare.

Other parrillada winners include spicy, falling-off-the-bone baby back ribs and full-bodied jalapeño sausage. One supposed luxury that seems out of place, though, is the beef tenderloin fajitas. Houston's love affair with the tenderloin and its tenderness is strange; no fat means no flavor. No flavor means lame fajitas. Chiles rellenos, meanwhile, might either burn your mouth or taste like bell peppers, but their peculiar, slightly sweet batter works, creating a funnel-cake aspect that plays nicely off the spice. The ground-beef filling has a great ratio of fat to meat, though it can often be underseasoned.

Beer is cold and consistent, while margaritas, especially after seven when the price goes up two dollars, will drive up the bill even further—but also, perhaps, help you forget about it. –SD

17

Meditate on the exquisite proteins at this hushed temple to simple, seasonal ingredients

9.3 Food | **8.6** Feel | **$100** Price | **New American**

Upmarket restaurant
Sun.-Thurs. 6:30am-10:30am, 11am-2:30pm, 5:30pm-10pm; Fri.-Sat. 6:30am-10:30am, 11am-2:30pm, 5:30pm-11pm.
Breakfast. Brunch. Date-friendly. WiFi.

Downtown
Alden Houston Hotel
(832) 200-8888
www.17food.com

Bar Full
Credit Cards Visa, MC, AmEx
Reservations Accepted

Watch out, because downtown is coming. For one thing, one of Houston's best restaurants is here—even if it's hidden away in a chi-chi boutique hotel, the Alden—and more are on their way. And the truth is that it's even easy to park.

On a larger scale, Houston food is happening, too. And nowhere is it happening more than it is at 17, whose ever-changing menu shows off seasonal local produce, Gulf seafood, and Texas game. The flavors of this kitchen speak in clear, expressive tones, simply but deeply reinforced by patient stocks and carefully reduced sauces, with the consistent understanding that fusion works best in moderation. The result is the kind of big-city restaurant that would go over well in San Francisco or even Paris.

You'd think it would go over better than it does in Houston, where you'll see a lot of the seats—which are done up in cutting-edge shades of gray against bright red walls and a network of hanging crystals whose sparkle challenges the minimalism of the aesthetic—empty, even on busy nights. People might be scared off by the high prices: $115 for the tasting menu with wine pairings puts you above $150 a head after tax and tip.

But the food and service absolutely sparkle. A compelling argument that soft-shell crab can be successfully grilled—not just fried—comes in the form of a preparation that bathes the crab in a delicious green-curry sauce whose heat and presentation seem less Asian than modern French. Homemade pastas—lobster "Love Letters" with spring peas, shaved fennel, and Meyer lemon, say—are elevated to excellence, as are simple medallions of pan-seared duck breast, glazed with honey and ras el hanout (a Moroccan spice). Decent lump crabmeat with avocado, grapefruit, and ponzu might show up at any number of restaurants—no fireworks there—but you probably have to travel to eastern Spain to find this good a version of a straightforward paella, our favorite dish on the menu, which employs house-made chorizo and saffron rice that's spot on, deeply infused with the richness of the stock. This dish alone is worth the trip downtown. Sorbets, too—green apple, cherry, mandarin—are sublime, like spooning frozen fruit straight into your mouth.

And how about salted caramel ice cream?

In a word: delicious. –RG

59 Diner

A Texan's answer to the almighty diner...or not

B Total pleasure grade

7.0 Food | **8.0** Feel | **$18** Price

American

Casual restaurant
Daily 24 hours.
Breakfast. Kid-friendly. WiFi.

Upper Kirby
3801 Farnham St.
(713) 523-2333
www.59diner.com

Bar None
Credit Cards Visa, MC, AmEx
Reservations Not accepted

North Houston
17695 Tomball Pkwy.
(832) 237-7559

Town & Country
10407 Katy Fwy.
(713) 984-2500

In the northeast, diners are pretty much the blue-collar version of the men's country club, a place where everyone knows your name, how you like your eggs cooked, and how your coffee will be taken. Your kids probably learned their swagger there—and also, probably, how to curse there. Houston's 59 Diner means well, emulating an old-school diner atmosphere with the greasy grub to boot, but that diner aura just isn't there. So while 59 Diner isn't a diner per se, it is, at the very least, a well-orchestrated theme restaurant.

The Fifties retro theme means checkered floors, neon lights, and booths. While the Johnny Rockets of the world can go overboard on their themes, 59 Diner has the place toned down enough not to annoy you—unless, that is, you're annoyed by droves of teenagers complete with screams, giggles, and freshly minted driver's licenses.

The three-page menu is several dozen menu items too short to actually be a bill of diner fare; however, true to diner form, best are the burgers, fried stuff, and thick shakes. The plain burger ain't much, but upgrade to an avocado burger or the "Down and Dirty" burger, and you'll wind up with plenty of flavors to go around: grilled jalapeños, onions, chili, and so on. Fried mushrooms are an earthy way to start, especially with a side of ranch—delicious. Onion rings are small, girly, thin cuts rather than manly, butch, diner cuts; still, they make a good burger anchor. Shakes come at a perfect consistency, though their taste can be too milky and slightly wimpy; still, taking a chance on a shake is better than trying the classic egg cream, which is likely to lack the desperately needed fizz.

While you should trust the 59 Diner cooks with the spatula for burgers, every other "Diner Favorite" here is disastrous. Chicken pot pie might be better renamed "Frozen Vegetables and Lots of Gravy with Bits of Chicken Pot Pie," while a "classic" meatloaf is like a dry void on the plate, covered in a ketchupy sauce. But again, if you really want to go to a diner, grab a flight to New York. Down here, our diners are called "taquerías." –JY

Abdullah's

A Hillcroft standby for legit Lebanese at below-reasonable prices

B *Total pleasure grade*

7.8 *Food* **6.9** *Feel* **$14** *Price* **Middle Eastern**

Casual restaurant
Mon.-Sat. 9am-9pm;
Sun. 9am-6pm.
Date-friendly. Outdoor dining. Wine-friendly.

Hillcroft Area
3939 Hillcroft Ave.
(713) 952-4747

Bar None
Credit Cards Visa, MC, AmEx
Reservations Not accepted

This Middle Eastern restaurant, bakery, and general store serves up some of the best, quickest Lebanese plates in Houston; it is a favorite amongst locals in the know for easy lunches. The location on Hillcroft just north of Westpark makes it easy to get to from anywhere. A huge cafeteria-style spread opens daily around 11:30, and it goes fast. Get there early to enjoy the fresh dishes like whole grilled fish, and tabbouleh. Braised lamb shanks, on the other hand, get better as the day goes on, so you'll have to take your chances with the potential tradeoff between availability and deliciousness.

Outside, like many ethnic restaurants, the building could use some work—but, at these prices, who cares? Upbeat Middle Eastern pop music adds to the experience, and a general store adds an old-world charm to the dining room: think bulk bulghur wheat, tahini, a myriad of pickled vegetables, and of course their freshly baked pita bread and pastries. The store also has all necessary ingredients to light up your hookah, including the pipes themselves. One part of the dining room is used for storage of empty boxes, but if you can ignore it, that's where the problems end. Abdullah's bakery produces most of the Middle Eastern pastries and breads for the local restaurants, but of course they're fresher at the source.

The beef shawarma wrap is as good as any in Houston. At $4.99, it's also one of the cheapest. For an ovine treat, order the lamb kebab with a choice of 2 side dishes and rice or lentils. Every once in a while, the store will offer bottles of the family's first-press olive oil, which comes from their own orchards in the old country. Unfiltered and cloudy, this oil is a steal at $20 a bottle, especially compared to American-made rip-offs that lurk in certain "specialty" stores.

If you can bear to stuff anything more in your belly after the gigantic portions, try a sweet baklava with some Arabic coffee. Abdullah's is a great place for a quick lunch—especially if you're in the mood for a quick whole grilled fish. And we're virtually always in the mood for a whole grilled fish. –SN

Adrian's Burger Bar

An unassuming Fifth-Ward dive with an unordinary burger

B *Total pleasure grade*

6.2 *Food* **7.6** *Feel* **$9** *Price* **Southern**

Counter service
Mon.-Fri. 11am-6pm;
closed Sat.-Sun.

East Houston
5309 Sonora St.
(713) 674-1488

Bar None
Credit Cards No credit cards
Reservations Not accepted

Great things have come out of Houston's Fifth Ward: the Geto Boys, Scarface's solo projects, and one of Houston's greatest burgers. In a small shack flanked by a laundry joint lives Adrian's Burger Bar, home to one of the heaviest and flava-most house-made patties in Houston. Bring an appetite, and be prepared not to mess around, because these burgers are a pound apiece.

Adrian's is old school, with a distinct family-business feel. You place your order with a lady in the corner, and she yells to one of her employees to make it. Whether you choose a hamburger, cheeseburger, or bacon burger, your patty will come out least an inch thick, griddled and served on a plain white bun with your choice of toppings. "All the way" is with mustard, lettuce, tomato, pickle, and mayo. The patty is so good, though, that everything else is rendered more or less obsolete—your mouth, too, as it probably won't be able to stretch itself around the burger. And be forewarned that the weight of the sandwich in your brown take-out sack might render your gait lopsided.

The building is respectable; imprinted on its side are the words "Adrian's Burger Bar," and the restaurant within—if you want to call it that—is honest, honest, honest. Walk in and you will see a small dining room with tattered walls and a small television that is usually playing daytime soap operas. There's no self-aggrandizement here, no adjectival nonsense: if you want to-the-point service and to-the-point, fill-your-stomach food, then you are definitely in the right place.

Beyond burgers, Adrian's also serves soulful soul food: braised oxtails in a thick brown sauce, crispy fried chicken, and stewed greens, among other Southern standbys. The soul food sits on steam tables behind a glass counter, but don't fret: the braised items, like the oxtails and the pork only get better with time. Not so for the burger: once you impose some method upon your jaw-wrenching madness, you should get going right away, because you're bound to be in it for the long haul. –SD

Al's Quick Stop

Where else can you get spark plugs, toilet paper, light bulbs, and a falafel sandwich in one stop?

B+
Total pleasure grade

7.2
Food

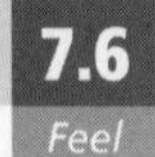
7.6
Feel

$8
Price

Middle Eastern

Counter service
Mon.-Sat. 11am-5pm; closed Sun.

Montrose
2002 Waugh Dr.
(713) 522-5170

Bar None
Credit Cards Visa, MC, AmEx
Reservations Not accepted

Food marts are a subculture all to themselves. Some sell the standard cold beverages and the occasional microwaved burrito and hot dog. Then there are some that up the ante by selling shirts and hats. And then there's Al's Quick Stop, which, besides being a standard quickie mart, also conceals a quality Middle Eastern restaurant and a carnicería within its walls. But you wouldn't know this at first glance; walking in to this unassuming muraled building next to Rudyard's Pub on Waugh, it looks like the first category: an everyday quick mart equipped with a heavily-accented cashier, three types of breakfast cereal, and ice cream bars for the occasional lift-off. But then you'll notice pictures of dishes on the wall; and then you'll notice their incredibly low prices. And look behind you at the above-average wine selection. Take a second to behold that: decent wine at a so-called "quick stop." Super-friendly cashiers make it all the more pleasant.

The Middle Eastern menu here boasts gyros, kebab plates, and hummus. A falafel sandwich with yogurt sauce, lettuce, tomato, and pickled vegetables runs a fantastic $2.99. Crispy and hot, the falafel mingles nicely with the acidic vegetables and yogurt. If you don't want a sandwich, each of the proteins can come deconstructed with hummus and vegetables for a dollar more. The carnicería right next door offers queso fresco, marinated skirt steak, and whole chickens. Homemade chorizo is linked up and has just the right amount of fat-to-meat ratio; garlic and paprika shine through. The fajita meat, marinated in a garlicky mix, is delicious, well worth the asking price.

Time after time we find ourselves amused by the happy coexistence of everything at Al's. Food cultures meld as well as those of the people coming in; foodies who've trekked out to give it a try mingle with anyone who happens to have stepped in for a quick quick-stop purchase. So the next time you need some tampons and cat food, stop by Al's and prepare yourself for a whole lot more. –SD

Aladdin Mediterranean

C
Total pleasure grade

You'd think that with such a spread, they'd at least get something right

4.1 *Food* | **5.3** *Feel* | **\$8** *Price*

Middle Eastern

Counter service
Mon.-Fri. 11am-10pm;
Sat.-Sun. 11am-11pm.
Live music. Outdoor dining. Vegetarian-friendly.

Montrose
912 Westheimer Rd.
(713) 942-2321
www.aladdinhouston.com

Bar BYO
Credit Cards Visa and MC
Reservations Not accepted

Does anyone out there really know what "Mediterranean cuisine" is? There are 21 modern states that have coastlines on the Mediterranean Sea, and each has a unique climate, landscape, culture, and above all, cuisine. While there are a few areas of overlap—the simple preparations of whole fish drizzled with olive oil, for instance, that are shared by coastal Italy, Spain, and Greece—the indigenous recipes far outnumber the communal ones. So why is Aladdin restaurant, at Montrose and Westheimer, claiming to serve "Mediterranean cuisine"? What's really being proffered here is a haphazard hodge-podge of dishes that might charitably be described as Americanized pan-Middle Eastern and Greek: shawarma, falafel, tabbouleh, kebabs, and such. The highlight is a nice selection of cold, occasionally fragrant salads.

Aladdin is a tray-and-take place: you grab your tray, order, and then take. It's an open space with rustic colors and a giant, eye-catching (if not exactly romantic) vase in the middle of the dining room. Shawarma is hardly tongue-catching, though; the sandwich features meat, lettuce, and tomatoes. Bland yogurt sauce makes scarcely any sense. Falafel balls themselves, on the other hand, are delicious, crispy and earthy, but they, too, come in a boring wrap with the usual suspects…and pickles. Whatever.

Cold salads (tabbouleh, lentil, vegetable, and so on) can tend toward the overly acidic, but at their best, the flavors are refreshing. The best part of Aladdin is the fresh juices that are made daily. Watermelon is a favorite, but the pineapple-papaya needs more of the sweet-and-sour flavor of pineapple.

In the end, you're best not show up to Aladdin at all, but if you do, you'd really better not show up in a hurry. Some dishes, such as giant kebabs, can gobble up 20 minutes from order to table. On the other hand, the kebabs come skewered with giant silver daggers that might come in handy if you are hanging around Montrose and Westheimer after dark, walking off your dinner, and happen to encounter an armed "Mediterranean" mobster. –SD

Alamo Drafthouse

A rare chance to experience film as it was meant to be experienced: with a beer

B Total pleasure grade

4.2 Food **8.7** Feel **$22** Price

American

Movie theater
Hours depend on movie times.
Date-friendly. Kid-friendly.

West Houston
1000 W. Oaks Mall
(281) 920-9268
www.drafthouse.com

Katy
531 S. Mason Rd.
(281) 492-1455

Bar Wine and beer only
Credit Cards Visa, MC, AmEx
Reservations Not accepted

The Alamo Drafthouse is a quintessential extension of Austin, and Houston is lucky to have a couple of its own (there's one in the West Oaks Mall and one in Katy). None of them have the notched wooden benches and vaguely criminal air of the downtown Austin original, but anyway, that might not play as well in Houston.

The concept does, though. Why, the Drafthouse seems to ask the world, aren't there more movie theaters that bring food and drinks to your seat? Yet the cinema does not rest at that mere gimmick. In addition to well-chosen first-run options, Alamo also shows some wacky second-run and oldie stuff, often timed with holidays, Hollywood milestones, and so on. The promotions seem never to end: there are weirdo horror flicks on Thursdays, when admission is free (you get what you pay for, unless you're a cult horror fanatic). Tuesday matineés are baby-friendly (under 6 allowed…you'd better watch out not to end up there by accident!). And there are Texans games screened for free every Sunday (as they should be—after all, we saved a lot of money by not drafting Reggie Bush).

But first, a primer: Once you enter the theater, you peruse the menu using darkroom-style yellow lights that hide beneath the narrow bar in front of you. Next, you scrawl your order in freehand onto a piece of paper, which you then place in the notch along the back of the bar, carefully positioning it such that it sticks up and can be spotted by one of the servers, who will confirm your order with a flashlight. (The waitstaff is incredibly good-natured given their arduous task.)

As for the food, it's just okay, but would you expect eye-rolling creations? You can barely see the plate, and, anyway, you're busy watching the little green men. Alamo's menu items are a little more earthbound. Pizzas have a nice, tangy sauce but humdrum toppings and an overdone crust. Fries are crunchy but can come cold. Stay away from queso (strange, to put it charitably), avoid the mealy Portobello sandwich, and opt instead for the chicken pesto, which is herby and moist. Beers on tap are lively and broad-ranging, and, of course, there's Austin's favorite, Amy's ice cream, for dessert. –FC

Alexander the Great

B-
Total pleasure grade

Good-hearted Greek food in a gaudy room that ranges from raucous to strangely lonely

8.0 *Food* **4.7** *Feel* **$63** *Price* **Greek**

Upmarket restaurant
Mon.-Thurs. 11am-10pm; Fri. 11am-11pm; Sat. noon-11pm; Sun. 11am-9pm.
Brunch. Kid-friendly. Live music. Outdoor dining.

Galleria
3055 Sage Rd.
(713) 622-2778
www.alexanderthegreatgreek.com

Bar Full
Credit Cards Visa, MC, AmEx
Reservations Accepted

With the unfortunate passing of Mykonos Island, Alexander the Great is just about the only real upmarket Greek restaurant left in Houston, even if the fontage of the restaurant's sign is as downmarket as they come, with that comic-Greek font that makes you think of Disney's Hercules, or a dumpy diner. The stripmall doesn't help appearances, either, nor does the enormously tacky Greek statue with whose Platonic form you're bombarded immediately upon stepping into the restaurant.

In this case, upmarket Greek translates to pricey fishes and meats, prepared on big platters, and served in a festive weekend atmosphere, with live music and belly dancers. (Weekends are just about the only time people come here—come on a weekday and be prepared for a lonely room.) It also translates to a unique opportunity to try an array of Greek wines, even if they're not world-class.

But here's the unexpected secret: amidst all the kitsch, Alexander the Great's food is actually pretty good. Saganaki, the greek cheese flambéed at the table, is irresistibly good. Moussaka is silky, with an addictive balance of flavors from potatoes, eggplant, and beef. Grape leaves, kefta, gyro—they're beautifully seasoned, moist, and careful. Lemony oven-roasted potatoes are rich with olive oil, and very good. Amongst proteins, rack of lamb is tender and delicious, and a whole char-broiled snapper is successful, too, as is a butterflied trout if you can find it on special. Shrimp and quail don't lose a bit of juiciness on the grill. The difference between these preparations and the ones you'll find at your everyday Greek-American dives couldn't be any more pronounced.

You'll have to come to Alexander the Great ready to pay the price: up to $39 for mains at press time, with the midrange options hovering in the low-to-mid $20s. It's probably more than you're used to spending on Greek food, and it's certainly more than you'd expect to spend for such an iffy atmosphere (be forewarned: don't bring a date here on a weeknight). Still, the refreshing change—and the chance to try something approaching real Greek food in a town now almost completely bereft of it—justifies the cost. –RG

Amazón Grill

Nuevo cafetereño

4.4	3.0	$28
Food	*Feel*	*Price*

Latin American

Counter service
Mon.-Thurs. 11am-10pm;
Fri.-Sat. 11am-11pm;
Sun. 11am-9pm.
Kid-friendly. Outdoor dining. WiFi.

West U
5114 Kirby Dr.
(713) 522-5888
www.cordua.com

Westchase
9600 Westheimer Rd.
(713) 933-0980

Bar Full
Credit Cards Visa, MC, AmEx
Reservations Not accepted

This giant cafeteria-style venue aims to bring Nuevo Latino to a very mainstream audience. You'll have to hunt a bit to find much that's authentically Latin American about the cuisine, though; even the name of the place is curiously adulterated (for some reason, they accent the "o" in the American spelling of the river; in Spanish, it's "Amazonas"). But maybe adulteration is what Nuevo Latino is all about.

In any case, people love it—especially big groups—and at times the wait can be up to 45 minutes. The space inside is airy and open, with the amusing addition of a giant, superfluous exposed pipe snaking haphazardly across the ceiling for aesthetic purposes. Otherwise, walls are pale, yellow, and empty. With the masses queuing up at the salad-bar-and-salsa station in the middle of everything, the place ultimately comes off like a mess hall at a children's camp in the woods.

Amazón's surprisingly pricey menu straddles pseudo-South American and bland North American fare. Chicken, spinach, and artichoke empanadas, with a well-seasoned filling and slightly undercooked dough, are comforting in that frozen-pizza-pocket way. "Peruvian-style" tilapia ceviche has a dried-out texture, with scarce lime juice and little else. The tilapia is better fried, with a nicely crunchy plantain crust. Creamy, spicy chicken flautas pair well with Amazón's ubiquitous cilantro dressing (have a look around—squeeze bottles full of the stuff are all over the restaurant, and everyone seems to be putting this dressing on something).

A poorly presented pulled-pork sandwich is boring, with sweet, chewy meat and a "miso slaw" that's almost undetectably scarce. A dish called "Amazón"—presumably a specialty—is described as "oven-roasted chicken crusted with fire-roasted corn and crema," which would perhaps suggest an actual chicken leg and thigh. Instead, it's just a spongily industrial breast on a pool of Latin-style cream, topped with corn niblets that reveal no hint of a fire anywhere in the vicinity. It's like an ill-fated Nuevo Latino spin on creamed corn.

A much-touted tres leches cake is sweet and wet, and tastes strongly of vanilla. Its whipped cream is overabundant, and tastes cheap and artificial. Certainly the overpriced dessert is popular. We'll stop there, because there's nothing we're going to tell you about Cordúa tres leches that you don't already know. –FC

Américas

A tried-and-true Nuevo Latino formula in Houston's most psychedelic setting

B Total pleasure grade

7.8 Food **9.6** Feel **$75** Price

Latin American

Upmarket restaurant
Mon.-Thurs. 11am-10pm; Fri. 11am-11pm; Sat. 5pm-11pm; closed Sun. *Date-friendly.*

Galleria
1800 Post Oak Blvd.
(713) 961-1492
www.cordua.com

Woodlands
21 Waterway Ave.
(281) 367-1492

Bar Full
Credit Cards Visa, MC, AmEx
Reservations Recommended

Picture a Gaudí art-nouveau mansion transplanted into a South American rainforest, then repurposed as an Amsterdam coffeeshop. Walk into Américas, and you'll wonder if the architect was just completely 'shroomed-out when he designed this room. But we're not complaining: hardly a bad table hides amidst these rock tunnels and archways of cascading colors, floods of mysterious light, and psychedelic glass lamps.

It's understandable why Américas was so exciting in 1993, when Nuevo Latino cuisine was just breaking ground. But the upcoming Woodlands branch is a testament to the staying power of Cordúa's Galleria flagship, even if its concept has barely changed since then. Américas' ingenious marketing ploy begins with the placement of plantain chips and chimichurri on the table, something so easy yet so endlessly crowd-pleasing. The menu's flavors are similarly bold, dominated by simple flavors, smoke, and strong salsas. Irrepressibly smoky, but otherwise unremarkable (except in price), are the "marineros" (crab claws), a Cordúa mainstay. Although they surround a deliciously sticky, starchy yuca cake that tastes like McDonald's hash browns might in heaven, they're a financial big gulp at $16. Ceviche is inoffensive but not great, tackily served in a carved-out pineapple, and even more tackily served with those same smoky crab claws.

The tender churrasco steak, which is equally touted here and at Churrascos, is well seasoned and carefully cooked, if overvalued. At $56, the 16-ounce churrasco has to be the most overpriced piece of meat in the city (although at $6, the decent side dish of jalapeños and onions "flambéed tableside" might secretly be the highest-margin item—percentage-wise, anyway—on the menu). We also like the grilled quail, with great texture and crispy skin, available in a mixed grill on some nights or as a "taquito" side. Pargo (pan-seared red snapper) is a total disappointment, though, medium-dry and uninteresting, with lump crabmeat and shrimp adding prestige but not flavor.

And then there's that famous Cordúa tres leches: so much hype, so much sugar, so little condensed-milk flavor or complexity. It's not that Américas is bad. It's that they're so good at psychological marketing that you feel like walking in with one hand protecting your wallet, like you would in a 'hood full of muggers. –FC

Amy's Ice Cream

Total pleasure grade

An Austin-based dessert classic, now and forever—we have a crush on Amy

8.6
Feel

Sweets

Counter service
Sun.-Thurs. 11:30am-midnight;
Fri.-Sat. 11:30am-1am.
Date-friendly. Kid-friendly.
Vegetarian-friendly.

Upper Kirby
3816 Farnham St.
(713) 526-2697
www.amysicecream.com

Bar None
Credit Cards Visa, MC, AmEx
Reservations Not accepted

Amy's Ice Cream has long been Austin's favorite place to get dessert. Since 1993, it's been one of Houston's, too. Now they're even in San Antonio. (At least it's still a Texas thing.) They're all equally wonderful places to end a first date or take the kids, with a fun, funky atmosphere featuring neon signs, a cow motif, and—sometimes—local art for sale. One of Amy's main attractions is the friendly "scoopers" with their eclectic headgear and behind-the-counter antics.

But let's get down to business. Amy's is the sui generis of ice cream. At 14.9% butterfat, it's rich and creamy, and the flavors change often. Then there are the "crush-ins"—candy, fruit, excellent cookie dough, and dozens of other treats that are ruthlessly whacked and beaten into submission—and into your ice cream—in a spectacular scoop-flipping display that rivals the knife-throwing chefs at those Japanese teppanyaki steakhouses like Benihana. The "smoosh-in" technique was first invented in Massachusetts in the 1970s by Steve Herrell, of Steve's and Herrell's fame, but Amy's renamed it and made the process more visually oriented.

The subtly flavored "Just Vanilla" is always on the menu, as is the sweeter, almost cinnamony "Mexican Vanilla," which can be cloying for some tastes but is absolutely adored by others. "Sweet Cream" is ideal for those that enjoy simplicity—it places the focus on Amy's creamy base. Watermelon is as close to the real thing as it gets—it actually tastes like watermelon, not like artificial candy. We also love oatmeal raisin, with dense, chewy chunks of cookies that taste freshly baked. A real surprise is the Shiner ice cream, made with local Shiner Bock beer. It looks like vanilla but has a sweet, delicate, fermented flavor that grows on you with each lick.

As fabulous as the ice cream is, here's the downside: this is not DQ, and it ain't cheap. Also, Amy's is very popular and therefore often crowded. But once you've spooned some, you'll forget the suffering. And if you're an Austin transplant, you will swoooooon. –FC

Antica Osteria

B-
Total pleasure grade

Romantic, but not quite cheesy, Italian-American that makes for a mainstream hit

7.3 *Food* **9.2** *Feel* **$67** *Price* **Italian-American**

Upmarket restaurant
Mon.-Sat. 5pm-10:30pm; closed Sun. *Outdoor dining. Date-friendly.*

West U
2311 Bissonnet St.
(713) 521-1155
www.anticarestaurant.com

Bar Full
Credit Cards Visa, MC, AmEx
Reservations Accepted

If you've been to this romantic, strategically located hideaway on Montrose, the first word that will probably come to mind when you think of it is "cozy." There are few restaurants in Houston that are this obviously positioned to be a date place—with all the kitschy accessories that such an aesthetic implies—yet manage not to be overbearing about it. That sense of balance enables the staff to, say, roll out a chalkboard—a move that, at most places, might seem cheesy—and have it come off as charming, not contrived. The ceilings are low, waitpeople are friendly but don't appear more often than you want, and the music isn't quite as cheesy as it is elsewhere at places with these kinds of vibes.

The cuisine of Antica Osteria is "Italian-American 2.0." This is a term we've introduced in this book (pages 6-7), and we'll define it again here: it's the upmarket Italian-American cuisine (eggplant with sun-dried tomatoes and goat cheese, veal chop in mushroom sauce, chicken breast with prosciutto in wine sauce—all of these appear on Antica Osteria's menu) that is no less authentic, but certainly more expensive, than its predecessor, Italian-American 1.0 (checkered-tablecloth cuisine: red-sauce spaghetti and meatballs, lasagne, and so on).

Other hallmarks of Italian-American 2.0 include frequent, often Spanish-tinged misspellings of Italian words (after all, the city's Italian kitchens are pretty much all run by Latin Americans, right?); wine lists with plenty of big American Chardonnays and Cabs, plus Tuscan and Piedmontese heavy hitters; phrases like "romantic dreamy Tuscan paradise" in the promotional literature; and perhaps some attempt at terra cotta in the interior and/or exterior. And Antica Osteria fits the bill on all of these fronts.

But the food here is better than you might expect. There's a good level of quality control in simple preparations. A grilled veal chop with mushrooms comes out slightly more tender than you expect. Sausages burst with flavor. Some pastas are homemade, and few—if any—are overcooked. If you come expecting an authentic regional Italian meal, you should turn around and go right back home. But if you're looking for some decent Italian-American 2.0 in a fun neighborhood with a carefully balanced date vibe under warm, low lighting, here's your spot. –RG

Aquarium

Swimming in bad seafood

1.1 *Food* **8.3** *Feel* **$30** *Price* **Seafood**

Upmarket restaurant
Sun.-Thurs. 11am-10pm;
Fri.-Sat.11am-11pm.
Kid-friendly.

Downtown
410 Bagby St.
(713) 223-3474
www.aquariumrestaurants.com

Bar Full
Credit Cards Visa, MC, AmEx
Reservations Recommended

The Aquarium is a great restaurant for people who care more about looking at fish than eating them. The food is not great—especially at these prices—but there is a lot of it. What you're really paying for is the view of the fish tank, which is spectacular. Sadly, all of our requests to pick our dinners from the tank have been rebuffed.

The Downtown Aquarium is an ambitious venture by the Landry's "casual dining" seafood empire that ranges in quality from the sublime (Pesce) to the ridiculous (Joe's Crab Shack). The link to Joe's, which Austin musical legend Cornell Hurd has described as "an apocalyptic embarrassment to every man, woman, and child in the state of Texas," explains the general mediocrity of the food at Aquarium, too: a chain whose procurement people are buying for dozens of restaurants at a time is going to focus more on volume than quality, and the result is that nothing tastes like it just came out of the sea—or the fish tank, for that matter. The plus side of the Joe's connection is that Landry's had the resources to put together an impressively Disneyesque complex.

The buildings incorporate the old Fire Station #1 and the Central Waterworks, spanning 17 acres on the west side of downtown where the Buffalo Bayou passes under I-45. The complex contains a ferris wheel, a train ride through a shark tank, dancing fountains, a temple with tigers, and assorted carnivalesque fun for the kids (you have to pay for most of these; there's a $15.99 all-day pass, not including tax, if you plan to spend some time). Inside the main dining area, the central stair curls around a 3-story cylindrical fish tank leading up to the main dining room, in which the tables are arranged around a 200,000-gallon tank full of rays, eels, and tropical fish. We can attest that kids love it.

Which is pretty much the point of this place. If you think of it as a trip to an aquarium with your dinner bill as the price of admission, then it's a good value. If you think of it as a trip to a seafood restaurant, then you're in deep, deep trouble. –FC

Arcodoro

Authentic Sardinian that leaves you shrugging your shoulders and rubbing your wallet

B- *Total pleasure grade*

7.2 *Food* **8.0** *Feel* **$75** *Price* **Italian**

Upmarket restaurant
Sun.-Thurs. 11am-11pm;
Fri.-Sat. 11am-midnight.
Brunch. Date-friendly.
Outdoor dining. Vegetarian-friendly.

Galleria
5000 Westheimer Rd.
(713) 621-6888
www.arcodoro.com

Bar Full
Credit Cards Visa, MC, AmEx
Reservations Accepted

Authenticity is a funny thing. It's hard to dislike a restaurant that strives for as authentic a regional food experience as Arcodoro does—and we salute its menu, which brings bottarga (cured roe) and wild boar ragú to Houston. But with a location so prime, a dining room so sophisticated, and a price point so high, it's hard not to wish that the food tasted better, the service were more intimate, and that your wallet didn't feel so violated as it does when you exit the doors of Arcodoro.

Advertising that you import bresaola or bottarga raises the expectation of quality. At Arcodoro, the food is not sharply executed—not bad enough to send back, but just not executed well enough to really enjoy. A special of simply pan-roasted blue-nosed bass, at one visit, was slightly overcooked, making it a bit dry and sapping its flavor. Gnocchi di patate e ricotta salata tend to be just a bit overworked, making the dumplings toothsome instead of fluffy, a frustrating problem because the dish has great flavor. And how a wood-burning oven, which should have temperatures in the thousands, managed—at one visit—to undercook the slices of eggplant that rested on top of our Genovese pizza is beyond us. The simple, delicate food that Arcodoro strives to create needs quality sourcing and spot-on cooking—neither of which seems to be a forte here. The claim of authenticity is compromised, too, by straight-up American dishes like whole-wheat fettucine with grilled chicken, roasted vegetables, and tomato sauce.

Arcodoro has a classic dining room, elegant but with a personality. The open kitchen area with a wood-burning oven brings comfort and sophistication to the place. However, the service is the exact opposite. Though staff are expertly trained and technically flawless in the act of service, the act comes off as soulless, indifferent, and on cruise control the entire night. For appetizers up to $24.50 and a check that can easily reach past a C-note per head, quality is even more important than authenticity. Your Sardinian grandmother would execute much better than this—and surely charge far less. –JY

Armadillo Palace

We'll take good ol' fashioned Texas pride, even if it's remanufactured

B- *Total pleasure grade*

6.2	9.0	$22
Food	*Feel*	*Price*

American

Bar
Mon.-Wed. 11am-midnight; Thurs.-Sat. 11am-2am; Sun. 11am-10pm. *Date-friendly. Live music. Outdoor dining.*

West U
5015 Kirby St.
(713) 526-9700
www.thearmadillopalace.com

Bar Full
Credit Cards Visa, MC, AmEx
Reservations Accepted

"A Disneyesque homage to Texas" would be the charitable way to describe it (charitable if you don't mind Disney, that is). "Totally fake" would be the uncharitable way. Either way, we'll take Jim Goode's Western-themed joint on Kirby, whose presence is trumpeted by a giant stainless-steel armadillo out front, over most other downmarket bars-and-grills in town. Even if you have a hard time not giggling at the rows of saddles, the longhorns, the paraphernalia at every glance, the live music is killer, the service is smiley, and some of the waitresses are drop-dead Texas gorgeous.

It's the sort of place you can't help but bring out-of-towners: people hang out on the nice, relaxing patio, drinking beers, downing outdoor food like boiled crawfish or brisket, depending on the day. The Aggies come out to watch Aggie games, knowing that they'll find friends here. And on many, many nights, there's dancin', and singin', and a good time is had by all.

Our favorite app—and many, if not most, people here focus on apps—is the smoked chicken-and-cheese flautas, which are deeply battered, satisfying comfort food. Buffalo wings are decent, fairly moist and appropriately vinegary, although the blue cheese dressing is totally smooth and wimpy, more like a ranch. We don't mind the green chile empanadas. We don't like them, either. Still, they're better than the boring, brittle nachos with a smear of mediocre refried beans, and the venison chili that doesn't have enough depth of flavor; nor does it lend itself well to nachos. Among mains, steaks tend to come too well done; burgers are better, if hardly notable. But hey, you're here for the beer and the tunes, right?

Weekend performances often require a cover, usually $5, not bad for a rocking party. There's pool, there's dominoes, there's shuffleboard—it's hard to argue with that—and there's two-stepping. We do wish the draft beer selection were better, given that this is such a beer kinda place. But another seductive smile from that bare-midriffed waitress, and we'll probably shut the hell up. –RG

Armandos

Standard Tex-Mex on gilded platters for the rich—and those who pretend to be

B- Total pleasure grade

7.5 Food **8.0** Feel **$64** Price **Tex-Mex**

Upmarket restaurant
Mon.-Thurs. 5pm-11pm; Fri.-Sat. 5pm-midnight; Sun. 5pm-9pm.
Date-friendly.

Upper Kirby
2630 Westheimer Rd.
(713) 520-1738
www.armandoshouston.com

Bar Full
Credit Cards Visa, MC, AmEx
Reservations Essential

It's not clear what's more amusing—watching the high rollers and the oilmen with young girls on their arms, or watching the people who are impressed by that and trying desperately to emulate it. The whole process is made even more amusing when it takes place at Houston's most conspicuously upscale Tex-Mex joint, Armandos. Eighty-six the enchiladas and margaritas, and you would guess this is one of Houston's classic steakhouses, or perhaps a new French brasserie, with its deep reds, dark golds, plush carpet, and even plusher curtains. And until recently, it was. The upmarket River Oaks Grill occupied this space until the legendary Armandos came out of retirement to take over its space.

Generally, upscale Mexican or Tex-Mex means you're dining in an hacienda-like space, whose aesthetics, more than anything, put you at ease. Armandos is more or less the opposite. They're so pretentious that they see it fit not to label the restaurant—on the door or anywhere else. If you're exclusive enough to find the way in, servers look sharp in close-fitting black clothing—the new, sexier take on the unisex tie. We love the large, secluded banquettes, especially great for two. Snag one in the corner and you've got the best view in the house.

Another phenomenon we get a kick out of is how every expensive restaurant in Houston thinks that all anyone really wants is a steak; clearly, it's sign that you're a success in life when you walk in and order the most expensive thing on the menu. It sometimes seems like every single upmarket restaurant, whether French, Italian, New American, Asian, or even Tex-Mex, seems to think that its flagship dish should be an expensive steak. And worse still, most of them think the cut should be filet mignon. Here we have the "Armandos Cut," the only time his name graces the dinner menu (aside from the delicious margaritas, to which he absolutely should lay claim).

We don't buy it. We like Armandos for its Tex-Mex, and, above all, those stellar margaritas. Queso shines, its consistency just thick enough. Beef fajitas come with well-seasoned meat that we wish were just a touch more tender. Chicken verde enchiladas, recommended by our server at our last visit, had dry chicken but competent sauce. (All things considered, would we trust them with a steak?) In the end, though, we find Armandos' kitchen not up to the standard set by Chuy's next door. And you'll certainly spend less on those equally delicious Mexican martinis. –AH

Artista

Upscale but disappointing Nuevo Latino, whether the theater audience mixes or matches

C
Total pleasure grade

5.9 *Food* **8.3** *Feel* **$69** *Price*

Latin American

Upmarket restaurant
Mon. 11am-2pm; Tues.-Thurs. 11am-9pm; Fri.-Sat. noon-11pm; Sun. 11am-9pm.
Live music. Outdoor dining. WiFi.

Downtown
Hobby Center
(713) 278-4782
www.cordua.com

Bar Full
Credit Cards Visa, MC, AmEx
Reservations Recommended

Within and without these pages, we've often railed against the customer-driven mix-and-match theory that is becoming so popular in the restaurant world these days. If that's the right-wing position, then we're far left—or if that's the left-wing position, then we're far right. We're not sure which it is, but regardless, we believe in omakase: we believe that the chef knows better than the customer what the customer should be eating, that the best restaurant doesn't even have a menu, and that the best customer should come in and eat whatever the chef happens to be making that day.

Cordúa's Hobby Center venture falls somewhere between the do-it-yourself and chef-knows-best extremes, offering a conciliatory middle ground. The main menu features a dozen or so proteins, plus an equal number of "accompaniments" (vegetables and starches, from grilled asparagus to cheese ravioli to yuca fries) and sauces (spanning the spectra of acidity and fat, from habañero-citrus to morel foie gras). It's middle-ground in that you can either play chef or stick with the house-recommended pairings.

This is the very definition of a captive-audience theater district restaurant—being attached to the theater itself—and as such, it automatically fills up before, and then again after, the show. Beyond that, though, Artista has a prime location, with scenic outdoor seating overlooking downtown.

Unfortunately, and unusually, it doesn't much matter whether you do it yourself or let the chef decide, because nothing we've tried has been particularly impressive, or particularly terrible. Maybe the theater crowd is conservative, cooking-time-wise. But we doubt they're conservative enough to want all the meats and fishes overcooked. What we do love, however, at Artista, are the angel wings with blue cheese aïoli, which are like buffalo wings on crack, expertly fried and one step removed from all chicken-wing bone issues—the lazy man's lobster of buffalo wings, perhaps. Soft-shell crawfish taquitos are comfort food, but Artista does less well when it tries to go Asian fusion, as in Miso soup with shrimp, avocado, and wonton crisps; or basic eclectic American dishes like Caesar salad, baby spinach and crabmeat salad. Mixed greens with cilantro drizzle come in at a shocking $9—still nothing compared with the $16 "crab caprese," an ill-conceived mess with underripe tomato. At these prices, Artista undershoots even its captive-audience expectations. –FC

Asia Market

A deliciously authentic Thai grocery store where farang are welcome, if scarce

A- Total pleasure grade

8.7 Food | **5.0** Feel | **$8** Price | **Thai**

Counter service
Mon. noon-7pm; Tues.-Sat. 10am-7pm; Sun. 11am-7pm.
Breakfast.

Heights
1010 W. Cavalcade St.
(713) 863-7074

Bar None
Credit Cards Visa, MC, AmEx
Reservations Not accepted

If it's true, generally, that the best Asian food in the city is often the cheapest, then that principle is doubly true for Southeast and South Asian. The cheapest Thai, Vietnamese, and Indian places in obscure Houston strip malls often seem to be twice as cheap, and twice as good, as their upmarket competitors. (Not that the upmarket places are, strictly speaking, even real competition—they're reaching out to a totally different audience.)

Contributing editor Tatiana Schnur showed us the way to this simple Thai grocery store, which just might be the most extreme data point supporting that hypothesis. The store, which caters to the local Cambodian, Lao, and Thai communities, looks like a condemned 7-11, with bars over it doors, but if your vision of heaven is filled with dried shrimp, tamarind, and kaffir lime leaves, then Asia Market will make your knees wobble. The aisles hold treats like Thai chilies, authentic Thai basil, fresh galangal, ginger, mint, mung bean sprouts (50 cents a pound), fresh noodles, and three types of house-roasted chili pastes for good measure.

Meal service happens in the back of the store, where you'll join members of the local Cambodian, Lao, and Thai communities, and perhaps a monk here and there. Som tam (that classic green papaya salad, the backbone of northern Thai cuisine, that's rarely found in the US) is prepared to order, and it's good, acidic, and spicy; but if you're a farang (the Thai word for Westerner), you'll have to be pushy to get it Thai-spicy (it's worth the battle). Pad Thai isn't nearly as common in Thailand as people think, but Asia Market's is easily the best in town, made with proper doses of spice and the fermented tang of dried shrimp, peanuts, lime, and fresh noodles with a refreshingly resilient, al-dente, texture. Sticky rice, that cheap Thai mainstay (pair it with the som tam), is better here than it is at Vieng, Asia Market's authentic-Thai competitor in town. (On the other hand, Vieng has better som tam.)

Desserts might include a challenging tamarind jelly wrapped with banana leaves and a dried nut-paste center, or homemade bean-paste cakes and pastries. Every visit to the Asia Market brings an opportunity to enter uncharted territory: a tripe dish has shown up, or an authentic fish curry over those wonderful homemade noodles—yet another treat that's utterly unfamiliar to farang tastes. –TS

Avalon Drug Company

An American culinary time capsule with a great big mouth

B
Total pleasure grade

6.6	6.9	$16
Food	*Feel*	*Price*

American

Casual restaurant
Mon.-Fri. 6:30am-5pm;
Sat.-Sun. 7am-4pm.
Breakfast.

Upper Kirby
2417 Westheimer Rd.
(713) 527-8900
www.avalondiner.com

Bar None
Credit Cards Visa, MC, AmEx
Reservations Not accepted

It's great when the staff takes control of the meal, and you're just along for the ride. Diners all across America the Beautiful tend to serve the food you're comfortable with, without much commitment needed. Avalon Drug Co. & Diner serves dishes that don't take a lot of thought, but do come packed with subtle, nostalgic flavors. It's a humble diner, but one with a big ego. The sometimes attitude-sporting staff is nothing if not genuine: if you're off to them, they'll probably be off to you, but hey, you probably deserve it. Soups, salads, hamburgers, and hot dogs all come out to play, but don't forget the genre that has withstood the test of time: blue-plate special.

In a small strip mall, this joint recalls days when life was easier and restaurants were humble places to eat and converse. Patty melts, chili cheeseburgers, and onion rings are what to expect at the Avalon Diner. Best of all, perhaps, is the crispy, delicious chicken-fried steak, made not with the shoe-leather meat that takes three days to chew, but rather with moist, tender, flavorful beef. The porky, peppery gravy is a triumph of sensuality, one of those erotic sins that you dream of when you get into a bathtub. There's a "Vienna Beef Dog" with chili and cheese, and well-executed fried chicken. The fried-egg sandwich is another Avalon home run: two fried eggs on your choice of bread with lettuce and tomato. Fork over the extra cash to throw on some pig for good measure. When you bite into the sandwich, the yolk oozes out and drips off your chin for a mess that will leave you delighted.

The famous-diner experience wouldn't be complete without malt or a flavored soda. The butterscotch malt with a bit of pineapple might seem like an unlawful entry, but it is in fact a combination for the record books. Alternatively, enjoy a cherry or vanilla Coke with two straws—the second for the significant other that will escort your bloated body home. –SD

Azuma and Azumi

Sushi, sashimi, robata, and sex appeal

B-
Total pleasure grade

7.6	8.5	$55
Food	*Feel*	*Price*

Japanese

Casual restaurant
Mon.-Thurs. 11:30am-2:30pm, 5pm-10:30pm; Fri. 11:30am-2:30pm, 5pm-11pm; Sat. noon-11pm; Sun. noon-10pm.
Date-friendly.

Rice Area
5600 Kirby Dr.
(713) 432-9649
www.azumajapanese.com

Downtown
909 Texas St.
(713) 223-0909

Bar Full
Credit Cards Visa, MC, AmEx
Reservations Accepted

Hold on, Houston: all hope may not be lost in the sushi scene after all. A Kirby mainstay, Azuma is one of the most balanced Japanese restaurants in town. The designer jeans and little-black-dress crowd are a strong presence at Azuma, perhaps for its dim-lit, trendy-sexy vibe, but thankfully, this is not a place where food is overlooked. The specialty rolls continue to be some of the best in town, while the robata—a style of Japanese grilled meats with super-heated stones—does well to satisfy the appetites of the raw-a-phobes; they're almost all good, even if overcooking can be a problem.

Azuma has its feng-shui in order: wood tones and running water seems to be a running motif. The space itself is sparse, but welcoming, sexy, but not over the top. The tightrope of trendiness is walked without the place feeling like a club—don't expect bells, whistles, or loud music. Unfortunately, though, the service has never been good at Azuma; they play by the rule that everything is fine as long as the food gets to your table. Order things separately, and the things will almost never show up at the same time, leaving one person watching others eat.

The food, however, has always been a strong point. We wince to recommend the specialty rolls—possibly the most anti-cultural, pro-American things you could order off the menu—yet they have long been a forte here. Hey, if we can ruin (and love) interpretations of the French tarte tatin by making apple pie and melting a Kraft Single on it, we can love the bastardization of Japanese cuisine, right? Azuma's famous "Red Devil Roll" is an addictive combination of spiciness and crunch, but the dobin mushi, a teapot soup with seafood in a highly concentrated broth, is often made with too much MSG, impelling you to drink a glass of water immediately. The hamachi kama (yellowtail collar) is heavenly, with soft grilling applied to both the crispy and fleshy parts of this little-used part of the fish. And the sashimi at Azuma is always served at the correct temperature, fresh, with large, glistening slices.

Azuma can quickly get pricey, but in this Zen setting, for quality—if not extraordinary—food, it's one of the places in town where you won't feel like you've overpaid for food that wasn't even cooked. –FC

Baba Yega

B-
Total pleasure grade

A flamboyant, euro-cute, garden-blessed brunch favorite in the heart of Montrose

7.7 *Food* **8.0** *Feel* **$14** *Price*

American

Casual restaurant
Mon.-Thurs. 11am-10pm; Fri.-Sat. 11am-11pm; Sun. 10am-10pm. *Brunch. Kid-friendly. Outdoor dining. Vegetarian-friendly.*

Montrose
2607 Grant St.
(713) 522-0042
www.babayega.com

Bar Full
Credit Cards Visa, MC, AmEx
Reservations Accepted

Named after a witch, Baba Yega brings on a potion of great sandwiches, grilled items, and burgers that use fresh and sometimes unusual ingredients. This converted bungalow, spot in the heart of the Montrose area, has been flamboyantly entertaining customers since 1975. From the outside, the restaurant looks like a converted Houston house, which it is, but on the inside it has the feeling of a little old European cottage. Brown wood, old paintings, and mementos clutter the walls, endowing the space with a vintage feel, and a beautiful garden and pond in the back of the structure team up to generate a view that's man-made but well worth it. Considerable crowds can sometimes show up here at random times—except brunch, when they're guaranteed to show up; nonetheless, there's usually room enough for everybody.

The menu is divided between appetizers, veggie-tailored selections (vegetarians will be quite happy with the selection here, from fruit plates to mains to desserts), and evil carnivorous mains, burgers, and sandwiches. The mainstays on the menu, however, are really the last two. A smoked turkey and brie sandwich with tomato and vinaigrette is delicious, light and filling at the same time, served on a multi-grain bread that's nutty and fresh. The burgers feature huge, grilled, house-made beef patties with fresh veggies and your choice of french fries or potato salad. The potato salad is spiked with dill that gives it a refreshing brightness.

All that said, if you go to Baba Yega, you should probably go for brunch. Get there early, because it gets crowded, and the food tastes better before the kitchen gets in the weeds (for the uninitiated, our Undercover Chef explains that this is a cook's term referring to the point when your station becomes untenably messy after hours of high-pressure meal service, and your cooking falls apart). Eggs, salmon, brisket...it's all fresh, well-executed, and on the $17.95 brunch buffet, which—after a trip through the line, and if Houston summers and tropical storms cooperate—can be enjoyed in the idyllic garden, which you might find more idyllic still after your fourth or fifth Bloody Mary (no mimosas for our Undercover Chefs). –SD

Baby Barnaby's

No need to change these diapers—this comforting breakfast place is established

6.0 Food | **5.0** Feel | **$10** Price | **American**

Casual restaurant
Daily 7am-noon.
Breakfast. Kid-friendly.

Montrose
602 Fairview St.
(713) 522-4229
www.barnabyscafe.com

Bar None
Credit Cards Visa, MC, AmEx
Reservations Not accepted

There are not too many places you can go to in the city for breakfast, which, some might argue, is what promotes Baby Barnaby's from the okay category to the good category. But our Undercover Chefs declare that this promotion is hardly *ex officio*: even if there's nothing that really blows us away about the place, but we like it. In a small room connected to the original Barnaby's they serve traditional breakfast foods. Eggs, pancakes, coffee, and fresh fruit: this place serves its purpose by neither turning anyone on nor rubbing them the wrong way.

The hours are early, so don't fret if you don't quite make breakfast; after all, breakfast is Houston's most challenged meal. If you do get there bright and early, sign the little paper book to get in line for a table, because space is limited, and there will be a wait no matter who you are. The coffee is hot, service is fast and polite, (no attitudes that early in the morning is a plus), and the portions are big enough to get you through (or past) the lunch crunch. Fast, furious business can sometimes mean chaos, but it's all part of the experience.

Baby Barnaby's atmosphere isn't as horrifically life-changing as is the psychedelic Barnaby's, but it still might make you think about the Brady Bunch on hallucenogenics. Mexican breakfasts—migas, huevos rancheros, and lowfat breakfast burritos—taste good, but also, in some weird way, all taste the same. The pancakes are delicious, and the tasty pork products that we all worship inexplicably in the early morning (thick bacon, link sausage, and so on) won't let you down, but rather deliver clear, greasy, porky satisfaction.

Parking is a bit crazy; unless you really luck out with a good spot, plan on a healthy breakfast walk-off (and its more unfortunate brother-in-law, the foggy breakfast walk-on). Baby Barnaby's is a great place for breakfast dates, whether flirty or postcoital. It's intimate in the sense that the tables are close, but once you start eating, you'll quickly realize that the bacon is your real date. Luckily, pork fat doesn't come with baggage or issues. –SD

Backstreet Café

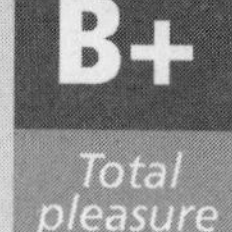

Total pleasure grade

A graceful, if hardly groundbreaking, society place awash with aesthetics

8.0 Food | **9.4** Feel | **$71** Price | **New American**

Upmarket restaurant
Sun.-Thurs. 11am-10pm;
Fri.-Sat. 11am-11pm.
Brunch. Date-friendly. Live music. Outdoor dining.

River Oaks
1103 S. Shepherd Dr.
(713) 521-2239
www.backstreetcafe.net

Bar Full
Credit Cards Visa, MC, AmEx
Reservations Essential

This River Oaks restaurant is lovely. Lovely for its gracious garden. Lovely for its effortless interior; for its keen sense of lighting and of server deference; for its stylish, older clientele; and for the graceful charm of the cute little bar. And it's lovely, too, for the elegant balance of its menu, which manages to traverse a fair bit of European and Texan thematic material without either scaring off the culinary conservatives or rolling the foodies' eyes.

The Backstreet Café menu begins with a sort of Texas version of that notorious culinary zone known as 1990s French-inflected New American. This yields some recipes that range from dated to trite to disastrous, like angel-hair pasta with shrimp, pine nuts, olives, and sun-dried tomatoes; a grilled beef tenderloin over Portobello mushroom with creamy spinach; or bacon-wrapped shrimp over mashed potatoes and spinach.

The frustrating thing is that the virtuoso French technique is clearly there. It shows through everything that comes out, in the way a chicken dish is deboned or trimmed, for instance. But the talent is wasted when it's put to use creating your lump crab cakes, which many upmarket Houston restaurants seem to think they can't live without. Better than any of the above, for sure, have been the dishes that are straight-ahead Southern: a salad of fried green tomatoes, blue cheese, and pecans (try finding that up North); crispy bacon-wrapped quail (Houston's pride) with jalapeño cornbread—yum—or a delicious "shrimp cheesecake" with house-made chorizo, roasted garlic, and peppers that seems vaguely Louisianan. We're not sure if we're just free-associating with Jacques-Imo's in New Orleans, but regardless, we mean that as a compliment.

Loveliest, however, have been fish mains, like a rainbow trout expertly crusted with hazelnuts and cleverly paired with salsa verde, in a judicious rendition of something Southwestern. At press time, this dish was priced at just $19, which—given the setting, the service, and the pricing of the competition nearby—seems just as lovely as the rest. There's also a well-put-together, deservedly popular brunch. At those moments—especially if you're sitting out in the garden—it can feel, momentarily, that Backstreet is just about the only way to dine in this city. If the rest of the menu caught up, its glory could be greater. –RG

Baker Street Pub

Hotties, beers, and burgers that actually aren't that bad

B- Total pleasure grade

7.0 Food **7.4** Feel **$17** Price **American**

Bar
Daily 11am-2am.
Live music. Outdoor dining. WiFi. Additional locations.

Rice Area
5510 Morningside Dr.
(713) 942-9900
www.bakerstreetpub.com

Bar Full
Credit Cards Visa, MC, AmEx
Reservations Not accepted

Sugar Land
15970 City Walk
(281) 494-0774

Woodlands
25 Waterway Ave.
(281) 362-7431

Any time the word "pub" is in a place's name, it's pretty safe to assume that's where the focus lies. The grill tends to be a mere afterthought, a concession to customers who get hungry after a few beers and whose taste buds at that point won't be the most discerning. The story is similar with service: publick house means, first and foremost, a place for people to convene—not to be coddled—so expect distracted service.

In all of these senses, Baker Street is a textbook pub, in the classic American-emulation-of-the-imagined-Irish-pub style, with far more Guinness paraphernalia than there would actually be in Ireland, and TVs everywhere screening the latest Astros defeat. This is hardly a crowd of Celtophiles, though. Rather, the Rice Village clientele is quick to reveal its Houston provenance: it's a beefy, fratty crew. There's quite the pickup scene on weekends, when the crowds spill onto the surrounding sidewalks; and unless you're Yao Ming or Beyoncé, it's next to impossible to get a pint when the place is busy.

That said, the food here does hit the spot as pub grub. Buffalo wings (available with or without the bone) strike a delicate balance of deeply vinegary buffalo sauce with rich blue cheese. Burgers are basic and good, cooked as ordered, and made with decent ground beef; we recommend adding bacon and cheddar. Of course, British classics—shepherd's pie and bangers and mash—are available, at your own risk. "Baja Tacos" have somehow managed to find their way onto the menu as well, but you should know better than to order that at a pub.

If you do actually find a place to sit down (later on an off-night, for instance, or mid-afternoon), you'll find the booths cozy and far more conducive to conversation than the rest of the place (where it's easier to communicate by groping than by talking—and probably more honest, too). Moral of the story: come early if you want to eat in peace, but have a few beers and the food will start to seem much, much better. So will the clientele. –AH

Bamboo House

Asian fusion that prides itself on simplicity and flavor

B- *Total pleasure grade*

7.0 *Food* **8.5** *Feel* **$23** *Price* **Pan-Asian**

Casual restaurant
Sun.-Thurs. 11am-9pm;
Fri.-Sat. 11am-10pm.
Vegetarian-friendly.

Montrose
540 Waugh Dr.
(713) 522-3442
www.bamboo-house.org

Bar Wine and beer only
Credit Cards Visa, MC, AmEx
Reservations Accepted

Blending a bunch of regional dishes into one bastardized fusion cuisine takes talent, especially if you want it to make sense rather than turning out a sloppy compendium of ideas with no focus. Bamboo House is the rare restaurant that pulls it all together with grace and ease. This simple, relaxed establishment on Waugh attempts dishes from Vietnam, Japan, and elsewhere in Asia—a classic recipe for disaster—yet the resulting flavors, though not supremely authentic, are clean, not too muddled, not too up-front, and soothing to the palate. The space is simply designed, with dark colors, nicely spaced tables, and minimalist décor. The service is much like the menu—clean and welcoming—and parking is not an issue, this being the classic Houston strip mall.

All the usual suspects are on the menu, but they are fresh, light, and modestly priced; miso soup, seaweed salad, crab dumplings, and a number of noodle dishes jointly represent America's takes on pan-Asia with knowledge and respect. Bamboo House's dumplings are decent, whether pork, vegetable, or crab; they're steamed and served with a sweet spicy dipping sauce that complements flavors rather than masking them. Shrimp tempura are gently fried, with a batter that's unusually light and crispy. Thai noodles are pleasantly spicy, with heat that doesn't sit on your tongue to spoil the meal, but rather accents the noodles before softly fading into a whisper. Rice, too—so often a pan-Asian afterthought—is delicious at Bamboo House, with hints of lime and cilantro. And it would normally be cringe-worthy to see sushi on a menu together with Thai and Vietnamese, but here, the basic assortment of raw fish is surprisingly fresh and crisp.

Dessert options include mochi, little balls of ice cream wrapped in rice paper; flavors vary from red bean to strawberry. Don't expect anything too memorable here, but Bamboo House's simple, modest understanding of fusion is refreshing in an age where food fads can so often turn out too trendy for their own good. –SD

Bank

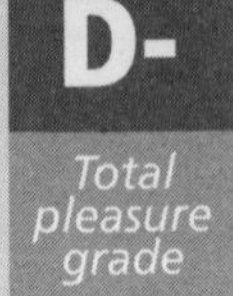

Beautiful, boring, and bumbling: keep your money out of this Bank

3.9 *Food* **5.6** *Feel* **$91** *Price* **New American**

Upmarket restaurant
Mon.-Fri. 7am-10:30am, 11:30am-2:30pm, 5:30pm-10:00pm; Sat. 7am-11am, 5:30pm-11:00pm; Sun. 7am-noon. *Breakfast.*

Downtown
Hotel Icon
(832) 667-4470
www.hotelicon.com

Bar Full
Credit Cards Visa, MC, AmEx
Reservations Recommended

It's hard not to like Bank's concept—even if that's all there is to like. The crowning achievement of the space is its creative conversion from an old bank lobby, circa 1911, into the Hotel Icon's restaurant. And what would a bank be without a vault? Here it's a wine cellar and private dining room conceived with a giddy cleverness, with an intimate window onto the restaurant's bustling kitchen. Outside the vault, 30-foot columns soar through a sleekly glowing dining room, which blends seamlessly into the hotel lobby. It will all definitely remind you of money—this is the sort of place the robber barons (or at least corporate bigwigs) would have peeled off rolls of cash to buy ribeyes for the whole crew to celebrate the latest heist (or hostile takeover).

Unfortunately, and for good reason, the crowds have thinned noticeably since the reins transferred from maverick-serial-chef-entrepreneur-pretty-boy Jean-Georges Vongerichten and his protégé, Bryan Caswell, to a twentysomething former apprentice who is clearly in way over his head. The marks that Jean-Georges has made on New York and Shanghai may be as indelible as the red ink will be on your post-meal Bank balance, but he seems to have peeled out of our own Icon without even a set of tread marks. It's unclear whether JoJo fled a sinking ship, or whether the vessel was diverted toward disaster by his departure itself.At press time, however, a new chef from South Carolina had been hired, so stay tuned.

Either way, while the Master Chef jumped into a luxury lifeboat bound straight for Vegas, Bank's kitchen headed straight for iceberg upon iceberg. Bland crab salad, unseasoned avocado, tasteless grapefruit. Seven-spiced rack of lamb? We had trouble tasting one. A highly touted surf-and-turf ("I'm from Texas, so this is the way I like it," said our server inexplicably) featured a lobster tail as rubbery as the Goodyears screeching up to the valet station, and a miniature filet mignon cooked to a masochistic well done, turning it to a stump about the color of a decayed gray tree trunk. Bumbling service, incompetent execution, and mediocre mains up into the $40s? Save your own wad of bills, because this food is not FDIC-insured. –RG

Barbecue Inn

Want some gravy with that nostalgia, honey?

B- *Total pleasure grade*

7.3 *Food* **8.3** *Feel* **$18** *Price*

American

Counter service
Tues.-Sat. 10:30am-10pm; closed Sun.-Mon. *Kid-friendly.*

North Houston
116 W. Crosstimbers St.
(713) 695-8112

Bar Full
Credit Cards Visa, MC, AmEx
Reservations Not accepted

At the Barbecue Inn, the waitresses call you "Honey," the salad dressing outweighs the salad, and the chicken-fried steak is covered in about an acre of thick country gravy. It's a restaurant that perfected its formula in the '50s, and, fortunately for us, hasn't budged since.

The "Barbecue" in the name is a bit misleading. While the Inn serves up some serviceable brisket, links, and smoked chicken, it's not one of the better barbecue offerings in town. The real geniuses at the Inn are the fry cooks, who are able to walk that fine line of crispiness between too hard and too soggy. In lesser hands, the chicken-fried steak can taste mostly like fried batter, but here, the batter plays a more deferential role, adding a crisp texture and providing an obliging surface for the artery-clogging goodness of the gravy. Fried chicken and fried shrimp are also standouts, with the batter properly locking moisture and flavor into the meat. The Barbecue Inn's french fries are some of the best in town: hand-cut, well-seasoned, and with a perfect texture for gravy-dipping. Baked potatoes are also fun, if only because they come with those three-cup serving carousels of cheese, sour cream, and bacon that seem to have disappeared everywhere else two decades ago.

Salads are a bit of joke here, unless you really, really like mediocre salad dressing, and a lot of it. We're not really sure what a vegetarian would do if they happened to wander in, but some fries and pie would probably be a good out. The chocolate cream pie and lemon meringue come right out of an era in which pie was the pinnacle of American dessert technology, so you might as well indulge—everyone else does.

At lunchtime and early dinnertime you could have a bit of a wait (who eats dinner at 5 o'clock? Oh, right…), but don't worry: the Barbecue Inn isn't going anywhere. It's been around more than half a century, and its fiercely loyal clientele will probably see to it that it's around for quite a while longer. –RH

Wiener schnitzel? Cotoletta alla milanese? Parmo? Tonkatsu?

They're all chicken-fried steaks.

Barnaby's Café

B
Total pleasure grade

Who ever said reliable comfort food couldn't be psychedelic?

7.1 *Food* **8.2** *Feel* **$20** *Price* **American**

Casual restaurant
Sun.-Thurs. 11am-10pm;
Fri.-Sat. 11am-11pm.
Kid-friendly. Outdoor dining.

Midtown
414 W. Gray St.
(713) 522-8898
www.barnabyscafe.com

Midtown
604 Fairview St.
(713) 522-0106

Bar Wine and beer only
Credit Cards Visa, MC, AmEx
Reservations Not accepted

Upper Kirby
1701 S. Shepherd Dr.
(713) 520-5131

It is widely known that dogs appreciate good value, and Barnaby's Café—likely the only restaurant in Houston named after a dead dog—is unquestionably one of the better value propositions in town. The food is predictable, but not in a bad way; it's just that you know what it's going to taste like before it enters your mouth. And you know that you and your dogs will leave full and happy. Giant salads, tasty hot sandwiches, and a few house specialties like ribs, meatloaf, and salmon don't hold any secrets to the universe or life; rather than trying to break culinary barriers, Barnaby's communicates in a common culinary idiom that just about any diner can understand.

The only thing likely to weird you out is the décor, especially at the original branch on Fairview, which is like a bad acid trip. Walk in and you will begin to wonder if your morning omelet was prepared with 'shroomz of the psychedelic variety. The walls and even ceilings are covered with paintings of flying dogs, dog bowls, and cartoon ribeye steaks. Go to the bathroom, and you might wonder if Pee-Wee is going pop out of nowhere and welcome you to his playhouse. Disturbing, yet kinky!

Luckily, the friendly, informative service will calm you down while you're tripping out, waiting to see if Barnaby the dog is going to pop out of the wall. And the menu is simple, focused, and consistently good. Surprisingly tender ribs, for instance, come with barbecue sauce that's not too sweet. Vaguely Southwestern hamburgers (skip the dry buffalo burgers and boring turkey burgers) might come well-dressed with sneakily hot green chiles, guacamole, or heartburn-happy Texas chili. We're fans of the smoked chicken tostada, and of the big, cheap, and tasty breakfasts. The roast beef, however, is strictly for the dogs—it's well done and dry—and if you're a soda-guzzling American, you might be disappointed by the small soda bottles. Best of all at Barnaby's, however, are the french fries: crispy, golden, hot, they're everything a potato could be and more. Imagine these in line, and you'll be panting just like everyone else. –SD

Barry's Pizza

Never underestimate college pizza—just stay away from the apps and drafts

6.9 Food **6.8** Feel **$15** Price

Italian-American

Casual restaurant
Mon.-Fri. 11am-11pm; Sat. noon-11pm; Sun. noon-10pm.
Delivery. Outdoor dining.

Galleria
6003 Richmond St.
(713) 266-8692
www.barryspizza.com

Bar Wine and beer only
Credit Cards Visa, MC, AmEx
Reservations Accepted

If you're the type of person who wears your college class ring around town like you just won the Super Bowl, then you're going to love Barry's Pizza. Geared toward all varieties of college types, Barry's brings back pride in your alma mater, perhaps reminding you of that day when you woke up in a pool of beer with an itching sensation that you later found out was called crabs (not on the menu). What *is* on the menu is surprisingly great pizza, chicken-centric college-town favorites like buffalo wings, and assorted salads and subs that are easily recognizable and delicious.

Decked out with a Wonder-Years-meets-the-Olive-Garden motif, Barry's stands alone in an unpretentious building with college and sports pennants hung throughout. But there's no need for a secret handshake or pledge name to enter; this is a welcoming joint that doesn't do too much preening, but quietly serves some of the best pizza in town. The thin, crispy crust comes out brown and airy, enabling it to serve as a substantial platform for the raft of classic American mix-and-match toppings. The "Barry's Special" is basically a pizza with everything—sausage, pepperoni, ham, onion, peppers, and so on—with a great balance between sauce, cheese, and toppings.

That's where most of the fun ends. Appetizers like fried mushrooms and spinach dip are merely predictable, while the chicken wings—disappointing for a college place, where wings are of paramount importance—are a total letdown. They're neither crispy nor juicy, they're small, and they're so utterly lacking flavor that even ranch or blue cheese dressing can't rescue them from disaster. Don't bother with the draft beers like Hefewiezen or other artisanal brews, because they all taste like they come from the same "King of Beers" tap (perfect for keg stands, but not very well paired with pizza). It is remarkable for an establishment to actually mess up draft beer, but it happens here, so stick to the bottles for all your adult libation needs.

Again in keeping with the college gig, Barry's has great promotional deals (half off appetizers for happy hour, and so on). And if you happen to have a wool sports pennant lying around, you can bring it in and get a free medium pizza. Brothers for life. –SD

Becks Prime

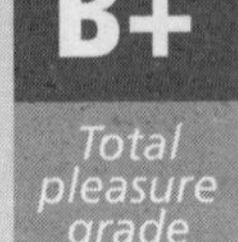

Total pleasure grade

The never-ending best-burger-chain-ever hype at this fast-food favorite is arrogant...and justified

8.5 Food **3.7** Feel **$13** Price **Burgers**

Counter service
Mon.-Fri. 10:30am-4am; closed Sat. and Sun.
Kid-friendly. Outdoor dining.
Additional locations.

Downtown
919 Milam St.
(713) 659-6122
www.becksprime.com

Spring Branch
1001 E. Memorial Loop
(713) 863-8188

Bar Wine and beer only
Credit Cards Visa, MC, AmEx
Reservations Not accepted

Upper Kirby
2902 Kirby Dr.
(713) 524-7085

When a man walks into a fast-food restaurant, he's going to buy food. He's not just a warm lead—he's already sold. So why must Becks subject its customers to a meal-long visual barrage of self-aggrandizement, from *Texas Monthly* kiss-ups to chocolate-shake hyperbole to six-square-foot food-porn images of burgers, steaks, and chicken? Even the sandwich-basket paper is striped with laudatory quotes from the *Houston Press* and *USA Today* absorbing the fry grease. (Somehow, we doubt that after this thesis paragraph, this publication will join their ranks.) The propaganda would be less jarring if there were anything else on the walls or tables. But other than the occasional splash of red paint—perhaps a counterpoint to the ketchup bottles on the formica tabletops—self-promotion is this restaurant's sole interior-decorating motif.

Just calm down, you want to say to Becks, and let the food speak for itself. Because these burgers sing in tones rich and satisfying enough to justify the hype. The ground beef is not Prime, as per the chain's name, but it's Choice, which is itself a rarity in the burger universe. The meat is ground and pattied in-house, well seasoned, and grilled over mesquite, and the indulgent results are full of meaty flavor. Sweet buns, lined with the excellent mayonnaise-based "Prime Sauce," absorb the juices well. The kitchen-sink-style "Bill's Burger" adds grilled onions (soft but not caramelized), jalapeños, bacon, cheddar, and lettuce along with that sauce, but the burger is meaty enough to render the bacon and onions superfluous—go with the basic cheeseburger. Fries, crisped to a deep, dark ochre color, are an everyday wonder.

Shakes are too thick; but grilled, butterflied hot dogs are good. Steaks (aimed at the take-it-home-and-pretend-you-cooked-it-yourself market) follow suit, but charging $24.50 for anything at a fast-food restaurant is still a ballsy move. Burgers, too, though enormous, are pricier than you'd expect at a lunch counter; at our last visit, one with fries and an iced tea cost $13.42—not prohibitive, but definitely toeing the line. Is all the self-promotion, then, meant to reassure sticker-shocked customers that their money has been well spent?

It has. But the proof is in the basket on the table, not in the writing on the wall. –RG

Benjy's

This Rice Village hotspot is deservedly popular—just not wholly for the food

B *Total pleasure grade*

7.3 *Food* **9.3** *Feel* **$54** *Price*

Southwestern

Upmarket restaurant
Sun.-Mon. 11am-9pm;
Tues.-Thurs. 11am-10pm;
Fri.-Sat. 11am-11pm.
Brunch. Date-friendly. Vegetarian-friendly.

Rice Area
2424 Dunstan Rd.
(713) 522-7602
www.benjys.com

Bar Full
Credit Cards Visa, MC, AmEx
Reservations Essential

The food's not bad, but the crowning achievement at this hypersuccessful Rice Village hotspot is the dramatic but warm interior design. The look is kind of retro-mod-meets-industrial-chic, with browns, greens, and yellow surfaces; splotchy modern paintings; and tables and chairs mixing wood with metal. Brick and pipes are exposed; floors are concrete. Little hanging lamps are like teardrops, punctuating the space; and a palm fern hogs the middle of the room, but it's a welcome distraction, as is the bustling open kitchen, which helps keeps things from feeling sterile. So does the reliably lively crowd.

The food on this menu is complex but direct Southwestern. Nothing's just for show, and most plates are piled with enough flavors to be pleasurable, if not sublime. Beef arepas are a great choice, with tender (if not melting) cumin-laced braised steak, ingeniously topped with an expertly fried egg for brunch (it's an app on the dinner menu, sans egg). The steak is served over tasty "Masa-Jack Cheese Cakes" with "Voodoo Cream," which is like crema mexicana, and there's corn everywhere. "Crunchy Chicken" comes undersalted but has fantastic texture from its pecan and pistachio coating; a sweet corn reduction works, but a combination of melted onion and marbled potato gratin is just OK, and spinach is also underseasoned.

Going back to that brunch, it's a good way to do Benjy's, if you don't mind the wait, which can be quite long on certain Sundays. They'll start you out with sweet, warm muffins, bagels, and miniature biscuits, along with a sweet apple butter. It's also a good excuse for a small but good Bloody Mary with faint wasabi and Absolut Peppar, or for the much-loved "Crunchy French Toast," which is delicious and also probably the only $14.95 French toast in town (although it does come with egg, sausage, and potatoes). Skip the overcooked burgers, though, and the crispy but bland fries.

Banana tres leches tastes more like coffee than banana, and it's quite moist but with little condensed milk flavor. A better dessert might be a drink in the sleek, if TV-laden, lounge upstairs. It's popular amongst the cocktail crowd for pomegranate cosmos and such, though it shouldn't be underestimated; they're pouring some of Houston's best and most creative drinks up here. –RG

Berryhill Baja Grill

Good fried fish tacos and periodic parties in a chainish Mex atmosphere

B- Total pleasure grade

7.1 Food **4.2** Feel **$12** Price **Tex-Mex**

Counter service
Mon.-Thurs. 11am-11pm; Fri. 11am-midnight; Sat. 10am-midnight; Sun. 10am-11pm.

Kid-friendly. Live music. Outdoor dining. WiFi. Additional locations.

Montrose
3407 Montrose Blvd.
(713) 523-8226
www.berryhilltamales.com

Heights
702 E. 11th St.
(713) 225-2252

Bar Full
Credit Cards Visa, MC, AmEx
Reservations Accepted

River Oaks
2639 Revere St.
(713) 526-8080

"Since 1928," proclaims Berryhill's logo and web site. Um, that's a bit of a stretch. Okay, it's true that a man named Walter Berryhill used to roll a tamale pushcart around River Oaks in those days. But calling this multiple-branches-in-Houston Tex-Mex mini-chain 80 years old because it supposedly uses his recipe is like claiming that the Astros date back to Sam Houston's era.

In any case, the musical atmosphere is far more festive than a tamale cart's: although you order at the counter (food is later brought to your table with suspicious rapidity), the feel is fun, and there's a full bar, complete with margarita specials, which often hops at happy hour with after-workers. At the Montrose location, the local gay community shows up to party on Sunday evenings. The dinner vibe's not quite there, though. (Maybe it's the super-gloss on the tables, or the queue at the counter.)

You'd think, given the history and domain name (berryhilltamales.com), that tamales would be the thing to eat at Berryhill. You'd be wrong. It's not that the tamales are terrible; it's just that they're no better than average, slightly underseasoned, served with a comfortable reddish brown sauce that you'd expect to see dumped atop Tex-Mex enchiladas. Rice and charro beans are good, the former well-cooked with stock, the latter undersalted but so porky that their smell practically jumps off the plate. Above average, too, are enchiladas, smothered in a deliciously green tomatillo sauce and plenty of cheese. Do the enchiladas with chicken or beef, not with the overwhelmingly rich filling of corn, red onion, chile, and cream cheese. Now there's something that wasn't getting served in 1928—and for good reason.

But the pride of this chain is fried fish tacos, whose culinary epicenter is found in little shacks along random coastal highways around San Diego and northern Baja California. Berryhill's excellent approximation is described as "tempura-fried," hinting at the thickness of the batter surrounding the fresh, mild, bright white fish. Cabbage adds a welcome crunch, and creaminess comes from a "special sauce" that tastes like chipotle mayo. Keep in mind, though, that the batter greases out after a few minutes, so eat the taco quickly. You'll want to, in any case. –RG

Bibas (One's a Meal)

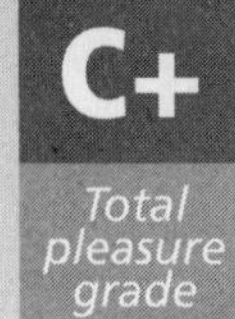

Legendary 24-hour post-bar Greek-American that will meet your expectations—if they're low

6.7 *Food* **6.0** *Feel* **$16** *Price* **Greek, American**

Casual restaurant
Daily 24 hours.
Breakfast. Outdoor dining.

Midtown
607 W. Gray
(713) 523-0425

Bar Wine and beer only
Credit Cards Visa, MC, AmEx
Reservations Accepted

Everybody has their go-to late night restaurant after a night at the bars, and Bibas is probably half of Houston's. This 24-hour Greek-American joint off West Gray in Midtown looks like your Jewish grandmother's house after having been converted first into a brothel, and then, 20 years later, into a restaurant. The colors are dark, with a couple of televisions playing in the corners—every last inch of which will be packed with people on a late Friday or Saturday night. If you come on one of those nights, prepare yourself for the show: drunks will entertain with vulgar remarks, transsexuals will work the crowd, yuppies will gape, and slicked-out scenesters will inspect scraps of paper with real or fake phone numbers scrawled across them, reliving their least failed conquests of the evening.

The fantastically amusing clientele aside, the food at Bibas is actually decent. Traditional Greek-American fare like gyros shares the menu with simple salads and greasy, delicious American and Italian-American favorites that aim straight for the pleasure centers. "Greek fajitas" are a cute idea, with slices of lamb, peppers, tomatoes, onions, melted feta cheese on pita. Fried calamari, served with spicy marinara sauce and a salad of olives, lettuce, and feta, is not bad for a fried-food fix. Gyros, served with a great acidic yogurt sauce, consistently rival the best in town.

Sometimes the service can be a bit slow, and if the owner is there, you might find yourself listening to his thoughts and opinions about life while you wait. He might even cap the amount of iced tea that you are drinking at two glasses, because he believes that more would be bad for you. At least someone's looking out for your health at that ungodly hour. –SD

Driving down I-95, somewhere in central Virginia, you'll cross an invisible real-iced-tea border. Nowhere south of there will you find tea that's not freshly brewed.

Bice

We'll take this classy, elegant Milanese chain any night of the week for reliably authentic Italian

A- *Total pleasure grade*

9.1 *Food* **8.2** *Feel* **$96** *Price* **Italian**

Upmarket restaurant
Sun.-Thurs. 11:30am-10:30pm;
Fri.-Sat. 11:30am-11pm.

Galleria
5175 Westheimer Rd.
(713) 622-2423
www.bicehouston.com

Bar Full
Credit Cards Visa, MC, AmEx
Reservations Recommended

Bice, you might say, is the Nobu of Italian cuisine; the original, founded in Milan in 1926, has since fathered over 40 locations worldwide. From Dubai to Buenos Aires to Singapore, Bice's slowly expanding presence makes us wonder just how they're dealing with the growing pains, and just how they're pulling it off with such style and a seeming lack of dilution—in Houston, that is. (We can't really speak to the level of success the kitchen is having in Brazil.)

The elegance is a constant. Bice might be one of Houston's most classy dining experiences. It's in the Galleria—where people already have no qualms about spending money—and it most certainly makes the best of a location in a mall. Beiges and woods are the main decorating themes; light coming from the shaded lamps is like being outdoors on a late October day. Servers are excellent, and we like to trust them to guide us to what's good on a given night. They're also great with the lengthy wine list; the breadth in Italian whites and reds is truly impressive.

The food seems to be handling the culture shock well. It's not that anything is Americanized, just that there are some dishes being served in Milan that, for whatever reason, are not here, like foie gras, which is fine by us—this is an Italian restaurant. What is here, in season, is white truffle, which might come shaved over pasta or risotto for $60.

A caprese salad comes with mozzarella di bufala—made from water-buffalo milk, it's got that really creamy, slightly funky flavor; unfortunately, tomatoes, as is the norm in Houston, are underripe. A special of spaghetti frutti di mare (clams, squid, and shrimp) has deep, deep flavors infused into the pasta strands. It's not overly aggressive, just addictive. Our favorite, however, is the cotoletta alla milanese; it's simply excellent. A veal chop is breaded oh-so-delicately and pounded oh-so-violently, making it less than half an inch thick. It's also enormous, more than enough for two people. And don't worry, the servers won't force dessert on you, though you probably will manage to procure some room for it anyway.

So no, Bice is not Nobu; they haven't yet dumbed themselves down to his ridiculous extent. Instead, this is true Italian, content with itself, speaking volumes in a whisper. –FC

Big Bowl

It's filled with slightly-above-average noodles

5.2 Feel | $6 Price | **Chinese**

Casual restaurant
Mon.-Thurs. 11am-10pm;
Fri.-Sat. 11am-midnight.
Brunch. Date-friendly.
Vegetarian-friendly.

Chinatown
6650 Corporate Dr.
(713) 776-2288

Bar None
Credit Cards Visa, MC, AmEx
Reservations Not accepted

Tucked away on Corporate Drive, Big Bowl is an eccentric little noodle nook off the main strip of Bellaire Chinatown. Its affordable-food-in-a-lively-atmosphere niche is clearly defined; delivering on such a promise is harder, however, because if you are charging lower prices than you can afford to, quality fails, and customers stop coming back…and then you start losing money, and have to cut even more corners. Once that happens, you're stuck in the restaurant equivalent of a drug habit: the whole operation is a vicious cycle that spirals into a slow, painful death.

Walking into the multi-colored room that Big Bowl inhabits is like stepping into the sunlight after having been indoors all day; these bright, schizophrenic colors take some getting used to. Service has always been friendly, and if you wind up with a long wait for the food—as can happen, given the tiny kitchen capacity—the staff will at least warn you apologetically. Fortunately, you can entertain yourself in the interim with Chinese pop videos on the flat screen.

Still, the noodles are better than most of what you'd get at Chinese-American joints elsewhere in the city. They come to your table steaming and warm along with manageably large plates of rice. Stir-fried flat noodles with beef and gai-lan come exceptionally dry and sparse in meat; they lack that seared, wok-breathed flavor that can make the dish so good in expert hands. Satay noodles come in a promising-looking murky broth that appears to be full of flavor; but unfortunately, in this case, looks aren't everything; in fact, the depth of the liquid is slight, and its meat more or less disintegrates into your mouth.

And then there are the secrets: our Cantonese-speaking Undercover Chef reports that the Chinese-only "specials" menu reveals—to Chinese speakers only—that between 3pm and 5pm you can get a main course and a huge cup of milk tea or iced coffee for $3.95 and up. But that's only if you want to bear the often interminable wait for noodles that are no better than the Chinatown norm. –FC

Bistro Lancaster

A Theater District hotel legend that's still comfortable after all these years

B- *Total pleasure grade*

6.6 *Food* **8.0** *Feel* **$70** *Price* **American**

Upmarket restaurant
Mon.-Thurs. 6:30am-10pm;
Fri.-Sat. 6:30am-11pm;
Sun. 7:30am-10pm.
Breakfast. Brunch. WiFi.

Downtown
701 Texas Ave.
(713) 228-9500
www.thelancasterhouston.com

Bar Full
Credit Cards Visa, MC, AmEx
Reservations Accepted

We love the old-school vibe of the Lancaster. Even when it's empty, it feels proper and relaxing, like a worn-around-the-edges upmarket bistro in Europe, the sort of place that's been serving the same regulars for decades. Although a new chef has recently come in and revamped the menu, the place still feels like it's thumbing its dusty nose at some of the irritatingly trendy joints that stomp into town and expect to do $5 million in the first year.

At the moment, Bistro Lancaster is still precisely the opposite. For ages, it's been serving the dignified crowd of hotel guests that come to stay here, year after year. Symphony conductors. Crusty couples. Or, perhaps, lawyers or oilmen with a spot of business to do downtown and a desire to be treated with a certain level of respect—the respect that befits their social standing and loyalty—rather than as a revenue number on some hotel-management computer.

That said, the Lancaster is reportedly due for a large-scale renovation, but the details and dates are uncertain. Probably, the restaurant's concept will be reinvented and updated, from menu to aesthetic theme to physical space. Without details, we are unable to evaluate its culinary prospects. We're ambivalent about the prospect of a newer Bistro Lancaster (or whatever it will be called). We look forward to a new concept, but we'll miss the old space, which feels, to us, more timeless than dated.

In the meantime, don't expect culinary fireworks. But a simple crab cake, with the emphasis happily placed on lump crabmeat rather than breadcrumbs, is quite competent. A hamburger with bacon burnt black is less so. Come for an excellent after-work Bloody Mary at the bar, and you won't be disappointed. Just relax, take it in, and savor the moment, because there aren't very many Bistro Lancasters of the world left these days, and Houston's trendy march to the tricked-out New-American scaffold is leaving fewer and fewer of them to survive. –FC

Bistro Le Cep

A restaurant of our Francophile past—with today's prices

5.3 Food | **5.5** Feel | **$42** Price

French

Upmarket restaurant
Mon.-Fri. 11am-10pm;
Sat. 5pm-10:30pm;
Sun.10am-9pm.
Brunch. Date-friendly.
Vegetarian-friendly.

West Houston
11112 Westheimer Rd.
(713) 783-3985
www.bistrolecep.com

Bar Full
Credit Cards Visa, MC, AmEx
Reservations Recommended

Enter the world of country French cooking, American-style: dated dishes that, when executed well, can satisfy your most romantic calf's-liver-and-kidney cravings. But when rushed, carelessly executed, or done with poor-quality ingredients, country French cooking can turn into a train wreck. Bistro Le Cep doesn't hit either one of those extremes; its tastes are mostly okay, but the earthy, almost mystical French country tradition that's capable of making these dishes taste so good is not really in evidence.

It's hard to miss Le Cep's standout building on the west side of Houston: giant white letters spell out its name against a field of bright red, and a fake cow welcomes diners at the front of the building. Inside, the dining room is modest, with wooden floors and a wooden wine rack suspended above the bar. The food is old-school French, and there's absolutely nothing modern or trendy about the place. Not that that's a bad thing—except in cases when the old school dictates customs like tacky plating with sprigs of non-functional garnishes that stick out of the food you are supposed to eat. (They don't even do that in France anymore.)

In classic faux-Francophile format, menu items are listed in French, with explanations in English. They seem to come straight from the recipes of Escoffier. The duck pâté is a good, creamy start, accompanied by an acidic Cumberland sauce—a classical combination that has withstood the test of time. We wish we could report equally good news about the escargot, but alas, they're chewy, oily little buggers, lacking flavor and thought. Get your calf's liver—served with apple, bacon, and french fries—medium rare, and you'll want another. It's the best thing on this menu. Not so for the abominably overcooked coq au vin, which, at our last visit, came out so dry that even an intentional drowning in braising jus couldn't save it.

Prices here might not be quite as astronomical as they are at some of the other French restaurants in town, but they are certainly up to date, and ultimately, Bistro Le Cep asks for more than what it can deliver. Even amidst moments of comfort and tastiness, the combination of pomposity, unevenness, and prices delivers a clear message: time has passed this place by. –SD

Bistro Vino

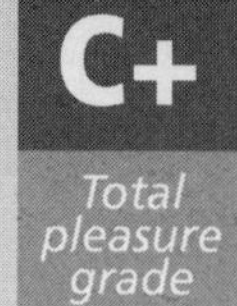

A tree-shaded garden that gets better with age—and tired Euro-American fare that doesn't

C+ Total pleasure grade

5.3 Food | 8.4 Feel | $60 Price

French, American

Upmarket restaurant
Mon.-Sat. 11:30am-midnight; closed Sun.
Live music. Outdoor dining.

Montrose
819 W. Alabama St.
(713) 526-5500
www.bistrovino.net

Bar Full
Credit Cards Visa, MC, AmEx
Reservations Accepted

It's hard to mess up cream of mushroom soup. And Bistro Vino doesn't mess it up; their version is rich, well reduced, and well seasoned. Nor do they mess up the other simplest dishes on the menu, like a brothy beef-and-vegetable soup that transports you, immediately and urgently—whoever you are—to the neediest moments of your childhood. And that is where Bistro Vino excels. And that is also the end of where Bistro Vino excels—from a culinary perspective, at least.

It's the lovely, verdant garden out back that bumps Bistro Vino from a C- to a C+. It's what makes the place recommendable. It's also what makes the place booked up for events on many evenings, negating its potential charm. Call ahead and plan accordingly. Big, round tables make the ideal spot for a mid-afternoon plot (over coffee and dessert) of a hostile takeover, say, or a reunion with long-lost college buddies—the sort of event for which people don't need the buzz of a trendified Houston hotspot to feel comfortable.

Okay, that was all the good news. The bad news is that most of the food at Bistro Vino—those comfort soups aside—is pretty bad. None of it, perhaps, is worse than the disastrous salade Niçoise, whose chunks of tuna are utterly dry and flavorless, whose leaves and beans are useless and underdressed, and whose everything else is bad, too. Only slightly better, at our last visit, was a preparation of veal atop overcooked pasta with weird, congealed cheese and underdeveloped pesto, and a totally dissociated, incoherent grilled vegetable lasagna. As for dessert, Bailey's ice cream was a great idea, with good flavor, and texture so granular as to render the dish inedible. But the freezer-burn problems don't end with the ice cream: we've actually tasted butter here—the kind that comes with the bread at the beginning of the meal—that, in spite of its spiral pattern, was full of funky fridge notes.

We wouldn't have accepted that even in the neediest moments of our childhoods. –RG

Black Labrador Pub

Total pleasure grade

Cobblestones, saucy barmaids, and low ceilings can't save this food—but do drink upstairs

3.6 Food | **7.5** Feel | **$26** Price | **British**

Bar
Mon.-Thurs. 11am-11pm;
Fri.-Sat. 11am-midnight;
Sun. 11am-10pm.
Brunch. Date-friendly.
Vegetarian-friendly.

Montrose
4100 Montrose Blvd.
(713) 529-1199
www.blacklabradorpub.com

Bar Full
Credit Cards Visa, MC, AmEx
Reservations Not accepted

We really like the vibe here: the Montrose location is beautiful. Old-world, ivy-covered buildings and cobblestones line the parking lot, transporting you, for a moment, to an old alley in Oxford. The interior sports just the cramped tables and low ceilings that are vital to a good British pub atmosphere, and occasional live music at the upstairs jazz club, Cezanne, cheers things up further.

But good British pub grub is hard to come by in this city, and at The Black Labrador Pub, it's even harder to come by. Great British traditions like fish and chips, bangers and mash, and steak and kidney pie are massacred beyond recognition. You're going to have to have a closed casket at the funeral for these dishes—think of the children. The flavors in, and execution of, this thoughtless mix of Tex-Mex favorites and British standards are as dry as the humor. The food tastes fake, and amazingly enough, a hefty asking price adds insult to injury.

The modern London restaurant scene notwithstanding, British food has hardly gotten a good name in the past, but places like The Black Lab just might make it worse, helping to reverse all the good work done by Gordon Ramsay and Heston Blumenthal. And the Black Lab hardly does justice to one of the greatest culinary accomplishments of all time: the sausage. These bangers are dry, underseasoned, and won't spark your (or at least our) libido in the way that the almighty pig usually does (we have a very serious relationship with him). We don't know if the mashed potatoes are boxed, but they certainly hint at that soulless taste that takes us back, way back, to the culinary inferno that is the school cafeteria. Fish and chips, too, leave a lot to be desired. We don't even know where to begin with the steak and kidney pie, whose thick brown sauce tastes of nothing but flour.

At least they don't mess up the booze, though. A nice selection of British and domestic beers are poured into personalized silver tankards that hang over the bar for their frequent customers. (We somehow doubt they will be offering us such a coveted spot.) The barmaids and servers are decked out in short plaid skirts and knee-highs, but unfortunately, nice legs don't make the food taste any better. –SD

Black Walnut Café

A Rice Village favorite that's got its audience pegged

C *Total pleasure grade*

6.1 *Food* **7.6** *Feel* **$12** *Price* **Italian-American**

Café
Mon.-Thurs. 8am-10pm;
Fri.-Sat. 8am-11pm;
Sun. 8am-9pm.
Breakfast. Outdoor dining. WiFi.

Rice Area
5510 Morningside Dr.
(713) 526-5551
www.bwcafe.com

Woodlands
2520 Research Forest Dr.
(281) 362-1678

Bar Wine and beer only
Credit Cards Visa, MC, AmEx
Reservations Not accepted

The appeal of Black Walnut Café spans generations; their to-go menu appeals to those that are "too tired to cook" (stressed-out working women), "not in the mood to clean the kitchen" (college boys), or those "yearning for a quite evening at home" (recent divorcées, perhaps?). Inside, you'll see small groups of sorority girls planning their next event, old friends catching up and taking advantage of the super-comfortable chairs, and, during the lunch rush, office workers looking for something quick. It's a surprisingly modern, hip interior, so it's a shame many people just grab take-out.

That said, this restaurant does have the dreaded counter-service-buzzer-tray system that we so dislike, especially at this price point: a few salads on the menu break the $10 barrier…or so we think. The menu here is a typographical joke gone horribly awry. Prices have four digits following the decimal—not your standard two. Thus a sandwich might cost $8.7263, or lasagna might run you $10.5567. Fonts change with wild abandon, and nearly every word is set differently from its neighbor. It's not funny; it's not cute; it's just annoying.

The menu looks too extensive to be good; we're always a bit wary of a place that claims to make a mean Greek pasta as well as a "Creole Bowl." But if you stick with the simpler options here, you'll end up eating happy. The "Potato Lil' Bacon Soup" ($5.3163) is made from surprisingly rich, creamy stock. Textures play off one another, as gobs of melted cheese (it's hard not to love that) mingle with soft potatoes, and crunchy bacon adds a whisper of smoke. It's as if each of the individual ingredients turns into a caricature of itself, making the soup a bit more complex. The "Lemon Chicken à la BW", however, is a lifeless, if lemony, linguine dish that spins toward bland disaster until you rescue it with a liberal dose of salt, which brings back some zesty, tart, and peppery flavors.

The listed hours here are equally silly; they open every morning at 7:57am. And they close a bit later than their neighbors in Rice Village—10:03pm on weekdays. –AH

Blue Fish House

Sake bombs, inconsistent service, and serviceable sushi

7.0 Food **8.5** Feel **$19** Price **Pan-Asian**

Upmarket restaurant
Mon.-Thurs. 11am-3pm, 5pm-9:30pm; Fri. 11am-3pm, 5pm-10:30pm; Sat. noon-3pm, 5pm-10:30pm; closed Sun.

Upper Kirby
2241 Richmond Ave.
(713) 529-3100
www.bluefishhouse.com

Bar Wine and beer only
Credit Cards Visa, MC, AmEx
Reservations Accepted

Blue Fish House is certainly not the best sushi joint in town, but it may be one of the most fun, even if the service is pretty bad. The space is cozy and convivial, and the food looks and tastes good. The menu is haphazardly pan-Asian, centering on sushi but also integrating significant Thai elements.

Names of dishes range from the stupid ("Udon It This Time," stir-fried udon with shrimp and vegetables) to the amusing ("Spicy Old Lady Tofu," with stir-fried roasted eggplant) to the racially offensive ("Fry Me to the Moon," fried teriyaki tofu with vegetables), but all are relatively well prepared, and all are under $10. The prices are excellent, particularly at lunch; "Some Young Guy" (stir-fried pork with vegetables—no comment) comes with miso soup and ginger salad for $6.50. Like the Hobbit Café next door, Blue Fish is particularly strong in vegetarian options.

High turnover results in fresh sushi fish, and presentations here tend to be beautiful and creative. The "Jade Roll" is particularly pretty, with dollops of seaweed and roe on top creating an interesting color contrast. The "Spiral Roll" is covered in large chunks of salmon, shrimp, and avocado; we're not fans of avocado on maki, although word has it they're even starting to do it in Japan these days. People seem to love the "Volcano Roll," too, but we find it too cream-cheesy.

As for the service, our experience on a recent trip pretty much sums it up: of four main courses, three arrived at different times, and one order of spicy escolar never arrived at all. We are also turned off by the several signs stating that misunderstood orders cannot be returned. In our experience, misunderstandings are not always the fault of the customer.

That said, the place is still enjoyable. Blue Fish does a thriving business at lunch and dinner, and on weekends it gets packed with a young crowd throwing down sake bombs. If that sounds like your idea of a sushi place, grab a bomb and join in. –RH

Blue Nile Ethiopian

Authentic Ethiopian food that tests even the most adventurous palates

B- Total pleasure grade

7.1 Food **7.5** Feel **$25** Price **Ethiopian**

Casual restaurant
Daily 11am-11pm.
Date-friendly. Vegetarian-friendly.

Westchase
9400 Richmond Ave.
(713) 782-6882

Bar Full
Credit Cards Visa, MC, AmEx
Reservations Accepted

It's not like Houston is bursting at the seams with Ethiopian restaurants, but we wish people were less skeptical of a cuisine that's so foreign in our fair town. Some find Ethiopian food less approachable due to by its spice-heavy fare that's often considered an acquired taste; people either love or hate it. In a world where "vegetable" can mean a baked potato and "seasoning" can mean mesquite flavoring, the food at Blue Nile is both figuratively and literally on the other side of the world.

While the food is foreign, the aesthetic of the place is consistent with most people's preconceptions about African design. Brightly zig-zagging fabrics in orange, yellow, turquoise, and other colors of the sun, sky, and land brighten up the otherwise dimly lit spot. The menu is delightfully not dumbed down, using exact Ethiopian words for dishes, leaving the burden of explanation on the unbelievably patient staff. (They're probably quite envious of their colleagues in DC, where Ethiopian cuisine is mainstream.) Service this caring translates across any barrier.

The vegetarian combination is the most popular, as it uses preparations that aren't a far cry from good ol' Lone Star cuisine. Baby steps, baby steps. Kik Alicha (split peas) have a smooth, yet biting texture, and just enough onion flavor. The gomen (collard greens cooked with peppers and garlic) could have a place on any Southern table; scoop them up as a sandwich between a bit of injera, a thick, salty, spongy sourdough bread that also doubles as a grabby utensil. Just pinch off a bit and shovel away. Meats are a little harder to understand, like the Kitfo, an intimidating mound of minced meat made gamey by its blend of spices. However, the Doro Wot, dark chicken meat, is fall-off–the-bone tender with a smoky, robust combination of spices.

Allow the naysayers to contemplate the flavors of their meal as they enjoy freshly brewed, tableside-prepared coffee and a satisfied stomach, and they'll likely find it hard to harumph. –JY

Bob's Steak & Chop House

B-

Total pleasure grade

A formidable new entry in the identical-overpriced-steakhouse sector

8.3	7.9	$101
Food	Feel	Price

Steakhouse

Upmarket restaurant
Mon.-Thurs. 5pm-10pm;
Fri.-Sat. 5pm-11pm;
closed Sun.

Galleria
1801 Post Oak Blvd.
(713) 877-8325
www.bobs-steakandchop.com

Bar Full
Credit Cards Visa, MC, AmEx
Reservations Recommended

We are amused trying to picture what the strategy meeting for Bob's Steak & Chop House looked like. "Wait, I've got an idea," says the up-and-coming SVP of the restaurant group. "A spark of inspiration. You know what Houston really needs? A high-priced steakouse that feels 20 years old, with a black, leathery feel, low lighting, TVs at the bar, $50 steaks, martinis, shrimp cocktail, four-pound lobsters, big overpriced red wines. You know, a corporate-expense-account type of place. We'll have deferential service, try to upsell everyone on wine, get 'em drunk, get 'em ordering the First Growths. A buck twenty a head. Five hundred a head. Sky's the limit. What do you think, Bob?"

"Brilliant!"

"Uh, wait," stutters a more junior man at the table. "Don't you think Houston has enough of those identical overpriced corporate-credit-card prime steakhouses, like, uh, say, Vic & Anthony's, Morton's, Ruth's Chris, Brenner's, Smith & Wollensky, Fleming's, Capital Grille, Strip House, Palm, Sullivan's, Spencer's St..."

"No way," Bob interrupts sharply. "Oil is above $90 a barrel," he barks. The naïve, idealistic young restaurant strategist cowers before the man, clearly wiser than he. "You'd have to be an idiot to open anything else." The board nods in unison, the employee hangs his head in shame, and another overpriced steakhouse is born. I'd go to work for Monica Pope, the junior guy says to himself. But there's no money in independent restaurants these days, is there?

In any case, as chain steakhouses go, this newcomer (the group calls Dallas home, though there's also a branch in San Francisco) is a good one. Bob's Prime steaks are appropriately seared and caramelized at extreme heat, and they come out tender and precise, cooked exactly as ordered, with melting bites of fatty goodness near the bone. Unusually, the steak comes with one side dish, and the creamed spinach—should you go in that direction—is excellent. There seems to be only one major blunder: what's that giant, super-sweet carrot doing there in the middle of the plate like an orange phallus, its sticky juices oozing aggressively across the plate and interfering with the other more delicate, refined flavors?

Maybe it's another subtle nod to the corporate execs. –RG

Bodard Bistro

A bright, bouncy Bellaire dive that can deliver—as long as you skip the discounted phô

B
Total pleasure grade

6.9 *Food*

6.6 *Feel*

$9 *Price*

Vietnamese

Casual restaurant
Daily 9am-midnight.
Kid-friendly.

Chinatown
9140 Bellaire Blvd.
(713) 541-5999

Bar Beer only
Credit Cards Visa, MC, AmEx
Reservations Not accepted

We'd be wary of any restaurant that advertises food deals like "buy three bowls, get one free." And Bodard's phô, which is huge in stature but filled with mediocrity, would justify that wariness. This isn't an outlet store, and we're not interested in buying culinary seconds at a discount. Fortunately, Bodard Bistro, even with its shady sales discounts, overly bright setting, and less-than-bright service, boasts a few non-phô menu items that make it worth the trip.

The place is tucked into the furthest corner of Chinatown's Welcome Supermarket complex. Walking in is like finding yourself stuck in a pinball machine, with neon flashing lights, frenetic music, and a steaming, Asian-looking waterfall. We wouldn't expect fantastic service at such a joint, but Bodard seems to try extra hard to keep staff-customer contact to a minimum, with a walk-up cashier's counter and 7-11-Big-Gulp-sized water cups that might well rupture your bladder if finished.

Be adventurous, though, and you'll be rewarded. Nem nuong nha trong (spring roll with grilled pork paste) is delicious and hearty, with the surprise element of a fried spring roll wrapper in the middle of it all adding unexpected texture. It's served with "Bodard Sauce," a slightly tomatoey, slightly eggy mixture. The catfish hot pot, complete with the fish head grotesquely poking out, is heavy on the sweet-and-sour, but has a salty finish, cutting all those muddy catfish flavors; the dish almost tastes Thai.

If the phô is why people first come, it's probably not often the reason they return. Offered in a mammoth-sized vessel that's dubbed a "Super Bowl," it's filled with clumps of rice noodles, broth that tastes like tap water, and little meat. Still, it seems to appeal to starving college students on the prowl for a deal. Maybe the buy-three-get-one-free bowl of phô fits into their double-date schemes—or, for the romantically bumbling, their refrigerator-stocking missions, enabling a week's worth of PS3 or Wii without leaving the dorm. For the rest of us, it's just another bum deal.

The lesson here: sometimes the most obvious good deals are the worst, and at Bodard Bistro, the best deal is the one that wasn't made. –JY

Bombay Brasserie

Ceiling doilies, a predictable menu, and yet some of the better Indian food inside the Loop

B- *Total pleasure grade*

6.9 *Food* **4.8** *Feel* **$33** *Price* **Indian**

Casual restaurant
Mon.-Thurs. 11am-2:30pm, 5:30pm-10pm; Fri. 11am-2:30pm, 5:30pm-10:30pm; Sat. 11am-3pm, 5:30pm-10:30pm; Sun. 11am-3pm, 5:30pm-10pm. *Outdoor dining. Vegetarian-friendly.*

Rice Area
2414 University Blvd.
(713) 355-2000
www.thebombaybrasserie.com

Bar Full
Credit Cards Visa, MC, AmEx
Reservations Accepted

Groundbreaking this restaurant is not. Its logo appears stenciled from an Indian-American restaurant catalog. Its interior design is relentlessly conformist. The ceiling is so out of touch with aesthetic reality that it appears to be lined by doilies that were dipped in bright white plaster and affixed into a grid. White tablecloths display rows of glasses stuffed with elaborately folded napkins, perhaps to remind you just how many more people would be sitting in the restaurant were it not half empty. The best place to sit is outside.

Bombay Brasserie's menu, however, deviates subtly from the Indian-American norm. There's a high percentage of vegetable dishes that often vary from day to day, and beef is completely absent—an authentic Indian touch, given that cows are less common than water buffaloes in South Asia. Still, this menu is hardly a work of creative genius; one of the few less-common dishes is fish masala, amusingly spelled as "maki-mahi" on one menu (now there's a thought: a roll of Indian fish masala wrapped in that delicious sushi rice from Kubo's next door in the Rice Village Arcade).

But it is with chicken, lamb, and vegetables that Bombay Brasserie shines. Deep chicken flavor bursts through the soft onions and rich spices of the well-developed stews and curries. Chicken tikka masala is surprisingly leggy, enabling it to stand up to its copious dose of cream in a way that bland white breast meat could not. Saag paneer, that other ubiquitous Indian-American favorite, has equally creamy, if undersalted, spinach and homemade cheese cubes that balance resilience with softness. Vegetable dishes—jalfrezi, chana masala, and so forth—are good, too, with sweet finishes.

Even the clouds have silver linings: Gamey lamb korma has some tough bites, but other pieces are meltingly tender. Tandoori chicken is overcooked but unusually smoky. Tandoor-fresh naan has a short half-life, but plenty of salt and oil. For dessert, kheer is simple and delightful, almost like arroz con leche, free from the aggressions of raisins or excessive cardamom. Atmosphere aside, this is one of the better Indian kitchens outside of HIllcroft, whether for dinner or the well-maintained $10.95 lunch buffet. –RG

Bombay Sweets

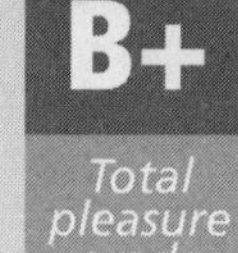

Total pleasure grade

A South Indian vegetarian buffet with a serious following

7.8 Food **3.1** Feel **$9** Price

Indian, Vegetarian

Counter service
Daily 11am-9:30pm.
Live music. Outdoor dining. Vegetarian-friendly.

Hillcroft
5827 Hillcroft St.
(713) 780-4453

Bar None
Credit Cards Visa, MC, AmEx
Reservations Accepted

With apologies to Washington, Midtown, and Montrose, Hillcroft might just be Houston's true culinary epicenter. What's indisputable, at least, is that for South Asian and Middle Eastern food, the area reigns supreme. Curiously, Bombay Sweets seems to be one of the best-known Indian restaurants in the area, with only London Sizzler slightly more renowned in the non-Indian-community oral legend of Hillcroft.

We say "curious" because we don't think this place does nearly the best of its vegetarian-lunch-buffet genre. Perhaps Bombay Sweets was so anointed for its bakery, which pretty much focuses on sweet things (and they're very sweet here). As such, you'll see a lot of take-out dessert or big-event orders. As for the food, well, the members of the local Indian community, who know their strip of restaurants better than any media outlet—ourselves included, of course—tend to mob Udipi Café at mealtimes, sending a queue out the door…but not Bombay Sweets.

Why not?

The answer: although it's still a worthwhile place for vegetarians, better than Madras Pavilion, Bombay Sweets cannot quite rise above the "good for vegetarian" stigma and emerge as a citywide-level destination restaurant. When you take your buffet, for instance, Udipi gives you a spectacular masala dosa. Bombay gives you decent naan (not that there's anything wrong with naan). The highlights at Bombay Sweets include a well-executed samosa and lassi. The buffet table—one of the cheapest all-you-can-eat lunches anywhere in Houston—almost always features palak paneer (spinach with homemade cheese cubes), that Indian-restaurant-in-America North Indian staple. Here, it's dark, less creamy and less rich (the purists prefer it this way) than the version at your average Indian buffet in a non-Indian neighborhood. We've had better-seasoned versions of channa masala, and better rice. On a slow day, fried food and vadas (doughnuts) might sog up at the buffet table. Northern à la carte dishes—for example, the Bombay-style chats like pani poori—fare better, although the à la carte menu can be bewildering and the staff behind the counter far from helpful.

To be fair, though, Bombay Sweets does not deserve to be judged against the superstar that is Udipi—it deserves to be judged against Houston Indian restaurants in general, and on that axis, it is above average, and definitely worth a visit. –RG

Bonga

Well-priced Korean food with the barbecue refreshingly not the star

A- *Total pleasure grade*

8.7 *Food* | **6.9** *Feel* | **$19** *Price* | **Korean**

Casual restaurant
Daily 10am-10pm.

Spring Branch
9861 Long Point Rd.
(713) 461-5265

Bar Wine and beer only
Credit Cards Visa, MC, AmEx
Reservations Accepted

Not many people know Korean food beyond the barbecue that you see at so many restaurants. Yet there are myriad flavors and textures to which few Americans have been exposed. While the barbecue at Bonga "Garden Restaurant" isn't a bad way to go, it's the other foods that really get your juices flowing. Going to Bonga is like re-reading a literary novel that you hadn't read since 9th-grade English and discovering an adult subtext that redefines the entire story.

It's not exactly clear what Bonga has to do with a garden—or exactly what a garden restaurant is, for that matter (this place clearly isn't vegetarian, nor does it have a garden). The restaurant is tucked away in an unassuming shopping center next to the residential areas of Long Point. With so many borderline health-code-violation restaurants around that area, it's a refreshing touch to see the dining room so clean and tidy at Bonga. Service is smartly push-button—no joke, you actually have a call button at your table, allowing the whole place to run with only a couple of waitpeople, if you consider that to be a good thing. (You should probably keep an eye on your trigger-happy children.) The restaurant is family-owned, with the chef a frail-looking, middle-aged woman with a warm smile and a deft hand at seasoning.

The food at Bonga hits all the Korean food groups: savory, meat, kimchee, spicy, and really spicy. The banchan, or small sides that come with every meal, are one of the better sets in town; sweet, glazed potatoes are surpassingly delicious. Bibimbap is flawless, with fresh and pickled vegetables and well-marinated meat coming together to form a sweet, savory, filling, but still light, perfectly-sized lunch. Get it in the super-heated stone bowl so you can mix in the crusty cooked rice, adding another dimension of texture. Tofu stews are another specialty, with a freshly cracked egg adding extra body to a haunting, spicy broth. But the real kicker is the freshly rolled beef soup dumplings that taste hand-made and deeply meaty.

Though the portions look substantial and you'll never leave hungry, this cuisine won't stuff you the way carnivorous Korean barbecue might. So consider yourself advised to come taste Korean food again…for the first time. –JY

Brasil

D-

Total pleasure grade

Bad food and a bad attitude ruin a great alternative coffee atmosphere

4.6 Food

1.5 Feel

$13 Price

Light American

Counter service
Mon.-Sat. 7:30am-11:30pm;
Sun. 7:30am-midnight.
Breakfast. Brunch. Live music. Outdoor dining. Vegetarian-friendly.

Montrose
2604 Dunlavy St.
(713) 528-1993

Bar Wine and beer only
Credit Cards Visa, MC, AmEx
Reservations Not accepted

A proud representative of the alternative scene that has sprung up along Westheimer, Brasil teems at lunchtime and throughout the afternoon with people that look like they'd be more at home in Austin than in Houston. Vegetarians seek out the veggie-heavy menu here, while others come just to hang out with a cup of bitter but passable coffee. Whoever they are, they're generally treated poorly by the legendarily standoffish owner.

They come anyway, however, for the enjoyable atmosphere: exposed brick at every turn, interesting artwork, industrial-chic exposed pipes and beams, and an outdoor patio whose explosion of greenery distracts you from the busy street noise a few feet away. This is a member of the new school of counter-meets-table-service restaurant: you order at the counter, then your food is brought out to you after a (long) while. The airy vibe works well for lunch; the place is dimly lit at night, but not really suited to dinner.

At press time, the kitchen was being expanded, but until now, it's been simple. Personal-sized pizzas, thick, cheesy, and airily crusted, are its best work. Spinach and feta is a good choice, with slivers of garlic and a sweet but undersalted tomato sauce that's balanced out by salty feta and copious mozzarella.

Salads utilize fresh ingredients, but the tastes are predictable. Sandwiches, thick and bready, are mostly formulated for vegetarians. There's a crusty, oil-absorbing ciabatta bread, but unfortunately, fillings are underseasoned, and generally more miss than hit. A "spicy chicken salad" sandwich isn't spicy, which is unsurprising given that its so-called "spicy poblano peppers" are actually amongst the mildest chilies known to man. Better are a turkey sandwich, to which you can add bacon (do it), and a BLT, which profits from aïoli and blue cheese.

Best of all, perhaps, would be just to come for coffee. But don't come to study: there's no WiFi, and the outlandishly rude owner seems to have nothing better to do than to go around from table to table admonishing laptop users for their patronage of his establishment. In the history of the *Fearless Critic* and its predecessor, *The Menu*, this is the first coffeeshop owner we've ever seen who is actually brazen enough to kick people out of his establishment, in the middle of the afternoon, for staying too long. His time would be better spent paying attention to his kitchen. –FC

Brasserie Max & Julie

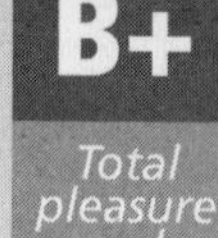

Total pleasure grade

French authenticity redefined at Houston's best brasserie

8.2 Food **8.8** Feel **$71** Price **French**

Upmarket restaurant
Mon. 5:30pm-10pm; Tues.-Wed. 11am-2:30pm, 5:30pm-10pm; Thurs.-Sat. 11am-2:30pm, 5:30pm-11pm; closed Sun.
Breakfast. Brunch. Live music. Outdoor dining. Vegetarian-friendly.

Montrose
4315 Montrose Blvd.
(713) 524-0070

Bar Wine and beer only
Credit Cards Visa, MC, AmEx
Reservations Not accepted

An easy dinner at a classic French brasserie is one of the world's most honest, engaging gastronomical experiences, and we think it was exactly what Houston was missing when Brasserie Max & Julie opened on Montrose. Rarely have we seen a restaurant so cleanly fit such an obvious culinary need in a city, and for the most part, it's executed well. Warm red fabrics adorn the interior, and bright gold railings provide contrast and add an air of authenticity. The look is exactly right, the menu has all the French standards, and the wine list is simply, deliciously extensive, made up entirely of French wines, many of them relatively obscure and eminently worthwhile: Cahors, Madiran, and a large selection of rosé wines (not the fruit punch that is White Zinfandel) make us particularly happy.

Thankfully, the menu won't remind you of that tourist-trap bistro that gouged you on the Champs-Élysées. Instead, the focus is on real French food, though it's pretty too; even the presentation of bone marrow is well thought out. You spoon the indulgently rich, creamy marrow out of its giant bones, sprinkle on some salt, and spread it onto toast—which, unfortunately, is too thin and brittle to serve that purpose; that's when the outstanding, crackly baguette slices from the table basket come to the rescue.

Rognons (kidneys), at our last visit, came out too tough, but we love the well-seasoned steak tartare, and we savor every lovely bite of a balanced Salade Landaise, with frisée, delectably seared chicken liver, juicy lardons, an expertly poached egg, and impeccable vinaigrette. Steak au poivre gets a lot of kick from its coarse peppercorns, and comes with french fries that approach earthly perfection, although we question the use of filet mignon, a notoriously flavorless cut of meat, for such a robust country dish.

The biggest weak spot at Max and Julie is the service. One day, you feel rushed; another day, you're just plain annoyed when your wine is overpoured in hopes that you'll buy a second bottle. In such a comfortable and understated space, bad service can kill some of your buzz. But from the concept and execution, we're still buzzing. We could eat here just about every day. –FC

The Breakfast Klub

A-
Total pleasure grade

Fried chicken and waffles for breakfast? Count us in!

8.2	8.0	$11
Food	*Feel*	*Price*

American

Counter service
Mon.-Fri. 7am-2pm;
Sat. 8am-2pm; closed Sun.
Breakfast. Kid-friendly.

Midtown
3711 Travis St.
(713) 528-8561
www.thebreakfastklub.com

Bar None
Credit Cards Visa, MC, AmEx
Reservations Not accepted

Already a Houston classic (or is it klassic?) after less than a couple of decades, the Breakfast Klub has a Southern charm that's hard not to like, especially in breakfast-starved Houston. While many kitchens play with a fusion of cuisines, the Breakfast Klub plays with a fusion of meals, bringing Southern classics such as grits, fried catfish, and the classic fried chicken and waffles into the limelight. While the novelty of eating such heavy foods in the morning wears off mid-plate for some people, the place is genuinely filled with generosity. Customers from different walks of life actually seem to be glad to be rubbing elbows with one another; it's a fun tradition, if not a healthy one.

That camaraderie extends to the line that runs outside the door at the Breakfast Klub—that's how popular this place is. Some of the most eye-opening conversations that you'll ever have might be with people craving the same wings and waffles that you are. Inside, large tables meant for groups and families stuff the room; warm colors and wood tones bring together a sense of calm, while the lively art brings an excitement to the space.

The food at The Breakfast Klub is a cardiologist's worst nightmare. The specialties of "katfish," along with grits and wings and waffles, all come in huge portions and immediately suggest hot sauce, maple syrup, and ketchup. If that combination sounds odd to you, well, it is. Everything is heavy, and much of it is off-puttingly savory-plus-sweet—though if you manage to keep everything separate, you'll have great success. Fried chicken and maple syrup, for instance, is a hard taste to acquire. But it's also a delicious one. French toast and pancakes are teeth-numbingly sweet, especially before they're set off against the savories, while the pork chop and eggs and biscuits and gravy are as salty as the maple syrup is sweet, leading to a mischievous sort of balance.

Even if your mother would disapprove of all this—and there's little doubt that she would—you might reassure her that breakfast is the most important meal of the day. As for yourself, even if you might want to nap after a visit to The Breakfast Klub, you'll also get your share of the heavy servings of heart, fried tradition—not to mention a glorious morning or afternoon spent immersed in one of America's only true, indigenous culinary traditions. –JY

Brennan's of Houston

High-flying, unbelievably overpriced New Orleans food, prepared tableside

B- Total pleasure grade

7.7 Food **9.0** Feel **$105** Price **Southern**

Upmarket restaurant
Mon.-Fri. 11am-1:30pm, 5:45pm-9:30pm; Sat.-Sun. 10am-2pm, 5:45pm-9:30pm.
Breakfast. Brunch. Live music. Outdoor dining. Vegetarian-friendly.

Midtown
3300 Smith St.
(713) 522-9711
www.brennanshouston.com

Bar Full
Credit Cards Visa, MC, AmEx
Reservations Recommended

Sharing nostalgic origins—but not ownership—with its namesake in New Orleans, this exorbitantly expensive restaurant serves similar Creole food to the original, but with a slight local twist. For instance, peaches and pecans (both preceded by the word Texas) are on the menu. Turtle soup, certainly a Brennan's original, has rabid fans who insist they love the meager chunks of turtle meat floating about; we've got news for them. It's not the little chunks of tasteless turtle they like—it's the super-enriched stock, copious cream, and other delicious sins. Remember "Stone Soup"?

Large, plump shrimp with biscuits and gravy rest atop a sweet onion-biscuit pudding in a pool of bisque. Don't forget to use some bread to sop up the remaining bisque after you've polished off the dish; it's all good in that lounging-in-cream sort of way. Seared foie gras, though, has been an utter disaster: veiny, stringy, and difficult to chew. Much better is "Redfish Ponchartrain, with an aggressive but enjoyable sauce of shrimp, crab, and fried oysters; it's the very essence of the Gulf, and does justice to its house-specialty status. It's unbelievably overpriced, but what isn't here?

Also overpriced, but also delicious, is bananas foster, the marketing ploy to end all others, the original tableside gimmick, but one we can excuse, if only for its longevity. It remains a giggly pleasure to watch the bananas go up in flames and caramelize before your eyes. The gimmick we can't excuse, though, is the special icon on the menu that indicates which items are prepared tableside—like a salad that is—get this—tossed before your very eyes! Fancy that.

Wine stewards are knowledgeable, and service is warm without being stuffy, except for the irritating requirement that men wear jackets, even in the heat of the Houston summer—an unbelievably snotty tradition that's been euthanized almost everywhere else. The interior, though, manages to avoid pomposity; warm colors and dim lighting create quite a romantic atmosphere, but also one that could work for a business meeting. The best tables for dates are in the lovely outdoor garden, a French Quarter replica that works to Disneyesque perfection. But the prices? They're way too high. Perhaps you're helping to cover the costs of bringing in that ston—uh, exotic turtle meat. Fancy that. –FC

Brenner's

High price, high cheese factor, and (sometimes) high taste—next up, Bayou Bend

B- *Total pleasure grade*

8.4	7.9	$90
Food	Feel	Price

Steakhouse

Upmarket restaurant
Mon.-Thurs. 11am-2pm, 5pm-10pm; Fri. 11am-2pm, 5pm-11pm; Sat. 5pm-11pm; Sun. 5pm-10pm. *Outdoor dining.*

Memorial
10911 Katy Fwy.
(713) 465-2901
www.brennerssteakhouse.com

Bar Full
Credit Cards Visa, MC, AmEx
Reservations Recommended

At press time, this meaty outpost of the Landry's empire was slated to move into a space vacated by Rainbow Lodge, then occupied and quickly vacated again by the Lodge at Bayou Bend. The new space, whose soaring, two-floor atrium has a surreally beautiful flow, is far more dramatic and less arcane than the current one, but there's also a similarity between the two: that time-frozen, Frank-Lloyd-Wrightish woodsy integration with nature.

In the current space, however, the nature in question is possibly the cheesiest, most hilariously overdressed garden in Houston, and the textural elements of stone and wood clash with the tacky Victorian style of the mirrors, lamps, glassware, and chests that would feel more at home in your great aunt's house than in a high-priced steakhouse. Choose a windowside table for the best view of that over-the-top garden, apparently modeled after the original in Mr. Brenner's German homeland. (Brenner's was taken over by Landry's after the family closed it in '02.)

Brenner's comically precise service quickly starts to seem like play-acting. There are many restaurants in the Houston area that engage in the farcical ritual of grinding black pepper onto your food tableside, but this is the only one we've seen where the waiter asks how coarse you'd like your grind. Pomposities aside, Brenner's does steak well, other things less so. A bone-in New York strip comes medium rare as ordered, with (thankfully) no sauce or jus, just salt, its outside surface appropriately charred, the fatty end of the strip richly melting, close-your-eyes transportative, as good a forkful of meat as any in Houston. (At market price, which was $48 at our last visit, it should be.) A peppercorn sauce (steak au poivre style) is well developed, though priced at a shocking $6.

What's frustrating about Brenner's are the starters, sides, and such, beginning with embarrassingly supermarket-ish bread and continuing with a wedge salad whose "signature Roquefort" doesn't really come together well, whose carrots add nothing, and whose long, flavorless chives are just in your way. Creamed spinach is challengingly tough, its creamed component gummy and clammy, with a taste that strongly evokes Knorr's onion soup packets, and the highly self-touted apple strudel is just okay.

But oh, that bite of meat. –RG

Brown Bag Deli

Mix-and-match sandwiches redeemed in restrained fast-casual format

7.0 Food | **5.5** Feel | **$7** Price

Light American

Counter service
Daily 11am-6pm.
Kid-friendly. Outdoor dining. WiFi.

Montrose
2036 Westheimer Rd.
(713) 807-9191
www.thebrownbagdeli.net

Bar None
Credit Cards Visa, MC, AmEx
Reservations Not accepted

Rice Area
2540 Amherst St.
(713) 520-6100

Spring Branch
13169 Northwest Fwy.
(713) 690-8600

Generally speaking, we're hardcore opponents of the customer-driven mix-and-match model of cuisine. But never has it taken on a more innocuous form than it does at the Brown Bag Deli, where simplicity rules. You take a brown bag, which is printed with sandwich options. You tick off your selections of bread, meat (the American deli essentials and nothing but: decent roast beef, turkey, creamy egg-studded chicken salad, and so on; pimento cheese is the only veggie option), and toppings. You pencil in your name, you pay, and you pick up your sandwich when the sirens sing. (The unconnected Which Wich? has franchised the bag-writing concept, but Brown Bag remains a Houston-only chain; the Westheimer location is the original.)

Whatever you create, it will be short, sweet, and straightforward. There is no other path. Rolls are soft and fresh but overly sugary; ask for them toasted (an off-the-menu open secret favored by Brown Bag insiders). Toppings are extremely basic: lettuce, tomato, onion, mayo, mustard; unaggressive, thickly sliced cheddars and jack cheeses; and so on. A mild horseradish sauce might be the most exotic thing on the entire menu. The overall sandwich comes out a bit too pliable, in some cases almost soggy, but it's still fresh, filling, and easy to eat. Any combination (unless you double up ingredients) costs an eminently reasonable $4.50, and the sandwich isn't any bigger or smaller than it needs to be. Iced tea and such underprice the competition, too. This place is all about value.

You expect the design of a place that's built around a gimmick—as the Brown Bag Deli is—to be, well, gimmicky. But aside from the trite faux-manual-typewriter font, it's not. The walls are simple and brown. Tables are dineresque, comfortable, laid-back. There's WiFi. And nowhere are the chainesque self-promotions or the overuse of adjectives that you might expect. In a brave new world of sandwich self-aggrandizement, from the fake folksiness of Jimmy John's to the smarmy smugness of Beck's Prime, Brown Bag seems not to see the need for brainwashing rhetoric, preferring, perhaps, to let the food speak quietly for itself. –RG

The Brownstone

C-

Total pleasure grade

Don't get too excited (although one couple once did) about this dated American fare and décor

5.3	6.2	$84	**American**
Food	*Feel*	*Price*	

Upmarket restaurant
Mon. 11:30am-9pm;
Tues.-Sat. 11:30am-10pm;
closed Sun.

Upper Kirby
2736 Virginia St.
(713) 520-5666
www.brownstone-houston.com

Bar Full
Credit Cards Visa, MC, AmEx
Reservations Recommended

Absurdly dated yet amusingly quirky, stuffy yet potentially haunted, the Brownstone occupies an auntie-style, antique-filled house, complete with a romantic front patio, on a little-traversed side street off Westheimer. It's full of exposed brick walls, archways, and bric-a-brac curiosities, some of which are for sale.

Food's for sale too, and it varies in quality, as does the service, which is certainly attentive but not overly knowledgeable. Some traditional starters are surprisingly good, like a light, smooth avocado soup, cleverly matched with black caviar. Well-seasoned lobster bisque comes with an overzealous tableside drizzle of sherry, while vichyssoise, a cold potato-leek soup, benefits from a solid chicken-stock backbone but comes out too thin.

Things go further downhill when you hit the mains. They make a big deal about beef Wellington, but who orders that these days? Maybe you should, because the "Creole Seafood Pasta" pairs mushy penne with an incoherent mess of sausage, vegetables, and tomato sauce; a preparation of Coho salmon comes terribly overcooked; and vegetable sides are boring. Bread pudding is decently executed, but we've also encountered strawberry crêpes that looked and tasted like our whipped-cream nightmare.

There's a private wine room (as if the main dining rooms weren't done up enough). If you plan to propose, pray for better luck than one unfortunate man we're told about whose would-be fiancée said no—and then walked out with the ring.

Happily, others through the years have found the Brownstone's Victorian-antique setting to be much more of a turn-on, perhaps none more so than the couple that, as reported by the *Houston Press* in 1999, had sex right in front of a full-out dinner crowd, then relaxed with a postcoital cigarette. The *Press* quotes one astonished customer as follows: "'The woman kept jumping up and doing this seductive dance, then she would literally bump and grind on the man's lap. Whenever he went to the restroom, she'd lick her lips, leer at us all and flash the teenage boys—she wasn't wearing underwear. Then they went outside and actually did it.'" Some of their fellow diners were offended, but the *Press* notes that "the valet parking staff appeared greatly entertained." –RG

Buca di Beppo

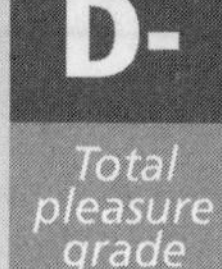

Giant portions for giant parties where almost nobody leaves happy

3.1 Food **3.7** Feel **$30** Price **Italian-American**

Casual restaurant
Sun.-Thurs. 11am-10pm;
Fri.-Sat. 11am-11pm.
Kid-friendly.

Upper Kirby
5192 Buffalo Speedway
(713) 665-2822
www.bucadibeppo.com

Bar Full
Credit Cards Visa, MC, AmEx
Reservations Accepted

If an Italian-American culinary Hell on earth existed, it might look like Buca di Beppo. This chain restaurant with its tentacles everywhere seems to embody everything that is soulless and wrong with the restaurant business: mass production of family-style food, prioritizing volume over quality, without doing justice to any culinary tradition—not even the Italian-American one.

Mass-reproduced posters, faux-old-world memorabilia, and everything else fake-Italian is flaunted at this cluttered mess of a restaurant that pretends to highlight the cuisine of Italy's south. Buca di Beppo will have your southern Italian grandmother rolling over in her grave to think that her descendants might be experiencing this as somehow Italian. She'd also be appalled by the behavior of the kids—with all the running, jumping, and screaming, Buca di Beppo can look like a daycare center where the supervisor forgot to show up. Hardly a date spot, this.

The menu is like a roll call of so-called "Italian" dishes that were actually invented in America: chicken parmigiana, fettuccine alfredo, stuffed shells, and so on. We call this cuisine "Italian-American 1.0" (as defined on pages 6-7 of this book). Granted, Little-Italy apologists might argue that Italian-American 1.0 *is* an authentic cuisine in its own right. But what would they say about Buca's attempt to look creative, too, by throwing together ill-executed dishes that cluelessly amalgamate trendy ingredients, like apple-and-gorgonzola salad or grilled polenta with gorgonzola and walnut spread? We're not sure if that's Italian-American 2.0, but it sure is gross.

The large portions at Buca are meant to be served family-style; this is one of the chain's gimmicks, a nod to gluttonous American eating habits. But even a glutton wouldn't want this much bad food. Lasagna tastes reheated, its tomato sauce strangely minerally, lingering in the back of your mouth for the duration of the meal. Gnocchi are too dense, and spaghetti comes spectacularly overcooked, although fist-sized meatballs are actually tasty and surprisingly flavorful. Chicken parmigiana (also available in individual portions) is the dark-horse winner here. It's everything you want it to be: flavorful, cheesy, and delicious. For once, poultry comes through!

If you must swallow your pride and eat this food in these portions, our advice is to starve yourself for at least two days beforehand. As Cervantes once said, hunger is the best sauce. –SD

The Buffalo Grille

Sometimes following the (Buffalo) herd isn't the best choice, but on some mornings, it is

C
Total pleasure grade

4.6 *Food* **6.9** *Feel* **$11** *Price*

American

Counter service
Mon. 7am-2pm; Tues.-Fri. 7am-9pm; Sat. 8am-9pm; Sun. 8am-2pm.
Breakfast. Kid-friendly. Outdoor dining. Vegetarian-friendly.

West U
3116 Bissonnet St.
(713) 661-3663

Memorial
1301 S. Voss Rd.
(713) 784-3663

Bar Wine and beer only
Credit Cards Visa, MC, AmEx
Reservations Not accepted

Ever since that hopped-up teddy-bear chef named Emeril showcased the Buffalo Grille's pancakes and bacon on his Food Network show, the place hasn't had much trouble raking in the customers, despite its around-par breakfast items and crowded corridors. Though the place has always had fans and a pleasant updated-Southern-comfort feel, its TV time brought it to the forefront of Houston's breakfast scene.

Even with wood-paneled walls, hand-written chalkboard menus, and hunting trophies, Buffalo Grille seems to somehow maintain a modern feel while retaining that gritty, down-to-earth Texan quality. In good weather at the Voss location, a morning breakfast on the shaded patio will get you in a good mood to start the day. Indoor tables at both locations are hard to come by at peak hours, and snagging one normally means cramming yourself into a smaller-than-intended table.

For all the families that have been swearing by Buffalo's hotcakes and eggs for ages, the taquería-meets-Continental-breakfast menu has never fully quite worked out its kinks. Traversing Buffalo Grille's extensive menu of sunup specialties also means facing its inconsistencies. Scrambled eggs in different forms, from cheddar-and-bacon to cream-cheese-and-chive scrambles, rarely lack in the flavor category, but often come out unfortunately overcooked and dry; this goes double for the migas, which scream out for pico de gallo or Tabasco. Hotcakes suffer from the same inconsistencies, at times coming out light and fluffy, but at other times needing to be submerged in their fake maple syrup.

The only real consistencies aren't worthy of much pride: cups of coffee are as reliably weak as Paris Hilton's vocabulary and taste like a big gulp of the Gulf of Mexico, and the lunch menu is like a consistently contagious epidemic of overcooking. Fortunately, when it's on—and when is hard to predict—the Buffalo Grille is a great place to spend mornings with the family, enjoying the most important meal of the day. When it's not, at least you'll have good scenery. –FC

Buffalo Wild Wings

Trivia question of the day: how many buffalo-wing sauces are too many?

5.7 Food **5.8** Feel **$22** Price

American

Bar
Sun.-Mon. 11am-11:30pm;
Tues.-Sat. 11am-1:30am.
Outdoor dining. WiFi.

Rice Area
2525 Rice Blvd.
(713) 521-1100
www.buffalowildwings.com

Bar Full
Credit Cards Visa, MC, AmEx
Reservations Accepted

West Houston
11803 Westheimer Rd.
(281) 497-9464

North Houston
17195 Tomball Pkwy.
(281) 955-7800

Since when did buffalo wings mean wings with mango habañero sauce? Or parmesan and garlic? We like our buffalo wings as they're meant to be: with buffalo sauce and blue cheese. Buffalo Wild Wings, a nationwide mega-chain, might be one big homage to that greatest of American bar-food inventions, but its proliferation of wacky flavors leaves us scratching our heads. Regardless of the intentions, by offending our collective buffalo-wing sensibilities, are they doing more harm than good?

Perhaps that's a philosophical question. In any case, the wings here are good, and come not only in a myriad of flavors, but also at different spice levels—great for those who don't want tears streaming down their faces as they eat. They also come with or without the bone. Culinary purists will, of course, want bone-in wings; infidels will choose the buffalo-tender version (here they're called "boneless wings," but it's white meat). Buffalo Wild Wings can be a bit stingy with the sauce, and presentation is subpar. Service is far more what-can-you-do-for-me than what-can-I-do-for-you; at least in the Rice Village location, tracking down your waitperson for something as simple as ordering another beer, even when the place is relatively empty, can be next to impossible.

Stray from the wings, and the menu is a minefield. Burgers are notoriously bad, and ribs are generally a disappointment. Given that Buffalo Wild Wings is also a bar, you should have a beer, though the beer selection isn't the greatest in town. The interior is bare-bones, but in an oddly deliberate way; lighting is strangely bright. The crowd tends to be young, and composed primarily of college students, for whom wings are a staple. There's also a distinct sports-bar need being filled here, with numerous well-endowed TVs consistently screening whatever games matter.

For the older (or nerdier) crowd, the TV trivia games are also popular—you ask your waitperson for a little game computer and compete against other teams at the bar and at other bars across the country. Trust us, it's fun. This place feels like a bar in the suburbs anyway, so you might as well distract yourself with some trivia. –AH

Buon Appetito

Old-world charm and competent Italian-American cooking in an unlikely setting

7.2 Food | **6.1** Feel | **$34** Price

Italian-American

Casual restaurant
Mon.-Fri. 11am-2pm, 5pm-10pm; Sat. 5pm-10pm; closed Sun.
Breakfast. Brunch. Live music. Outdoor dining. Vegetarian-friendly.

Medical Center
2231 W. Holcombe Blvd.
(713) 665-4601

Bar Full
Credit Cards Visa, MC, AmEx
Reservations Accepted

You can easily miss Buon Appetito, as it's tucked away in a run-down house next to its bigger and more boisterous neighbors: Mister Car Wash and Taco Bell. Even in the most modest of settings (and modest is being charitable), Buon Appetito delivers one of Houston's most honest, rustic, and charming "Italian-American 1.0" dining experiences. (For our definition of Italian-American 1.0, see pages 6-7.)

From the outside, it's wholly possible for you to have the "who would want to eat *there*?" reaction. Inside, Buon Appetito is exceptionally rugged. The floorboards creak under your feet, it's dark, and it's way too warm. The space seems cramped, and the chairs are straight-backed and pretty uncomfortable, but as the waiter approaches the table, everything changes.

There's a certain charm to the waitstaff. They seem absolutely enthused to be doing what they're doing, ready to give you a taste not just of their food, but also of their Italian-American culture. However, at times they are a bit bullheaded. The restaurant calls itself Sicilian, and if you make the mistake of calling the food Italian, they'll correct you—which is amusing, given that there is scarcely an authentic Sicilian dish on the entire menu. That aside, the staff is extremely welcoming, and as you sit down to eat, an elderly gentleman will often wander the rooms playing classical guitar and singing Italian and Spanish love songs.

Every bite at Buon Appetito tastes like someone spent hours stirring the pot lovingly with a wooden spoon. This is food that's rustic and homey. The minestrone soup is hearty and tastes every bit as homemade as they claim. A main course of cannelloni with ricotta and tomato sauce is expertly balanced, with the creaminess of the cheese cut slightly with the spring of acid from the tomatoes. For something covered in cheese, it is exceptionally light. Pastas suffer a bit from over-saucing, as some plates come swimming in sauce, but that's a chronic problem in Houston, anyway.

Don't be fooled by first impressions, because as you're enjoying a light tiramisù, sipping on coffee, satisfied from your meal, listening to the flow of Italian love songs in the air, and staring into your significant other's eyes, you won't be sorry you gave this Houston gem a chance. No matter how ugly the package was. (The restaurant, that is, not your significant other.) –JY

Cabo's Mix-Mex Grille

Bad food and good drink late night in downtown

D *Total pleasure grade*

3.0 *Food* **5.7** *Feel* **$25** *Price* **Tex-Mex**

Casual restaurant
Mon.-Fri. 11am-11pm;
Sat. 11am-1am; Sun. 11am-10pm.
Outdoor dining.

Downtown
419 Travis St.
(713) 225-2060
www.cabomixmex.com

Bar Full
Credit Cards Visa, MC, AmEx
Reservations Not accepted

It's frustrating trying to eat a late dinner in Houston. So few places are open, and at those that are, you often feel bad for keeping everyone around when they clearly just want to go home. There's nothing fun about being the only table in a restaurant. After an Astros evening game, the choices are bleak if you want to eat anywhere in the area. No one's around; offices are closed, and so are the few eateries downtown. Except for Cabo's Mix-Mex, that is. And we can't help but wonder what percentage of Cabo's business is driven simply by the fact that it has no real alternative. Sure, the atmosphere is fun; there's a lively deck where people raucously sip margaritas—even if they are just drowning their sorrows over the loss of Craig Biggio and a subpar season from Lance Berkman, whose lethargic waddle looks to be a far cry from his glory days at Rice.

But would we come here for any reason other than convenience?

No. "Cabo Queso"—to which you can add picadillo, though we find it does little to help—is disappointing. It's poorly presented and has record-breaking skin-forming abilities; queso this bad is inexcusable in Texas. Fajitas, too, leave us seriously underwhelmed. They're underseasoned and overcooked—a fatal combination—and their accompanying tortillas are a hardened disaster. Even in chip form, they're still off, often (but not always) too brittle. It takes skill to mess these things up on such a level. There's little to redeem Cabo after its balcony. Certainly the fake-cantina vibe doesn't do much to boost the indoor atmosphere, nor do the antiseptic, plasticky booths.

The margaritas, however, save the day; they can be called in to save any kind of meal. Awkward social situations, bad food—they can fix it. And if you look around, that's what everyone here seems to be doing, really: downing margaritas. If you're going to drink the night away downtown, this deck really isn't such a bad place to do it; it's lively enough, it's tucked into the shadows of all the big buildings, and it reminds you what downtown Houston could, and will, someday become. –AH

Cadillac Bar

Total pleasure grade

A Landry's Tex-Mex joint whose execution is as tired as an Eldorado

Food

Feel

Price

Tex-Mex

Casual restaurant
Sun.-Thurs. 11am-10:15pm;
Fri.-Sat. 11am-11:15pm.
Kid-friendly.

Heights
1802 Shepherd Dr.
(713) 862-2020
www.cadillacbar.com

Bar Full
Credit Cards Visa, MC, AmEx
Reservations Accepted

Cadillac Bar has the hallmarks of a restaurant that's fun for all ages: a fun motif and mass-produced food. They claim "it's the best time you'll ever have." We're skeptical. A Landry's soldier, Cadillac offers Tex-Mex food with few or no surprises; a run-of-the-mill menu has queso, fajitas, and overstuffed burritos. This leaves the burden on pure taste to deliver an over-the-top experience. Which it doesn't.

Take a look around—no bars on the windows, the servers are smiling, and the place is blowing A/C like it's nothing. (Who's paying the electric bill here?) Everything looks too generic—a common problem at volume restaurants where numbers reign supreme. You have the obligatory pictures of Hispanic men with giant sombreros, and also some pictures of a sparkling Cadillac in the rear.

If only the menu were as eclectic as the décor. Your choices are pretty limited to chiles rellenos, flautas, chalupas, enchiladas, and tamales. "Cadillac Nachos" with beef or chicken, cheese, guacamole, and pico de gallo taste like the other countless versions of this moneymaker appetizer around town. The best item on the menu, hands down, is the sopa de tortilla. (Putting the item's name in Spanish makes it taste better, right?) It's a hearty chicken soup with avocado, cheese, and tortilla strips.

When Cadillac Bar tries its hand at more ambitious items, the results aren't so pleasing. They try enchiladas suizas, stuffed with chicken and topped with a tomatillo sauce, but the results are not exciting: just the same ol' Tex-Mex dressed up in a different way. The redfish del mar, blackened to the point of being burnt, comes so overcooked and dry that even its cilantro cream sauce can't help it. So if you do decide to Cadillac over to the Cadillac Bar, do it when drink specials are in full effect and you won't stress about what the food tastes like. The kiddos, anyway, will amuse themselves and be happy regardless. –SD

Café 101

A dressed up, over-priced, under-substanced, shoot-for-the-trend mix of Asian cuisine

4.5 Food | **6.3** Feel | **$14** Price

Vietnamese

Casual restaurant
Daily 11:30am-2am.

Chinatown
9889 Bellaire Blvd.
(713) 272-8828

Bar Wine and beer only
Credit Cards Visa and MC
Reservations Accepted

Dear Café 101,

We are aware of the possibility that by installing a bright purple shaded sign, hiring pretty waitresses, and serving things in trendy bento boxes, you thought you might then be able to charge a premium for food that's produced with little to no thought. Still, we struggle to understand your business plan. What is it about the combination of bad food, slow service, and an environment that guys refer to as "the place to go to look at all the pretty girls," and that women are therefore intimidated from patronizing, that seems like such a strong business concept?

Was your aim to recreate Al Bundy's No Ma'am Club, perhaps?

If so, we must compliment your cheesy, loungey, cheap décor. We have certainly taken note of the faux-kindling-hanging-off-the-ceiling look. Whether you were going for Hong Kong cool or Asian Hooters, we commend your ingenious plan to distract the customers with hot female bodies while they wait for 20 minutes to be acknowledged and another 20 minutes for their food.

Which reminds us, we're also impressed that all you have to do is write up a huge list of tapioca-ball drinks and shaved ice, and you've suddenly got low overhead and high income. As for the hot food, does the name Café 101 refer to the number of different cuisines on your menu? Are they—along with the short skirts—intended to confuse people to the point of being apathetic about how much cash they're coughing up? Are you then able to fry up fish and slather it in what seems to be honeyed soy sauce, and serve cold broccoli, chewy pieces of sushi, and still have nobody complain? Brilliant.

You might have to watch your back on the beef noodle soup, though. San Dong Noodle House across the street serves the same thing, but it's actually good, so the fact that yours tastes like nothing but boiled beef in a tinted broth with noodles could potentially come under fire. Otherwise, keep up the good work. One day, we too hope to take people's money without actually offering them a dining experience.

Yours,

The Fearless Critics

Café Adobe

Don't believe the hype: this margarita hotspot serves some of the worst Tex-Mex in town

D
Total pleasure grade

2.1 *Food* **8.7** *Feel* **$24** *Price* **Tex-Mex**

Casual restaurant
Mon.-Fri. 11am-10pm;
Sat.-Sun. 11am-11pm.

Live music. Outdoor dining. WiFi. Additional locations.

River Oaks
2111 Westheimer Rd.
(713) 528-1468
www.cafeadobe.com

Spring Branch
7620 Katy Fwy.
(713) 688-1700

Bar Full
Credit Cards Visa, MC, AmEx
Reservations Accepted

Sugar Land
2329 S. Hwy. 6
(281) 277-1757

If you come into a city knowing absolutely nothing about its restaurants, a good rule of thumb is to avoid the ones that advertise the most. Nowhere is this more true than it is at Café Adobe, whose splashy ads—which you'll see all over Houston—speak of superlative margaritas, canonical Tex-Mex, and the best whatever in town.

Now, there is something to the Café Adobe margarita, especially the frozen version with both Cointreau and Grand Marnier, which has plenty of alcohol and manages to steer clear of that dreaded sour-mix taste. Also irreproachable, at least if you have a taste for kitsch, is the caricatured, Disneyish faux-Mexican interior. It's an enjoyable place to come just for cocktails, and its pleasant outdoor garden, which directly fronts Westheimer and suffers from road noise, is still set off from the street enough to feel like an unexpected urban Mexican courtyard.

It's the Tex-Mex food at Café Adobe that is deranged. Even the chips and salsa that show up to start are terrible. Red salsa transports you immediately into your jarred nightmares. Green salsa is not quite as bad as the red, but it isn't good, either. Chile con queso, that Tex-Mex standby, is one of the worst versions we've ever seen, forming a thick skin within seconds after each bite. Fajita beef is darkly marinated, with an almost teriyaki-like flavor—it's the least of the evils on the plate—but chicken enchiladas with sour-cream sauce are horrible, with underseasoned chicken, tasteless gravy, and copious, quickly congealing cheese. A pico de gallo garnish, amazingly, is actually the best part of the dish.

And the culinary blooper reel continues. Rice has no taste of stock; beans have no taste of pork. If you want to go for a happy-hour drink, fine, but for a restaurant that trumps itself up as famous, popular, and best of this or best of that, you'd think they could afford to divert a few of those marketing dollars into the kitchen. –RG

Café Annie

Famously high-concept Southwestern that's sometimes successful, but not worth the tab

B *Total pleasure grade*

7.6 *Food* **9.3** *Feel* **$106** *Price* **New American**

Upmarket restaurant
Mon. 6pm-10pm; Tues.-Thurs. 11:30am-2pm, 6pm-10pm; Fri. 11:30am-2pm, 6pm-10:30pm; Sat. 6pm-10:30pm.; closed Sun.

Galleria
1728 Post Oak Blvd.
(713) 840-1111
www.cafe-annie.com

Bar Full
Credit Cards Visa, MC, AmEx
Reservations Essential

The crowd is as elite as they come at Café Annie, Houston's sumptuous Southwestern showroom. Even on a weekday night, you'll walk in past a long row of black limos queued up outside the restaurant, the chauffeurs whiling away the time while the business-class passengers roar it up in an imperious dining room that absolutely oozes with money and privilege. (The newer, more casual Bar Annie, where you can come without a reservation, is a lite version of the power-dinner scene.)

But even if the soaring ceilings, traditional lamps, and spectacular service evoke 1940s aristocracy, Café Annie manages not to feel clubby in that masculine, Vic & Anthony's sort of way. This is the more modern, metrosexual face of the oil-business expense account, a world where women are welcome in the boardroom and green chile welcome on the ambitious menu, which road-trips down to Mexico via Tucson, Albuquerque, Santa Fe, and Taos.

Although the menu changes frequently, fowl is Annie's strongest suit, as in grilled quail or roasted pheasant, whose leg and thigh pieces sizzle with savory fat and swim in a chile arbol sauce with golden raisins. Irreproachable steaks are served properly to temperature, while starches—perhaps a meat-decorated, delicately chunky polenta or surreally silky mashed potatoes—are even more addictive. Seafood tends to be less successful: red snapper might come out slightly dry; and daring but disastrous, at one visit, was tough kampachi (amberjack) sashimi curiously topped with barbacoa far less tender than versions at your average one-dollar taco stand; it's a sort of Japanese-Mexican surf 'n' turf, if you will.

Populist but good, though, are enchiladas of red chile beef, whose homemade tortilla, cabbage slaw, fragrant green sauce, and bright cilantro speak in the idioms of the central Mexican marketplace rather than nouvelle Tex-Mex. And desserts shine, as they should in this town; a sweet, moist banana tamal in a plantain leaf is paired with walnuts. Even more memorable is a berry cobbler whose dough is raw and velvety on the inside, like a cobbler version of molten chocolate cake. In the end, the meal is not really worth the money, but few who come here care. –RG

Café Caspian

A taste of everything Persian—including soft drinks

B *Total pleasure grade*

7.4 *Food* **7.8** *Feel* **$19** *Price* **Middle Eastern**

Casual restaurant
Tues.-Thurs. 11am-10pm; Fri. 11am-11pm; Sat. noon-11pm; Sun. noon-10pm; closed Mon.
Delivery. Outdoor dining.

West Houston
12126 Westheimer Rd.
(281) 493-4000
www.cafecaspian.com

Bar None
Credit Cards Visa, MC, AmEx
Reservations Accepted

Houston is pretty receptive to other cultures and cuisines—especially when it's light, flavorful, and cheap. Such is Café Caspian. The people here rely on the dishes of their former homeland to let them make a living in this country, and they've got a strong following of Middle Eastern expats who come for a taste of home—like some of the best hummus in town. Even those totally unaccustomed to Persian food will find this cuisine accessible and find themselves reaching for thirds. And everyone can appreciate the fact that the food is healthy and guilt-free.

Bring your appetite; the portions are big, and the flavors are bold without being overstated. Hummus is creamy, with just the right amount of garlic and deep flavors of tahini. Tabbouleh, heavy on the bulghur and parsley, is moist and delicious, spritzed up by lemon juice, olive oil, and fresh mint. Mains are limited, but the mahicheh is wonderful; it's braised lamb shank that is cooked until it's falling off the bone, served with sabzi polow (an herbed basmati rice), and the natural lamb jus. The lamb has the flavor of cardamom and anise, and the sabzi polow, which is usually served with fish, works wonderfully.

A unique part of the menu at Café Caspian is the "House Stew" section. The ghormeh sabzi (herb stew) makes a tasty and light meal; fresh herbs are stewed with kidney beans, dried limes, and beef to make a delicious broth. Also good are the esfenaj-o alu (spinach and prune stew) and fesenjan (pomegranate and walnut stew). Authenticity is key here at Café Caspian, so keep it up even after you've finished eating. Enjoy some post-prandial Persian hot tea with cardamom, or doogh, a naturally carbonated yogurt drink that aids in digestion. Whatever you pick will probably be a winner, because the folks at Café Caspian serve the food of their country not only with pride, but also with intense flavor. It'll get you hooked. –SD

Café Express

If this is what the American restaurant has become, then there's a dark age ahead

D-
Total pleasure grade

4.7 Food | **2.8** Feel | **$16** Price | **American**

Counter service
Daily 11am-11pm.

Kid-friendly. Outdoor dining. Vegetarian-friendly. Additional locations.

Upper Kirby
3200 Kirby Dr.
(713) 522-3994
www.cafe-express.com

River Oaks
1422 W. Gray St.
(713) 522-3100

Bar Wine and beer only
Credit Cards Visa, MC, AmEx
Reservations Not accepted

Hermann Park
Museum of Fine Arts
5601 Main St.
(713) 639-7370

The customer knows best. The chef is but a server. Mix and match your salads, your proteins, your starches, your sauces. Have it *your* way: it's *your* palate, *your* body.

That's the driving philosophy behind the Café Express movement: the customer knows best. Customers don't like pork, because it's too fatty? Make it with chicken. Customers don't like dark meat, because it tastes too much like chicken? Make it with a slab of pasty white breast that tastes like nothing at all.

This is America! Free our imprisoned restaurant customers from the shackles of the paternalistic chef—we're grown-ups now! Why should we have to subject ourselves to those ugly meats that actually look like they came from animals? Why should we put up with bitterness, challenging textures, unusual spices, or foreign foods? Why should we ever have to try anything raw, anything fatty, anything new?

Free us from the shackles of a thousand years of culinary tradition, and deliver us to a brave new culinary world where the evils of all strong flavors have been eradicated, where the guilt of feeling like you're actually consuming animals has vanished along with their skins and bones. Take us to the promised land of milk and honey mustard, of grilled-chicken-breast Caesar, the fillet of salmon cooked to white, the penne pasta with sautéed spinach and mushrooms with "Turkey Bolognese" sauce, the "Grilled Chicken & Pasta Pesto Deli," the mushroom-and-spinach turkey burger. Take us to Café Express!

And why should we have to put up with service anymore? With servers who might get our order wrong? Why take suggestions, specials of the day? We know what we want! Put it all on LCD monitors above the counter, and go from customer straight to computer. Let us choose—*ourselves*—between the 11 grilled chicken dishes, and six turkey dishes! If we want wine, let us choose—*ourselves*—between Yellow Tail white and Yellow Tail red! Let us obtain our receipt from the register and then get the wine—*ourselves*—from the bar. This is America, the land of choice, the land of self-sufficiency, the land of grilled chicken!

If this is what the famous Del Grande himself, owner of Café Annie, sees as our culinary future, then a dark age lies ahead. –RG

Café Japon

An apathetic staff and mediocre sushi at a restaurant seemingly run by robots in Dallas

D- Total pleasure grade

2.3 Food | **1.0** Feel | **$27** Price | **Japanese**

Casual restaurant
Mon.-Thurs. 11am-midnight;
Fri. 11am-2am; Sat. noon-2am;
Sun. noon-midnight.
Outdoor dining.

Upper Kirby
3915 Kirby Dr.
(713) 529-1668
www.cafejapon.com

Bar Full
Credit Cards Visa, MC, AmEx
Reservations Accepted

In Japan, sushi is all about the interaction between restaurant and customer, between sushi chef and sushi-eater. The restaurant business is a human business, because what's more human than eating?

Café Japon, a Houston branch of a Dallas restaurant, doesn't seem to share in that philosophy. When we showed up for lunch at the big, airy, impersonal space at 2:35pm one day, our first clue to stay away should have been the fact that we were the only ones in the house.

Untrained in the local customs, we requested the lunch menu, but were coldly rebuffed: lunch ended at 2:30 on the dot, and "last call" was 2:25. We were, of course, allowed to order the same exact dishes as were on the lunch menu, which were then prepared by the same exact kitchen staff as they would have been five minutes earlier, because the restaurant stays open all afternoon. But the same dishes cost nearly twice as much, because, at 2:35pm, we were clearly in for dinner, not for lunch. After a long discussion with our server, we were informed that they were actually banned by their computer system from serving us lunch, and that there was nobody in the house who could override it. Next time, we were told, we should arrive earlier.

Now, our point here is not to emulate an irritating b4-u-eat post. It's to call attention to the last, and most interesting, part of the story: *there's nobody in the restaurant who even has control over the computer system.* Which means there's nobody in the house who has the power of a restaurant manager. Which means the restaurant is not being managed. Which, in turn, might help explain many other things about Café Japon, such as why the food, like the service, is so unbelievably bad.

As it turns out, computers aren't very good sushi chefs, either. Maybe their software can't detect when the tuna is stringy, the yellowtail fishy, the surf clam rubbery, or the uni skunky. Maybe no syntax error appears when the spicy sauce tastes foul, when the sushi rice has no structural integrity, or when the nori is old and chewy.

We're comforted, at least, by the fact that the human automata that work at this restaurant seem to share our concerns: as we departed one afternoon, we noticed the Asian staff of Café Japon, sitting at a nearby six-top, eating their lunch: big bags of take-out from Taco Cabana next door. –FC

Café Le Jadeite

Awkward, sorta-Asian-French fusion in an over-the-top setting

C+ Total pleasure grade

7.4 Food **7.9** Feel **$73** Price **Pan-Asian**

Upmarket restaurant
Mon.-Thurs. 11am-10pm;
Fri. 11am-11pm;
Sat. noon-11pm; Sun. 5pm-10pm.
Date-friendly. Live music.

River Oaks
1952 W. Gray St.
(713) 528-4288
www.cafelejadeite.biz

Bar Full
Credit Cards Visa, MC, AmEx
Reservations Recommended

If there is one restaurant in Houston that has the most extreme version of the interior-design-on-crack, they-probably-spent-way-too-much-money-on-this setting that you would expect to see in a Vegas casino, this is probably it. Never mind that the Asian fusion food isn't really fusion, or that high-flying presentations conceal food that doesn't taste all that good. Café Le Jadeite's flamboyance and faux-sophistication are so bewildering that they almost manage to cover up for the poor quality of food.

Why anyone would want to dine in what feels like the Asian Arts exhibit at the MFAH is questionable, but even more puzzling is the fact that there's a live jazz pianist in the same area as what looks to be stoic stone carved Chinese relics. Some might call the décor stunning, but they'd probably say the same thing about the Bellagio, and at least that establishment has roulette and blackjack to justify its sleaze. Yet it's all so dramatic that we have to respect it, even if we don't like it.

"Fusion" has given birth to some of the most ill-conceived, disgusting dishes the world has ever seen, but your frightened taste buds might actually relax when they realize that Café Le Jadeite seems to have misunderstood its meaning: generally, French and Asian merely coexist on this menu, rather than overlapping. The Asian dishes, meanwhile, show up under "House Specialties," which include surprisingly good renditions of Chinese-American standbys like the sprightly, bright-tasting orange beef. Spicy green beans have a good balance of garlic and jalapeño flavor, but this is something for which you expect to pay $7.95, and it's hard to convince yourself that these double-digit price tags are fair for glorified take-out Chinese.

Appetizers suffer most from the fusion treatment, with the "grilled" oysters actually fried and sauced with a ginger-scallion mix that only slightly cuts their muddy, not-very-recently-shucked taste. "Chef's Favorites" include French dishes like a dinosaur-sized, sticky-sweet bone-in short rib that's cursed with dry, mealy mashed potatoes.

Presentations are gimmicky; some dishes are flambéed with 151. The point of the flambé is supposed to be to add flavor, but this merely leaves a trail of burnt garnishes. Speaking of garnishes, those adorning the Chilean sea bass are inedible—a cardinal sin—except for the wooden skewer of impaled shrimp rammed into the fish. At least it's not fusion. –JY

Café Lili

A casual Lebanese find where you should stick to the chalkboard specials

B Total pleasure grade

7.5 Food | 5.0 Feel | $23 Price

Middle Eastern

Casual restaurant
Mon.-Thurs. 11am-9pm;
Fri.-Sat. 11am-10pm; closed Sun.
Date-friendly. Kid-friendly.
Vegetarian-friendly.

Galleria
5757 Westheimer Rd.
(713) 952-6969
www.cafelili.com

Bar Wine and beer only
Credit Cards Visa, MC, AmEx
Reservations Not accepted

Specials are such an endlessly unpredictable aspect of the restaurant world. At times, they can be an amalgam of leftover ingredients that the kitchen's trying to dump before they go bad. Other times, they showcase a chef's talented treatment of an ultra-fresh item that's just come in. But sometimes, as on Café Lili's chalkboard, the specials represent the most authentic portion of the kitchen's culinary background—preparations that people wouldn't buy otherwise. The regular menu at Café Lili is passable, if sometimes in need of salt and pepper. But the chalkboard is the true heart of this soulful Middle Eastern restaurant.

Café Lili has that distinct aura of a family-run business. Sitting down at the table makes you feel like you're a part of the family, and staff members have no problem ribbing each other even while serving. It's easy to share jokes and be loud at Café Lili—in fact, the place practically demands it. The TV, the close-knit corners, and thick, clunky wine glasses make you feel arm-in-arm camaraderie with your dining neighbors. The several Lebanese wines on offer are high on Bordeaux varietals and pair interestingly with the food. While many ethnic restaurants focus on culture, this place just seems like one big, happy family.

Acidic hummus and smoky baba ghanooj are perfectly fine starters, though nothing out of the ordinary. Tabbouleh salad is a brighter spot than usual, with a tangy, mouth-clearing flavor of fresh parsley. Amongst mains, chicken and rice is unfortunately reminiscent of a 1970s English preparation, with chicken breast meat that tastes boiled. A beef shawarma comes tough, overcooked, and tasteless, although the accompanying side of fried eggs is a delicious match.

That chalkboard, though, is where you should live. On one day, a simply grilled redfish had the perfect amount of bitter char to it to go with its sweet, flaky flesh, and a lamb kibbeh of raw ground meat and raw onion sections was like a better, more powerful Lebanese version of a good French steak tartare. And that's no small compliment, because a good French steak tartare is one of the best things there is. –JY

Café Malay

An authentic taste of the Straits in a strip mall—how's that for culinary transportation?

A- Total pleasure grade

8.5 Food | 7.1 Feel | $15 Price | **Malaysian**

Casual restaurant
Sun.-Thurs. 11am-9:30pm;
Fri.-Sat. 11am-10pm.
Date-friendly. Delivery.
Kid-friendly. Vegetarian-friendly.

Westchase
10234 Westheimer Rd.
(713) 785-7915
www.café-malay.com

Bar BYO
Credit Cards Visa, MC, AmEx
Reservations Accepted

Ah, strip-mall food. In Houston, it's normally quick, it's normally simple, it's normally greasy, and quite frankly it's normally not that great. There are several exceptions to this, one of them being Café Malay, located on an unassuming corner of Westheimer. While décor and atmosphere are severely lacking here, the food is tasty, exotic, and thankfully out of the ordinary.

Walking into Café Malay is like walking into a 1980s-Chinese-restaurant throwback. There are pink tombstone-looking rows of chairs, mostly barren walls with a few works of vaguely Asian art and novelties, and white panels on the ceiling that make you feel like you're in an office building rather than a restaurant. The white tablecloths are misleading; Café Malay is as casual as they come, and that's probably for the better. Given that in Malaysia, this sort of food is most authentically served in tiny restaurants or even on the side of the street, it seems absolutely appropriate.

The fare at Café Malay is the sort that makes you want to get out of the city and travel the world. The flavors are different and exciting. Anything labeled a "specialty" is normally more authentic and usually a sure-on hit. Roti canai, a Straits dish you'll see all over Malaysia, Singapore, and Indonesia, is influenced by both Indian and Chinese flavors; it's a fried piece of thin dough that's served with a penetrating curry dipping sauce. The buttery pancake, almost like a lighter Indian paratha, takes on coconut-curry flavors while still maintaining its crispness. Nasi lemak simultaneously highlights many of the various components of what Malaysian food is; with its coconut rice, boiled egg, crispy anchovies, and curried chicken, it's sweet, sour, and salty, with a lot of emphasis on contrasting textures. That theme follows throughout the menu, with the banana-leaf-steamed fish that's fantastically tender with an insane amount of spice. Even the simple coconut drink has an unexpected tang. The menu is all about balance: if it's sour, it's sour, but it's never offensively so. There's always something to offset the extreme flavors and textures.

Before Café Malay, to get the real flavors of the Straits, you'd have needed hours of flying and fighting through airports. Now all you have to do is deal with Westheimer traffic. –JY

Café Montrose

Total pleasure grade

A urinating statue, moules frites, great Belgian beer, and lackadaisical European service

6.9 Food | **5.9** Feel | **$43** Price | **Belgian**

Casual restaurant
Mon.-Sat. 11am-10pm; closed Sun. *Date-friendly. Live music. Outdoor dining.*

Montrose
1609 Westheimer Rd.
(713) 523-1201
www.cafemontrose.com

Bar Full
Credit Cards Visa, MC, AmEx
Reservations Accepted

You know you're in for a good night when your first sight is a statue of a kid peeing. It's the icon of Brussels—the manneken pis—and you should take it as evidence that the mussel dishes and other Belgian fare aren't watered down here. Café Montrose isn't trying to appeal to Houston, but rather waiting on Houston to come to it. You won't see Belgian fajitas or a mussel burrito on the menu; the deal here is food that is unique to their country, with universal appeal to taste buds.

The national dish of Belgium is moules frites, in which mussels are steamed off in a variety of aromatics and served with fries. Café Montrose's version of the latter is one of the best in the city, especially when the fries are dipped in their creamy and delicious mayonnaise. A variety of moules frites is served: mussels in white wine, mussels in curry sauce, mussels in escargot butter. The moules marinniere see mussels with white wine, celery, and onion presented in the pot they were cooked in. The mussels are always on, but the other mains are a bit hit-or-miss. Waterzooi de poulet is a stew of chicken with vegetables in a thick sauce that has little flavor, and leaves a lot to imagination. Filet and ribeye steaks make an appearance, but with hefty asking prices and poor execution, they can be easily passed over.

The waitstaff come complete with thick French accents, and we sometimes wonder if then language gap is bigger than it might seem at first; service lacks at times. Nonetheless, the beers make up for it. Great Belgian beers on tap are offered at a good price, and they accompany the food wonderfully, just like a nice glass of wine would. In sum: go for the mussels, fries, and mayo. The beer will make you happy if the service gets you in a statuesque mood, and the food is easily worth the prices. –SD

Café Piquet

Cuban food: the only gift we can legally enjoy from this rich culture

B-
Total pleasure grade

7.4 *Food* **7.5** *Feel* **$13** *Price* **Cuban**

Casual restaurant
Mon.-Thurs. 11am-9pm; Fri.-Sat. 11am-10pm; Sun. 11am-7pm.

Bellaire
5757 Bissonnet St.
(713) 664-1031

Bar Full
Credit Cards Visa, MC, AmEx
Reservations Accepted

Whatever its political merits, the embargo against Cuba is a culinary loss, because when it's good, Cuban food can be delicious. It's better understood in places like Miami (Cuba is to Florida as Mexico is to Texas), but little is known about the cuisine in Houston.

It's a shame when a Cuban restaurant opens and tries to mold into a Cuban-Mexican concept to stay in business. Café Piquet, however, serves bona fide Cuban food without any sort of posturing. Yuca frita and croquetas are available, as well as pargo entero frito (whole fried snapper) to make you feel like you're Cuba—without the whole diplomatic debacle such border-hopping would entail.

But Café Piquet is situated a lot closer by: in a small strip mall on Bissonnet. Inside you'll find a fairly small restaurant that is modern and clean with a few tables and chairs, and Cuban pictures and memorabilia grace the uncluttered walls.

Appetizers consist of papas rellenas—balls of mashed potatoes that are stuffed with seasoned beef and fried—and empanadas with ham, beef, or cheese. The ham empanadas are particularly delicious; the dough is light and wrapped around seasoned ham, and it doesn't weigh you down and leave you too full for your mains. The yuca frita is wonderful, lightly fried and served with mojo that is pleasantly packed with lots of garlic.

The fryer gets a lot of use at Café Piquet. Masitas fritas are lightly fried chunks of pork that are seasoned with mojito sauce and served with onions and rice. Even though they're fried, they're still a nice, light dish that focuses on seasoning and protein.

Dispense with those ideas of sneaking away to Cuba to guarantee yourself a steady supply of this food; service is friendly, even during the busy lunch rush, and you'll manage to have a nice time. If you're not too high-maintenance, that is. –SD

Café Pita +

Showstopping, painstakingly homemade Balkan food in an unlikely spot

Total pleasure grade

9.1	8.0	$17	**Bosnian**
Food	Feel	Price	

Casual restaurant
Mon.-Thurs. 11am-9pm;
Fri. 11am-10pm;
Sat.-Sun. noon-10pm.

Westchase
10890 Westheimer Rd.
(713) 953-7237

Bar Wine and beer, BYO
Credit Cards Visa and MC
Reservations Not accepted

You'd have to be a true culinary nerd (the kind of guy who would stay after cooking-school class to watch the stock form its raft) to know much about this delicious culinary genre, of which Café Pita + is one of greater Houston's only faithful practitioners. Either that, or you'd have to hail from the former Yugoslavia—like our friend who thankfully escorted us to this out-of-the-way gem.

Bosnian cuisine begins with lepinja, the doughy bread, and here it's deliciously homemade. But it is also only one amongst house-made wonders that define this devoted, disciplined, diminutive kitchen, which serves a stark but still somehow cozy room. Maybe it just feels cozy because of the Bosnian guy sitting by himself in the corner, reading the paper and sipping his Turkish coffee, giving you the sense that you've just stepped from a random Houston strip mall into some street café in Sarajevo. Or maybe it's the warm, genuine staff, who import—from Chicago—such rarities as a Bosnian version of feta, which has a more sour, fermented flavor than the standard Greek stuff. There's also the deepest-flavored "pastrami" we've ever tasted, a cured beef cut that plays off like Italy's air-dried bresaola, except for the smokiness (and except that it's not made from horsemeat, as is top bresaola).

Then there's expertly fried cheese, homemade in the halloumi style and delicately battered. We've developed a curious obsession with its texture, which—in an unexpected turn of events—actually becomes more irresistible as it cools off and congeals, revealing more of its trademark squeak. More addictive yet, though, is the evap, ground-beef-and-lamb sausages that are served on lepinja as a sandwich—they sing with transportative, meaty flavor.

Some menu items exist only to accommodate American tastes (think chicken Caesar salad), and you should avoid them. Beef and chicken shish kebabs can come dry and relatively flavorless. But the rest is solid gold: the city's most moist, flavorful rice; butterflied grilled sardines and their delightfully forward marine flavor; comforting sarma (stuffed cabbage in a flavor-forward broth); and soft pirjan (meltingly braised lamb shank with potatoes and vegetables). This is one of the most honest, heartfelt restaurants in the city. –RG

Café Rabelais

Great wine and decent mussels by candlelight

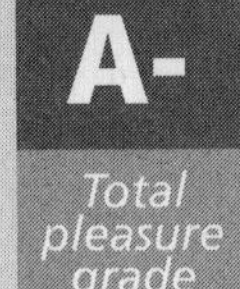

7.7 Food | **9.8** Feel | **$55** Price | **French**

Upmarket restaurant
Mon. 6pm-9pm; Tues.-Wed. 11am-2:30pm, 6pm-9pm; Thurs.-Sat. 11am-2:30pm, 6pm-10pm; closed Sun.
Date-friendly. Wine-friendly.

Rice Area
2442 Times Blvd.
(713) 520-8841
www.caferabelais.com

Bar Wine and beer only
Credit Cards Visa, MC, AmEx
Reservations Essential

It doesn't get much more romantic or transportative than this. Imagine: the only light in the place comes from tall candles in old empty wine bottles on the tables. The walls are lined with bottles of wine lying on their sides, working their magic, softening through the years—until somebody chooses one of them as their own for that evening. In fact, everyone here seems to be under some sort of spell. Couples lean over the table that much closer, or stare off dreamily into the dark corners of the restaurant. Servers do their best to provide just what's needed without being overly attentive. The only jerk back to reality is some of the food, and even then, it's not too disruptive.

The menu is scrawled onto a large chalkboard hung high; it's a painfully cute and provincial touch. The only print menu available is the extensive, almost sacrificially well-priced wine list, refreshingly half-bottle heavy, whose older vintages you can easily get carried away with. For starters, escargot à la Bourguignonne are a good option. Plump, green, and herby, they have an earthy taste that's big, yet delicate. Foie gras—strangely square, strangely smooth—doesn't have the texture of a fresh, house-made mi cuit foie gras; it leaves us wanting for something richer and denser. Mussels "Rabelais" seem logically to be a good choice, and their texture is tender, although their broth is a bit thin and wimpy, lacking the rich, creamy concentration that you're supposed to be so excited to sop up with bread. A dish of beef medallions topped with semi-melted goat cheese is a crowd-pleaser that, at one visit, was strongly pushed by our server, but its flavors were thin and predictable. You're better off with fish mains, especially the whole loup de mer, when it's available.

But let us shut up, and let this atmosphere take you to a faraway place. A good bottle of wine (which the particularly knowledgeable wine stewards can help you select) makes everything taste better. Just be forewarned: the exit into the SUV-filled parking lots of Rice Village will be a shock. By now, your date might well be imagining lanterns and cobblestones. –AH

Café Red Onion

Chicken Belize, Chicken Fiesta, Chicken Brazil, and Chicken Tikal. Get the message?

C *Total pleasure grade*

5.5 *Food* **5.9** *Feel* **$37** *Price* **Latin American**

Casual restaurant
Mon.-Thurs. 11am-10pm;
Fri.-Sat. 11am-11pm;
closed Sun.

Upper Kirby
3910 Kirby Dr.
(713) 807-1122
www.caferedonion.com

Bar Full
Credit Cards Visa, MC, AmEx
Reservations Not accepted

West Houston
1111 Eldridge Pkwy.
(281) 293-7500

Northwest Houston
12440 Northwest Fwy.
(713) 957-0957

What is fusion cuisine? Is it as simple as creating a menu with mixed origins and calling it fusion? You combine 10 genres of cuisine without any connection to each other, you get a cool sign, you commission business cards on nice stock, you jack up the menu prices, and you get promoters to invite the beautiful people from around town.

That's Café Red Onion at its worst. Café Red Onion tries to touch on every Latin American niche, and it often backfires. But that's not all that the restaurant stands for. Half the menu peddles of dishes that are well thought out and make sense, while the other half just seems like filler to make the menu long enough.

The restaurant has seen it fit to open multiple locations around Houston, so this concept has obviously been working for them. Amongst starters, ceviche is good; packed with shrimp, it's acidic and refreshing. Miniature crab cakes, however, leave a lot to be desired; their unique, mushy texture makes them taste more like bread than like crab. And anyway, haven't we had enough crab cakes in Houston?

You should also pass on the salads, which, at press time, started at $12.50 and went up from there. Pupusas revueltas, with bland pork and jack cheese stuffed inside, are a far cry from what you find in El Salvador (or even at a decent pupusería in Houston); they're a total letdown. "Chicken Belize" has a star next to its name on the menu, indicating that it's critically acclaimed by food critics. Not these: it's a perfectly dry chicken breast with watery pineapple salsa. Chicken, in fact, clucks all over the menu; there are eight different preparations of the dreaded chicken breast, all with different names, and served with different relishes or rice and beans. Prices are high in general, and beware the $2.50 charge to split dishes. Certain locations do to-go orders, but if the food isn't that great at the restaurant, there's no reason to believe it would be any different after you get it home.

If you want to steer clear of the whole minefield, go with the fajitas. Their sizzling platter is like a breath of fresh air into this fusion disaster; as long as our fajitas still sizzle, then all is right with the world. –SD

The Cajun Greek

B-
Total pleasure grade

The Cajun Gulf breeze blows in from Louisiana at the best seafood spot on Galveston Island

5.3 *Feel*

Seafood, Southern

Casual restaurant
Mon.-Sat. 11am-10pm;
Sun. 11am-8pm.

Galveston
2226 61st St.
(409) 774-7041

Bar Wine and beer only
Credit Cards Visa, MC, AmEx
Reservations Not accepted

This Galveston classic is the old home of the Seafood Depot, which locals used to rave about. It was bought a few years back and turned into the Cajun Greek, which serves up typical Cajun and Gulf Coast cuisine, with a few clichéd Greek items thrown into the mix. You should stay away from the latter and seek out the former: fried shrimp platters, gyros, gumbo and po' boys are a few of the delicious Gulf specialties to look for.

You maybe confused about the name when you walk in. You may still be confused when you walk out. We generally are. Fusion might be the first thing that comes to mind, but happily, that's not the deal. This is really just a Cajun restaurant with gyros and Greek salads. Parking is about as hard to come by as a table during the rush, but if you're not lucky enough to snag a table, a horseshoe-shaped bar in the middle of the restaurant is a great place to enjoy your meal, grab a Shiner, and watch the game—or the kitchen. The front of the menu notes that your food may take up to 45 minutes, but that good food isn't about speed. Great first impression.

The Cajun Greek is one of the only well-established places to eat on Galveston Island that is not owned by Landry's. We chose not to list the outposts of the latter in the *Fearless Critic* for cause: if you are going to drive all the way down to Galveston for a meal, why should you dig on the same seafood you can get in Houston? Some of the Cajun Greek staples include crawfish pie, when available; good gumbo; and an eminently well-priced fried oyster po' boy; you can feel the Gulf breeze blowing in from Louisiana here. Mounds of fries garnish most everything.

If you've got a beach house waiting, take-out is a great way to go. Just call ahead well in advance. As for service, the place was once much better for groups than it is now, but it's gotten more distracted lately. With a few tweaks to the speed of the food, friendlier servers, and a parking lot, this place could be great. Still, it might be Galveston's best easy, downmarket fish solution. –SN

Cali Sandwich

No money, no problem: $2 sandwiches

B *Total pleasure grade*

7.7 *Food* **7.6** *Feel* **$5** *Price* **Vietnamese**

Counter service
Mon.-Sat. 9am-9pm;
Sun. 9am-7pm.
Outdoor dining. Vegetarian-friendly.

Midtown
3030 Travis St.
(713) 526-0112

Bar None
Credit Cards Visa, MC, AmEx
Reservations Not accepted

This humble Vietnamese restaurant has traditional bahn mi, noodle bowls, and great shakes that are flavorful—and all of this at no markup, so to speak. But if you're looking for attentive service with a smile, then you are at the wrong place. People at Cali Sandwich aren't rude or mean; they're simply efficient and to the point. Don't expect to be fawned over, and don't look anywhere else; these are some of the best Vietnamese sandwiches in the city. The building has a dingy charm to it; a bit of paint is chipping off the walls and there are a few cracks in the molding, but this isn't the place to be critical about the décor—Cali sandwiches are two dollars.

Two dollars.

The well-prepared, well-executed sandwiches stuffed with your choice of pig, bird, cattle, or fermented bean curd are works of art for your mouth. They are served on wonderfully crisp bread with an assortment of air holes snaking throughout the bun, highlighting the skill of the baker. Fresh jalapeños, cucumbers, carrots, and a secret sauce are deliciously presented in that all-too-familiar package that is the sandwich. Have we mentioned that they are two dollars?

Even though sandwiches are their namesake, they also serve other Vietnamese fare. But stay away from the Chinese offerings; they are just boring and incoherent. As with all great Asian restaurants they have numbers for the menu items for the Ameri-can'ts, who can't pronounce the names of the dishes.

We'll keep it simple for you too: the number 11 is delicious. It's a spot-on vermicelli bowl with grilled pork and Vietnamese egg roll, and the $4.25 price makes it taste even better. Smother it in fish sauce, or douse it with the kick-you-in-the-ass chili sauce and go to town. And no, you don't need to have your eyes examined; these are the real prices. Honest food at a razor-thin markup is what this restaurant prides itself on. Just don't be scared if someone starts yelling at you in Vietnamese; it's a compliment, really. –SD

Candylicious

Venture into the magical land of sugar, where the Idaho Spud and Big Hunk roam

Sweets

Specialty grocery
Mon.-Wed. 10am-9pm; Fri.-Sat. 10am-10pm; Sun. noon-6pm.
Kid-friendly. Vegetarian-friendly.

Montrose
1837 W. Alabama St.
(713) 529-6500

Rice Area
2515 University Blvd.
(713) 874-1988

Bar None
Credit Cards Visa, MC, AmEx
Reservations Not accepted

About four out of every five pieces of candy sold in the United States were made by either Hershey's, Mars, or Nestlé. Check out the candy aisle at any convenience store to see what we mean. Candylicious exists to show you that there's a whole world out there beyond the big three. It's not that you can't buy a Snickers bar at Candylicious; it's that you'd be crazy to do so when you can try a goopy Valomilk or a multi-flavored SkyBar. You might go back to the Snickers for your regular sugar fix, but do you want to live your life without ever having sunk your teeth into a chewy Big Hunk?

Candylicious reaches beyond industrial candy distribution to bring you regional candy specialties and downright weird stuff that you'll never find at a Wal-Mart (sadly, America's leading candy retailer). Surely this is one of the few places outside of Idaho where you can find the Idaho Spud, a homely confection that looks kind of like an old potato and tastes like a cocoa-covered marshmallow. More tasty is the GooGoo cluster, a renegade disc of chocolate, marshmallow, caramel, and peanuts from Chattanooga, Tennessee. It's only available in the winter months, as there's no way it would survive the journey in the heat of a Texas summer. International offerings from Cadbury and strange German and Japanese confectioners provide worldly variety.

Candylicious does a thriving business in nostalgia sweets, offering '80s standards like Big League Chew and Pop Rocks (don't worry, they're still being manufactured), as well as a wild array of Pez dispensers. They offer freaky stuff too, like chocolate covered bugs or hard candies so sour you'll choke. They've got 21 colors of M&M's and 16 variants of Haribo, so somewhere in there you should be able to fill up your candy bowl. The store features some colorful candy "cakes" with assortments of packaged candies arranged in artful tributes to the sweet tooth.

Candylicious isn't exactly a restaurant, but you can eat the goods in the store after you buy it, so it sort of qualifies for this book. And, anyway, it deserves a salute for its attempt to elevate the candy dialogue in this country. –RH

Canino's

A vast array of the cheapest local produce around

Gourmet wonderland

Specialty grocery
Daily 6am-8:30pm.
Vegetarian-friendly

Heights
2520 Airline Dr.
(713) 862-4027

Bar Full
Credit Cards Visa, MC, AmEx
Reservations Not accepted.

In some towns—Austin, for instance—a farmer's market is a place where local farmers proudly display their rapturously imperfect organic produce and grass-fed hormone free beef. The Airline farmer's market isn't like that. This covered market is where local restaurants go when they need to buy very large quantities of produce from local farm operations at very competitive prices. Intrepid consumers can get in on the volume pricing too—if they dare.

Canino's, the face of the farmer's market that non-commercial buyers mostly see, is the store facing Airline where you can park and pick up a shopping basket. The difference between Canino's and the monster market behind it is that at Canino's you can buy *an* onion, whereas in the back you can buy a 40-pound bag of onions. Canino's buys directly from the mostly local farming operations that fill out the farmer's market. The selection is vast; you won't see the organic produce and the exotic imported stuff that you'd find at a Whole Foods or Central Market, but you will find local produce like freshly shelled black-eyed peas. "Local" means that your tomatoes haven't necessarily spent the last week traveling in a truck, as the ones in your average corner grocery store probably have. In addition to the wide selection of fruits and vegetables, Canino's has locally produced eggs, honey, and salsas. Connoisseurs know to pick up an ice-cold glass medio litro of Mexican Coke (made with sugar, not corn syrup) on the way out. In front, a separate business sometimes sells melons and berries in season.

The farmer's market can be a bit of an adventure; it helps if you speak Spanish. You can buy spices in bulk—how many pounds of cumin do you go through in a month?—and very large quantities of just about any fruit or vegetable. The market is also a good spot for snagging Mexican specialties like sacks of pozole or dried chili peppers—which, after all, are really as Texan as anything else. –RH

In San Juan Chamula, Chiapas, Coca-Cola is an integral part of the spiritual healing ritual in the town church. (At least Mexican Coke is made with cane sugar.)

Cantina Laredo

Decent upmarket Tex-Mex, straight outta Dallas

C *Total pleasure grade*

6.7 *Food* **7.3** *Feel* **$44** *Price* **Tex-Mex**

Upmarket restaurant
Sun.-Thurs. 11am-10pm;
Fri.-Sat. 11am-11pm.
Brunch.

West Houston
11129 Westheimer Rd.
(713) 952-3287
www.cantinalaredo.com

Bar Full
Credit Cards Visa, MC, AmEx
Reservations Accepted

Cantina Laredo, waaaay down Westheimer, is one of the most ambitiously upscale Tex-Mex restaurants in the city. However, we must first disclose that it is not only a Dallas-based chain but also, unfortunately, a subsidiary of Consolidated Restaurant Operations (the name alone makes us shudder), of Spaghetti Warehouse and El Chico fame. However, designers seem to have done a nice job of avoiding that chain-restaurant feel; although furnishings are distinctly new, they're soothing and intimate. We are booth fans, and particularly like the cozy two-person booths here. Lighting is dim, and there's a certain pleasant bustle to the space.

It's kind of amusing that Cantina Laredo seems to have successfully propagated the myth that it is "authentic Mexican." Is a restaurant serving chile con queso and fajitas, and whose name platter consists of a cheese chile relleno, a tamal, a chicken enchilada, and a beef taco, anything but Tex-Mex? And that's not to mention such ill-inspired fusion dishes as raspberry spinach salad, filet mignon with a Portobello mushroom cap, and, most frighteningly of all, the "Pollo Laredo," a grilled chicken breast topped with sautéed artichoke hearts, peppers, mushrooms, and onions in a chipotle-wine sauce. If not for the pepper, it would sound like bad Italian-American.

Guacamole prepared tableside, an overblown fad that might have started at New York's Rosa Mexicano, is a total gimmick; still, the guac's taste is fresh and cilantro-forward and the seasoning pleasant, if salt-hungry. It goes well, too, with margaritas, which are strong, tasty, and not overly sweet. Easily the most impressive thing on the menu, though, is the "Camarón Poblado Asada," a favorite of controversial Chicago journalist Emma Graves Fitzsimmons, with sautéed shrimp, mushrooms, onions, and jack cheese all stuffed inside a grilled poblano pepper, which is itself wrapped in a tenderized carne asada steak. It sounds like overkill, but the combination is cheesy and harmonious. The steak might be recommended medium-well, but ordered rare, it is juicy and delicious. Watery spinach enchiladas and fairly dry mole enchiladas are much less impressive, probably more in line with your chain-generated expectations. But, anyway, that's what Cantina Laredo is.
–RG

Capital Grille

Dry-aged steaks derailed by unnecessary jus at Darden Restaurants' latest acquisition

C *Total pleasure grade*

6.4 *Food* **7.7** *Feel* **$92** *Price* **Steakhouse**

Upmarket restaurant
Sun.-Thurs. 5pm-10pm;
Fri.-Sat. 5pm-11pm.

Galleria
5365 Westheimer Rd.
(713) 623-4600
www.thecapitalgrille.com

Bar Full
Credit Cards Visa, MC, AmEx
Reservations Recommended

The pride of RARE Hospitality International, Inc. (which, at press time, was in the process of being acquired by Darden Restaurants, parent of the Olive Garden and Red Lobster chains), this steakhouse pulled in more than $8.1 million in revenues per chain branch in 2006, according to its annual report.

You'd assume a giant metal bald eagle, regally perched between kitchen and dining room, to be tongue-in-cheek at most restaurants. Likewise for a room full of somber Americana, like pious John-Singer-Sargent-like portraits of dead white men, and sweeping manifest-destiny landscapes. Not here. Maybe there's something about listing on the Nasdaq that renders the restaurant business a touch less wacky. Here's a taste of the annual report: "The increase in same-store sales at the Capital Grille restaurants was primarily attributable to an increase in average check of approximately 4.8%...Management believes that a number of factors have contributed to the increase in check-average, including price increases on menu items of approximately 3.0%." This particular American culinary Dream—$986,914,000 in FY2006 revenues—seems about as humorless as the expression on the eagle's face.

Lighting is appropriately dim, service appropriately fawning, and seating appropriately posh, but culinary fireworks don't often result when a restaurant group is run by businesspeople, not chefs. Rather, the focus is on producing nothing out of the ordinary. Amongst starters, fried calamari aren't bad, getting a welcome kick from hot cherry peppers. That's where the fun ends, though. The cold shellfish platter is a pricey disappointment, and lobster and crab cakes are bland. In a sad concession to small-town tastes, they hard-boil the egg in the steak tartare instead of using the proper raw egg. Prosciutto-wrapped mozzarella is flavorless, and lobster bisque is creamy but not very complex or interesting. Juicy lamb chops are actually better than steak here. We can only wonder which member of the Board was behind the fatal mistake of drowning dry-aged ribeyes and sirloins with Capital's "jus," an aggressive, cheap-tasting glaze that distinctly evokes cafeteria roast beef. Broiled, dry-aged steaks, including Capital's, deserve deferential treatment: they should be served with nothing but salt, pepper, and perhaps butter.

Darden stock might make a good addition to your portfolio, but at dinnertime, your corporate credit card would be better used elsewhere. –RG

Carrabba's Italian Grill

C+

Total pleasure grade

A Houston original—which makes the chain thing even more frustrating

6.9 *Food* **6.9** *Feel* **$52** *Price*

Italian-American

Casual restaurant
Mon.-Thurs. 11am-10pm;
Fri. 11am-11pm;
Sat. noon-11pm; Sun. noon-10pm.
Kid-friendly. Additional locations.

Upper Kirby
3115 Kirby Dr.
(713) 522-3131
www.carrabbas.com

Galleria
1399 S. Voss Rd.
(713) 468-0868

Bar Full
Credit Cards Visa, MC, AmEx
Reservations Not accepted

Katy
11339 Katy Fwy.
(713) 464-6595

Carrabba's is a difficult, ambiguous restaurant. It's a Houston original, yet it's a big chain. It certainly enjoys economies of scale, and prices are still lower than much of the competition, yet most of its ingredients are fresh, and most everything is made in-house.

Carrabba's is very Houston, eternally kid-friendly and adult-friendly, as comfortable as an old pair of shoes. Its menu is built around the decent execution of unambitious Italian-American pleasures: linguine with spicy clam sauce; fried calamari with hot peppers and marinara; not-bad pizza. The menu is also foodie-friendly enough to feature oak-and-pecan-grilled, pancetta-and-sage-wrapped quail on the menu, but not embarrassed to serve fried mozzarella or spaghetti (sometimes overcooked) and meatballs (not bad). And then there's that most fake of all fake Italian customs: garlic-laced olive oil for bread-dipping. Completely inauthentic, completely American, and completely delicious.

There's also something to eating in the original, vintage-1986 Kirby branch of a chain that now claims at least 230 branches. Interestingly, this branch is still locally owned, and doesn't answer to OSI, the parent company of Outback Steakhouse, like most of the chain does. In 2007, with declining same-store sales, OSI was taken private in a $3.1 billion takeover by a group led by Mitt-Romney-founded Bain Capital. At press time, the status of Carrabba's hung in the balance; it was seen as a divestiture target.

A deep tension arises, of course, once restaurants are the subjects of CNBC gossip. The artistic goals of the good chef are at fundamental odds with the growth goals of shareholders, whether public or private. In a 20-table restaurant, there is a real channel of communication between chef and customer. When you're closer to 10,000 tables, shareholders are happier—in part because there *is* no chef to impose his margin-thwarting personality. We choose willingly to eat at these chefless restaurants; it's rational to eat consistent, good-value, comfort-food Italian-American. And yet we don't like where it's all going.

So who *do* we blame for America's relegation of the real chef to the realm of the very expensive or very cheap? Could it be the amorality of the free markets themselves? That rational choices aren't always the right ones? That what the industry really needs from its customers, to keep the chef-artists alive, is a little dose of spirituality? –RG

Catalan

Creative iterations of delicious fats, and a wine list straight from Heaven

A
Total pleasure grade

8.8 *Food* **9.1** *Feel* **$70** *Price* **New American**

Upmarket restaurant
Tues.-Thurs. 11am-10pm; Fri. 11am-11pm; Sat. 5pm-11pm; Sun. 5pm-9pm; closed Mon.
Brunch. Wine-friendly.

Washington
5555 Washington Ave.
(713) 426-4260
www.catalanfoodandwine.com

Bar Full
Credit Cards Visa, MC, AmEx
Reservations Essential

Don't show up at this trendy, high-ceilinged, wine-centric restaurant—with its rows upon rows of bottles, glassy modern lights, and open kitchen—expecting to experience the cuisine of Catalunya. Spain is more of a nouvelle inspiration than a real genre here, yet it successfuly ties together what is really a menu of chefs' favorites—pig fat, duck fat, eggs, and innards—with delicious wines at bargain prices. The pro-cholesterol lobby would do well to choose Catalan for its annual meeting. But so would anyone else.

The much-talked-about "foie gras bon bons" are fried balls of the stuff, unbelievably rich and certainly fun...yet perhaps also wasteful, melting the duck liver into pure fat without the delicacy or body of a terrine or torchon. But we unconditionally love the cubes of pork belly sweetly crusted with cane syrup, impaled by sugar cane spears (we've once had them come out tough and overcooked, but this was the exception to the delicious rule). Delicious, too, are piquillo peppers deliciously stuffed with braised lamb; and morcilla (rich, black blood sausage), here tricked out with fennel kraut, a brilliant pairing of fat with acid. And then there are the superlative marrow bones, whose fatty, gelatinous goodness you scoop out, spread on toast, sprinkle with salt, swallow, and roll your eyes back into your head.

What's lost in the shuffle, sometimes, is a periodic inability to execute on the basics, like a paltry portion of marinated Spanish white anchovies and olives; a charcuterie plate that comes too cold; an unexciting Spanish tortilla (omelet); or a simple "pressed, brined, and pulled chicken"-and-slaw sandwich of little interest. We've had EggsGarlic soup, a smooth, balanced version that might be the dark horse of this menu. But stick with the upmarket small plates, drink lots of wine, don't expect too much, and for the most part, you'll wind up very, very happy.

Two keys to happiness here: First, try to get a good seat; we hate the unromantic rows of tables in the middle of the space. Second, lose yourself in the spectacular wine list, which reads like a work of creative literature, not only demonstraing a welcome focus on lesser-known regions, but also claiming little more than retail markups (around 1.6x wholesale, which beats most other restaurants two to one). This alone makes the restaurant eminently worthwhile. And don't worry about all the fatty food; you're in the best city for hospitals. –RG

Cava Bistro

Where's the Cava?

C
Total pleasure grade

5.7 *Food* **8.0** *Feel* **$54** *Price*

New American

Upmarket restaurant
Mon.-Thurs. 11am-10pm; Fri. 11am-11pm; Sat. 5pm-11pm; closed Sun.
Date-friendly. Live music. Outdoor dining. WiFi.

Downtown
301 Main St.
(713) 223-4068
www.cavabistro.net

Bar Full
Credit Cards Visa, MC, AmEx
Reservations Recommended

Cava is Spain's version of Champagne, made in the same traditional, laborious, bottle-fermented method as its prestigious French counterpart. Certainly there are many great Champagnes, but it's the unequalled marketing clout of the region, above all else, that has succeeded in convincing consumers the world over that it's the *only* proper bubbly to drink at an upscale wedding, a graduation, a victory celebration. All of this has left Cava (perhaps accompanied by France's Cremant d'Alsace and Italy's Franciacortia Brut) as perhaps the most underappreciated sparkling wine in the world. Enter Cava Bistro (or "Cava Bristo," as it's repeatedly called on the web site). It looks like a replica of a Cava cellar, with arched stone ceilings, dim lighting, and so forth. So far, so good. You're elbow-to-elbow with a good quotient of pre-clubbing weekend revelers and yuppies who have taken the plunge into downtown loft living. You soak in the warm lighting, the healthy buzz. You ignore the spotty service.

Now, how about a glass of Cava?

Sorry, try again. *The Cava Bistro does not serve a glass of Cava*. There are, however, two bottom-end supermarket Cavas (Freixenet and Segura Viudas) that you can get by the bottle, if you must.

Right then. On to the "Moroccan pizza," which is, just, well, pizza, with a bit of unremarkable sausage that's said to be merguez, but tastes more like your basic hard spicy sausage; plus onions, tomatoes, and unwelcome black olives. There's a pretty bad baked brie, and even worse wild mushroom spring rolls.

When there's whole fish on the menu, it's almost always a decent choice; here, the whole, oven-baked red snapper in a preserved-lemon-tomato charmoula sauce comes overcooked, but still not bad. But expect a sinking feeling from most of this menu. It's studded with booby traps like pork tenderloin with Granny Smith apple chutney, "Chicken Napoleon" (grilled chicken breast in a "mushroom herb demi cream sauce"), and the absolutely frightening "Cava's Rice Noodles" (sautéed chicken breast, pea pods, cherry tomatoes, baby corn, and water chestnuts in a "soy coconut cream"). We know that there's culinary talent somewhere in this restaurant group, because Saffron is pretty good, but clearly, it's not being effectively deployed here.

So go elsewhere for Cava—and while you're at it, go elsewhere for food, too. –RG

Central Market

Quite simply one of the best gourmet supermarkets in America

Gourmet wonderland

Specialty grocery
Daily 8am-10pm.
Breakfast. Kid-friendly.
Outdoor dining.
Vegetarian-friendly. Wine-friendly.

Upper Kirby
3815 Westheimer Rd.
(713) 386-1700
www.centralmarket.com

Bar Wine and beer only
Credit Cards Visa, MC, AmEx
Reservations Not accepted

Westheimer's Central Market is a dazzling, world-class gourmet marketplace. This is a candy store for gourmet home chefs: every single hunk of cheese, jar of salsa, bottle of olive oil, or bin of shrimp is selected with a deep underlying commitment to "foodie" principles. Whatever the department, Central Market always seems in relentless pursuit of the best ingredients available, whether it's USDA prime dry-aged beef from our backyard, dried pasta from Puglia, queso from San Antonio, or sultry, exotic sauces from Sicily.

After a trip here, you may well find it difficult to return to your local corner grocery for anything at all. If you ever return, that is; it's possible to lose yourself completely at Central Market, spending hour upon hour tasting breads and cheeses, ordering thinly cut pounds of spectacular hams from Italy or Spain, surfing for obscure sauces, pouring bags of fresh coffee beans, wandering through the wines…and suddenly, you look at your watch, and you've spent the entire afternoon at Central Market, missing the very dinner for which you came here to shop.

Speaking of wines, the wine program here has an extraordinary commitment to quality, finding value producers from around the globe and—just as importantly—pairing them with in-store wine consultants that can explain their wines to you.

The Central Market Café, which has a pleasant, underappreciated set of second-floor tables, has long been not only a convenient place for hungry shoppers to stop by for a bite to eat while shopping, but also a worthwhile dining destination in its own right. The seat-yourself spaces are clean and well lit, with flowers on the tables and works by local artists for sale on the walls. There's often live music, as well as periodic food festivals, for which they set up outdoor grills. Food is reasonably priced and the portions are substantial. Strong points include simple sandwiches, salads, and smoothies, plus selections for vegetarians and vegans that are nothing less than excellent.

The coffee counter also makes one of the best espressos in Houston—yet another feather in this legendary food store's delicious cap. –FC

Chacho's

Chacho's enjoys success in the highly profitable world of twenty four hour Tex-Mex

B- *Total pleasure grade*

6.0 *Food* **5.7** *Feel* **$19** *Price* **Tex-Mex**

Casual restaurant
Daily 24 hours.
Breakfast. Date-friendly.
Outdoor dining. WiFi.

Galleria
6006 Westheimer Rd.
(713) 975-9699
www.chachos.com

Bar Full
Credit Cards Visa, MC, AmEx
Reservations Not accepted

Why do we like this place so much? Why do we enjoy waking up feeling like we ate and digested an atomic bomb that exploded somewhere between our trachea and lower intestine? It must have something to do with their operating hours: 24 hours a day, every day. For years, Chacho's, in all of its Tex-Mex glory, has been setting the bar for all other late-night restaurants in Houston.

At peak times, which is often after bars close, the parking lot becomes an absolute zoo (you might find yourself circling and circling, looking for a spot), and lines snake out the door. Inside is a madhouse—in the most enjoyable way possible. It's loud with everyone's chatter; a few tables outside are equally noisy, as they front Westheimer. And it's exactly what you want, given that the sudden curfew has just summarily halted the carousing at whatever bar you just came from.

Every combination imaginable of meat, cheese, tortillas, avocados, pico de gallo, rice, and beans is present on Chacho's menu, from the very humble bean and cheese nachos that just want to be taken seriously, to the gluttonous, ultimately greedy "Monster Kong Nachos" (just use your imagination). Burritos, too, are unbelievably large, and finishing one in one sitting is the stuff legends are made of. Queso is utterly addictive; it's creamy with a nice kick of chile. If it's still before the witching hour, giant margaritas make the perfect accompaniment; they're well-balanced—even the frozen version isn't too sweet—and their strength will sneak up on you.

If you're on the South Beach diet, Chacho's offers a low-carb menu, so when you scarf down your three-meat plate (beef, pork, and chicken with cheese and sour cream) in record time, you can rest assured knowing that there aren't any horrible fruits, vegetables, or whole-grain breads trying to ruin your waistline. (For everyone not already needing to be on a diet, Chacho's seems to be trying its hardest to get them there.)

Ultimately, this is a place for everyone: insomniacs, happenin' scenesters looking for a bite to eat after curfew, and even—believe it or not—families. –SD

Chapultepec

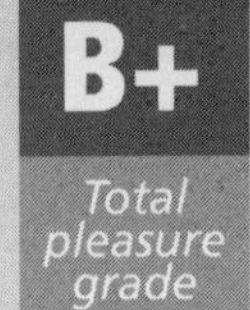

Queso and fajitas, once self-salted, serve as sincere Tex-Mex solace—all night long

7.5 Food | **8.3** Feel | **$15** Price | **Tex-Mex**

Casual restaurant
Daily 24 hours.
Date-friendly. Outdoor dining.

Montrose
813 Richmond Ave.
(713) 522-2365

Bar Full
Credit Cards Visa, MC, AmEx
Reservations Accepted

Let's set the stage: It's 3:30am on a Saturday. (Or 10:30pm on a Monday, which is more or less the same thing in Houston.) You don't feel like entering sleazy-motel purgatory at Spanish Flowers, and Rico's Triangle Café is closed even when it's supposed to be open. You don't have the stomach for the disgusting food at Ruchi's, and Chacho's is so full of some post-Beyoncé-concert crowd that you can't squeeze your way in.

It is at moments like these that even a hardcore Houston hedonist might well shed his skepticism and thank every deity he can think of that Chapultepec is here—and open. This restaurant's soothing combination of sincere service, windowside (if plastic) tables, cooling ceiling fans, appropriate kitsch, a Christmas-lit bar, well-conceived color paints, and well-constructed margaritas would be welcome even at prime dinner hour—which is why it's such a delight to find them equally functional 24 hours a day, seven days a week. Chapultepec will make a believer out of anyone.

The newfound believer might begin with an ideally executed queso, whose only slight flaw is the quickly forming skin. Otherwise, this smooth, buttery bowl offers more of a welcome chile kick than most in town, and the ground beef with which it is optionally adorned is unusually well seasoned; it's the kind of taco meat that would actually stand up on its own as picadillo, rather than serving as an afterthought of an accoutrement.

Fajitas come out with a surreal skillet sizzle—like, perhaps, you might imagine fajitas in a movie soundtrack, as fine-tuned by the boom man—and they deliver a meaty punch, although their central flaw is a lack of seasoning (salt, in particular). Beans are also undersalted and have a disappointingly wimpy flavor, shrimp are boring, flour tortillas have a short half-life, and guac feels more mushy than fresh. But the vibe, the queso, and the fajita meat (once self-seasoned) still make this place one of the MVP contenders in the all-night all-star game. Especially once you start swaying to the Mexican music, which provides companionship even to the loneliest diners at the loneliest times of the loneliest nights. –RG

Charlie's Hamburger Joint

Big on Texan pride, not so big on Texan burgers

C- Total pleasure grade

3.3 Food | **6.6** Feel | **$9** Price

Burgers

Counter service
Mon.-Fri. 10:30am-8pm; Sat. 11am-8pm; Sun. 11am-5pm.
Kid-friendly.

River Oaks
1440 W Gray St.
(713) 520-1744

Spring Branch
9747 Katy Fwy.
(713) 932-1462

Bar Wine and beer only
Credit Cards Visa, MC, AmEx
Reservations Not accepted

Meyerland
14610 Grisby Rd.
(281) 870-9682

If you're going to have a huge Texan flag as a wall made in industrial sheet metal, and a fake crocodile named Pickles hanging from your ceiling greeting your guests, your burgers had better resonate with Texas. They'd better be big, juicy, flame-licked patties like you'd find home on the range, where the deer and the antelopes play. Your food had better be high on flavor, and served with a cold beer.

Charlie's somehow didn't get the memo. What looks so wholeheartedly Texan is really pretty far from it, with decent-at-best burgers and wimpy food. It looks the part. Texas flag, booths, wooden chairs. Plastic squirt bottles for ketchup, fresh limes for your Corona. Charlie's Hamburger Joint is dressed to be just the Texas grillery that it claims to be. It looks like a joint. It feels like a joint. Neon beer advertisements reflect off the bottles of hot sauce on the table. Tex-Mex influences—guacamole, pico de gallo—invade several burgers and salads. When you see the cooler of beers, it looks like you've made it. Until your number is called, and you saunter up to pick up your food.

That's when the house of cards collapses. Dainty burgers? GRIDDLED patties? Texas didn't sign up for no GRIDDLED patties. Without fire, there can't be the charred little bits on the patty that make a burger a Texas burger. It's like telling OutKast's Andre 3000 to sing Sinatra and wear a gray suit. It doesn't work. The fries fare no better. Whatever happened to big, this-belongs-with-a-steak cuts of fries? What's with the matchsticks? What's with the seeming lack of even one shake of salt? Okay, they're crispy, but contrary to popular belief, brunette is more in than blonde, especially when it comes to fries—and the fries at Charlie's definitely need more time in the fryer to bring out their earthy, crispy goodness. Shakes are better—thick, filled with chocolate—but, truth be told, beer is probably the most Texan thing served at Charlie's. So embarrassing is this place that one might consider sneaking in when nobody's looking and hoisting, say, a California state flag.

Just a thought. –JY

Chez Georges

These are still the good old days—but how long will they last?

B- *Total pleasure grade*

7.4 *Food* **8.2** *Feel* **$75** *Price* **French**

Upmarket restaurant
Tues.-Sat. 5:30pm-10pm;
closed Sun.-Mon.
Wine-friendly.

Midtown
219 Westheimer St.
(713) 529-7788
www.chezgeorgesrestaurant.com

Bar Wine and beer only
Credit Cards Visa, MC, AmEx
Reservations Accepted

You might very well drive past Chez Georges every day and never have noticed it. An innocent blue house on Westheimer, near Bagby, gives no indication as to what lies within. You might assume the French flag, which flies unassumingly next to an American one, to belong to some old expat or an avid Francophile. But it's Chez Georges, one of Houston's remaining bastions of fairly pricey, very traditional French food and service.

Not that the interior doesn't sometimes feel homey; you'll find an old family photo here and there. But stuffiness mostly reigns; chandeliers light some of the rooms, and you'll see gilt-framed Impressionist paintings. Light, breezy curtains keep the busy street out of sight, and out of mind. So is this a romantic place?

Decidedly not. Lighting is strangely bright, and all of the artifacts in the house don't add up to quirky charm; rather, it seems as though years of neglect have allowed them to pile up. It's kind of like dining in your pack-rat aunt's house—though presumably your aunt isn't cooking quite on this level. The menu changes seasonally, but in the past we've had a wonderful "Soupe de Crustacés 'Astrodome.'" A well-developed, but not in-your-face seafood flavor permeates the broth; shrimp within are delicious. The "Astrodome" is a puff-pastry dome atop the soup—and, perhaps, another gentle reminder of how outdated the place is (not that we'd want a Minute Maid soup).

Ris de veau (veal sweetbreads), served with Morel mushrooms in a brandy cream sauce, hit a bit of a snag the last time we tried them. We're not sure if the dense mealiness of the unusually large, thick glands were the result of a tough specimen or of slight overcooking, but they missed the boat.

The wine list is great, focused strongly on French wines; it is complete with maps and label images for the uninitiated. A larger than normal selection of half bottles, too, is refreshing, as is the $38 three-course dinner that's a relative bargain. Yet we can't help but wonder if Chez Georges is on its way out. It's not that there are many critical errors in the kitchen; rather, it seems that for better or for worse, time has just passed this place by. –AH

Chez Nous

Overrated, overpriced, overdressed meals in a not-so-Humble setting near IAH

5.9 Food **2.4** Feel **$94** Price **French**

Upmarket restaurant
Mon.-Sat. 5:30pm-10pm; closed Sun.

Humble
217 S. Ave. G
(281) 446-6717
www.cheznousfrenchrestaurant.com

Bar Full
Credit Cards Visa, MC, AmEx
Reservations Recommended

For restaurants as for personal relationships, we each draw our own lines between attentive and overbearing, enthusiastic and arrogant, discriminating and pompous. The warm, low-lit house in which Chez Nous has lived since 1984, with its twirly Impressionist paintings and the restaurant awards wall of fame, feels cute, at least. What crosses our line—by far—is the constant stream of supercilious chatter that's force-fed to you by the formidable army of servers, who just won't shut up about how "delicious," "beautiful," or "stunning" your mediocre meal is. Someone might even stop by your table for that reason alone.

Perhaps they must speak so loudly for the food because it fails so miserably to speak for itself. A recent five-course tasting menu (which frequently changes)—presumably a showcase for the chef's talents—followed sleazy dinner rolls with a sweet garlic soup whose deep, thickly reduced, viscous, well-seasoned stock was ruined by gross, chewy "house-made" croutons. Vinaigrette is an underappreciated topping for white fish, but it still didn't manage to save a fillet of grouper from boring flakiness. Good veal-beef meatballs in an open-faced raviolo were brightened by lemon zest, but defeated by the villains of the dish: watery, overcooked pasta; thin, wimpy béchamel; and a "concassée" of uselessly underripe tomatoes.

Even more bothersome is how gullible Chez Nous seems to think its customers are when it comes to wine. An $85 tasting menu pairs five wines with different courses, but they're plonk, plonk, plonk, plonk, and plonk: for example, a cloying, chemical-tasting Leaping Horse Chardonnay that sells for about $6 at grocery stores, or an undrinkable Muscat Beaumes de Venise whose offensive odors of nail polish remover fought with a harsh burn of alcohol.

Serving sorbet between courses is pompous enough in itself, but it is downright absurd when a cucumber ice "intermezzo" is so sugary that its aftertaste is more intense than what it purports to cleanse. Chez Nous is a relic from an old American culinary era in which you paid more for dinner-jacket pomp than for execution in the kitchen. Nowadays, it's not even the best dinner choice if you're stranded at IAH in tropical storm season—we prefer the food at Pappadeaux in Terminal E—and Chez Nous should be laughed out of town. –R

Chilos Seafood

A Mexican refuge that fries everything that swims

Total pleasure grade

Food | Feel | Price

Mexican, Seafood

Casual restaurant
Daily 10am-midnight.
Live music. Outdoor dining. WiFi.

Southeast Houston
8334 Gulf Fwy.
(713) 643-3505

North Houston
4606 N. Shepherd Dr.
(713) 697-3784

Bar Full
Credit Cards Visa, MC, AmEx
Reservations Accepted

Chilos Seafood is a likeable place whose many charms include lunch specials, happy hour, and the feel-good, rocking sounds of mariachis on weekends. Even if the spacious, relaxingly downmarket restaurant looks as if it would be at home on the coast of Mexico somewhere—blues, yellows, whites, seashells, and fishing vessels are the motifs—its food manages to taste more like Long John Silver's. A stage to the right hosts the live mariachi music, which will no doubt urge you toward more tequila.

The specialty here is fried seafood—shrimp, scallops, crabs, and whole tilapia—which makes up most of the menu and just about all of the lunch specials, which start at $4.95 and go up. There's a normal selection of fruits of the sea, too, but poor ingredients and excessive frying plague the dishes; much of the shellfish tastes as if it were pre-breaded and frozen. Mexican favorites are on the menu as well: caldos, quail, tortas, tacos, and even whole lobsters displayed in a glass case.

The problems with this joint aren't so severe that booze can't help—especially when happy hour consists of two-dollar margaritas. After a few of these, you'll probably find yourself warming up to the fried food, to your fellow patrons, and maybe even to your server; the service tends to be nice and very polite. Even though very little English is spoken, they try their best to help you along in the ordering process; nonetheless, you might want to revisit that old Spanish textbook. Numbers accompany the names of the dishes for the monolingual diner.

Chilos is one of those places that seems to fill a need for people who don't speak English and want something other than enchiladas and beans every day. It is a safe haven where customers are amongst friends, and where everyone seems to feel at home with some good music and mediocre food. And if you're in the mood, sometimes there's nothing wrong with that. –SD

The Chocolate Bar

Very, very rich chocolate cake for the very, very rich

Sweets

Specialty grocery
Mon.-Thurs. 10am-10pm;
Fri.-Sat. 10am-midnight;
Sun. noon-10pm.
Date-friendly. Kid-friendly. Live music. Outdoor dining. Vegetarian-friendly. WiFi.

Montrose
1835 W. Alabama St.
(713) 520-8599

Bar None
Credit Cards Visa, MC, AmEx
Reservations Not accepted

Some people might balk at the idea of a $10 slice of chocolate cake. Fair enough, but if any slice of chocolate cake were worth $10, it would probably be the foot-high monsters of chocolate richness they serve here. The Chocolate Bar, like Candylicious next door, is dedicated to the proposition that when you yield to your sweet tooth, you should yield all the way.

The Chocolate Bar has three distinct lines of business: chocolates, ice cream, and baked goods. All are fine examples of their respective genres. The homemade chocolates come in all sorts of cutesy shapes like calculators and tennis rackets that are clearly intended as gifts—no one buys a chocolate tennis racket for themselves (although the chocolate tooth brush is tempting…). They've got chocolate-dipped fruits and pretzels behind the counter that are extremely expensive (up to $4 per unit, in some cases), but far better than your average candy. Chocolate-covered Rice Krispies treats are like super-evolved Kit-Kat bars, while caramel-coated-chocolate-dipped pretzels are simultaneously salty, crunchy, sweet, and gooey. Yum.

Ice cream selections come in some inventive flavors, like "Root Beer Float" or "Chocolate Cape Cod" (with cranberries and dark chocolate chips). The specialties are the chocolate flavors, of which they usually have three or four variants at a time, and the chunky mixes, which all find some way to include more chocolate. "Candylicious Junkyard" is worth a taste: they take handfuls of candy bars from Candylicious next door and smash them up into the ice cream, the result being a wild ride of chocolate, caramel, nuts, and assorted crunch. We find it a bit busy, but its adherents are legion.

Finally, there are the baked goods. The cake display is like diabetic porn; grab some ice cream before you go back there or you'll wind up buying one of the $75 cakes. The German chocolate cake is dense, rich, and dark. The "Mississippi Mud Pie" is delightfully messy. You might suffer from sticker shock when you first encounter the slice price face-to-face, but can you put a price on gooey chocolate goodness?

Yes, you can. It's $10. –RH

Christian's Tailgate

A shabby but charming old shack with a good, honest burger

B-
Total pleasure grade

6.2 *Food* **8.6** *Feel* **$9** *Price* **Burgers**

Bar
Mon.-Sat. 11am-9pm; closed Sun. *Outdoor dining. WiFi.*

Heights
7340 Washington Ave.
(713) 864-9744

Midtown
2000 Bagby St.
(713) 527-0261

Bar Full
Credit Cards Visa, MC, AmEx
Reservations Accepted

Houston is blessed with many shabby shacks whose owners, over time, turn them into real dives. A true dive is of the people, for the people, and, above all, loved by the people. Christian's Tailgate is that dive that people know, love, and find themselves coming back to time after time.

Well, sort of. There are two locations of Christian's in Houston: the original, which is a really soulful shack-like structure on Washington; and the new edition—a commercialized, confused place that has let its hip location in Midtown go to its head, and is anything but charming. Many people prefer the original location because of its comfortable outdoor patio and long storied history; perhaps there's a real sense in which the intrigue just makes the food taste better.

Christian's is known for legendary burgers and simple food, like fried chicken tenders and fried catfish po' boys. However famous they are, though, the burgers are really no big deal, just good and honest: a well-seasoned patty piled with lettuce, tomato, pickles, onions, mustard, and mayonnaise on a fluffy bun. People go crazy for the meat, which is ground and formed in house. It's a fairly easy task, and one that should be standard operating procedure for a burger house, but there are plenty of places that just buy the frozen patties and call it a day. Christian's claims to honor rare orders, but in practice, they won't do one less than medium, failing the true test of a hamburger joint; on the bright side, at least they don't kill the burger by cooking it 'till it's even deader than dead.

All in all, this is a great place to watch the game or just enjoy a lazy afternoon playing hookey. The regulars are a scrappy bunch that don't take lightly to the riff-raff walking in off the street, but the staff are, for the most part, nice and helpful—until the place gets really packed, in which case, look out. Also, a word to the wise: at the Washington location, a cop generally sits right at the traffic light. Be very careful with those rolling stops; you don't want him to win. –SD

Churrascos

Decent steaks and good times at Cordúa's simplest, most down-to-earth outpost

B- Total pleasure grade

7.6 Food **7.8** Feel **$63** Price

Latin American

Upmarket restaurant
Mon.-Thurs. 11am-10pm;
Fri. 11am-11pm;
Sat. 5pm-11pm; Sun. 11am-9pm.
Brunch. Outdoor dining.

Upper Kirby
2055 Westheimer Rd.
(713) 527-8300
www.cordua.com

West Houston
9705 Westheimer Rd.
(713) 952-1988

Bar Full
Credit Cards Visa, MC, AmEx
Reservations Recommended

This is the granddaddy of the Cordúa chain—the groundbreaking restaurant that put Houston on America's earliest Nuevo Latino map. Twenty is old age in restaurant years, but Churrascos is still going strong, pleasing the crowds with the same tender, if overpriced, marinated tenderloins—a cuisine that's bold but hardly daring—that helped establish an entire culinary genre in the late 1980s.

The décor still works, the service still works, and the whole package, however predictable it has become, still works. You also have to salute Michael Cordúa for his business savvy. His restaurant group could serve as a first-year business-school case study. For example:

Economies of scale: the bigger you are, the lower your costs.

Leverage: whereupon you draw upon an existing customer base to generate traffic at your newest venture.

Synergies: whereupon the profitability of multiple business units working together is greater than the sum of the units by themselves.

On the other hand, even the stodgy management professors that teach these theories to their students probably don't appreciate the upshot of the strategy in edible form: it means that the many outposts of a single restaurant group, in spite of their different branding strategies, visual themes, and target markets, are going to be doing a lot of the same things. And we're not just talking about the tres leches, or the fried plantain chips and chimichurri that greet you when you sit down (great the first time you taste them, but they get monotonous). We're also talking about the marineros, those smoky crab claws—which aren't bad, but aren't exactly good either, that showed up on a recent special. We're also talking about the underperforming ceviche, or the mixed grill of seafood (here called "Opereta") in which every single piece of fish on the platter comes overcooked.

Roasted maduros are hard to mess up, and yuca fries are fun, but seafood and meats beyond churrasco are far too often overcooked. But if you haven't yet experienced this first—and still most down-to-earth—branch of the Cordúa chain, it's an experience you should have, because Churrascos will remain a permanent footnote in the history of Latin American cuisine in America. –FC

Chuy's

Good Tex-Mex in a finely realized, self-consciously retro environment

B+ *Total pleasure grade*

8.4 *Food* **8.8** *Feel* **$30** *Price* **Tex-Mex**

Casual restaurant
Sun.-Thurs. 11am-11pm;
Fri.-Sat. 11am-midnight.
Date-friendly. Kid-friendly.

River Oaks
2706 Westheimer Rd.
(713) 524-1700
www.chuys.com

Bar Full
Credit Cards Visa, MC, AmEx
Reservations Accepted

It's well established that the original Chuy's, in Austin, was the place where, in 2001, the underage Bush daughters got caught in a humorously well-publicized episode that vaulted Tex-Mex onto the front page of every newspaper in America. Jenna and Barbara had good taste, though: the margaritas at Chuy's are as reliable as any in town, and we have no doubt that the episode actually wound up boosting business at this well-loved 1950s-retro-themed Tex-Mex joint, even in its far-flung branches like the one in Houston, which are just as much fun as the original. The only downside is parking—their lot's too small, and neighbors have lately posted signs threatening to tow Chuy's customers.

Even better than the 'ritas are the Mexican martinis—a true Texan invention. It's not just an excuse to order three at once: we think the flavor mix is better, with less sweetness. The Chuy's version comes in a plastic shaker with that not-quite-attached lid that must be held down while pouring, as it's the only tenuous barrier between the drink and the outside world. Needless to say, somebody always forgets this fact, and the result is a sudden flash hailstorm of ice, tequila and Cointreau all over the table and, no doubt, somebody's lap—a natural check, perhaps, on the person who probably didn't need the rest of that drink anyway.

The '50s paraphernalia works pretty well as a theme—it's carefully done up with Disneyesque detail. As for the food, it's much better than we expect from a chain. The queso (which you can serve yourself for free out of a faux-'50s-car hood during happy hour) is absolutely top-notch, with more seasoning than most, while hatch green chile enchiladas hit just the right balance of Tex with Mex. So do the tomatillo sauces, although we wish the chicken were somewhat less dry; nonetheless, the joint has a solid grasp on the essence of comfort food. Beef fajitas are well seasoned, remarkably tender, and come with tasty flour tortillas. The only real headache here is the wait: an hour or more on weekend nights. Sometimes fame has its costs. –RG

Ciro's Italian Grill

A displaced family favorite still does decent pizza and puttanesca

C- *Total pleasure grade*

4.5 *Food* **7.0** *Feel* **$35** *Price* **Italian-American**

Casual restaurant
Sun.-Thurs. 11am-10pm;
Fri.-Sat. 11am-11pm.
Kid-friendly.Outdoor dining.

Memorial
9755 Katy Fwy.
(713) 467-9336
www.ciros.com

Bar Full
Credit Cards Visa, MC, AmEx
Reservations Accepted

A collective groan, with plenty of cursing, was heard from the Memorial area when the long-loved original Ciro's closed on Campbell Road due to the expansion of I-10 to eight lanes. When a new Ciro's down the freeway finally opened, anticipation was high. But just as it was a bad idea for Michael Jordan to sign with the Wizards, maybe Ciro's would have been better advised to stay retired than to come back and not live up to the memories.

These were never culinary works of art—certainly, with chipotle and crawfish, Ciro's was far from authentic—but it was once tasty. Thankfully, the wood-burning oven still churns out solid pizzas, with crisp crusts and herbaceous sauces; the puttanesca, too, is an enduring choice, with chunky bites and the trademark salty-sour-savory flavor, but every other old house specialty is now down in the dumps. The "Pasta Gina" once had a luscious alfredo sauce, with plump, prosciutto-wrapped shrimp, but the sauce is now watery, slipping the pasta between fork tines, and the shrimp often come out rubbery. Plating seems to be drop-and-slop, and seasoning is an afterthought, as in the dry, tasteless, waste-of-a-chicken parmigiana.

The current location, near Memorial City Mall, was Ciro's second take on a larger space. Much like their previous Galleria experiment, the quality of this current rendition conceals but a whisper of what the Campbell-era Ciro's once was. Its outer façade is a neon orangish-pinkish eyesore that looks like a Tuscan countryside painted by someone who was colorblind. Service was a high point of the previous Ciro's, where turnover seemed extraordinarily low, but now the service bombs. Servers are either timid or cocky, with some as pushy and overbearing as used-car salesmen. The signature bocce grounds, which followed Ciro's from the old location, once made the long waits more bearable; nowadays, the bocce is the highlight of the meal.

The owners themselves still make regular appearances at the tables, but it's hard to give them an honest answer to their "how was your meal?" these days. Don't be fooled by full tables; nowadays, they're fueled by nothing but long-lost memories. –JY

Cleburne Cafeteria

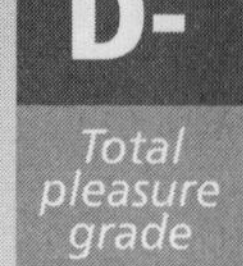

Total pleasure grade

One of Houston's worst restaurants—what is everyone thinking?

1.3	2.3	$17	Southern
Food	Feel	Price	

Counter service
Mon.-Fri. 11am-8:30pm; closed Sat.; Sun. 10:45am-8:30pm.

West U
3606 Bissonnet St.
(713) 667-2386

Bar None
Credit Cards No credit cards
Reservations Not accepted

There are plenty of bad restaurants in the world. But it's rare to find an establishment this highly acclaimed by the media that is this consistently awful. The Cleburne Cafeteria's glowing reviews invariably lyricize the after-church queues on Sundays, the radioactively large slices of cake, and the restaurant's longevity—it opened in 1941. The problem is, 1941 was in America's culinary dark ages, an era that brought up a generation to believe it unwise to eat anything foreign or spicy, unsafe to order anything less than well done, and unsanitary to come in contact with any meat, fish, or fowl whose form suggests that it has ever actually come from an animal.

At least this throwback is authentic, ambrosia and all. Jell-O is bright green, fried fish patties are perfectly rectangular, hunks of salmon evoke petrified science-museum rocks, and a standing rib roast has a center the color of slate. The exotic option is "teriyaki"—tough stumps of meat formerly known as chicken breast, glazed in something sugary. After overcooking, this food then sits there, tray-aging, until someone is unlucky enough to order it.

Cleburne's much-heralded chicken-fried steak measures approximately one square foot, covering twice the surface area of its plate with tasteless, sinewy meat. Its breading is crispy, but salt—so essential to breaded-and-fried anything—is undetectable, and the cream gravy's most prominent feature is its floating clumps of congealed flour. Much better—almost average, even—is creamed spinach with parmesan, but artichoke-heart salad is overwhelmed with poor-quality olives and meaningless chunks of bell pepper and celery, all of this wrought with the metallic acidity of industrial artichoke liquid.

This terrible food is consumed in two brightly lit rooms with ugly institutional furniture beneath an extensive array of even uglier ocean and sea paintings. As for service, the brazenly rude staff seems to think it's cute and quirky to refuse credit cards, to yell at you if you take too long deciding, or to treat you like an idiot for asking what's in one of the trays of buffet-aging gloop. You'll feel like one, regardless, for having bothered with this colossally overrated disaster. –FC

Cliff's Hamburgers

Flat-top cooking equals flat burgers, if not bad ones

6.3 *Food* **6.4** *Feel* **$8** *Price* **Burgers**

Casual restaurant
Daily 10am-9pm.

Breakfast. Delivery.
Kid-friendly. Outdoor dining.

Galleria
1822 Fountain View Dr.
(713) 780-4010

North Houston
3335 FM 1960 West
(281) 580-0126

Bar Wine and beer only
Credit Cards Visa, MC, AmEx
Reservations Not accepted

Who first propagated the myth that Cliff's served the best burgers in town? Does anybody know?

Whoever it was, they must not have owned a grill or a mind of their own, because the griddled patties at Cliff's should drive any burger aficionado up the wall. Ground meat needs caramelization. It needs to have as many dips and dives in flavor as the Hill Country has in its terrain. That is to say, it needs to be *grilled.* Not that Cliff's doesn't serve a decent burger; it's fine, in fact, but with so many other quality places in town, the recent drop-off in attendance has been noticeable, making the already barren room look even more deserted.

With more than a decade under its belt, Cliff's has taken the role of the "joint" and run with it. Aging gracefully doesn't really matter for "joints," because people who frequent "joints" have tunnel vision: they come to eat, and that's about it. Seen through more skeptical eyes, Cliff's may look a little ragged—but come on, the place is old.

We do have to give the staff here some credit, though, for their seasoning of the meat, and for their even buttering and griddling of the bun, which adds an extra dimension of crunch to an otherwise boring burger. The skin-on fries are good only when they're fried crispy, but at other times, they can come out slightly limp. Management has also figured out that by offering other menu items, they can get off the peg leg that is their griddletop. Breakfast, with its discounted coffee if you bring your own mug, is a breath of fresh air in the morning—if mainly because that breath of fresh air includes the potential for devouring the well-seasoned sausage (okay, there's the griddletop again) and soft, fresh biscuits that actually taste as good as they smell. And they smell good.

While Cliff's dropped in quality after being bought out a few years back, it's still not a bad choice—as long as you don't come expecting a contender for best burger in Houston. –JY

Collina's Italian Café

Sometimes even BYO and goodhearted Italian kitsch can't rescue a failed kitchen

D
Total pleasure grade

3.4 *Food*  **5.7** *Feel* **$34** *Price* **Italian-American**

Casual restaurant
Mon.-Thurs. 11am-10pm; Fri.-Sat. 11am-11pm; Sun. 11am-9pm.

Delivery. Outdoor dining. WiFi. Additional locations.

Heights
502 W. 19th St.
(713) 869-0492
www.collinas.com

West Houston
12002 Richmond Ave.
(281) 679-5800

Bar Wine and beer, BYO
Credit Cards Visa, MC, AmEx
Reservations Not accepted

Greenway Plaza
3835 Richmond Ave.
(713) 621-8844

We're always fans of a BYO policy—or even a small corkage. But it's amazing when a BYO policy singlehandedly rescues a restaurant from obscurity, and oblivion, and keeps it going even when it wouldn't otherwise. Perhaps it's because most restaurants would rather close than lose that precious wine markup. So bravo to Collina's for their generous policy. We only wish that we had more nice things to say about the food.

In a city increasingly overrun with "Italian-American 2.0" restaurants, Collina's is staunchly "Italian-American 1.0." (Allow us to explain our nerdy terminology, which is fleshed out more fully on pages 6-7: Italian-American 1.0 is the original strand of Americanized red-sauce Italian food that was created by the wave of immigrants in the early 1900s, drowning spaghetti, lasagne, and meats in heavy tomato-based sauces, melting cheese, serving giant portions of comfort food on red-checkered tablecloths.)

Collina's pretty much sticks to that 1.0 formula, but it executes more poorly than average on almost all of it, with a particularly inept hand when it comes to seasoning. Tortellini stuffed with sausage and spinach, and covered with alfredo sauce, is not bad for comfort food—the seasoning's right and the sausage tasty. But there are serious flaws in many of the other pasta dishes. The kitchen displays an incompetence with even the most basic preparations, overcooking spaghetti and brutally butchering pizza. The biggest and most consistent problem here is underseasoning. Get your wrists in shape before you come to Collina's, because they'll get quite a bit of exercise correcting everything with the table salt shaker. Pizzas' problems, however, go beyond woeful underseasoning. They're thick but not in the good way, weighed down by grease and gobs of quickly congealing cheese. Ingredients are of poor quality, and in the balance we find it difficult to eat more than half a slice under any circumstance.

We kind of like the kitschy décor, which goes with the Italian-American 1.0 menu: scenes of a mythical Italian countryside where everybody grows their own grapes and the young'uns have never heard of Grand Theft Auto. And speaking of grapes, wine industry people still find solace in Collina's for BYO. They're willing to overlook the food in order to taste their cases of wine—blindly, we hope. –RG

Connie's Seafood Market

B- *Total pleasure grade*

Cheap, tank-fresh fish—Mexican-Chinese-American style

6.8 *Food* **4.0** *Feel* **$24** *Price* **Mexican**

Counter service
Sun.-Thurs. 10:30am-10pm;
Fri.-Sat. 10:30am-midnight.
Kid-friendly.

Heights
2525 Airline Dr.
(713) 868-2144

Southeast Houston
8520 Gulf Fwy.
(713) 641-5003

Bar Beer only
Credit Cards Visa, MC, AmEx
Reservations Accepted

There is something viscerally satisfying about looking a catfish in the face before eating him. At Connie's, we like to find the meanest-looking catfish in the tank and then tell the cook to fry the sucker up. This Mexican-style seafood restaurant across from the Heights Farmers Market offers some of the best-value seafood in Houston.

Connie's was once mostly a seafood market, but the restaurant portion has expanded over the years as more and more customers ate the fish in-house. What we like about this place is the freshness, which comes not just from the tanks but also from the combination of a relatively small stock and high turnover. You'll probably get better service if you order in Spanish. They'll sell you fish whole or filleted (hint: go for whole), fried, grilled, or cooked up ranchera style (in a spicy red sauce). They'll do this with catfish, flounder, shrimp, lobster, or whatever else is on ice or in the tank.

The prices are eminently reasonable, far more so than at the similar Tampico: Special #1 is six decent-sized shrimp, two pieces of fried fish, and shrimp fried rice for under $6. Specials offer more shrimp than you'd expect for the price. There is a curious Asian element on the menu with the fried rice (again mimicking Tampico) and egg rolls; these are just okay. We aren't thrilled with the gumbo here, either, which has too much tomato. Better are the classic Mexican seafood cocktails—if that's your thing—served fresh in a mix of tomato, onion, cilantro, avocado, and lime juice. Connie's is also one of the best places in town for a michelada (beer mixed with a spicy cocktail sauce in a frozen mug).

Connie's is a festive, family-friendly place. You'll often catch Mexican soccer on the television, and sometimes you'll even run into mariachis. If mariachis don't frequent your regular seafood joint, you owe it to yourself to give this one a try. But don't pick out the mean catfish in the corner of the tank, terrorizing the others. They're saving that guy for us. –RH

The County Line

Kitschy, Austin-based barbecue way up north—overpriced, but wow, those beef ribs

C Total pleasure grade

5.9 Food **8.0** Feel **$29** Price **Barbecue**

Casual restaurant
Sun.-Thurs. 11:30am-9pm;
Fri.-Sat. 11:30am-10pm.
Kid-friendly. Outdoor dining.

North Houston
13850 Cutten Rd.
(281) 537-2454
www.countylinehouston.com

Bar Full
Credit Cards Visa, MC, AmEx
Reservations Accepted

Knock, knock. Who's there? Interrupting cow. Interrupting co…? Moo.

The cow interrupting in this instance is the large, stuffed longhorn variety that hangs from a wall at one or more of the County Line's branches and occasionally blurts out insufferably bad jokes. She is an apt spokesperson for this oddly conflicted business that has fought hard to join the ranks of Texas' barbecue elite—it cannot quite decide between low-brow kitsch and pricier, high-brow ambitions.

Although outposts of this Austin original dot all of Texas and now even grace New Mexico and Oklahoma, they still manage not to feel too chainish, even if the interior décor seems cribbed from a western-themed Vegas casino, complete with loud wall-to-wall carpeting, multi-colored lighting, and disco-ball-cum-wagon-wheel fixtures. The north Houston branch, which feels like a house in the Old Western woods, has a bar covered with cowhide and nice, shaded outdoor tables out back.

The food, for its part, more or less gets the job done. The County Line is not Houston's best overall spot for barbecue, but it's easily the best for beef ribs. They're enormous and unusually meaty. We also love their tender, subtle sausage. Pork ribs are decent, but the beef brisket is considerably drier than the humor of its wall-mounted cousin. Slaw is interestingly big and chunky, but beans are bland, and barbecue sauce is too vinegary and lacks complexity. The County Line does its less classic sides well, though: sugary bread costs extra, but it's worth it—you can't put it down. And side salads come well dressed (we particularly like a creamy pecan-herb vinaigrette).

The problem is, with all the pretense, this restaurant simply prices things too high. Dishes cost around one-and-a-half times as much as they do elsewhere, and the all-you-can-eat barbecue combos climb shockingly high into the $20s. And that, friends, is a poor joke. –FC

Courses

Students at the Art Institute of Houston deliver flavorful food, albeit with trainee service

7.5 Food | **7.4** Feel | **$51** Price

French

Upmarket restaurant
Mon.-Tues. 11am-1pm; Wed. 11am-1pm, 6:30pm-9pm; Thurs.-Fri. 6:30pm-9pm; closed Sat.-Sun.

Galleria
1900 Yorktown St.
(713) 353-3644
www.artinstitutes.edu/houston

Bar Wine and beer only
Credit Cards Visa, MC, AmEx
Reservations Essential

Like back in the day when Mom took you to the barber college to get the reduced-price haircut, Courses at the Arts Institute offers discounted upmarket food if you're willing to expose yourself to the occasional mistakes of chefs-in-training. Luckily, unlike that barber shop, Courses won't leave you scared for life and with a bad haircut. Better yet, the supervision by real chefs is excellent, not least because cooking here is actually a required part of the associate's degree in culinary arts, so you can rest assured that at least they're trying.

What the students deliver is a modest, well-thought-out menu that's generally honest and well executed. To a lot of people's surprise, the food and the quality of the ingredients are high, and the prices are low for what you're getting, which is often a four-course prix-fixe with wine pairings. Menus change sometimes each quarter. Note that you have to reserve a table in advance to dine here—even for lunch.

Sometimes you'll even get to try dishes that are specific to certain famous chefs, like Daniel Boulud to Nobu Matsuhisa, but prepared by students. For instance, crusted pork tenderloin with spaghetti squash and a cherry sauce has come out surprisingly succulent, cooked to the right temperature and, most importantly, seasoned well. On another menu, a tomato lemon tart was flavorful and refreshing. This experience will leave you with the satisfying observation that most Houston restaurants are getting one-upped by students (food-wise, that is).

Not everything is peaches and cream, though. The atmosphere and service can often leave a lot to be desired. It's clearly a school first and a functioning restaurant second. The performance of the waitstaff can get quite shady at times. Sometimes the students have never waited on a table before, and are suddenly thrust into French-style service. As such, this place isn't ideal for a date or special occasion, but it is a good place to try creative, well-executed dishes cheaply. These menus would cost an arm and a leg at other so-called "fine dining" restaurants (and too often, at those places, the chef could stand to go back to school himself). Here, at least you can get in on the cheap. –SD

Cova Wine Bar

A pair of refreshingly obsessive strip-mall-wine-stores that go upmarket with the food

B- Total pleasure grade

7.3 Food **8.2** Feel **$47** Price

New American

Wine bar
Mon.-Thurs. 11am-11pm;
Fri.-Sat. 11am-12:30am;
Sun. noon-10pm.

Date-friendly. Live music. Outdoor dining. Wine-friendly.

Washington
5555 Washington Ave.
(713) 868-3366
www.covawines.com

Rice Area
5600 Kirby Dr.
(713) 838-0700

Bar Wine and beer only
Credit Cards Visa, MC, AmEx
Reservations Not accepted

Cova has an obsession with wine and all things that are wine. They have two locations around Houston, but the one on Washington is unique. It's a prime example of the raging—but hardly new—trend in Houston of nice restaurants opening in strip malls. We respectfully dissent to this school of thought, but it is what it is, and for what it is, Cova's not bad. Certainly, the wine-shop concept makes the experience more palatable.

Cova looks like a small boutique specialty wine shop with a few tables here and there; the main interior-decorating attraction is the rows of wooden wine racks. The Rice Village location has a few pleasant outdoor tables. Upon entry, you should head straight for the tasting bar. It's good fun to sit around and taste—but it's better yet to munch a bit. We don't suggest the place for an elaborate dinner, though. Sit at the bar to enjoy some food or take a seat at one of the small tables. Cova's menu is divided in two: tapas (small plates) and raciones (twice the portion). We recommend trying more of the former, rather than gorging on fewer of the latter.

At either location, given the retail-store aspect, you wouldn't know from first glance that they're actually serving decent food here. The kitchen focuses on simple preparations using fresh ingredients. A lot of the food is prepared on induction burners in a small kitchen. Starters include great wine food like artisanal cheese plates (you choose four cheeses from their list) with cured meats, or smoked salmon. Cova certainly brandishes its fair share of prestige ingredients—foie gras, lobster, caviar, and so on—but the standouts are tortilla española and braised oxtail. (Don't expect a Mexican tortilla; tortilla española is more like an potato-and-onion-studded omelet.) Oxtail generally comes falling off the bone, yet not overcooked, with a well-executed bordelaise.

Do take advantage of the wines and the wine-shop setting. Use the opportunity to try different wines paired with good food and at a great price. Cova has some wines that you'll be hard-pressed to find anywhere else, so do some shopping. Sunday nights also see live jazz performances. Wine, tapas, and jazz on Washington Avenue—does it get any hipper than this? –SD

Craiganale's Italian Deli

C-
Total pleasure grade

A quaint sandwich shop with a bit of an identity problem

5.2 *Food* **4.5** *Feel* **$11** *Price*

Italian-American

Counter service
Mon.-Fri. 9am-3pm;
closed Sat.-Sun.
Breakfast. Delivery.
Outdoor dining.

Downtown
415 Caroline St.
(713) 237-0000

Bar None
Credit Cards Visa and MC
Reservations Not accepted

Don't pee on our legs and tell us it's raining, and don't give us a turkey sandwich and say it's Italian food. And you can't fool us with plastic cold cuts hanging from the ceiling, either. An Italian name doesn't guarantee Italian food, even if it can bring people through the door. Craiganale's is a deli that serves childhood favorites (what we liked back before we knew what real Italian was) such as spaghetti and meatballs, po' boys, and sausage sandwiches. The sandwiches are all right, with a sprinkle of good execution, but hardly memorable.

In a distinctive space downtown, Craiganale's manages to catch the foot traffic from the surrounding businesses. This is a place downtown where business men and women converge, taking a break from the rat race to fuel their stomachs. Spacious and well lit, the cafeteria-style interior has plenty of seating, but most of the business is to-go orders. The mufaletta is a popular choice; it brings together salami, ham, cheese, and a unique olive mix that rounds it out nicely. It's not the best in the city, nor is it the worst. The roast beef sandwich is a bit dry, with meat that's frighteningly well done—not the juicy rare sort that packs in so much flavor. Most of the sandwiches come with a sweet mayonnaise and boring pickles. It's all a little too simple; you might find yourself opening the sandwich to see if everything's really there.

Spaghetti and meatballs are a surprise. The spaghetti is purposefully overcooked in that classic Italian-American way, but moist and flavorful meatballs save the day. They come bathed in a nearly imperceptible red sauce. There's also a weak side salad sitting sorrowfully in its Styrofoam bowl. Better, comfort-wise, is the garlic bread, with a bold aroma and flavor, but it can get a bit hard if not consumed immediately. The place is only open for lunch; parking can be an issue, so come prepared to walk a few blocks—even in the Houston heat. –SD

Crescent City Beignets

Total pleasure grade

As close as you'll get to Café du Monde in Houston

6.9 *Food* **4.9** *Feel* **$12** *Price* **Southern**

Fast-food chain
Mon.-Thurs. 7am-11pm;
Fri.-Sat. 7am-1am; Sun. 8am-11pm.
Breakfast. Kid-friendly.
Outdoor dining. WiFi.

Greenway Plaza
3260 Westheimer Rd.
(713) 520-8291

Bar None
Credit Cards Visa, MC, AmEx
Reservations Not accepted

In the history of man, every culture that has invented dough has eventually reached an epiphany: if you deep-fry it and cover it in sugar, it tastes good. The Ancient Greeks invented loukoumades, in Mexico they've got churros, and in Portugal it's malasada; the Italians have their zeppole, the Midwestern fairs their fried dough, the South Africans their koeksuster, the Okinawans their sata andagi; Tex-Mex places serve sopapillas, and in New Orleans you order beignets. Rectangular, crispy, chewy, and covered in powdered sugar, the beignet has let the good times roll for over 200 years.

Crescent City models itself after Café du Monde, the famous, if touristy, French Quarter coffee shop. Sorry, but you can't get that kind of gritty ambience until generations of feet have trampled powdered sugar into the floor. They try to make up for it with exposed brick walls and posters of old New Orleans. But prices are 50% above Louisiana levels. Maybe that helps cover repairs after a 1999 incident, reported in the *Houston Press* as follows: "Around noon on Friday, May 21, a woman driver described by witnesses as a 'little old lady' mistook her accelerator pedal for her brake and slammed through the front of the store at high speed. 'And as if that weren't enough,' said a store employee, 'once she smashed through the front, she made a hard left turn inside and wiped out our whole serving line.'"

If you can avoid the oncoming traffic, go for the classic big rectangular model rather than the skinny little finger beignets, which are too oily and not quite chewy enough (but we've noticed that kids tend to prefer the fingers). Cinnamon- and chocolate-sauce-enhanced beignets are a total waste of your menu-reading time; New Orleans savories like gumbo and po' boys are also less exciting than the basic beignets.

As at Café du Monde, the café au lait is spiked with root chicory, giving it a slightly bitter, spicy flavor that's offset by the hot milk. We can only wonder about the developmental consequences these coffees and beignets will have on the hordes of students who come over from Lamar High School across the street. Maybe they'll someday trample on enough sugar for this place to hit its stride. –RH

Cyclone Anaya's

Come get swept away by Midtown (or Heights) mania

Total pleasure grade

7.0 Food | 8.7 Feel | $35 Price | **Tex-Mex**

Casual restaurant
Mon.-Thurs. 11am-10pm; Fri. 11am-11pm; Sat. 8:30am-11pm; Sun. 8:30am-10pm.

Brunch. Date-friendly. Outdoor dining.

Heights
1710 Durham Dr.
(713) 862-3209

Memorial
5761 Woodway Dr.
(713) 339-4552

Bar Full
Credit Cards Visa, MC, AmEx
Reservations Accepted

Midtown
309 Gray St.
(713) 520-6969

Reporting on Cyclone Anaya's, we almost feel as if we should create two separate entries, one for the Midtown location, and one for the Heights, because they couldn't be more different. The Midtown branch is the scene to end all scenes, while the branch in the Heights is still quite lively, but is a dose of refreshing calm in comparison to its raucous brother. It seems that about half of downtown's offices empty into the Midtown Anaya's after work so everyone can unwind with margaritas. And generally speaking, they stand as they unwind; getting a table outside is a Herculean feat—whether for dinner or for drinks.

Cyclone Anaya's was once a Tex-Mex joint run by the former professional wrestler himself, but came upon hard times in the mid '90s; by 1996, they had filed for Chapter 11 bankruptcy three times. Clearly, whatever Cyclone himself hadn't figured out, his wife and sons, who run the new Cyclones, did; we're still not clear on how they managed to make the spot so unbelievably popular, but seeding the crowd might have helped. In other words, part of what's so fun about coming here is that everyone's already here. Whatever they did to drum up these amazing crowds, it's tough to argue with.

In the Heights, however, they let the patio work its magic; it's spacious, and getting a seat is a snap. You're not likely to run into that cute guy you flirted with on the elevator at work that morning, but after a couple of their enormous margaritas you might find someone nonetheless. Not only are these drinks large; they're also strong. We'd recommend sharing them—and it's quite rare that we would issue a word of caution about a margarita.

The food here is Tex-Mex comfort food, more Tex than Mex. We put it in the same category as Chuy's. It's nothing that spectacularly innovative or even tasty, yet it's something we find ourselves going back to time after time. It's Tex-Mex like this—a cheesy aesthetic with a bit of spunk, combined with giant margaritas and a great outdoor space—that makes us proud to be Texans. –AH

D'Amico's

Dish after bland, disappointing dish in a pleasantly jumbled market

C- *Total pleasure grade*

3.8 *Food* **6.9** *Feel* **$18** *Price*

Italian-American

Counter service
Mon.-Thurs. 11am-10pm; Fri.-Sat. 11am-11pm; Sun. 5pm-10pm
Outdoor dining. WiFi.

Rice Area
5510 Morningside Dr.
(713) 526-3400
www.damico-cafe.com

Bar Wine and beer only
Credit Cards Visa, MC, AmEx
Reservations Accepted

It's not clear whether it's deliberate nonchalance or simple negligence that allows D'Amico's, which dubs itself an "Italian Market Café," to feel harried and haphazard even when not crowded. The cramped Rice Village space contributes to that sense of chaos, too, but also to a certain coziness that makes it a pleasant place to sit. Boxes of surplus materials line shelves high up on the walls, and old Italian posters overlap each other down below. For sale, aside from lunch-centric food, are olive oils, vinegars, and other Italian specialties in a little market area, which also stuffs in a few eat-in tables and chairs. A small bar generally hosts a few solo diners, who might sit there sipping a glass of wine like old Italian widowers while they wait on a take-out order.

Some probably favor D'Amico's for its shaded outdoor patio, which is watched over by cheesy statues facing the bars across the street. Sitting outside in Rice Village is not exactly atmospheric—there are parking lots everywhere—but at least it doesn't suffer from the whizzing street noise of Westheimer or Montrose. The menu jumps around Americanized notions of Italy, while managing to avoid anything that would actually be served in Italy, from "Sandwiches and Panini: (Italian Style)" that include cheese steaks, po' boys, and a muffaletta that's more like an olive sandwich, dripping with olive brine, its supermarket-esque salami, mortadella, and provolone completely drowned out by the aggressive olive flavor. Salads are international atrocities, from a honey mustard chicken, romaine, tomato, cucumber, and mushroom disaster to the blandest of all blandnesses, the grilled-chicken Caesar. Avoid at all costs the steam-table buffet, whose "Daily Steamtable Menu" might include such atrocities as deep-fried, breaded cauliflower in an advanced state of sog, and scary manicotti.

And then there is pizza: we don't understand why Italy's margherita has been so often reinterpreted by Americans to include big slices of raw tomato with no sauce, and D'Amico's "Margarita" is one of the worst offenders, with thick, underripe, pinkish tomato slices that are better thrown away than eaten. Not that you'd be left with much: an undercooked, doughy crust and thick goops of cheese. When will the pizza fairies save Houston from this? –RG

Da Marco

A+

Total pleasure grade

Simple, honest, and dazzling taste sensations at one of the best Italian restaurants in America

9.7 *Food* **9.1** *Feel* **$77** *Price* **Italian, Pizza**

Upmarket restaurant
Tues.-Thurs. 11:30am-2pm, 5:30-10pm.; Fri. 11:30am-2pm, 5:30-11pm; Sat. 5:30pm-11pm; closed Sun.-Mon.
Date-friendly. Wine-friendly.

Montrose
1520 Westheimer Rd.
(713) 807-8857
www.damarcohouston.com

Bar Full
Credit Cards Visa, MC, AmEx
Reservations Essential

Houston's best restaurant is often mislabeled as "northern Italian" by the local press. Though virtuoso chef Marco Wiles is from Friuli, Italy's northeast, the restaurant is not. Buffalo-milk burrata, for instance—a profound, cream-spiked version of mozzarella, paired with exceptionally ripe tomatoes—derives from Puglia, in Italy's deep south, on the heel of the boot. Campania, another southern Italian region, is where you'd see the most wood-fired brick ovens of the sort that Chef Wiles uses for his traditional margherita pizza, whose balance of ripe, reduced tomato flavor with sharp, brick-seared ash approaches a level of perfection rarely found in the United States, though there is an extra pool or two of olive oil.

To traverse Da Marco's menu is to span much of Italy. An old Jewish recipe from Rome is the basis for a delicately fried artichoke alla giudea, dressed in olive oil with mint, lemon, and a touch of orange; the citrus is almost too acidic here, but not quite. And you might find a whole roasted branzino—a sweet, firm white fish also known as spigola—absolutely anywhere along Italy's extensive coastline, especially during the summer holiday season. Chef Wiles' treatment of the branzino is just as deferential as it should be: that same wood-burning pizza oven sears and burnishes its skin, locking the moisture within. The whole fish is later deboned at the table to produce sweet meat that sings with flavor and delicacy. This is the best fish dish in the city.

The only un-Italian taste you'll have at Da Marco is likely to be the first one: bread dipped in a dish of olive oil. This is an American custom that might have vague roots in southern France or North Africa, but certainly doesn't exist in Italy. Not that there's anything wrong with that: the bread (fresh and correctly crusted) and Tuscan oil (grassy and spicy) are both best-in-class.

So although Da Marco is one of Houston's only two truly authentic Italian restaurants—the other is Dolce Vita, Chef Wiles' other venture—what separates it from the pack is not its regionality. Rather, it's the obsessive quality and provenance of the ingredients, the honesty of the recipes, and the elevated yet balanced taste sensations that result from their irreproachable execution. A dazzling plate of prosciutto San Daniele embodies this mix as well as any dish on the menu, setting the salt and softness of rosy, paper-thin cured ham against the sugar and crispness of wood-oven-seared slices of flatbread stuffed with fig jam, which play with the palate like the Fig Newtons of your dreams.

A big, open-faced raviolo of homemade pasta mixes ricotta, egg yolk, and truffle to take you somewhere else, far away from Houston or America or even Italy. This recipe wasn't Chef Wiles' idea, but his execution makes this earthly union—of wheat, fruit of the fields; cheese, aged nourishment from the breast; truffle, sniffed out by pigs from deep within the earth; and egg, the symbol of rebirth—into an elemental, almost pagan experience.

And then there is the panna cotta, easily the best in Houston. A judicious mix of gelatin imparts the cooked cream, as it should, with what Gordon Ramsay once called a "sexy wobble." In an inspirational touch, it's balanced by a pool of saba, a syrupy cooked grape must that's similar to aged balsamic vinegar. It is simple in conception, composition, and color, a white slab that sits on the plate in flabby modesty. And it is sublime.

Yet, into the second page of our only two-page review, there remains one aspect of Da Marco that needs to be explained: its accessibility, its casual sense of propriety, and above all, its shockingly fair prices. The atmosphere is nothing special; like the kitchen, it's authentically Italian, with well-dressed, but not overdressed, tables; cozy, low ceilings; an airy porch-style room; and servers that are on the ball, if sometimes less warm than Houstonians probably expect. The specials of the day come out on a chalkboard, adding a folksy, if slightly contrived, angle to the experience.

This is nowhere near the most expensive restaurant in town, and you, whoever you are, should not think that it's out of your range for a special occasion. It is neither too elaborate nor too unusual, neither too challenging nor too pompous, for a party that has no experience with this level of cuisine. And when we say that the prices are disarmingly reasonable, we're excluding the $22 three-course business lunch. That's beyond fair: it is a gift to the city.

To call Da Marco the best restaurant in Houston is to underrate it, because nothing else even comes close. This kitchen is better judged on a national or international scale. The worst dishes on Da Marco's menu are some of the best in the city.

The best will take your breath away. –RG

The Daily Grind

Jerky service at a quirky Austi—er, Houston coffee shop

C
Total pleasure grade

4.0 *Food* **7.0** *Feel* **$8** *Price*

Light American

Café
Mon.-Fri. 6am-10pm;
Sat.-Sun. 8am-10pm.
Breakfast. Outdoor dining. Vegetarian-friendly. WiFi.

Washington
4115 Washington Ave.
(713) 861-4558

Bar None
Credit Cards Visa, MC, AmEx
Reservations Not accepted

When you first step onto the dusty floors of the Daily Grind, you might be possessed by the temporary sense that you've just stepped off of Austin's Guadalupe Street rather than Washington Avenue. It's not just the cups of coffee that seem tailor-made for students with stacks of books; it's that the Daily Grind just gives off that very liberal, very Austiny, very this-place-is-poorly-kept-but-that's-just-part-of-our-personality vibe. If only the staff could imitate Austin's friendly, laid-back service, rather than giving off a distinct I'd-rather-be-anywhere-but-here-and-I'm-going-to-take-it-out-on-everybody feeling, the Daily Grind could really be one of those hipster hangouts.

The scattered tables, overworked espresso machines, and super-self-serve areas with tattered menus and do-it-yourself water and coffee area give this place a certain charm. Even if the staff weren't mean, service probably wouldn't be a strong point of the place just because it wasn't meant to be. But they go above and beyond the call of duty. Near closing time, you can expect a rigid "get out or I'll make you get out" mentality, even if your food hasn't arrived yet. Approaching the counter or asking for silverware might elicit the sort of sharp glance you might get from your mother when you've done something wrong.

The place is first and foremost a coffee shop. The breakfast items in the morning are serviceable, but most people come for a good cup of coffee and a newspaper. Waffles are a little soggy, but bacon tastes like…well…delicious bacon, and waffles can always be cured with loads of syrup. Eggs go on and off from being cooked nicely to being overcooked and brown. During later hours, sandwiches and pick-your-ingredient pastas are available, but they taste like food prepared by a frazzled babysitter: either nothing comes in fresh, or they're just good at making things taste canned. While this place does make the many Houstonian UT Alumni yearn for their Austin heyday, we'd still rather make the two-and-a-half-hour drive. –JY

Ask for a "latte" in Italy,
and you'll get a glass of milk.

Daily Review Café

You pay for tasty food, not creative food

B- *Total pleasure grade*

7.1 *Food* **7.4** *Feel* **$31** *Price* **American**

Casual restaurant
Mon. 11:30am-2pm; Tues.-Thurs. 11:30am-2pm, 5:30pm-10pm; Fri. 11:30am-2pm, 5:30pm-10:30pm; Sat. 11am-2:30pm, 5:30pm-10:30pm; Sun. 11am-2:30pm, 5:30pm-9pm.
Breakfast. Brunch. Date-friendly. Live music. Outdoor dining. Vegetarian-friendly.

Montrose
3412 W. Lamar St.
(713) 520-9217
www.dailyreviewcafe.com

Bar Full
Credit Cards Visa, MC, AmEx
Reservations Accepted

When it comes to menu prices, restaurants figure in the quality of the products, demographic of their clientele, and how much the competition is charging. The DRC, as it is known, is a simple restaurant that has withstood the test of time, and time has enabled the place to begin charging uncomfortable prices for its comfortable bistro food. It might still be dubbed a "hidden treasure" in the vernacular, but the DRC seems to have won enough awards to feel justified charging $16.25 for chicken-fried chicken—a price that can test your temper, even if, in all fairness, it tastes fantastic. Favorites like a margarita shrimp cocktail, pork chops with fried green tomatoes, and chicken pot pie are represented on the menu in great nostalgic fashion. Daily Review also boasts one of Houston's favorite brunches, equipped with migas and jumbo lump crab cakes with chipotle hollandaise. Slated as a hidden treasure, it has won many awards throughout the years for the food.

The restaurant's interior has a quaint, modest look to it. A very small dining room isn't that exciting, but the outside seating is brilliant. The food is not breaking any barriers, nor is it cutting any corners. The Southwestern egg rolls (here they have some stiff competition from Chili's) are filled with black beans, corn, peppers, cilantro, and cabbage, and are crispily delicious. But never leave, under any circumstances, without trying the pork chop. Though it sounds just like every other restaurant's preparation in Houston, the summer squash and fried green tomatoes bring it up a notch. Power to the pig.

Mains are sometimes unimaginative, but almost always delicious. The chicken-fried chicken is fried 'till golden and crispy, topped with black peppercorn gravy, and served with a selection of fill-your-stomach sides that will remind you of Sunday dinners. It's served every day for lunch, but only Tuesday through Thursday for dinner, so mark your calendar; you don't want to miss out. As far as Houston's favorite protein goes, the DRC chicken pot pie, surprisingly, is extraterrestrially good. Get any notions of school-cafeteria-style chicken pot pie out of your head; you're in for a treat with this version. However much it costs. –SD

Damian's

We're waiting for the day they'll actually serve cucina italiana

B-
Total pleasure grade

7.7
Food

8.7
Feel

$73
Price

Italian-American

Upmarket restaurant
Mon.-Fri. 11am-2pm,
5:30pm-10:30pm;
Sat. 5pm-11:30pm; closed Sun.

Midtown
3011 Smith St.
(713) 522-0439
www.damians.com

Bar Full
Credit Cards Visa, MC, AmEx
Reservations Recommended

There are two main strands of Italian-American cuisine, neither of which has much to do with the food you'd find in Italy. We call them versions 1.0 and 2.0 (see pages 6-7). Italian-American 1.0, often mislabeled "southern Italian," is the red-sauce stuff that you would have grown up with in an American town in the 1950s through the 1980s: spaghetti and meatballs, veal and chicken parmigiana, baked lasagne.

Italian-American 2.0, which has often been mislabeled "northern Italian" since it got going in the late 1980s and early 1990s, is focused less on tomato and cheese, and built more around proteins like veal chops, chicken breasts, shrimp, and lobster, sometimes served over pasta, generally smothered in complicated sauces and toppings that bring together nominally Italian-derived ingredients like balsamic vinegar, prosciutto, Marsala, gorgonzola, and sun-dried tomatoes.

Damian's is clearly Italian-American 2.0. The few 1.0 dishes on the menu (garlic bread, fried calamari, sausage and peppers, eggplant parmigiana), though well-executed, are far outnumbered by creations like "Linguini di Amore" [*sic*], with crab, shrimp, asparagus, and sun-dried tomatoes in pesto sauce or aglio olio, and "Branzino Azzurro" (grilled sea bass topped with jumbo lump crabmeat, Pinot Grigio sauce, and sautéed spinach). The problem is, as with Microsoft Office, the expensive version upgrade isn't necessarily an improvement; the old version can actually be less confusing, less weighed down by unnecessary features, and easier to enjoy.

Damian's atmosphere, too, is classic Italian-American 2.0—out go the red-and-white checks, and in come the discreet white tablecloths, low lighting, intimate atmosphere, and deferential service. There are some classy touches, like the table full of antipasti—cured meats, cheeses, olives, Tuscan white beans, caponata, and so on—and we like the rich, hearty ribollita soup. Pastas, too, are well executed, if generally rich and heavy, and proteins come off the grill with the kiss of flame but the subtlety of their flavor intact. The wine list is strong in high-end Italian reds like Barolos and Brunellos, generally with severe markups, though there are some decent values from southern Italy.

After two decades, Damian's remains one of the best Italian-American 2.0 kitchens in the city. The question is whether Houston has outgrown Italian-American 2.0, and is ready for Italian that's not American at all. –RH

Demeris Barbecue

B-
Total pleasure grade

A forgettable entry in a state filled with barbecue heavyweights—but one we still love

6.7 *Food* **6.7** *Feel* **$10** *Price*

Barbecue

Casual restaurant
Mon.-Sat. 11am-8:30pm; closed Sun.

Delivery. WiFi.

Montrose
2911 S. Shepherd Dr.
(713) 529-7326
www.demeris.com

Spring Branch
9552 Hempstead Rd.
(713) 681-7204

Bar Beer only
Credit Cards Visa, MC, AmEx
Reservations Not accepted

Bellaire
6722 Marinette
(713) 776-0088

Driving down Shepherd, past Richmond, it is easy to miss this barbecue restaurant that has been feeding Houstonians for more than 35 years. Demeris Barbecue, tucked away in plain sight, smokes, grills, and fries barbecue for the masses. Diehard barbecue fans will complain that the 'cue here tastes more of hickory than the all-knowing post oak, but non-aficionados who just want smoked meats that taste good will be happy. Sausage, brisket, and ribs are just a fraction of the selection that you can enjoy at Demeris Barbecue. They also do quite a bit of catering and delivery business—grab a menu by the door.

The menu, like most barbecue joints, is quite simple: smoked meats, beef brisket, chicken, and even ham, offered on a bun or as a meat plate with a couple of sides. The beef barbecue sandwich is mediocre; the beef itself has little smoke flavor, and the bun looks and tastes like a poor mass-produced piece of bread that was not loved as a child. Sides include potato salad, and beans; you know the drill. French fries are poorly fried, lying there lifeless, limp, and not crispy—but with good seasoning.

Demeris does offer juicy hamburgers, fried jumbo shrimp, and believe it or not, fajita dinners. Half pound burgers with your choice of topping are juicy and delicious. Also, Demeris is one of the few places in town where you can find an old favorite—the Frito pie. Known colloquially as the B-Man, it's off the menu, but you can ask for it with your choice of one, two, or three meats. It's the greatest Frito pie in town, but you will probably be incapable of doing anything very active afterwards. This is neither the best nor the worst barbecue in town, but spirited regulars worship the joint, and the product is consistent. Enjoy it every day but Sunday, and revel in the smokehouse scent that bombards you before you even open the front door. –SD

The Dessert Gallery

Where young love and sugar highs overshadow powerfully sweet cakes

C
Total pleasure grade

6.7
Feel

Sweets

Counter service
Mon.-Thurs. 11am-9pm;
Fri.-Sat. 11am-midnight;
Sun. noon-9pm.

Date-friendly. Kid-friendly. Outdoor dining. Vegetarian-friendly. WiFi.

Upper Kirby
3200 Kirby Dr.
(713) 522-9999
www.dessertgallery.com

Galleria
1616 Post Oak Blvd.
(713) 622-0007

Bar None
Credit Cards Visa, MC, AmEx
Reservations Not accepted

It must be that crackish aspect of sugar that leads clamoring crowds to pay such high prices for sticky-sweet cakes scarcely better than those your reasonably competent aunt could turn out. Or maybe it's the cushy couches. Or the city's singular obsession with sweets.

Whatever the reasons for the Dessert Gallery's success, the joint's bright interiors are consistently overpowered by herds of people on weekend nights. Couches are taken over by groups of friends, while tables are used for high-school dates whose awkwardness is smoothed out by the provided board games—what's more romantic than "accidentally" bumping hands while grabbing for a game piece? You have to watch your step here; loud, rambunctious children, seemingly propelled by sugar-fueled jet engines that enable them to outrun their frantic parents are everywhere. Nonetheless, staff manage to remain calm and collected, even if they sometimes have a hard time keeping track of who has orderered which cake. In the end, the Dessert Gallery seems more about the frenzy than the actual dessert.

Strong showings in down-home, and huge, classic cakes is what the Dessert Gallery is; Houston's best pastries, as some suggest, they are not. Variety notwithstanding, the cakes are certainly a better option than buying a box of Betty Crocker and following the instructions at home, but that doesn't translate into world-class taste. The popular "Chocolate Euphoria" cake is decadent, with textures of smooth and chunky dark chocolate dominating the palate for about three bites, at which point your euphoria turns to sloth. The cheesecake works in the same manner. Other cakes, such as a well-made carrot version, hold out better, but their flavors get boring half-cake through, and most of the tooth-numbingly-sweet cream-cheese icing winds up scraped off to the side. But if your idea of a fun Saturday night is to buzz on sugar, slink around the couches, and move in rhythm to the shouts of "Jenga!," then Dessert Gallery is definitely your place. –JY

Dharma Café

A cozy, intimate bistro whose menu explores the disastrous side of diversity

C Total pleasure grade

4.1 Food | **8.7** Feel | **$38** Price

New American

Casual restaurant
Tues.-Thurs. 11am-3pm; 6pm-9pm;
Fri.-Sat. 11am-3pm; 6pm-10pm;
Sun. 10am-2pm; closed Mon.
Brunch. Outdoor dining.
Vegetarian-friendly.

Washington
1718 Houston Ave.
(713) 222-6996
www.dharmacafehouston.com

Bar Full
Credit Cards Visa, MC, AmEx
Reservations Accepted

The haphazard eclecticism of this menu is frightening. It flies from a blue-cheese pizza with mango to a tuna with wasabi miso vinaigrette, with a Mediterranean stopover of hummus and tabbouleh. Even if the place isn't as bad as its schizophrenic assortment of recipes might lead you to believe, Dharma Café is overstretching its abilities. The kitchen is simply not up to its menu's ambition; in fact, few kitchens would be up to such a complicated task.

A spicy tuna wrap combines foods from approximately four continents into one appetizer, stuffing a tomato-basil tortilla with ahi tuna, cream cheese, cucumber, red onion, jalapeños, wasabi, and fresh spinach. The tuna is fresh and soft, and surpirsingly the overall effect pleasant, if 21st-century-gourmet-supermarket-ish. Scallops are overcooked—a common problem here—and come with a totally wimpy red curry coconut sauce and a big, unappealing salad. The culinary trip around the world continues with shrimp with garlic basil mojo on a bed of fettuccine; these shrimp are in bed with some unlikely company—basil, capers, and sun-dried tomatoes, and the noodles, though homemade, are pasty and overcooked. A chicken-fried filet mignon, the "steak of the day" on one visit, was an entertaining but ill-inspired idea with even worse execution. We ordered it rare, and it came medium-well, with random bits of crunchiness all over the filet, adding nothing more than a bizarre texture to the overcooked hunk of meat.

The space, however, is quite cute; it's got high ceilings with exposed beams, and extremely casual service, hidden in a yup-and-coming neighborhood on the edge of downtown where fading sketch meets nouveau middle-manager (and still sometimes mugs him). The out-of-the-way location and down-to-earth environment strike an appealing vibe. Dharma Café manages to woo people, it seems, with its cuteness and local base, even despite a lack of culinary fireworks. Perhaps they have developed a devoted local following among suckers for the superficial excitement of an overambitious "world cuisine" menu. Clearly, given their relative success, Dharma Café understands its audience—but maybe not its food. –RG

DNR European Café

It's not a gyro, it's not a shawarma—it's a DNR wrap

C Total pleasure grade

6.2	6.5	$11
Food	Feel	Price

Middle Eastern

Counter service
Sat.-Thurs. 11am-8:30pm; closed Fri.
Delivery. Kid-friendly. Outdoor dining. WiFi.

Montrose
4621 Montrose Blvd.
(713) 529-0367
www.dnrfoods.com

Bar BYO
Credit Cards Visa, MC, AmEx
Reservations Not accepted

The Greeks and the Turks have a bitter past. Nowadays, their cuisines are extremely similar, with dish names often the only difference, though neither camp will admit to this. DNR tries to avoid any confusion and stay out of this battle by labeling itself as "European cuisine," although a light investigation reveals the menu to be Turkish. The name DNR is short for döner, a Turkish word meaning "turning roast." The meat for döner sandwiches is placed on a turning spit that roasts the meat as it turns; the meat is then shaved off to order.

Think this sounds similar to a gyro or shawarma?

Right you are.

This cozy establishment serves sandwiches, wraps, and plates in different combinations with different sides. The wraps are nothing special, good enough to get by; they're big and filling, stuffed with the classic beef-and-lamb mix—or, alternatively, bland grilled chicken breast—plus the most boring of cookie-cutter accoutrements: lettuce, tomato, onion, and parsley. The meat tends to get a bit dry, so grab some yogurt sauce to help it along. A big salad bar with hummus, pickled red cabbage, and other light cold Turkish salads is in the middle of the restaurant. The hummus is delicious. Nutty, smooth, and acidic, the DNR version does justice to this chickpea spread's reign as king of all dips.

Unfortunately, DNR makes a lot of concessions to Americans' taste buds and sensibilities along the way, diluting the overall quality as so many Turkish, Greek, and Middle Eastern places in America do. This translates to multi-colored meal-deal specials, which are loudly advertised all over the restaurant and web site; the latter even seems to insinuate that the owners have their eye on franchising, with a "Locations" tab in spite of the existence of only one. It also translates to serving such abominations as baked potatoes stuffed with meat or vegetables. A kids' menu tries even harder not to offend picky palates, and to complete the deal, WiFi is available for all those who want to sit in a fast-food restaurant and the great Turkish novel while downing their combo. –SD

Dolce Vita

A

Total pleasure grade

Breathtakingly authentic, affordable regional Italian that's flawed in all the right ways

9.0 *Food* **9.2** *Feel* **$38** *Price*

Italian, Pizza

Casual restaurant
Tues.-Fri. 5pm-10pm;
Sat.-Sun. noon-10pm;
closed Mon.
Date-friendly. Outdoor dining. Wine-friendly. Vegetarian-friendly.

Montrose
500 Westheimer Rd.
(713) 520-8222
www.dolcevitahouston.com

Bar Full
Credit Cards Visa, MC, AmEx
Reservations Accepted

Like an old lover, we keep coming back to Dolce Vita, again and again, forgiving it every one of its faults. And the faults are many: the crust is perfectly seared one night, but it's too thick, doughy, and undercooked the next. Yesterday, orecchiette with escarole and sweet sausage was the porky, glutinous, slightly bitter pasta dish of our dreams; today, a plate of spaghetti, clams, and chickpeas is dry and incoherent. On one evening, our waitress is perfect; on another, she goes AWOL for 45 minutes.

Yet still we love Dolce Vita with all our hearts. Granted, the whole thing is a carbon copy of Mario Batali's Otto. But we love Otto, too—so what's the problem?

Sometimes the very qualities that most attract you to lovers, or restaurants, are the same ones that irritate you. Maybe the service is spotty because they cram in so many tables, so that they can keep down waits and accommodate as many people as possible. Maybe the kitchen is occasionally inconsistent because they're operating on a cost base that allows them to keep every single item on the menu under $15. The truly unusual thing about this restaurant is its principled devotion to certain priorities, like preparing strictly authentic Italian dishes, without a single concession to American tastes; serving them in a warm, bustling, effortlessly enjoyable two-story space with a patio; and doing it at prices that are accessible even to starving students.

As such, we take an off-night at Dolce Vita as just another excuse to come back the next: to dip another piece of crunchy fennel into bagna cauda, the vegetable dip to end all others, made simply and gloriously from garlic, anchovies, and oil; to revel in another plate of spectacular marinated whitefish, or of delicately fried baby artichoke; or to relax once again with a simple pizza margherita, made with buffalo-milk mozzarella, which—when it's on—is rivalled in Houston only by the pizza at Marco Wiles' other restaurant, Da Marco. And then there is the truffle egg toast, whose elemental pleasure can only be experienced, not written about.

So come to Dolce Vita expecting that something will go wrong, and when it does, just take it as it is. The city is still lucky to have this restaurant, and so are you. –RG

Don Café

Crave-worthy Vietnamese sandwiches at pocket-preserving prices

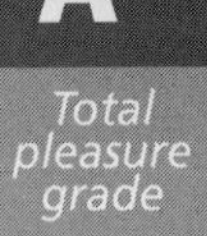

Total pleasure grade

8.6 Food | **3.9** Feel | **$5** Price

Vietnamese

Counter service
Daily 8am-9pm.
Kid-friendly.

Chinatown
9300 Bellaire Blvd.
(713) 777-9500

Bar None
Credit Cards No credit cards
Reservations Not accepted

It's hard to miss Don Café: it's probably the only free-standing restaurant on Bellaire Boulevard, where shopping centers normally swallow up restaurants and conceal them from outside-world view. In the building that was once the bright-pink, ill-fated Venus Café, Don Café now serves delicious, quick Vietnamese fare at reasonable prices, much to the delight of those who work in the area.

Don Café is the baby of a family who used to work at Givral Hoang's (not to be confused with Les Givrals in Midtown), a cramped hole of a Vietnamese sandwich shop behind Don Café that has taken a huge nosedive over the past few years. Here, the space is large and energetic, relatively undecorated, but comfortable and well lit. The counter is normally manned with one of the family members ready to take your order with a welcoming smile. Even if there's a long line of customers, many of which bring huge to-go-order lists at lunchtime, the food will come quickly, and you'll be in and out within thirty minutes.

Don serves several Vietnamese classics, like bowls of hot noodle soup, crispy Vietnamese egg rolls, and rice plates with charcoal grilled pork. But the star of the show is the Vietnamese sandwich. What comes out is an absolutely fresh, warm, and tasty sandwich that's probably worth double the $2.20 that you're charged. The pièce de résistance is the baguette, which has a thin, crunchy crust and that holds in carrots, jalapeño, cilantro, a perfect spread of yolk-heavy mayo, and grilled pieces of meat that are like flavor crystals ready to explode in your mouth.

For a place this affordable, you wouldn't expect things to be so beautifully marinated and seasoned, but it seems that Don Café has their food down to a science, getting it right every time. Even packaged spring rolls, sitting on the counter, are as moist and fresh as any. For the quality and variety of food, Don Café has to be one of the best bangs for your buck in town. –JY

Doneraki

Spectacular execution in the least likely of quarters—unpretentious Tex-Mex at its best

A Total pleasure grade

9.0 Food **7.7** Feel **$30** Price **Tex-Mex**

Casual restaurant
Sun.-Thurs. 8am-midnight;
Fri.-Sat. 8am-3am.

Brunch. Delivery.
Kid-friendly. Live music
Outdoor dining. Additional locations.

Westchase
7705 Westheimer Rd.
(713) 975-9815
www.doneraki.com

South Houston
300 Gulfgate Ctr.
(713) 645-6400

Bar Full
Credit Cards Visa, MC, AmEx
Reservations Accepted

Heights
2836 Fulton St.
(713) 224-2509

Tex-Mex is up and down in Houston, but Doneraki, in its big friendly incarnations, is up and up. Warmth defines the experience here, from the Spanish-language welcome at the door to the effects of the strong margarita pitchers. According to the management, the place is named after a man called Eraki, who invented tacos al pastor, that pineapple-basted Mexican version of the Greek gyro or the Middle Eastern (drumroll please…) döner. Putting aside all the coincidences and dubious stories, though, the Tex-Mex menu here, if predictable in content, is dead-on.

We'll begin with the few weaknesses of the kitchen: chips can show up brittle, particularly as the night drags on, and the salsa is just okay, with a decent flavor but little kick. Queso is not the best version in town, either; it's American-cheesy, without much chile aspect, although the consistency is pleasantly balanced between liquid and solid. Things only get better as you move through to the mains. Grilled quail on the fajita spread is one of the unique joys of Houston Tex-Mex, and Doneraki's version—which comes à la carte or on a parrillada—scales the heights of char-grilled supremacy, its skin crisped without its juicy meat exposed to heat for a second too long.

Other fajita meats—particularly beef and sirloin adobada—perform well too, their marinades informing the flavor but not dominating it. Chicken breast can be slightly dry, but you should know better than to ever order chicken breast. The various forms of enchiladas perform their comfort-food duties with consummate skill: the cheese is melted but not congealed, the salsa verde has the right degree of tang, the Tex-Mex chili gravy is rich and guiltily good. Margaritas aren't quite tart enough, but they're not absurdly sweet either, and they pack a surprisingly good punch.

Of the three locations, Gulfgate is the original and most interesting, sporting an enormous, room-sized replica of a Diego Rivera mural that portrays the artist strolling through the Alameda Park in Mexico City, past illustrious figures of Mexican history. Central Houstonites, however, will find the also-affable Westheimer location more convenient. –RG

Dry Creek Café

Total pleasure grade

Come to this BYO spot for its limeade and one-hit-wonder burger

5.5 *Food* **3.6** *Feel* **$15** *Price* **American**

Casual restaurant
Sun.-Thurs. 7am-9pm;
Fri.-Sat. 7am-10pm.
Breakfast. Kid-friendly. Outdoor dining.

Heights
544 Yale St.
(713) 426-2313

Bar BYO
Credit Cards Visa, MC, AmEx
Reservations Not accepted

We've heard that when life gives you lemons, you find someone to whom life gave vodka, and have a party. But what happens if you're in the dry area of the Heights? Well, live gave Dry Creek Café limeade, and with their BYO policy, a party is still doable.

And this laid-back joint is just the place to host; it's been transformed from an old gas station, and it's got just enough rust and grunge to make almost anyone feel comfortable. There are some uninvited guests, however, in the form of flies; when you eat, they multiply exponentially.

But get a burger anyway. The "Triple Bypass Burger" is all it's cracked up to be: a sloppy, delicious, glorious mess to eat. With its Tabasco mayo moistening the bun, its bacon and fried egg try desperately to stay together; the end result is yolk dripping down your hands as you eat, and frankly, we don't mind—it's that much less to clog our arteries. Though burgers call for beers, go for the limeade; it's got the sprightly freshness of good wheat ale, so it's close enough. Stay away from the Paris Hilton-like fries, though: they're thin, blonde, and lacking in substance.

Unfortunately, the choice of breads in many of the sandwiches doesn't work. The brioche bun that comes with the veggie burger is untoasted, making any sort of freshness from the cucumber, sprouts, and mushroom-based patty chewy and heavy. The focaccia used for a mozzarella and tomato sandwich is too flimsy to handle all the juice squishing from the tomatoes, and it crumbles in your hands. The whole dish is undersalted, leaving a bit to be desired.

As does the service. It's hit or miss, but if you miss, look out, because these people can be downright gruff. And it's especially irritating when they're clearly doing a subpar, inefficient job. We'd like our service with a smile (and maybe even a fly zapper). –FC

> People complain about $15 corkage fees, but the cheapest bottle on the average wine list has about an $18 markup. And it's usually terrible.

Dynasty Supermarket

Some of the city's best Chinese barbecue in one of its dingiest markets

Chinese

Specialty grocery
Sun.-Thurs. 9am-9:30pm;
Fri.-Sat. 9am-10pm.

Chinatown
9600 Bellaire Blvd.
(713) 995-4088

Bar None
Credit Cards Visa, MC, AmEx
Reservations Not accepted

Dynasty Supermarket, like DiHo Supermarket, is one of the oldest Asian grocery stores on Bellaire. The sounds, smells, and yellow hue of Dynasty haven't changed much over the last couple of decades. Walk in, and be prepared to be serenaded by the high-pitched sound of whole primals of animals being taken apart in the butcher shop. Push around your rickety cart, and you'll experience the spray and smell the brininess of fish being cleaned and taken apart in the seafood department.

Although its prices are still competitive, Dynasty has really started to show its age over the last decade or so, and this has been detrimental to their business. Newer markets have popped up left and right, offering the same products in the same price ranges, but in buildings whose roofs don't seem about to cave in.

What keeps people coming back to Dynasty is something else entirely: the little hole of a prepared-foods shop, where greasy, withering cooks chop up cheap, surpassingly delicious Chinese roast duck, barbecued pork, and crispy-skinned pigs. This is downmarket Cantonese meat at its finest, and anyone nostalgic for Hong Kong's Mong Kok neighborhood will be in love.

Dynasty's produce rarely seems to be in top form, nor does it boast much variety. Mustard greens and watercress smush up against one another uncomfortably, concealing something else underneath. The meat and fish department—aside from the barbecue—are nothing special, either. A fair bit of the business here is in cheap ramen.

And yet, tucked in a nook in the back corner, hanging medievally on hooks, slabs of sticky-sweet lacquered char siu, or barbecued pork, crisp-skinned ducks, and sometimes whole fried pigs is a gruesome but mouth-watering sight. PETA would probably go insane if they did a thorough inspection of the joint, but for the rest of us, taking home a box of meat to our families is a moment proud enough to be worthy of a primal roar. And maybe a box of 99-cent ramen, too. –JY

El Hidalguense

Festive Mexican that will leave you surprised—and full of goat

B- *Total pleasure grade*

7.3 *Food* **8.9** *Feel* **$37** *Price*

Mexican

Casual restaurant
Mon.-Fri. 6am-9pm;
Sat.-Sun. 8am-10pm.

Breakfast. Live music. WiFi.

Spring Branch
6917 Long Point Rd.
(713) 680-1071

Hillcroft Area
3631 Hillcroft St.
(713) 781-6656

Bar Full
Credit Cards Visa, MC, AmEx
Reservations Accepted

Most Mexican restaurants in Houston fall into one of three main clusters: the simple, authentic, bare-bones taquerías; the comforting, cheesy Tex-Mex cantinas; and the sleek, pricey top-shelf-margarita yuppievilles. El Hidalguense manages to exist totally outside this trimodal distribution. The food is authentic, but the service is attentive; you can eat very cheaply, or very expensively; you can duck in for take-out meat by the pound, or spend hours getting musically drunk.

The restaurant's simple, bright room vibrates with authenticity and tradition. It echoes with extended-family Spanish-language crosstalk. And it sizzles from open fire, above which the dramatic carcasses of goats, lambs, and cows are mouthwateringly impaled. On weekends, you'll likely dine to the tune of mariachis, yet the genuineness of the quirky waitstaff somehow prevents you from dismissing the whole thing as over-the-top. These are not patronizing black-tie waiters singing Verdi arias to an awkward anniversary-date couple during their tiramisú course in hopes of boosting the tip to 22%. It's just fellow members of Houston's Mexican community enjoying each other's easy company.

Your arrival is first acknowledged with something far beyond the regular chips-and-salsa hello: complimentary, but unfortunately dry, chicken flautas accompanied by a thick chile sauce that rescues them with a happy heat sinking into their crackly fault lines. Charro beans, which come out before your mains, have enough pork backbone to eat them like soup. But the main event is the enormously overpriced portion of cabrito asado (which three signs remind you is the best in town—decide for yourself). The baby goat, grilled over an open fire, shows up tender and juicy, basted by its own juices, but in need of a liberal salting; the meat closest to the big, long rib bones brandishes the best flavor. Grilled lamb (borrego) is far less impressive, fairly underseasoned, and comes with an equally underseasoned but deeply enriched lamb consommé floating with large chunks of hominy. Better is the winning "mixteca" preparation, in which the meat is steamed with a chile-based sauce in a leaf—a method that will be familiar to cochinita pibil freaks.

Free tequila digestifs are yet another gesture that's nothing but genuine. If more Houston restaurateurs treated their customers this way—like neighbors, not covers—this city would surely be a more neighborly place. –RG

El Mesón

Schooling Rice Village in the intricacies of paella

B- Total pleasure grade

7.0 Food | **6.5** Feel | **$42** Price

Spanish, Cuban

Upmarket restaurant
Mon.-Thurs. 11am-10pm;
Fri. 11am-11pm; Sat. 11am-10pm;
Sun. noon-10pm.
Date-friendly. Live music.

Rice Area
2425 University Blvd.
(713) 522-9306
www.elmeson.com

Bar Full
Credit Cards Visa, MC, AmEx
Reservations Accepted

El Mesón seems in the midst of an identity crisis. It sometimes calls itself Cuban, but its menu is largely Spanish. Meanwhile, its décor features proudly hung Mexican flags, and its menu features a number of Tex-Mex items.

What do we make of all this? We'll take it as it is, as El Mesón proudly owns up to its multiple personalities; they're just trying to please as many palates as possible. Instead, we're urged to focus on its cute, cozy, quaint qualities, which are especially unique given its Rice Village location. Not to mention the great wine list, and the decent food, which beats the pants off neighboring Mi Luna.

You'll be amazed by how quickly a carafe of sangría will disappear here. Sweet and fruity, it goes well with most tapas selections…as do many of the Spanish wines they have on hand, which the knowledgeable (but not know-it-all) staff is happy to discuss with you at length. The tapas menu is pretty straightforward in its Spanish focus. Gambas al ajillo leave us wanting for a bit more ajillo, though shrimp are nice and bouncy. Piquillo peppers come "del mar" or "de la tierra"; we recommend the land version, with tender, flavorful lamb, raisins, and pine nuts. The menu also takes a brief, ill-inspired foray into Tex-Mex with offerings such as beef fajita nachos and spinach quesadillas; stay away from that stuff. Paella is good, though, especially the "Paella del Mesón," which integrates delectable shrimp, chicken, and spicy, tight chorizo. None of it will knock your socks off, though.

Still, there's something about El Mesón that is quintessentially Rice Village. It appeals largely to college students, who come, perhaps, to get their first taste of "nice" "world" cuisine, or, later in their careers, to satisfy a paella craving after that semester abroad in Barcelona. Young dates come here to woo in the low lighting, although things get less romantic as the place empties out, which happens around 9pm, even on weekends. The good news is that the food isn't compromised as much as it is in other college-area eateries. There are missteps, but the people behind this restaurant are serious. We wish this would have been part of our college education. –AH

El Pueblito

Bad Tex-Mex in the mouth can still be music to your ears

4.9 Food | **8.7** Feel | **$20** Price

Tex-Mex

Casual restaurant
Mon.-Wed. 11am-10pm; Thurs. 11am-midnight; Fri.-Sat. 11am-2am; Sun. 11am-11pm.
Breakfast. Date-friendly. Live music. Outdoor dining.

Montrose
1423 Richmond Ave.
(713) 520-6635
www.elpueblitopatio.com

Bar Full
Credit Cards Visa, MC, AmEx
Reservations Accepted

The border between Texas and Mexico is less well defined here than it is at most Mexish places in town, primarily because of the hard-to-pin-down dinginess of the décor and the totally mix-and-match clientele. Look at the menu, and you'll think "Tex-Mex"—and, we're sorry to report, it's bad Tex-Mex, beginning with the terribly sweet salsa and continuing on through bland chicken dishes, tough fajitas, flavorless enchiladas, gummy melted cheese, and so on. Chile con queso is one of the worst versions we've ever had, practically unseasoned and skin-happy from the moment it arrives. It's difficult to find a high point on this low-lying menu.

But you'll see that that's hardly the point at the moment you take your place in the delightfully shabby backyard—perhaps at a rickety table in the middle of everything, or perhaps—if you're lucky, or if you have a larger party—in one of the more secluded, shaded tables on the edges of the space, which are slightly raised and offer a certain degree of seclusion yet plenty of exposure, too, to the liveliness of the garden.

Basically, what happens here—after you walk through the main restaurant, which is mostly full of raucous, fun-loving Mexicans at bare-bones tables—is that people old and young get drunk, sometimes spectacularly so, and sway to the tune of reliably bizarre live music, which seems to happen more or less every night.

Turn your attention back to your plate, and you'll kill the musical buzz, contemplating the mini-disasters that are your tacos. Think too much about your sickly-sweet margarita, which has enough tequila but hardly another good quality, and you'll lose track of why you're here. But keep focused on the main event—and you might lose yourself in the sensation of being at a Mexican friend's garage party. Which means, by the way, that you should be drinking beer, not margaritas. –RG

El Pupusodromo

The pupusa, the pride of El Salvador—in a word: delicious

8.5 Food | 8.1 Feel | $12 Price | **Salvadoran**

Casual restaurant
Daily 9am-9pm.
Breakfast.

North Houston
13235 Veterans Memorial
(281) 587-2800

Southwest Houston
6817 Bissonnet St.
(713) 270-5030

Bar Beer only
Credit Cards Visa and MC
Reservations Not accepted

Hillcroft Area
5902 Renwick Dr.
(713) 661-4334

It's great when you stumble upon a hidden gem that is reproducing the flavors and dishes of another's homeland. El Pupusodromo is one of those terrific examples. Pupusas, tamales, plátanos fritos con crema, and thick corn tortillas are just a few of the offerings of this humble restaurant. Although they try to please the Houston audience with novelty dishes, stick with the Salvadoran basics and you won't be disappointed. With multiple locations around Houston, they are all consistently delicious, flavorful, and salvadoreño.

Blue is the color of choice here, as it's one of the colors of the Salvadoran flag. The color happens to work, too, creating a relaxing and comfortable atmosphere. Each table has its own jar of curtido, the pickled cabbage condiment essential to pupusas; its reliable presence conveys the sense that they're serious about these Salvadoran staples, although this particular curtido could stand to be a bit more acidic. Fresh juices like maracuyá (passion fruit) and pineapple contribute a sense of freshness to a soda-and-caffeine society. The natural juices also aid in digestion.

Food is exact and to the point. Salvadoran tamales are fluffier and lighter than their Mexican cousins. Sweet tamales de elote (corn tamales) are lighter than air. Flavorful and packed with kernels of corn, they come with thick cream that really kicks your taste buds into overdrive; it's a fantastic dish. The same can be said for the fried plantain with cream; with some refried beans, it's a perfect way to start your day, Salvadoran style. Pupusas are good, authentically revueltas (stuffed with bean, cheese, and chicharrón—fried pork rinds). Thankfully, they're not as greasy as other versions, and they're still flavorful.

This place is a success story of immigrants coming to this country and pleasing discriminating palates with their simple comfort food—food you might find on any street corner back in El Salvador, but not here. Each branch of El Pupusodromo is a small operation, with what appears to be only one cook in the back and one server in the front, but the size and pace don't seem to stress them out at all. Day after day, they turn out stack after stack of piping pupusas.

Revueltas, indeed. –SD

El Rey Taquería

Maybe not the king of taquerías, but the Cuban specialties stand out

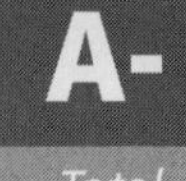

Total pleasure grade

8.8 Food | **6.0** Feel | **$11** Price

Latin American

Counter service
Mon.-Thurs. 7am-9pm;
Fri.-Sat. 7am-3am; closed Sun.
Breakfast.

Downtown
233 Main St.
(713) 225-1895
www.elreytaqueria.com

Bar None
Credit Cards Visa, MC, AmEx
Reservations Accepted

Washington
910 Shepherd Dr.
(713) 802-9145

North Houston
3330 Ella Blvd.
(713) 263-0659

El Rey distinguishes itself from the taquería hordes by offering Cuban specialties along with generally well-executed Tex-Mex standards. The Mexican food doesn't particularly stand out for Houston, and the Cuban food wouldn't be a star in Miami, but the prices are good, service is fast, and the overall combination fills a tasty niche in the local taquería scene.

You can get tacos anywhere around here, so let's consider the ropa vieja ("old clothes"), the stewed and shredded beef standard of Cuban cuisine. The meat is stringy, which is actually kind of authentic, and it has a lot of tangy flavor, although we would prefer more garlic. The old clothes are served with black beans, rice, and fried plantains, which bring a filling sweetness to the meal. Cuban rotisserie chicken is well-seasoned and not overcooked, which puts it a step above grocery-store rotisserie, but, unfortunately, it's generally not much different from the chicken at Taco Cabana (other than the plantains and black beans). The Cuban sandwich packs a lot of flavor with its roast pork, Swiss cheese, and pickles. You might start putting pickles on your ham sandwiches at home. Then you'll buy a sandwich press. And then the next thing you know you're booking a flight to Havana, (hoping they don't stamp your passport), and sipping mojitos...

On the Mexican side, the menu bridges authentic Mexican with Tex-Mex, along with some fusion dishes like a "Tejano Torta" made with rotisserie chicken, avocado, cheddar, and chipotle, and the audacious but tasty "Torta Diablo," with ham, cheese, tomato, onion, avocado, mustard, and jalapeños. There's also an amusing "Cuban Taco" with beef or chicken fajita, black beans, plantains, and sour cream. We also like the breakfast tacos (egg, chorizo, and cheese, for instance), and the shrimp tempura tacos are above average. Coffee specialties are simple and strong; the Café Cubano double packs a lot of punch. All three locations are small, so seating can get cramped. The drive-thru is a decent option; it's slower than the drive-thru at McDonald's, but then McDonald's doesn't serve old clothes, does it? –RH

El Tiempo Cantina

Fun, fratty Tex-Mex, with a glorious garden and spikes of talent on the parrilla

8.6 Food | **8.7** Feel | **$58** Price | **Tex-Mex**

Casual restaurant
Mon.-Tues. 11am-9pm;
Wed.-Thurs. 11am-10pm;
Fri. 11am-11pm; Sat. 9:30am-11pm;
Sun. 9:30am-9pm.

Breakfast. Date-friendly. Delivery. Outdoor dining.

Greenway Plaza
3130 Richmond Ave.
(713) 807-1600
www.eltiempocantina.com

Washington
5602 Washington Ave.
(713) 681-3645

Bar Full
Credit Cards Visa, MC, AmEx
Reservations Recommended

El Tiempo has just the kind of festive atmosphere that makes us love Tex-Mex joints. Outside seating is at picnic tables under a covered patio under a canopy of palm trees, which transport you to the Mexican coast (at spring break, perhaps, given the loud, fratty clientele). You'll be greeted with chips and a salsa that bears a striking resemblance to Italian red pasta sauce; it hasn't the least bit of spice, just sugary stewed-tomato sweetness.

The first two tests of Tex-Mex are margaritas and queso. Here, El Tiempo is one for two. The former are excellent, even the cheaper versions, although you should pass on the Mexican martinis, which are missing the trademark three-refill shaker. Queso is a big letdown: it's basically just undersalted melted cheese with Velveeta-like qualities and practically no chile flavor, and it's served with messy baked flour tortillas that crumble and don't stand up to the queso.

Beyond that, the menu is completely overwhelming. Pages upon pages of the same meats arranged in different forms—tacos, enchiladas, flautas, fajitas, parrilladas—leave your head spinning. Our advice is to stick to those last two; the kitchen at El Tiempo Cantina has a way with grilled meat. Everything on the parrillada (mixed grill), which highlights all of these, is good: deeply flavored beef, sausage, and bouncy shrimp; juicy, smoky pork tenderloin cubes (a pleasant surprise); and tender quail. Parrilladas for one person are actually enough to feed four—as they should be, given that versions for one cost up to $60. Everything on the menu, in fact, seems a bit too expensive, even given the gargantuan proportions. One parrillada actually costs $159 (could the most expensive dish in Houston actually be served at a local Tex-Mex joint?). Granted, it would feed the Texans' entire sorry Reggie-Bush-less offense.

A meal at El Tiempo Cantina marks only the beginning of your evening; a copy of your receipt gains you and your family free admission into next-door Diamond Cabaret, where you can take the young'uns to admire a collection of strippers that range from anorexic to obese to just plain sad-looking. –RG

Empire Café

Stick to coffee and cake at this ever-popular icon of Westheimer hip

Total pleasure grade

5.8 Food | **8.0** Feel | **$14** Price

Light American

Counter service
Sun.-Thurs. 7:30am-10pm;
Fri.-Sat. 7:30am-11pm.
Breakfast. Brunch. Date-friendly. Outdoor dining. Vegetarian-friendly.

Montrose
1732 Westheimer Rd.
(713) 528-5282
www.empirecafe.net

Bar Full
Credit Cards Visa, MC, AmEx
Reservations Accepted

There are the successful coffeeshops whose atmosphere is so dim and romantic that people crawl in and nestle like baby birds. There are the successful coffeeshops so central or ubiquitous that people wind up walking in because they almost can't avoid it. And there are the successful coffeeshops that function as surrogate study halls, replacing the antiseptic ambience of a university library with a place to pop open your laptop to a soundtrack of good tunes and milk-steaming whistles. But then there is a fourth kind of successful coffeeshop—and Empire Café, like its neighbor Brasil, belongs to this group—that attract and maintain a loyal clientele through simple harmony. Here, it's the balance of a laid-back vibe, a hip location, folksy service, plentiful shaded outdoor seating, chill music, and an anything-but-chain neighborhood feel.

Empire Café does this so well that it's able to go through morning, noon, and night with a constant queue at the register. (There's only one, and it can get frustratingly slow at peak times, especially if all you want is coffee.) It's all the more remarkable given that, in spite of the proliferation of intellectuals that populate this hip Westheimer neighborhood, Empire has made the (clearly conscious) choice not to provide WiFi. As a result, you'll see fewer laptops and more conversations: groups of two, three, or four are much more common at Empire than at its contemporaries.

That is also because Empire doubles as an afterthought of a restaurant. You'd have to assemble a crack squad of Jersey mafia restaurant consultants to come up with a more pedestrian Italian-American menu than this, from minestrone to eggplant parmigiana. Bland chicken breast inhabits every corner of the menu. Pastas come in bowls, dissociated from their sauces. There are also some ill-fated attempts to assuage vegetarians, as in a $10 main composed of nothing but grilled vegetables and potatoes, or a doomed Portobello-and-goat-cheese panino. If you must, omelets and pizza might be least offensive. But if you are looking for a sweet pick-me-up, one of the huge, shareable pieces of cake is the way to go—especially coconut and lemon (appallingly, many people eat one solo). But you should really come, as most do, just to sip coffee and catch up with a friend. –RG

Escalante's

"Fine Tex-Mex" that gets a bit more attention than it deserves

B- Total pleasure grade

7.2 Food | **6.8** Feel | **$44** Price

Tex-Mex

Upmarket restaurant
Sun.-Wed. 11am-10pm;
Thurs.-Sat. 11am-11pm.

Brunch. Date-friendly. Outdoor dining. Additional locations.

River Oaks
4053 Westheimer Rd.
(713) 623-4200
www.escalantes.net

Memorial
6582 Woodway Dr.
(713) 461-5400

Bar Full
Credit Cards Visa, MC, AmEx
Reservations Not accepted

Meyerland
590 Meyerland Plaza
(713) 663-7080

The Infinite Monkey Theorem states that a monkey randomly pounding keys on a typewriter (or—let's be current here—a computer keyboard) for an infinite span of time will, at some point, wind up typing the entire text of Shakespeare's *Hamlet* by complete chance. However, the probability that the monkey would actually produce the manuscript during a span of time on the same order of magnitude as the age of the universe is virtually—but not quite—zero.

We're not sure whether Escalante's employs any monkeys on its graphic design team, but the possibility did occur to us that its staff might well have been the first to use the phrase "Fine Tex-Mex" since the Big Bang. As it turns out, though, we were proven wrong by the following portion of the *Merriam-Webster* definition #5 for the word "fine":

> Fine *adj.* ...
> **5 a:** ornate <fine writing>
> **5 b:** marked by or affecting elegance or refinement <*fine* manners>
> **5 c:** filet mignon inexplicably drowned in a mismatched sauce involving champagne and frozen lobster meat <*fine* dining>
> **5 d:** marking the anniversary of a doomed marriage celebrated in an American restaurant that's decorated like a Rococo ballroom <no, nothing's wrong, I'm *fine*>
> **5 e:** guacamole prepared tableside for no reason <*fine* Tex-Mex>

What Escalante's—whose light, airy room, which is cheerfully done up with a beige-and-yellow Maya fetish and sports a visible tortilla station—isn't quite getting is that Tex-Mex has always been unpretentious, and people want its evolution to be unpretentious, too. As arguably the second-most-upmarket Tex-Mex establishment in town, this restaurant should be looking to improve on the cheesy, elemental flavors of its tradition, not trying to sell its customers on the idea that the avocados are worth $12 just because they've been melodramatically scooped out by the waiter. Fajita chicken and beef are well marinated here, and Tex-Mex enchiladas do come out sufficiently cheesy. But "chipotle-glazed" quail shouldn't be; chile con queso "blanco" might actually be better yella'; and rice and beans would *definitely* be better with some good, ol' fashioned seasoning. We'd prefer that our chiles rellenos be stuffed with more meat than hot air. Or, for that matter, even cheese could help pick up the slack. –RG

Fadi's Mediterranean

B-

Total pleasure grade

Hesitatingly educating Houston's palates in the art of Middle Eastern food

7.3 *Food* **6.6** *Feel* **$15** *Price*

Middle Eastern

Counter service
Mon.-Thurs. 11am-9pm; Fri.-Sat. 11am-10pm; Sun. 11am-8:30pm.

Delivery. Kid-friendly. Vegetarian-friendly.

Meyerland
4738 Beechnut St.
(713) 666-4644
www.fadiscuisine.com

Southwest Houston
8383 Westheimer Rd.
(713) 532-0666

Bar None
Credit Cards Visa, MC, AmEx
Reservations Accepted

Fadi's Mediterranean Grill has been introducing Houston to Middle Eastern food for some time now. What once was relatively unknown and just a bit too foreign is now a dining mecca for businessmen, families, and people from all walks of life. They come for the fresh pitas, kebabs, falafel, and other traditional staples from that part of the world.

A long buffet greets you as you walk into Fadi's, but the place manages to feel surprisingly family-ish, even given the cafeteria-style system by which you're made to carry your food to your table on a tray. The buffet dominates the room and entices you with the smells of cardamom and clove. One of the few virtues of a buffet is that looking at the finished product before you make your final choice puts the ball in your court; and with this hefty selection of items, winning isn't a given. A selection of cold salads starts off the buffet. Tabbouleh and dolmas have a great balance of flavors, but fattoush needs a heavy salting. Kebabs are always fresh and incredibly well seasoned. The vapors rising up from them are just a taste of how delicious the meat is. Whenever braised lamb shank is on the buffet, snatch it up fast; it's braised in a dark brown sauce and served with cabbage salad, and the lamb is succulent and flavorful.

Fresh juices are offered at the end of the buffet. Mango is best, with an aromatic, fruity taste that is refreshing and quite satisfying, though it can be a bit thick at times. The baklava is a bit too sweet, but the date cookies are the ideal marriage between pastry and fruit. Braised vegetables in a curry sauce, or big chunks of potatoes served with cauliflower and eggplant, make this a great place for vegetarians. The lunch crowd can pack it in, so beware on weekdays. Dinner and weekends are a better option; they're just crowded enough to ensure that food doesn't sit on the buffet table too long. –SD

Farrago

The original Midtown fusion spot, still serving better food than many of the new hotspots

B-
Total pleasure grade

7.7 *Food* **8.3** *Feel* **$38** *Price* **New American**

Casual restaurant
Mon.-Wed. 11am-10pm;
Thurs.-Sat. 11am-11pm;
Sun. 11am-3pm.
Brunch. Date-friendly. Outdoor dining. WiFi.

Midtown
318 Gray St.
(713) 523-6404
www.farragohouston.com

Bar Full
Credit Cards Visa, MC, AmEx
Reservations Accepted

If "regionally inspired" is the new "fusion," then Farrago is the old, not the new. And yet, after seven successful years, it still feels like a trendsetter. Farrago was a key player in the West Gray renaissance, opening on the street-level space of a trendy apartment building-to-be in Midtown way before it was cool to do so. And in many ways it defined, and still defines, the Midtown-yuppie aesthetic: the wide-open, inviting, dual-dining-roomed space is one of Houston's only restaurants that can actually snag walk-ins. Even if Farrago's not the hippest kid on the block anymore, many of its newer neighbors still seem to take it as inspiration.

And even if the catch-all fusion seems more dated by the year, Farrago shows no signs of giving up anytime soon—or of letting itself go downhill, as restaurants usually tend to do. Farrago's menu of "world cuisine" (a term that induces fright in foodies the world over) globe-trots with abandon from Vietnam to Jamaica, Lebanon to Mexico. At least the folks at Farrago have a sense of humor about their ADHD: the name of the place actually means "confused mixture." This is the serve-one-dish-from-every-country model of fusion, which is safer, at least, than the disastrous mix-all-the-world's-ingredients-in-one-pot version. The kitchen avoids most of the haphazard-fusion pitfalls by following recipes faithfully and steadily, and bringing out flavors that will smack you in the face and awaken your taste buds.

Don't be shy about drinking or sopping the deep, cilantro-spiked coconut-curry-and-lemongrass broth that sits in a delicious bowl of steamed mussels. Hamburgers are juicy but one-dimensional; too much melted blue cheese, for instance, can be overbearing. Fries, however, are crispy and salty. The Vietnamese noodle salad is a good idea, but is poorly executed. A bright, well-seasoned pozole, however, is right on the money.

As on the food menu, beer and wine from all parts of the world are featured, from New Zealand Sauvignon Blanc to Italian Peroni. (We don't recommend either.) Amazingly enough, parking is not an issue, even on this fashionable block; the restaurant has its own parking garage. And it's free, too. No tow trucks or tickets today—just easy, old fusion dining that's convenient and still mostly delicious. –SD

Felix

Just because it's a Houston tradition doesn't mean it's good

D
Total pleasure grade

1.4 *Food* **2.9** *Feel* **$18** *Price* **Tex-Mex**

Casual restaurant
Tues.-Thurs. 11am-8:45pm;
Fri.-Sat. 11am-9:45pm;
Sun. 11am-8:45pm; closed Mon.

Montrose
904 Westheimer Rd.
(713) 529-3949

Bar Wine and beer only
Credit Cards Visa, MC, AmEx
Reservations Accepted

Human beings are supposed to adapt over time, to improve upon their past mistakes, to elevate the fate of humanity—in whatever small way—into something slightly better. Changes in food service and style have improved Tex-Mex drastically in the past 50 years, and as a society, we are better for it. So our question is this: why do people like Felix Mexican Restaurant? People swear by the chile con queso, enchiladas, and fajitas. Maybe there's something fun about time-warping back to an era when tobacco was just an excuse for a social gathering; canned food was cutting-edge; and a culture's cuisine from south of the border was being mutilated to satisfy the tastes of red-blooded, God-fearing Americans. It was into that era that Felix Mexican Restaurant was born; but it wasn't a happy one for food.

It's not that we don't love good Tex-Mex. The problem is that nostalgia only goes so far when you're using sub-par ingredients. It seems as though Felix's two main kitchen staples are the #10 can and the can opener. It's not bad enough that the place looks like a school cafeteria; the food, too, actually tastes like a frozen TV dinner nuked to "perfection." There is probably still a fully functional fallout shelter somewhere in the restaurant, just in case the Reds get wise again.

Tortilla chips—one of the only bright spots here—are outstanding, but the salsa tastes of canned tomato purée and onions. What they make their chile con queso out of is anyone's guess, but it is incredibly greasy, leaving your entire mouth saturated. Cheese enchiladas would likely have a better chance at solving world peace than being good. (Remember, those pinkos could return at any moment.) The chicken fajitas come so overcooked as to be on par with the texture of sand. And why does it take almost twenty minutes to prepare a chile relleno?

Perhaps that's the exact amount of time it takes for all of the flavor to be cooked out.

The stone-cold supporters of Felix are almost exclusively old-timers. Rumors have circulated that they've chained themselves to the front door amidst threats of the building's implosion. Sounds like the Commies might have already struck: there must be something radioactively brain-washing in this Tex-Mex. –SD

Field of Greens

Wholesome, healthy, and very, very green

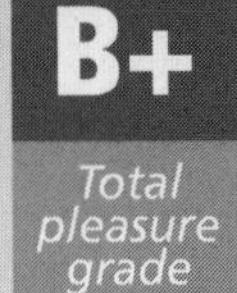

B+ Total pleasure grade

8.2	5.9	$11
Food	Feel	Price

Light American

Counter service
Sun.-Thurs. 11am-9pm;
Fri.-Sat. 11am-9:30pm.
Kid-friendly. Vegetarian-friendly.

Upper Kirby
2320 W. Alabama St.
(713) 533-0029
www.fieldofgreenshouston.com

Bar BYO
Credit Cards Visa, MC, AmEx
Reservations Not accepted

In a small secluded area off of West Alabama, Field of Greens is a palace of vegetarian, vegan, and macrobiotic fare. In a town where a menu without the holy trinity of cheese, beef, and bacon fat might induce a heart attack, Field of Greens responds with heartwarming and heart-healthy food that might actually save you from one.

Clearly, the positioning is strategic: an alcove a stone's throw from Whole Foods is ideal for attracting the health-conscious, organic-buying, farmer's-market-frequenting, Croc-footed, family-in-tote customers. The place looks industrial-deco-meets-family-café, with springtime-green walls, fake shrubbery, monochromatic paintings, and the Flaming Lips flowing from iPod-rigged speakers. If it weren't for the dry-erase board for a menu and the self-serve water station equipped with both ketchup and Sriracha, the place would be pure Zen.

While the owners are Asian, the health grub at Field of Greens is straight-up American-Continental. Offerings range from faux-meat burgers to vegan fajitas to a wild salmon sandwich (their concession to the fact that some claimed "vegetarians" still eat fish). Even with the starred and striped offerings, Asian touches make their way into the meal, as in the "Village Tofu Burger," in which seared pieces of tofu skin cleverly envelop a patty of tofu to give that grilled meaty-savory taste that soft tofu doesn't inherently get upon cooking. It's touches like this that make the food so often successful—even the odd-sounding tofu-chocolate pie, whose tofu adds silkiness and nuttiness.

Not every Asian inflection is spot-on; a barbecue burger's sauce is overwhelmed by ginger. Not that it's bad, but when you're expecting the taste of barbecue, it's not a pleasant surprise. Seitan and tempeh make several appearances on the menu, as in the fajitas, but tend to have a disagreeable chewiness. But with so many places trying to kill you these days, it's hard to eat out without getting an earful from your mother or an eyebrow raise from your doctor. And Field of Greens is one of the rare places that you can actually enjoy without having to lie to them. –JY

Finger Licking Bukateria

Cow's knee, goat, and tripe at one of Texas' only Nigerian hangouts

B *Total pleasure grade*

8.0 *Food* **4.7** *Feel* **$14** *Price* **Nigerian**

Casual restaurant
Mon.-Sat. 11am-11pm;
Sun. 11am-8pm.
Delivery.

West Houston
9817 Bissonnet St.
(713) 270-7070

Bar None
Credit Cards Visa, MC, AmEx
Reservations Not accepted

Houston's big enough to have representation from myriad ethnic groups, although sometimes you have to head out to the far-flung regions of the city to find the hangout of a particularly small one. This bukateria (the word is roughly translated as "informal restaurant") is flanked by Afghan and Middle Eastern eateries on a stretch of way-west Bissonnet. It's one of those Houston places that transports you to another country immediately upon entry. If you're white, you'll get stares, because you'll probably be the only one. Everything is foreign; customs are different, the menu is totally disorienting. And we like that.

Forgetting about skin color, be prepared for a struggle unless you're actually Nigerian. Your overly protective waitress will inevitably push you towards boring chicken with rice. She will assure you that you won't like the authentic meats on the menu. She'll go to any lengths to steer you toward chicken, overcooked beef, boring tilapia in tomato sauce, or competent but uninteresting fried rice.

Fight the good fight. Don't let it happen. Getting the goat will be an uphill battle, but trust us, it's worth it. It's the most flavorful meat on the menu, and, after all, you came here for something new, right? We also like eggy egusi (a seed) and spinach, with undertones of dried shrimp. Tripe is soft and tender, and springy cubes of cow's knee (gelatin) are worth the fight, too. All of it comes with fufu, a starch with a texture similar to gnocchi that's made from white yam flour pounded into a tight ball, which is brought to you in a plastic bag. You lubricate your hands in a metal water bowl, pinch off a small piece of fufu, and dip it in your stew.

Delicious.

There's also something else up at Finger Licking Bukateria: by day, a disco ball hangs innocently from the ceiling, an empty dance floor begs to be used, and large televisions show African music videos. We've got a suspicion that on weekends after dinner, it turns into a Nigerian expat rager—and if you *really* want to feel foreign, try coming then. –AH

The Fish

Put on your dancin' shoes for this sushi

6.9 Food | **6.0** Feel | **$58** Price

Japanese

Upmarket restaurant
Mon.-Wed. 11am-2pm, 5pm-11pm; Thurs.-Fri. 11am-2pm, 5pm-midnight; Sat. noon-midnight; Sun. 5pm-10pm.
Outdoor dining. WiFi.

Midtown
309 Gray St.
(713) 526-5294
www.fishhouston.com

Bar Full
Credit Cards Visa, MC, AmEx
Reservations Accepted

It's quite clear that a lot of money has been spent styling this restaurant. It falls in the sushi-bar-as-dance-club model of interior decorating, the result being that you don't fully get a real restaurant experience here. Thump-thump-thumping music requires that you shout to be heard. Strangely colored lights complete the look, ensuring that you can't really see your fish, either. (We're just waiting for the day they employ the use of a strobe light. At least then we'll get the occasional glimpse.) Solo diners should forget it, as the experience of sitting here is quite lonely, akin to showing up at a bar alone; you might as well go eat dinner in a disco. Even for midtown, the Fish stands out as being hip. Too hip.

Remember the days when sushi was brave and daring? Raw fish? It sounded scary. Nowadays, everyone has their favorite roll (even if any taste of the fish is drowned out by a gloopy, creamy sauce, as it sometimes is here). Kids eat it, exhibiting an impressive deftness with chopsticks—sometimes better than their parents. Grocery stores sell pre-prepared favorites in mass quantities; rarely is it edible, but that's beside the point.

Pretty people demand pretty sushi, and here we find that it's generally artfully presented. They're not really hiding much here as far as the food goes; what you see is what you get, and prices are high for what you get. The sushi's not bad, but not great, maybe a little above average. Rolls and nigiri are largely unremarkable, and all the usual suspects are there—never fear, they've got California rolls.

Service is generally shoddy; it's more akin to what you would expect in a busy pub. That said, at least the drinks are decent. And pricey—like everything else at the Fish. Because, just like a nightclub, part of the point in being here is showing others that you can afford to be.

And maybe that's the essence of hip, in the end.

If only hip meant delicious. But nothing could be further from the truth. –FC

Fleming's

Chain steakhouse that's big on cheddar—in all its forms

7.6 Food | **8.0** Feel | **$88** Price | **Steakhouse**

Upmarket restaurant
Sun.-Thurs. 5pm-10pm;
Fri.-Sat. 5pm-11pm.

Outdoor dining.

River Oaks
2405 W. Alabama St.
(713) 520-5959
www.flemingssteakhouse.com

Woodlands
1201 Lake Woodlands Dr.
(281) 362-0103

Bar Full
Credit Cards Visa, MC, AmEx
Reservations Accepted

Eh. What can we say about Fleming's? It's your average corporate-expense-account chain steakhouse that has managed to sprawl across most of the US—and quite quickly, we might add. The original branch was opened only in 1998. And the power of this name recognition cannot be underestimated. Traveling executives come to know and trust it, ordering the same thing every time, every location, knowing there won't be any deal-spoiling surprises. People who just eat there because they like it do the same—"My husband always gets the ribeye, and I get the filet mignon." And this, ultimately, is what chains really provide us with: consistency nationwide. Service invariably varies, but when you get the trusted "Fleming's Potatoes" or Chili's "Awesome Blossom," you know exactly what you're going to get.

The sad thing is that this is still an incredibly successful business model in the Houston restaurant scene, even for restaurants as high-end as Fleming's. Surely a large part of it is all the visiting businessmen; but we need restaurants for ourselves, too. We need human chefs behind our food.

The Fleming's web site, for instance, reads like a corporate document—because it is. The visitor is wooed with numbers, commitments to this and that, and if you're looking for a job, rest assured; Fleming's understands the importance of balancing work with play. And for the executives, at least, there probably is quite a bit of time to play.

Enough teasing, though. The space is well-executed: they have good booths, large and comfortable. A few sides here are out of the steakhouse norm: chipotle cheddar macaroni and cheese, potatoes with jalapeños and cheddar cheese. They make for the sort of steak dinner we would have imagined as kids, unabashedly hitting all the pleasure points in one meal. But it's the steak that defines the place, and Fleming's are decent, but they're wet-aged, not dry aged. Boo hoo.

The chain also claims to undersell other steakhouses, and it's true by a few dollars, but after a nice bottle of wine—which you wind up ordering at a place like this—what's the difference between $88 and $94? And anyway, if it's not on your dime, what does it matter? –FC

The Flying Saucer

Come for the beer...stay for the chili-cheese fries

Total pleasure grade

6.2 Food | **8.1** Feel | **$18** Price

American

Bar
Mon.-Wed. 11am-1am; Thurs.-Fri. 11am-2am; Sat. noon-2am; Sun. noon-midnight.
Date-friendly. Outdoor dining. WiFi.

Downtown
705 Main St.
(713) 228-7468
www.beerknurd.com

Bar Full
Credit Cards Visa, MC, AmEx
Reservations Not accepted

It's lovingly referred to as the Saucer, and it's many different things to many different people. For the one-dollar-Lone-Star crowd, it's too snooty and expensive, with too many confusing beers. For beer connoisseurs, it's a tipsy trip around the world. For the normal working Joe, it's a good place for a couple of brews and a quick bite. And for the haggard lech, it's a dreamland, with all the "beer goddesses" walking around in all-too-Catholic-schoolgirl-like knee-high socks and short skirts. But as far as the Fearless Critic is concerned, it's the home of a well-loved basket of chili-cheese fries, which are wildly variable.

The Saucer seems to cater to all different sorts of people, so picking your poison doesn't end at figuring out which beer you want to enjoy. The expansive space has a nook and cranny for every person: comfortable couches, hard wooden tables, booths that are strategically located near the Golden Tee machine, and the cramped and cozy Pub of Love that's in an upstairs loft. And while the beer goddesses' attire may exude vapidity, every single one of them is a walking encyclopedia of yeast and hops knowledge. It's hard, even for the upstanding male (or female) citizen, not to fall in love with any one of them, except when they deny your team on trivia night (Tuesdays, at press time) with an impossible question on a double-point round.

Certainly, beer carries the spotlight, with every corner of the world represented by its ales and lagers; the food at the Saucer plays second fiddle. It deserves consideration for a decent lunch downtown—as long as that lunch includes a beer. Pizzas are served by the slice, and they're serviceable. The barbecued chicken is a bit dry, but its BBQ tang goes well with the cheesy goodness. The "Steak Wrap," a star, is now off the menu, but they'll still make it on request; its fatty mayo and serious beefiness make for hand-held deliciousness.

We once loved these chili-cheese fries dearly, but lately, they've been variable, sometimes showing up soggy, with large chunks of tomato, cheese overcooked to dryness, and the chili beneath scarce. On a good night, it's salty, it's fatty, it's cheesy, and it's good enough use your fork to stab the hand of your friend who's trying to steal some of it. –JY

Fogo de Chão

C
Total pleasure grade

An all-you-can-eat chain steakhouse where the carefully conceived financial joke's on you

6.7 *Food* **6.7** *Feel* **$77** *Price*

Steakhouse, Brazilian

Upmarket restaurant
Mon.-Thurs. 11am-2pm, 5pm-10pm; Fri. 11am-2pm, 5pm-10:30pm; Sat. 4:30pm-10:30pm; Sun. 3:30pm-9pm.
Kid-friendly.

West Houston
8250 Westheimer Rd.
(713) 978-6500
www.fogodechao.com

Bar Full
Credit Cards Visa, MC, AmEx
Reservations Accepted

One of the most eternally popular and exalted steakhouses in the city, Fogo de Chão probably owes less to its kitchen or its ingredients than to its "Brazilian" concept, which scales the heights of themed gimmickry. Turn your table's token onto its green face, and the meat-shavers (dressed humiliatingly as gauchos), who roam the restaurant with enormous skewers and long knives, will keep stopping by to shave hunks of deliciously fatty ribeye and "house special" sirloin, along with dozens of other lesser cuts of meat, onto your plate. Turn the token red, and the barrage will subside.

Fogo has hit upon the same crowd-pleasing formula as Benihana, combining interactive cuisine and faux-exotic theming with utterly familiar, kid-friendly tastes. There are other versions of the Brazilian steakhouse in town, but this is probably the highest-revenue practitioner of the art. The genius of the sprawling salad bar, and of the irresistible little hot cheese buns that show up first at your table, is that you spend the first part of your meal filling up on high-margin items like starches, salads, and beans. If you actually measure the amount of (lower-margin) meat you wind up eating, the $46.50 you're paying for "all you can eat" (not including drinks or dessert) starts to look like less and less of a good deal.

Our advice is to save virtually all of your appetite for the meat, because the salad bar is a minefield. The few highlights include intensely smoked salmon of the cooked-through variety, which comes with pleasant dressing; decent giant asparagus; and equally enormous hearts of palm, which are always a welcome delivery system for salt, acid, and bright textural punch. But potato salad is underseasoned and mealy; artichoke hearts, meanwhile, are enormously overmarinated and oversized, dominated by the classic taste of jar juice. Many meats are problematic too—bacon-wrapped chicken is terribly dry, filet mignon is cooked to oblivion, and so on. In the end, we'd take one simple, competently prepared steak, and perhaps a simple salad and side, over the many different manifestations of mediocrity that adorn this overrated, spectacularly profitable chain. –RG

Frank's Pizza

Not your average Houston pizzeria; this late-night favorite would be more at home in NYC

C+ Total pleasure grade

6.8 Food **5.8** Feel **$15** Price **Pizza**

Counter service
Sun.-Wed. 11am-9pm;
Thurs. 11am-1am;
Fri.-Sat. 11am-3am.
Delivery. WiFi.

Downtown
417 Travis St.
(713) 225-5656
www.frankspizza.com

Bar Wine and beer only
Credit Cards Visa, MC, AmEx
Reservations Not accepted

Take a stroll down Travis Street, and you will come across one of the better New York-style pizza joints in Houston, maybe the best. Of course, pizza is polarizing. Everyone has his favorite—his go-to—and it may or may not be correlated with taste. In our book, in the later evening—that is, once Dolce Vita and Da Marco close—this is a pretty good standby. So get a babysitter and make your way over to this lively, dively late-night hotspot.

Frank's also has the look and feel of a real New York pizzeria, the sort of place where you'd enjoy a giant slice back east. No matter where you're from, you should relish the fact that Houston manages to serve a pizza with restorative properties; it will absolve your sins, iron your pants, and fix that nasty rash that's been around since the last time you strolled down Travis Street late at night.

A little hole in the wall, Frank's makes everyone feel a little more edgy. The space itself is long and thin, but still maneuverable; the people are nice—that is, until all the drunks roll in after last call at the bars. You can order a whole pizza or just by the slice; also available are sandwiches, but they're less impressive. Frank's crust is above average. Thin (but not thin-crust thin), but with multiple crispy layers, it holds up to the sometimes-too-copious toppings and sauce that round out the pizza. People say New York crust is so good because of the city's tap water; we can't help but wonder if Frank's has been co-opting one of our precious oil pipelines to suck over some of that delicious east-coast sewage, because the crust here is an uncannily close approximation.

Frank's is open late night, so after you're done polluting your body with your vice of choice, stop by and admire the organized chaos that is this busy pizzeria. Big deck ovens will reheat your pizza and give it that crucial crunch factor.

Surely, it's partly the late hour that makes it taste so good. But hey, we'll take it. –SD

Freebirds World Burrito

The burritos aren't free, but there's freedom of choice

C Total pleasure grade

6.2 Food **3.9** Feel **$8** Price **Tex-Mex**

Fast-food chain
Sun.-Thurs. 11am-9:30pm;
Fri.-Sat. 11am-10:30pm.

Kid-friendly.
Vegetarian-friendly.

Upper Kirby
3745 Greenbriar St.
(713) 524-0621
www.freebirds.com

North Houston
6940 FM 1960 West
(281) 444-3336

Bar Beer only
Credit Cards Visa, MC, AmEx
Reservations Not accepted

Webster
528 W. Bay Area Blvd.
(281) 557-2300

Who knew that lair of maroon madness known as College Station could generate such burrito genius? Even the Longhorns in Austin—when Freebirds moved in there—quickly realized that it was worth swallowing their Aggie hatred for long enough to swallow a bite or two of those famous burritos.

The Freebirds burrito is a simple thing, made in the assembly-line style popularized by Subway, but decidedly better than fast food, and spiked with local flair. The formula: take an enormous tortilla (flour, wheat, cayenne, or spinach), stuff it to the bursting point with anything and everything (chicken, steak, or roast veggies, plus beans, pico de gallo, guacamole, jalapeños, cilantro, and so on), drench it in sauce, and then wrap the whole mess in a tidy aluminum package so that you can actually eat it without bringing a change of clothes.

This is more Tex than Mex, and it's not *good,* exactly, but it's not exactly *not* good, either: the taste is fresh, the toppings perky, the mood affable. Odd little aluminum-foil sculptures pop out of the walls for a peek (you can add your own creation when your aluminum wrap is done with its other duties), and a mad Statue of Liberty, having crashed through a wall, soars overhead on a motorcycle wielding a particularly large burrito. Freebirds is veggie-safe (they never use lard, which creeps silently into so many Tex-Mex dishes), but for carnivores, we recommend the steak burrito. Although the barbecue sauce is a signature option, skip it—it's too sour to complement the fillings.

Freebirds' burritos come in a variety of sizes, from the "half-bird," which is bigger than half a standard burrito and a good deal, to the "super monster," which weighs a pound and a half—and, in the right hands, well aimed, could take the legs out from under a large Longhorn (we're not naming names). –FC

If everything that went into a large burrito were placed on a plate without the tortilla, people wouldn't even try.

Freeway Hamburgers

C+
Total pleasure grade

Fantastic customer service makes up for forgettable burgers

6.5	7.1	$9
Food	*Feel*	*Price*

Burgers

Counter service
Mon.-Sat. 11am-9pm;
Sun. 11am-3pm.
Kid-friendly.

Memorial
8800 Katy Fwy.
(713) 468-4111

Bar None
Credit Cards Visa, MC, AmEx
Reservations Not accepted

In the old Southwell's Hamburgers spot, where the burger-mongers didn't ever even look you straight in the eye and would probably have rather left you for dead than given you any sort of customer service, Freeway Hamburgers and Grill served as a breath of fresh air for the Memorial area. The fair fare off the grill is well-intentioned, but never spectacular; rather, it's the owner's attitude toward guests that makes you want to come back, if only because you feel good about yourself for giving the guy some business.

Freeway didn't bother to do too much physical touching up after Southwell's moved out; they're still using the same wood-backed booths and small, rigid chairs and tables. But the newfound service mentality of the place was like a Cultural Revolution and Renaissance rolled into one. The owner never seems to remember names, but he also never forgets a face, always welcoming whoever walks through the door as if he or she were an old family friend. Even if the food isn't the best part of Freeway Hamburgers, its quick meals and smiling staff make it easy to not hesitate to come back.

The hamburgers, panini, and other sandwiches here at Freeway are more or less of the type that sort of make you shrug your shoulders and go, "eh." From the patty melt to the tried-and-true cheeseburger, the beef lacks enough caramelized, roasted meat flavor, probably because they don't let the meat sit on the grill for long enough on one side. Fries often need an extra shake of salt or two; seasoned fries are better, if hardly the best in the city. The double-pattied "Big Tex" burger seems to taste better and meatier than the other burgers, though most of it can be attributed to the novelty of eating two patties. It has even reached cult status amongst surrounding high school students, who enjoy trying to get their names on the wall for having eaten the most of them in one sitting.

When we look over at the owner and consider the smiling service once again, we have no problem eating at least one. –JY

Frenchy's Chicken

Feelgood fried chicken served with sass

A- *Total pleasure grade*

8.7 *Food* **6.5** *Feel* **$8** *Price* **Southern**

Counter service
Sun.-Thurs. 10:30am-1am;
Fri.-Sat. 10:30am-3am.
Date-friendly. Outdoor dining.

Downtown
3919 Scott St.
(713) 748-2233
www.frenchyschicken.com

Bar None
Credit Cards Visa, MC, AmEx
Reservations Not accepted

Additional locations
(at your own risk).

Southwest Houston
11631 Southwest Fwy.
(281) 495-4415

North Houston
757 W. Little York
(713) 691-1001

When it's on, this is some of the best fried chicken we've ever had. This is a very bold statement, but this is a very bold piece of chicken. There are multiple locations of Frenchy's Chicken around Houston, but be forewarned: the one by the University of Houston on Scott Street is the best of them all. It's a favorite of students and chick-o-philes alike. This is fast food, but it's local fast food with soul. It isn't commercialized with rules, regulations, corporate mission statements, and "diversity training"; it's just good, wholesome chicken that is fried to its crispy ideal and is to-the-point delicious.

Don't be scared away by this shack of a restaurant that looks like it could crumble at any minute; just place your order at the window, and hope the ladies are in a good mood that day. They're nice to you if you're nice to them, but if you have any attitude at all, then you will most certainly be put in your place.

The waits are sometimes long at Frenchy's, but be patient, because they pay off. Also, words to the wise: credit cards are only accepted for purchases of five dollars and up. Don't say we didn't warn you; remember, you don't want to make these ladies cross. Now that you've successfully ordered and gotten your food, get ready for the best part: the crispy, pleasantly spicy batter is the kind of thing that dreams are made of, and Cajun seasoning adds a nice kick. Thighs and drumsticks are best: juicy dark meat releases steam when the crusty exterior is cracked, filling the air with the aroma of poultry. Sides range from buttery biscuits to just-average french fries, which hardly do justice to the joint's name.

And we remind you again to stick with the Scott Street location, and avoid the other impostors around Houston, that call themselves "Frenchy's" by mere virtue, we imagine, of some back-room franchising deal that didn't seem to involve the exchange of recipes. These outlets have been commercialized with speed-ridden mascots and bright color schemes that will attempt to brainwash your children. If you know what's good for them, you'll take them to the real deal. –SD

FuFu Café

Total pleasure grade

Solid, casual Chinese fare in need of better service

7.1 Food | **4.0** Feel | **$10** Price | **Chinese**

Casual restaurant
Wed.-Mon. 11am-2am; closed Tues. *Kid-friendly. Vegetarian-friendly.*

Chinatown
9889 Bellaire Blvd.
(713) 981-8818

Bar None
Credit Cards No credit cards
Reservations Not accepted

While eating at FuFu Café, a pint-sized hole-in-a-shopping-center restaurant, something like this will probably begin ringing in your head: "Can you hear me now? No? Can you here me *now*? Can a man get some service over here?"

Perhaps FuFu is still suffering from the effects of the customer barrage that followed from certain positive reviews in the press, or perhaps all of Houston has suddenly developed an irrepressible craving for soup dumplings. Whatever the reasons, Fufu Café is up to its gills in customers without the space or the staff to serve them, even if the food remains above average.

It would probably help if FuFu were not totally devoid of any sort of atmosphere whatsoever, so you could at least look at something while you're waiting for your food to come, but we can forgive this: the management probably never imagined it would come to be considered Houston's leading provider of xiao long bao (Chinese soup dumplings). These little packages are filled with warm soup and flavorful meat, rendering them a bit of a novelty food item, albeit a tasty novelty food item. With the media anointment of FuFu as *the* place to go for these popular little dumplings, the waitstaff looks almost timid and afraid to serve at times, looking straight down to avoid the vicious stares of people who've been sitting at their table for thirty minutes without their food. It's hard not to feel sorry for them, unless you're doubling over from hunger pains.

Once you finally do get your food, Fufu is easy to like. It's equally well suited to a simple lunch or a late-night alcohol sopper. The ma po tofu, tastefully oily green beans stir-fried with ground pork, is fiery, but full of flavor—a treat if you're into the burn-your-mouth sort of dish. Pan-fried pork dumplings are cooked just right, with a liberal saltiness mixed in with the crusty, seared underbelly of the dumpling. Try the xiao long bao too, but skip most of the lunch specials, as they're normally run-of-the-mill dishes that are only there for the looks. Otherwise, though, if FuFu Café could get a grip on the service, it could really shine. –JY

Fung's Kitchen

Confucius says: stop aiming for class and be more consistent

A-
Total pleasure grade

8.6 *Food* **7.8** *Feel* **$46** *Price*

Chinese, Seafood

Upmarket restaurant
Sun.-Thurs. 10:30am-10pm;
Fri.-Sat. 10:30am-11pm.
Date-friendly. Vegetarian-friendly.

Chinatown
7320 Southwest Fwy.
(713) 779-2288
www.fungskitchen.com.

Bar Wine and beer only
Credit Cards Visa, MC, AmEx
Reservations Accepted

Fung's Kitchen serves Houston's best Chinese food. Well, sometimes. And, well, only if you're willing to pay for it. While there's an argument to be made for more affordable restaurants with homier food, it's like comparing a Michelin-starred restaurant with your good ol' mom-and-pop place: while how *good* Fung's Kitchen is can always be debated, it can't be denied that the place is the *finest* strictly Chinese restaurant in Houston, and if you want to put up the money, you can have a spectacular meal here.

While most Chinese restaurants budget for decorating about as much as a blind man, Fung's Kitchen's gleaming marble tiles and live seafood display defy most stereotypes about dirtiness and dinginess. That's not to say that it's tasteful, though; its huge running waterfall, self-important awnings, and over-the-top regal interior seem more suited to a state banquet than a relaxing dinner. Not so for the service: most of the waitstaff—minus the lovely owner, who always seems to be covering for them—pay little attention to tables.

When kitchen is on, the Chinese food at Fung's is second to none in Houston. The cuisine is as freewheeling as the streets of Hong Kong, with the chef at times shunning the expected tradition of Chinese cuisine in favor of new techniques. A visit to dim sum one day yielded a lotus leaf-wrapped package of kudzu starch and red beans, which was sweet with the taste of a good tea. Presentation is not an afterthought: a body-warming bitter-melon-and-pork soup came in a hollowed-out gourd with Chinese characters carved into its side. Live seafood is sourced well, with Maine lobsters and Alaskan king crabs, and the flavors show through.

The kitchen's rough spots are very annoying, though, given how much they charge. Fish can come out over-steamed, more mushy than tender. And you shouldn't expect much more than average from the restaurant's traditional cuisine, like simple stir-fried vegetables or noodles. But you know better than that, right?

Going to Fung's and ordering noodles would be like going to New England to try the Tex-Mex. –JY

Fuzzy's

An old sports favorite that still serves good pizza, though with some attitude

C *Total pleasure grade*

6.2 *Food* **3.5** *Feel* **$12** *Price* **Pizza**

Counter service
Sun.-Thurs. 11am-10pm;
Fri.-Sat. 11am-11pm.
Delivery. Kid-friendly.
Outdoor dining.

Westchase
2727 Fondren Rd.
(713) 787-5200
www.fuzzyspizzafondren.com

Memorial
823 Antoine Rd.
(713) 682-8836

Bar Wine and beer only
Credit Cards Visa, MC, AmEx
Reservations Accepted

Back in the day, Fuzzy's was the home base for Houston sports fans, a place where they could loosen their ties and enjoy the game. One would have been hard-pressed to go during a game and not find a whole bunch of hootin', hollerin', half-drunk, pizza-in-hand carousers. Fuzzy's serves a fine American-style pizza, and still has the biggest televisions around; we can only attribute the thinning crowds these days to an uncaring, how-can-you-help-me staff with little flexibility and a bad attitude.

If it weren't for the wafting smells of baking crusts and Italian sausage, you'd assume yourself to be in your everyday sports bar, with nothing but bar snacks on offer. The main lighting comes from the neon wattage of the beer signs, and the rest comes from the comforting glow of the televisions. During peak hours, the line at Fuzzy's gets long and the waits even longer. Don't even consider complaining about how long you've been waiting, unless you want a huffy cashier to add to the fun.

Sour service normally brings sour food, but not here: the food at Fuzzy's is solid. The best of the menu is a mile-high tossed salad that looks like it has an entire garden of vegetables in it, and a pizza. Soggy crusts and over-sweetened sauces are normally a problem for American-style pizza, but at Fuzzy's, the crust is dense enough to hold the large pile of toppings; its edge double as a breadstick, and the tomato sauce isn't bad, either. Specialty combination pizzas are safe bets—save for the two Bush family contributions: both George (not dubya) and Barbara have namesake pizzas here, each displaying a penchant for artichokes. (No broccoli, though.) Unfortunately, the artichokes have that overwhelmingly briny, tinned-like taste. We've had waitstaff not honor our requests for a pizza split between two toppings, although the restaurant denies that this policy exists. Whether this was done out of pure laziness, or because Fuzzy's doesn't have the business sense to charge more for such a pie, there are clearly—as a consultant might say—"management issues" here. Even if the food-and-sports reputation is still well deserved, it might be time for a hostile takeover.
–JY

Garson

If it ain't broke, don't fix it

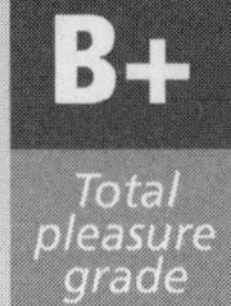

7.5	8.6	$29
Food	Feel	Price

Middle Eastern

Casual restaurant
Daily 11am-9:30pm.

Hillcroft Area
2926 Hillcroft St.
(713) 781-0400

Bar BYO
Credit Cards Visa, MC, AmEx
Reservations Accepted

We sometimes need to take a step back and realize how spoiled we are living in Houston. So many great, authentic, regional cuisines are all in easy reach here, especially along this wonderful strip of Hillcroft, where you'll find stores selling saris, halal meat markets, and the random Colombian bakery. For a sampling of Iranian cuisine, come to Garson, a casual and traditional Persian restaurant that educates and feeds Houston with delicious stews of braised meats and the light, acidic flavors of yogurt and hummus. Kebabs, braised lamb, and stew with lentils are just a few of the numerous fresh menu items. Go on a good night (generally a weekend) and you might even catch some belly dancing.

You can't miss this place; there's a huge sign out front with the name of the place in big caps. Although the atmosphere is inviting and comfortable, the service can be hit-or-miss. An easily flustered waitstaff can't deal with the place if it's really busy, although they're up to the task when the crowd is only moderate. And if it's dead, they'll be nearly flawless. The food, on the other hand, is far more consistent no matter how busy the place is.

Crispy-bottomed flatbread is served with feta cheese and parsley to start your meal. Stews are the stars of the menu, no matter the season. The braised lamb shank is wonderfully tender, with a pleasantly gamey flavor that is accented with seasonings like cinnamon and coriander; don't forget to dig out the bone marrow for a palate cleanser. Other stew ingredients are beef, lentils, greens, and kidney beans, along with a few more unexpected treats that we'll leave you to discover for yourself. Garson displays an uncommon talent with non-stewed meat, too.

Persian teas and yogurt drinks are offered to accompany the meal. Desserts are pretty disappointing; there are no real Persian sweets, even if the rest of the menu is refreshingly authentic. A BYO policy is enticing—you'll have some fun pairing wines with your stews. There is no shortage of parking here: there's plenty of space for Houston's famous SUV population. –SD

Glass Wall

Total pleasure grade

Glass, smoke, mirrors, and tildes: meet the dark side of Heights hip, html and all

6.0 *Food* **5.8** *Feel* **$78** *Price* **New American**

Upmarket restaurant
Tues.-Sat. 5:30pm-10pm; closed Sun.-Mon.
Outdoor dining.

Heights
933 Studewood St.
(713) 868-7930
www.glasswalltherestaurant.com

Bar Full
Credit Cards Visa, MC, AmEx
Reservations Essential

Even the menu of this Heights restaurant screams "yupped-out:" it's done entirely in lower case, with tildes and slashes to give it an HTML sort of feel. The interior, too, makes you think of the tech boom (as does all the money in the room): an open kitchen, avant-garde columns, and enormous linen curtains angled across the ceiling like a tarpaulin descending over the dining room. The environment is jovial, though, with warm yellow walls and a loud buzz. If you don't mind sitting amidst a lot of 328i-driving-twentysomething first dates, you'll probably get a kick out of it. (If that describes you, try to avoid the unromantic middle tables and get something along the edges. And speaking of BMWs, go valet; the local neighbors may kick your ass if you park on their streets.)

The kitchen's artfully presented handiwork changes seasonally, so don't bet on finding the same pretentiously named dishes we have sampled: the "duck tart~spinach~manchego~pinenuts~piperade," for example, is smoky duck leg meat and stringy spinach on a buttery Southern biscuit with an incoherent roasted red pepper sauce, none of it even lukewarm. Slightly more successful, if underseasoned, has been a "risotto~mushrooms~dry ricotta~leek~tarragon pesto" in which leek was the only prominent flavor.

A fatty, deliciously seasoned "ribeye~arugula/blue cheese salad~potato crisps~beet/apple jam ribeye" came with perhaps a few too many subdirectories; the blue cheese and jam were good ideas, but sweet potatoes were superfluous and shoestring potatoes just an unexciting crunch. Ironic given chef/co-owner Lance Fegen's claim that his menu is an "homage to his other life as a surfer" and "inspired by the natural lifestyle of coastal regions" was the appearance, on one dish, of a root vegetable called romanesco—a genetic hybrid of broccoli and cauliflower with the benefits of each, also known as "fractal broccoli." It's neither natural nor coastal, but it's also one of the most interesting things we've tried at Glass Wall, beautifully and simply prepared with lemon zest and parsley. And for dessert, delicious cobblers overshadow their precursors, rescuing Glass Wall from being dismissed as a total waste of money, pomp, and valet. –RG

The Golden Room

25 years strong and the service is still the only reason to come

5.9 *Food* **7.9** *Feel* **$24** *Price* **Thai**

Casual restaurant
Mon.-Thurs. 11:30am-2:30pm, 5pm-9:30pm; Fri. 11:30am-2:30pm, 5pm-10:30pm; Sat. 5pm-10:30pm; closed Sun.
Date-friendly.

Montrose
1209 Montrose Blvd.
(713) 524-9614

Bar Wine and beer only
Credit Cards Visa, MC, AmEx
Reservations Accepted

There's something about the service at The Golden Room that makes you overlook the fact that the food really isn't that good. It's like the heartfelt, well-meaning look your mother gives you when she puts down a plate: the feeling is so intoxicating, like a drug, that you can't help but enjoy your meal, even if it's Shake n' Bake and Rice-a-Roni. In that sense, for more than 25 years, the Golden Room staff has been drugging people.

The restaurant is set in a small house, and you're guaranteed to be greeted like a houseguest—even though there are only a few waiters, someone usually comes running to the door at the sound of a car pulling up outside. The escorted route to your table will then take you through what feels like someone's ornate, Southeast Asian-derived living room. The walls are a faded, dark gold, and much of the furniture feels like it was recycled from an old house, too. Unsurprisingly, a good portion of the customers are return visitors.

If this were any other restaurant or any other staff, The Golden Room probably wouldn't have lasted 25 years, because the food on its own doesn't taste like anything special. Mee krob, which is supposed to be a fragrant, textured fried-rice-noodle concoction with sweet tamarind sauce, turns out far too sugary, with the sauce tasting more like that red sweet-and-sour sauce from Chinese take-out places; bean sprouts and green onions contribute nil. Pad Thai noodles are more of an American craze than a Thai one—they do exist in Thailand, where they're generally topped with an omelet—but this rendition is exceptionally dry, and lacking much peanutty flavor.

Thai flavors are more apparent in the salads like the yum pla muk, which combines sour lime and aromatic basil flavors with refreshing cucumber and charred squid, but overall the menu has more under-achieving dishes than most. And yet, even after a so-so meal, the send-off is so gracious, so endlessly hospitable, with the smiling and waving that you'd expect might accompany an extended-family reunion, that it won't just allow you to forgive the kitchen's trespasses—it will actually bring you back. –JY

Goode Co. Taquería

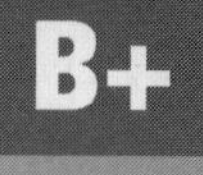

Total pleasure grade

The mesquite does Goode work at this character-less joint

8.2 *Food* **4.4** *Feel* **$16** *Price*

Tex-Mex, Burgers

Counter service
Daily 11am-10pm.
Kid-friendly. Outdoor dining.

West U
5109 Kirby Dr.
(713) 522-2530
www.goodecompany.com

Spring Branch
8911 Katy Fwy.
(713) 464-1901

Bar Wine and beer only
Credit Cards Visa, MC, AmEx
Reservations Not accepted

First things first: the Goode Company Taquería, whose kitchen is dominated by the mesquite grill, deserves serious praise within the Houston Tex-Mex universe for keeping the menu to such a manageable number of options. Coming off the mesquite-burning fire are deliciously marinated, tender, but undersalted fajitas, which come on plates or in tacos; chicken breast, dry and bland compared to other meats, but still grill-kissed; plus ribeye, pork chops, and even quail—a rare delicacy in the rest of the world but a mainstay in Houston Tex-Mex.

In a city overflowing with mediocre queso—at least vis-à-vis Austin and San Antonio—Goode Company's is decent, with a lot of seasoning, though it smacks slightly of the nacho cheese in Combos and develops a thick skin after only about fifteen seconds of neglect. Burgers are more flavorful than most around, taking on quite a bit of mesquite. At the toppings bar, you can pile on such sensory counterpoints to the meat as jalapeños, pico de gallo, and a delicious, dark roasted-tomato salsa, in addition to the standard lettuce, tomato, mayonnaise, and so on. It all makes for a burger well above the local average. Here, the mesquite grill proves itself not just powerful but versatile.

There's also a full breakfast served on weekends, including eggs with quail or venison sausage, but sadly, it shuts down at 12:30pm, shutting out the party crowd to whom it might otherwise hold vast hangover-cure appeal. Frozen margaritas are strong and well balanced, although the plastic-cup presentation takes away from the effect (there's something not that fun about licking salt off of plastic). Service is cafeteria-style, in the great Houston tradition; as such, the atmosphere is what it is. No romantic Tex-Mex cantina this; the characteristic Goode Company theming, which here takes on the form of neon signs and contrived hand-painted menus, is drowned out by all the open space, and the Taquería basically winds up feeling like a big, empty Tex-Mex warehouse—but one with a great mesquite grill whose luscious burning scents waft through the airy space even at the loneliest of hours. –RG

Goode Co. Bar-B-Q

An overrated reminder of how far Houston lags behind Central Texas in the Lone Star BBQ wars

C- *Total pleasure grade*

4.5 *Food* **3.2** *Feel* **$14** *Price* **Barbecue**

Counter service
Mon.-Thurs. 11am-10pm;
Fri.-Sun. 10:30am-10pm.
Delivery. Kid-friendly.
Outdoor dining.

West U
4902 Kirby Dr.
(713) 520-9153
www.goodecompany.com

Bar Wine and beer only
Credit Cards Visa, MC, AmEx
Reservations Not accepted

This set of highly touted barbecue siblings is full of boasts, from the self-congratulatory wall paraphernalia to the overuse of the Copperplate Gothic font to the larger-than-life banner of long-bearded Jim Goode, "still at the reins" since 1977.

Perhaps unsurprisingly given its Houston location, Goode Company does not live up to the hype. The best options are the unusually moist smoked chicken, with a peppery skin that's fun to eat, and jalapeño pork sausage, which is juicy and full flavored, if not the least bit spicy. But beef brisket, a dish you'd expect to be good at a place whose motto reminds you to "thank your lucky stars you're in Texas"—lacks flavor, even when ordered fatty; this stuff wouldn't fly in central Texas. Pork ribs, too, are merely serviceable.

Goode's barbecue sauce is spooned on stingily by the indifferent staff, but you might not mind, because it's not very good. The sauce is mild, sweet, and tomato-forward—more like a jarred pasta sauce than an acidic balance for the meat—and lacks salt. Sides, too, cry out in a sodium-deprived chorus. It's amazing that so many sides in one buffet could be undersalted, from overly eggy but okay potato salad to liquidy pinto beans to dry jambalaya to boring cole slaw.

As for the experience, we don't expect much out of counter-service bar-b-queue, but still, we expect basic politeness, or at least a willingness to tell you what is and is not available. The Goode Company staff fails to deliver even on these basics. Sidle up to the line and you might be treated like a criminal for being there; you could dismiss this as quirky charm, perhaps, at a world-class destination joint, or at a dirt-cheap hole-in-the-wall, but not at a just-okay place whose marketing concessions include a line of (those same bland) barbecue sauces and a glossy catalog.

And that might just sum it up: underneath all the Texana, and tattered-chic attitude lies a barbecue restaurant that is not nearly as good as it thinks it is. –RG

Goode Co. Seafood

B+ *Total pleasure grade*

Canned kitsch and surprisingly good fish in a done-up diner

8.3 *Food* **5.7** *Feel* **$40** *Price* **Seafood**

Casual restaurant
Sun.-Thurs. 11am-10pm;
Fri.-Sat. 11am-11pm.

West U
2621 Westpark Dr.
(713) 523-7154
www.goodecompany.com

Memorial
10211 Katy Fwy.
(713) 464-7933

Bar Full
Credit Cards Visa, MC, AmEx
Reservations Not accepted

Each of Jim Goode's restaurants is themed in its own way, but the common motif is the carefully synthesized aura of an age-old local institution. This one opened its doors in the 1980s, but the décor would have you believe it's been around for the better part of a century: black-and-white fishing photos and hand-painted signs bearing paternalistic messages like "FOOD'S BEST JUST WHEN IT'S COOKED; We Serve Each Plate When It's Ready" (maybe that's why appetizers come out with mains). Then there are gracious comments like "High-Back Chairs Are Reserved For Patrons Wishing to Dine at the Counter. Thanks, Jim." Is this there to insinuate that Sir Jim himself is still running the kitchen? To remind us how lucky we are to have a seat? Or just to sound rude, because that's supposed to be part of a local institution's quirky charm?

In spite of what the trying-too-hard signage might suggest, the staff is perfectly friendly, and the train-car-diner interior is otherwise cute. You can sidle up to the long counter for fresh oysters, sway to the blues, and enjoy the bustle during the lunch or dinner rush. Best of all, and perhaps surprisingly, this is one of Houston's better places for fried fish: oysters, catfish, and flounder are done not a minute too much or too little, locking in moisture and crusting the fish beautifully, although an extra shake of salt is generally needed.

Po' boys—a much better deal than platters, at about half the cost—are excellent, with judiciously toasted French bread absorbing well-integrated lettuce, tomatoes, and mayo. Grilled redfish and shrimp are almost as good, with mesquite fire donating black notes of wood and smoke yet leaving the fish moist. Seafood "pies" (also called "empanadas" as a smaller platter accoutrement) are stuffed with a well-seasoned gumbo-like stew. Other sides fare less well: seafood rice and garlic bread are both dry and tasteless. But Goode's highly-(self-) touted pecan pie is hard to argue with. It's made with larger-than-normal pecans and softer-than-normal goo, so the thing's structural integrity disintegrates after the first bite. Your palate won't care. –RG

Gorditas Aguascalientes

A traditional Mexican restaurant with a motherly touch

A- Total pleasure grade

9.0 Food **6.1** Feel **$9** Price **Mexican**

Casual restaurant
Mon. noon-3am.; Tues.-Sat. 7am-3am; Sun. 7am-midnight.
Breakfast. Brunch.

Bellaire
6102 Bissonnet St.
(713) 541-4560

Heights
4721 N. Main
(713) 863-9915

Bar Wine and beer only
Credit Cards Visa, MC, AmEx
Reservations Not accepted

After a good meal, you should feel energized, satisfied, and happy. This authentic Mexican kitchen will get you there with its lovely renditions of not just gorditas, but also tacos, sopes, and even hard-to-come-by huaraches, which are like griddled masa pizzas stacked high with toppings, so named for their sandal-like shape. All of it is done with a motherly touch: the kitchen staff is almost entirely comprised of women, which would hardly be a surprise in Mexico, but it's a pleasant one in Houston. (Although within these walls, you're more in Mexico than you are to Houston.) You can taste soul, tradition, and—we dare say—femininity in each of these dishes.

Gorditas Aguascalientes is not yet the go-to regional Mexican shop for most Houstonians, but it's getting there. Obviously they're doing something right, because both locations are graced with a steady human flow all day long. The Bellaire outpost delivers flavor through the vibe, too, with Banda playing on the jukebox, pictures of mothers cooking for their families cluttering the walls, and clay pots hung at odd angles. Lunch is when Gorditas Aguascalientes is in full swing; great specials hover around four dollars, while for a bit more you can get a deliciously sizzling platter of onion-laced fajitas (a Tex-Mex detour on this menu, perhaps, although you'll see Mex-Mex customers ordering them, too). Other lunch specials—flautas, carne guisada, and so on—are also shockingly cheap and consistently satisfying. Do try to go at the tail end of lunch to miss the crowd; you don't want to be harried as you eat.

The produce at the front of the restaurant is worth a look. And you must, of course, try the gorditas. Stuffed with nopales (cactus), chicharrón (pork rinds), or shredded beef, they come with lettuce and a spicy salsa to add to the mix within; they're a great taste of Mexico. Gorditas Aguascalientes also serves one of the biggest bowls of soup we've ever seen; even the small size is enough for two. Every day—not just on weekends—menudo, pozole, and different caldos are served, in yet another authentic corner of this menu. Service is friendly and happens—just as authentically—in Spanish. By this point, you'll expect it; you might even find English a bit jarring. –SD

Grand Lux Café

A generic Cheesecake Factory offshoot specializing in baked desserts and doggie bags

Total pleasure grade

6.2 Food | **7.4** Feel | **$28** Price | **American**

Casual restaurant
Mon.-Thurs. 11am-11pm;
Fri.-Sat. 11am-midnight;
Sun. 10am-11pm.
Brunch. Kid-friendly. Outdoor dining. Vegetarian-friendly.

Galleria
5000 Westheimer Rd.
(713) 626-1700
www.grandluxcafe.com

Bar Full
Credit Cards Visa, MC, AmEx
Reservations Not accepted

It may be the atmosphere, which has an ebb and flow like Grand Central Station. It could be the uniformly garbed army of a staff, who are more cheery than caffeinated kindergarten teachers. It might be the fact that the portions are huge, and the flavors of food are elementary. But somehow, Grand Lux Café almost seems like it belongs in a shopping center; it's a place where there is something for everyone—except anyone who really cares about quality or execution.

Grand Lux Café is smack in the middle of the road. The place is not slummy, but it's not nice. It's not cheap, but it's not that expensive. The service isn't horrendous, but it's never really good either. Nothing on the menu is terrible, but there aren't items that you would go back for. A great example of this is chicken, which seems to be on—or can be added to—more than half of the menu. Sandwiches, pastas, mains…the list is endless. And it all tastes like chicken. Grilled chicken, at that. Which tastes like nothing at all.

One thing you can count on though is that you'll get your food, and you'll get a lot of it. The food is more Asian-tinged than its Cheesecake counterpart, and both seem to play by the rule that you can make anything taste good if you slather it in butter, or sauce, or both. A mains-sized appetizer of chicken lettuce wraps—surprisingly one of the better dishes at Grand Lux—has three different sauces, which you can mix and match with cilantro, carrots, fried noodles, and peanuts; you may get so distracted amusing yourself that you won't even notice how the underlying protein tastes. (Hint: it tastes like chicken.) Baked-to-order desserts are a star, like a warm, rustic, comforting, and delicious apple pie; but the size of the sweets often leave you walking out of the restaurant on an extreme sugar high, disgustingly stuffed, and with a five-pound to-go bag in hand. Shopping center, indeed. At least you know you don't have far to walk. –JY

> If we want everything to taste like chicken, then why do we so often make our chicken taste like nothing?

Grappino di Nino

Total pleasure grade

An Italian-American 2.0 wine bar that's stuck in the endless past

5.4 Food **6.6** Feel **$36** Price **Italian-American**

Upmarket restaurant
Mon.-Sat. 3:45pm-11pm; closed Sun.
Live music. Outdoor dining. Vegetarian-friendly.

River Oaks
2817 W. Dallas St.
(713) 528-7002
www.ninos-vincents.com

Bar Full
Credit Cards Visa, MC, AmEx
Reservations Not accepted

Our award for the worst service in Houston goes to (drum roll, fiddle with the envelope, pretend we don't know who won)...Grappino de Nino. We would like to thank the fifteen minutes it took for our waiter to acknowledge us at our last visit, the wrong order delivered with a fake smile, and the disappearance of any signs of human life at thirty-minute intervals. Keep up the good work. We don't have the space to go through the entire list of our grievances with Grappino de Nino, nor do we want to bore our readers.

So, a bit about the place, then: Grappino de Nino is a spawn of another Mandola spawn that serves pretty good Italian food—that is, if you consider Prego to be pretty good. It's the most casual branch of a trio of restaurants that share a garden, and similar homey, family-oriented, country-Italian décor that's cheesy but fun; this is the so-called "wine bar" counterpart to Nino's and Vincent's.

The atmosphere is the best thing these places have going for them; too bad the atmosphere can't cook our food. You might start with the classically overplayed, underwhelming bruschetta, or tough crab claws with lemon butter and garlic, before moving onto overcooked, unsatisfying pasta. Grilled salmon might be good if the fish had any decent flavor, because the artichoke, crabmeat, and roasted-red-pepper sauce, though over-complicated, tastes good. On the other hand, we do like a wood-roasted chicken with rosemary potatoes and panzanella salad—the moist chicken is a deservedly renowned Mandola forte in which the leg and thigh wisely upstage the dreaded breast.

In the end, though, this is a pretty disappointing restaurant with bad service and food that does nothing out of the ordinary. It does seem that Grappino de Nino wants to be a serious Italian restaurant, yet it's stuck in that classic mindset that has, over the past few decades, brainwashed everyday Americans into thinking that what we call "Italian-American 2.0" (see pages 6-7 for the definition)—from Caesar salad to seafood-and-mushroom cannelloni, from grilled shrimp over "angel hair marinara" and spinach to sautéed veal with artichoke hearts, lemon butter, and fettucine alfredo—are in any way Italian. Why can't we just take credit for our own cuisine, and call it American? –SD

Gravitas

A refined American bistro where substance meets style

9.0 Food | **9.1** Feel | **$72** Price | **New American**

Upmarket restaurant
Mon.-Thurs. 11am-10:30pm;
Fri.-Sat. 11am-11:30pm;
Sun. 10:30am-9:30pm.
Brunch. Date-friendly.
Outdoor dining.
Vegetarian-friendly.

Midtown
807 Taft St.
(713) 522-0995
www.gravitasrestaurant.com

Bar Full
Credit Cards Visa, MC, AmEx
Reservations Recommended

With creaking wooden floors, minimalist design, and—somehow—a comfortable, hearth-filled ambience in such a wide open space, Gravitas resonates with a rustic yet stylish motif. The food follows suit with updated twists on traditional bistro fare that favors the less-is-more attitude.

It's hard to consider this as a true bistro. Whereas you expect a traditional bistro to be filled with simple soul, Gravitas resonates with trend and style—and prices to match. But food is hard to deny: most dishes are simple and fantastic, and you'd be hard-pressed to find anywhere else in Houston where you could eat cordon bleu while still feeling sexy.

Gravitas is a chef-driven restaurant with a seasonal menu headed by super-chefs Scott Tycer and Jason Gould. There is no mind-blowing, creative genius that goes into the menu, but the Gravitas chefs don't hold back, serving versions of old bistro standbys like a pan-seared calves' liver—rich, yet still light enough to be an appetizer because of a twang of acid to cut it—and beef tartare, a smack in the mouth with every bite of beef, shallot, mustard, and tarragon. Appetizers and pastas strike a high chord, with the pastas being the highlights. Lush buttermilk pierogis are bathed in brown butter, contrasting with a combination of cream cheese and buttermilk; you'll only wish they'd given you more than the six or seven units. Mains, on the other hand, sometimes suffer from too much restraint. None of them are bad, and virtually all are expertly executed, but dishes like steak frites and trout almondine can seem boring compared to the surroundings. Desserts are well thought out, with most on the lighter side to contrast the heavier main meal, but that same slight boredom can come into play. A fluffy, not-too-sweet berry clafoutis (made with pancake-like batter), though, is a hit.

One bone we have to pick with Gravitas is their wine program. Though the list is exceptional, including hard-to-find California producers like A. Rafanelli, the markups are not reasonable at all. That aside, the simple and well-executed menu will still keep us regulars here. –JY

The Grotto

Is this what happens to artichokes when they're Landryified?

D *Total pleasure grade*

3.8 *Food* **7.3** *Feel* **$55** *Price*

Italian-American

Upmarket restaurant
Sun.-Mon. 11am-10pm; Tues.-Thurs. 11am-11pm; Fri.-Sat. 11am-midnight; Sun. 11am-10pm.

Galleria
4715 Westheimer Rd.
(713) 622-3663
www.grottohouston.com

Bar Full
Credit Cards Visa, MC, AmEx
Reservations Accepted

There are plenty of bad dishes in Houston. But the Grotto's artichokes might be the worst of all. The last time we ordered this appetizer, it couldn't actually be chewed and swallowed. The inedible outer leaves of the large artichoke had not been removed before the thing was stuffed and sautéed whole. You chew and chew, it doesn't break down, and you eventually have no choice but to spit it out, which isn't so classy in River Oaks/Galleria circles. If you're not adept with the discreet-spit-in-the-cloth-napkin move, you can always try to hold it in your mouth and fake a trip to the bathroom. But how, then, do you excuse yourself politely with your mouth full of food? Our recommendation is to stash the chewed leaves between teeth and cheek, like chewing tobacco, and feign a mild speech impediment.

We're not sure why the Grotto claims to serve "Neapolitan" cuisine—this is straight-up Italian-American—but the place competes with La Griglia, its Landry's sister (both were bought from Vallone in the early '90s), for the title of most dramatically soaring faux-terra-cotta ceiling in the city. The centerpieces are a big, wood-burning pizza oven with a copper chimney rising to the ceiling, and a set of plate-glass windows revealing the kitchen to onlookers. Colorfully bizarre murals of Italian scenes complete the scene, which buzzes on most nights.

Unfortunately, the antipasto problems don't end with that artichoke train wreck. The house antipasto spread might include mouth-puckering, ice-cold spinach with minced garlic; soggy, tasteless breaded and fried cauliflower; and grilled vegetables marinated in one-dimensional vinaigrettes. Some pastas are a positive diversion—especially well-textured homemade pappardelle, which is great in its simplest preparations, like cacio e pepe, with grated cheese and a lot of black pepper. Fine, too, is vitello alla valdostana, a thin veal cutlet with melted cheese, mushrooms, and a well-reduced, not-too-sweet mushroom marsala sauce. But many other sauces fall flat—especially the ones with grilled chicken—and the foofy cakes and other desserts that roll over on a cart are too much to handle after the enormous portions. Then again, if you've started with those artichokes, you'll have probably burned extra calories from all the chewing. –RG

Guadalajara

One of the good guys in the Tex-Mex scene, with the fajitas and fonts to prove it

B+ *Total pleasure grade*

8.5 *Food* **7.7** *Feel* **$34** *Price* **Tex-Mex**

Casual restaurant
Sun.-Thurs. 11am-10pm;
Fri.-Sat. 11am-11pm.

Brunch. Delivery.
Kid-friendly. Outdoor dining.

Memorial
9799 Katy Fwy.
(713) 461-5300
www.guadalajarahacienda.com

Greenway Plaza
2925 Southwest Fwy.
(713) 942-0772

Bar Full
Credit Cards Visa, MC, AmEx
Reservations Not accepted

Woodlands
27885 IH 45 North
(281) 362-0774

Given the striking similarities between the décor, menu, and clientele of so many Tex-Mex restaurants, it can be easy to assume that they're all created equal. That assumption couldn't be farther from the truth: for every two seemingly identical restaurants, with sombreros and Corona paraphernalia lining the walls and a "Cadillac" or "top-shelf" margarita on the menu, one of them is probably brilliant—with careful comfort-food execution—and the other terrible, with dried-out, flavorless meats filling crackly tortillas topped by insipid salsa and congealing cheese. Tex-Mex is more challenging than a lot of restaurateurs seem to think.

The people behind Guadalajara, on the other hand, take that challenge quite seriously. Few places in town execute Tex-Mex this comfortably and this consistently, with so many unexpected winners amongst a broad range of dishes (and the Friday and Saturday night crowds know it—expect a wait). It is also one of the few places in town where chicken breast—here, because of its smoke-kissed flavor—is not a bad thing to order, where refried beans become platforms for pork fat, where even chips and salsa are better-textured and more complex than you expect them to be, and where the marinade for fajitas is so intense that you almost wish it imparted *less* fruity complexity than it does.

The "Guadalajara enchilada" is a delicious creation, with a "roasted corn" salsa that has a buttery, creamy goodness whose deep appeal is almost impossible to explain. The dryish shredded chicken within, meanwhile—normally a recipe for disaster—takes on the unexpected flavor of wood fire. Queso, tamales, and tortillas perform as well as or better than expected, too.

We're befuddled by the aesthetic: why has a three-branch local restaurant group in Houston adopted over-the-top, Disneyish fonting and a menu with the graphic-design look of a Chili's, creating the illusion that it's a huge chain when it's really just a three-branch Houston institution? At least the space works—it's got that faux-hacienda look, which works pretty well as escapism when the room is full of people (when it's not, it just feels depressing). At the Greenway Plaza branch, a pleasant patio stands ready to take you away from the "neighborhood," which consists basically of the swish and zoom of a massive highway. Gotta love the urban planning. –RG

Guy's Meat Market

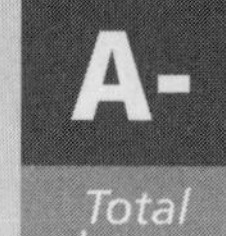

Total pleasure grade

High demand, limited hours, smoke that penetrates car doors...it must be good, and it is

8.5 Food **8.5** Feel **$8** Price

Barbecue, Burgers

Counter service
Tues.-Fri. 9am-5:30pm;
Sat. 9am-3:30pm;
closed Sun.-Mon.

Medical Center
3106 Old Spanish Trail
(713) 747-6800
www.guysseasoning.com

Bar Beer only
Credit Cards Visa, MC, AmEx
Reservations Not accepted

Creativity has taken on a different form at an unassuming meat market in the Medical Center. No extra adjectives on the menu, no neatly folded napkins, and no self-obsessed chef. None of that jazz—just meat, smoke, and seasoning, coming together to make a smoked hamburger. This is one of the greatest culinary creations of our city; it must be humbling for some of Houston's chef-driven restaurants to come here and find themselves one-upped by a meat market. Unsurprisingly, they run out of these burgers every day, leaving Houstonians hungry for more.

Pulling up to Guy's you can smell the smoke through the car door, making your car smell like the erotic aromas of smoldering wood and meat. Not only is Guy's known for their "BBQ Burger," but also for house-made sausage with various fillings, and for good ol' Texas barbecue. Walking in, the faint haze of smoke deludes you into thinking that either this is hamburger heaven or the depths of Hell. We'll take Hell if it smells and tastes like this.

The mad rush for the BBQ Burger begins at 11am and ends at 1pm. There is no guarantee that you get one if you show up after noon, though, because they'll sometimes sell out in an hour. Two hundred half-pound patties are smoked each day, with no intention of producing any more, so the mystery and mystique remain firm; the creation of artificial shortage is a great marketing gimmick. These burgers stay juicy, and the smoke gives such a unique flavor that you would swear you're eating something else. Given the demand and shortage, it's surprising they keep the price so low; at press time, it was $4.38 for a burger. So enjoy yourself, and let the moment take you away. The regular barbecue (brisket, ribs, sausage) is more hit-or-miss, but jalapeño sausage, with a pleasantly burning flavor in the back of your mouth, is seasoned well and smoked beautifully. You won't find fancy plates with fifteen garnishes here. This is a meat market, and you are a Neanderthal. Get your food, then go devour it. –SD

Harlon's Barbecue

Just what you imagined succulent, fatty, flavorful barbecue could be

Total pleasure grade

7.8	8.4	$10	Barbecue
Food	Feel	Price	

Counter service Mon.-Sat. 10am-9pm; Sun. 11am-6pm.	*North Houston* 5404 Alameda Rd. (713) 533-1230 www.harlonsbbq.com	*Bar* Beer only *Credit Cards* Visa, MC, AmEx *Reservations* Accepted
Additional locations.	*Southeast Houston* 6930 Martin Luther King (713) 733-5687	*Galleria* 5085 Westheimer (713) 629-0447

Sadly, more people have probably heard of Harlon's because they've seen the dumbed-down outposts at Hobby and Intercontinental Airports than because of the humble, well established smokehouse on MLK in Southeast Houston, which has been feeding the city for more than thirty years now. The original location was in a converted service station. Known for their ribs and house-made sausage, these folks clearly know what they're doing with beef. The menu is constructed just like that of any other smokehouse, but with the addition of some fun daily specials. A "Save Your Soul Sunday" meal consists of oxtail, steak, turkey wings, and sides that offer salvation. The meat here speaks volumes with just the right smoke-to-seasoning ratio, and the hickory that is used for smoking takes center stage with its subtle but effective smoke flavor.

The inside of Harlon's is a bit intimidating; it's like a cross between a church and the inside of a casino in Laughlin, Nevada. This place screams old-school. An out-of-date television is propped up in the corner, and it's usually playing reruns of "The Price is Right." Vinyl chairs are scattered throughout the dining room, but you have to place your order at the bar. And when you do, order the brisket, because it's a thing of beauty. When sliced, the giant hunk of charred beef lets its fatty, smoky juices run everywhere, retaining the entirety of its natural flavor. Rarely does one find a brisket that's as juicy and tasty as the version at Harlon's.

The sausages are also legends in the making. They are made in-house, with a mix of pork and beef that endows them with a crumbly texture and markedly robust flavor. Order a ring or two, or just get one sliced up on a meat plate. Turkey is another crowd pleaser, and ribs are tender and never tough; you won't walk out of here with rib shreds stuck in between your teeth, because the fatty meat just falls off the bone. Get your plate with one, two, or three meats, or just slap anything on a sandwich and call it a day. Harlon's is satisfying and traditional. It doesn't get much better than low prices, humble hospitality, and fantastic barbecue. (Needless to say, don't expect any of the above at the airport.) –SD

Himalaya

A Pakistani food revelation that fires on all cylinders

A *Total pleasure grade*

9.2 *Food* **6.5** *Feel* **$14** *Price* **Pakistani**

Casual restaurant
Tues.-Thurs. 11am-11pm;
Fri.-Sat. 11am-midnight;
Sun. 11am-11pm; closed Mon.
Kid-friendly. Vegetarian-friendly.

Hillcroft Area
6652 Southwest Fwy.
(713) 532-2837

Bar None
Credit Cards Visa and MC
Reservations Not accepted

Chef Kaiser Lashkari should run for mayor of Houston. His engaging personality alone could probably win him the vote, but the food at his glorious palace of Pakistani food, Himalaya, would make him a shoo-in. Stuck in one of the city's least auspicious locations—a shopping center off the corner of Hillcroft and Southwest Freeway—Himalaya has been wowing the pants off customers with breathtaking food, even in a "wait, is this a restaurant?" setting. If you don't want to know what your dining companions look like when they have sex, we suggest not bringing them here, because after they take a bite of any of the masalas, biryanis, or naans, you're definitely going to see their O face.

While Da Marco has its white-suited waiters, and Tony's its air of old money, Himalaya has its own one-of-a-kind atmosphere. The ratty, bare-bones tone is set by Chef Kaiser's office, which is literally in the middle of the dining area, its PC fully loaded with a Himalaya screen saver and, presumably, the restaurant's financial records. The dry-erase board of a menu is covered with unheard-of treats, but just trust Chef Kaiser, whose oil-stained shirt proves that he knows what's best out of his kitchen that day.

In our many experiences here, we have not come across a single dud. The cuisine is like a lesson in spices: fennel seed, fenugreek, cardamom, and anise are amongst a vast, rotating cast of characters. Grilled fish is expertly perfumed and grilled until the flesh flakes, but is not mushy. Goat masala is a deep revelation. Paratha is exceptional, but you haven't had naan until you've had Himalaya's. How any bread can be so crispy and airy at the same time is mind bending. Even the salty lassi is flawless.

Kaiser is known for his fragrant, fluffy biryanis, which are huge plates of rice, scented with spices and studded with hearty meats, from chicken to lamb, and any choice is good, even the vegetarian version. But Himalaya isn't only vegetarian friendly, but even vegetarian-forward, with stars like the malai kopta (a potato dumpling with a creamy, spicy sauce) that even make carnivores forget about meat. Ending with the creamy, pistachio-topped rice pudding will send you into overdrive. Who needs foie gras, fine wine, and big bucks when you can have a meal by Kaiser? –JY

Hobbit Café

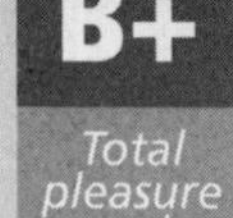

Total pleasure grade

A funky dive that with food that would make Frodo proud

7.5 Food **7.0** Feel **$20** Price

American, Vegetarian

Casual restaurant
Mon.-Thurs. 11am-9:30pm; Fri. 11am-10:30pm; Sat. 10:30am-10:30pm; Sun. 10:30am-9:00pm.
Brunch. Date-friendly. Kid-friendly. Outdoor dining. Vegetarian-friendly.

Upper Kirby
2243 Richmond Ave.
(713) 526-5460
hobbitcafe.verycool.at

Bar Wine and beer only
Credit Cards Visa, MC, AmEx
Reservations Accepted

Tucked away in the back of a parking lot on Richmond, Hobbit Café is not a money-grabbing knock-off intent on capitalizing on the recent success of J.R.R. Tolkien's *Lord of the Rings* trilogy at the box office. Rather, this quirky hobbit hole has been an institution for years, serving heaping portions of health-conscious food while serving as a simultaneous ode to all things Tolkien.

You may be taken aback by the amount of Lord of the Rings memorabilia that lines Hobbit Café, with the most jarring piece of the Tolkien relics being a life-sized figurine of Golum, staring at you as you walk through the door, but don't be deterred by either the mutant creature or the large crowds: this restaurant and its food do not lack in flavor or soul.

The health conscious fare at Hobbit Café harkens back to the dive-ish hippie hallows that are common in Austin, but rare in Houston. With light recipes that favor herbivores over the omnivores, and cuisine that veers into several different cultures, Hobbit Café screams brunch at all hours of the day. Most plates include either a low-fat this or a wheat that, but whether you're watching your waistline or not, the food is tasty and comforting. Avocado and alfalfa sprouts seem to be a fallback, with bombs of each on many of the dishes. Sandwiches are a strong point, with a straightforward Portobello mushroom burger being everything that it should be: savory, toothy, and with a twang to it; this burger is no longer on the menu, but if you ask, they'll make you one. An avocado omelet is fantastic for the first half, but a struggle for the second half, as it seems like it's made with at least two whole avocados. The spinach and mushroom enchiladas have a nutritious, nutty taste, and although we doubt anything covered in cheese can be good for you, we nonetheless feel better about ourselves after eating it.

Service is friendly but sometimes incompetent, as the large number of customers at times can turn the waitstaff into a frenzied bunch whose movements imitate the Astros' outfield when Jason Jennings is pitching. But Hobbit Café is a fun place. It has good, straightforward food that won't break the bank, and you'll leave with both your mouth and your stomach smiling. –JY

Hollywood Vietnamese

Late-night, gay-friendly Asian fare in the 'trose

Total pleasure grade

6.0	7.0	$24
Food	Feel	Price

Vietnamese, French

Casual restaurant
Sun.-Thurs. 11am-2am;
Fri.-Sat. 11am-4am.
Delivery. Live music.
Outdoor dining.

Montrose
2409 Montrose Blvd.
(713) 523-8808

Bar Full
Credit Cards Visa, MC, AmEx
Reservations Not accepted

Here's the scenario: you've just gotten into town from some trip and you're hungry. It's late, so your options are quite limited. Hollywood Vietnamese-Chinese is one of the only places open. Given its eclectic menu of French, Vietnamese, and Asian-ish items, dare you try it? We say yes. You'll be pleasantly surprised. And the place is superbly gay-friendly.

Even at the latest hour, you'll find Hollywood full of people. Many are simply enjoying what's coming from the bar, while others are devouring untold quantities of vermicelli. A festive atmosphere makes it all feel even livelier. The outdoor patio is large and inviting, set a safe distance back from the busy street; fun little twinkle lights are strung about. It's a great place to hang on a warm night.

As for the food, at least you can't complain about the choice. The menu is incredibly extensive—it would take the better part of an hour to truly inspect it—covering Vietnamese, Chinese, and French (!) food. We recommend sticking with the Asian side of the menu. (A sample of the elaborate but disastrous French menu: chicken with raisin Madeira sauce, lobster thermidor au gratin. We'll pass.) Instead, we'll take their vermicelli bowls, which are appropriately balanced between quantities of noodle, meat, and broth. Black pepper scallops or tofu also come highly recommended.

But back to that atmosphere. It reminds us why we love Montrose so much. Everyone here seems so comfortable being there and being with the company the place provides. The bar is a friendly scene; people sit around sipping the elaborate tropical drinks, making friends with whoever's next to them—at any hour. After the bars close, Hollywood actually turns into a pickup scene, like a surrogate nightclub. Even in the late afternoon—that dead time when some restaurants, this one included, stay open, and their employees try hard, if unsuccessfully, to look busy—you'll find regulars, bringing each other up to date, and just chatting about life. –AH

Hong Kong Food Market

An Asian supermarket mega-mart offers up Wal-Mart-like variety

Chinese

Specialty grocery
Daily 8am-9:45pm.
Vegetarian-friendly.

Chinatown
11205 Bellaire Blvd.
(281) 575-7886

North Houston
13400 Veterans Memorial Dr.
(281) 537-5280

Bar None
Credit Cards Visa, MC, AmEx
Reservations Not accepted

Westchase
5708 S. Gessner Dr.
(713) 995-1393

Of all the supermarkets on Bellaire, Hong Kong Food Market, in the Hong Kong Shopping Center on the corner of Boone, is probably the only one in whose aisles you can lose yourself for hours without ever covering the entirety of the store. Even if high quality and low prices aren't its foremost attributes, where else can you walk in the door and grab a spirally bamboo plant sort of thing; walk down the aisle, pick up some fresh-baked pork buns; stroll over to the produce aisle, find your knob of galangal; and end up at the checkout counter with live geoduck clams, a porcelain tea service, a giant durian, and a rice cooker?

While most of Chinatown's other markets, on the other side of the Sam Houston Tollway, have at least some of these components to their markets, only Hong Kong Supermarket seems to have them all. The bakery is iffy at best, with dried-out breads and poorly made egg tarts, but the soft, brioche-like buns with several varieties of fillings like ham and cheese, onion, and dried pork make for an easy, tasty snack or lunch. Just stay away from the Spam bun.

Produce is more impressive in variety than quality. There seems to be a lack of care for seasonality, so you can get almost everything year-round even if it's not in top form. If you're looking for sprouts, Chinese stir-frying greens like bok choy, gai lan, and pea shoots, and water chestnuts, it'll be there. Fruit is plentiful but hit-or-miss in quality, although when they're in season, you can't get better mangos anywhere else. The seafood aisle has the best selection, with stacks of tanks of crabs, tilapia, and so on, but some of the creatures look mighty lethargic; we prefer the Welcome Supermarket.

In the frozen food section, you can even find balut, the half-developed duck embryo in an egg that's prevalent in Vietnamese, Filipino, Cambodian, and Laotian cuisine.

And you thought you were an adventurous eater. –JY

Hong Kong's Café

A little Bellaire dive with big variety

C
Total pleasure grade

6.1	4.9	$7	Chinese
Food	*Feel*	*Price*	

Casual restaurant
Daily 10am-9pm.
WiFi.

Chinatown
9108 Bellaire Blvd.
(713) 772-9633

Bar None
Credit Cards No credit cards
Reservations Not accepted

Buried in one of the several corners of the Welcome Supermarket center, Hong Kong's Café is a tiny restaurant with no more than 10 elbow-to-elbow tables. While the place is small in stature, its menu of noodles, rice, and congee mixed in with interesting takes on American food is large and free-wheeling. The price column is agreeable, so although there are hits and misses, none of it will set you back much, and you can keep coming back until you find your go-to dish.

This is really more of a nook than a restaurant. But it's a bit like a short bald man hopping out of a Hummer H2: it tries to make up for its size with flash. The idea, we suppose, is an ode to the night-lit streets of Hong Kong, with all the lights and bright colors. Male waiters look like Asian pop stars, and female waiters look like they just walked out of the Sanrio store, though neither is likely to pay much attention to you unless you're Yao Ming.

The obligatory bowls of noodles with fish balls, shrimp, throngs of vegetables, or roasted meats aren't anything special here, and should pretty much be taken as eye candy: we wish the broths were more dense and flavorful, but instead, they taste rather like flavored water. Barbecued duck tastes old, dried out, and without that sweet stickiness that's so good in Chinese barbecue.

Shockingly, Hong Kong's Café riffs on American food are actually better, like surprisingly light, flavorful baked spaghetti with a pork chop. No joke. This isn't your red-sauce-and-Chianti-bottle spaghetti restaurant, so the dish isn't oversauced or cheesy, as it's aimed more at the Asian palate. An eyebrow-lifting "shrimp toast" is a baked, thick-cut piece of bread with shrimp paste schmeared on for a crusty, shrimpy, surprisingly crave-worthy treat. Roasted tilapia with sweet corn sauce is flaky, and though it's suspect whether or not the corn comes from a can, its thick sauciness and sweet crunchy kernels complement the fish admirably. Even if the American food at Hong Kong's is sometimes clumsy, there's something fun, sometimes tasty, and definitely heartfelt about it. –JY

House of Pies

Wait—shouldn't it be House of Corned Beef Hash?

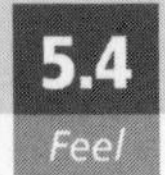

$11 *Price*

American, Sweets

Casual restaurant
Daily 24 hours.
Breakfast. Kid-friendly.

Upper Kirby
3112 Kirby Dr.
(713) 528-3816
www.houseofpies.com

Galleria
6142 Westheimer Rd.
(713) 782-1290

Bar None
Credit Cards Visa, MC, AmEx
Reservations Not accepted

With its late night availability and mish-mash of a menu, House of Pies has been a favorite of the late-night-breakfast crowd for a long time. Given that probably more than half the crowd is under the influence of something, the scene can get loud in a hurry. The food ranges from not good to edible, with their "famous" pies—which are like something that a group of twelve-year-old girls would throw together during a slumber party—being the worst. (Fresh fruit pies are a hyperglycemic's worst nightmare, and the cream pies taste like they come from a Jell-O pudding box.) All in all, House of Pies is a good place for a buzz-kill, with acceptable breakfast items and cups of lukewarm coffee.

Front-room pie displays; old, shabby booths; and a selection of stool-and-counter seats make House of Pies feel like a New-York-diner-meets-middle-of-nowhere Ohio-truck-stop-meets-Denny's mix. It's often an after-party destination where price takes precedence over food, and scantily clad bodies scatter the booths. More often than not, the waitstaff is uncaring and swamped with too many tables—not the best of combinations—but at this point in the night, as long as the food gets to the table, you'll be happy.

Without looking, you can probably be sure that the two most-used pieces of equipment in the kitchen are the griddle and the fryer. Really, the lunch and dinner options should be ripped out of the menu: steaks and burgers come out looking steamed, and salt is clearly not taken seriously here. Breakfast items are more successful because there's more room for error, and, of course, there's always ketchup and Tabasco to help. You look for fluffiness in a good pancake, and these don't have it, but they're still a decent choice; stay away, though, from the flimsy waffles. The highlight is corned-beef hash and eggs. Order your eggs poached so you can break them over the top, forming a delicious pile of meat, potatoes, and runny yolk. The plate is later fit for toast-sopping. Maybe they should consider a name change to the forte: who knows, maybe renaming the place House of Hash will bump up business, and not just amongst the stoners. –JY

Houston Tamales Factory

B-
Total pleasure grade

A charming restaurant in the Heights serves up careful, moist versions of these masa treats

7.3 *Food* **5.6** *Feel* **$10** *Price* **Tex-Mex**

Casual restaurant
Daily 8am-6pm.
Breakfast.

Heights
1050 Studewood St.
(713) 802-1800

Bar None
Credit Cards Visa, MC, AmEx
Reservations Not accepted

The tamale is probably not Mexico's most misunderstood dish—that title would be a tight race between mole and menudo—but the tamale might be the dish that is most often ruined by inferior execution. It's a delicate balancing act, steaming masa without overcooking it, maintaining the moistness of the corn flour and meat stuffing at the same time, and managing a balance of lightness and richness.

Houston Tamales Factory is one of the few places that gets it right. This little family-owned place has been open for about three years, and in those three years, they've developed quite the committed following. Serving Monterrey-style Mexican food, which is closer to Tex-Mex than to most regional cuisines further south, Houston Tamales Factory also does a decent job with breakfast tacos; flautas, too, come out well above average.

Don't consider the menu limited to what you see, because on demand, for the right price, the staff here will produce just about anything, stuffed with just about anything else. Special-order bulk tamales, for example, are a popular holiday-season order.

You can't miss the bright orange exterior of this place. It's a small establishment whose owners work the counter, so you are guaranteed to get good service—no tamale jerks here. The moist tamales are stuffed with a number of different meats, and there's also a vegetarian version with cream cheese and jalapeño. It sounds a little like what you might find under a heat lamp at 7-11, but cream cheese is an easy-to-enjoy taste and texture, and adds even more moistness from within the masa, a starch that can so easily dry out; we'll take it. The masa is also not as dense as some the other well-known places around town, and we like these lighter, fluffier versions. Certainly they're not the greatest in the world, but they're definitely the best in the Heights. And they're refreshingly not over-hyped (except by us, of course).

If you're up for breakfast, the Houston Tamales Factory can fit into that plan, too: competent breakfast tacos integrate standard eggs, bacon, potato...you know the drill. They'll get your day off to a good start—although barbacoa might get it off to an even better one. Salsas, however, are a bit flavorless, and fajitas should be skipped. Stick to the tamales and breakfast tacos, and you'll be satisfied. –SD

Houston's

A night of family, fun, fries, and freeloading off our city's reputation

B *Total pleasure grade*

8.2 *Food* **8.2** *Feel* **$62** *Price*

American

Upmarket restaurant
Sun.-Thurs. 11am-10pm;
Fri.-Sat. 11am-11pm.

Upper Kirby
4848 Kirby Dr.
(713) 529-2386
www.hillstone.com

Galleria
5888 Westheimer Rd.
(713) 975-1947

Bar Full
Credit Cards Visa, MC, AmEx
Reservations Not accepted

You probably won't encounter much skepticism if you try to pass off this ultrapopular restaurant as a Houston original—most of its considerable cult following already assumes that to be so. In reality, the warm, well-loved, upmarket-yet-moderately-priced chain actually started in 1977 in Nashville, Tennessee (although for some reason, the LA-based Hillstone Restaurant Group, the chain's current owner, seems mighty protective of that fact).

Its success since then (Houston's branches now grace most big American cities) has been legendary, owing largely—but by no means solely—to the delicious grilled burger, the icon that Houston's cult following tends to worship most. It comes in several configurations of accoutrements (a California version, for instance, includes avocado, jack cheese, and arugula), but all of them taste of a good smokehouse grill, rather than the dirty griddle you might find in lesser hands. Get it medium-rare, and it will really come that way. Don't miss some of the best fries in the city, either—they're crispy, salty, and exemplary.

You should probably start with an inspired version of spinach dip, whose followers are legion. A filet mignon is unusually flavorful and beefy, although we wish a fattier cut were available. Still, this is top-steakhouse quality in a less pretentious atmosphere, at a price that undersells the big names by a bit. The menu continues with almost caricatured straightforwardness, with reliable meats, from chops to ribs.

The outlandishly energetic, almost disturbingly attentive waitstaff does our city's name proud: it's all Texan, and all feel-good. The restaurant's inoffensive decorative theme integrates some elements that seem almost faux-Navajo; shiny, curvy red banquettes are a bit too brightly lit but certainly comfortable. All of it works well for families or groups, less well for romantic dates.

Houston's can get crowded and busy on the weekends, so expect a wait; but this is a volume restaurant, so it won't take forever. They bring 'em in and push 'em out with a smile and a complimentary mint. Wait it out at the bar and enjoy a good cocktail—or, if you simply can't take the wait, order at the bar and eat there. It's not a culinary temple, but for a chain, it does an unusually good job of pleasing a lot of different palates with uncanny reliability. –FC

Coming Attractions

Oil's up, Houston's booming, and we've got a lot to look forward to on the culinary scene. These are three of the more high-profile restaurants that were on their way into town at press time.

Beaver's: Pope strikes again

Beaver's, Monica Pope's newest venture, is reviving the idea of the classic Texas icehouse. The beer list aims to achieve the level of detail of a good wine list. Food will be equally Texas-and-beer-centric; think chili, hush puppies, and cole slaw. Its location is set for the edge of the East End, at the intersection of Decatur and Sawyer. We can expect appropriately kitschy, tongue-in-cheek beaver décor, including a "Beaverabilia" wall (devoted to the old incarnation of the old Beaver's icehouse, which inhabited this same space).

De La Vega: Mexico's celebrity chef Iliana de la Vega moves to Houston

Oaxaca's loss is Houston's gain: celebrity chef Iliana de la Vega is set to open De La Vega, focusing on the regional cuisine of her native Oaxaca, in a location still to be determined. Darling of the *New York Times* and *Bon Appétit*, de la Vega was considered by some to be the best chef in Mexico. Her renowned Oaxaca restaurant, El Naranjo, was forced to close in late 2006 after a series of riots ravaged the city. The cuisine will be Oaxacan *cocina de autor*, thus saving Houstonians the four-hour flight to sample her famous regional moles. Expect ceviche, duck, whole fish, and a creative wine, tequila, and mezcal list.

The Grove: Schiller and Del Grande back Discovery Green restaurant

The Grove, set to be the flagship restaurant of the new Discovery Green park-entertainment complex downtown, is set to be one of Houston's most eco-friendly dining destinations. Schiller del Grande is also backing this project, making it their their first upscale launch since Café Annie. The menu will be a mix of Spanish and Mexican.

Hugo's

Brilliantly packaged, ideally situated: it's everyone's favorite Mexican—except ours

B+ Total pleasure grade

7.3 Food | **9.2** Feel | **$53** Price

Mexican

Upmarket restaurant
Sun.-Thurs. 11am-10pm;
Fri.-Sat. 11am-11pm.
Brunch. Date-friendly.
Live music. Outdoor dining.

Montrose
1600 Westheimer Rd.
(713) 524-7744
www.hugosrestaurant.net

Bar Full
Credit Cards Visa, MC, AmEx
Reservations Recommended

Exceptionally high ceilings, low lighting, exposed brick: Hugo's, on a hip corner of Westheimer, has all the elements of the upmarket-warehouse look that has become (deservedly) popular over the last decade. It's a transportative atmosphere that's particularly romantic at dinnertime. Insofar as it's hard to find lesser-known regional Mexican dishes in Houston, the menu is as modern and exciting as the environment: you'll find roast rabbit, cabrito (goat), cochinita pibil (baked pork with achiote), quesadillas with huitlacoche, and mole everywhere.

Hugo's is extremely popular for its Sunday brunch buffet, an enormous spread evocative of Austin's Fonda San Miguel but at a somewhat lower price. The concept is great, and you're serenaded by live music as you stuff your face; unfortunately, the ambitious food doesn't hit all the right notes. Especially at brunch, but at dinner too, there are particular systematic problems with dry, overcooked meats (from pork to chicken to duck); rampant underseasoning; and arid, flavorless tortillas.

On the dinner menu, a starter of "sopesitos" is three small masa (corn) cakes, each topped with a different slow-cooked meat. One has chicken with a sweet black mole; another has flavorful cochinita pibil; and the third has somewhat dry beef rib meat with green salsa. Hugo's touch is to serve it with habañero salsa, but we can't fathom how habañero peppers could be rendered this mild.

"Filete de Campesino" is a beef tenderloin stuffed with mushrooms, huitlacoche, squash, and Chihuahua cheese and topped with tomatillo sauce. As elsewhere, this dish's execution is like a lite version of the menu's bold description. None of these tastes really manages to come together, and the huitlacoche—a corn fungus which, at its best, evokes earthy notes like black truffle—is too scarce to taste.

The experience is marred slightly by indifferent service, but the excellent drinks menu will make you forget. Mezcal, for instance, is a liquor similar to tequila but rendered more smoky and complex by the agave plant's roasting over wood fire. This is one of the only restaurants in Houston to serve authentic mezcal (i.e. no worms). The Del Maguey mezcal flight is three small clay cups of "single-village" mezcal from different towns around Oaxaca. Ultimately, the allure of Hugo's isn't the food; it's the drinks, atmosphere, and ambition. –FC

Hungry's

News flash, circa 1989: iceberg lettuce with creamy salad dressing is less healthy than meat

C-
Total pleasure grade

6.7 *Food* **3.5** *Feel* **$18** *Price*

Light American

Casual restaurant
Mon.-Thurs. 11am-10pm;
Fri. 11am-11pm; Sat. 9am-11pm;
Sun. 9am-10pm.

Brunch. Delivery.
Vegetarian-friendly.

Rice Area
2356 Rice Blvd.
(713) 523-8652
www.hungryscafe.com

West Houston
14075 Memorial Dr.
(281) 493-1520

Bar Full
Credit Cards Visa, MC, AmEx
Reservations Accepted

Hungry's seems to be one of those places that everyone knows about but has never really been to. Either that, or they've been there, but it was so bland and forgettable that they've erased it from their memory. It's a café-type setting that resembles every other so-so café, and its menu is full of items similar to something you might have made at home.

It's not as though Hungry's, with its stark whiteness and unique walk-up step design, is unnoticeable. It's just that the exterior sums it up; it's plain, it's white, and it's boring. The interior straddles quaint and IKEA, pulling off neither well; paintings from local artists, metal grating, and weird, modern, cataloggish lights are the only adornments to an otherwise-vanilla room with office-style ceilings. Waiters hardly crack a smile and lack any sort of obvious zeal.

Lunch is the specialty, and everyone's looking for a healthy lunch these days. Hungry's tries to fit the bill, but its idea of healthy seems stuck decades in the past. A "whole wheat wrap" sounds healthy, but it's full of calories, not the least from its big iceberg wedge drowned in a creamy feta dressing that's not bad, but would be better suited as a steakhouse appetizer than as a light-lunch side. The array of bland sandwiches and wraps include a "Baja Chicken" version that might feel at home on a Quizno's menu, overstuffed with black beans and feta cheese that adds some twang. House mains sound like TV dinners, with names like "Rigatoni Rustica with a creamy marinara sauce." The kicker is that desserts are colossal, too big for their own good—or yours.

Again, we fail to see what's so healthy about it all. Maybe in the 1980s, the world believed that salad with creamy dressing, or anything whole wheat, was diet food. In the modern era of health-consciousness, Hungry's just looks like a not-very-healthy, not-very-good place to waste your appetite. It's the worst of both worlds. –FC

Don't count calories,
but do make every
calorie count.

Ibiza

Bottle nerds, gastro-hip Hummers, and a wine list to end all arguments

A
Total pleasure grade

8.5 *Food* **8.7** *Feel* **$72** *Price* **New American**

Upmarket restaurant
Tues.-Thurs. 11am-10pm; Fri. 11am-11pm; Sat. 5pm-11pm; Sun. 5pm-9pm; closed Mon.
Date-friendly. Live music. Outdoor dining. Wine-friendly.

Midtown
2450 Louisiana St.
(713) 524-0004
www.ibizafoodandwinebar.com

Bar Full
Credit Cards Visa, MC, AmEx
Reservations Recommended

Between its sleek, trendy lines and its obscure, low-markup wines, Ibiza manages to strike an equally appealing note with goombas and wine geeks. The resulting Midtown parking lot, at least on a warm weekend evening, is an unlikely mixer of H3s with Hondas—with anyone's guess as to which is more likely to wind up with a DUI. On a nice night, we highly recommend sitting outdoors, where you can observe the V-12 roars and parking-lot shouts and take in the warm breeze; the candlelit indoors, if slightly pretentious, amuses you with the hum of the open kitchen and a wall of wine bottles glowing from recessed lighting.

But don't make the mistake of writing off Ibiza as an esoteric wine bar or singles scene, because its kitchen is surprisingly competent, with moments of wine-pairing genius overshadowing the sometime snags. In spite of the irritating valet-parking hijinks, the whole thing comes together remarkably well, especially given the cultural circumstances. A piquillo appetizer is one of the most memorable individual dishes in the city of Houston, with ground pistachios and smoked duck breast melding together into a sort of mousse that bursts from within a roasted red pepper with all the savory smokiness of Texas. Other starters tend to be less impressive: peppercorn-crusted tuna with seaweed and "cucumber-red chili ponzu" is tired, and a Caesar salad with big romaine hearts is merely satisfying, lacking much anchovy kick.

Beyond that, things tend to progress well. Local goat cheese is the star of the crispy, personal-sized pizza show, though its bedfellows—oven-dried tomato and apple-smoked bacon—also do admirable work. A fillet of beef, however, has inexplicably come sliced in three, drastically taking away from the tenderness that's the hallmark of a fillet (it's certainly not flavor). A so-called "eight-hour" braised lamb shank winds up more tender and melty in some bites than others, but the preparation pairs well with the Burgundies and expressive Rhône wines on the list. There are other hits and other misses, but the real guarantee is the quality of the quaff: French, Spanish, and American bottles from great vintages at prices often only a few dollars—if that—above store or auction prices. We can only hope that more Houston restaurants will jump aboard this bargain-basement wine bandwagon. –RG

India's Restaurant

Classic, generic Indian-American with more misses than hits

C *Total pleasure grade*

5.2	5.4	$20	Indian
Food	Feel	Price	

Casual restaurant
Mon.-Thurs. 11am-10pm;
Fri.-Sat. 11am-10:30pm;
Sun. 5pm-10:30pm.
Delivery. Vegetarian-friendly.

Galleria
5704 Richmond Ave.
(713) 266-0131
www.indiasrestauranthouston.com

Bar Full
Credit Cards Visa, MC, AmEx
Reservations Accepted

Many of the big Indian restaurants in central Houston—the Hillcroft area is the exception—serve up Americanized Indian dishes at prices are even less authentic than their recipes. Indian food is based on spice, off-cuts, grains, and vegetables, so why are the asking prices so high for such predictable outcomes?

One such offender is India's Restaurant on Richmond. Their classic menu consists of dry kebabs and other such disappointments, although the curries are generally on point with flavor and execution. It's best to go for lunch, when there's a much cheaper buffet; at that time, the food's also got something of an alibi.

India's is a modest establishment tucked away in plain sight on the ever so popular Richmond strip. The space is clean, organized, and well kept—in short, everything we don't like in a good Indian restaurant. The atmosphere and the table settings could pass for a chain or corporate restaurant; it seems they are really trying to appeal to a certain crowd.

The food is not memorable by any means. Saag paneer, cubes of cheese and spinach, is very watery, both texturally and flavor-wise; dum aloo, however—potatoes with herbs and spices coated in a brown sauce—is delicious. The potatoes are cooked right, and the sauce is packed full of flavor. Curry here is good, flavorful, and everything that a curry is supposed to be. Lamb vindaloo, on the other hand, is a disappointment. Granted, Indian restaurants usually cook proteins until well done, but this lamb comes out exceptionally dry, tough, and flavorless; no amount of heat can save it.

India's is a great place for vegetarians; even the reasonably-priced lunch buffet sports many veggie selections. It's during dinner service that prices creep higher; most of India's main courses start above ten dollars. It's not exactly highway robbery, but things look even worse if you figure in the opportunity cost: Houston is a city with a remarkably good range of Indian options, from the cheap, authentic South Indian and Bombay-style dives in the Hillcroft area to cutting-edge nouvelle Indian in Montrose. Either of these extremes is totally worthwhile; we just don't quite see where this middle ground fits into the equation.
–SD

Indika

Show-stopping, occasionally pompous Indian that lives up to its lofty reputation

A *Total pleasure grade*

9.1 *Food* **9.0** *Feel* **$65** *Price* **Indian**

Upmarket restaurant
Tues.-Thurs. 11:30am-2:30pm, 6pm-10pm; Fri.-Sat. 11:30am-10:30pm; closed Sun.-Mon.
Brunch. Date-friendly.
Outdoor dining. Vegetarian-friendly.

Montrose
516 Westheimer Rd.
(713) 984-1725
www.indikausa.com

Bar Full
Credit Cards Visa, MC, AmEx
Reservations Accepted

Believe the hype: the flavors of Indika will punch you straight in the nose. Bold, beautiful, and exotic, this once-hidden Indian restaurant has moved to a hip new location in Montrose, hiked up its skirt, threw on five-inch stiletto heels, and in fabulous Montrose style, is ready to spend a night with the prom/drag king/queen. Although the interior looks pieced together from a home-furnishings magazine, the subtle colors, flowing curtains, and airy spacing of tables make diners feel relaxed and ready to consume these multifarious takes on modern Indian cuisine, which brandish creative, sexy, up-to-date appeal.

Start with one of Indika's signature libations. The "Kama Sutra" (passion fruit, gin, and lime) is a refreshing, acidic palate cleanser for the meal ahead. Appetizers feature more hits than misses. There are a few foul-tips, though, like crab samosas, which feel like a concession to those who feel it's blasphemy for any restaurant not to serve the almighty crab cake. The heat of chilies and the sweetness of papaya chutney mask any crab flavor trying to fight its way from samosa to tongue. Far more interesting is "Absolut pani poori," a nouvelle version of the Indian street food that spikes tamarind-broth-filled fried dough pockets with vodka. Best of all, though, is goat-brain masala (don't be scared) on peshawari naan with mango and cucumber. The ferrous, liver-like, delicious, creamy flavor of the brain really breaks through the up-front masala spices.

Mains—like lamb shank braised in tomato, onions, and roasted garlic, and naan-crusted goat curry—are creative takes on tradition. Goat curry might remind you of an Indian pot pie, with spicy chunks of goat bathed in a dark curry sauce in a bowl topped and sealed with naan bread; a cold beet and yogurt salad extinguishes yet still accents the spiciness of the curry. The "carnivore tasting plate" does wonders with venison, while on the flip side, the many vegetarian options are well executed.

The food and drink at Indika will definitely get you going. Once you get past the fact that the restaurant has the same track lighting as everyone else in town, you'll recline and revel in the fact that you've just eaten goat brains—and enjoyed it. –FC

Inversion Coffee House

A funky, wired spot for froofed-up coffee drinks and unexciting baked goods

B- *Total pleasure grade*

6.5 *Food* **8.9** *Feel* **$9** *Price*

Light American

Café
Mon.-Thurs. 5:30am-11pm; Fri. 5:30am-midnight; Sat. 6:30am-midnight; Sun. 7:30am-10:30pm.
Breakfast. Vegetarian-friendly. WiFi.

Montrose
1953 Montrose Blvd.
(713) 523-4866
www.inversioncoffee.com

Bar None
Credit Cards Visa, MC, AmEx
Reservations Not accepted

Houston coffee shops—when they're not corporate clones—tend more toward the urbane than the funky. Inversion is straight-up funky. Even if its red velvet couches were full of Fortune 500 finance executives eating its red velvet cake, it would still be the funkiest coffee shop in town.

Let's start with some history. Inversion gets its name from the wacked-out art house that stood on the same spot until Hurricane Rita wrecked it in 2005. The outer wall of Inversion has a picture of the original – it looked like a house that a tornado had sucked through sideways (evidently, a giant gaping hole in the wall makes a house vulnerable to hurricanes—who knew?). Fortunately, the folks at the Art League of Houston who had built the first Inversion turned out to be a creative lot, and on the ashes of the old Inversion they built an art-filled coffee shop with a shocking dearth of right angles. One wall is covered with photographs of coffee beans and a series of abstract finger paintings. Other walls sport a changing display of paintings and sculpture-type things. Up high, thick beams and air conditioning conduits are displayed in all their post-industrial glory.

Inversion offers free WiFi, which you might somehow be able to guess from all the Macs on the scene. The clientele is heavy in students and strange-looking characters who are presumably artists. The coffee is good and strong. Some of the specialty coffee drinks, such as the "Chocolate Cherry Bomb" and the caramel macchiato, are sweeter than we'd like, but perhaps we should have been warned by the name: the former, for one, does not suggest a lack of sugar. The pre-packaged sandwiches from Kraftsmen Bakery (turkey, tuna, and so on) are fresher than you'd expect because they're made just up the street. The baked goods they bring in aren't the best in town (they discontinued a Chai tea cupcake we adored), but they're good enough to keep the artists, graphic designers, and funky finance executives coming back. The seven-layer bar is particularly big and messy—just the thing, perhaps, to pair with a cup of joe while you formulate your plans for art-world domination. –RH

Irma's

Don't try to rebel against the years at this stadium-area standby

B
Total pleasure grade

7.6	8.1	$26
Food	*Feel*	*Price*

Tex-Mex

Casual restaurant
Mon.-Fri. 8:30am-3pm;
closed Sat.-Sun.
Breakfast. Delivery. Kid-friendly. Live music. Outdoor dining.

Downtown
22 N. Chenevert St.
(713) 222-0767

Bar Full
Credit Cards Visa, MC, AmEx
Reservations Accepted

The assumption, when you step inside Irma's, is that you will be having the lemonade. Everybody has the lemonade. The lemonade is legendary. The people that don't have the lemonade, but instead opt for iced tea, are considered by the Irma's community to be idiots, or at least malinformed miscreants. That's the shtick of this cult Tex-Mex favorite, and it's been inordinately successful: in spite of (or perhaps because of) opening only at lunchtime—a bit later when the Astros are playing at home—and in spite of (or perhaps because of) treating even older customers like naïve children, Irma's is as much of a sure bet to fill its tables as any restaurant in Houston.

You'll start with the salsa (hot, not cold, with an unusually deep roasted-tomato flavor) and top-notch chips. If there even is a printed menu at Irma's, you're unlikely to ever see it. Your waitperson will come to your table and recite a list of what's available, which will likely focus on Tex-Mex. You might need to coax the authentic Mexican specials of the day out of the staff: tamales, caldo de pollo (chicken soup), braised pork stew, and such stuff. It's all delicious, but so, too, are the world-class beef enchiladas: corn tortillas that actually taste like corn tortillas, stuffed with picadillo that actually tastes like beef; and, to boot, a bunch of unexpected, welcome flavors to punctuate the dark, deeply flavored red sauce. Need we elaborate? Okay: chopped green chiles, cheese, fresh tomato, cilantro, and onions. These might well be the best enchiladas in Houston. Too bad their accompanying rice is relatively flavorless, even if the refried beans are done righteously, with plenty of pork-fat depth.

Taste the food, and you'll excuse the gimmicky nature of the over-the-top, mother-you-never-had service, even if it's not your thing. Ditto for the walls, a living archive of Houston—and American—history: newspapers from JFK's assassination, Ann Richards headlines, movie-star posters, a Yorx 8-track player (remember Yorx?), *Gourmet* magazines from the 1980s, sports memorabilia, and so on. We do wish the tablecloths felt a little less cheap, flowery, and plasticky. We also wish that the Astros would win the World Series. Some things never change. –RG

Istanbul Grill

Killer lamb and döner at the granddaddy of Houston Turkish cuisine

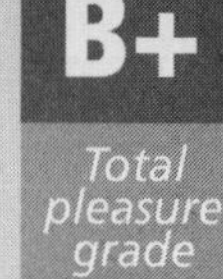

8.1 *Food* | **7.2** *Feel* | **$51** *Price* | **Turkish**

Casual restaurant
Tues.-Thurs. 11am-10pm;
Fri.-Sat. 11am-10:30pm;
Sun.11am-10pm; closed Mon.
Outdoor dining.

Rice Area
5613 Morningside Dr.
(713) 526-2800
www.istanbulgrill.com

Bar Wine and beer, BYO
Credit Cards Visa, MC, AmEx
Reservations Not accepted

Istanbul, Constantinople, Istanbul, Constantinople. Istanbul Grill is the king—the granddaddy of Turkish cuisine here in Houston. Meat pies, tabbouleh, hummus, and sandwiches are all here, but the specialty of the house is kebabs. Döner kebabs, sliced meat kebabs, and ground meat kebabs—they're all here, and they're all good. Yet the meal manages not to be heavy; almost everything is served with pilaf rice and cabbage, making you feel fairly food-coma-free afterward.

There are deep colors all over the restaurant; Turkish rugs hang from the walls, and the nazar (evil eye) is found everywhere, doing its job of warding off evil spirits. A big brick oven and a vertical turning spit roast are the other main aesthetic elements. However, people come not for the aesthetics but for the döner—thinly sliced, highly seasoned strips of beef and lamb turned on that legendary self-basting spit, over an open fire, and then sliced to order. Kebabs of baby lamb, beef, or chicken are grilled or are cooked in a brick oven, its wood imparting them with a great smoky flavor. We love the flavorful adana kebabs, which are made with chopped lamb, seasoned with Aleppo red pepper, and char-broiled on the skewer.

Turkish cuisine is also built on light flavors and ingredients, and as such the cold salads and appetizers here are refreshing and delicious. Dolmas (rice-stuffed grape leaves) hit you with a big, herby impact when the leaf wrapper is first pierced. Other Turkish specialties include Ayran (an acidic, salty yogurt drink), and Turkish coffee.

There's an interesting Turkish wine list—certainly one of the only ones in town. Even if you're a devoted wine snob, we guarantee grapes you've never heard off, like Bogazkere, Öküzgözü, and Kalecik Karasi. They're fairly light in style, and a lot more fun for experimentation than another big California red.

The Istanbul Grill has managed to maintain consistent quality for about a decade, which is quite an accomplishment in the highly competitive Rice Village market. It remains one of the neighborhood's most versatile standbys. –SD

James Coney Island

It may be a big chain—but its hot dogs are hard to argue with

6.4 Food **5.4** Feel **$8** Price

American

Fast-food chain
Mon.-Thurs. 10:30am-11pm;
Fri.-Sat. 10:30am-midnight;
Sun. 10:30am-10pm.

Delivery. Kid-friendly. Additional locations.

Upper Kirby
3607 S. Shepherd Dr.
(713) 524-7400
www.jamesconeyisland.com

Bar None
Credit Cards Visa, MC, AmEx
Reservations Not accepted

Town & Country
701 Town and Country Ln.
(713) 973-9143

Chinatown
6633 Fondren Rd.
(713) 772-5862

Quick: where do you go to get a great frank in this town? Houston isn't known for having a great hot dog stand, or anything else in the way of hot dogs—unless you wanna grab a pack from the supermarket or go to a fast-food restaurant. Some people dub chain fast-food restaurants the death of cuisine, and we generally tend to concur, but in the few cases where the food is well executed and pleasing to the taste buds, we can't really complain. Nonetheless, the stereotype hangs over 'em all.

James Coney Island is certainly fast food; you know it from the all-too-common question from the cashiers: "Would you like that with fries and a drink?" And this chain certainly tries pretty hard with its in-your-face nostalgic faux-'50s-diner graphic aesthetic, with bright colors and contrived fontage. Still, this is that delightful exception to the fast-food rule. First of all, it's been around since 1923, when two Greek immigrant brothers opened a stand in downtown Houston (although we wish they still served the "goose liver and Roquefort" sandwich that they reportedly once did.) Second of all, we appreciate their focus and we can forgive them the requisite kid-pleasing hot-dog mascot.

You're rarely far from one of these joints in the Houston area, and in respectable fast-food style, most of the buildings look identical, with good ol' red, white, and blue colors to make you feel safe, relaxed, and American. Hot dogs reign supreme, and they'll dress them up or down; our favorite is the "Chicago-style" dog, garnished with tomato slices, hot peppers, relish, cucumber, and the ever-so-important celery salt, which gives it a good twang of seasoning. Lemonade is so sugary that you might have to visit the dentist afterwards. Doesn't matter—it's worth it. Fries are standard, but they're better when slathered with chili and cheese.

Service is surprisingly friendly and outgoing at most locations. But it's still fast-food service. And, in the end, this is still fast food, hardly a special treat for your palate. It's not even a B-. Nonetheless, it is a welcome stereotype-breaker. In a sea of increasingly disconcerting fast-food-chain antics, James Coney Island is still the real deal. –SD

Jasmine Asian Cuisine

C+
Total pleasure grade

Seven-course beef served with a side of frustration

7.2 *Food* **3.6** *Feel* **$19** *Price* **Vietnamese**

Casual restaurant
Daily 11am-11pm.

Chinatown
9938 Bellaire Blvd.
(713) 272-8188

Bar Wine and beer only
Credit Cards Visa, MC, AmEx
Reservations Accepted

Jasmine Asian Cuisine proves two things: first, that meat is good, beef is better, and beef in seven courses is best. Second, that bad service can make good food taste lousy. The phrase "seven-course beef" is a cherubic call to any red-blooded Texan, but even in its well-designed outfit, Jasmine throws a bitter aftertaste into your mouth with shoddy, unwelcoming service that overshadows its exciting, well-formulated Vietnamese flavors.

Comfortable wood tones and a modern design—though not rambunctiously juvenile—are both a sight and a decoy here. The room is meticulously decorated with enough embellishments to give the room an Asian feel. Unfortunately, the service is a ticking time bomb. It's one thing to not offer utensils, water, or even a smile, but with the food being so different and hands-on, it is truly amazing that the staff at Jasmine could seem genuinely annoyed at having to explain how to eat the food placed (or rather clunked) in front of you, as if you were some great mound of stupidity to which they must unwillingly impart important information. This attitude has been repeatedly confirmed, even when the server has no other tables.

The food, though, is a triumphant display of Vietnamese cuisine. While there are some homey dishes, it would be a shame not to partake in seven courses of bovine succulence at least on your first visit. (For later visits, there's a good fish seven ways too.) Really, the seven courses are two, as six of the courses are served at once. These include thin slices of raw beef to be dipped in an oniony broth and wrapped in rice paper with fresh cuts of cucumber and carrots. Ground, seasoned beef is wrapped with Hawaiian herbs and grilled, endowing the meat's grilled char with a bright tropicality. A meatball with peanuts and vermicelli has come out dryly overcooked, even though its mushroomy, savory flavor was still apparent. The biggest surprise comes last: a thin but densely beefy flavored broth served with bits of alphabet pasta—probably the best glorified alphabet soup you'll ever lap up. Unfortunately, the check will arrive even if you're still hungry, reminding you once again that a deal so sweet will eventually have some sort of bitterness to it. –JY

Jenni's Noodle House

Even the noodles try too hard to be trendy here

B- Total pleasure grade

7.2 Food | **7.7** Feel | **$14** Price

Pan-Asian

Casual restaurant
Downtown hours Mon.-Fri. 11am-3pm; closed Sat.-Sun.
Vegetarian-friendly. WiFi.

Montrose hours Mon.-Sat. 11am-10pm; closed Sun.

Downtown
2130 Jefferson St.
(713) 228-3400
www.noodlesrule.com

Montrose
3111 S. Shepherd Dr.
(713) 523-7600

Bar BYO
Credit Cards Visa, MC, AmEx
Reservations Not accepted

There are so many reasons to go to Jenni's Noodle House besides the food: they have great shirts with the Srirachi logo on them; it's BYO (which means whiskey to boys); and they have those fun (or stupid, depending on your position) menu titles like "Stir Me Crazy" or "Sexy Salad." This is a good noodle house that doesn't focus too heavily on tradition; rather, they have fun with the food while still making it taste great. The atmosphere is fun too, with a spunky staff bopping their heads to the music playing; that also happens to be what the youngsters like.

Starters are pretty predictable, with spring rolls, egg rolls, and dumplings, but the stars are the seaweed salad and the crispy tofu. The seaweed's mellow saltiness blends nicely with the pepper vinaigrette dressing, and the tofu is the crispy fried kind that is great alone, but has some house soy to accompany. Jenni's also has curry and vermicelli salads to add to the somewhat haphazard pan-Asian attack. The "Infernal Chicken Curry" is studded with potatoes and swimming about in a coconut chile shrimp broth that will leave your mouth desperate for rice to extinguish the flames, though we find that we just keep dousing them with more of the fiery goodness that is the broth. But you can't leave Jenni's without having some noodles. The "Angry Udon" are thick udon noodles with tofu and mushrooms in a spicy tamarind broth that is a wonderful complement to the tofu.

Remember the BYO policy: you can bring whatever you want into Jenni's, and it is free. No corkage fee. Good times. After a few drinks, those Jenni's shirts might suddenly look a lot more appealing, and you'll find yourself spending even more money here. With the good comes the bad; Jenni's has two locations, and the one on Jefferson only serves lunch. Gone are the days that they were open late-night—we guess you'll have to find another place to gorge yourself at such an hour. –SD

Jerusalem Halal Deli

A gem of a Middle Eastern lunch spot; plain, simple, and cheap

B+ *Total pleasure grade*

7.6 *Food* **6.1** *Feel* **$10** *Price*

Middle Eastern

Counter service
Daily 8am-9pm.
Breakfast. Vegetarian-friendly.

Hillcroft Area
3330 Hillcroft St.
(713) 784-2525

Bar None
Credit Cards Visa, MC, AmEx
Reservations Not accepted

"Hole in the wall" might be an incredible cliché. It also might be the ideal description for Jerusalem Halal Deli. Not only do they serve up some of the most traditional Middle Eastern food in town, but it must be the cheapest. Who wouldn't love a lamb shawarma that rings in at $3.50? Who wouldn't love well-seasoned sliced rotisserie lamb, tzatziki, raw onions, cucumbers, and some kind of red chili sauce all wrapped up in crispy grilled flatbread, with none of the ingredients drowning out any of the others? We want it. Now.

One of our Undercover Chefs first stumbled into the place looking for some pickled lemons for a recipe he wanted to try. The deli is in the back corner of a meat market/grocery that is about as organized as a freshman-year locker before final exams. With enough time and patience, however, you will probably be able to find just about any canned or jarred item that exists in the Middle East. The center of the store is a working meat market where sub-primals are broken down by a team of five men. The smell is one you must get used to, but if you want authentic, it's a small price to pay.

During lunch, you'll find Middle Eastern businessmen lined up for the daily specials, kebabs, and salads. If you want a menu, you'll have to ask—most people who eat there know exactly what they want. Olives, hummus, and marinated feta are a few standbys to munch on with your main course of choice. As you'll find with so many places like this, the meat seems to be a bit dry, but at these prices it's hard to complain—and, anyway, with enough hummus you won't even notice.

This place is a real gem of a lunch spot. Take the surroundings lightly and enjoy Jerusalem Halal Deli for what it is. Dinner is less than busy, which is a nice change, although this is hardly a romantic date spot. They run daily specials, so it behooves you to ask what's cooking. Otherwise, try the mixed vegetables with lamb. And on your way out, grab a pound of their fresh feta cheese. It makes for a great midnight snack after a few beers. –SN

Josephine's

The food your Italian grandmother would cook—if she had a microwave

C
Total pleasure grade

6.0 *Food* **6.5** *Feel* **$17** *Price* **Italian**

Counter service
Mon.-Thurs. 11am-9:30pm;
Fri. 11am-10pm;
Sat. 5pm-10pm; closed Sun.
Delivery. Kid-friendly.

Downtown
1209 Caroline St.
(713) 759-9323
www.josephinesitalian.com

Bar Wine and beer only
Credit Cards Visa, MC, AmEx
Reservations Accepted

If Luby's Cafeteria grew up in the Italian-American mecca of New Jersey, it might look a lot like Josephine's. This place puts a red-sauce twist on cafeteria-style service, with food that starts out bad and gets even worse at the steam table or in the microwave. However, while we would normally advise against any restaurant that uses "nuking" as one of it cooking techniques, Josephine's is actually one of the better midday options in its neighborhood, if only for the solid decision-making on what to nuke.

Both the green awning and the fact that Josephine's has both "Italian" (to clear up any confusion for English speakers) and "Ristorante" (to make it Italianissimo) in its name has the garlicky smell of New York's Little Italy about it. Red-checked tablecloths confirm this. You half expect to see candles sticking out of wicker Chianti bottles and a fat man with a twisted moustache singing "That's Amore."

Skip any mention of an appetizer, because the salads are iceberg-lettuce-based, and soups suffer from the tortured fate of being held warm too long. To wit: an ill-advised minestrone soup whose vegetables disintegrate with the first bite. Pizzas need major reworking; their crusts come thick and bready, with toppings straight from the book of Pizza Hut. In fact, a so-called "supreme"—olives, peppers, and several meats—is actually a poorer rendition than the chain's. As for pastas, one of the commonly nuked items is a so-called "pomodoro" sauce that feels like tomato-flavored water, making your noodle choice irrelevant. Surprisingly, po' boys are a good way to go, as in a meatball version with moist balls of ground beef sandwiched in crusty but soft bread. Eggplant parmigiana sports a thin coating of breadcrumbs that give the eggplant just enough crunch, along with a thankfully less-than-generous portion of mozzarella melted on top. It's a solid rendition of an "Italian-American 1.0" classic. (See pages 6-7 for the definition of "Italian-American 1.0.")

If only because mid-priced Italian-American dining in Houston is so often even worse, for a quick lunch of such heritage, Josephine's, for all its faults, actually manages to do a decent job with the genre—at least by neighborhood standards. –JY

Joyce's Ocean Grill

A Houston gem that takes you back to the good old days with fresh seafood

B+ *Total pleasure grade*

7.3 *Food* **8.5** *Feel* **$26** *Price* **Southern, Seafood**

Casual restaurant
Galleria hours Mon.-Fri. 11am-10pm; Sat. noon-10pm; closed Sun.
Greenway Plaza hours Mon.-Fri. 11am-10pm; Sat. noon-10pm; Sun. noon-9pm.

Galleria
6415 San Felipe St.
(713) 975-9902
www.joycesoceangrill.com

Greenway Plaza
3736 Westheimer Rd.
(713) 850-7738

Bar Full
Credit Cards Visa, MC, AmEx
Reservations Accepted

You know that warm feeling inside your body that's awakened when you revisit a worn old memory? That's the feeling that you'll get at Joyce's. It'll take you back to a time when time didn't matter and good friends were always around. (At least that's what it did, as you might have gathered, for one of our Undercover Chefs.) This is a wonderful little restaurant that serves Louisiana seafood, with some interesting Gulf-Mex dishes, like blackened catfish enchiladas, that actually turn out pretty well. Joyce's is an honest restaurant that isn't trying to set any trends or blow your mind with fancy plating techniques; they just want to serve good food at a good price. Sign us up.

Nicely tucked away from prying eyes on a busy street, this place serves up seafood and hospitality. The inside of the small restaurant is soothing, if hardly cutting-edge, with blue and green dominating the color scheme; it entices you to relax and focus on the food—or your delightful company. The service is over-the-top nice, from hostess to bartender to owner; they've definitely got Southern hospitality down.

And the food will treat you right, too. Joyce's serves an array of cooked-your-way seafood, and, of course, crab cakes. Even the bread and butter to start with is good; butter is sweet, delicious, and addictive. An array of—believe it or not—enchiladas are on the menu, and as iffy as they might sound, they end up tasting good. Mussels steamed in white wine are flavorful, and even the steam coming off the dish is intense and intoxicating; the mussels, most of the time, are big and plump. Joyce's missteps are mainly limited to stuffed items, like shrimp and fish; the stuffing is too bready, and it totally overpowers the delicate sea flavors. But you know better than to order that, right?

The wine list is a bit light and poorly stocked, but you didn't come here for wine. Gulf oysters are fresh and juicy, and are offered at the right price. This is hardly the best seafood in town, as the 7.3 food rating indicates. But service, warmth, and a deep sense of place can sometimes elevate a B- to a B+, and here, they do.

Back in the day, when you could smoke at the bar, they used to use old oyster shells as ashtrays. So come to engage in some escapist time travel—even if it's to a time and place you were never around to remember. –SD

Julia's Bistro

A lot of effort behind little done right

C- Total pleasure grade

4.9 Food **5.8** Feel **$60** Price **Southwestern**

Upmarket restaurant
Mon.-Thurs. 11am-2pm, 5pm-10pm; Fri. 11am-2pm, 5pm-11pm; Sat. 5pm-11pm; closed Sun. *Outdoor dining. Vegetarian-friendly. WiFi.*

Midtown
3722 Main St.
(713) 807-0090
www.juliasbistro.com

Bar Full
Credit Cards Visa, MC, AmEx
Reservations Recommended

You can just feel the enthusiasm here as Julia's Bistro aims to please. A polished interior, taking the minimalist route to hipness, screams out for a bit of attention. Silver angular chairs are nothing special, and shades of pink and mauve on the walls add a decidedly feminine element; this isn't Julio's, after all. And yet there's something lonely about the place. They have impressive dimensions to work with, but something about the layout makes you feel isolated and dwarfed by the high ceilings and huge glass windows. Even when the restaurant is full and packed with people, it still feels empty.

Sloppy service doesn't help either. Servers try their best, but their attempts at getting it right come across as forced and ultimately bungled. Sometimes there are communication kinks, and apéritifs ordered upon arrival might not show up until after the appetizers do. All this misdirected energy adds up, and with what's coming out of the kitchen, we find Julia's Bistro committing a faux-pas too many.

The cuisine here is based on, ahem, "Latin heritage cooking—featuring Mexican, Central American, South American, as well as Spanish-Mediterranean dishes with a Continental flair." That just about oughta cover it. As such, we have ceviche—a dish whose origins and manner of preparation are clear and simple—that verges on inedible. Shrimp are marinated to rubbery oblivion, yet still manage to maintain muddy off-notes; they float sadly in sour, unappealing citrus juice, with mounds of avocado on top. Crepas de huitlacoche (a Mexican corn fungus whose taste is—or rather should be—strong and earthy) are dominated by a "light cream sauce", such that none of the delightful wet-earth-after-the-rain elements shine through. Plantain-crusted snapper, with its ginger mango butter sauce, turns too sweet after a couple of bites; the roasted maduros (plantains) on the side hold absolutely no appeal in the face of the other sugars. One of your better options, however, is the "Camarones Criollos"; they're sautéed in an orange mojito marinade that also flirts with sweetness, but they take on a char that counterbalances that flavor.

And speaking of mojitos, they're not bad here. Given the sugar required of them, we think this should be right up Julia's alley, and it is. A Picojito is a girly version with Bacardi Coco and pineapple juice. Maybe it's just the pink walls getting to us, but we like 'em. –AH

Jungle Café

A modern Chinatown café whose Black Forest cake serenades the sweet tooth

7.8
Feel

Sweets

Counter service
Daily 10am-9pm.
Date-friendly. Vegetarian-friendly.

Chinatown
9110 Bellaire Blvd.
(713) 272-6633

Bar None
Credit Cards Visa and MC
Reservations Not accepted

French pastry chefs, culinary school programs, and sugar-holics, cover your ears. (What's with the tooth-numbing amount of sugar in desserts these days?) We get that sweets should be sweet, but it's too hard to get an appointment at the dentist's office these days to eat them that often. Enter Jungle Café, an unassuming little nook of a café in Chinatown, of all places, that caters to the Asian palate, which is a bit more sensitive to sugar. With above-average tea, a rock star of a Black Forest cake, and interestingly Asian-tinged desserts, Jungle Café, without meaning to, has turned into one of the most balanced (both business- and flavor-wise) pastry cafés in town.

Most places in the Welcome Food Center off of Bellaire are stuck in one of two extremes: either they're a hole in the wall, or they're an ultra-super-hip-cool-modern place. As with their pastries, Jungle Café has struck a happy balance. The place is at once sedate and modern with clean-cut lines. Staff at the counter don't speak much English, so don't be afraid to just point to what you want.

Though they also serve it in a mini-plated size, you'll probably want to pre-order a large Black Forest cake for yourself and hide in the corner of a room eating it. No one thing can be so mysteriously light while still being decadent, with layers of chocolate sponge, butter-cream, and rum-soaked cherries. The mango mousse cake is a signature of the shop, with inexplicably airy layers of cake sandwiching a mousse made of fresh, sweet-and-sour mangoes. The taro cake is an acquired taste, with earthy woodiness cutting through the sweet flavor. Aside from the black forest cake, chocolate and mocha desserts are probably their weakest points, as in a chocolate-hazelnut pyramid that lacks definitive bold flavor. Coffee- and espresso-based drinks are served in various forms; most impressive is the milk tea, with tea that's not over-brewed or sickly sweet. Jungle Café is no high-end haute French pastry temple, but it's an ideal place to have your cake and eat it too. –JY

Just Dinner

A home-grown BYO restaurant-speakeasy that breaks ground more atmospheric than culinary

B
Total pleasure grade

7.3 Food | 9.1 Feel | $30 Price | **American**

Casual restaurant
Tues.-Sat. 6pm-9:30pm;
closed Sun.-Mon.
Date-friendly.

Montrose
1915 Dunlavy St.
(713) 807-0077

Bar BYO
Credit Cards Visa, MC, AmEx
Reservations Essential

If you haven't heard of it, don't be surprised—most people haven't. This small house on Dunlavy only seats thirty people, and has a kitchen that is a cross between a professional and a home kitchen. A professional gas stove stands right next to white countertops and a standard home refrigerator.

Charming.

With only two cooks in the kitchen, the menu focuses on quality and friendly, laid-back service in a unique environment. Like a restaurant speakeasy, this place is mysterious and hidden. Dark colors and hardwood floors play off white tablecloths and white chairs. The owner lives in the house behind it, and some of the produce comes from his giant vegetable garden, which hints at his commitment to artisanal ingredients. The menu is limited, but it's well executed and works well in its small surroundings. Spring mix salads and wedge salads play nicely against the endlessly crowd-pleasing house-made ranch with chunks of gorgonzola folded in. Soups change seasonally. (Does that even really mean anything in Houston? Let's just say it won't be the same each time you visit.)

The main weakness of Just Dinner is its uncreative menu, which centers around banal Italian-American recipes that you've seen a thousand times before. With the access to good ingredients and good execution, it is frustrating that they don't do more with the cuisine. Expect the usual suspects like a tender, broiled filet of beef topped with blue-cheese butter and served with classic mash and zucchini to add crunch and texture. Daily fish specials are flavorful, with different fish brought in from the Gulf during the day to be prepared that night; this is probably some of the freshest fish in Houston.

Crème brûlée is overplayed but still delicious; creamy, sweet, and with a hard topping that is oh-so-fun to crack, it's one of the better versions in the city. Parking can be an issue, but all the friendly neighbors are cool with the parking situation—except, that is, for the Guild shop next door; beware. The best thing of all about Just Dinner is that it's BYO, with a five-dollar corkage fee; you can enjoy a great dinner, wonderful atmosphere, and your own bottle of wine at an unusually low price. –FC

Kahn's Deli

Total pleasure grade

Hit-or-miss sandwiches and Jewish fare that seem further from New York than we really are

Food

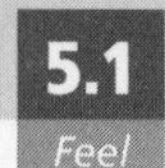

Feel

Price

Jewish Deli

Counter service
Mon.-Fri. 10am-5pm;
Sat. 10am-4pm; closed Sun.

Rice Area
2429 Rice Blvd.
(713) 529-2891
www.kahnsdeli.com

Bar Wine and beer only
Credit Cards No credit cards
Reservations Not accepted

The 1,415-mile hop from Houston to New York only takes about three hours in the air on Continental (America's best airline, hands down), but Kahn's deli makes New York City, which it has purported to emulate for the past half-century or so, seem a whole lot farther than that.

What's even more surprising, perhaps, than Kahn's failed food is the fact that it's the object of such adoration on the internet. CitySearch, as farcical and clueless as ever, calls Kahn's a "real winner," waxing poetic about the "bona fide kosher-style food" at a restaurant whose declared specialty is the Reuben, a sandwich that combines corned beef with Swiss and American cheese (the most basic rule of kosher food, followed by even the most laid-back of kosher folk: you can't mix meat and dairy).

The atmosphere at Kahn's is nothing much: you order at the counter, pay, wait a few minutes, and your sandwich appears—to go or to eat at one of the few bare-bones tables and chairs. Still, there's some character in the brusque service, the chalkboard-and-local-lore feel, and so on. That character is sapped, however, by the uniformly poor quality of the sandwich board, from cold, congealed cream cheese and one-dimensional lox on a sorry excuse for a bagel to chopped liver with disturbingly tangy off-notes.

And as for that Reuben—dubbed "world-famous" by the presumptuous menu scribe at Kahn's—it's imbalanced: the decent sauerkraut, Russian dressing, melted cheese, and toasted rye turn into faint voices in the wind amidst a grotesquely overstuffed pile of mediocre meat. Granted, there are some shops in New York that also pile on mountains of corned beef, but at least it's *good* corned beef; Kahn's thin, wimpy, and salty stuff doesn't even taste like a distant relative of those fresh slices of thick, well-marbled brisket. But then again, nothing much here reminds us of New York. –RG

Kaneyama

A classy dose of authenticity with faithful renditions of Japanese sushi and onigiri

B+ *Total pleasure grade*

8.5 *Food* **7.5** *Feel* **$33** *Price* **Japanese**

Casual restaurant
Sun.-Thurs. 11:30am-10:15pm;
Fri.-Sat. 11:30am-10:45pm.

Westchase
9527 Westheimer Rd.
(713) 784-5168
www.kaneyema-houston.com

Bar Full
Credit Cards Visa, MC, AmEx
Reservations Accepted

Kaneyama's website claims that even after a dozen years of being open, the place is still "sparkling new"; the fact that it was probably opened on a wing and a prayer means that its barren décor and high ambition are easy to maintain. So in that sense, Kaneyama is as good as when it first opened, with the same straightforward menu that's low on the frills and never fails to deliver.

If chef-owner Keeper Lin were a movie star, he'd be Clint Eastwood, with his straight shooting, hard charging, gruff attitude, and unwavering enthusiasm for hard work. While many other sushi bars in Houston expect you to throw back sake bombs and go gaga over complicated rolls that end up tasting like nothing but mayo, cream cheese, or avocado, Keeper has cultivated sushi that's worthy of a following, even absent the confusion of flashy lights, pounding music, or scantily clad bodies.

Kaneyama has probably birthed more sushi-lovers than any of their club-wannabe counterparts around town. Little touches show how much they care; yellowtail and yellowtail belly are served separately, with the belly a gorgeous, fatty cut that melts in your mouth. Flounder is cut thin to display the white fish's unique texture; another treat is the sea trout, as oily as salmon, but with smaller, sweeter flakes.

Hot food is not an afterthought, and might be good for those trying to get their feet wet with Japanese cuisine. A starter of seafood tempura is beautifully fried, except for the squid, which would have benefited from a higher frying temperature; scallops are still juicy, plump, and briny. Onigiri, or grilled rice balls, aren't seen anywhere else in town; they have a firm texture, benefiting from a nice char that takes real skill to achieve.

Kaneyama won't be the best Japanese restaurant you'll ever go to, and it doesn't have aspirations to be. While there aren't fireworks, there is good quality and hard work here, and you can taste that in every single bite. –JY

Kanomwan

Good—if sometimes overrated—Thai, served up by the surliest owner in town

$19 *Price* **Thai**

Casual restaurant
Mon.-Fri. 11:30am-10pm;
Sat. 5pm-10pm; closed Sun.

East Houston
736 1/2 Telephone Rd.
(713) 923-4230

Bar BYO
Credit Cards Visa, MC, AmEx
Reservations Not accepted

Kanomwan has acquired cult status among many office workers downtown. Its fans generally agree that it has some of the most vividly flavored Thai food in the city. Its detractors, on the other hand, point out—rightly—that it's more expensive and less authentic than Vieng Thai. But there's one thing everyone agrees on: that the owner, who takes orders and works the cash register, might just be the surliest dude in the Houston restaurant business.

Many people call the restaurant "Telephone Thai" because of its location on gritty Telephone Street, southeast of downtown, near the University of Houston. When Kanomwan moved from its original location a few years ago, many of the faithful were worried that it would lose its divey flair. They shouldn't have worried; the new spot just down the street is slightly larger, and the posters of Thailand are vaguely brighter, but it's still a straight-up dive.

People come for the food, which isn't the most authentic in town, even if it's a bit more Thai than some Thai-American joints. On the good side, the flavors are bold, direct, and well developed. Fried spring rolls arrive at your table crispy, burning hot, and strangely addictive. The ubiquitous tom kha gai soup has more flavor here than it does at most Thai-American joints, mixing slivers of chicken with coconut milk, lime, and lemongrass in a way that fills your mouth with flavor. Shrimp soup, too, is complex, offering elements of heat, sweet, and sour in each spoonful. The curries, though, are where Kanomwan really excels—if by "excels" you mean "kicks your ass." The green chicken curry is one of the hottest dishes we've sampled anywhere. Ask for it spicy, and get ready for tears. Ditto for the chicken with cashews and red chili paste, which some people make a really big deal about. We don't quite get it.

Nor do we get the owner's surliness. Whether it's an act or the guy is deeply depressed, the whole thing would be a bit more charming if his Thai food were as authentic as its reputation would have it. –RH

Katz's Deli

Katz's never kloses, but we wish they would

D

Total pleasure grade

3.6 *Food* **5.1** *Feel* **$20** *Price* **Jewish Deli**

Casual restaurant
Daily 24 hours.
Breakfast. Kid-friendly.
Outdoor dining.

Montrose
616 Westheimer Rd.
(713) 521-3838
www.ilovekatzs.com

Bar Full
Credit Cards Visa, MC, AmEx
Reservations Not accepted

You can sell a million shirts and have maps of New York City plastered throughout your restaurant. You can open two locations, one in Houston and one in Austin, that publicly proclaim that you're connected by family and license to the famous New York deli. But if the food's not good, then none of it matters.

We will pay good money for a great sandwich, but anything less than greatness between two slices of bread for eight to ten dollars is a deal-breaker. Bad food plus high prices can't even be fixed by great service—not that Katz's has that, either. Nonetheless, the giant restaurant on Westheimer flaunts its New Yorkiness at every turn. Disastrously chewy bagels with terrible cream cheese and stringy, chunky lox make you feel further away from New York than the actual 1,500-mile flight. They can't even slice onions properly. Other sandwiches, overstuffed with dry pastrami, salami, and so on offer equally little to answer your Jewish deli cravings. The pastrami needs to be warm, and the fat on the meat needs to be succulent. Here, it's neither. Pickles, broccoli-cheese soup (not available every day), cole slaw, and potato knishes are better than the sandwiches—moving up toward almost acceptable—but it's not nearly enough to rescue this place. Stuffed cabbage, if done right, can be a beautiful thing, perhaps bringing up memories of a lovely childhood. But when your childhood favorites are adulterated and poorly executed, then the emotions run wild. Here, the cabbage's sauce is way too sweet, the meatballs show up dry, and the results are a disaster.

The only thing Katz's really has going for it are the drinks specials and specialty drinks. They've got three-dollar draft beer all day, every day, and giant Bloody Marys that rival any in town. And they're open 24 hours a day. Otherwise, when it comes to Jewish delis, it's not hard to blame New Yorkers for pronouncing "Houston" differently from us, because this Katz's has nothing in common with the one on Manhattan's Houston Street. –SD

Kenneally's Irish Pub

There's some truth to the hype; just don't socialize with the regulars

B *Total pleasure grade*

7.2 *Food* **7.5** *Feel* **$17** *Price* **Pizza, American**

Bar
Mon. 4pm-1am; Tues.-Sat. 3pm-1am; Sun. 3pm-11pm.
Outdoor dining.

Montrose
2111 S. Shepherd Dr.
(713) 630-0486
www.irishpubkenneallys.com

Bar Full
Credit Cards Visa, MC, AmEx
Reservations Accepted

Walking into this Irish pub, with sports on the many televisions and tons of testosterone, you might be predisposed to like it. But there's a hook here: the pizza is famous throughout Houston. It's often spoken about like a myth or a tall tale, its qualities exaggerated in the literature—especially the thin crust, which does admittedly hold up beautifully to cheese and tasty toppings. Lots of pictures of the who's who of the sports and entertainment world clutter the walls here, and in the pre-smoking-ban days, there was a haze of smoke constantly suspended in the air. Patrons, on your average night, might include anyone from a suit on his cell explaining to his wife that he's working late at the office to the stereotypical backwards-baseball-hat-wearing, all-American guy.

A nice selection of standard draft beers from around the globe—Stella Artois, Guinness, and so forth—will put you at ease. Kenneally's doesn't offer pub grub from the other side of the pond; rather, they serve good ol' American bar food. House-made potato chips, burgers, and pizza are what keep 'em coming back. Those artisanal potato chips are so thin as to be practically non-existent; they dissolve instantly upon being crunched. The fry job can be a bit poor; we've gotten them still raw in the middle, though they are seasoned very well.

We've all heard all the hype about Kenneally's pizza; some say it's the best in the city and others say it's the best in the country. Does it live up to the hype? The pizza arrives on a silver disk that is supported by a four-pronged stand—a typical pizza accoutrement—and it's cut into squares. It's hot, crispy, with well-developed flavor in the sauce, and plenty of porky topping options. The crust is pleasantly thin, but it comes off slightly dense, slightly crackly, slightly under-flavored—crackery, if you will. But these complaints are minor: the pizza does deliver. Best in the city? No. For one thing, it's not even close to the pies at either of Marco Wiles' joints. If you're looking for a good pizza and fresh draft beer, though, Kenneally's is your place. You'll have a lot more fun here if you don't come with such weighty expectations. –SD

Kenny & Ziggy's

Only the lofty New York prices are authentic at this Manhattanish deli

C+ Total pleasure grade

4.8 *Food* **4.3** *Feel* **$20** *Price* **Jewish Deli**

Casual restaurant
Mon.-Fri. 7am-9pm;
Sat.-Sun. 8am-9pm.
Breakfast. Brunch. Delivery.

Galleria
2327 Post Oak Blvd.
(713) 871-8883
www.kennyandziggys.com

Bar Full
Credit Cards Visa, MC, AmEx
Reservations Not accepted

New York delicatessens in Houston have had a bad reputation for a while. The reasons for this are twofold: one, most of them are horrible; and two, New Yorkers who relocate to Houston are tough critics, understandably, of their own cuisine. (Of course, we Houstonians do the exact same thing when it comes to critiquing Tex-Mex or barbecue in other parts of the country.) A good pastrami, corned beef, or tongue sandwich is going to be hard to come by in Houston, and most people have accepted that fact. But when a place advertises that it's a real New York delicatessen, and gussies up their restaurant with Midtown Manhattan gear, they'd better bring the goods. Kenny and Ziggy's does a mediocre job of that. It definitely couldn't hold its own elsewhere—especially in New York—but by default, it is the best in Houston.

Kenny and Ziggy's is brown and wide open, with plenty of noise at peak lunch hour to recreate the New York deli experience. The décor is ghastly in its inauthenticity, however; fake-New-York everything decorates the walls, and a predictable clear glass case of spinning cheesecakes tempts you to spoil your appetite. Giant sandwiches of the usual pastrami, corned beef, and salami are offered, as well as some typically Jewish food like whitefish salad and chopped liver (both are good). The sandwiches are expensive, many breaking the $10 barrier, which builds up expectations. Unfortunately, they're not met by the meat between the bread. Pastrami and corned beef are dry, too lean, and flavor-deprived. The franks, with sauerkraut and fries, are thin and poorly represented. If they make you happy at all, it will be by jogging your memory—not by tasting good.

The onion rings are some of the best in town, crispy, brown, and delicious. But the cole slaw feels like cabbage swimming in milky mayonnaise, and the pickles taste overly pickled. Do ask the waiter to bring some pickled green tomatoes; they're free and full of garlicky, acidic goodness. But it's garlicky, acidic goodness doesn't quite transport you to New York City. –SD

Khyber

It's not good Indian, it's not bad Indian, so what is it? Slightly overpriced Indian

C+

Total pleasure grade

6.1 Food

7.0 Feel

$26 Price

Indian

Casual restaurant
Daily 11am-2pm, 5:30pm-10pm.
Date-friendly. Vegetarian-friendly.

Upper Kirby
2510 Richmond Ave.
(713) 942-9424

Bar Full
Credit Cards Visa, MC, AmEx
Reservations Not accepted

Here we have yet another Indian buffet that will occasionally surprise you with an exciting flavor, but most of the time it's just all right. The trend nowadays is to do a buffet for lunch and à la carte during dinner, but your concept is irrelevant if you don't have the food to keep people interested.

Khyber, on Richmond, has everything in place to be a great restaurant: a great location, tasteful interior design, and warm service. But the food is just too unpredictable. Vindaloo dishes, curries, cold salads, and rice pudding grace the buffet daily, and there are lots of delicious vegetarian options keep the herbivores happy. It's just that it's so easy to get better for cheaper in this city.

Khyber is sandwiched between two Pappas restaurants. A sign outside of Khyber changes almost every week making fun of the two other restaurant's signs. We're quite amused by the game, but unfortunately, you can't run a restaurant on jokes alone.

The inside of the place is simple and warm. The walls aren't cluttered with items that look like they were pulled out of a basement, and the service is professional and hospitable without being too pushy. The food, on the other hand, disappoints. It's not terrible, but it could be so much more.

Best amongst the options are vegetarian dishes, but vindaloo dishes are one-dimensional (and the dimension is heat). Rice pudding is flavorful, but eat fast, because it suffers from Viagra syndrome—it can get stiff and hard quickly and easily. Naan is good, with a crusty bottom and a fluffy top, making it ideal for dipping into the decent curries. Unfortunately, there's not much to dip it in; the meek gravy could use more depth of reduction and spice—or, for that matter, just more of *itself*. The flavors have a "short finish," as a wine snob might put it; they disappear too quickly. Although, in principle, we like the notion of differentiating oneself through subtle variations in the execution of otherwise familiar dishes, we prefer it when the method of differentiation doesn't amount to a reduction in flavor. –SD

Kim Son

Lukewarm dim sum and overpriced buffet isn't a good combination

Total pleasure grade

6.7 Food | 7.0 Feel | $32 Price

Vietnamese, Chinese

Casual restaurant
Sun.-Thurs. 11am-11pm;
Fri.-Sat. 11am-midnight.
Kid-friendly. Vegetarian-friendly.

Downtown
2001 Jefferson St.
(713) 222-2461
www.kimson.com

Chinatown
10603 Bellaire Blvd.
(281) 575-0140

Bar Full
Credit Cards Visa, MC, AmEx
Reservations Accepted

Chinatown
12750 Southwest Fwy.
(281) 242-3500

You know that one hot girl that everyone wants to get with? The one who seems so nice on the outside but that the guys can't help but continually wonder if, on the inside, she's got dirt for a heart? That's the Bellaire-Chinatown branch of Kim Son. In spades. In the newest of the mega shopping centers springing up, the place looks eminently bright and shiny, with reaching arches and a golden reputation. Once you're inside, though, it's like a bad joke. Like a punch-you-in-the-mouth-just-for-fun joke. How could a place with such underperforming food really be so popular?

You'd think that one would heed the warning signs: the overly grandiose white buildings, say, or the fact that "Dim Sum," "Buffet," and "Fine Dining" are all inscribed on one restaurant. The behemoth Bellaire Kim Son is split into two dining rooms, neither designed well: the buffet room has only the buffet tables to take away from its emptiness, while the dim sum room, which also serves à-la-carte food, looks like an oversized Holiday Inn banquet hall. Now, when your buffet is better than your dining-room food, you know you have a big problem. The problem here is overproduction. Stir-fried beef with flat noodles tastes as if it was cooked in large batches in too small of a pan, rendering it soggy and flavorless. Dim sum is standard at best; underseasoned siu mai, open-faced pork dumplings, lack a certain firmness and savory aspect. Sweet dishes can be decent: steamed buns with yellow coconut custard are a nice, not-too-sweet way to finish up your meal. At the downtown branch, the rooms are more similar to each other, and the clientele is trimodally split between Vietnamese families, old Houstonians, and groups of cops. (Needless to say, the latter two groups stick with the Chinese-American fare: egg rolls, beef with broccoli, and so on.)

The downtown location specializes more in Vietnamese options like bo kho: braised beef stew with French bread for dipping. In the end, though—like that girl that looks so good on the outside—you're probably just going to be used for your money. –JY

Kiran's

Standard Indian-American meets ill-executed nouvelle French

C Total pleasure grade

6.2 Food | **7.5** Feel | **$60** Price | **Indian**

Upmarket restaurant
Sat.-Mon. 5:30pm-10pm;
Tues.-Fri. 11am-2:30pm,
5:30pm-10pm.
Vegetarian-friendly.

Galleria
4100 Westheimer Rd.
(713) 960-8472
www.kiranshouston.com

Bar Full
Credit Cards Visa, MC, AmEx
Reservations Accepted

In much of the popular literature, Kiran's and Indika are mentioned in the same breath. They're both Indian restaurants that are understood to be venturing beyond the norm, striving to create something new, different, modern, connected to New American cuisines and New York tasting menus, in tune and in touch with the foodies, the critics, and—at least in the case of Kiran's, it seems, from the collage of multi-page kiss-ups in glossy, full-color national magazines—the freelance food writers. The problem is, in spite of its ambition, Kiran's can't execute on what it sets out to achieve. It's nowhere near Indika's level.

The idea, anyway, is to serve a high-priced, multi-course menu in a strangely steakhouse-like setting that shatters the Indian-restaurant norms and fits itself out for oilmen, CEOs, and Texans quarterbacks. To go with it, they'll happily sell you a pricey bottle of wine—although they might uncork it clumsily and overfill your glasses. They'll definitely scale the heights of ambition with a highly touted nouvelle Indian tasting menu.

Unfortunately, the menu comes out worse than the spread at your average bargain lunch-buffet Indian. Get ready for a parade of muted Indian spices on a bad date with haphazardly-executed modern French food, beginning with undersalted "goat cheese tikka," and progressing through a lowlight reel of overambitious, underperforming fusion dishes. "Vindaloo aïoli," just a name, not a taste, that comes with mediocre crab cakes (Can you get any more boring than mediocre crab cakes?) is a flavorless green salad, adorned with goat cheese and pomegranate seeds whose only purpose seems to be to strut around and look pretty, like a struggling fashion model.

No would-be Persephone would stay in the underworld to eat these. Then comes fatally chewy "Tandoori Portobello" with mushy "sweet peppers and red onions." Cashew-and-paneer-stuffed eggplant in desperate need of salt. "Tandoori quail" with mission figs, black currants, and pine nuts plopped onto a bed of watery baby spinach, with a port wine reduction, that comes out to so much less than the sum of its parts. Overcooked duck, and underseasoned rack of lamb.

It's sad, because if you stick to the Indian-American (or Indian-British) classics like tikka masala, saag paneer, and so forth, the food's not half bad. But we must define Kiran's as the restaurant defines itself, and given what this kitchen is going for, it's disastrously out of its league. –RG

Kona Grill

D-

Total pleasure grade

An Asian-inspired mega-chain that fails to live up to its shine and glamour

3.3 Food **7.2** Feel **$54** Price

Pan-Asian

Casual restaurant
Mon.-Thurs. 11am-11pm,
Fri.-Sat. 11am-midnight;
Sun. 11am-10pm.

Outdoor dining. WiFi.

Galleria
5061 Westheimer Rd.
(713) 877-9191
www.konagrill.com

Sugar Land
16535 Southwest Fwy.
(281) 242-7000

Bar Full
Credit Cards Visa, MC, AmEx
Reservations Accepted

When the main attraction for a restaurant is its location, then you're probably looking at a moderately priced, over-decorated, food-for-the-masses type of place. And that's what Kona Grill is—to a T. In the Galleria, where taste is often secondary to how fast and full you can get before running back to Coach or Nordstrom, Kona Grill's so-called "Hawaiian" food touches many bases, none of which are on the way to an extra-base hit. Some dishes are gum-rottingly sweet, and some are super-salty, but most are just bland. The idea is to give shoppers a prettier and more appealing option than food-court grazing, but after a meal at Kona, you'll probably wish you'd spent your money at Chili's or the Golden Arches.

Kona Grill is a public company (Nasdaq: KONA)—which doesn't exactly engender confidence in its kitchen—but it's also a beautiful place, with an impressive collection of the avant-garde restaurant trinity of wood, stone, and oversized fixtures. Large banquettes accommodate big parties with bigger shopping bags, and the bar is spiced up by the countless beautiful faces of Galleria shoppers pounding sake bombs and trying to look cool.

The menu looks like what might have emerged if the Cheesecake Factory took a detour to Chinatown. We understand that many Americans have developed quite a tolerance for high-fructose corn syrup, but much of this food might leave a healthy elephant crumpled and quivering on the ground from sugar shock. A chicken satay starter feels steamed, though it's grilled, and comes with a dipping sauce that claims to be hoisin but tastes like salted honey. The signature "Macadamia Chicken" comes with a sickeningly rich cream sauce that's supposed to be offset by a pineapple-papaya marmalade, except that the off-colored pile tastes like candied fruit. And it takes talent to mess up a spicy tuna roll, but Kona manages to do it, overcooking the sushi rice to such an extent that the roll disintegrates in your mouth.

The best thing we've tried at Kona has been avocado egg rolls, an attempt to be Cheesecake Factory chic—which reminds us: if we're eating bad food in a mall anyway, why don't we just *go* to the Cheesecake Factory, and save our wallets from Kona Grill's prices? –JY

Korea Garden

An aging restaurant that can still bring the heat

B
Total pleasure grade

6.9	7.7	$32
Food	*Feel*	*Price*

Korean

Casual restaurant
Daily 11am-10pm.
Vegetarian-friendly.

Spring Branch
9501 Long Point Rd.
(713) 468-2800

Bar Full
Credit Cards Visa, MC, AmEx
Reservations Accepted

Korea Garden doesn't just look and feel old—it *is* old. It's probably been years since any water has flowed through the former fish tank that anchors the middle of the restaurant, and possibly even longer since either the décor or the menu was refurbished. Still, there's a quality about Korea Garden that makes it feel time-honored rather than senile—and if you choose carefully, it still has the chops to deliver a swift, size-12 boot kick in the rear with surgingly spicy food and long-marinated meats.

The water-tank void in the dim, gloomy room conveys a clear message: the restaurant's best days have definitely passed it by. But you're somehow made to feel as if it'll close down on its own terms rather than being forced into closure, especially since the place had such a glorious golden age. Not that the staff seem like they would much mind retirement; they come off as bored, delivering attentive but unenthusiastic service with pressed smiles.

Lunch specials deliver Korea Garden's worst food—overcooked bulgogi, soggy tempura, and over-honeyed teriyaki chicken hold court—but they still seem to be the restaurant's best-business meal, perhaps because no one can resist the allure of the bento box, even if a mayo-heavy potato salad occupies a whole compartment. Ordering food off the real menu is better; Korean barbecue is good, but the collection of Korean-style hot pots is best. The complimentary banchan, or side dishes, sometimes include a dried salt fish that's slightly fishy and—once you acquire the taste—slightly addictive. Unlike its counterpart, Seoul Garden, whose barbecued meats have taken a noticeable nosedive in quantity and quality, Korea Garden still has a kalbi that's heavy on the soy-and-onion flavor and well-acidulated squid that takes on a char well while staying tender. If you're looking for the quintessential, ass-kicking, don't-need-no-Viagra-'cause-I-got-spice flavor, however, a haemool jungol, or seafood hot pot loaded with shellfish and clear noodles, is heart-warming with its spiced broth. There's spicy, and then there's Korean spicy. And with so many years under its belt, it's no question that Korea Garden has this part down right. –JY

Kraftsmen Bakery

If you want a good sandwich, start with good bread

B- Total pleasure grade

7.5 Food | **7.5** Feel | **$12** Price

Light American

Casual restaurant
Mon.-Fri. 7am-7pm;
Sat. 8am.-7pm;
Sun. 8am-5pm.
Breakfast. Outdoor dining. Vegetarian-friendly. WiFi.

Montrose
4100 Montrose Blvd.
(713) 524-3737
www.kraftsmenbaking.com

Bar None
Credit Cards Visa, MC, AmEx
Reservations Not accepted

The Kraftsmen Café on Montrose is the retail outlet of Kraftsmen Bakery, a wholesale artisanal provider of breads and assorted baked goods to upscale restaurants and hotels in town. The Café serves standard café fare—soups, salads, sandwiches—but its greatest strength, not surprisingly, lies in the baked goods. Muffins and scones are top-notch, and the sandwiches benefit from bread that's still well above average. That said, the place has gone downhill since first opening, tasting flatter than it once did.

The breads are certified kosher, and the bakers claim to use organic ingredients whenever possible. All baked goods are cooked that day, and the result is baguettes that are crunchy on the outside and moist and chewy on the inside; rye that's dense, with a distinct caraway flavor; and buttery scones that crumble when your teeth sink into them, not before. The sandwiches are assembled to order from ingredients that look and taste fresh. The turkey and brie sandwich, with avocado and bacon on a baguette, is filling, if unspectacular. The Reuben has less meat than a Reuben really should have, but the quality of the rye bread puts you in a forgiving mood. They throw in your choice of chips, which you can then throw away.

If you're not into the baked goods, the Mediterranean salad will hook you up with olives, tomatoes, and red peppers—but, honestly, who orders a salad at a bakery? Breakfast choices make more sense, particularly the croissant sandwich with scrambled eggs, cheddar, and bacon on a flaky croissant.

Kraftsmen also serves up strong coffee and teas to accompany the pastries; iced chai is a good choice in summer months. They also stock a decent selection of Illy coffee products, should you desire to take your espresso at home. More elegant, however, is to have your muffin and cappuccino out on the shady brick patio. If you stick around long enough, it could be beer o'clock, at which point you can head over to the Black Labrador next door for a pint. –RH

Kubo's

Surprising sushi and nouvelle Japanese in bland Rice Village packaging

B- Total pleasure grade

7.5 Food | **7.4** Feel | **$44** Price

Japanese

Casual restaurant
Mon.-Thurs. 11:30am-10pm; Fri. 11:30pm-midnight; Sat. noon-10:30pm; Sun. noon-9pm
Outdoor dining.

Rice Area
2414 University Blvd.
(713) 528-7878
www.kubos-sushi.com

Bar Full
Credit Cards Visa, MC, AmEx
Reservations Accepted

The tacky storefront and clumsy logo of this highly touted second-floor Japanese restaurant in the Rice Village Arcade reveal little of what lies within: strange works of modern art with an aboriginal fetish, an orange wall glow that evokes a postapocalyptic Hong Kong, and one of Houston's better sushi bars.

Your first clue that Kubo's is something different comes from the billboard out front. There, those classic Asian-restaurant scrawls of neon lime and peach announce the unusually authentic daily specials, which might include salmon-and-sea-bass carpaccio or spicy scallop soup.

Go for such specials. At one visit, braised pork belly—a melting tower of spectacular pork fat and browned meat that's also on the regular menu by itself, came with juicy but bland shrimp; jarring parsley; sinus-searing wasabi dabs that, when applied, overwhelmed other flavors; and a sweet, one-dimensional "reduction sauce" that tasted teriyaki-ish. Still, the fatty pork belly shone gloriously through.

Ample nigiri sushi pieces sing with freshness, especially springy suzuki (sea bass); sweet, pasty ama ebi (sweet shrimp); delicate seared white tuna; buttery salmon; simple, clean tuna; and soft, mild mackerel. Skip the gelatinous, slightly metallic-tasting eel, though, and the rubbery, challenging awabi (abalone). Sushi rice is expertly vinegared and textured, but wasabi dabs are applied too liberally, stealing the spotlight from beneath the milder fish slices. Sometimes we sneak in a chopstick and carve them out.

The big, yuppie-chic room generally works, its dim sleekness interrupted only by a glaring glass exit door in one corner, and by a giant blue curtain that seems to promise a stage show that never begins. The bar can get lively, and booths and round banquettes are warm and intimate. Not so for the erratic service; on our last visit, the main arrived two bites after the appetizer. You're better off at the sushi bar, where you'll have private chef access to the most special pieces of fish. And at their best, they really can be special. –RG

La Fendée

Total pleasure grade

Confused Mediterranean dishes that come with quite a price to pay

4.9 Food **3.0** Feel **$30** Price

Middle Eastern

Casual restaurant
Mon.-Thurs. 11am-10pm; Fri.-Sat. 11am-11pm; Sun. noon-10pm.
Outdoor dining.

Montrose
1402 Westheimer Rd.
(713) 522-1505

Bar None
Credit Cards Visa and MC
Reservations Not accepted

Walking into this small, flashy restaurant, you wouldn't expect anything unexpected. And you'd be right. With its large-screen television and dry-erase board, La Fendée, with a prime Montrose location, looks much like the other small Middle Eastern joints around town that are trying to update their concept and décor to bring it in line with the 21st century. This attempted catapult into the future comes with a price, though—and that price is covered by you, dear customer. Aside from a few outrageously priced salads, La Fendée offers classics like falafel, baba ghanooj, shawarmas, and kebabs. By keeping their menu small, they strive for consistency and quality.

Strive, that is.

La Fendée looks like it was designed by a Tele-Tubby; with its bright colors, it bears a striking resemblance to the play area at McDonald's. Service seems to get more disorganized with every request. Still, baba ghanooj is delicious, with an earthy flavor that's spiked with acid in all the right places. Use the accompanying pita to shovel it all into your mouth. The falafel performs well, too; its dipping sauce has just the right level of acidity to balance it all out.

But ugh, those prices. Mains tend to creep into the double digits, which is especially egregious in the case of the incredibly dry deconstructed chicken shawarma. Gyros, blander than average, are piled up with onions the size of Tennessee—exercise caution if you're on a date.

La Fendée does offer nice fresh juices, usually two different ones a day. The mango and strawberry versions are refreshing and thick. Desserts, though, are pretty lame, with baklava, espresso, cake, and sorbet the only principal players. But in spite of the good baba, falafel, and juices, there aren't many compelling reasons to come here, and even if you happen to be driving right through Montrose, the high prices will keep you away. –SD

La Griglia

We'd trade in the slick, colorful scene for some decent Italian food

Total pleasure grade

4.9 Food | **8.4** Feel | **$60** Price

Italian-American

Upmarket restaurant
Mon.-Thurs. 11:30am-2:30pm, 5:30pm-11pm; Fri. 11:30am-2:30pm, 5:30pm-midnight; Sat. 5:30pm-midnight; Sun. 5:30pm-10pm.
Outdoor dining. WiFi.

River Oaks
2002 W. Gray St.
(713) 526-4700
www.lagrigliarestaurant.com

Bar Full
Credit Cards Visa, MC, AmEx
Reservations Accepted

It's a testament to Houston's dynamic dining scene that when restaurants become bad, they don't often remain popular. The exceptions to that rule are few, but La Griglia is one of them. Although the restaurant might have had a bright past, the only thing rosy about its future is that nobody seems to have noticed how far downhill the food has fallen. Sometimes, reputation is everything.

Thankfully, the delightful atmosphere at La Griglia hasn't changed; it's in the Wolfgang Puck school, a striking, soaring, warmly lit space with huge, colorful murals and mosaics that create an atmospheric buzz out of thin air, even when the place is mostly empty (which is basically never). Few moments of the experience here aren't finely tuned and enjoyable, beginning with the lively bar scene by the entrance. The place can really churn through covers on a busy night. La Griglia has almost no bad seats. Even in corners that might be forgotten at most other restaurants, you'll see graceful archways, smoking pizza ovens, rainbows of tiles, flow, and movement.

Unfortunately, that slickness isn't replicated in the wannabe-Italian kitchen. La Griglia executes poorly on just about everything it does, and when it tries to do too much—as it often does—things get even worse. We've sampled a roll call of bland starters not worth mentioning; a thin-crust pizza with sausage and peppers is not great, but it's probably the least of the evils here. Pasta performs poorly in these hands.

Amatriciana is a Roman pasta dish in which thickly reduced tomato, onion, and pancetta flavors are supposed to meld together into a sort of coating designed to tunnel into the holes of bucatini, or, alternatively, to stick to the ridges on rigatoni. Here, a watery, underreduced sauce sits pathetically on thin, overcooked cappellini, doing none of the above. It's a combination of the wrong recipe and incorrect execution. Braised and roasted meats, like a wild boar chop, have come consistently tough, overcooked, underseasoned, and underflavored. Fish fares even worse. The only excuse, perhaps, for a place this popular to serve food this bad is that they know they can get away with it. –RG

La Guadalupana

A place pulled right out of Mexico that serves simple, good food

7.9 Food | **6.7** Feel | **\$11** Price | **Mexican**

Casual restaurant
Mon.-Tues. 7am-3pm;
Wed.-Sun. 7am-9pm.
Breakfast. Outdoor dining.

Montrose
2109 Dunlavy St.
(713) 522-2301

Bar BYO
Credit Cards Visa, MC, AmEx
Reservations Not accepted

This hole in the wall on Dunlavy is, at first blush, a quaint, conservative bakery. But it doubles as a homey Mexican restaurant serving 19 meals per week. Its traditional regional dishes, like mole poblano, along with more pan-Mex comfort food like tortas and bistec ranchero (a thin, pounded steak with salsa), are served up in a small, plain, haphazardly decorated space that immediately transports you to Mexico in all its downmarket brilliance.

Enter, and you're first met with the bakery, which features all sorts of cakes and cookies. About ten tables are squeezed into another, minimalist room where you can sit down for meals (although take-out is not a bad option here). Warm, dark colors will comfort you as you browse the sometimes-hard-to-understand menu. Breakfast might consist of chilaquiles, breakfast tacos, or huevos rancheros, which are spot on, highlighting the salsa ranchera that gets its spice from chilies and tomatoes to help out the humble egg. There's also coffee and flavored milks.

Lunch and dinner share the same menu. Tortas with a choice of meat (pork, chicken milanesa, carnitas) come piled with beans, jalapeños, onion, lettuce, tomato, and avocado; it's hearty Mexican comfort food, one of the most common but underappreciated preparations in the Mexican repertoire. Remember, this is a bakery too, so the bread that's used for the tortas is delicious, a bit sweet and nicely spongy. A chicken breast with mole poblano (a dark, bittersweet dry-roasted chile sauce integrating pumpkin seeds and chocolate) is nutty and complex. The chicken can come overcooked, but the sauce adds extra flavor and moisture. Authentic, regional Mexican soups such as caldo de mariscos (seafood soup) and pozole (soup with hominy), are hot, flavorful, and will have you wanting more.

Prices are unbeatable—almost as authentically Mexican as the food—and juices and drinks tend to change daily. Carrot, orange, or a "Vampire" (carrot, orange, and beet) are refreshing and fresh. Then there's horchata (a Mexican rice drink) and Mexican Coke, which comes in the old-school glass bottles, and is made from sugar cane instead of corn syrup—the most paradoxical, you might say, of all authentic Mexican treats. –SD

La Mexicana

Some Tex-Mex standards seem certain to outlive us all

B- *Total pleasure grade*

5.0 *Food* **8.7** *Feel* **$27** *Price* **Tex-Mex**

Casual restaurant
Mon.-Sat. 7am-11pm;
Sun. 7am-10pm.
Breakfast. Delivery. Kid-friendly. Outdoor dining. WiFi.

Montrose
1018 Fairview St.
(713) 521-0963
www.lamexicanarestaurant.com

Bar Full
Credit Cards Visa, MC, AmEx
Reservations Accepted

Google the word "mexicana," and the musical website for this restaurant comes up in the first page of search results. Keep in mind that Google indexes the web sites in Mexico, too.

Need we say more about this restaurant's popularity in Houston?

La Mexicana has been a Houston tradition for more than a quarter of a century now, and people in the Montrose area swear by it. The reasons for this unbelievable renown are not entirely clear to us, although it's certainly clear that tradition—the first-mover advantage—played a serious role. But we can also point to a few other likely culprits: the patio is pleasant, the margaritas are tart and enjoyable, and the crowd is cheery and local. There's the convenient location, of course, and the ease of parking. The building has lots of fun, familiar flair. If the wooden chairs, paper cutouts hanging from the ceiling, and old pottery placed along the wall make the down-home Tex-Mex vibe seem generic, it might just be because so many other Tex-Mex restaurants in Houston have modeled themselves after La Mexicana, not vice versa.

A meal at La Mexicana might—should, actually—start well with good queso before moving on to the main Tex-Mex event. The menu does harbor some desire to pitch some Mex along with the Tex: menudo, mole, and tacos de barbacoa or chicharrón (fried pork skins, served on weekends only) squeeze their way in between the enchilada combination plates and such.

Fajitas arrive at your table still sizzling, but the beef and chicken slices often show up so dry that it takes extra moisture from the salsa to rid yourself of the ensuing cottonmouth. Yikes. Refried beans and rice are nothing more than standard. On a more positive note, fajitas for two come with tons of meat, and the price is surprisingly right—about $18. Cantaloupe juice is great, a wonderful non-alcoholic accompaniment, though the margaritas are hard to pass up. We only wish the food—like the prices, in recent years—were trending upward, rather than downward. Still, it's hard to argue that we won't be back, sooner or later. La Mexicana will probably outlive us. –FC

La Michoacana

A transportative Mexican-grocery empire offering cheap eats at a basic counter

B+ Total pleasure grade

8.0 Food | **6.3** Feel | **$6** Price

Mexican

Counter service
Daily 8am-10pm.
Breakfast. Outdoor dining.

Spring Branch
2030 Wirt Rd.
(713) 956-2974

Bellaire
6906 Atwell Dr.
(713) 668-3869

Bar None
Credit Cards Visa, MC, AmEx
Reservations Not accepted

La Michoacana doesn't probably come to mind when you think of Houston's chain empires. But it's one of the biggest. There are 47 La Michoacana groceries in the Houston area—more, by some measurements, than there are Burger King branches. They cater mainly to Latin American immigrants, offering dry-goods staples from Mexico and Central America, cheap prices on meat and produce, as well as in-house taquerías and panaderías to satiate immediate hunger.

Some locations are charmingly painted with murals of huge vegetables and cuts of meat on the outside. Inside space is generally at a premium; aisles allow only one small cart at a time, and every wall and surface is there for the selling of product. The meat department is particularly interesting, with cases stacked a foot and a half high with every cut imaginable, from head cheese to trotters.

When you're done browsing and are ready to eat, figure out what you want and head over to the registers to pay—you pay for everything in advance here. The cashier will give you a ticket with your order to be presented at the counter. A working knowledge of Spanish is a good thing here, as they might take some liberties with your order if they believe that a gringo wouldn't really order that. If you choose to eat in, there are counter seats and a few booths and tables that could certainly stand to be wiped.

Menu choices vary from simple breakfast items to tacos, tamales, stews, and more. Slightly soggy chiles rellenos are filled with mild asadero cheese. Beef fajita tacos are strangely tough, so we prefer tacos de lengua (tongue), barbacoa (beef cheek), and a faithful rendition of tacos de chicharrón (greasy, flavorful pig skin). The enveloping tortillas are thin and tasty. If you're a tamale fan, try the hoja de plátano, a Oaxaca-style tamal stuffed with chicken and steamed in a banana leaf, which is uncommon in these parts; it's big enough to be a whole meal. Homemade aguas frescas (fruit drinks) are excellent, and delicious menudo—prepared daily, not just on weekends, as it is elsewhere—makes a hangover cure available any day of the week. –FC

La Strada

Total pleasure grade

Flamboyant Bellinis and hit-or-miss Italian amidst beautiful brunchers

6.2	8.0	$59
Food	Feel	Price

Italian-American

Upmarket restaurant
Tues.-Thurs. 11am-9:30pm;
Fri.-Sat. 11am-3am;
Sun. 11am-6pm; closed Mon.
Brunch. Live music.
Outdoor dining. WiFi.

Montrose
322 Westheimer Rd.
(713) 523-1014
www.lastradahouston.com

Bar Full
Credit Cards Visa, MC, AmEx
Reservations Recommended

Like the high-class stripper whose work environment this restaurant's interior decorating suggests, La Strada conceals multiple personalities beneath its skin. First and foremost, it is the city's craziest gay-straight Sunday brunch scene. You must reserve in advance if you hope to get in. Once you're there, your challenges will be to drum up some semblance of service; to guzzle the famous Bellinis with floaters; and, finally, to take your place on the rocking outdoor terrace amidst a mass of hot-bodied scenesters. Up there, you can show off your wardrobe, dance to (or, if you're too close to a speaker, cringe at) hip-hop, and flirt with the beautiful people at what amounts to a morning (or afternoon) dance club.

This flamboyant Montrose mainstay re-opened in 2004 after a fire, and they've recently re-tooled their schedule to include a (somewhat less insane) Saturday brunch, and—best of all—a "mezza notte" brunch on Friday and Saturday nights from 10pm to 3am. Certainly the midnight brunch is a groundbreaking concept in Houston, and of that we approve. But on an average night, the relatively uninteresting food that's served with pretense in amusingly sexed-up early-'90s style—ultra-dim lighting, Vaudeville-esque curtains, exposed brick—doesn't really justify an expenditure of $60 or $70 a head.

That's not to say the food is terrible. Good—if disappointingly sauced—fried calamari and happy, well-textured crab cakes headline the starters; however, baked brie is as unexciting as usual, and spinach-and-artichoke dip is a merely acceptable version of a straightforward dish lessened by boring tortilla chips. "Fettucine La Strada" is the best choice amongst mains, with a roll call of full-bodied ingredients (sausage meatballs, mushrooms, sun-dried tomatoes, basil, and black-pepper cream sauce) generously lending flavor to otherwise bland grilled chicken. Almond-crusted snapper and other fish dishes aren't bad, but tend toward the overrich and overcooked; but avoid at all costs the disastrous plate of wild-mushroom ravioli with cremini mushrooms and a marsala reduction that offends the palate with aggressive sweetness. But forget about all that; you know what to do here, right?

Brunch. Morning, noon, or night. –RG

La Tapatía Taquería

A family standby more Tex-Mex than traditional, with tons of national pride

C+ *Total pleasure grade*

6.8 *Food* **6.4** *Feel* **$12** *Price*

Mexican

Casual restaurant
Daily 8am-2am.
Breakfast. Additional locations.

Midtown
1749 Richmond Ave.
(713) 521-3144
www.latapatiamexcafe.com

Bar Full
Credit Cards Visa, MC, AmEx
Reservations Accepted

Bellaire
6413 Hillcroft St.
(713) 995-9191

Westchase
3965 S. Gessner Rd.
(713) 266-4756

A taste of Mexico is not far away in Houston. We're not talking about the taco stands in the border towns that you stumble across, but rather a family-oriented joint that might not be authentic Mexican, but sure does taste pretty good. La Tapatía Taquería has many locations around the Houston area, and all are pretty consistent, flavorful, and open late. Local favorites like chile con queso, mole enchiladas, and assorted tacos fill the pages of the menu. A traditional fin de semana (weekend) menu sports classic hangover soups like menudo.

At any time of day, the Richmond location of La Tapatía Taquería is filled with construction workers, blue-and-white-collar gringos, and plenty of Mexicans in cowboy hats with giant belt buckles, indicating that this place must be good. Try out your Spanish at the bar and order a margarita—they pack a punch—or admire the giant mural of a bullfight in the back of the restaurant. Look closely and you'll see the name of the painter (Juan Navas) and his phone number below. Give him a call and invite him out for a drink if you like his painting.

Tacos, gorditas, and burritos all come with a choice of meats, like pastor (marinated pork), pierna (leg), or our personal favorite, lengua (tongue). Menudo (tripe soup), though, is bland and tastes like it was made from a can, packet, or by any other shoemaking method that is acceptable these days. Don't forget to sample the free escabeche: its pickled garlic, carrots, and jalapeños (which can sneak up on you if they're ripe) are equally delicious.

Traditional Mexican street food and Tex-Mex cuisine live in a harmonious marriage on this menu. Unfortunately, some of the food has been going downhill recently, especially the latter. We've had enchiladas come out dry, with bland shredded chicken and caked-on cheese; but we've also had tacos come out with uncharacteristic underseasoning. We hope La Tapatía recovers its former glory.

If you want to mingle with some real Mexicans, show up when Mexico is playing soccer on the big screen that lowers at game time. But take our advice and don't root for the opposition. –SD

La Vista

One of Houston's best-kept BYO secrets—if you can score a seat amongst the winos

B Total pleasure grade

7.5 Food **9.0** Feel **$35** Price

New American

Upmarket restaurant
Daily 5:30pm-11pm.
Outdoor dining. Wine-friendly. WiFi.

Galleria
1936 Fountainview Dr.
(713) 787-9899
www.fatbutter.com

Memorial
12665 Memorial Dr.
(713) 973-7374

Bar Wine and beer, BYO
Credit Cards Visa, MC, AmEx
Reservations Not accepted

La Vista's $7 corkage fee is like a gift to the city. Scratch that: the whole restaurant is a gift, the single place in town that best blends BYO with a fun, warm atmosphere. And, now, a new branch brings that same experience to Memorial, in a space once inhabited by Indika. Still, we're nostalgic fans of the almost-a-decade-old Fountainview locale, where neighborhood locals rub gregarious elbows with wine industry insiders. Armed with anything from Yellow Tail to Château Margaux, customers take their seats at one of the many pleasant, shaded outdoor tables in front of the restaurant's big, glassy entrance. At prime time, it might be a while before you can grab one—this restaurant doesn't take rezzies.

You might want to come with a Muscadet or a crisp German Riesling to pair with the superlative steamed mussels in white wine sauce, an irresistible mix of mussel juice, wine, garlic, tomato, and lemon that takes particularly well to the grilled bread that comes with the dish. It's La Vista's absolute best work. Gnocchi with venison ragout isn't: although notes of cinnamon in the tomato sauce are interesting, the potato doughballs themselves are too dense, the flavor deep but hard to get excited about.

Pappardelle with smoky roasted tomato, mushrooms, mint, and goat cheese is comfort food, little more; in "shrimp and grits," overcooked, prosciutto-wrapped shrimp sit atop tasty but unfortunately lumpy cheese-spiked polenta. Crusted rainbow trout, meanwhile, has only a thin film of cornmeal, not the crispy counterpoint you might imagine, and suffers as a result; its citrus sauce is too sweet, and the accompanying "crab and shrimp enchilada" reads like an underseasoned seafood crêpe.

BYO glasses, too, if you're bringing a reasonably expensive wine, because in spite of the wine-friendly policy, La Vista's wimpy glasses aren't swirl-friendly. In the end, it's the dynamite price point that gets La Vista so many extra points in our book. Only two mains are over $20, and many are as little as $13 or $14. The drink-in wine list, too, is short but unbelievably cheap (Viña Sol, a simple, totally drinkable Spanish white, goes for $11). Between BYO, prices, and ambience, a C+ kitchen turns into a B restaurant. –RG

Lai Lai Dumpling House

C-

Total pleasure grade

Despite borderline food, cheap prices keep Lai Lai's charging through

4.0 *Food* **3.1** *Feel* **$7** *Price*

Chinese

Casual restaurant
Daily 11:30am-10pm.

Chinatown
9262 Bellaire Blvd.
(713) 271-0080

Bar None
Credit Cards No credit cards
Reservations Accepted

If there was ever a restaurant that operated both literally and figuratively in a gray area, it would be Lai Lai Dumpling House. The whole place is so drab that it feels like you're living an old movie, with that light gray film across the entire screen. Figuratively, Lai Lai's food works in a gray area between passable and a train wreck. For a house that's long been the stuff of legend, the only things really legendary about Lai Lai these days are the prodigious portions and incredibly low prices.

You probably haven't seen a restaurant where people routinely walk in, take a look around, and then walk out. But this has probably happened more at Lai Lai than anywhere else in town. Lai Lai used to be *the* place for dumplings and Chinese food that bordered on American-style and authentic. The reputation has never needed upkeep, because for some reason, people just keep on coming. Yet the place looks like a living, breathing health violation (although they only had one this past year), which doesn't exactly whet your appetite.

Thankfully, for a dumpling house, Lai Lai makes a fair dumpling: it's as large and plump as a baby's bottom. Steamed beef dumplings are a good call when it's cold or rainy outside, because they'll leave you feeling nice and warm; both the steamed version and the pan-fried version have thicker-than-average skins. The rest of the food here is edible, but just barely; for some reason, much of it comes out lukewarm and covered in cornstarch-thickened gravies. Chicken lo mein is greasy, with about 10 times more noodles than chicken, and the General Tso's is sweet enough to be a chicken dessert. The plates are huge, so variety is pretty much out of the question. And trust us when we say you probably won't want a doggie bag, because you don't want to see what happens when food that's already bad degrades further. Nevertheless, Lai Lai does its job of giving you a lot of food for a little money, even if its legend really is a myth. –FC

Lankford Grocery

Total pleasure grade

A time warp of a little burger shack stuck in the middle of the real world

6.6 Food **7.5** Feel **$12** Price **Burgers**

Casual restaurant
Mon.-Sat. 7am-3pm; closed Sun.
Breakfast. Kid-friendly. Outdoor dining.

Midtown
88 Dennis St.
(713) 522-9555

Bar Wine and beer only
Credit Cards No credit cards
Reservations Not accepted

Sometimes, atmosphere and mystique come first, and food second. Lankford Grocery & Market's definitely got the atmosphere (housed in a converted garage cluttered with Texas and southern memorabilia) and mystique (hard to find, tucked away in Midtown amongst all the generic McTownHouse developments that are have become legion in the neighborhood). In short, it's got all you want from a hamburger shack: friendly service that will tell you stories of life in the Forties; a space that's charmingly in shambles, yet organized; good prices; and a word-of-mouth reputation that makes those in the know feel quite savvy.

Walking up to Lankford, you'll first notice a deck with large shade umbrellas; it's an irresistible place to be on nice days. Inside, there's the atmosphere of an effortless dive: neon Lone Star signs, a sit-down diner-style counter, and a two-car garage, all of it steeped in history. Everybody seems to know everybody at Lankford's; on any given day you will overhear snippets of conversations: "Bubba was in here yesterday," "Oh hi, Bob," "Thanks for everything, Jimmy." It's like a little time warp of a community in a garage.

The menu is basically sandwiches and a few daily specials. But it's the hamburgers that Lankford is known for; they're not bad, by any means, but with all the hype that is behind them, they can't help but disappoint, given what they are. The homemade patty is as thin as it is in everybody's favorite fast-food burger, cooked a bit past the medium that the menu specifies. Daily specials include delicious fried chicken, crispy and succulent, as underrated as the burgers are overrated; and enchiladas that are only acceptable if you've never had a good enchilada before. If you're going to do dessert, you'll have to like cobbler, because they have cherry, peach, blackberry, and chocolate; all are pretty good, and at only $3 they're well priced. –SD

Laredo Taquería

Dirt-cheap tacos with green salsa that will light you up

C
Total pleasure grade

6.3 *Food*

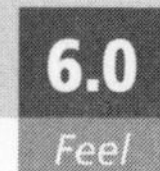
6.0 *Feel*

$8 *Price*

Mexican

Counter service
Mon.-Sat. 6am-5pm; closed Sun. *Breakfast.*

Washington
915 Snover St.
(713) 861-7279

Bar None
Credit Cards No credit cards
Reservations Not accepted

It is one of the great ironies of American cuisine that cow cheeks can only be found at ultra-high end restaurants—think braised veal cheeks for $37.50—or at places where the tacos go for $1.25 each. Laredo Taquería falls in the latter category. Laredo's barbacoa tacos are totally unpredictable—not all parts of a cow's head are equally delectable—but they're always cheap, they're sometimes spectacular, and with a dash of the homicidal green salsa it won't matter what you're eating.

Laredo can be a bit of an experience for the neophyte. The "parking lot" off of Washington Street is basically gravel and dirt, and the line out of the shack-like restaurant often snakes out the door. Service is of the brusque variety, and we'd be lying if we said it didn't help to speak Spanish. But when you see a line snaking out the door composed of Hispanic construction workers mixed with business dudes in suits, you should guess you're onto something. The drill goes like this: you first tell the taqueras whether you want flour or corn tortillas (both freshly made); next, you tell them if you want refried beans spread on your tortilla (you do); finally, you point to one or several of the vats of fixin's, and they'll do the rest. It's pretty simple, and for $1.25 a taco, you can afford to experiment. The taco fillings are varied and muy auténtico. In addition to the barbacoa, we recommend the calabaza con pollo (squash with chicken), the nopalitos (spicy cactus pads), and the picadillo (ground beef with potato). But really, if anything looks good to you, just point and eat. And don't expect fireworks, unless you go crazy with the hot sauce.

The breakfast tacos are worse, if even cheaper (just $1 per taco at press time). The fillings go through all the permutations of eggs, bacon, chorizo, potatoes, and peppers. At both breakfast and lunch you can spice up your tacos with the very spicy red salsa and the wickedly hot salsa verde. Still, not much can rescue terrible scrambled eggs. If you want the respect of those construction workers in line, and some flavor in your tacos, you'd better pile on the verde. –RH

Las Alamedas

An I-10 stalwart whose leafy gardens overshadow the pricey, dumbed-down Tex-Mex

C- *Total pleasure grade*

4.7 *Food* **8.1** *Feel* **$42** *Price* **Tex-Mex**

Upmarket restaurant
Mon.-Thurs. 11am-10pm;
Fri. 11am-11pm;
Sat. 6pm-11pm; Sun. 11am-9pm.
Brunch. Kid-friendly. Live music.

Spring Branch
8615 Katy Fwy.
(713) 461-1503
www.lasalamedas.com

Bar Full
Credit Cards Visa, MC, AmEx
Reservations Accepted

Beside a planned maze of identical homes in a faux forest just off I-10, not far from IKEA, is where you will find the imposing building that houses Las Alamedas. As you exit your car, you will feel dwarfed by everything around you; the highway dominates, too, with its noise. Las Alamedas is a gentle reminder that everything is indeed bigger in Houston—cars, buildings, serving sizes. Inside, the place has the feel of a large and slightly neglected hotel; it's dark and dim, decorations are outdated, colors are muted. Still, the large-but-not-cavernous dining room manages to feel comfortable, even inviting. Large windows look out onto a wooded area, and tables beneath them are the best seats in the house. Friendly service helps, too.

Culinary highlights, though, are scarce. One version of cheese enchiladas comes out more like enfrijoladas, smothered in a refried-bean sauce and stuffed with Swiss-like cheese that hardens quickly into a cheese block (eat fast!). Still, perhaps because of their lack of refinement, they hit all the pleasure points. But this acceptable preparation floats in a stormy sea of failures. Chilaquiles, an item on the famous Sunday buffet brunch, contain hilariously overcooked chicken. Fish comes morbidly dry. And so on.

As for that brunch—which is popular with the after-church crowd in their Sunday best—it's, well, diverse. Concessions to unadventurous palates (ham salad, shrimp boiled to oblivion, and a carving-station beef round that appears to have roasted since the Mexican-American War) might share the table with Mexican dishes like cochinita pibil (dry and overcooked pork, with a decent sauce), snapper "Guanajuato" (dry and overcooked fish, with a decent sauce), and pollo en mole (dry and overcooked chicken, with a decent sauce). Included in the $26-per-person fee are bottomless mimosas (hint: that's not Krug mixed with your orange juice). As you make your way past other tables, you might see such unexpected and disturbing sights as tuna salad intermingled with eggs benedict and flan, roast-beef stumps and omelet shreds in used melon-water, and bagels resting in pools of mole. But such are the risks of attending a buffet brunch. –RG

Last Concert Café

Dreads, dreamers, and Tex-Mex—what a trip

B- Total pleasure grade

6.5 Food **9.5** Feel **$16** Price

Tex-Mex

Casual restaurant
Mon. 11am-2pm, 5pm-9pm; Tues.-Thurs. 11am-2pm, 5pm-10:30pm; Fri. 11am-2pm, 5pm-midnight; Sat. 5pm-midnight; Sun. 3pm-9pm. *Live music. Outdoor dining. Vegetarian-friendly. WiFi.*

Downtown
1403 Nance St.
(713) 226-8563
www.lastconcert.com

Bar Full
Credit Cards Visa, MC, AmEx
Reservations Accepted

In a land where Birkenstocks and beads rule supreme, you will find that everyone's favorite hippie haven and Mexican Restaurant is Last Concert Café. The place started out as a humble Mexican restaurant, but it was slowly taken over by the alternative-lifestyle types. Nowadays, you can go to the Last Concert Café not only to enjoy tostadas and enchiladas, but also to partake in a drum circle or take in a psychedelic hula hoop show. The menu is simple Tex-Mex peppered with the occasional award-winning burger and (hippies take note) vegetarian options, but it's dominated by the enchilada, which is hardly a hippie dish. Cheese, beef, spinach, or chicken—you name it—and they will roll it up in a tortilla and smother it in sauce. The Last Concert Café will definitely leave you scratching your head at times—but the food satisfies more often than not.

You don't have to change your name to Moonchild or Earthwoman when you step inside, but be ready for an alternative lifestyle, especially when the sun goes down. This compound, hidden on the edges of downtown on Nance, is very unassuming during the day, but at night everyone comes out to play. Appetizers are normal Tex-Mex; we like the botana platter, with its quesadillas, jalapeños, chicken flautas, and guacamole. It'll definitely fill up those used to alfalfa sprouts and organic tofu. The potato with green chile soup is one of the best items on the menu. Chunks of potatoes, simmered in chicken broth mix with poblano peppers, cheeses, and pico de gallo; the resulting dish is satisfying. The "Apolinar's Enchiladas" are delicious: two roast-beef-stuffed enchiladas with chili gravy and rice and beans.

On any given night you'll hear music coming from out back. Order a beer and head back there to enter a different universe. Vendors are selling beads and jewelry, hula hoops are being whipped around gracefully, and it all turns into a mellowed-out party. It would be hard to conjure up an atmosphere for Tex-Mex in Houston that's more transportative than this one. So wipe the dirt off the kids' feet, strap 'em to your chest in a hemp carrier, and come on down. –SD

Late Night Pie

Total pleasure grade

Somebody's gotta give the whole town indigestion

Food

Feel

Price

Pizza

Counter service
Daily 5pm-3am.
Delivery.

Midtown
502 Elgin St.
(713) 529-5522

Bar Wine and beer only
Credit Cards Visa, MC, AmEx
Reservations Not accepted

Antacid consumption went up ten-fold when Late Night Pie opened. They have been providing Houston with late night pizza and indigestion for years now, claiming that "somebody's gotta do it." Fresh dough, toppings, and sometimes unusual combinations combine to create Late Night Pie's mystique, which is compounded by their anti-establishment charm. Their place in Houston nightlife tradition is cemented in stone; every weekend there are waits of up to an hour, even at three in the morning. With prices that are comparable to other pizza joints around town, Late Night Pie does offer a slightly better quality of product to its patrons, who consist largely of bikers, rednecks, dazed and confused teens, and sometimes the Stanky Whore.

Late Night Pie looks like a mechanic's shop, equipped with the front end of a truck sticking out of the building and the ever-so-popular garage doors that welcome most customers. The inside is organized chaos on a good day, with video games and beer. The service is sometimes friendly, and other times you'll struggle to get someone even to look at you. But the main attraction here is the pizza. People swear by this pizza and come from far away lands, usually inebriated, to get it, because late-late-night delivery takes forever.

The truth is, the pizza is not very good *unless* you're in an altered state. The two main components of a good pizza are crust and sauce, and Late Night Pie at least pays attention to both: the crust is thin, and the sauce is subtle and not too sweet. Toppings are subpar, however. You've got the standards, of course (cheese, pepperoni, and vegetarian). And then you've got the uniquely named pies like the Bossman and the Stanky Whore (there she is!), with goat cheese, garlic, anchovies, and a side of garlic butter: it's deliciously dangerous, and perhaps the most antacid-anticipating of all. –RG

Most Americans grow up thinking they hate anchovies, which makes sense given how they taste here.

If that's you, try bagna cauda at Dolce Vita, then come talk to us.

Latina Café

A lazy Cuban Sunday

B *Total pleasure grade*

7.2 *Food* **8.6** *Feel* **$22** *Price* **Cuban**

Casual restaurant
Mon.-Thurs. 11am-9pm;
Fri. 11am-10pm;
Sat. 10am-10pm; Sun. 10am-3pm.
Delivery.

Montrose
1972 Fairview St.
(713) 521-2611
www.latinacubancafe.com

Bar None
Credit Cards Visa, MC, AmEx
Reservations Accepted

On a late Sunday morning—okay, early afternoon—you'll find locals reading the newspaper, sipping coffee, and starting the day off with some plantains at this cute, old-school Cuban café. And we think that's the ideal way to start a day. Or end it, as we really can't say enough about how cute and comfortable the interior is here. Complaints of sluggish service are common—and accurate—but for us, it just adds to the laid-back Montrose vibe, which is the whole point of the place.

The menu has been severely tampered with to suit American tastes, but it doesn't have any pretense of being otherwise, so you can just enjoy its comfortable, unchallenging flavors and textures. Appetizers include decent meat empanadas; addictive stuffed, fried mashed-potato balls; and your first taste of Latina's magical garlic sauce, which integrates orange for an addictive blend of salt, sugar, and acid that improves everything it touches. Ropa vieja, a house specialty and Cuban mainstay, is slow-cooked shredded beef in a tomato sauce; it's bland and chewy, though, well below average for the dish. It's brought up by the sides: fried yuca, a simple pleasure, though one in need of a heavy dose of salt; soupy, nicely seasoned black beans; and plantains—either maduros (sweet and soft) or tostones (salty and crispy). We recommend the former, which are slightly and sweetly caramelized; they also make a great dessert. And then, of course, there's the magical garlic sauce to make it all better. The Cuban sandwich has decent bread, but its filling comes out too dry, as is so often the case. What's the fix?

You guessed it.

If all is said and done, and you feel unsatisfied with the inauthenticity or the less-than-stellar food—which is certainly possible—just calm down. Sit back, grab a newspaper, and think of it as a café. That's what it's called, after all. And that same coffee that's so great to start the day with is also great to end your meal with. It's rich and dark, and you'll feel ready for the world—and to forgive the kitchen its faults—after a few cups. –AH

Laurier Café and Wine

A relatively unnoticed bistro that delivers consistently, but shines a bit too dimly

B
Total pleasure grade

7.3 *Food* **7.7** *Feel* **$44** *Price* **New American**

Upmarket restaurant
Tues.-Thurs. 11:30am-10pm;
Fri. 11:30am-11pm;
Sat. 5:30pm-11pm; closed Sun.-Mon.
Date-friendly. Outdoor dining. Wine-friendly.

Greenway Plaza
3139 Richmond Ave.
(713) 807-1632
www.lauriercafe.com

Bar Full
Credit Cards Visa, MC, AmEx
Reservations Accepted

This odd-looking restaurant, which—on the outside—screams small, local, and intimate, houses a modest yet overpriced kitchen that turns out pleasant, unimaginative bistro food. Laurier Café has been flying under the radar for a while now. It's a small operation that's for the most part consistent, but prone to the occasional slip-up.

Laurier really is a small place that is, for lack of a better word, cute; bright yet subtle colors fill the restaurant's walls with relaxing images. The food could hardly be any simpler. The menu changes with the seasons and focuses on local ingredients—as local as possible, that is, in an urban empire. We like the appetizers, which tend to single out the usual frou-frou seasonal suspects; the rest of the menu focuses on overplayed classics.

The food is not dressed up, by any means, although at its best, it could certainly be classified as refined. Applewood-smoked bacon salad, though overplayed, is well-executed, with a nice mustard vinaigrette, but the Gorgonzola kills the delicate taste of the greens. (Believe it or not, greens have flavor; they are not just for texture.) The vegetable tart is delicious: eggplant, artichokes, beets, fennel, and carrots all come together with the help of goat cheese to create a nice, healthy pastry. A good steak frites is hard to beat, and Laurier has a great one. Even if $24 is hard to swallow for a cut of meat that you know is cheap, we love the choice of hanger steak: it's what a steak frites should be, and Laurier cooks it properly as ordered. (As filet mignon proves, more expensive cuts of beef aren't always better.)

Laurier has a nice selection of wines by the glass and even, refreshingly, some half bottles—something we wish there were more of. The desserts, however, are a weak point. And at the end of your meal, you might well understand why Laurier has escaped notice for so long: there's just not a whole lot to remember. Absent any new innovations, the place remains solid; it's just not ready for the spotlight. –SD

Le Mistral

It's certainly cheaper than a ticket to Provence, or memory implants

A Total pleasure grade

9.1 Food **9.6** Feel **$74** Price

French

Upmarket restaurant
Tues.-Thurs. 11am-3pm, 5pm-10pm; Fri. 11am-3pm, 5pm-11pm; Sat. 5pm-11pm; Sun. 11am-3pm, 5pm-9pm; closed Mon. *Brunch. Outdoor dining. Wine-friendly.*

West Houston
1420 Eldridge Pkwy.
(832) 379-8322
www.lemistralhouston.com

Bar Full
Credit Cards Visa, MC, AmEx
Reservations Essential

When you think of immigrant communities in the Houston area, you rarely think of rich oil executives from France that moved here for business. But they too have their cliques, their shared haunts. Homesickness does not discriminate by class.

Le Mistral serves the same purpose for the many French and other Western European expats who have been brought to Houston by the oil business as the neighborhood pupusería does for the Salvadorans craving a taste of home. Go to Le Mistral, and English might well be the language you hear least—just like at the pupusería. Co-owner/manager/sommelier Sylvain Denis is making the rounds, cajoling with customers in French. His brother David is in the back, cooking. You might hear German, some Italian, or some other sounds from the Old World. And the interior is what you would find in a casual bistro in southern France, with bright yellow curtains keeping the outside world of parking lots and industrial parks a safe distance away.

These brothers, who hail from Provence, really get it. And we mean "get it" on every level. It's not just that their menu and preparations are totally authentic; they also understand their audience. They grew up around good food and wine; their mother and grandmother owned brasseries. The two opened up Le Mistral in the cutest way possible: David in the kitchen, and Sylvain designing the wine list and amassing the notable collection. What really proves their savvy, though, is their clever choice of location, way out West along Eldridge Parkway in the Energy Corridor, flanked by—surprise, surprise—gas stations. It's where many of those European oil execs work. A lunch break here means temporary teleportation back to their home continent.

The food is soul-warming. French onion soup is addictive, its beef stock deep and rich, its onions adding a brown, caramelized taste that's exactly as it should be, its Gruyère melting into the soup in an exemplary fashion. A Provençal lamb stew, on one day, came laced with the unexpected brightness of preserved lemons. For brunch, the béchamel-rich croque madame is a flawless meld of warm, comforting flavors of ham, cheese, egg, and crusty bread, which will take you directly to the French country home of your childhood in an alternate universe. It's a trip we love taking. –FC

Le Peep

Stupid name, good breakfast

B- Total pleasure grade

7.0	5.8	$14
Food	Feel	Price

American

Casual restaurant
Mon.-Fri. 6:30am-2:30pm;
Sat.-Sun. 7am-2:30pm.
Breakfast. Brunch. Outdoor dining.

Rice Area
6128 Village Pkwy.
(713) 523-7337
www.lepeephouston.com

Westchase
11199 Westheimer Rd.
(713) 861-0497

Bar None
Credit Cards Visa, MC, AmEx
Reservations Not accepted

Greenway Plaza
4072 Westheimer Rd.
(713) 629-7337

Like a nicer version of Denny's, Le Peep is fun for the whole family. This is a national chain that's got systems in place to keep your children safe and silent for longer than ten minutes—it's even better than Ritalin.

Le Peep's décor is so unassuming as to come off as neo-politically correct; there's no way they'll step on any toes. In fact, the atmosphere is very calm and soothing—so much so that it is a bit unnerving. Carafes of water are on every table, leaving you with the power to refill without looking and hoping your server's around—or worse yet, dealing with a hovering server who refills your glass after each sip.

The food is not going to knock your socks off; it'll just fill you up. This is a pure breakfast, brunch, and lunch play; they've got a big menu with enough lines to ensure that everyone will find at least something they like (or think they will). There are eggs galore, French toast, salads, and sandwiches. The appearance of south-of-the-border fare, like migas, seems weird and out of place, but daring to test them yields surprising Southwestern rewards. The "Desperado," for instance, with potatoes, chorizo, and green chile, is an egg creation that will catch fire in your mouth. Avoid the eggs benedict, though, whose Hollandaise sauce is often too cold and too thick, the consistency of wallpaper glue. Giant, stuff-your-gut skillets, meanwhile, can definitely pack on the pounds. They combine eggs with potatoes and a meat in a big scramble that's certainly not the most innovative, but turns out tasty and flavorful.

Basically, this is your typical, conservative restaurant that doesn't want to try anything out of the ordinary, insult anybody, or offend any palates—or emotions, for that matter; servers tend to walk around with jarringly big smiles. Parking is never an issue here; the big bank account of a chain seems to have helped their various branches secure prime real estate. Still, given its overly sterile atmosphere and food, Le Peep will have you feeling like you live in the 'burbs, even if you have been living out of a friend's closet in the 'Trose for six months, starving-artist-style. It's hard to walk out of here not feeling well-adjusted. –SD

Lee's Sandwiches

Total pleasure grade

You'd think a Vietnamese sandwich chain would make good Vietnamese sandwiches

3.2 Food | **7.5** Feel | **$5** Price

Vietnamese

Fast-food chain
Sun.-Thurs. 5am-midnight;
Fri.-Sat. 24 hours.
Kid-friendly. WiFi.

Chinatown
11210 Bellaire Blvd.
(281) 933-9988
www.leessandwiches.com

West Houston
8338 W. Sam Houston Pkwy.
(281) 988-5788

Bar None
Credit Cards No credit cards
Reservations Not accepted

For almost a year, the population that frequents Bellaire Boulevard watched in anticipation as Lee's Sandwiches built its first outpost in Houston. Everything seemed so promising. The chain was from California, serving Vietnamese sandwiches, making their own baguettes, and opening late into the night. That was all for naught. Lee's serves a joke of a banh mi (Vietnamese sandwich). Its only possible selling point is the modern feel, with bright flashing lights, flat-screened monitors, gadgetry, and WiFi. It's like they think that they're attracting moths to a light.

When you walk into a place and you're not sure exactly if you walked into a restaurant or just a really fancy, Asian-themed gas station store, you probably know you're in for some trouble. But that's what Lee's looks like. There are several open-faced refrigerators with cold, pre-prepared foods and drinks. Walking around, you may find some interesting Euro-Asian boxed cookies, crackers, or candies, but they're mostly ridiculously priced compared to what you can find in the Asian markets that surround Lee's.

It's hard to believe that in California there are lines out the door at Lee's, because the banh mi here is nothing special. The baguette that's supposed to be light and fluffy is hard and dense. The vegetables inside aren't fresh, the cilantro is wilted, and the meats, whether you choose the barbecue pork, the pâté, the shredded pork, or the meatballs, are always surprisingly sweet (not in a good way) and especially sparse. The sandwiches' ratios are approximately 70% bread, 30% filling. The European-style sandwiches fare no better, with disgusting, sweet croissants and dry cold cuts and cheeses.

However, if somehow you are stuck there on one of Houston's 100-degree-plus summer days, you can get an ice-cold, kick-you-in-the-butt, stay-up-for-the-next-week Vietnamese iced coffee. Again, the ratios are off, with about eighty percent of the cup being occupied with ice, but at least you can sit down, people-watch, and enjoy the air conditioning. That is, if you don't mind feeling like you're people-watching in a gas station. –JY

Lemongrass Café

Pan-Asian can work when it's focused and refined by a devoted Thai CIA grad

B *Total pleasure grade*

7.4 *Food* **8.4** *Feel* **$25** *Price* **Pan-Asian**

Casual restaurant
Mon.-Thurs. 11am-9:30pm; Fri. 11am-10pm; Sat. noon-10pm; Sun. noon.-9pm.
Date-friendly. Outdoor dining. Vegetarian-friendly. WiFi.

Bellaire
5109 Bellaire Blvd.
(713) 664-6698
www.lemongrass-café.com

Bar Full
Credit Cards Visa, MC, AmEx
Reservations Accepted

Chef Srifah Vorattinapa is said to have bucked tradition by pursuing her career in the culinary world, heading to the legendary Culinary Institute of America in Hyde Park instead of getting her MBA, as her Thai parents wanted. Her food, too, bucks tradition. It isn't classic Thai-American, nor is it authentic Thai; rather, it draws inspiration from a myriad of techniques and flavors and melds them into something familiar. We are in Texas, after all. Thus, Americans' Thai favorites like pork dumplings, pad Thai, and yakiniku don (actually a Japanese dish, but still a favorite) find themselves on the menu with scallops and beef, rosemary potatoes, coriander-crusted rack of lamb, baked sweet potatoes, and asparagus. And many of these dishes totally shatter your nervous Pan-Asian expectations.

The Bellaire location is full-on strip mall; thankfully, parking is plentiful, and there are no annoying valet parkers swarming around to do you the favor of parking your car a few feet from the entrance. In spite of the strip, Lemongrass Café looks hip enough, yet without feeling not too flashy or fake. Flatware is attractively heavy; strangely amusing thick silver forks and knives are almost a workout to lift. When you sit down, you'll get some small sweet buns at your table with chili oil for dipping—a nice hello. Pork dumplings, steamed and then seared on one side, are wondrously fresh. Hints of ginger, spice, and pig bounce off each other then melt together in your mouth. Delicious.

Pad Thai is uniquely presented here: noodles and tofu are wrapped in a very thin egg crêpe with srirachi chili sauce on the sides of the plate. The noodles brandish a good balance of salty and sweet flavors. "Sesame Chicken Milanesa" is supremely unique, too: a thin chicken breast is breaded and fried with sesame seeds, giving it a nutty flavor and an extra crunch; it's served with lemon beurre blanc, haricots verts, and grape tomatoes. There's a full bar, which, of course, means specialty drinks. The dessert menu is weak, although there's a bright spot in the rice cake with fresh mango and mango ice cream. We haven't tried anything here that quite rose to the level of the sublime, but the execution has been surprisingly good, shattering our Pan-Asian expectations. –SD

Little Hip's Diner

A dive diner serving selections from the four food groups of Texas

C+ *Total pleasure grade*

6.5 *Food* **7.5** *Feel* **$10** *Price* **American**

Casual restaurant
Mon.-Thurs. 10am-9pm; Fri. 10am-10pm; Sat. 9am-10pm; closed Sun. *Breakfast.*

Washington
1809 Washington Ave.
(713) 861-4411

Bar BYO
Credit Cards Visa, MC, AmEx
Reservations Not accepted

No street in Houston can compare with Washington Avenue for its variety of quality dives. Little Hips, at the east end of Washington close to downtown, is one of the diviest. From the name and dubious exterior, you might guess that this place is some kind of unfortunate cabaret, but it's actually a diner in the mode of those little country places you might find if you wandered off the interstate on the way to San Antonio. The inspiration for Little Hips is actually an old diner by the name of Hipps, which used to sell burgers and fried shrimp in San Antonio. Although Little Hips is practically brand new, if you don't look closely, you'd swear it dates back to the days when the Oilers were in town.

The menu goes all the way from burgers to fried catfish to barbecue to tacos, which pretty much captures the four main food groups of Texas. The half-pound burgers are big, greasy examples of what a diner burger should be. The Cajun-style burger has a dash of Tony Chachere's seasoning, just like they do it over in Lafayette. We like the hand-cut fries, which aren't as crisp as we like but brandish the sort of sweetness you'll only find in a fresh-cut potato. Onion rings have a pleasant crunch, and aren't too oily.

The owner and chef, Daniel Brieg, smokes the brisket and chicken himself in small batches, and the result is some quality barbecue—not championship level, but moist, with a strong, smoky flavor. We're much less impressed with the shrimp po' boy; while the shrimp are big and taste fresh, there are usually only about four of them, and we just can't figure out why they still have their tails on. Shrimp tails in a sandwich make no sense.

Best of all are probably the desserts, mostly because they're so appropriate to the concept of the place: chocolate cake from an honest-to-God Bundt cake that someone has baked and slathered with icing that very morning, and a slice of cherry pie that would make Warrant cry. We hope Little Hips sticks around; it'll be interesting to see how it turns out once it's as old as it looks. –RH

London Sizzler

An unexpectedly rocking Brit-Indian party

A-
Total pleasure grade

8.4	9.0	$32
Food	Feel	Price

Indian

Casual restaurant
Tues.-Fri. 5pm-11:30pm;
Sat.-Sun. noon-11:30pm;.
closed Mon. *Date-friendly.*
Live music. Vegetarian-friendly.
WiFi.

Hillcroft Area
6690 Southwest Fwy.
(713) 783-2754
www.londonsizzler.com

Bar Full
Credit Cards Visa, MC, AmEx
Reservations Not accepted

It's a breath of fresh air—spicy fresh air—to find an Indian restaurant that's both authentic and festive, even if its authenticity is more faithful to the British tradition than to the Subcontinent itself. The hidden strip-mall location of London Sizzler—just off Hillcroft and I-59, caddy-corner from another Fearless Critic favorite, Himalaya—is why most mainstream Houstonians still don't know about it. But amongst those that do—including not only much of the local Indian community, but also a bunch of local chefs and foodies—it has acquired a cult following.

It's not hard to see why. First of all, the place is just fun: there's a full bar; the staff is friendly; and the dark, gregarious atmosphere is worlds apart from that of the many downmarket Indian joints in the same area. Long tables work well for big groups, too. Second of all, a lot of the food is delicious, from the classic Brit-Indian dishes like deep, creamy chicken tikka masala, to the grand, sizzling platters of meat for which the restaurant is best known. Surprisingly for a grilled-meat restaurant, vegetarians love it just as much as carnivores do. The kitchen does great work with "Chili Manchurian," described as "Indo-Chinese vegetable dumplings stir-fried in a light Manchurian sauce," which doesn't really mean anything; just trust us and try them—they're toothsome, savory delights. Equally good is "Mogo and Paneer Pili Pili," homemade cheese cubes and fried potato root simmered in an East African-inspired sauce that's spicier than most on the menu.

Lamb vindaloo is delicious, as is smooth, mild, and absolutely addictive butter chicken. We're far less impressed with other chicken dishes—stay away from chicken tikka—and don't come here for biryani; go to Himalaya instead. But vegetarian curries hit just the right spot; wash it all down with a beer, or three; invite a bunch of friends to maximize the number of dishes that each person gets to taste; and let the secret Brit-Indian party begin. –RG

López

Death, taxes, and Tex-Mex

C Total pleasure grade

4.2 Food | **6.5** Feel | **$19** Price

Tex-Mex

Casual restaurant
Mon.-Sat. 11am-9:45pm; closed Sun.
Kid-friendly.

West Houston
11606 S. Wilcrest Dr.
(281) 495-2436
www.lopezmexicanrestaurant.com

Bar Full
Credit Cards Visa, MC, AmEx
Reservations Not accepted

Nostalgia connects us almost involuntarily to things we would otherwise shun: peculiar people, obscure objects, and arbitrary places that, if not for the singular human obsession with that which we have left behind, we would have long ago cleansed from our memories like bedrooms full of old junk. Why are we such relentlessly nostalgic creatures, so deeply uncomfortable with our ability—perhaps unique within the animal kingdom—of reinventing ourselves, and our tastes, in real time? Whatever the reasons, it is so, and so it is that even our geniuses spend their days circling like buzzards over their carcasses of youth, fancying those lost moments more vital than anything ahead.

And so it is that nostalgia maintains mediocrity. And so it is that people still go to López Mexican Restaurant. For almost 30 years, the restaurant has been serving milder-than-mild Tex-Mex (these days, your Texan grandmother probably uses more chipotle than this) at fairer-than-fair prices. But on the plate, even the highlights are flawed. That good ol' brown enchilada gravy ain't bad, but their rice and beans are; chiles rellenos have a decently textured egg batter, but their picadillo tastes practically unseasoned. Even given the restaurant's legendarily friendly, familial service, and the portions so large they should be FDA violations, it's remarkable, and telling, that—in a city with Lupe Tortilla, Doneraki, and other Tex-Mex competitors that better marinate their fajita beef, better squeeze their margaritas, better spice up their queso and salsa, and better flavor their refried beans—many people still swear by López, whose atmosphere, with rows of cafeteria-style chairs and tables, feels more like a food court in a university student center than a festive place for margaritas.

Why are we still so addicted to López, addicted to turning the imperfect meals of our youth into moments of revisionist perfection? Maybe these gargantuan combination plates of enchiladas oozing with the irresistible cheese of our childhoods still manage to distract us, if only for a moment, from the fear that death is as indelibly inked in our future as our childhood memories are in our past; that López will someday close its doors and go dark; and that when it does, nobody knows what, if anything, will replace it. –RG

Los Guanacos

Great Savadoran food that hits all the right notes

B *Total pleasure grade*

8.1 *Food* **7.2** *Feel* **$10** *Price* **Salvadoran**

Casual restaurant
Hours vary.

Northwest Houston
16282 Loch Katrine Ln.
(281) 550-3467

Bar Wine and beer only
Credit Cards No credit cards
Reservations Not accepted

If you've got to drive a long way for a meal, the restaurant had better be really delicious. Well, trust us: we aren't leading you astray when we say you should check out Los Guanacos. The word "guanaco" is slang for a person from El Salvador, and this humble little establishment will introduce you to hte wonders of Salvadoran food, which, for most people, comes as a refreshing change of pace from Mexican or Tex-Mex (although there are enough similarities that it's unlikely to shock your system). Here you'll find all that's good about homestyle Salvadoran cooking, beginning with pupusas, tamales, and pasteles.

Los Guanacos is way out in northwest Houston in a modest and humble shack that is clean and respectable. And their prices are most definitely low—which is good, considering the gas money it takes to get out here. The smell of lemons hits you as you walk into the spacious and usually full dining room, which will generally be full of a steady flow of regulars. The pupusas, a mainstay of Salvadoran cuisine, are tasty; they're small discs of hand-patted masa (corn flour), stuffed with a choice of cheese, chicharrón (fried pork skins), or loroco (a green, mild Salvadoran flower). Here, they're fluffy, and surprisingly, not greasy. (Even in El Salvador, we've had many versions weighed down by too much grease.) Curtido—pickled cabbage and carrots—is an essential condiment for the pupusa, adding a much-needed crunch of salty acidity. Tamales are good, too. Not to be confused with the denser Mexican version, the Salvadoran tamal is made from a light, fluffy masa. Simple elote, chicken, or poblano are good filling options. Ask for Salvadoran crema to accompany whichever you choose; it's thick and somewhat akin to sour cream, and you'll get that much more pleasure from your tamal.

Service is on point here. There's enough Salvadoran food in Houston—and enough of a Salvadoran community—that we see no reason why the whole city shouldn't soon be hooked on El Salvador's ultimate street food, or why "pupusa" shouldn't someday become a term as recognizable in Houston as "pork belly." –SD

Lucky Burger

In the mood for both Chinese and American food? Today's your lucky day

5.0 *Food* **5.6** *Feel* **$6** *Price* **Burgers**

Counter service
Mon.-Sat. 11am-9:30pm; closed Sun.
Delivery.

Montrose
1601 Richmond Ave.
(713) 522-5650
www.luckyburger.com

Bar None
Credit Cards Visa, MC, AmEx
Reservations Not accepted

Hamburgers and fried rice don't exactly sound like star-crossed lovers, but don't dismiss them as an unlucky combo. Lucky Burger, a modest burger shack in the Montrose area, has been cashing in on this concept for years. And we say "shack," but we really mean "barrel"; the place is housed in what looks like a giant barrel. How's that for quirky charm? Smiling food items perched atop their blue building are ready to give your kids nightmares at first glance. And with so many potholes, this could very well be the worst parking lot in Houston. Serving everything from cheeseburgers to fried rice, teriyaki chicken burgers to egg rolls, Lucky Burger embraces unity and equality among dishes; there are no hateful or racist food sentiments here.

Lucky Burger brings back the red-and-white-checkered tablecloths and nostalgic pictures of the past to a younger crowd of yuppies, hippies, and rednecks; there's also a roomy counter, with plenty of elbow and knee room. They're known for their burgers, which are exactly what you'd expect for $3.39. You won't find fresh, hand-formed patties here, but rather thin, griddled patties that are seasoned well and are accompanied by crisp lettuce, thick tomato slices, dill pickles, and American cheese. For a simple burger, it is both executed and presented well.

And don't fret, you are reading the menu right; fried rice is indeed making an appearance in a fast-food hamburger restaurant. Rice is fried to order with your choice of shrimp, chicken, or pork; it will remind you of the suburban Chinese meals of your youth, but without the paper placemats bearing the animals of the Chinese New Year. Remember giggling about the year of the cock?

The friendly Asian staff deals well with their largely Caucasian crowd. They close at 9:30pm, and all day on Sunday, so get your fix early; angry mobs do sometimes form. –SD

Lucky Pot

B+

Total pleasure grade

A simple, quality Northern Chinese find with great green-onion pancakes

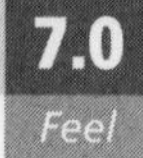

$15 Price

Chinese

Casual restaurant
Daily 11am-9:30pm.
Vegetarian-friendly.

Chinatown
9888 Bellaire Blvd.
(713) 995-9982

Bar None
Credit Cards Visa and MC
Reservations Not accepted

Don't walk into Lucky Pot looking for a $3.99 special of General Tso's chicken, fried rice, and an egg roll; if you do, you may elicit stares of contempt, or possibly have the waitstaff pretend not to speak English just so they can ignore you. Lucky Pot, as the name may suggest, serves an addictive, authentic style of Northern Chinese cuisine—one which emphasizes crispiness and crunchiness in texture, and heartiness in taste. The décor may not suggest much, but the magic is all in the food.

Your first glance at Lucky Pot will reveal little. The place is clean and tidy, but the interior looks like it's the product of a single $100 shopping trip to a Chinese supermarket and a roll of Scotch tape. Service is a bit harried, and because of the lack of English, you'll likely be stuck pointing and saying "that one" to your waiter. Asking for an explanation of dishes is out of the question.

If you're not expecting a lot, however, you're in for a pleasant surprise. Lucky Pot adapts well to both of Houston's two seasons; nothing is complicated, and every flavor is versatile. For hot days, there are fantastic cold appetizers. The special sliced beef shank is marinated, slow-cooked, then chilled, turning gelatinous from the tendons that are common on the shank. It's an odd texture contrast at first, but then quickly becomes a habit-forming one. Steamed pork and vegetable dumplings have thicker-than-normal skins, but they're still light and far tastier than others in town (such as Lai Lai). For colder days, tofu casserole with a steaming, mushroomy broth warms you up more than a shot of tequila. But it's the savory, crunchy, tastefully greasy pan-fried green-onion cakes that you should really come for. This is food that's absolutely at ease, hitting the brain's pleasure centers like your first sip of beer after work. Same goes for the pan-fried vegetable cake and spicy stir-fried eggplant, with penetrating flavors that work hand in hand.

Sometimes, food isn't supposed to be complicated, just good. Not every restaurant has to be fru-fru. Lucky Pot clearly realizes this, working hard to do what it does simply—and right. –JY

Luling City Market

A moist, beefy taste of the Tex-German Hill Country in a concrete jungle

8.6 Food | **6.5** Feel | **$15** Price

Barbecue

Counter service
Mon.-Sat. 11am-9pm;
Sun. noon-7pm.
Kid-friendly. Outdoor dining.

Galleria
4726 Richmond Ave.
(713) 871-1903
www.lulingcitymarket.com

Bar Full
Credit Cards Visa, MC, AmEx
Reservations Not accepted

Luling City Market is an offshoot of the original meat market in Luling, Texas. Its German-style barbecue is done in a specific style, hard to find in Houston, that relies on lots of smoke, low temperatures, and zero sauce on the meat. A mustardy, peppery sauce, again characteristic of this style, sits on all the tables. You'll find turkey, chicken, and pork ribs on the menu, but beef is king in this house, because German-Texas barbecue revolves around beef sausage and beef brisket. Welcome to Texas!

Luling City Market is off Richmond right before 610, in a strip mall that feels nothing like the Hill Country, but when you step inside, a burst of smoke will transport you to hog…or, rather, cow heaven. With Post oak logs surrounding most of the restaurant, Luling is a place for those that find immense pleasure in simple, powerfully smoky flavors, aromas, and textures. The brisket is the star of the show, with a nicely charred crust but a moist and tender interior that pulls apart with little effort and tastes like three things: beef, fat, and smoke. Delicious. Get it on a plate or place it on an onion roll—either way you will be satisfied. Other options are beef sausage, which can be bit dry and crumbly, if only because of a lack of fat from the beef, and ribs with a great smoke flavor and texture.

Luling is strictly counter service. Grab a red tray, pick a drink, pick a side, and bring it home with the meat. Raw onion, pickles, and relish, all standard for the genre, are there for the taking. The potato salad is also some of the best in the city. It has a nice mustard flavor but it doesn't mask the creaminess of the potatoes. Because of the place's fame, unfortunately, the pricing has gotten a bit out of control. This is country food, and they shouldn't be charging more than five dollars for a brisket sandwich; brisket is one of the cheapest peasant cuts of any animal. But the food is good enough that we're happy to be price-gouged whenever we feel a craving for simple, sensational smoke. –SD

Lupe Tortilla

Block your eyes and ears to enjoy some of America's best fajitas and flour tortillas

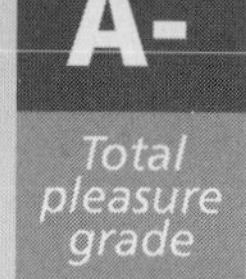

A-

Total pleasure grade

8.7	7.3	$26
Food	Feel	Price

Tex-Mex

Casual restaurant
Sun.-Thurs. 11am-9pm;
Fri.-Sat. 11am-10pm.

Additional locations.

Greenway Plaza
2414 Southwest Fwy.
(713) 522-4420
www.lupetortilla.com

Bar Full
Credit Cards Visa, MC, AmEx
Reservations Not accepted

West Houston
318 Stafford St.
(281) 496-7580

North Houston
15315 North Fwy.
(281) 873-6220

Every branch of this Tex-Mex granddaddy is almost always packed. The popularity of Lupe Tortilla has long transcended the generations: at 59 and Kirby, for instance, the playscape-sandbox area sees a ton of action; children are everywhere, throwing sand at one another, while inside, their parents try vainly to buzz from the weak margaritas. Service seems to grow ever more chainlike by the day, especially at busy times, when it ranges from distracted to just plain rude: requests are shrugged off, food can take forever to come out, few apologies are offered. Maybe they've been wearing those goofy Hawaiian shirts for far too long.

The restaurant was founded in 1982 in Addicks (at I-10 and Highway 6, west of the city, about halfway to Katy), but in 1995, the family's younger generation returned from the Culinary Institute of America to get involved in the business. In the years following, Lupe Tortilla was born again as a mini-chain all over Houston. The pace hit breakneck (for a family business, anyway) with 2006 openings in the fast-growing areas of Sugar Land and the Woodlands, reinforcing Lupe's new status as one of the biggest players in a city known for fajitas. If more of the city's Tex-Mex places pressed them like this, Houston might be known for flour tortillas, too. Here, they're humongous, homemade, warm, and delicate.

The menu has an annoying, patronizing, borderline offensive habit of writing some things as a non-native speaker of English would say them. Thus, chicken becomes "cheekin", fish is "feech", and mixed fajitas are "meexed"; it'll make you cringe, especially when you learn the restaurant was created by an American couple who, according to the restaurant, spoke no Spanish when they launched Lupe. Despite their linguistic shortcomings, however, they clearly knew, and still know, their way around the parrilla. Beef is meltingly tender and well seasoned; chicken, marinated in lime, is of the spongy breast variety, but its smoky sear still hits all the right points. Rice and beans are delicious, too; in the end, this Tex-Mex is simply irreproachable, and when you're in the midst of one of America's best fajitas, nothing else really matters. –AH

Lynn's Steakhouse

The wine list is like a candy store for wine freaks, while the steak just sorta *is*.

8.1 *Food* **8.7** *Feel* **$90** *Price* **Steakhouse**

Upmarket restaurant
Mon.-Fri. 11am-2pm, 5pm-10pm; Sat. 6pm-10pm; closed Sun.
Date-friendly. Wine-friendly.

West Houston
955 Dairy Ashford St.
(281) 870-0807
www.lynnssteakhouse.com.

Bar Full
Credit Cards Visa, MC, AmEx
Reservations Accepted

One of the most unexpected joys of Houston dining is the wine list at Lynn's, a straightforward, traditional steakhouse way out west. The 17,000-bottle volume is as enthralling as a classic literary novel, and it's as steeped in history as one, too, replete with old vintages that are being given away roughly at auction prices.

The wine list is not cutting-edge or innovative; don't expect many Grüner Veltliners (not that you'd want that with steak) or Niagara Vidal ice wine (not that you'd want to pay what that costs under any circumstances). Rather, it is steady, strong, and relentlessly reasonable in the traditional sweet spots: Bordeaux, Burgundy, Piedmont, and Tuscany. It's also a list that rewards those who spend a bit more than the entry level. Markup percentages go drastically down as you move up in price, and the best bargains are in the $50-100 range—above the entry level but before you get to the prestige pricing of first growths and such. Somewhere in that range might buy you, for instance, a ready-to-drink 15-year-old Médoc or Côte d'Or from a reliable producer—something that's virtually impossible to find elsewhere in town. Catalan and Ibiza aren't even in this league on the older vintages, while Mark's, Tony's, and the other steakhouses sometimes have the prestige vintages but can't compete in price. Not even close.

Which leaves Lynn's the undisputed champion in the older-vintage division. But it's a steakhouse, not a wine bar, so what about the steak? It's just fine, not the best in town, nor the cheapest ($32-40 for most steaks), but priced a notch below Pappas and such. Think of it as an accompaniment to the wine.

And then there's the $19.95 business lunch special. Sounds like a good deal, right? We'll let the menu items speak for themselves:

"Black bean soup or House salad / Beef stroganoff over fettuccini, or filet of salmon with dill cream sauce, or grilled chicken breast with stewed vegetables / Crème Brûlée or Strawberries Romanoff."

And there you have it. You win some, you lose some. But at Lynn's, you win more than you lose, because we'd pay $19.95 for a plate of saltines in exchange for the honor of ordering off this beautiful wine list. –RG

Madras Pavilion

A vegetarian and kosher, if not Hillcroft-quality, Indian dive in Upper Kirby

C+ *Total pleasure grade*

6.2 *Food* **4.5** *Feel* **$20** *Price*

Indian, Vegetarian

Casual restaurant
Sun.-Thurs. 11:30am-9:30pm;
Fri.-Sat. 11:30am-10pm.
Vegetarian-friendly.

Upper Kirby
3910 Kirby Dr.
(713) 521-2617
www.madraspavilion.us

Bar Wine and beer only
Credit Cards Visa, MC, AmEx
Reservations Accepted

Madras Pavilion serves primarily South Indian specialties, presenting an interesting alternative to the majority of central Houston's Indian restaurants, which are focused on other parts of India and Indian-American food. There are some joints of this sort—better ones, in fact—on Hillcroft. But it's rare to find a proper vegetarian Indian place in a district like Upper Kirby. Madras Pavilion is an exception. There's a buffet steam table, but the rest is mostly unadorned. Service can be a bit gruff.

The menu is entirely vegetarian and has a section of kids' offerings, as well as a lunch buffet. Much of the food is fried, as evidenced by the appetizer combo plate, which is served with five condiments—a curry, the standard tamarind and mint chutneys, a grainy coconut sauce, and something boring and unidentifiable. Bland, donut-like medhu vada has a light fennel flavor, and paneer pakoda, a battered and fried cheese, is chewy and uninteresting. We like the bonda, a fried potato concoction with a creeping heat, and the very similar veggie cutlet: mashed and fried vegetables seasoned with coriander, curry, and lemon.

Madras Pavilion is known for two things: it is one of the few truly Kosher restaurants in town, making for a lively mix of saris and black suits, and it has tremendous dosai—foot-and-a-half-long rice-and-lentil-flour crêpes rolled like burritos around a variety of fillings. They are deliciously light, served crisp and hot, again with a variety of condiments, like chutneys and strong lime pickle. We love the creamy butter masala dosa, filled with curried potatoes, onions, and nigella seeds. Curries are also a good choice—palak paneer has an unusual nutty flavor to its spinach, and the paneer (homemade cheese) comes in nice, big cubes. Spicy malai kofta has sliced almonds and is so rich, you might not even realize that the "meatballs" are vegetarian. L'chaim. –FC

Mai Thai

Run-of-the-mill Thai food in a pink-themed room

6.6 Food | **5.3** Feel | **$23** Price | **Thai**

Casual restaurant
Mon.-Thurs. 11am-2:30pm, 5pm-10pm; Fri. 11am-2:30pm, 5pm-11pm; Sat. noon-11pm; closed Sun. *Date-friendly. Vegetarian-friendly.*

Upper Kirby
3819 Kirby Dr.
(713) 522-6707
www.maithaihouston.com

Bar Wine and beer only
Credit Cards Visa, MC, AmEx
Reservations Accepted

Sure, Mai Thai looks like a shoddy old tiki bar, but your mother always said it's what's on the inside that matters, right?

Unfortunately, things don't get too much better inside, with a dining room that's in serious need of an update. But remember, some of the best food in the world comes from places that look less than appetizing, right?

Regrettably, Mai Thai doesn't fit that bill either, serving mediocre, forgettable food of a cuisine that's normally pretty exciting.

To say that Mai Thai just didn't age gracefully would be an understatement. The dining area looks like a 1980s banquet room. Aside from the pictures of Thailand on the walls, everything is pink. Very, very pink. In fact, it's so pink that you may think that you're in the dream world of your Barbie-crazed five-year-old niece. Still, the service is nice enough, even if you sometimes feel as if they're paying more attention to the small TV that they have on one side of the dining room than to you.

At Thai restaurants, your ordering rule of thumb should be that if you don't know what it is or have never heard of it before, it's probably good. While, following that rule, Mai Thai has its bright spots here and there, most of the food is watered down. Tom yum goong soup is flooded with fantastic spices, sweetness, and loads of fragrant lemongrass, but it could use more of the shrimp that the menu promises. Phad kra pow could be one of the best items on the menu, with flavors of stir-fried beef with kick-you-in-the-butt spice rounded out by vegetables and the exotic flavor of Thai basil, making the dish exciting and tasty. Unfortunately, many other dishes fail. The good ol' pad Thai lacks any sort of pizzazz, and desperately needs more sauce or cilantro or peanuts. Curries suffer from the fate of being flooded with too many vegetables, losing the flavors in a sea of green. At least the veggies are probably good for your health. Except that you'll probably want to find a real tiki bar afterwards and counteract their effects. –JY

Mai's

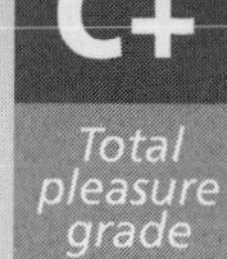

Total pleasure grade

Spring rolls, phô, and (if you're lucky) pig's blood, all into the wee hours

5.9 Food | **7.6** Feel | **$25** Price

Vietnamese

Casual restaurant
Sun.-Thurs. 10am-3am;
Fri.-Sat. 10am-4am.

Midtown
3403 Milam St.
(713) 520 7684

Bar Wine and beer only
Credit Cards Visa, MC, AmEx
Reservations Accepted

Who's a man gotta bribe to eat some pig's blood around here? This is one of the dilemmas at Houston's favorite local Vietnamese restaurant. Established in 1978, Mai's has been educating midtown yuppies and insomniacs on the ins and outs of Vietnamese cuisine for three decades. Vietnamese egg rolls, noodle bowls, phô, and classic Chinese food populate the menu; the blandly lit place is open until 3am (4am on weekends), drawing in restaurant-industry and post-bar crowds, and for the price and quality of service, expectations are met.

We'd compare Mai's to the circus: it's loud, fast, and argumentative (you might just be charged extra for a lemon wedge). Business practices aside, Mai's offers good Vietnamese food at reasonable prices. "Vietnamese egg rolls"—crispily deep-fried pork rolls served with lettuce, cilantro, and mint to wrap everything up—are a crunchy, fresh, and succulent start. Other favorites are the vermicelli noodle bowls, and the phô noodle soup offering an array of proteins to add, like brisket (which can be tough), fatty tendon, or tripe.

If you're in the mood for pig's blood, then Mai's is your spot, but there is a stipulation: to get the elusive #12 on the menu—chao huyet, a rice porridge with coagulated pig's blood, the only one of the 177 menu items at Mai's that's not translated into English—you or your dining companion must be Vietnamese. In the past, apparently, too many non-Vietnamese people have sent it back, so now, they're playing it safe. If you're not Vietnamese, don't even bother groveling, threatening a 14th-amendment lawsuit, or posing as an experienced huyet-lover. It won't work. Instead, call up a Vietnamese friend and take him or her out to dinner.

Mai's also caters to the guests who believe that every Asian restaurant is a Chinese restaurant, offering classic Chinese-American food like General Tso's chicken and beef and broccoli. Happily, though, they spike some of it up a bit—the spicy beef and garlic is pretty tasty, with whole cloves of garlic roasted in their shells, so you can squeeze the cells of hot, nutty paste into your mouth one by one. Just don't exhale for the rest of the day. –SD

Mak Chin's

Total pleasure grade

Ambitious Asian fare that aims for trendy roti, but just ends up bland

4.2 Food | 7.9 Feel | $25 Price

Pan-Asian

Casual restaurant
Sun.-Thurs. 11am-10pm;
Fri. 11am-11pm;
Sat. 5pm-11pm.
Brunch. Date-friendly.
Outdoor dining. Vegetarian-friendly.

Washington
1511 Shepherd Dr.
(713) 861-9888
www.makchins.com

Bar Full
Credit Cards Visa, MC, AmEx
Reservations Accepted

The original Mak Chin's concept was a counter-service restaurant not unlike Pei Wei, with a trendy, sleek setting and iffy service. Less than a year later, Mak Chin's changed its concept to a full-service restaurant with a trendy, sleek setting and iffy service. Start with something unimpressive, and no matter how much you buff it up, you'll still end up with something unimpressive.

While the interior design at Mak Chin's is the biggest plus, it's still not without its head-scratching elements. Tables are stylish and naked, bringing on a sense of high-class casualness, but a red-painted, stone-blocked wall dividing the dining room and bar area looks like it belongs in a middle school boys' locker room, and low-hanging lights might as well have been swiped from a Chili's. Service is well intentioned and pleasant, but not really helpful; asking them to recommend a dish has them spouting off about half the menu, and looking at the wines is like walking down the beer and spirits aisle at Kroger's.

Gone from Mak Chin's is its signature condiment bar, a favorite element that was actually the smartest selling point of the restaurant. The pan-Asian menu at the new Mak Chin's melds numerous cuisines that are heavy on roaring spices, fragrant herbs, and aromatics, generating a menu that actually looks enticing. Unfortunately, though, the food at Mak Chin's has remained as bland as it was before its price bump. Sweet-and-sour soup is neither sweet nor sour, and tastes like thickened soup base with fried noodles and scallions. There is one high point to the restaurant: light, crunchy, delicious roti chanai, served with a thick, spicy curry sauce (as opposed to the thin curries that you'll find at many Malaysian places). Beef rendang, on the other hand, showcases the kitchen's ability to braise a piece of beef and have it taste like absolutely nothing. Yellowish rice is overcooked to a textureless, flavorless mush; the best part of the dish is its cute little clay pot and pickled onion garnish.

In the end, Mak Chin's just doesn't have it. The atmosphere is one step back, and the food is several steps back, so maybe you should just step to somewhere else. –JY

Malay Bistro

Fantastic Malaysian lunch deals

B- *Total pleasure grade*

7.6 *Food* **3.2** *Feel* **$10** *Price*

Malaysian

Casual restaurant
Sun.-Thurs. 11am-10pm;
Fri.-Sat. 11am-11pm.

Chinatown
8282 Bellaire Blvd.
(713) 777-8880

Bar Wine and beer only
Credit Cards Visa, MC, AmEx
Reservations Accepted

Malaysian cuisine is a fiery mixture of Chinese, Thai, Indonesian, and Indian. It's sweet, sour, spicy, and savory all rolled into one and pumped up with steroids. It shouts rather than speaks, runs rather than walks. So how does Malay Bistro get off serving Malaysian food with such gentle flavors? We're guessing that price point has got something to do with it. The Malaysian community in Houston is perhaps not big enough to support the restaurant by itself, so they reach out to a very broad Bellaire crowd with less-than-six-dollar lunch specials.

Malay Bistro's atmosphere is flat and boring; there's an odd-looking brown-painted wall, several plastic-covered tables, and that's about it. More exciting is the Asian windpipe music and the ornately dressed waitstaff with their frosted hair and imported fabric aprons—but most importantly, hard-to-understand accents that make you wonder if they got the order right. These little signs of authenticity are reassuring.

Eating Malaysian food for the first time is like doing a full body workout you've never done before; you'll discover new muscles that you've never used before, new taste buds you didn't even know you had. If you want a warm-up, the food at Malay Bistro is subdued compared to its neighbors down the street, K.L. Malaysian and Café Malay, so it's good entry-level Malaysian cuisine. A plate of Hainanese chicken is the best way to start, with absolutely tender pieces of chicken that you practically don't even have to chew and rice that's cooked with the same broth that the chicken was poached in; it ties the dish together, though some extra cilantro does help to bring it along. Asam laksa is a fragrant and powerful, fish-based, sweet-and-sour broth with coconut milk and thick noodles; if you want a heartier dish, try the beef curry. It needs an extra kick in the pants, but its sweet, coconut-curry-based sauce and bowl of rice are still delicious.

And at six bucks a pop, you don't have much to lose. So it's a good choice for anyone who's in the early stages of experimentation with the profound flavors that lie beneath real Malaysian cooking. –JY

Mama Ninfa's

If this is the original fajita, then we welcome progress

3.8 Food | 6.6 Feel | $17 Price

Tex-Mex

Casual restaurant
Daily 8am-5pm.
Breakfast. Delivery.
Kid-friendly. Outdoor dining.

Downtown
2704 Navigation Blvd.
(713) 228-1175
www.mamaninfas.com

Bar Full
Credit Cards Visa, MC, AmEx
Reservations Accepted

Supposedly the place where fajitas were invented, Mama Ninfa's has multiplied into a sizeable chain. The various attempts to recreate the kitsch and dingy character of the original Navigation Boulevard location come off like Disney without the good execution—and, strangely, even the menu items wind up adulterated and homogenized. Household-name status should not be abused in this way. (The Ninfa's chain is reviewed separately in this book—see "Ninfa's.")

The original Mama Ninfa's, in a run-down neighborhood that's still mostly Hispanic, is well within the city limits; certainly you should visit this locale before stooping to dine at any of the chain's branches. The shacklike exterior suggests rural Mexico, but the interior looks more polished and put together—a recent facelift, perhaps, to bring the original in line with its squeaky-clean offspring. Still, the place feels legit, and a shaded garden area in the back is ideal on a beautiful day, even if it borders a dusty parking lot.

If this is indeed the birthplace of the faijita, then that dish has been improved upon elsewhere, with innovations like proper seasoning and cooking time. Mama Ninfa's tough, overcooked versions cry out for salt, although carnitas are not as bad, with a pleasant, crunchy fattiness. A better legacy for Mama Ninfa's than grilled meats, perhaps, would be the "queso puff"—an ingenious, truly Tex-Mex invention. Queso is drizzled on top of a razor-thin tortilla that's puffed out like a balloon; upon first cut, the sphere crumbles to pieces, creating a light, fork-edible, non-messy delivery mechanism for queso (which is itself some of the best in Houston, creamy and skinless, with a chile taste that's actually perceptible—a rarity in these parts). Not bad, either, is the chile relleno, just spicy enough, though brought down by a somewhat soggy egg batter. Enchiladas, tacos, and such are barely average—Old El Paso-style all the way. Margaritas, best frozen, are too sweet. In the end, even the mother branch of this Houston legend is not worth the pilgrimage. In a city full of great fajitas, the original just doesn't cut it anymore. –RG

Mama's Café

King Ranch chicken: a south Texas classic comes home to roost at this down-home eatery

6.9 Food | **5.9** Feel | **$15** Price

American

Casual restaurant
Mon.-Wed. 6:30am-1am; Thurs. 6:30am-3am; Fri. 6:30am-4am; Sat. 8am-4am; Sun. 8am-1am.
Breakfast. Outdoor dining.

Galleria
6019 Westheimer Rd.
(713) 266-8514
www.mamascafe.net

Bar Full
Credit Cards Visa, MC, AmEx
Reservations Accepted

A restaurant chain with six branches, all of them in San Antonio except this one, Mama's Café has managed to keep the already-average quality of the food from slipping even further while expanding slowly but surely. The inside looks like an exploded antique shop, with a lot of disturbing and unattractive clutter and memorabilia on the walls—maybe it's there in a misguided attempt to keep people's eyes off the food.

The menu is plagued by a lack of focus, trying to go in so many different directions that it obscures the occasional well-executed dish. Mama serves us everything from breakfast, soups, and salads to burgers. Starters include fried cheese, mushrooms, zucchini, and wings, giving the fryer a workout. They're nothing special, but they're well executed; the fried cheese is exactly what we want when we bite into a crispy, breaded, and fried piece of mozzarella.

People come here mainly for the great burgers, as well as Mama's comfort-food specialties: meatloaf and such. We were delighted to discover Mama's to be one of the only places in town to get King Ranch chicken, a south Texas staple. Here, chunks of chicken are sandwiched in between corn tortillas and smothered with a spicy cream sauce, and the results are delicious. Liver and onions, on the other hand, is a heroic but sorrowful attempt; it's poorly presented with overcooked liver and undercooked onions.

And, of course, what Mama wouldn't wake up early and serve breakfast? Here, it's rib-sticking skillets and breakfast staples like eggs and bacon, biscuits and gravy. It's perfectly competent, and good therapy for anyone who has to be up early against his or her will. Still, approach the place with caution: Mama's is a commercial-looking space serving food that is sometimes way off the mark. And we can only imagine what's going to happen as the chain grows. –SD

Mardi Gras Grill

Total pleasure grade

New Orleans right in your backyard...got any beads?

7.8 Food **7.9** Feel **$17** Price

Southern

Casual restaurant
Mon.-Thurs. 11am-10pm;
Fri.-Sat. 11am-11pm;
Sun. noon-10pm.
Outdoor dining.

Heights
1200 Durham Dr.
(713) 864-5600
www.mardigrasgrill.net

Bar Full
Credit Cards Visa, MC, AmEx
Reservations Accepted

Nowadays anyone can take a prehistoric bug (or, if you prefer, crustacean); suck its brains out; and be accepted into our society. We praise our barbaric crawfish-eating ways with high fives and slaps on the back; most everyone has seen the shot glasses that explain the process, stressing the importance of sucking the head and swallowing.

Certain establishments in Houston accommodate these needs, and one of the best is the Mardi Gras Grill. Formerly known as Floyd's Cajun Shack, this...well, shack...was renamed, but kept all the character that we need to be brought down to earth. Serving chicken-fried chicken, crawfish, gumbo, and oysters, Mardi Gras Grill delivers a New Orleans experience without putting you at the risk of strangulation by twenty pounds of beads around your neck.

With all the trendiness in the Heights, Mardi Gras Grill stands alone, looking something like a shed with a deck built on to it. The deck is huge, and on a nice day a seat out here can't be beat. The chicken-fried chicken is "off the hook," according to a reliable source: the kiddos. (Their taste buds don't lie.) Its crispy batter, smothered in thick white gravy, will have you selling your stock in the Black-Eyed Pea in no time. The gumbo is dark, rich and flavorful, packed with loads of the Gulf coast's finest offerings. Then comes the main event—the crawfish. Only available when they are in season, they are spicy and delicious. Corn and potatoes take a back seat to these unusually big and plump mudbugs.

If you have a name like the Mardi Gras Grill, then you're required by law to have a party every once in a while. Not a bunch to disobey, they've got parking lot parties during crawfish season and Mardi Gras that are a drunken haze to most, and a gluttonous experience for all. They bring out a sidecar band, shut down the parking lot, and rage. Adult libations, along with tons of prehistoric bugs, of course, are on hand. –SD

María Selma

Slightly creative, slightly pricey Montrose Mexican plus good tequila

6.8 Food | **6.3** Feel | **$32** Price | **Mexican**

Casual restaurant
Mon.-Thurs. 11am-10pm; Fri. 11am-midnight; Sat. 10am-midnight; Sun. 10am-9pm.
Outdoor dining.

Montrose
1619 Richmond Ave.
(713) 528-4920
www.mariaselma.com

Bar Full
Credit Cards Visa, MC, AmEx
Reservations Not accepted

How common is authentic Mexican food in Houston? Is it a huge gamble for a restaurant to venture beyond the realm of Tex-Mex? Should we turn away if the only Mexicans in the restaurant are the staff? And what do we make of a restaurant like María Selma, whose chef was born in Mexico City? Off Richmond in the Montrose area, the restaurant offers toned-down Mexican cuisine for the gringo palate, but with a bit of nobility. You can get all your abuela's favorites like enchiladas, tacos, and tortas, and they're no better than average, but also more exciting cuisine like duck flautas and pork loin with green mole, even if they're only slightly better than average.

Prices here imply excellence. (Hey—they've got to pay the rent somehow.) With a giant palapa that greets the eyes and covers the patio, the restaurant is dressed in warm colors evocative of the Mexican desert; here, the taste buds awaken and the mind relaxes. Thicker-than-usual tortilla chips are accompanied by an intensely fiery salsa. Amongst appetizers, try the duck flautas with adobo sauce. Gamey duck meat delivers a bold flavor that holds up against rich, deep adobo sauce. Fajitas that sit atop a live flame at the table though, are more for novelty than enjoyment. The menu is hit-or-miss, in the end.

One thing that separates María Selma from the rest of the overpriced Montrose-area south-of-the-border restaurants is the tequila. This is not the stuff that comes in the quart plastic bottles, but the real deal. More than 120 different kinds of tequila are available on any given night. There are also frequent tequila dinners, where tequila is paired with each dish to accent the food. There is plenty of parking, but here as ever, valet parking is a superfluous, pompous, annoying waste of money. –SD

Mark's

The prices, ambition, and adjectives don't add up at this hyped-up disappointment

B- Total pleasure grade

7.5 Food **9.3** Feel **$112** Price

New American

Upmarket restaurant
Mon.-Thurs. 11am-2pm, 5:30pm-11pm; Fri. 11am-2pm, 5:30pm-midnight; Sat. 5pm-midnight; Sun. 5pm-10pm. *Date-friendly.*

Montrose
1658 Westheimer Rd.
(713) 523-3800
www.marks1658.com

Bar Full
Credit Cards Visa, MC, AmEx
Reservations Recommended

An apt preview of Mark's, perhaps, is its web site. Many restaurants try too hard with tacky Flash graphics and haughty-looking photos of empty dining rooms with overdressed tables, so that's hardly surprising. But then, suddenly, your computer speakers are blaring with cranked-up Baroque, exuding all the class of a late-night TV commercial: it's Vivaldi's Four Seasons. Spring, at that. You're baffled: you thought Mark's was an understated, chef-owned, market-driven restaurant, tops in the city according to some guidebooks. Now you're wondering if it's just a $100-plus-per-head dinner show on cheesy overdrive.

The reality is somewhere in between. As with Vivaldi's melodies, there is something legitimately wonderful about the building blocks of Mark's. It's set in an original 1920s church, converted into Houston's most elegant dining space. The organ "Loft" now holds wine racks and a few choice tables. Graceful lines gently balance deco with Protestantism, and muted orange walls envelope you with warmth and calm—a remarkable feat given the high ceilings. Expert service is neither condescending nor doting, but rather as warm as the colors.

As a shopper, Chef Mark Cox is very good at his job, often sourcing praiseworthy ingredients from artisanal producers. The menu, awash with prose, changes daily, and its variable results range from unexpected comforts like extraordinarily good bread and some of Houston's best oysters to unremarkable pomposities overwrought with needless adjectives, like a $22.95 crab-tasting appetizer that took 29 words to describe on the menu but wasn't worth half its price. A Kobe special, on one night, featured a sirloin that was recommended—and ordered—medium-rare, but came out medium-plus, along with short ribs that weren't tender. It was a tough, uninteresting way to spend just shy of $50.

As you depart, you'll gaze upon the anteroom's proud display of cheesy accolades—from its induction into some "Fine Dining Hall of Fame," to the boast of "extraordinary to perfection," to the suspect *Wine Spectator* "Award of Excellence" (which it sometimes seems all you need to win is a check for $250 and a self-addressed, stamped envelope). It makes you think about how carefully they've cultivated their high-end reputation over the years—and about how suggestible people sometimes are. It's not that Mark's is a bad restaurant. It's just that the adjectives, ambitions, and prices set the expectations well above the reach of this kitchen's vertical leap. –RG

The Mason Jar

The food and service remain solid at this aging standby

B- Total pleasure grade

6.6 Food | **4.6** Feel | **$24** Price | **American**

Casual restaurant
Mon.-Thurs. 11am-10pm; Fri.-Sat. 11am-11pm; Sun. 10am-10pm.
Brunch. Kid-friendly.

Memorial
9005 Katy Fwy.
(713) 461-9005

Bar Full
Credit Cards Visa, MC, AmEx
Reservations Accepted

There aren't many places left where you can feel peanut shells crunching beneath your feet at the bar, food that you can enjoy whether you're eight or 80, and service that actually makes you feel cared for. Houston's trend toward cool and steely restaurants has run rampant over the last decade, but the Mason Jar, on its perch off of I-10, shows exactly why a restaurant that hits closer to home—rather than the club—can stay in business for so long.

While the décor is outdated, it doesn't seem out of place—rather, it contributes to the distinct aura of rough edges in all the right places. Lighting is dim, but that's probably to cover up the Mason Jar's age. Even with servers turning over like a revolving door, with many of them looking fresh-faced, perhaps right out of high school, the personable service has remained constant. These aren't your five-star, wooshing, snooty servers, but rather people who don't mind giving you a warm smile to go along with your meal.

The menu is pretty limited, with a couple of soups and clumsily tossed salads to go along with your run-of-the-mill burgers, sandwiches, and main courses. Burgers have the most consistency, like the hickory burger, which comes with a mound of bright yellow sharp cheddar, onions, and enough smoky barbecue sauce to make the taste spike without dampening your bun. Shoestring onions and seasoned fries are a smart choice for sides; the latter come crunchy, tinted red from their seasonings.

Whatever you do, stay away from any of the vegetables, as al dente is a mere memory in their distant pasts. That can happen to the mains, too, but inconsistently; a pork chop or a prime rib might be cooked just so on one evening, and overcooked to oblivion on another. Inevitably, someone at your table will order the chicken-fried steak, and inevitably, it will be a fine rendition, with a good breading-to-meat ratio and thick, creamy white gravy that isn't too heavy on the salt.

What the Mason Jar lacks in innovation and style, it makes up for with consistent service. Many people have fond memories of this place going back decades, and they'll probably still have them for decades to come. –JY

Masraff's

An admirable, if undifferentiated, crack at New American in a dramatic setting

B- *Total pleasure grade*

7.8 *Food* **7.5** *Feel* **$76** *Price* **New American**

Upmarket restaurant
Mon.-Thurs. 10am-10pm;
Fri. 10am-11pm;
Sat. 6pm-11pm; Sun. 10:30am-3pm.
Brunch. Live music. Outdoor dining. WiFi.

Memorial
1025 S. Post Oak Ln.
(713) 355-1975
www.masraffs.com

Bar Full
Credit Cards Visa, MC, AmEx
Reservations Accepted

We don't have a particular problem, exactly, with catch-all eclecticism that has become the hallmark of the haute cuisine experience in Houston. But to pull it off, a restaurant needs to make your dinner coherent, too. There needs to be some connective thread, some guiding culinary or cultural concept—even if it's a vague one—to anchor the flights of ingrediental fantasy.

The space at Masraff's is pleasant enough, with high ceilings and warm terra-cotta-colored walls. The service is professional. The chef is skilled. But the menu has a terminal case of ADHD. Leaping from crabmeat bruschetta to sesame-crusted tuna with shiitake mushrooms and wasabi to Caesar salad, skipping from a salmon burger to cranberry-ginger chutney to pesto to Armenian rice pilaf, the Masraff's menu surfs so many countries so quickly that it's overwhelmed by jetlag. Even a kitchen as competent as this one can't redeem such ill-inspired juxtapositions as cheddar cheese cannelloni and red grape ragout, or the overbearing surfeit of ingredients (crab, salmon, scallops, shrimp, and asparagus) that overwhelms the delicate point of a risotto.

Take an appetizer of roasted quail stuffed with molasses-caramelized onions and walnuts, pear-celery-compote-stuffed crêpe, and Madeira sauce: it is totally misguided, less than the sum of its adjectives. The overambitious gâteau-style presentation falls apart immediately upon fork contact, and it's almost impossible to get a bite that brings together the many ingredients—not that they complement each other well, anyway. It feels as if the menu was created on paper, without feedback from tasters.

There are redeeming counterpoints, so to speak: a bar-style "Chef's Counter," for instance, where tasting menus are served. And there are some rousing successes, like seared (if not quite "caramelized") scallops over polenta laced with truffle oil. Regardless of your position on truffle oil (the Italian chefs hate it), this dish succeeds because it only has three basic ingredients, and they don't fight with each other. Likewise for foie gras, properly seared, vein-free, and meltingly delicious, paired wisely with pears and a port wine glaze. And wild mushroom ravioli from good homemade pasta, excellent flavor, and a barely "truffle-scented" broth that's nicely reduced. –RG

Massa's

Like an old-school steakhouse, but with fish

B- *Total pleasure grade*

7.0 *Food* **7.0** *Feel* **$42** *Price* **Seafood**

Casual restaurant
Mon.-Fri. 11am-9pm;
Sat. 5pm-9pm; closed Sun.

Downtown
1331 Lamar St.
(713) 655-9100
www.massas.com

Downtown
1160 Smith St.
(713) 650-0837

Bar Full
Credit Cards Visa, MC, AmEx
Reservations Accepted

Massa's Restaurant and its sibling, Massa's Seafood Grill, are traditional high-end seafood restaurants that don't try anything too fancy, but maintain high standards for what they put on the table. They're standbys for downtown business lunches, where lawyers and energy-industry types can be sure that the reliable seafood and discrete service won't get in the way of business, and might just help things along. Both restaurants get quiet at night and on weekends once the power lunchers have gone home.

Massa's specialties are based on the seafood of the Gulf Coast region. "Redfish Ponchartrain" is like a dish you'd find in almost any high-end Louisiana seafood restaurant: a substantial cut of redfish (when they can get it) in a tawny-port mushroom sauce, topped with shrimp and crabmeat. They don't skimp on the crabmeat either. Meatatarians can get the same dish with ribeye instead of redfish. The fried shrimp are large and cooked just right, so the crisp batter locks in the fresh flavor of the shrimp. On a recent visit we enjoyed a key-lime rainbow trout special that achieved a nice balance of the delicate flavor of the trout and the lime and butter they cooked it in. The considerate staff had taken out all the bones, which is a tough task even for the most meticulous line cooks at the top restaurants. We're also fans of the seafood gumbo, which is thick with shrimp and crabmeat and has a smoky dark-roux flavor.

The two restaurants are similar, although the original Massa's on Smith is a bit more formal than the Seafood Grill on Lamar. The décor at the Grill is more fun, with a big wall-mural reminding you how beautiful fish can be before you eat them. The Grill also gets a little more adventurous with the menu, generating unimpressive results with items like jerk catfish and Asian tuna with ginger-soy and wasabi. We wouldn't expect either Massa's to get much more adventurous than that, though; the original has stuck around since 1944 by meeting downtown expectations of what a fish restaurant should be, so unless those expectations change, we don't expect Massa's will either. –FC

Max's Wine Dive

B-

Total pleasure grade

Overpriced food and wine that the see-and-be-seen love to pay for

7.4 *Food* | 7.7 *Feel* | $46 *Price*

New American

Wine bar
Tues.-Wed. 4pm-midnight;
Thurs.-Sat. 4pm-2am;
Sun. 11am-midnight; closed Mon.
Brunch. Outdoor dining. WiFi.

Washington
4720 Washington Ave.
(713) 880-8737
www.maxswinedive.com

Bar Wine and beer only
Credit Cards Visa, MC, AmEx
Reservations Accepted

How wine became the "in" thing in Houston is beyond us. In the land of Buds and Bocks, somehow the yuppies that overflow Washington Avenue's burgeoning restaurant row have found their new gold with the likes of Pinot Noir, Riesling, and Cabernet Sauvignon. Such is Max's Wine Dive: a conundrum, because after taking care of the check and heading out to the parking lot, you're not sure if you just walked out of a trendy restaurant or just a really pricey bar.

For a place that stresses fun with a sense of gourmet class, everything in print is a wreck. The menu reads like a pubescent teenager wrote it, looking for a cheap laugh with items such as "Three Big Balls" and the "BMF Bread Pudding" (use your imagination). The wine list talks as if it were a rhyme-time with a two-year-old. There's such a thing as making food and wine more accessible, but the menus make it seem like they want to treat their customers as toddlers.

Though at times it might feel like it's overlooked, the food at Max's is sometimes good, sometimes not bad, but most of the time grossly overpriced. The portions are huge, and the menu changes seasonally with what seems like very good raw product coming in, but a lack of execution can often creep in. The fried chicken is disappointing. When we have ordered it, the chicken had been fried too long, over-caramelizing its buttermilk marinade and creating a slightly burnt aspect. Appetizers fare better than mains, and (chicken aside) most of the best food at Max's comes out of the fryer. One of the only things worth the money is the spiced "frites," an addictive version, melding just enough salt with just enough spice. Fried oyster nachos, too, are a nice twist on an old classic, and it's hard to argue with the mac-and-cheese (although you can argue with the price).

The wine program, however, has no redemption. The list is filled with well-priced, but boring, mid-level wines that are served either too warm, or way, way too cold. For a wine dive, the wine really does take a dive. We have no doubt that Max's really does mean well, but for price and execution—and, sorry Max, even wine—you and your money should go elsewhere. –FC

Mayuri

North-meets-South Indian in a random location that gets it mostly right

B
Total pleasure grade

7.6	7.3	$33	**Indian**
Food	*Feel*	*Price*	

Casual restaurant
Sun.-Thurs. 11am-2:30pm, 5:30pm-10pm; Fri.-Sat. 11am-2:30pm, 5pm-10:30pm.
Vegetarian-friendly. WiFi.

Galleria
5857 Westheimer Rd.
(713) 975-6565
www.mayuri.com

Bar Wine and beer only
Credit Cards Visa, MC, AmEx
Reservations Accepted

Indian food is best eaten early here. You're well advised to clear out before 10pm, at which point the lights progressively brighten, and the cleaning staff emerges from the woodwork to stare you down. You'll need to budget your time throughout dinner if you want dessert; they won't stick around for you otherwise. Still, they're nice about it; you sympathize with them. These people just want to go home.

And after spending a bit of time in the strange, expansive interior of Maturi, you just might want to as well. It's not that it's particularly miserable; it's just large and not that cozy. Little to no thought is put into the appearance of the place, leaving you to feel like you're eating in an abandoned banquet room. Small attempts here and there try to make it feel borderline upmarket, but they ultimately fail. But doesn't this describe most of Houston's Indian restaurants?

It's the food that redeems Mayuri. Saag paneer is earthy and creamy, exacting a delicate balance that's neither watery nor heavy. Lamb dishes will fire you up further; they're tender, lamby, well seasoned. Rice and breads are unusually good here. Poori come out slightly thicker than usual, which works to their toothsome benefit, while good, spongy idli (rice-and-lentil-flour cakes), one amongst many southern Indian dishes on the menu, come with spicy, refreshing chutneys.

Vindaloo has decent flavor but could use a bit more kick, though spice-sensitive patrons will find it just right. Goat biryani, too, is lacking in that distinctive flavor that makes us love goat so much. One baffling starter of breaded and fried chili peppers reminds us of poppers, the likes of which you can find easily in the frozen-foods section of any grocery store; that said, they still hit all the pleasure points. Mango lassis aren't cloyingly sweet here—sometimes we order them as dessert because they can be so saccharine—and have a pleasant taste of fresh mango. They actually serve their purpose of helping neutralize the fire the food started. If only the Vindaloo had such flammable properties. –AH

McCormick & Schmick's

B
Total pleasure grade

Houston's independent seafood restaurants should watch out for this local-fish-serving chain

8.2 *Food* **7.5** *Feel* **$61** *Price*

Seafood, American

Upmarket restaurant
Mon.-Sat. 11am-11pm;
Sun. 11am-10pm.
Brunch. Outdoor dining.

Memorial
1151 Uptown Park Blvd.
(713) 840-7900
www.mccormickandschmicks.com

Bar Full
Credit Cards Visa, MC, AmEx
Reservations Accepted

Even if you love to hate upscale chain restaurants, it's hard to hate McCormick & Schmick's. For one thing, they serve local fish. In Houston, that might include reasonably-priced cornmeal-fried catfish from Palacios, amberjack from Flower Garden Banks, or grouper from Galveston. These fishes are underrepresented in town, and it's bizarre to see a chain taking up the slack. Salty, peppery blackened redfish from Palacios, Texas, for instance, is a rousing success, juicy, cooked not a moment too long. Its rich, nutty citrus butter works surprisingly well, even if the blue crab on top is superfluous, and wild rice is sweet and inexplicably addictive. Your mother makes an unexpected appearance on the plate in the form of bitter asparagus and useless carrot slices, but your childhood ghosts will be exorcised, because she's powerless to make you eat them.

Another good reason not to hate McCormick & Schmick's is the happy-hour deal at the dark-wood bar tables—and we actually prefer their pubby atmosphere to the more sedate, romantically lit, but generic main dining room.. If you're drinking—not just from 4-6:30pm, but also during the Euro-Argentine dinner hours of 9-11pm—they give away giant appetizer plates for two, three, or four bucks: fried calamari, blackened ahi tips, seafood tostadas, and so on. There's a $1.95 cheeseburger. It's one of the cheapest dinners in town. Don't expect service, though—what's attentive in the dining room turns disastrous in the bar.

There's also a commitment to seasonal raw oysters, which are right on the money. As for those fried calamari, they're very salty, not quite rubbery but not quite tender, and their sauces are subpar; it's best with a simple squeeze of lemon or dash of malt vinegar, whose acidity balances out the salt. It's not worth anywhere near its $9.95.

In an effort to appease the lowest common denominator, this restaurant dilutes its quality by crowding the menu with too many losers: Asian short ribs? Spinach salad with basil Dijon dressing? Blackened chicken linguine with peppers and onions?

Chains will be chains. But this one could hold a fish seminar for some of the independent restaurants in town. –RG

The Men's Club

Surprisingly good specials with an atmosphere that will rival the Vatican

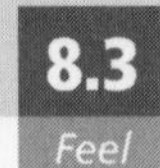

$20 Price

American

Strip club
Daily 11am-2am.
Breakfast. Brunch.
Date-friendly.

Galleria
3303 Sage Rd.
(713) 629-7900
www.mensclub.com

Bar Full
Credit Cards Visa, MC, AmEx
Reservations Not accepted

What's better that eating cheesy scrambled eggs at two in the morning just to satisfy a craving? If you're a single, sleazy man, it's eating them in a strip club with a pair of breasts being jiggled in front of your face while you miss your mouth with your fork because you're preoccupied, that's what. Eggs and estrogen is what the Men's Club excels at.

Yes, the Men's Club is a gentlemen's club; yes, they have a breakfast buffet that runs circles around IHOP; and yes, they do have one of the best happy hours in town. It surprises many people that the Men's Club actually has good food. Also, surprisingly, the atmosphere rivals some of the old-boy steakhouses in its aesthetic, and not just because of the topless women.

Housed in a cult-like compound with white walls protecting the perimeter from the morally superior masses, the Men's Club offers extravagance and lavish living with only a small asking price. They offer a happy hour from 4-7pm, Monday through Friday, with free cover and $1.50 drink specials. A free buffet, which accompanies that deal, changes from time to time, with the usual salads and finger foods for the taking. The main event, though, is on Wednesdays and Fridays for lunch; at those times, you pay $10 for a buffet with more than 70 items.

Amongst them—surprise, surprise—the food is hit or miss. The buffet game of "whose is longer" focuses on quantity, not quality. From pasta salads to mains like surprisingly delicious meatloaf, decent pork chops, and less decent steak and potatoes, there's something to please even the pickiest palate. On Mondays, you can get a steak-and-shrimp dinner for only $7.95, which includes a beef tenderloin that's helped out in the flavor department by blue cheese butter. The shrimp, meanwhile, are overcooked, but have good flavor. What a deal—if all you do is eat, that is. Suffice it to say that the buffet is not the Men's Club's cash cow. –SD

Mezzanine Lounge

B-
Total pleasure grade

$2.50 you-call-its all night long—please exercise caution

7.3	7.6	$16
Food	*Feel*	*Price*

American

Bar
Mon. noon-2am; Tues.-Fri. 4pm-2am; Sat. 3pm-2am; Sun. 3pm-midnight.

Upper Kirby
2200 Southwest Fwy.
(713) 528-6399
www.mezzaninelounge.com

Bar Full
Credit Cards Visa, MC, AmEx
Reservations Not accepted

One of Houston's best drink buys happens on Tuesdays at Mezzanine, where a measly $2.50 will buy you any drink you want all night long. This dive bar off 59 is frequented by drunks, college folk, sports fanatics, and poor line cooks who need their after work drink for cheap. Aside from liquor, they serve sports-bar food in all its greasy glory. Burgers, wings, dips, and fried anything-and-everything will make you believe that you can drive home, but remember—that's just the grease talkin'. Specials are in place every day to keep you coming back; what might keep you away, on the other hand, is the sometimes-obnoxious college folk measuring the size of their manhood with yells and chants.

But good bar food, cheap prices, and cheap drinks? Sign us up. There are no multiple-course tasting menus here, just food for the common man. After the booze, burgers are the second main attraction; patties are seasoned nicely and paired with crisp lettuce, tomato, and pickles. The fries are outstanding; they're the thick kind that will take you back to school cafeteria days, and they come out crispy and pleasantly salty. Indulge yourself by putting cheese and chili on top of the fries for a party in your stomach. Just be careful what other drinks you invite to this party; it can easily turn into a brawl.

No great bar experience is complete without buffalo wings, the fried gems of the culinary world. Here, they're crisply fried and then coated in a tangy sauce that will make you feel great—until you hear your own arteries clogging. Don't worry, it's all part of the experience. Served with ranch or blue cheese (we always go for blue cheese), they're a nice way to round out your night. Then, for the palate cleanser: vodka, whiskey, brandy, or Jägermeister—you'll be satisfied no matter what you pick. Remember, spirits aid in digestion. –SD

Mi Luna

One of Houston's most popular restaurants is also one of its worst

D- Total pleasure grade

2.8 Food | **4.5** Feel | **$63** Price | **Spanish**

Upmarket restaurant
Sun.-Tues. 11am-10pm; Wed. 11am-11pm; Thurs. 11am-midnight; Fri.-Sat. 11am-1am.
Brunch. Live music. Outdoor dining.

Rice Area
2441 University Blvd.
(713) 520-5025
www.mi-luna.com

Bar Full
Credit Cards Visa, MC, AmEx
Reservations Recommended

Sugar Land
2298 Texas Dr.
(281) 277-8272

Woodlands
6777 Woodlands Pkwy.
(281) 419-0330

Tapas are festive by nature. The format encourages convivial sharing, and the salty, garlicky flavors pair well with sangría, the ideal party drink. Customers come ready to have fun, and primed to love it all. Witness the immense, contagious popularity of Mi Luna, a vaguely Middle Eastern-Spanish red-and-gold-themed, romantically boothed space in Rice Village. Amidst Spanish lanterns, latticework, tacky Renaissance murals and bullfighting posters, and even live-band salsa on certain nights, each party—large or small—manages to feel simultaneously secluded and completely a part of the restaurant.

But rarely does a place this popular serve food and drink this spectacularly bad. Mi Luna starts with tables full of happy people and manages to send many of them home feeling totally ripped off—if not by the overpriced food then by the service, which is so incompetent on a busy night that it can come between old friends, put a damper on a family reunion, or ruin the chemistry in a budding date. We've seen it happen.

Beginning with the vile sangría—which tastes like powdered Kool-Aid with the instructions followed improperly—and the terrible, expensive margaritas and mojitos—which are like shooting up sugar—we haven't tasted anything liquid or solid at Mi Luna that was even vaguely palatable. Expect leathery jamón serrano; rubbery shrimp al ajillo with off-notes instead of garlic; mushrooms with less flavor than those dumped straight out of a supermarket can; tasteless patatas bravas; small, boring, chewy tortilla española; overly sweet b'stilla, a Moroccan pie stuffed with bone-dry chicken; and more nightmarish apparitions.

Amazingly, things get even worse with mains. "Paella Mi Luna" is more maimed than any we've ever seen, with dry rice, barely detectable saffron, horrible shrimp, and dry meats. It's really, really hard to mess up chorizo, so we're left wondering what the family secret is here. And the inexplicable rudeness of the service even extends to pricing logic: you wind up spending far more on the tapas-and-paella combo samplers for the whole table than you would if you ordered everything à la carte. It seems just another way that this inexcusable farce of a restaurant has discovered to stick it to a captive crowd that started the evening in a good mood. –FC

Michelangelo's

A tacky Italian-American snooze that is inexplicably still popular

C- Total pleasure grade

3.4 Food | **5.8** Feel | **$52** Price

Italian-American

Casual restaurant
Mon.-Thurs. 11am-10pm; Fri.-Sat. 11am-11pm; Sun. 11am-9pm.
Brunch. Live music. Outdoor dining.

Montrose
307 Westheimer Rd.
(713) 524-7836
www.michelangelosrestaurant.com

Bar Full
Credit Cards Visa, MC, AmEx
Reservations Accepted

Dear Michelangelo's Restaurante' [sic]:

Having recently dined at your establishment, we find that our visit has left us with a few questions. First: Restaurante'? We have consulted both our Spanish-English and our Italian-English dictionaries, and it seems to us that you have used a Spanish word in reference to your Italian restaurant. More importantly, why is there an apostrophe at the conclusion of the word? Is it a botched attempt at an accent? But neither "ristorante" nor "restaurante" have an accent. Is it the remnants of a vestigial possessive, perhaps? As a policy, we don't generally pick on bad spelling, but this is your restaurant's actual name.

A second question: why do you add a 15% gratuity to all parties, regardless of size, but do not leave any room for patrons to tip any more than that on a credit card? We would strongly advise rethinking this policy. Have a little more confidence in your servers; they're capable of earning a solid 20%. You do have a live piano player on occasion, after all, even if his repertoire derives largely from *Phantom of the Opera* and *Titanic*. And you should capitalize on those $6.95 bottomless mimosas for brunch. Even if your eggs benedict are made with gummy hollandaise and chewy Canadian bacon, we're sure you'll find that your patrons are more generous after a few glasses.

Finally: Where do you get your bread? It bears a striking resemblance to that of our neighborhood Kroger bakery. And what are you doing to your cannoli? Because we like it. The texture of the blended spinach and veal is pleasant. Your fettuccine alfredo, on the other hand, is disappointingly lackluster, and your chicken parmigiana is dry and flavorless. Perhaps your kitchen has been running low on seasoning, or perhaps on culinary expertise?

Can you remind us, again, why anyone goes to your restaurant? Because, on our last visit, we spent all afternoon trying to figure that out.

Thank you very much in advance for your time.

Sincerely,

The Fearless Critics

Mission Burrito

Big burritos, San Francisco-style, and a kid-friendly patio

B *Total pleasure grade*

6.9 *Food* **5.6** *Feel* **$9** *Price* **Tex-Mex**

Counter service
River Oaks hours daily 10am-10pm. Heights hours Mon.-Sat. 11pm-10am; Sun. 11am-9pm.
Kid-friendly. Outdoor dining.

River Oaks
2245 W. Alabama
(713) 529-0535
www.missionburritos.com

Heights
1609 Durham Dr.
(713) 426-6634

Bar Wine and beer only
Credit Cards Visa, MC, AmEx
Reservations Not accepted

Any self-respecting burrito joint should have at least one burrito on the menu so big that no normal person could finish it without pain. The twelve-dollar "Mission Super Burrito" fits the bill. Weighing over three pounds and requiring two hands to maneuver, the Super Burrito is composed of such quality ingredients that you'll probably enjoy yourself up until the pain starts. Unless you've got something to prove, go with the "Regular."

Downmarket, San-Francisco-wannabe burrito places are distinguished by (A) quality of ingredients, (B) competence in preparation, and (C) degree of customizability. Mission Burrito gets decent marks in (A) and (B), and even higher marks in (C). The char-grilled chicken and beef have a real grill flavor that carries through the whole burrito. The veggies taste freshly chopped, and the salsas provide real fire; we like the smoky flavor of the chiles de arbol. In terms of customization, if you don't want lots of rice, they won't load it on as filler, as some places do. If you want your burrito smothered in cilantro, by God, they'll smother it in cilantro. We sometimes load up on the vegetables just to feel virtuous while chomping down on a three-pound burrito.

The non-burrito options are a step back from the burritos, but still decent value Tex-Mex. Fish and shrimp tacos are tasty, while tortilla soup and quesadillas are just average. You can pick up free chips and salsa at a side table. The former are a bit thick for our taste, but the birds outside seem pretty fond of them.

The patio area facing Alabama is shaded by a noble old oak tree that, unfortunately for you, hosts whole avian families. There's a small playground area for kids, complete with Tonka trucks. The kid-friendly vibe is continued with munchkin meals for $3.50, as well as the cute practice of giving out toy animals and pirate swords as claim-checks for your order. It's the little creative details like that—"munchkin meal and two fish tacos for the elephant"—that make Mission Burrito stand out from the Chipotles of the world. –RH

Miyako

Late-night sushi and so-so Japanese food in a sea of awkward first dates

5.5 Food | **6.8** Feel | **$38** Price

Japanese

Upmarket restaurant
Mon.-Thurs. 11am-11pm;
Fri.-Sat. 11am-midnight;
Sun. noon-11pm.

Outdoor dining. WiFi.

Upper Kirby
3910 Kirby Dr.
(713) 520-9797
www.miyakosushibar.com

Meyerland
728 Meyerland Plaza
(713) 838-7500

Bar Full
Credit Cards Visa, MC, AmEx
Reservations Accepted

Galleria
6345 Westheimer Rd.
(713) 781-6300

Miyako is one of a few proud sushi joints that broadcast their dedication to freshness, quality, and all things good across the World Wide Web. Fair enough—don't most sushi places strive for those ideals? Regardless, the attitude seems to reflect at least somewhat in the food; while the sushi isn't top-notch, it's not bad either. Bizarrely—especially at the dark, often empty Upper Kirby location—there's something about the place that makes it a date destination. Perhaps it's the late hours, as Miyako is open until midnight on weekdays. (Maybe some are exercising wishful thinking in hoping their date will continue that long.) So, if you're not trying on someone new, enjoy the show: surface-level conversations and attempted jokes that fall flat, and a display of each individual's personal take on the make-you-wanna-do-me costume.

They're certainly not focusing on the food. Unfortunately, we are. An entire section of the menu is devoted to vegetarian sushi, an interesting concept and a sign of the times. None of the selections look that appealing to us, but, then, we're not vegetarians. Maki (cut rolls) are also a big part of the menu. The ubiquitous maki that haunts our sushi combinations, the California roll, is strange here; it's not made in a style we care for. It's just a bit too creamy, making the texture too one-dimensional. An extensive dinner menu covers heavy dishes that aren't as interesting (or as good) as the sushi. Some of it just seems bad and sadly overambitious. Green mussels baked with caviar cream sauce? No thanks.

The sushi is what you should come for here, and prices are refreshingly low (or should this frighten us a bit?), making it that much more appealing. Red snapper nigiri is $1.50, and nigiri prices reach their peak at $2.25. Seasonal items are market price, but worth a try—ama ebi, uni, and toro are generally worth the small price increase. Still, it's really only worth coming here after better sushi options like Nippon and Sasaki have closed. –AH

Mockingbird Bistro

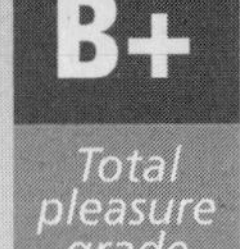

Total pleasure grade

This old-Guard Texas-style bistro food is solid—if you can get past the first course

8.0 Food | **9.0** Feel | **$80** Price

New American

Upmarket restaurant
Mon.-Fri. 11am-2pm, 5:30pm-10pm; Sat.-Sun. 5:30pm-10pm.
Date-friendly.

River Oaks
1985 Welch St.
(713) 533-0200
www.mockingbirdbistro.com

Bar Full
Credit Cards Visa, MC, AmEx
Reservations Recommended

Houston's celebrity chefs seem to do best in bistro settings: the now-defunct Boulevard Bistro and the happily-chugging-away Gravitas are two good examples. Another is the Mockingbird Bistro, serving sensible, close-to-the-vest bistro fare to a River Oaks crowd that's flush with cash. The food is consistent, if unspectacular, and the wine list is intriguing enough to keep the landed gentry coming back regularly—and for good reason.

Like the cuisine at Mockingbird, the atmosphere is practical with a touch of old-world class. Large, medieval-looking chandeliers evoke old France, while the sill-to-ceiling windows and crisp white linens bring a reasonable amount of upmarket fluff to the space. The staff are very measured and careful, though not quite technically proficient. There's some clunking of the large and heavy plates onto tables, rather than delicate presentation, but we're not sticklers for such matters. More importantly, there's a high bar for the staff's general knowledge of wine, which is either excellent or, at the very least, well rehearsed.

There's nothing wrong with the food at Mockingbird Bistro; the kitchen is technically proficient beyond reproach. Our complaints, such as they are, are more about what they *don't* do than what they do. Well-executed, run-of-the-mill bistro fare has a notable Texan twist; we just wish we could see a bit more of the chef coming through. The time-honored calamari with remoulade and spicy glaze gets rave reviews, but it tastes the same as most well-fried calamari around town—only with fancier dipping sauces. (Not that there's anything wrong with well-fried calamari.) A seasonal tomato soup is tasty for the first few spoonfuls, but it doesn't inspire you to lick the dish clean or to meditate on the flavors; that is, it hits neither the pleasure centers of the brain nor the intellectual ones.

Mockingbird Bistro seems to have missed the boat on the portion-size aspect of the nouvelle movement; huge first courses are followed by even heavier mains. Diver scallops come judiciously seared, but seem better suited to a lighter preparation than their in-your-face red-wine risotto and beurre rouge sauce. The starch-heaviness continues with a salmon dish with lentils and a hearty curry sauce that's perfect for winter; in summer, however, you just find yourself tugging at your collar. That said, this kitchen is steady, and Mockingbird's wine selection happily traverses the globe. But may we suggest sharing? –JY

Molina's

A disappointing Houston tradition since 1941

Total pleasure grade

4.3 Food **3.8** Feel **$30** Price **Tex-Mex**

Casual restaurant
Mon.-Tues. 11am-9pm;
Wed.-Thurs. 11am-10pm; Fri. 11am-midnight; Sat. 11am-11pm; Sun. 11am-10pm.
Kid-friendly. Outdoor dining.

Washington
4720 Washington Ave.
(713) 862-0013
www.molinasrestaurants.com

Bar Full
Credit Cards Visa, MC, AmEx
Reservations Not accepted

Westchase
7901 Westheimer Ave.
(713) 782-0861

Greenway Plaza
5227 Buffalo Speedway
(713) 432-1626

This Tex-Mex is as pedestrian as it comes, but at least there's a story behind it. The restaurant was begun by Raúl Molina, originally from Laredo. Upon arriving in the US, he took a job as a busboy, eventually saving enough money to buy his own restaurant. If only there were some clause in the American Dream ensuring that "making it" as a restaurateur in America requires serving good food.

The Molina's we have today is total Tex-Mex: think sour-cream chicken enchiladas, chips, and salsa—but without that good execution that makes us love Tex-Mex. Even the slam dunks are bungled here. "José's Dip," for instance—chile con queso with taco meat—is a real disappointment. How we love our chile con queso, but oh, how they've managed to mess it up here: no flavor, practically no chile, pretty much no nothin'.

Servers wear strangely pseudo-formal attire that might be better suited to Chippendales dancers. Maybe that's what brings in all the female office workers; it certainly couldn't be the "Ladies' Special," a cheese enchilada, guacamole, and chile con queso combo that is certain to return them to their offices in a post-Tex-Mex food coma. (Just because it's a small lunch doesn't mean it ain't fatty. Not that it's a small lunch, anyway.) The lunch specials here are gigantic—surprise, surprise—but bad. "Enchiladas à la Michael" are crackly enchiladas in an underseasoned tomatillo sauce with chicken that's unpleasantly dry. Bone dry. Spit-it-out dry. A section of the menu marked "Comidas Tejanas," meanwhile, includes a "Mexico City Dinner" (don't worry, we don't get it either) that consists of a dry taco, a dry enchilada, a dry tostada, a dry tamal, flavorless guacamole, flavorless chile con queso, flavorless rice, and flavorless beans. And you thought the Ladies' Special was coma-worthy? Dios mío. After that, you might as well just pass out for the rest of the day. But, then, you were probably just checking Fantasy Baseball standings and deleting spam from your inbox all morning, anyway.

So how is it that Molina's is still around? Our best guess is that they generated a loyal following back in the day; as for the new converts, maybe it's just convenience. Or dressed-up hunks. –AH

Mom's Hand Restaurant

The Koreans are definitely on to something here

B *Total pleasure grade*

7.9 *Food* **6.9** *Feel* **$9** *Price*

Korean

Counter service
Mon.-Sat. 9am-8:30pm; closed Sun.

Spring Branch
1049 Gessner Dr.
(713) 468-5955

Bar None
Credit Cards No credit cards
Reservations Not accepted

There are many ethnic markets around Houston with delicious little food stalls. Whether Mexican, Chinese, or Korean, they have situated themselves to serve their people, as the vast majority of the people who shop at these markets are from the local communities. So it only makes sense that some of the greatest ethnic comfort food will be found at these markets. And this is also where some of the most rewarding eating experiences can be had. At their best, they can trasport you to, say, Korea, if only for thirty minutes. Mom's Hand Restaurant, inside of Komart, serves noodle soups, chicken wings, and dumplings; this is real food with real soul that is great for morale.

Speaking of the Komart, it's an incredibly authentic Korean food market off Gessner; even the smell is just like what you'd find in Asia. Each stall has its own specialties, and the thing to eat at Mom's Hand is the noodle soup. Homemade rice noodles accompany a spicy seafood soup that will satisfy all your cravings. It's spicy, but if you beg and plead they can make you a tamer version. Lots of seafood is in the soup; shrimp, squid, and octopus play nicely against each other in a fiery broth that has the essence of chilies. Get a slurp of noodle, broth, and seafood and indulge your taste buds in a food-induced high. Kimchee (fermented cabbage) is also served with the soup; it's a ubiquitous Korean side.

Aside from noodle soup, Mom's Hand has chicken wings and seafood scallion pancakes. The wings are disappointing in their dryness, and their sauce is frighteningly gluey, with little flavor. The scallion pancakes with squid and shrimp, on the other hand, are pretty delicious. But you know what to order here. If you have time, take a look around the Komart market and admire the totally foreign groceries and low prices. If you're running low on jarred kimchee, here's your chance. –SD

Monarch

An arrogant hotel restaurant whose modernity is just an expensive façade

D
Total pleasure grade

6.8 *Food* | **3.8** *Feel* | **$93** *Price*

New American

Upmarket restaurant
Daily 6:30am-10am, 11am-11pm.
Breakfast. Brunch. Live music. Outdoor dining. WiFi.

Hermann Park
5701 Main St.
(713) 527-1800
www.monarchrestauranthouston.com

Bar Full
Credit Cards Visa, MC, AmEx
Reservations Essential

Over the past decade, the American hotel industry has undergone a profound, long-overdue transformation. Some observers have dubbed it the "boutique hotel" revolution, but that's a misnomer, because the hotel brand that launched the new school—the W—is neither small, nor privately owned, nor niche-marketed.

What really changed in the late '90s was that, for the first time in decades, the booming hotel industry decided to respond to the real desires of business and leisure travelers. It turned out that they cared more about technology than shoe-shining; they fancied comfortable beds and flat-screen TVs more than giant rooms with Victorian furnishings; and they preferred hip, cutting-edge lounges to the tired, stuffy restaurants and bars that, until then, had dominated even the top American hotels.

Although the Derek and the Alden fit the genre, too, the ZaZa is Houston's foremost member of the W school, and its new restaurant-lounge, Monarch, is its culinary entry into this new game. It's dressed up in sexy shades of black and velvet-red, with warm yellow lighting and postmodern, hypnotically patterned upholstery. Monarch seeks to achieve what its bar scene already has: to become a real Houston hotspot, not just for visitors, but for locals.

And it fails spectacularly. From the incompetent hostess to the clumsy service to the embarrassingly inconsistent kitchen, we've rarely seen a restaurant this expensive that was this poorly run. Your table's ready, and then they take it back from you. They have the (overpriced) wine you ordered, and then they don't. Your "foie gras sliders" (in little hamburger buns), however, are deliciously hard to argue with; you order an enormously expensive steak medium-rare, and it comes out well done. And then you notice that the same thing has just happened to the table next to you. You each send your steak back, and you each get an eye-roll instead of an apology.

Sadly, the ZaZa doesn't really seem to understand its own genre, because when you strip the pompous adjectives from Monarch's menu, it turns out to be nothing but a tired old hotel restaurant in disguise: smoked salmon, overcooked steaks, and chops. The only thing that Monarch has really added to the equation is attitude. –RG

Morton's

Houston's dry-aged piece of the chain to end all chains

B
Total pleasure grade

8.7 *Food* **8.0** *Feel* **$102** *Price* **Steakhouse**

Upmarket restaurant
Mon.-Sat. 5:30pm-11pm;
Sun. 5pm-10pm.

Downtown
1001 McKinney St.
(713) 659-3700
www.mortons.com

Galleria
5000 Westheimer Rd.
(713) 629-1946

Bar Full
Credit Cards Visa, MC, AmEx
Reservations Recommended

One of the best meals we've ever had at a chain restaurant, anywhere in the world, was at the Morton's in Singapore. To get those Prime cuts of beef there from the American Midwest would have taken Singapore Airlines' new A380 about nineteen hours. The steakhouse décor (corporate luxe, plush booths, dark and elegant, you know the drill) and impeccable service were identical to their counterparts anywhere else. The execution was as good, or better, than it is in Chicago—and Singapore is hardly a city where they're used to broiling steaks at 1800°. That's how smoothly the Morton's machine is running at the moment. And it's running just as smoothly at Houston's two branches, both of which appear to be minting money.

One of the trademarks here is the plastic-wrapped beef ritual, wherein your server shows you all the different raw cuts of meat, covered in what looks like Saran wrap, as you're ordering. The idea is to let you choose your Prime weapon, although this steakhouse version of the tableside guacamole routine tends to make at least someone at the table squirm with squeamishness. (There's always someone that loves meat but wants to deny that it ever consisted of living muscle.)

It's pretty hard to go wrong here, except if you consider the effect on your wallet. The only steakhouse chain that compares to Morton's is Ruth's Chris, which is a local competitor in Houston as well. Capital Grille is trying, and failing miserably, to make a run for it. Houston's and Outback are more modest. Fogo de Chão, at the end of the day, is a buffet restaurant. Morton's does have one failing: we prefer the funkier flavor of dry-aged beef to the wet-aged version that they settle for. Regardless, three decades after its opening, this remains a genre-defying—or perhaps new-genre-defining—restaurant in the history of the American chain. Certainly Morton's is not the best steakhouse in New York, nor is it the best in Houston (we prefer Vic & Anthony's). But even wet-aging, it comes pretty darn close.

And you pay the price. You're best off experiencing all of this with an expense account at your disposal. After all, everyone else in the restaurant seems to be doing so. –RG

Mr. Gatti's

Why eat bad national chain pizza when you can eat bad Texas chain pizza?

C-
Total pleasure grade

5.0 *Food* **4.5** *Feel* **$12** *Price* **Pizza**

Casual restaurant
Daily 11am-10pm.
Delivery. Kid-friendly.

Southeast Houston
16607 El Camino Real
(281) 480-4800
www.mrgattis.com

Bar Beer only
Credit Cards Visa, MC, AmEx
Reservations Not accepted

East Houston
150 Uvalde Rd.
(713) 451-2866

North Houston
12155 Jones Rd.
(281) 807-3333

Founded in Austin in 1969, Mr. Gatti's has spread over much of the southern United States. They offer consistently decent pizza, reasonable delivery times, and an affordable buffet. Then there are the infamous Gattitowns—buffet-only establishments with game rooms, TVs, and battalions of wheeled high chairs for navigating your and your toddler's way through their vast expanses. These are understandably popular with kids—and even some parents.

The restaurants themselves are pretty short on ambience, most of which comes from whatever is playing on the closest TV (usually cartoons or sports). We prefer the regular Mr. Gatti's to the Gattitowns, if only because they seem to smell better (fewer little people, perhaps?).

The buffet includes salad, pasta, a variety of pizzas, and dessert pizzas as well, with larger buffets at the Gattitowns. The pizza crust is fairly thin but chewy, with a texture reminiscent of smashed white bread, sprinkled with fresh toppings and ample cheese (which comes in slightly unfortunate pellets). There are usually a half dozen types of pizza to choose from including a vegetarian sampler and a barbecued chicken pizza with an overly sweet sauce that is balanced with plenty of red onions. The pastas are sticky and served with a choice of bland sauces.

The salad bar is full of pickled items as well as the usual offerings, not always at their freshest. There's also fruit, Jell-O, and sometimes pudding, all of which helps with feeding the little ones. There's no reason to try most of the buffet, so we recommend that you stick to the pizza, which, while not terribly memorable, is actually kind of yummy, in an ashamed-to-admit-it kind of way. Mr. Gatti's is usually heavily populated by families, and while it's not the best pizza in town, it's certainly one of the easiest places to go for a meal with the kids.
–FC

Nam Gang

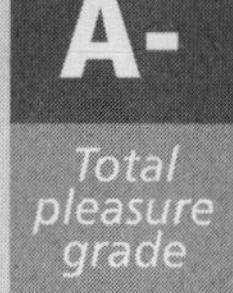

Where the marinating times are long, and the good times even longer

Total pleasure grade

8.1 Food | **8.6** Feel | **$23** Price | **Korean**

Casual restaurant
Daily 11am-10:30pm.
Vegetarian-friendly.

Spring Branch
1411 Gessner Dr.
(713) 467-8801

Bar Full
Credit Cards Visa, MC, AmEx
Reservations Accepted

Korean people may be the smartest people to ever open a restaurant. They give you raw pieces of meat, make you cook it on your own, charge you for it, and if you don't like it, it's most likely your own fault. It's a great idea, but Nam Gang doesn't capitalize on it. Food and service are both strong points in this Gessner restaurant, with well-marinated meats and a staff who seem more than happy to do the cooking for you.

There's something inherently homey about Nam Gang, sort of like you just walked into your aunt's house, where the smell of food cooking is in the air, and you're fussed about with cheek pinching and comments about how skinny you've become. To say that the staff is gracious would be an understatement. While they don't speak much English, the effort they put into a table does translate; they are willing to cook your meat in front of you if you would like, though this is a double-edged sword because at times they get so swamped that they forget about customers.

While anything that's been soaked in soy, sugar, and spice probably won't taste bad, there's something about Nam Gang's kalbi (beef shortribs) and bulgogi (ribeye) that has that extra kick. Flavor penetrates every protein cell and sinew of the beef, putting the flavor of Nam Gang's Korean barbecue a notch above the rest. They also use heated pieces of charcoal in a town where gas grills are almost exclusive. Charcoal grilling gives the meat a little more gumption, rendering every meaty bite the culinary equivalent of an orgasm. While Nam Gang's barbecue is more than top notch, they aren't a jack of all trades, as demonstrated by their poor, flimsy showing of a kim chee pancake. Most of the ban chan (side dishes) are fair, though several of them—including the marinated tofu skin—are way too aggressive with their heat. Drinking here can get expensive, as a recommended bottle of Korean brew called Hite tastes like a Bud Light with the cost of shipping tacked onto your bill.

Nam Gang isn't perfect, but on weekdays when it's slower and you can get better service, and with a group of friends that won't mind smelling of pickled cabbage and roasted meats after they leave. The place is a good spot to fill up your protein quota for the next month. –JY

Nelore Churrascaria

A Fogo de Chão knockoff that does the same thing: endless meat and awful gaucho costumes

C *Total pleasure grade*

5.7 *Food* **6.4** *Feel* **$58** *Price*

Steakhouse, Brazilian

Upmarket restaurant
Mon.-Fri. 11am-2pm, 5pm-10pm; Sat. 5pm-10:30pm; Sun. 11am-3pm, 5pm-9pm.
Brunch. Kid-friendly.

Montrose
4412 Montrose Blvd.
(713) 395-1050
www.nelorechurrascaria.com

Bar Full
Credit Cards Visa, MC, AmEx
Reservations Accepted

Do they *really* have to wear those gaucho outfits? We're embarrassed for the staff, just looking at them, so we can only imagine how embarrassed *they* must be when they get dressed for work. Do Nelore and its emulatee, Fogo de Chão, really fancy Houstonians so immature that they gain if their waitperson shows up in what looks like a Halloween costume?

Don't get us wrong: we aren't the sort of people who can't enjoy Disney World. It's just that we feel bad for these people. And anyway, Disney characters are dressed up mostly for the kids. Yet Nelore caters squarely to carnivorous adults.

The routine of Fogo de Chão is emulated here in every possible fashion, from the unbelievably appealing little cheesy popovers that show up at the meal's beginning, to the salad bar that can overfill you if you don't watch out, to the overwhelming array of meats shaved off the long spear by roaming meat waiters dressed as gauchos. Nelore has three advantages over Fogo, however: one, it undercuts the price by a bit. Two, it's more conveniently located for central Houstonites, snuggled between Montrose and the Museum District. Three, it's smaller, cuter, and locally owned (even if it's a carbon copy of a chain).

As for the meat itself, it lines up perfectly with Fogo's—that is, it's totally inconsistent. One bite of ribeye, on one particular visit, might be rare, fatty, and delicious. On another night, you'll get stuck with petrified lamb, useless pork sausage, meat the color and texture of cardboard. To some extent, you can manage the gauchos, directing them to cut off this part or that. You can sometimes judge if a whole slice is overcooked, and reject it outright. When it's not overcooked, top sirloin is our favorite cut.

Service at Nelore is inexcusably sloppy, given how little they need to do. On one visit, we never received our rolls, even after repeat requests. On another, no chimichurri (which is red, not green) ever showed up. The organizational problems don't extend to the meat-shavers, though; those guys come through with dangerous regularity. The keys to success here are pace and resisting most of the salad bar—although the not-very-filling hearts of palm are a welcome treat. –RG

Nidda Thai Restaurant

B

Total pleasure grade

Tell them you like it spicy—we dare you—and enjoy the eye-watering experience

7.4 *Food* **7.3** *Feel* **$17** *Price* **Thai**

Casual restaurant
Mon.-Fri. 11am-2pm; 5pm-9:30pm; Sat. noon-10pm; Sun. noon-9:30pm.

Montrose
1226 Westheimer Rd.
(713) 522-8895

Bar Full
Credit Cards Visa, MC, AmEx
Reservations Not accepted

The Montrose area is cursed with quite a few overpriced ethnic restaurants that jack up the prices to pay the rent. Nidda Thai Cuisine, however, is an exception to this rule. The cooking here isn't intrusive or forceful (unless you want it to be); the atmosphere is inviting, friendly, and flavorful; and service is awkwardly nice, but genuine. All the crowd pleasers are on the menu: red and green curries, panang, pad Thai, and steamed dumplings.

Situated in the same strip mall as a porn shop and a tanning salon, Nidda could easily be mistaken for a happy-endings Thai massage parlor. Little curtains shade the windows from the outside to give it a charmingly dingy appeal. Once inside, though, the restaurant is comfortable and intriguing. Dim lights and the solace of pans clanging on a stove bring everything together.

Boast of your tolerance for heat, though, and you will be punished—we still haven't learned our lesson. Heat and chilies are what this restaurant prides itself on. The elementary-titled "Surprise Beef" (with two chilies next to the name) should be treated with respect; thin strips of beef are tossed in an eye-watering Thai glaze. Red curry with chicken, served with bamboo shoots and steamed rice, is flavorful, with hints of coconut milk and ginger. Seafood is the weakest part of the menu, with tilapia getting most of the game time, and shrimp a close second. Pad Thai, which is unfortunately what many people order, is loaded with bean sprouts, crushed peanuts, and surprisingly good noodles. Not that it's bad, but why don't people branch out?

Servers are attentive, knowledgeable, and ready to give you all the spice you claim you can handle. If you look at them right and show them you're not scared of heat, they will light you up; a special concoction of fish sauce and crushed chilies is their secret weapon. And it's delicious—even if your tongue might hate you afterward. –SD

Nielsen's Delicatessen

B-

Total pleasure grade

The dirty playground kid who beats up all the rich boys, in deli form

7.6 *Food* **5.9** *Feel* **$11** *Price*

Light American

Counter service
Daily 8am-4pm.

Galleria
4500 Richmond Ave.
(713) 963-8005

Bar None
Credit Cards Visa, MC, AmEx
Reservations Accepted

Nielsen's Deli is a humble restaurant: no attitudes, no flair, just good food that speaks for itself. The place has made a name for itself almost entirely by word of mouth; they rely heavily on their devoted repeat customers. They're an independent establishment that focuses on providing the community with a good deli; you won't find a bald New Yorker spitting out ridiculous slogans, and, believe it or not, there's no website. It can get quite crowded at lunch time with the locals who sear by this little gem, and they will wait however long it takes to get their favorite cold cuts.

A small restaurant with limited seating, Nielsen's looks like they put the interior of the restaurant on the back burner—"drab" seems to be the central decorating theme. But the food does deliver. Sandwiches are the specialty of the house, and they do them well. They're made with your choice of meat piled high, but not obnoxiously so; you can specify "regular" or "junior" size. The "regular" is just the right size to get a normal human being satisfied and energized. (Isn't it nice not to have to overeat?) The house-made mayo here is a thing of legend. It complements the meat, not overpowering it at all, but rather blending in nicely to accent the real star of the show—the protein. Turkey breast is a favorite, as is the rare roast beef. Of course, the usuals, like corned beef and pastrami are featured. Bread is baked on site and you choose what you want per sandwich.

Not only are the sandwiches good, but the sides actually deliver with the same force. The potato salad, dressed in that same mayo, showcases the tuber in all of its glory. Also, the lowly beet, which doesn't get a lot of game time in the delis of today, is featured as a flavorful, sweet, and acidic salad; it's a nice surprise on the menu. Turns out you don't need neon lights and a full PR staff to run a successful local deli. –SD

Niko Niko's

A colossal Greek-American rip-off whose popularity grows more inexplicable by the year

D Total pleasure grade

3.4 Food | **4.1** Feel | **$20** Price | **Greek**

Counter service
Mon.-Thurs. 10am-10pm;
Fri.-Sat. 10am-11pm;
Sun. 11am-9pm.
Outdoor dining.

Montrose
2520 Montrose Blvd.
(713) 528-4976
www.nikonikos.com

Bar Full
Credit Cards Visa, MC, AmEx
Reservations Not accepted

Brutally honest though we may be, we still find Niko Niko's a tough restaurant to write about, because its supporters are legion. We do understand some of the reasons for the restaurant's vast popularity: delicious gyros, with complex, richly flavored meat folded into a thick, fatty, warm pita. A good location with a pleasant outdoor seating area, even if it's adulterated by road noise. Reasonably late opening hours. A proud tradition amongst customers of all ages that goes back 30 years in Houston.

But to those of you who consider it sacrilege to question the supremacy of Niko Niko's—that criticism of the joint is akin to a slur against Houston itself—we submit the following: please go, with an open mind, and order something other than the famous gyro sandwich. Taste the Greek salad, and see if the iceberg lettuce doesn't taste like tap water, that its green bell peppers serve any purpose at all. Tell us with a straight face that you really plan to finish it. Order the souvlaki, and find us one chunk of meat that's not amongst the worst you've ever had, tough, overcooked, gamey, juiceless, challenging to chew.

Show us some seasoning in the moussaka. Take a forkful of the oven-baked potato, and defend the position that it's not one of the blandest, mealiest tubers you've ever bitten into. Try a broiled filet of fish, and tell us it's not cardboardishly overcooked. Buy a portion of "Greek lasagna," and ask yourself if it doesn't taste like Chef Boyardee noodles with the instructions followed wrong. Produce a falafel ball from this kitchen that's not dry. Show us rice that's not flavorless aside from the little mounds of unevenly shaken seasoning.

Or, for that matter, find us one Niko Niko's counter clerk whose attitude is better than indifferent. But what's even more offensive than rudely serving some of the worst food in the city is gouging its loyal customers to the tune of around $11 for a large vegetable-only Greek salad, about $8 for a large order of tzatziki (yogurt sauce) alone, or $7.50 for six fried shrimp—and this at a bad restaurant without table service. With apologies to all those we've offended—and we have no doubt that there are many of you—Niko Niko's is wearing the Emperor's Greek clothes. –RG

Ninfa's

If Mama tried this food, maybe she'd impose some discipline on the kitchen

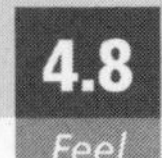

$21 *Price* **Tex-Mex**

Casual restaurant
Daily 9am-10pm.

Breakfast. Kid-friendly. Additional locations.

Downtown
600 Travis St.
(713) 228-6200
www.mamaninfas.com

Upper Kirby
3601 Kirby Dr.
(713) 520-0203

Bar Full
Credit Cards Visa, MC, AmEx
Reservations Accepted

Galleria
6154 Westheimer Rd.
(713) 781-2740

We're not exactly sure what Mama Ninfa was thinking when she sold her restaurant and likeness to the corporate world, but we're not convinced that she'd be happy that her smiling face is now the cover girl for what this place has become. (The original location is reviewed separately in this book as "Mama Ninfa's.")

Maybe it wasn't obvious that stores were going to open up left and right; that attempts would be made to squeeze quarters out of pennies; or that her heartfelt recipes and service might be lost somewhere in translation to careless cooks and even more careless waiters. Any way around it, Ninfa's is only famous for Mama's (and her fajitas') legend, and not for anything they're producing nowadays.

Not surprisingly, the interiors of most of the Ninfa's are quite pleasant; corporate-owned restaurants have the deep pockets needed to cheerily outfit all their restaurants. Most locations have the feeling of a Mexican indoor courtyard, with earth-toned tiles and straight-backed chairs. Careless (or maybe just clueless) service seems to be a chronic problem; both servers and hostesses like to drop menus, food, or drinks and speed off before you have a chance to even say anything.

Frozen margaritas are small and lifeless cups of yellow-green tinted slushies; expect to spend a fortune to get even a slight buzz—or just go with beer. Ninfa's salsa may be the only chips and salsa in town that aren't even mildly addictive; they just taste of watery tomatoes and vinegar. The famous fajitas, served on a sizzling platter, look and smell delectable, but the show is the best part; skirt steak always seems to come moist, but chewy and flavorless. Platos Mexicanos are Ninfa's answer to the value meal. "El Dannie" (three crispy tacos) comes with dry, tasteless beef, while "El Henry" has the most variety with a tamal, enchilada, and taco, all dominated by a yellow-orange film of grease.

But still, Ninfa's is Houston's own; Mama sold it, it grew, and homogenized. We wish we could taste even a whisper of her loving care in this food every now and then. But we can't. –FC

Nino's

A fading Montrose bastion of relaxing comfort food

C
Total pleasure grade

5.8 *Food* **7.7** *Feel* **$57** *Price*

Italian-American

Upmarket restaurant
Mon.-Thurs. 11am-2:30pm, 5pm-10pm; Fri. 11am-2:30pm, 5pm-11:30pm; Sat. 5:30pm-11pm; closed Sun. *Kid-friendly. Outdoor dining.*

Montrose
2817 W. Dallas St.
(713) 522-5120
www.ninos-vincents.com

Bar Full
Credit Cards Visa, MC, AmEx
Reservations Recommended

Nino's and its little brother Vincent's are the anchor restaurants in Vincent Mandola's chunk of the Mandola family restaurant empire. Nino's, Vincent's, and Grappino di Nino sit side by side on a tree-lined residential block in Montrose off West Dallas. Vincent Mandola opened Nino's in 1977, Vincent's in 1984, and Grappino di Nino in 1996. Like their cousin Carrabba's (which is now part of the Outback empire), they are among the most popular casual Italian spots in town. Nino's, as befits its age, is the most grown-up of the three Montrose restaurants, with a slightly more formal feel.

Nino's menu is solidly "Italian-American 2.0" (see pages 6-7 for our definition of this culinary category), served up with Texas appetites in mind. As Italian-American 2.0 goes, it's not bad. Among the appetizers, we recommend the carciofi fritti, crispy, fried baby artichokes in the Roman style (they don't mangle it like the Grotto does, though it doesn't have the subtlety of Da Marco's version). Nino's salads are pretty and interesting: a beet salad with avocado, fennel, and green beans is colorful and richly textured, while the arugula salad ($7.75), with gorgonzola, orange, and walnuts, provides a fresh flavor contrast. Tagliolini—thin, flat, freshly made noodles—come in a light sauce with ground veal rolled in fried eggplant; it's good comfort food, as is the mezzaluna, a big, half-moon-shaped raviolo stuffed with chicken and cheese and served with a creamy tomato sauce.

The menu sometimes crosses over into real authenticity, as in rigatoni alla Norma (a Sicilian dish with eggplant and sharp ricotta salata), but then quickly scampers back with sausage-and-cheese-stuffed chicken breasts and such. The medium-length wine list is moderately priced, although you can go up as far as Sassicaia.

Nino's is smaller than Vincent's, and it fills up fast. If they can't seat you, they can probably get you a spot at one of the sibling restaurants. If not, you can get similar food without the cozy ambience at Vincent Mandola's new fast-casual spot, Pronto Cucinino on Montrose and Holcombe. The empire continues to expand. –RH

Nippon

Central access to great sushi starts and ends at this underappreciated gem

Total pleasure grade

9.2 Food | **6.8** Feel | **$42** Price

Japanese

Casual restaurant
Daily 11:30am-10:30pm.
Outdoor dining.

Montrose
4464 Montrose Blvd.
(713) 523-3939

Bar Full
Credit Cards Visa, MC, AmEx
Reservations Accepted

Picture this: you're sitting at Nippon, wondering why the Fearless Critic likes it so much. The place is dark, dingy, aging, and mostly empty, aside from a few suited Japanese businessmen over by the sushi bar, shooting the breeze with the old chef. The menu looks just like every other Japanese-American menu in town. So what should you order?

Well, first of all, you're not even looking at the right menu. There's another, secret menu, handwritten only in Japanese, that lists a whole array of delicious, authentic daily small-plate specials, both raw and cooked, that aren't mentioned on yours. Unless you speak the language, it'll take some politicking even to get your hands on this furtive document. After all, what are you going to do with a Japanese menu if you can't read it?

The best strategy is to ask your waiter (unlike at most Houston Japanese places, most staff here are actually Japanese) to start translating for you. If it's a lazy day, and he likes you, this can work. Or ask him to selectively recommend a few of the Japanese-menu dishes, reminding him that—although you don't speak the language—you've "lived in Japan," perhaps, and "like unusual foods."

You don't really have to lie, of course. Just make friends with these guys. Because the real truth of the matter is that you shouldn't be choosing anything; the chef should. If you're lucky, he might be making tako wasabi (tender raw octopus, a slimy, salty delight); negitoro (a mound of chopped fatty tuna with a raw quail egg to mix in as you would in a steak tartare); sawagani (baby Japanese crabs, crunchy and flavorful when flash-fried with a squeeze of lemon); or fillet of silky aji (Japanese horse mackerel) tataki. Bluefin tuna and other fishes sometimes fly in from Japan, and if you're on a budget, even the banal sushi combinations are delicious, and priced aggressively.

Given Nippon's central location on Montrose just off Route 59, it's unclear to us why the place doesn't have a cult following amongst local sushi hounds.

It must be the language barrier. –RG

Nit Noi Café

Total pleasure grade

Good prices and helpful service save Nit Noi's offspring

5.8 Food | **7.6** Feel | **$13** Price | **Thai**

Casual restaurant
Sun.-Thurs. 11am-10pm;
Fri.-Sat. 11am-11pm.
Date-friendly.

Downtown
2020 Louisiana St.
(713) 652-5855
www.nitnoithai.com

Bar Wine and beer only
Credit Cards Visa, MC, AmEx
Reservations Not accepted

West Houston
1005 Dairy Ashford St.
(281) 496-9200

River Oaks
4703 Richmond Ave.
(713) 621-6088

As one of Nit Noi's more casual offspring, Nit Noi Café hopes to provide a more affordable, quicker spin on this Thai favorite. Though the prices are right, and servers are always more than happy to help and make you feel at home, Nit Noi—which means "a little bit" in Thai—could really do a little bit more to make you want to come back more often.

The newest Richmond location is a more casual, bright, and cheery incarnation of the original Nit Noi in Rice Village which was high in the faux-traditional finish. Half the menu comes with specials that are big on the rhyme, little on the actual explanation of the dish. To wit: "Thai Chili so Silly." Luckily, the waitstaff seems genuinely enthused to guide you along, explaining components of each dish—even if you feel like an idiot ordering your food.

A Thai tea, with its burnt orange hue, is the best way to start out. Its creamy base and smoky, not overbrewed, sweet-but-not-too-sweet taste primes the taste buds for the booming Thai flavors to come. Unfortunately, although the food means well, there's a sense that the restaurant has cut back to save themselves (and you) money. Spring rolls come with a too-thick peanut sauce that needs to be spooned on. Green curry with vegetables and tofu is too chunky and soupy; the extra liquid waters down its supposedly fragrant flavor, rendering it boring. A whole fried fish with sweet-spicy sauce is a treat—and a steal at $7.95—with crispy fins and skin and a bright sauce with plenty of Thai tang, but the choice of tilapia, at our last visit, was awful. It's hard to cover up that dirty taste that tilapia seems to carry, even if it is fried.

For the prices and the people, Nit Noi Café is worth a shot at least for a decent lunch spot, but probably doesn't have the chops to become your go-to Thai place. –JY

Nit Noi Thai

High-quality, inauthentic Thai food in an upmarket setting

B- *Total pleasure grade*

7.0 *Food* **7.6** *Feel* **$33** *Price* **Thai**

Casual restaurant
Mon.-Fri. 11am-10pm;
Sat.-Sun. noon-10pm.
Date-friendly. Outdoor dining. Vegetarian-friendly. Additional locations.

Memorial
6395 Woodway Dr.
(713) 789-1711
www.nitnoithai.com

West Houston
11807 Westheimer Rd.
(281) 597-8200

Bar Wine and beer only
Credit Cards Visa, MC, AmEx
Reservations Not accepted

Woodlands
6700 Woodland Pkwy.
(281) 367-3355

Nit Noi Thai, in its several locations, will always have its naysayers: for some reason, people tend to believe that Thai restaurants shouldn't have this much polish and shine. The dining room isn't old or faded, the prices are higher than normal, and the food has certain American touches to make it more appealing to the local clientele. Those touches tend to make Thai purists scream bloody murder. But pure or not, Nit Noi consistently delivers tasty food that generally doesn't hold back on Thai flavors, and its setting is refined enough for a date, making it worth the few extra dollars.

The hand-painted, full-wall Thai murals are a signature element of all the Nit Noi locations, bringing an additional layer of artistry to a classy, wood-studded (if too-brightly colored) dining room. Cheesy? Yes, but at least it's an enjoyable space to inhabit, which can't be said for much of the competition. Unfortunately, as it has expanded, Nit Noi's service has degenerated to barren-to-non-existent levels—unless, that is, you're the only one there (as has happened to us on several occasions).

Big bowls of steaming tom yum goong soup are the best way to start, with pangs of sourness and piquancy and the welcome aromas of fragrant kaffir lime leaves and lemongrass. You only wish its shrimp were plump rather than chewy. The "Nit Noi Chicken Wraps" are a lighter, fresher way to start, though they hearken more to PF Chang's cuisine than authentic Thai. Squid, which at many other places can come either chewy or overcooked, is prepared expertly here, especially in a dish that mixes the bright aroma of sweet basil and the light spice of peppers with the tender, briny sea creature. Stir-fried garlic eggplant is oily and not as light as you might expect, but full of garlic flavor, at least, and a nice accompaniment to any meal.

In conclusion, to the naysayers, we submit the following: Nit Noi is sometimes just okay, and certainly not the best Thai in town, but sometimes it's quite good, and its atmosphere is actually enjoyable. And you can't say the same for a lot of the other Thai-American places around. –JY

Noé

Consistently delicious food in its classics, consistently bad food in its improv

8.0 Food | **8.3** Feel | **$100** Price | **New American**

Upmarket restaurant
Mon.-Thurs. 5:30pm-10pm;
Fri.-Sat. 5:30pm-11pm.
Date-friendly. Vegetarian-friendly.

Galleria
4 Riverway Dr.
(713) 871-8177
www.noerestaurant.com

Bar Full
Credit Cards Visa, MC, AmEx
Reservations Recommended

Noé is the second incarnation of Robert Gadsby's successful LA location. While its minimalist aesthetic and flowing service are spot on, the wild variation between tried-and-true dishes and the ambition to tailor-make every experience tends to leave customers in one of two very different places: either in euphoria or feeling horribly ripped off.

Noé's sleek design comes dangerously close to creating an empty feeling in the room. The décor is definitively new-age Japanese, with simple Asian touches everywhere, like a single flower bud on each table. And then there are some touches that give off a vibe that's more Hong Kong hostess bar than cutting-edge nouvelle cuisine, such as glowing blue lining lights.

Service is an absolute strong point of Noé; both format and cuisine need to be explained, but the staff here handle every situation like they've faced it before. One trouble spot is the wine list, which is a clunky mix of old and predictable bottles; it doesn't seem to have been updated since its inception. Nonetheless, staff are more than happy to tell you what they do have in stock.

The cuisine at Noé can be a bit uneven; with a tasting menu, you'll get a combination of improvised dishes that meet your preferences and specifications, as well as Gadsby classics like his "Mimosa Salad," a beautiful stack of crispy noodles, sugar, spice, and fragrant cilantro. Though the bundle looks more or less like dog food after you press it down to mix it, the dish—especially with its accompanying shot of a mango lassi-like drink—is like a French-tuned take on southeast Asian flavors. It's when the kitchen starts to play with its food that things go downhill. A foie gras dish, at our last visit, came out with a cute, but poorly thought-out mini-toad-in-a-hole, so that the yolk fat bathed the liver fat. Even worse was a cous-cous-crusted pork tenderloin that tasted of old, burnt oil, and was desperately underseasoned.

As Gadsby's fame grew—even after getting stomped on by Mario Batali and his orange clogs on Iron Chef America—he left to pursue other Hollywood-dreaming endeavors. Noé's now left with no chef—just a frantic search for the stability that's never been there. –FC

North China Restaurant

B
Total pleasure grade

Refreshingly authentic Mandarin cuisine that's not-so-refreshingly buried in suburbia

7.6 *Food* **6.4** *Feel* **$19** *Price* **Chinese**

Casual restaurant
Tues.-Thurs. 11am-9pm; Fri. 11am-9:30pm; Sat. noon-9:30pm; Sun. noon-9pm; closed Mon. *Brunch.*

Memorial
879 Frostwood Dr.
(713) 464-6774
www.houstonnorthchina.com

Bar Full
Credit Cards Visa, MC, AmEx
Reservations Accepted

North China Restaurant is like the Cuban defector of Chinese restaurants. Somehow, this Mandarin restaurant squirted away from the Chinese-food hub on Bellaire Boulevard and escaped to the Memorial area, where it now serves a totally different crowd from the authenticity-craving first-generation Asian community that defines Bellaire. While most Chinese restaurants outside of Bellaire make their living off of General Tso's lunch specials and the like, North China also surprises its neighborhood by throwing in lot of reassuringly homemade, culturally heartwarming versions of Mandarin dishes.

The fiery, fast-paced Mandarin ideal is not very suited to this nondescript shopping center near Memorial Hermann Hospital, and as such, North China must first and foremost make concessions to its local clientele by catering to doctors on lunches, older couples, and families with young children. The dining room seems hushed instead of hurried, and wire wine racks filled with grocery-store wines and framed French-ified posters hanging on the wall seem oddly out of place. Service is unusually warm and personable for the genre.

While North China still couldn't resist the temptations of making an easy buck or two by offering Chinese-American food that spells out exactly what you're getting (think beef and broccoli or cashew chicken), the joint's Mandarin forte centers around zippy flavors, with vinegar and spice often ringing loudly. Sizzling rice soup, the house specialty, is only ordinary, with more bark than bite, although it's fun to watch the tableside preparation, in which the rice crackles as it's added to the broth. Ordering dishes whose names are even less transparent often yields the best results, like the chow ma mein, a bowl of robust chicken broth, cabbage, and noodles cooked in an almost al dente style that the Northern Chinese love. Boiled pork dumpings are plump and juicy, dribbling with juice after you bite into them, and with a dash of dark, red vinegar and shredded ginger, they make for a spectacular light meal. Yu shing chicken is well balanced between sweet garlic and spicy peppers, though it may need to be toned down with scoops of rice for those who can't handle the heat. Mandarin string beans are great as they are, though, exploding with soy and spice flavors like firecrackers on the plate. –JY

Ocean Palace

A mega-Chinese restaurant that's not the standard bearer people make it out to be

C
Total pleasure grade

5.7	6.0	$29	**Chinese**
Food	*Feel*	*Price*	

Casual restaurant
Sun.-Thurs. 10am-10pm.
Fri.-Sat. 10am-11pm.
Brunch.

Chinatown
11215 Bellaire Blvd.
(281) 988-8898

Bar Wine and beer only
Credit Cards Visa, MC, AmEx
Reservations Accepted

With all the fuss, press, and praise that Ocean Palace seems to get, it's hard not to compare it to another "mega" in town. Everything's bigger in Texas, and if Chinese food were a religion, Ocean Palace would be its Lakewood Church. Just like the Compaq Center and Lakewood Church, Ocean Palace reels people in by the hordes. But, comparison aside, Ocean Palace needs to be much better than it is, especially given the responsibility it carries as a main channel for the introduction of Chinese cuisine to Westerners.

Ocean Palace totally drops the ball here. It's hard to believe some of the swill that comes out of this kitchen. At least the setting is legit; if you can brave the blue fountains without losing your appetite, Ocean Palace does a good job in transporting you to Asia, if only by making you feel like a speck in a big, scary world. The place has two stories, with dining rooms that both seem like glorified banquet rooms (fish tank here, obligatory golden dragon there). The atmosphere really comes from the droves of dim-sum customers; if you can brave that storm, you'll be seated upstairs, where a holistic-feeling dome allows beautiful sunlight to shine onto the non-stop movement below. It may all evoke the hustle and bustle of Hong Kong, but the food isn't even close.

How do you control food quality at a place that seats over two hundred people? At Ocean Palace, the answer is that you don't. During its city-famous, weekend-morning dim sum, dishes come out lukewarm in both temperature and quality. Chong fun (meat or shrimp wrapped in a flat-rice-noodle envelope) is flimsy and lacks even subtle flavor. Barbecued pork buns are stuffed with honey-sweet pork with no savory balance. Almost nothing else coming off the carts has that flavor-forward, punch-you-in-the-mouth taste to it that you expect from Chinese cuisine. For dinner, ordering anything live out of the tank is a good idea. Simple preparations of fish, like flounder steamed just with soy sauce, make for a light, if pricey, meal. Still, you can get a cheaper, better rounded dinner somewhere else. –FC

Oceanaire

Fried, grilled, or chilled, none of it's good—or professional

D
Total pleasure grade

4.9 *Food* **5.1** *Feel* **$82** *Price* **Seafood**

Upmarket restaurant
Mon.-Thurs. 11:30am-10pm;
Fri. 11:30am-11pm;
Sat. 5pm-11pm; Sun. 5pm-9pm.

Galleria
5061 Westheimer Rd.
(832) 487-8862
www.theoceanaire.com

Bar Full
Credit Cards Visa, MC, AmEx
Reservations Accepted

Oceanaire, an elaborately fonted, carefully conceived upmarket seafood chain stuck inside the Galleria mall, shows a flashy façade—but ultimately disappoints. Its location virtually ensures a hefty bill, and given the pleasant vibe and healthy din of the room, it's one that we wish were justified. It looks nice enough; round comfortable banquettes afford a nice level of privacy, although you should make sure you stay away from the windows, whose views of the parking garage exit aren't the most romantic in town.

If there's a wait—assuming you don't take our first piece of advice, which would be to abort the mission and trek over to Bice instead—a bar area is nice, and you can have a cocktail and some good, fresh oysters while you wait. Ten or so different oyster provenances might grace the selection on any given day, and littleneck clams are generally available too. The cocktail list has all our old-time favorites: the rusty nail, the sidecar, and, most delightfully, the negroni (gin, campari, and sweet vermouth: the ultimate apéritif, packing a pleasantly bitter, subversively alcoholic punch).

The pleasantries end here. While most everyone can navigate a cocktail list, people often need some help with the wines, and the wine stewards here are utterly useless. Once, when we called over the resident wine expert to ask his opinion about a Meursault we'd been considering, he suggested a Marlborough Sauvignon Blanc as a similar alternative. We can't imagine two more completely opposite whites, on every possible axis, than these two. There's no shame in a waiter that's clueless about wine, but a restaurant selling bottles for up to $260 shouldn't send him out as the sommelier.

Oh right, the food. Are you wondering why we've waited so long to talk about it? That's because there's nothing to talk about. It's not terrible, but doesn't even come close to justifying the prices. You might think whole fish the way to go, but it comes out overdone, defeating its simple purpose. Fried seafood, like the "Fisherman's Platter," is somewhat better, but its batter is boring and underseasoned; only the salt-and-vinegar fries really succeed. Leave it to fries to swoop in and rescue a $24 dish. –AH

Onion Creek

It's not Austin hippie. No really, it's not. Get your bike out of the middle of the street

B- *Total pleasure grade*

7.9 *Food* **7.9** *Feel* **$18** *Price* **American**

Bar
Daily 6:30am-2am.
Breakfast. Outdoor dining.

Heights
3106 White Oak Blvd.
(713) 880-0706
www.onioncreekcafe.com

Bar Wine and beer only
Credit Cards Visa, MC, AmEx
Reservations Not accepted

The Heights feels a lot like Austin, and a lot of people there want to pretend that it *is* Austin. Well, it's not, but Onion Creek is an Austinesque escape of sorts; labeled as a coffee house, lounge, and bar, it manages to fill each role well. It's a friendly bar that will kill you with kindness and leave you satisfied. They've got great specials all the time, and they're an everyday man's kind of place that doesn't try to fancy things up.

Standouts on the menu are, of course, the sandwiches. The hummus wrap is a favorite with hippies the world over. Nutty hummus plays off creamy avocado and feta, with cucumbers thrown in for crunch factor. A tangy cilantro dipping sauce completes it and makes sense of the whole thing. (Just be careful not to spill any hummus on your Birkenstocks, or those of the other patrons.) The "Country Ass Ruben" is another crowd pleaser. Basically it's a corned beef sandwich that is kicked in the ass with some havarti cheese and sauerkrau; it delivers a kick to our ass when we need it, and it's delicious.

We don't recommend the goat-cheese salad. It's paired with underripe strawberries, almonds, assertive and overpowering red onions, and a strawberry vinaigrette that bears only a slight resemblance to strawberries.

Do go to Onion Creek for the specials, though. Wednesdays are steak nights, when you can get a decent marinated ribeye that's grilled to your liking and served with a baked potato. Good, simple, tasty, delicious, it's bar food 2.0. And, look out for drink specials. There's a farmers' market in the parking lot on Saturdays; foodies and hippies from all walks of life will gather and bask in its local-ingredient glory. It's really small, but after you get done browsing, you can always duck into Onion Creek for some breakfast. –SD

Osaka

On-par sushi bar that takes a note from upmarket restaurants

B- Total pleasure grade

7.7 Food **7.1** Feel **$42** Price **Japanese**

Casual restaurant
Daily 11:30am-10:30pm.
Date-friendly.

Montrose
515 Westheimer Rd.
(713) 533-9098

Bar Full
Credit Cards Visa, MC, AmEx
Reservations Accepted

Osaka, as it's often suggested, is not Houston's best sushi bar. Not that it's a terrible sushi bar, either. Really, more than anything, it's a smart sushi bar. With fish that's no better than average, and non-memorable hot food that's the most ordinary of ordinary, Osaka takes a page from the upmarket restaurants of the world with free tastes of food and large cuts of fish. The Osaka legend relies more on its goodwill than on good taste.

The atmosphere, even when busy, is the essence of Japanese culture—serene and controlled. While other Japanese restaurants feel that they need to do a song and dance for customers, Osaka realizes that its location doesn't lend itself well to sake bombs and eating sushi off of half-naked women. Thus, the dining room is singularly focused on simple woods, without much deviation in color—a stark contrast to some of the circuses that call themselves sushi bars in this town.

Somewhere along the line, Osaka realized that people didn't complain about quality as long as they got quantity. Size does in fact matter, and a lot of people can be fooled by their so-so sushi as long as they receive huge chunks of it. Some may call them generous, but we just think they're just smart in pegging this as a size-oriented culture; a glance out the window at a row of Hummers says it all. It's not that Osaka's food is all show and no taste, but the huge pieces tend to overwhelm, destroying any balance between sweet-sour-sticky sushi rice and the fish—except for the escolar, when available; it's a smooth, sweet, firm fish that is delicious in spite of this.

A better choice is the chirashi, with a bento box of rice and huge cuts of varying fish so that you can balance textures yourself. Hot foods include several renditions of udon and not-so-crispy tempura, but nothing stands out. Meals start and end with an upmarket touch—a complimentary roll as your "amuse bouche" and green tea or red bean ice cream to end with.

Lately, Japanese businessmen and foodies in the know have been skipping Osaka for the more authentic, if lesser-known, traditional Japanese restaurants in town, such as Sasaki for sushi, or Nippon for kaiseki. But Osaka probably isn't worried: they know that free food and huge portions will keep them one step ahead of the competition. –JY

Otilia's

Overrated Mexican that's still riding its original wave of hype

C-
Total pleasure grade

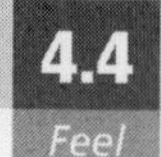

$21 *Price*

Tex-Mex

Casual restaurant
Tues.-Thurs. 11am-9pm;
Fri.-Sat. 11am-10pm;
Sun. 11am-3pm; closed Mon.

Spring Branch
7710 Long Point Rd.
(713) 681-7203
www.otilias.com

Bar None
Credit Cards Visa, MC, AmEx
Reservations Not accepted

On the way out to Spring Branch, you'll pass a variety of great Mexican restaurants to choose from. So why keep going to Otilia's? It's not terrible, but when it comes to paying the bill, you question everything. Were those flautas really worth $10? The answer is no; they're hardly mind-blowing. And that's a good description of the food here; it's good enough, but nothing all that special. Still, they do respectable versions of mole, cochinita pibil, and milanesa.

Otilia's has fallen into the trap of too much renovation, and too many new concepts. Once upon a time, they built up a wonderful reputation of quality and consistency, but now, after renovating and adding extra space, they have let the focus fall from the food. Otilia's soul has dissipated. The cochinita pibil is still delicious, though; pork tender enough for fork-eating is cooked with spice, and served with pickled red onions and a nicely complementary sauce. Beef milanesa, thinly breaded and cooked golden brown, is a bit chewy, but has good flavor. The mole is delicious and bittersweet. Rice and beans take a back seat to all the dishes, a common and annoying problem; just because they're not the focus doesn't mean they shouldn't be good. The nogada dishes are flavorful, a nice change from the usual. Chiles en nogada are good, too, their poblano pepper stuffed with walnuts and beef with a white cream sauce over the top. Yum. Desserts, however, leave a lot to be desired, though we rarely find ourselves hungry for more after a big Mexican meal anyway.

There are plenty of quality authentic Mexican restaurants in this town that are serving better food than this. Otilia's has a good reputation that's kept people coming, but they're going to have to do some serious rearranging to keep this going for much longer. –SD

Otto's BBQ & Hamburgers

B-

Total pleasure grade

A homegrown burger joint with a delinquent barbecue brother

7.0 *Food* **6.0** *Feel* **$11** *Price* **Burgers**

Counter service
Mon.-Sat. 11am-8pm;
closed Sun.

Kid-friendly. Outdoor dining.

Washington
5502 Memorial Dr.
(713) 864-2573

Downtown
1200 McKinney St.
(832) 553-6886

Bar None
Credit Cards Visa, MC, AmEx
Reservations Not accepted

Stafford
11222 Fountain Lake Dr.
(281) 313-6886

If the barbecue at Otto's is the problem child with bad grades, the chain-smoking addiction, and the nobody-understands-me attitude, then the hamburgers are the golden boy, all-state football player, valedictorian, and all-around good guy. The difference in quality between burgers and barbecue is night and day, although that's not to say that Otto's hamburgers are that good—it's just that the barbecue is that bad.

Atmosphere has never been an emphasis of Otto's; they've chosen instead to focus on its rough-around-the-edges, down-home, good-ol'-boy food. The smell of a barbecue joint is a thing to be cherished. Roasting meats atop smoldering wood brings back memories of camping with Dad. So why Otto's has an off-putting smell of disinfectant is beyond us. Counter service is fair enough, but obviously much more skewed towards the regular customers. But they can have it; we're not interested.

Otto's menu serves the usual suspects, all of which are pretty bad. George Senior was a frequent customer, giving his name to his favorite combination of brisket, ribs, and sausage. Eating these ribs is like chewing on rubber; even after 20 minutes of work in the mouth, it's hard to pick out any discernable flavor. Brisket, often the shining glory of a Texas 'cue joint, is also uniformly dry, whether lean or fatty. (Get it as a sandwich to soften the blow.) Dousing your food in BBQ sauce is also out of the question, as the liquid is cloyingly sweet and sour. (Memo to Otto's: sweet and sour goes on a Chinese menu. Smoky and robust is what a barbecue sauce should be.)

Hand-pressed burgers are haphazardly grilled, and "cheeseburger" means a bland, paltry Kraft-single-style slice slapped on top. Onion rings and fries are above average, although their crispiness can vary, and the kitchen is refreshingly not afraid of its salt shaker. This joint's not-so-secret secret, however, is the excellent breakfast with huge breakfast burritos. Somehow, even when they're visibly cooked on a griddle-top, the eggs come out fluffy and the packaged sausage actually tastes fresh and homemade. With a heavy dose of pico de gallo and a strong cup of coffee, breakfast at Otto's is a great way to start off the day—that is, if you stay away from the barbecue. –JY

Ouisie's Table

For this River Oaks crowd-pleaser, Southern comfort means fretting service and overcooking

C+
Total pleasure grade

6.1 *Food* **8.1** *Feel* **$61** *Price* **Southern**

Upmarket restaurant
Mon.-Thurs. 11am-10pm;
Fri.-Sat. 11am-11pm;
Sun. 10am-10pm.
Brunch. Live music. Outdoor dining.

River Oaks
3939 San Felipe St.
(713) 528-2264
www.ouisiestable.com

Bar Full
Credit Cards Visa, MC, AmEx
Reservations Accepted

Ouisie's Table, recently relocated to a new and incomparable location in the heart of River Oaks after a hiatus following the closure of the old location on Sunset, may now have one of Houston's most underrated dining rooms. Its space is elegant but not uptight, classy yet quaint, with a gruff chalkboard for specials. There's a definite sense of southern charm to it, and the outdoor tables absolutely scream out for brunch on a sunny Sunday morning.

If there's a drawback to this down-home atmosphere, it's that you feel almost as at-home as you would...well...at home, which means that the staff has the tendency to be as overbearing as your mother. Checking up once on the table is fine, but after the fourth or fifth time, you wonder if you'll start to get comments about how you've gained weight, or how you need to find a nice young lady or man to settle down with.

Yet for all the charm of Ouisie's Table, its food has stayed back in the last century. This is the menu that might have resulted if Escoffier met Robert E. Lee. For such a beautiful dining room, the food at Ouisie's isn't up to snuff. The idea of classier Southern cuisine is ingenious, especially in Houston, where even the upmarket crowd loves to dig down to its roots. True to Southern style, most every dish at Ouisie's is heavy, leaving you almost too full after appetizers to go on to your main courses.

The '80s idea of stuffing, wrapping, and crusting most every protein is still there from the old Sunset spot. Unfortunately, the kitchen's hand is often not sufficiently deft to avoid either burning or undercooking the proteins. A rib eye loses any sort of robust meaty flavor after it's blackened with spices, and a fried venison steak, on our last visit, lost all its novelty after one crusty, gamey, chewy bite. Not all is lost, though: lunch options, like a mozzarella cheese sandwich, are cheaper, lighter, and tastier than dinner. –JY

Paciugo Gelateria

A chain gelateria that fails to fulfill its shiny Italian promise

6.4
Feel

Sweets

Counter service
Sun.-Thurs. 10:30am-10pm;
Fri.-Sat. 10:30am-11pm.
Date-friendly. Kid-friendly. Outdoor dining. Vegetarian-friendly.

Greenway Plaza
5172 Buffalo Speedway
(713) 666-4958
www.paciugo.com

Bar None
Credit Cards Visa, MC, AmEx
Reservations Not accepted

The owners of this Italian gelateria may have just arrived in Texas from Turin, Italy, in 2000, but that hasn't stopped them from pursuing immediate dreams of a mega-chain in the Promised Land. For Paciugo (pronounced "pa-choo-go"), these freeways were indeed paved with gold: 24 Texas branches and kiosks will be open by 2007, a Mexico City branch is already in place, and Chinese branches are soon to follow.

The appearance of Paciugo in Houston has increased public fears that the city is being secretly infiltrated by Dallas spies (Cantina Laredo, El Chico…). What's next, imitation Mustangs of Las Colinas galloping across Hermann Park?

Dallas hasn't won yet, but sweet brown concoctions like hazelnut and tiramisù do relatively well here, and cinnamon is surprisingly creamy. Chocolate chocolate chip gelato, with the deep fudginess of Belgian chocolate, is good, as is mixed berry (a version of the Italian frutti di bosco). Not so for a slushy strawberry-balsamic sorbet; a banana flambé ice cream overwhelmed by an unappealing alcohol taste; German chocolate unimpressively paired with coconut; or a chocolate chip cookie dough ice cream with bits of dough so sparsely scattered you'd think they were as valuable as beluga caviar.

The most interesting offering at Paciugo is a mixture of extra-virgin olive oil, black pepper, and sugar that tastes exactly as described. It's appealing, although we're not sure we could get through a full dish of it.

The problems, though, are legion. From the mass-market fonting of the menus in the back to the antiseptic modern room in which a few minimalist tables and chairs have been set up, Paciugo frustrates its promise—and its product is just too Dallas for Italophile-trained taste buds. Still, it might be the best gelato in town. Is that praise for Paciugo, or a condemnation of Houston?

Both, perhaps. –FC

Palazzo's

Riding high on a wave of bland marinara sauce and southwest chicken lasagna

D *Total pleasure grade*

3.6 *Food* **4.7** *Feel* **$34** *Price*

Italian-American

Casual restaurant
Daily 11am-10:30pm.
Brunch. Delivery.

Upper Kirby
2300 Westheimer Rd.
(713) 522-6777
www.palazzoscafe.com

Galleria
2620 Briar Ridge Dr.
(713) 784-8110

Bar Full
Credit Cards Visa, MC, AmEx
Reservations Accepted

West Houston
10455 Briar Forest Dr.
(713) 785-8800

Palazzo's Trattoria is, at its heart, an Italian-American restaurant. In calling itself a "trattoria," however, it is giving itself the ability to charge a few more dollars for fried mozzarella sticks (just like the ones they eat in Italy, right?). But there's no posturing here; Palazzo's doesn't hide its pack 'em in, stuff 'em, and get 'em out volume-house mentality. Pastas, pizzas, salads, and overpriced mains populate the menu. A money-maker of a restaurant, it is concept-driven, and for that, the food suffers.

Palazzo's takes poor ingredients to create equally poor food—but the atmosphere is nice enough. It's a family restaurant that will keep the kids happy with fried calamari and cheese pizzas. It's also, of course, a clean restaurant with no burglar bars over the windows, and its calming colors reassure you that you are safe and abiding by all zoning laws.

Food, however, is where you need your guard up. They try to fancy up the menu by calling the appetizers "antipasti," but everyone knows what's going on. The chain-restaurant-favorite spinach artichoke dip makes an appearance; it's somewhat likeable, but marred by the fact that the chips are hard, not crispy, and seemingly stale. Other such antipasti are mussels in white wine, Italian sausage, and Portobello mushrooms. The famed "Southwest Chicken Lasagna" is one of Palazzo's signatures; jalapeño-cilantro pasta with layers of black beans, cheese, poblano peppers, and chicken successfully make the dish look simultaneously novel and desperate. It doesn't make sense; the texture of the pasta doesn't go with texture of the peppers—or, especially, of the beans. It's weird and unpleasant.

Service varies wildly. Some servers are seasoned vets, and can turn a bad meal into an enjoyable experience; others, however, are totally green. This can happen at any restaurant, of course, but here, people sometimes seem to be thrown into the mix without a clue. Trial by fire, we suppose. Not that any of this should matter to you, because you have no excuse for eating here. Period. –SD

The Palm

Total pleasure grade

Steaks and chops in a not-so-steakhouse-ish place

5.9 *Food* **7.3** *Feel* **$95** *Price* **Steakhouse**

Upmarket restaurant
Mon.-Fri. 11am-11pm;
Sat. 5pm-11pm;
Sun. 5pm-10pm.

Galleria
6100 Westheimer Rd.
(713) 977-2544
www.thepalm.com

Bar Full
Credit Cards Visa, MC, AmEx
Reservations Recommended

Ah, the Palm. Here we have yet another player in Houston's steakhouse scene, but this one has the force of an entire chain behind it—locations are everywhere, even Puerto Rico. Houston's branch is out on Westheimer. Unfortunately, although it looks, feels, and smells like the storied, still-delicious Manhattan original, the exemplar after which the chain is modeled—and, of course, costs as much, too—that's where the similarities end. Here, the atmosphere (wall cartoons and magnums of California Cab, mostly) is totally contrived, but at least it manages to feel slightly warmer and more casual than the competition, even if the heavily out-of-town business clientele plays the rude-corporate-credit-card-customer part perfectly.

It's not often that you'll find us raving about a salad, but the "West Coast Gigi" here does get us excited. Similar to a Cobb salad, it's rich with avocado, egg, and bacon. What don't get us excited are the Italian specialties on the menu; you don't come to a steakhouse for linguine with clam sauce. We wish prime steaks came out as we'd expect them to, but this kitchen seems to struggle a bit with cooking times; the all-around consensus about what exactly a rare steak is seems low. Creamed spinach, meanwhile, is excellent, but the wine list is disappointing. Wines by the glass aren't great to begin with, and presumably they're even worse when you get a glass of oxidized wine that was opened the last time someone ordered it, and since has been waiting around for someone to finish the bottle. Bottle options, obviously, are better, and you've got all your big reds on the list, but the markups are brazen.

The atmosphere is warm, not the least bit stuffy, and decidedly more casual than Houston's other steakhouses. A business lunch menu gets you a three-course meal for $22—if you want a steak in the middle of the day. (There are other options, like fish or chicken.) It's a great deal, but still, if we find ourselves with $22 burning a hole in our pockets at lunchtime, we're heading straight for Da Marco. –AH

Pappadeaux

Greek salad at a Cajun restaurant? Only in Pappas-land

B Total pleasure grade

7.5 Food | **8.0** Feel | **$45** Price

Seafood, Southern

Casual restaurant
Daily 11am-11pm.
Kid-friendly. Outdoor dining.
Additional locations.

Upper Kirby
2410 Richmond Ave.
(713) 527-9137
www.pappadeaux.com

Town & Country
10499 Katy Fwy.
(713) 722-0221

Bar Full
Credit Cards Visa, MC, AmEx
Reservations Not accepted

Galleria
6015 Westheimer Rd.
(713) 782-6310

With Dixie blasting in the background, an open bar where the tap flows constantly, and oysters being shucked onto crushed ice, you might not notice that this restaurant was Greek-owned—that is, until you see the streams of orders for the special tableside-prepared Greek salad, which would probably give Paul Prudhomme a heart attack if he saw it (though he's probably due anyway). If *you* get a heart attack here, it'll probably be from the reliable, tasty fried seafood. (You can also get your fish, shrimp, or crawfish blackened instead—although it's less fun and less tasty.)

It feels like there's a party every night here, with the perpetual floods of people clamoring to pay pretty high prices for pretty huge portions of okay seafood. The staff is well trained, if at times young and awkward, and the restaurant always seems to be brimming with excitement; a quiet night is out of the question.

Tampering with products seems a specialty at Pappadeaux—the goal, perhaps, is to make freshness count less, and preparation count more. As such, precious little on the menu—aside from decent raw oysters—is allowed to retain its natural flavor. Everything from fish to pasta seems to be Emeril-ized with "bam"s of spices many times before cooking. The fat-boy special is the "Pappadeaux Appetizer," a bypass-surgery sampler of everything from gator to oysters, and you can opt for all of it fried. Don't start with the gumbo: it's lukewarm and tasteless. Shrimp or oyster po' boys are your best bet, as they're the lightest of all the fried foods, and thankfully cut with lettuce and tomato. They're also the best value on the menu. Whatever you get, though, the food is what it is: salty, crunchy, creamy, sometimes tasty, and hell-bent on destroying your waistband.

Our favorite Pappadeaux is the one at Terminal E at IAH; this alone upgrades Pappadeaux from a C+ to a straight B. There, all past Pappas missteps are forgiven; snag a back table (hiding the terminal view), or sidle up to the gregarious bar, and you might even forget that your flight is boarding in half an hour. Equal parts relaxed, reliably tasty, quick, and fun, it's one of the best airport dining experiences in the country. And trust us, we spend way too much time at airports. –FC

Pappas Bar-B-Q

A black mark on the proud Pappas empire, in barbecue format

C- Total pleasure grade

5.0 Food **4.2** Feel **$12** Price **Barbecue**

Counter service
Mon.-Fri. 6am-10pm;
Sat.-Sun. 11am-11pm.
Breakfast. Kid-friendly.
Additional locations.

Hillcroft Area
7007 Southwest Fwy.
(713) 772-4557
www.pappasbbq.com

Downtown
1217 Pierce St.
(713) 659-1245

Bar Wine and beer only
Credit Cards Visa, MC, AmEx
Reservations Accepted

Downtown
1100 Smith St.
(713) 759-0018

One of the more downmarket outposts of the Houston casual mini-chain dining empire, Pappas BBQ is a cafeteria-style mess hall, with the tables and chairs lined into row after row in a big, open wooden barnlike roof structure to give it a certain mess-hall aspect; the blues soundtrack and faux-vintage neon signage countryfies the place a bit.

One of the enduring mysteries of Texas brisket is what motivates purveyors and customers alike to discard the delicious part—the edges of fat—and to eat the tough, overcooked, dry part—the lean brisket. Watching the knife-man is like watching a culinary train wreck in slow motion: he carefully separates all the good parts from the bad parts, and then serves you only the bad parts. Pappas' brisket is one of the foremost examples of this tragic mistake: the beef is delightfully redolent of wood smoke, with a dense, flavorful rub and that trademark red smoke ring in clear evidence on the edges of the meat. But unless you ask for it fatty, you'll get stuck with the driest, toughest, grayest slices, ruining everything; and rather than melting into tenderness, those parts of the brisket turn into virtual cardboard. Better than to order even the fatty sliced beef would be to sneak behind the counter and swipe a plate of the delicious morsels from their waste bin.

Turkey here is equally dry. Baby back ribs, though, are much better than the brisket and turkey, with the pork fat contributing nice flavor and the texture just right (with ribs, unlike with brisket, there's no easy way for the butchers to sap off all the flavor and fat, and the fat stays on the bone). It all comes with Pappas' BBQ sauce, which is deep, dark, sweet, fruity, and overbearing. Sides are slightly above average for Houston, slightly below average for Texas at large. Mac and cheese is Kraftesque, with very soggy pasta shells; a few dashes of salt improve the dish vastly. Cucumber salad is crunchy but too sweet. Potato salad, bright yellow and eggy, is studded with too many little bell pepper chunks to let the potato work its textural magic. To complete the tray is good Texas-sliced white bread and a toppings bar that adds some Tex-Mex touches like pico de gallo, jalapeños, and sour cream to the usual pickles and onions. –RG

Pappas Bros. Steakhouse

Where steak is a caricature of itself

6.9 *Food* **8.4** *Feel* **$105** *Price* **Steakhouse**

Upmarket restaurant
Mon.-Thurs. 5pm-10pm;
Fri.-Sat. 5pm-11pm; closed Sun.

Galleria
5839 Westheimer Rd.
(713) 780-7352
www.pappasbros.com

Bar Full
Credit Cards Visa, MC, AmEx
Reservations Recommended

The traditional way to serve steak
Is starting to feel a bit fake.
Soft leather, dark wood... it's not bad, it's not good,
But might it be time for a break?

The profits are surely prolific.
But the theory seems unscientific,
That a steak at this price cannot help but taste nice,
If the service is tux-butler-iffic.

"Market-driven" it is, without fail,
But we're not talking peaches or quail.
It's that credit cards fly, keeping Pappas' net high,
When the markets crave oil for sale.

The kitchen's too often lopsided—
Creamed spinach is deeply misguided;
They overcook meat, and desserts are too sweet,
Though the pre-strip-club fuel is provided.

All the Ts on the wine list are crossed,
But you'll have to be rich to get sauced;
Almost every Château, from Latour to Margaux,
Have price tags that mock their real cost.

Yet from Dubai, the Woodlands, or Jarrell,
They'll still come in their business apparel.
Cristal will still pop, and the thousands will drop,
When it's ninety-two dollars a barrel.

–RG

Pappas Burgers

The lowly humble burger all dressed up and ready for action

B *Total pleasure grade*

8.0 *Food* **7.6** *Feel* **$16** *Price* **Burgers**

Counter service
Sun.-Thurs. 11am-10pm;
Fri.-Sat. 11am-11pm.
Kid-friendly.

Galleria
5815 Westheimer Rd.
(713) 975-6082
www.pappasburger.com

Southeast Houston
7088 Airport Blvd.
(281) 657-6171

Bar Full
Credit Cards Visa, MC, AmEx
Reservations Accepted

Houston's Pappas Bros. are back at it, this time giving the burger of the past a makeover and updating it for the new millennium. Flat, well-done, "have-it-your-way" patties are a thing of the past; now it's all about fresh ground meat, seasoned and cooked to your liking. Pappas Burger is a Fifties-style burger joint, with early 21 century prices; you might debate if you want to spend up to eight dollars on a hamburger, but it's worth it. Once you put the beefy goodness to your lips, they will thank you for the heavenly feeling of the fat lubricating the inside your mouth with flavor—very erotic. (We might need a moment.)

There are two locations in Houston, but the one on Westheimer is the original. They try to take the look of a happy-go-lucky burger shack of the past and convert it into a happy-go-lucky burger shack of today. Bar seating; red, white, and blue colors; and creamy milkshakes all sell the concept, but the giant televisions and staff that look like a fashion nightmare snap you right back to reality. The menu, however, is simple; burgers can be plain or have bacon, blue cheese, chili, or a number of other condiments on them. But no matter how many condiments are offered, it is ultimately all about the meat. And seasoned generously and cooked with care, these patties are everything a hamburger should be. French fries, on the other hand, look homemade, but are limp and have no crunch factor whatsoever.

In addition to hamburgers, Pappas Burgers offers vegetarian sandwiches, fried shrimp, catfish, and salads. The catfish basket comes with giant fried catfish planks, french fries, and cole slaw, and is not as good as the versions at other soul-food restaurants in town. But would you expect the Pappas Bros. to know how to cook up soul food? Beer is sold to quench your thirst, as are margaritas, but save room for the pleasantly thick milkshakes made with fresh ingredients. You will leave pleased and thankful that the Pappas Bros. didn't screw this one up. –SD

Pappas Seafood

Cajun seafood cleaned up and given a white-wine-cream-sauce bath

B- Total pleasure grade

7.0 Food | **6.4** Feel | **$48** Price | **Seafood**

Casual restaurant
Sun.-Thurs. 11am-10pm;
Fri.-Sat. 11am-11pm.
Additional locations.

Upper Kirby
3101 S. Shepherd Dr.
(713) 522-4595
www.pappasseafood.com

Bar Full
Credit Cards Visa, MC, AmEx
Reservations Not accepted

Bellaire
6894 Hwy 59 South
(713) 784-4729

East Houston
12010 I-10 East
(713) 453-3265

The Pappas empire is all-encompassing, and they're not afraid to take on any cuisine—from Greek to steak to Cajun. That said, we think it's with seafood that they really shine, and they do it at both Pappadeaux and Pappas Seafood. The two restaurants' menus are quite similar, but at Pappas Seafood you find the emphasis more on the seafood—not the Cajun—and the vibe aims for something more upmarket than Pappadeaux's raging bar scene. You won't find people sucking the heads off crawfish here; rather, you'll find them civilly attacking a fried filet of fish with a fork and knife, napkin in their laps. Frankly, though, we kind of like the grittier Cajun feel better.

Not that there's anything wrong with Pappas Seafood; as you walk in you see a giant tank of beautiful and exotic fish, but you won't be eating any of these guys. Rather, what's in store for you might be a "Blackened Catfish Louisiana" topped with oysters, crawfish, and shrimp in a good lemon-butter-garlic sauce. As at Pappadeaux, the treatment is more hands-on than hands-off, but the balance of this sauce is perfect; the acidity of the lemon cuts through the butter, and we find we just can't get enough of it. Jambalaya, though, is boring; even the sauce can't revive it.

When choosing fish, the daily specials are generally a good way to go. Pappas is also proud of their margaritas, and for good reason. Made with both Grand Marnier and Cointreau and your choice of top shelf tequila, they avoid being sickly sweet or too tart. And their strength will happily creep up on you.

Staff here is warm and helpful, oozing with southern hospitality. And despite being part of such a large restaurant group, much of Pappas Seafood feels genuine. Décor is not over-the-top nautical, nor does it go out of its way to feign a downmarket feel. Rather, with its high-backed booths and bow-tied servers it's not hiding anything. You might say it's trying to be the seafood equivalent of a steakhouse.

Still, only Pappadeaux has that glorious Intercontinental branch. –AH

Pappasito's

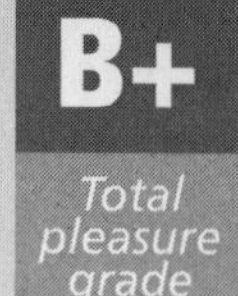

If this is an empire, then call us loyal subjects: the execution is right on the money

8.5 Food | **8.3** Feel | **$31** Price | **Tex-Mex**

Casual restaurant
Sun.-Thurs. 11am-10pm;
Fri.-Sat. 11am-11pm.
Date-friendly. Delivery.
Kid-friendly. Additional locations.

Upper Kirby
2536 Richmond Ave.
(713) 520-5066
www.pappasitos.com

Bar Full
Credit Cards Visa, MC, AmEx
Reservations Accepted

North Houston
15280 I-45 North
(281) 821-4500

Galleria
6445 Richmond Ave.
(713) 784-5253

One of Houston's most reliable Tex-Mex standbys, Pappasito's succeeds, first of all, because it has a tight focus; it takes one simple concept—fajita-centric Houston Tex-Mex—and it executes well, from acidically balanced, liquor-endowed margaritas to some of the most tender beef fajitas in town, even if their char doesn't have too much of the wood-smoke flavor we so cherish. Grilled quail comes out with a lot of flavor—it's a great way to impress the out-of-towners with the sophistication of Houston's Tex-Mex scene. Cheese enchiladas with chili gravy are just about flawless, spinning certain unwitting customers off into a nostalgic euphoria that takes them straight back to childhood outings with the family.

Just as importantly, Pappasito's also does the little things well, like charro beans that burst with pork-fat flavor from cubes of bacon, or chile con queso with more tomato-and-pepper texture to stand up to the creamy cheese than most versions have. And the servers have a way about them—good training doesn't seem to fully explain it—that represents the very best about easygoing Texas hospitality.

A fearless critic of our own restaurant criticism once accused us of being sanctimonious when it came to casual chain restaurants. And we do admit to having, on occasion, become engrossed in annual reports of NYSE-listed restaurant groups like Darden, at times even employing the finance-speak from quarterly earnings reports as an ironic literary device (as in Houston's Capital Grille review). But there are plenty of chains we like, too, and we submit Pappasito's as an example. Like Chuy's and Lupe Tortilla, two of its worthy competitors in town, it's the sort of chain that has the culinary rigor that's required to execute one regional cuisine faithfully —in this case, Tex-Mex—with remarkable consistency. Maybe that's because it's still at the relatively cozy (by Darden Restaurants standards, anyway) level of 20 stores. We like to imagine a future world in which Pappasito's were still this good when it had multiplied to 700. We want to believe that it's possible. But that's science-fictional rooting for the home team, and for now, let's just enjoy Pappasito's as it is: a local restaurant group that deserves every bit of its considerable success. –RG

Pappy's Café

Where the grunge-meter is high and smoked pork products rule

C *Total pleasure grade*

5.5 *Food* **4.8** *Feel* **$16** *Price* **American**

Casual restaurant
Mon.-Sat. 11am-10pm;
Sun. 11am-9pm.
Brunch. Kid-friendly.

Memorial
9041 Katy Fwy.
(713) 827-1811

Bar Full
Credit Cards Visa, MC, AmEx
Reservations Accepted

Pappy's has been a neighborhood feeding hole for many generations, one of those places where it feels like you're in a Lone-Star-State café made for families, quick lunches, and cheap meals for high school groups on a budget. The place isn't especially pretty or even comfortable like its neighbor, The Mason Jar, but they do hit the spot with certain menu items, most notably those that are wrapped with slices of pure ecstasy (otherwise known as bacon).

Between its rocky parking lot, unattended back entrance, and dark interiors, Pappy's feels like a place that should probably have a mechanical bull somewhere. It's one of those joints that has the grunge to be a one-horse-town café in east Texas or down near the border, a place at which the entire town's population has scraped its knees, eaten chicken-fried steak, and maybe even tasted its first beer. Families often come in from the surrounding area, so a quiet meal is normally out of the question. Expect scampering kids and screaming babies.

More often than not, the food that you'll eat here at Pappy's is homemade, inconsistent, but with plenty of character even when it's off. But when it's on, it's on, and its flavors pack a punch. Salad dressings tend to be either too thick or too thin, although their flavors (especially the garlic-heavy ranch) are always there. The non-industrial aspect—no shades of Sysco here—makes all the difference at Pappy's. Dense, flavorful homemade buns, for instance, are the key to their burgers—that, and the fact that they'll actually cook the patty to your requested temperature, which is amazingly unusual. There's a lot of hit-or-miss going on, too: meats often come out dry, and the chicken-fried steak has too much breading. But where Pappy's excels is in their ability to recognize that anything wrapped in bacon is a good thing. "Scorpion tails," for example, are bacon-wrapped shrimp with melty, gooey jack cheese, and the "Bubba's chicken" is prepared likewise. Some may regard that as redundant, or complain that such a treatment nullifies any merits of the underlying protein.

But we say, who cares? It's bacon. –JY

Paradise Café

Amidst chaos, drinks, and shouts, a shining gem of a Chinese soup dumpling

B+ *Total pleasure grade*

7.6 *Food* **7.0** *Feel* **$12** *Price* **Chinese**

Casual restaurant
Wed.-Mon. 10am-10pm; closed Tues.
Date-friendly. Kid-friendly.

Chinatown
9889 Bellaire Blvd.
(713) 774-8883

Bar None
Credit Cards Visa and MC
Reservations Not accepted

With a food menu that's dwarfed by its long selection of teas, juices, poorly made coffee products, and artificially flavored creams, all ready to be jellied, tapioca-ed, and sucked down with huge straws, it's not hard to see how Paradise Café is often overlooked as a food destination. So many incarnations of similarly premised restaurants speckle the Chinatown landscape, emphasizing fast, fun, cheap, and casual over delicious, giving away mangled food with the purchase of a drink. But there is one specific difference about Paradise Café, a singular detail that separates it from the other "crap-food-but-hey-a-drink!" restaurants.

The secret is hidden in a terrible translation on the menu that reads "pork bun with juice." Really, this is an order of Houston's highest-quality soup dumplings: simple, tightly wound packages filled with wads of plump pork and a gingery broth. With ideal thickness, skin, and size, these are one-bite virtuosos of flavor and gushing texture, excelling in an area where many of Paradise Café's soup-dumpling competitors (where a one-biter can often result in second-degree burns to your tongue and soup all over the front of your shirt) fall short.

The frustrating thing about Paradise Café is that, aside from soup dumplings, its kitchen is fickle; it's hard to predict whether the food will be good on a given day. On a recent plate of pan-fried pork and napa cabbage dumplings, half the dumpling bottoms came perfectly seared and the other half burnt black. "Beef La Noodles" are advertised with a picture of a noodle-kung-fu master hand-pulling even strands of pasta—a special art form that results in a delightfully rough, al dente noodle that normally sits in a hearty beef broth. Unfortunately, the Paradise version suffers from what we like to call the Arby's Effect: the picture looks nothing like the food that you get. Our noodles have often come uneven and flat, in a broth that looks beefy only because of the addition of soy sauce to the base.

The staff is young, and the crowd is even younger; as such, many opt for a communal, delicately priced hot pot. Lots of table-pulling and unnecessary space-cramming is required to squeeze into the poorly designed room, but sometimes, for the right soup dumpling, you need to work. –JY

Pasha

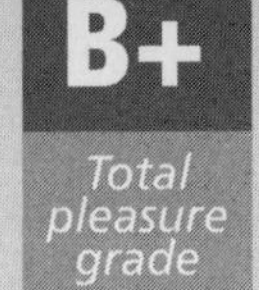

A simple but surprisingly formidable Turkish dining experience that's all about pleasure

8.3 Food | **7.2** Feel | **$34** Price | **Turkish**

Casual restaurant
Tues.-Sun. 11am-10pm; closed Mon.

Rice Area
2325 University Blvd.
(713) 592-0020
www.epasha.com

Bar Wine and beer only
Credit Cards Visa, MC, AmEx
Reservations Accepted

Pasha means "general" in Turkish, and the Pasha in Rice Village does indeed have us under its command. As a white-tablecloth restaurant, they serve traditional Turkish food with a few twists, and their prices are cheaper than most similarly tableclothed places. It's all about simple ingredients and fresh flavors here. Yogurts and hummus are deliciously done in-house, though the menu hits a bit of a roadbump with a section for Turkish pizza. This sounds like a tall order, but Pasha pulls it off with style.

A simple-looking dining room with folded napkins will make you think it's fancy and stuffy, but this is casual Turkish at heart. Dark walls and dark wood chairs ring the restaurant, spaced like little soldiers in a line. It's something of a safe haven for all of the Village lunchgoers who don't want to be surrounded by the entire Rice student body. Cold starters such as ezme (chopped tomatoes, onions, parsley, and crushed walnuts), imam bayildi (stuffed eggplant cooked in olive oil), and lebni (yogurt curd, walnuts, dill, and garlic), are refreshing, flavorful, and a great way to start a meal. They also act as palate cleansers, with their acidity helping to gear you up for the next course. Ezme is particularly delicious and light, and all of the individual ingredients' flavors blend nicely with each bite.

Like virtually any Turkish restaurant in America, Pasha serves kebabs. If you don't want the meat skewered you can order it as part of a plate; all mains come with Turkish rice, grilled tomato, and cabbage. But it's these surprisingly good Turkish pizzas that really set Pasha apart. Even though they only exist on the menu for novelty, they're not exactly bad; their thick crusts are piled high with specialty toppings, which can include lamb, feta, dill, egg, or Turkish sausage. There's Turkish wine, too, but any Italian will tell you that beer is the only thing to pair with pizza. We're not sure where a Turk would stand on the matter. –SD

Paulie's

A neighborhood sandwich shop that excels at more than just sandwiches

B *Total pleasure grade*

7.3 *Food* **8.1** *Feel* **$15** *Price*

Light American

Counter service
Mon.-Sat. 11am-9pm;
closed Sun.
Outdoor dining.

Montrose
1834 Westheimer Rd.
(713) 807-7271
www.pauliescookies.com

West U
2617 W. Holcombe Blvd.
(713) 660-7057

Bar Wine and beer only
Credit Cards Visa, MC, AmEx
Reservations Not accepted

A soulful sandwich shop that is now a Houston staple, Paulie's offers the community good food, good prices, and great service. People come not only for the sandwiches, but also for the salads, soups, pizzas, and pastas. They have two locations: the small, quaint flagship in the Montrose area with an artsy feel, and the other on Holcombe, which is a bigger spot to please the business crowd. Thus Paulie's draws in a diverse crowd—especially large during lunch—that's a healthy mix of businesspeople and starving artists.

First things first: the shrimp BLT is probably one of the best things here. It's a polygamous marriage of grilled shrimp, crispy bacon, sweet tomato, and lettuce, all served on one of the best buns in town. In fact, all of Paulie's bread is delicious. One of their sides is an Italian potato salad, but it isn't your everyday swimming-in-mayo potato salad; rather, it is dressed in olive oil and vinegar with olives and parsley, and you can actually taste the salad's namesake, with a light potatoey-ness coming through. The Portobello-mushroom-and-red-pepper sandwich is a surprisingly good vegetarian option; its marinated mushrooms, which have a meaty flavor, mingle with roasted red peppers and goat cheese for a bit of brightness. Pastas are nothing special, and they come with the usual suspects like meatballs, alfredo sauce, or grilled vegetables with olive oil.

Salads are ho-hum, but are generally well executed. The gazpacho, when available, is pleasantly acidic, with chunks of tomatoes that add some taste and texture for the tongue. We still don't understand why Americans don't follow the Spanish recipe and blend their gazpacho, but it's a refreshing soup for a hot day. Paulie's also serves steaks, veal chops, and roasted salmon for dinner; you should stay away from all of them. All mains are served with grilled vegetables, pastas, or potatoes. Finally, don't miss Paulie's famous cookies; they're a diverse bunch, decorated with different colors and icings. Not a bad ending, although we rarely follow a sandwich with a dessert. –SD

Pavani Indian Cuisine

A buffet that we will willingly go to...enough said

B Total pleasure grade

7.8 Food **8.4** Feel **$16** Price **Indian**

Casual restaurant
Daily 11am-10pm.
Vegetarian-friendly.

Southwest Houston
10554 Southwest Fwy.
(713) 272-8259

Bar Wine and beer only
Credit Cards Visa, MC, AmEx
Reservations Not accepted

When it comes to buffet-style restaurants, we find the all-you-can-eat price point a thing of interest. While it is nice to be able to sample many different dishes, sometimes we do just want to pay a little more for table service and a nice atmosphere. Pavani's well-executed Indian food, however, trumps our concerns. (After all, it sure beats The Golden Corral.) Selections change daily on the buffet, but there are mainstays like curries, naan, and biryani, and they rarely sit too long; a quick turnover keeps the food coming. With twenty selections to choose from, you can really get the feel of the place—and of Indian food, if you're a newbie.

Pavani is making the best of its awkward setting in an old Steak and Ale. They have exercised restraint in decorating; walls are uncluttered, with comforting colors—we don't need ornate, metallic icons watching over us as we attack a giant Indian buffet. If the food is labeled "spicy" at Pavani, take their word for it—they mean hot. Cold salads of lentils and marinated vegetables and creamy, acidic yogurt sauce work to put the fire out.

Tikka masala, dosai, and lemony basmati rice are the biggest crowd pleasers of all—but we think you can do better. Sometimes they have chicken, beef, and goat curries all at once and for the taking; those are the days. Goat curry is delicious, with a rich, dark curry sauce that adheres to the chunks of braised goat. Take it with rice and pickled cabbage, and you'll be on the road to satisfaction. Vegetarians are not outcasts here. Instead they're welcomed with open arms and plenty of vegetarian options, although labels are sometimes wrong on the buffet. They don't have much in the way of dessert, though they do offer rice pudding, cold or hot, which is enough for any sweet tooth.

Pavani has broken the curse of the buffet in flavorful fashion, even if you do leave feeling not so fashionable; your clothes will inevitably take on the aromas of cardamom and curry for the rest of the day. –SD

Peking Cusine

Northern Chinese cuisine that needs no boasting—just a call ahead of time

A Total pleasure grade

9.0 Food **5.2** Feel **$13** Price **Chinese**

Casual restaurant
Daily 11am-9:30pm.
Outdoor dining.
Vegetarian-friendly. WiFi.

West Houston
8332 Southwest Fwy.
(713) 988-5838

Bar Wine and beer only
Credit Cards Visa, MC, AmEx
Reservations Accepted

You're in Houston. You don't need to call ahead of time. You don't need reservations. Especially not way out West.

Right?

Sorry, friend, but in the spirit of Oliver Twist: Ahem…NO DUCK FOR YOU!

Peking Cuisine purveys the most authentic and tastiest renditions of Northern Chinese cuisine in Houston. But getting your hands on the piece de résistance—the Peking duck—at this place without a prior reservation (figure on one duck for every 3-4 people) is about as likely as Craig Biggio striking out in a clutch situation. But even if you consider calling ahead to be undignified, there's plenty of good food beyond the fabled duck at dirtier-than-dirt-cheap prices.

The epicenter of Houston's Peking duck scene is a clean, plain dining room that sits in a small shopping center off Southwest Freeway. Don't be annoyed by the call-ahead policy; this is not an elitist society that shuns any round-eye in sight [This was written by an Asian man. -Ed]; rather, the Peking duck crew is deeply in tune with the multiple steps of the process—which, when executed properly, as it is here, includes air-drying and slow roasting so as to generate extra-crispy, fatty skin ready to be sandwiched and stuffed into your mouth. Still, bringing along a Chinese acquaintance wouldn't hurt. While the staff means well, nobody in the dining room tends to be fluent in English. Pointing at a menu probably won't work either, as many of the descriptions are either spelled wrong or are missing important verbs or adjectives.

The duck is the be-all of the restaurant, but it's not the end-all. Discreet flavors are not a forte of northern Chinese cuisine, and the flavors in soft, spicy marinated beef aren't either, but its gelatinous, denatured tendons get just the right amount of spice and oiliness. Stir-fried spicy eggplant's flecks of red pepper make it look hot, but a surprising sweetness balances the dish. Still, if you hadn't been too lazy to pick up the phone and make a call, you could accompany all this deliciousness with a duck, too. –JY

Pesce

Showstopping seafood and warm vibes at Landry's only top-notch property

A

Total pleasure grade

8.8	9.4	$85	**Seafood**
Food	Feel	Price	

Upmarket restaurant
Mon.-Thurs. 5:30pm-10pm;
Fri.-Sat. 5:30pm-11pm;
closed Sun. *Date-friendly.*

Upper Kirby
3029 Kirby Dr.
(713) 522-4858
www.pescehouston.com

Bar Full
Credit Cards Visa, MC, AmEx
Reservations Recommended

Warmly lit, slickly packaged, and precociously priced, this is the sort of Landry's property that, upon first glance, could easily turn out to be a shining star or a colossal flop. Happily, the only thing flopping here is the remarkably fresh fish, which are anointed with an equally remarkable diversity of excellent preparations that help elevate Pesce to greatness.

So, too, does the layout. An expansively horizontal open kitchen bustles with sizzles and shouts, fish swim around in tanks, and jazz vocals serenade the round banquettes beneath flowing sail-ceilings in the style of a tech company, circa 1999. A wonderful waitstaff exudes an uncanny sense of calm, balancing expertise with modesty, warmth with restraint. This is the rare restaurant whose service and cuisine both do justice to an $85-per-head bill.

Things begin with an addictive tuna mousse, served in lieu of butter along with the assortment of delicious, fresh breads—one of the many touches here that evoke Le Bernardin, New York's legendary temple to fish. Don't miss the martini appetizer, a cascade of succulent picked lobster meat, lump crabmeat, and juicy shrimp frolicking happily on a bed of spice-forward mayonnaise-based slaw with hearts of palm. Impeccable, too, are oysters, whether raw or delicately battered and fried ("Damian").

Mains rotate regularly, but highlights have included a grilled fillet of mahi-mahi that expressed every ember of its oak fire, yet was cooked quickly enough not to allow even a drop of moisture to escape. The catch rotates daily, but its boring "seasonal vegetables" notwithstanding, this is generally one of the most delectable pieces of grilled fish in the city of Houston. Expertly pan-seared snapper "benestante" hosts a confusing mix of artichoke, shiitake, and crabmeat; its lemon butter sauce flirts with overrichness, as does its creamy orzo (rice-like barley pasta), which absorbs plume after plume of smoked cheese.

In this city of great desserts, the offerings here—apple "crostata" with buttermilk ice cream, for instance—could be improved upon. And such an ambitious wine cellar could do better with the dessert wine selection. But such complaints are minor: this is the best seafood restaurant in Houston. –RG

PF Chang's China Bistro

C-
Total pleasure grade

Homogenizing Asian food across America, one serving of lettuce wraps at a time

5.4 *Food* **6.0** *Feel* **$41** *Price* **Pan-Asian**

Upmarket restaurant
Sun.-Thurs. 11am-11pm;
Fri.-Sat. 11am-midnight.
Kid-friendly.

River Oaks
4094 Westheimer Rd.
(713) 627-7220
www.pfchangs.com

West Houston
11685 Westheimer Rd.
(281) 920-3553

Bar Full
Credit Cards Visa, MC, AmEx
Reservations Accepted

North Houston
18250 Tomball Pkwy.
(281) 571-4050

When PF Chang's opened in 1993, it was nothing if not an innovator. It was certainly the first restaurant to sell family-friendly Chinese-American food in a sleek, trendy, well-lit, un-Chinese-restaurant-like space, empowering people to fancy themselves cutting-edge eaters, movers, and shakers without actually having to expose their palates to anything more unusual than the dumbed-down Chinese they were already used to. And they didn't have to spend much more, either.

For better or for worse, it really took hold. Especially the lettuce wraps: when you think PF Chang's, you think lettuce wraps. People flocked here—and continue to flock here—for these craze-spawning "healthy" (or at least healthier than moo shu) do-it-yourself appetizers. The concept is a loose Americanization of a Korean concept, minus all the interesting flavor: you stuff crisp bowls of iceberg lettuce with chicken or vegetables; you mix them with rice noodles, peanuts, and water chestnuts; and dress them with the sauce prepared by your server tableside (a precursor, perhaps, to the tableside guacamole fad). They're easy to hate in conception, but hard to argue with on the palate; the texture is crunchy and fresh, the flavor supremely mild but somehow addictive.

Cocktails are fun and creative, though a bit over-priced. As far as the appetizers beyond lettuce wraps go, it's slim pickin's. Spare ribs are sad and tough, like the worst of corner Chinese fast-food, and everything else is what you'd expect: Steamed dumplings, fried dumplings, spring rolls. Bad, boring, bad. Mains are straight-arrow Chinese-American, even if they don't look like it. The American version of sweet-and-sour chicken, with its otherworldly color and tooth-coating, saccharine goop, is one of the greatest culinary atrocities ever committed against mankind, and here—with warm chunks of pineapple—PF Chang's carries on that noble tradition. Obviously, there's a bigger push to meet quarterly earnings than there is to be a culinary innovator. People know what they want, and don't want to order things they haven't heard of. Sad but true.

Salt-and-pepper prawns are a better choice than most mains, if usually overcooked. But what were you expecting, authentic Cantonese? This is a company based in Scottsdale, Arizona. And it's traded on the Nasdaq. –AH

Phô Danh II

I, not II, out of what seems like a million phô restaurants in Houston

A *Total pleasure grade*

9.0 *Food* **7.3** *Feel* **$8** *Price* **Vietnamese**

Casual restaurant
Daily 8am-7:30pm.

Chinatown
11209 Bellaire Blvd.
(281) 879-9940

Bar None
Credit Cards No credit cards
Reservations Not accepted

Phô this. Phô that. Phô everything. Houston has so many phô restaurants that try to cut their costs with watered-down broths, meats that could be mistaken for rubber, and clumpy noodles that you're wont to lose your phô faith before finding a good, hot, steaming bowl of this Vietnamese standby.

You'd think that Phô Danh II—buried in the side of Hong Kong Mall 4, which houses several of these offenders—would be no different. But Phô Danh II shatters all expectations.

Wait, can Phô Danh II even be in Hong Kong Mall? Walking into this sparklingly clean restaurant from floors caked with at least an inch of dirt is an utter shock. If the phô here weren't in mostly liquid form, you could probably eat it off the floor. Even the kitchen looks like it's been swept and buffed once an hour. The pots hanging on the wall don't even have that burnt carbon look to them, and floors are stark white.

Whereas most phô places have rice plates, spring rolls, and egg rolls, Phô Danh II doesn't deviate from what it does best: phô. You can actually pull apart the different flavors in this broth. It has a strong beefiness, with a base built on onions, yet pangs of anise flavor show up, too. Meats often come freshly sliced, and only slightly cooked before broth immersion, such that they begin their journey to your table rare to medium-rare. And as if that weren't enough, the accompanying vegetables come to the table triumphantly tall and impossibly fresh. Whereas side vegetables are an afterthought in most phô restaurants, every leaf here looks like it's hand picked. Chefs kill for freshness like this. There are bitter lettuces; there are exotically fragrant Thai basil leaves; crispy, crunchy bean sprouts come in huge piles. All of them are eagerly waiting to be warmed in your bowl.

Couple all of this with a bull-strength glass of Vietnamese iced coffee, and a meal at Phô Danh II is suitable for any day, any weather, and any mood. It's just... dare we say it? No, we won't say it... Okay, fine. Phô-nomenal! –JY

Phô Nga

Affordable, delicious, and authentic Vietnamese fare in Midtown

8.6 Food | **5.4** Feel | **$9** Price | **Vietnamese**

Casual restaurant
Daily 9am-9pm.

Midtown
2929 Milam St.
(713) 528-6055

Bar Wine and beer only
Credit Cards Visa and MC
Reservations Not accepted

It's always a good sign when 90% of the people that frequent a given Vietnamese restaurant are actually Vietnamese. They seem to have a sixth sense for detecting crappy food from a mile away. You may not fully understand why when you first walk through the doors, but you'll know before you leave. Phô Nga is not your average "Phô Something-or-other" restaurant. In fact, the Vietnamese beef noodle soup that's the namesake of this restaurant, although good, is actually one of the less impressive choices on this menu. It's the dishes that you can't get at other Vietnamese places that are the most memorable at Phô Nga.

This is hardly a hole-in-the-wall. The restaurant is pretty big and well known, even in Midtown circles, but it still carries the same qualities as a hole-in-the-wall might: it has a dingy, worn feel, almost glowing yellow from a lack of upkeep. But the service is accommodating and gracious—as long as you make sure they get your order right. Some things are lost in translation. But, then, that's part of the charm.

Unlike another Midtown Vietnamese legend—Mai's—Phô Nga doesn't stuff its menu with any Chinese-American placeholders. There's no General Tso's, and there's no beef and broccoli. The "Phoenix"—half a roast chicken, the meat mixed with the thin, crispy skin—is mind-bogglingly delicious, but the kicker is the dark sauce that comes with it, bursting with salty soy and spicy ginger. Though they do serve the normal vermicelli bowls, there's also a special vermicelli that's higher in gluten, stickier, and better able to take on the flavors of pickled vegetables than any other. There are grilled meats that are charred in the right places. There's fragrant cilantro. Put a spoonful of nuoc cham (Vietnamese fish sauce) in there, and you're in heaven. It's got spice, it's got zip, it's got rhythm, it's got a small price tag. Who could ask for anything more? –SD

Phô Saigon

Feeding hungry Houstonians with big steaming bowls of tripe and soft tendon for years

B *Total pleasure grade*

7.9 *Food* **7.5** *Feel* **$14** *Price* **Vietnamese**

Casual restaurant
Daily 9am-9pm.
Additional locations.

Midtown
2808 Milam St.
(713) 524-3734
www.phosaigonnoodlehouse.com

Westchase
2553 N. Gessner Dr.
(713) 329-9242

Chinatown
11360 Bellaire Blvd.
(281) 564-9095

Bar None
Credit Cards Visa, MC, AmEx
Reservations Not accepted

Phô Saigon Vietnamese Noodles is an institution in Houston—it's bordering on being a legend. Its many incarntions in strategic locations around the city have infiltrated the comfortable, suburban, chicken-fried-steak way of life with soft tendon, tripe, and fatty brisket in a broth of simmered animal bones. You might think that quality would suffer at the hands of quantity, given the current scale of the chain, but that's not the case; not only is quality as high as ever, prices are as low, too.

It's hard to write about the menus of phô places in Houston, because they're all virtually identical. Here, as elsewhere, it's not the menu that distinguishes the place: it's the delicious, authentic, fast, affordable noodle soup. Then, of course, there are the spring rolls (fresh or fried) and vermicelli rice bowls. Walk into Phô Saigon at lunch time, and the hustle and bustle that is the lunch rush seems ten times faster than anywhere else. Most locations are decorated identically with a mass-produced comfort feel to them, if that's possible. Each table has an ingenious push-button system with which you can alert the server if you're ready to place your order, need more water, or are ready for the check. Phô isn't as technologically advanced, though; it's just a good, simple soup. Select from beef noodle soup, egg noodle soup, or chicken noodle soup. Small bowls are big, and large bowls are giant. One of the best combinations is the beef noodle soup with round-eye steak (haha), well-done flank, fatty brisket, soft tendon, and beef tripe. The broth, made from both beef and chicken, is so clean yet so flavorful. Phô Saigon also serves seafood in egg broths. Beverages are almost as delicious as the phô, with a great selection of fruit smoothies, teas, sodas whipped with condensed milk and egg yolk, and a simply labeled "Chinese health drink".

We'll let that go unreviewed. –SD

Phoenicia

Far beyond its Middle Eastern roots, a globetrotting playground-superstore for foodies

Gourmet wonderland

Specialty grocery
Mon.-Sat. 8am-9pm;
Sun. 8am-7pm.
Live music. Outdoor dining. Vegetarian-friendly.

West Houston
12141 Westheimer Rd.
(281) 558-8225
www.phoeniciafoods.com

Bar None
Credit Cards Visa, MC, AmEx
Reservations Not accepted

Rarely do we quote from an establishment's web site, but this one is priceless: the store imports foods from countries "***including*** France, Greece, Spain, Bulgaria, Romania, Croatia, Hungary, Poland, Turkey, United Kingdom, Germany, Lebanon, Chile, Argentina, Portugal, Syria, Switzerland, Netherlands, Russia, Egypt, Iran, Saudi Arabia, Jordan, Armenia, Brazil, and Sweden."

Emphasis added.

This gargantuan space out west on Westheimer does justice to the image of the old Phoenician traders, evoking the days when boats would glide into ports of call bearing unheard-of goods from untold corners of the world—anything at a price. This Phoenicia begins with a quality lineup of Middle Eastern and Greek nibbles, from olives and feta to some of the best fresh-baked pita in the city. The bakery is outstanding, wowing customers from the Balkans to Egypt, Latin America to Greece. In fact, despite its slightly ungainly appearance both inside and out, Phoenicia can feel like a home away from home to expats from all over the globe. Its cluttered shelves accommodate just the right articles from every country: stout, middle-class Tetley's tea and digestive biscuits from England, sour cherries from Hungary, canned sprats from the Baltic, North African merguez, dried fish flakes from Ghana.

But the Middle Eastern products are the stars of the show. Many varieties of olives lie marinating in big vats in the counter. Several different feta cheeses are stacked in their salty brine (we find the Bulgarian particularly creamy and good). Phoenicia makes its own delicious hummus; smoky baba ganoush (an eggplant dip); terrific, lemony tabbouleh with a fresh parsley punch; and less impressive, too-hard dolmas (rice-stuffed grape leaves). Ready-to-eat sandwiches are cheap and terrific, herby, and fresh-tasting, wrapped in that amazing pita. It is often still warm when it arrives, and it is delicate, sweet, and chewy. The gyro is packed with tender beef and lamb shawarma, and perked up by a tangy yogurt dressing. Grilled zatar bread contains salty Kalamata olives and feta, marinated onions, and a symphony of herbs. The chicken kebab sandwich is another favorite. You can eat in, but we recommend taking your food to go. It's made it this far, after all. –FC

Pico's Mex-Mex

Finally, a pleasant Mexican restaurant that isn't stuck in the last century

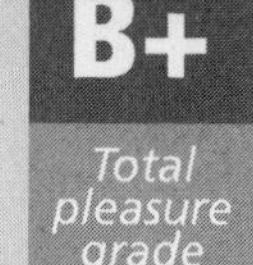

Total pleasure grade

Food

Feel

Price

Mexican

Casual restaurant
Sun.-Thurs. 9am-10pm;
Fri.-Sat. 9am-11pm.

Bellaire
5941 Bellaire Blvd.
(713) 662-8383
www.picos.net

Bar Full
Credit Cards Visa, MC, AmEx
Reservations Not accepted

In a humble building in Bellaire, sporting a cracked-out bird as its mascot, you'll find Pico's, an unassuming restaurant that doesn't inspire high hopes—especially when you find out that it fancies itself as "traditional yet contemporary". Adjective phrases like these often tip you off to a train wreck waiting to happen, but Pico's manages to stay on the tracks. Dishes traverse Mexican regions, from the Yucatán (huachinango Tikin-Xik, red snapper seasoned with achiote seed and wrapped in banana leaves) to Oaxaca (pollo en mole negro oaxaqueño, chicken served in Oaxacan-style black mole). But the dishes, while pan-Mex, are well chosen, so they make us happy.

From the outside, Pico's would look abandoned were it not for the cars in the parking lot. Outside décor is thrown together in a cluttered style, and upkeep is clearly not a priority. Not to worry, though; it's a Mexican restaurant, and it's all part of the charm. And the menu blows an unsuspecting visitor out of the water with seafood, poultry, and everybody's favorite animal (okay, ours, anyway)—pig. Queso flameado, packed with chorizo and peppers will have you wondering where queso has been all your life, and cochinita pibil is one of Houston's better versions, its achiote-seed-marinated pork steamed inside of a banana leaf and served with red onions. It shreds beautifully, and, unlike some lesser versions, is packed with porky flavor and moisture. The Pico's kitchen also turns out a mean batch of mole—dark, bittersweet, and flavorful, it has been hiding right under Houston diners' noses for years.

It keeps getting better with the great selection of tequilas. If you decide to drink your lunch or dinner, you'll be in good company, with high-end tequilas that will treat you right—maybe even through the next day. Margaritas balance sweet and sour well. In the evenings, a mariachi band makes the rounds. A note of warning, however: they do not take well to spontaneous accompaniment from would-be Mexican Frank Sinatras, no matter how beautifully harmonized. Instead, just enjoy the food, and bask in the consistency of flavors that attack your taste buds with a vengeance. –SD

The Pizza Guy vs. the Tamale Couple

C+ Total pleasure grade

Very fresh, six dollars; for you, only five dollars

6.0 Food **8.5** Feel **$5** Price

Pizza vs. Mexican

In your face
Late night, mostly on weekends
Date-friendly.

Anywhere
Everywhere

Bar Not on a good night
Credit Cards Not wise
Reservations You could probably negotiate something

In this corner, selling five-dollar pizzas that are "very fresh" (even if there's no telling how long they have been in that delivery case), we have the hard hitting, flavor-busting, you'll-remember-me-in-the-morning-as-you're-hugging-your-toilet-bowl dynamo: The Pizza Guy. And in this corner we have the very humble, soft-spoken, aluminum-foiled package from the gods, the dynamic duo of flavor: The Tamale Couple.

We don't know their names, nor do we know where they come from, but we do know that they appear at many of the bars in the Houston area throughout the night, and just when you thought that you were off their radar screen—that there's no way that they could *possibly* find you this far outside the Loop—there they are. How do they do it?

The Pizza Guy sells pizza that is, he claims, "very fresh, five dollars," but around the holidays, or if he just doesn't like you, it's six. Most of the time it's just pepperoni, cheese, or sausage, but on the good nights he has supreme. If you weren't drunk, you wouldn't eat the pizza, but after three shots of tequila and a few beers, it seems like a great idea. The thought process goes something like this:

Sober: The pizza is cold, the crust is doughy, and it looks like it's been sitting around for two days. There's no way I would eat that.

Intoxicated: The flavors are having a party on my tongue. A cold, doughy party. Delicious!

The Tamale Couple, on the other hand, is a little more subdued. Perhaps they have achieved a Zen state of calm from each other's companionship. They take pride in their work and they actually offer a good product. The tamales are not hot, but the flavors are good. They have chicken, pork, or beef, and they even have little containers of salsa as an added bonus. Again, to the sober palate, they're average, at best, but if you're hungry enough, it's better than taking your chances with the pizza guy.

Side effects can sometimes result from eating either food, but note that these are often indistinguishable from the raging hangover associated with the inebriation required to eat them in the first place. Split decision goes to...the tamale couple! –SD

Pizzitola's Bar-B-Que

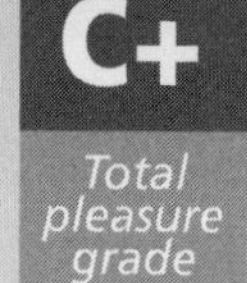

Friendly and authentic—if somewhat overrated—barbecue

Total pleasure grade

6.3 Food **7.5** Feel **$15** Price **Barbecue**

Casual restaurant
Mon.-Fri. 10:30am-8pm;
Sat. 10:30am-3pm; closed Sun.
Delivery.

Heights
1703 Shepherd Dr.
(713) 227-2283

Bar None
Credit Cards Visa, MC, AmEx
Reservations Accepted

It's easy to get excited about authentic, downmarket Texas barbecue. The sultry smell of smoke, as you enter Pizzitola's, takes such abstract excitement and turns it into anxious, giddy anticipation. Building upon that, the Texas-themed history and sports paraphernalia, the humble booths and tables, the cheap plates, the dishes of pickles and onions, the classic stack of Wonderish bread slices, and the what'll-it-be-Hon service are all absolutely faithful to the genre.

The menu, too, is as honest as they come, with family-style options, plates with one or two meats, sandwiches, and so on. Yet even amidst this ideal confluence of factors, and even amidst the smoky aromas, disappointingly few flavors come through on the plate. All of it lacks sadly in the trademark smoke flavors. Ribs, in spite of that deficit, are well seasoned, more tender and juicy than average, as is deboned chicken. Sausage has enough flavor of its own to survive without smoke, but the most dramatic underperformer of all is the beef brisket. It's dry, gray, and relatively tough, even when requested fatty, and even its fat lacks flavor.

Especially given the genuine warmth of the staff, you'd have to be a heartless bastard to hate Pizzitola's; we certainly don't. And its relative renown in the city might actually be well deserved. Still, that fact points to a larger problem: the lack of top-flight Texas barbecue within the city limits of Houston (the spectacular Luling City Market notwithstanding). It's sad, because you can get truly superlative brisket and sausage not just in the Hill Country, but also at Hinze's in Sealy, at one or two spots in La Grange, and at a few other random places on the road an hour or two in any direction from Houston.

We suppose you could say that Houston's loss is Pizzitola's gain, because the BBQ field is so weak here that the place stands out as a big fish in a little pond. Luckily, it's a friendly, nonthreatening big fish, content to keep serving reasonably priced, better-than-Goode barbecue with a smile. –RG

PK's Blue Water Grill

If this is blue water, then give us brown

D
Total pleasure grade

3.1 Food | **3.2** Feel | **$44** Price

Southern seafood

Casual restaurant
Mon.-Thurs. 11am-10pm;
Fri.-Sat. 11am-11pm;
Sun. 11am-9pm.
Kid-friendly. Live music. Outdoor dining.

Memorial
6401 Woodway Dr.
(713) 339-3663
www.pkbluewatergrill.com

Bar Full
Credit Cards Visa, MC, AmEx
Reservations Accepted

"Strictly blue water," reads the awning. The thing is, PK's might do well to take a trip out to Galveston and gaze upon the Gulf: the water there is brownish, not blue. Maybe that's the explanation for the disappointing seafood here.

The big, squat restaurant, located in the Memorial area near Second Baptist Church, probably intended to attract the highbrow customers with a nice Louisiana-style menu, clearly modeled after Goode Company, and a quaint dining room. But somewhere, something went wrong. Why anyone would hang up sheets of ridged metal lining, like the kind you would build a tool shack out of, is unexplainable. Have we missed out on the latest trend in interior decorating? Did the partners balk on a capital call halfway after the restaurant was built? Or did some construction wise guy hit up Home Depot and work out a kickback deal with a sales associate who needed to sell some sheet metal?

In true Gulf fashion, everything on the menu gives you a choice of being mesquite grilled, blackened, or fried; these are cooking techniques that, though laden with potential, often breed complacency. As such, more than half of the items that come to the PK's table tend to be overcooked. A fried shrimp platter isn't anything to haw about, but it's about the best thing on the menu. Even with the shrimp, though, we've had our plate come out chilly—which is about the worst thing there is. We've seen hard catfish, gummy oysters, and bacon-wrapped shrimp the texture of rubber balloons—even if their flavor winds up fine, smoky and fatty, just like anything covered in bacon fat. Worse still are the sides, from a tacky mashed potato-fest with three different types of mashed potatoes—each bad in its own way—to rice with bizarre off-notes.

The waitstaff here tends to look deflated, too—but then, bringing out this food in this dining room, and pouring a bunch of grocery-store wines, you probably would, too. –JY

Pollo Campero

B-
Total pleasure grade

Lots of hype and not enough delivery, but still a nostalgic Central American experience

7.4 *Food* **7.2** *Feel* **$9** *Price*

Latin American

Fast-food chain
Daily 10am-10pm.
Kid-friendly. Additional locations

Bellaire
5616 Bellaire Blvd.
(713) 395-0990
www.campero.com

Bar None
Credit Cards Visa, MC, AmEx
Reservations Not accepted

North Houston
7418 Airline Dr.
(713) 691-8922

Spring Branch
8358 Long Point Rd.
(713) 722-0592

Whenever restaurant chains from back home install themselves in new countries, they rarely taste the way you remember. Such is the problem with Pollo Campero. True, it is loved by many Central Americans as comfort food, and, true, when it opened in Houston, people were at first willing to wait for over an hour for fried chicken; alas, it doesn't strike that chord that propels people backward to their homeland when they taste and smell a childhood favorite. And a favorite is is indeed: board a flight to the U.S. that's originating in San Salvador or Guatemala City (the chain originated in Guatemala), and the plane will be as full of Pollo Campero (It's a tradition to bring a big bag of it to your American relatives) as it is people. Apparently they know, too, that the U.S. branches are but inferior copies.

A piece of fried chicken can be a thing of beauty when it's served right out of the hot oil; when the crusty coating is penetrated, a stinging vapor of chicken steam hits you in the face. And that's what Pollo Campero is lacking: that sexy, exciting crunch that only fried chicken can provide.

Nonetheless, with a hint of oregano in the flour, it is a better piece of poultry than the American chicken chains are capable of frying. Unfortunately, sitting under a heat lamp for the lunchtime rush, it loses all of its self-esteem—like a girl getting stood up on prom night.

The sides at Pollo Campero are meant to play supporting roles to the infamous chicken, but there are no award-winning performances here. Some locations have tostones (fried plantains), but they taste a bit too starchy. French fries are delicious, but the tortillas that come with every meal have little flavor and are sometimes hard, sometimes greasy. There are some places in Houston that are fast, cheap, and well worth it. In the end, you'll like Pollo Campero more if you haven't experienced the real thing in Central America. As for us, our fond memories of Pollo Campero, which we frequented in El Salvador, come mostly from the morbid fascination that comes from watching a grown man in a full-body chicken suit get on a scooter to make a delivery. "I've got a great new job," you imagine him stuttering to his wife. "There's only one catch." –FC

Pollo Riko

Bust of the barnyard has rarely looked or tasted this good

A- *Total pleasure grade*

8.5 *Food* **6.9** *Feel* **$7** *Price*

Latin American

Fast-food chain
Mon.-Sat. 11am-10pm;
Sun. 11am-9pm.
Kid-friendly.

Southwest Houston
14443 Bellaire Blvd.
(281) 498-4716
www.polloriko.com

North Houston
5532 Airline Dr.
(713) 692-2822

Bar None
Credit Cards No credit cards
Reservations Not accepted

Chinatown
7229 Fondren Rd.
(713) 271-4321

If you're the average reader, chances are you haven't been to Colombia on vacation. You're missing out: not just on the spectacular countryside of Boyacá and the coffee plantations of the Eje Cafetero, and on the unexpected vibrancy of Bogotá, but also on the vastly underrated cuisine. At least here, at Pollo Riko, you can taste a roast chicken that evokes the real thing. With super-crispy skin; plump, juicy meat; and that right-off-the-spit taste that nears perfection when it comes to the almighty bird, this specialty at Pollo Riko is one of the best chickens in town—as it should be. Roast chicken is the only thing on the menu here, aside from sides and sodas; there is thus only one focus, which is a good quality in a restaurant.

This isn't your mother's dry Sunday chicken that has been cooked 'till it tastes like sand whose soul has long ago clucked out. Notice the giant rotisserie right when you walk in, and you'll see that these guys mean business. At least 30 whole chickens are roasting at once on the giant spit, which rotates around a wood fire; their fat glistens and drips as it cooks, producing an extra-crispy chicken skin. The mesquite-charcoal mix over which they're roasted also helps out.

Pollo Riko is a fast-paced restaurant. Know what you want before you get to the counter, or else you risk disrupting the flow and making them cross. Prices are right at this humble chicken house; lunch specials run about three dollars, dinner specials about four dollars. The specials come with your choice of dark or white meat, two sides, and your choice of arepa or corn tortilla. (An arepa is a small griddled masa cake, like a fresh, double-extra-thick corn tortilla; it's common in Colombian cuisine.) Sides are all-American, but tasty: potatoes, coleslaw, red beans and rice, as well as tostones and fried yuca. Portions are reasonable enough to leave you feeling good about yourself—not feeling like you just swallowed a whole barnyard. After all, the Colombians are fit, too. And beautiful. –SD

Ponzo's

A great location with okay food and a pizza-tossing show to boot

C *Total pleasure grade*

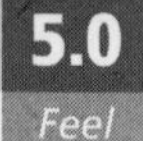

$14 *Price*

Italian-American

Casual restaurant
Tues.-Thurs. 11am-10pm;
Fri.-Sat. 11am-11pm;
Sun. 11am-10pm; closed Mon.
Delivery. Kid-friendly.
Outdoor dining.

Midtown
2515 Bagby St.
(713) 526-2426
www.ponzospizza.com

Bar None
Credit Cards Visa, MC, AmEx
Reservations Not accepted

Hot subs, especially hot meatball subs, are a thing of beauty; we'll take a good one anytime. Ponzo's is one of the better all-around fast Italian cafés that does only a few things, but does them well—like hand-tossed pizza, great hot subs, and surprisingly good salads. Your challenge, though, is to avoid the many pasta pitfalls that plague the menu, drawn from what we call the "Italian American 1.0" culinary repertoire (for a definition see pages 6-7). Still, it's a decent lunch spot in an unfortunate stripmall location, and it feeds mostly downtown businessmen and alternative patrons. Service is friendly and to the point.

Ponzo's has an industrial feel to it. There's no cheesy memorabilia hanging on the walls and none of the dreaded plastic vegetables hanging from the ceiling. What there is, though, is the good old pizza show. It'll bring back that same excitement as when you were a kid, watching someone throw handmade dough into the air and catch it like a pro; it's the same at Ponzo's, and it never gets old. These are experienced pizza tossers.

The pizza itself is not too bad, not too good; crispy crusts with the usual array of toppings arrive steaming hot, so be careful. The humble meatball sub makes an even bigger impact: house-made meatballs are stuffed into crusty bread and toasted with melted cheese on top (upon request—do it!). The meatballs aren't crumbly, but rather moist and flavorful. Equally good is a sausage-and-pepper sub with spicy and sweet Italian sausage paired with sweet peppers. "Ponzo's Original" is pretty delicious with salty salami, mortadella, and provolone. Come with an appetite, though, because the subs are nine inches long; and if you really haven't eaten in a long time, they have 15-inch sandwiches, too.

Pasta dishes are boring, one-dimensional, and definitely not a strong point of the kitchen. Manicotti is largely flavorless. Cannoli, the little crunchy pastry tubes, are unfortunately filled with pastry cream, like an éclair, instead of the ricotta cheese that makes cannoli so good. But this is Italian-American 1.0—what do you expect? –RG

Prego

B-

Total pleasure grade

Upmarket, slightly outdated Italian-Southwestern that can still hit the right vibe

7.3 Food | **7.6** Feel | **$57** Price

Italian-American

Upmarket restaurant
Mon.-Thurs. 11am-10pm;
Fri.-Sat. 11am-11pm;
Sun. 11am-10pm.
Brunch. Date-friendly. Live music. Vegetarian-friendly. WiFi.

Rice Area
2520 Amherst St.
(713) 529-2420
www.prego-houston.com

Bar Full
Credit Cards Visa, MC, AmEx
Reservations Recommended

Prego's early-1990s Italian-American affectations are nothing less than classic. The dish of olive oil infused with basil, peperoncino, and salt on the table for dipping your bread acts to form an amuse-bouche (contrary to popular belief, this has never been done in Italy). But it's delicious. We have fewer nice things to say about the waiter's polite offer to grind fresh pepper from a long, impressive mill onto absolutely anything you order, however mismatched it is with black pepper.

The thing is, it's not really Italian-American, this menu. It's barely even Italian-American 2.0. (That's our term for the new version of Italian-American cuisine invented by upmarket restaurants in the past couple of decades—its trademarks are expensive meats in complicated sauces with Italian-sounding ingredients, yet no more authentic than Italian-American 1.0. See pages 6-7 for a full definition of 1.0 vs. 2.0.)

Where Prego will surprise you is with the occasional addition of a Southwestern ingredient to the mix, as in a roasted red pepper and poblano cream soup that extracts contrasting flavors from the two different peppers—the mild bell and the spicier poblano. The creamy, well-reduced mixture is correctly seasoned and shockingly successful, though so rich that it could practically be a sauce for a Southwestern chile relleno, chicken, or some such; its plating is artistic too, the green side of the soup set off against the orange side, imitating, perhaps, a modern painting you might expect to have seen on the wall in one of those early upscale joints.

Pastas are decently executed, too; we've tried potato ravioli in a buttery (almost too buttery) sauce whose effect was similar to that of pierogi, but with an eggier pasta and a lemon kick. Sautéed spinach comes with plenty of salt and garlic. Less successful, generally speaking, are the protein mains like butterflied salmon, which—deboned—comes off more like steelhead trout. –RG

Prince's Hamburgers

The artist formerly known as Prince's is a shadow of his old drive-in self

C- *Total pleasure grade*

3.5 *Food* **7.0** *Feel* **$9** *Price* **American**

Counter service
Mon.-Fri. 11am-10pm;
Sat.-Sun. 11am-11pm.
Delivery. Kid-friendly.

West U
3899 Southwest Fwy.
(713) 626-9950
www.princeshamburgers.com

Bar Beer only
Credit Cards Visa, MC, AmEx
Reservations Not accepted

Southeast Houston
11460 Fuqua St.
(281) 464-6611

Spring Branch
9535 A Katy Fwy.
(713) 722-8822

Houston was quite a different town in 1934, when Prince's "family style drive-in" opened. By 1940, this place had been featured—in the form of a leggy, uniformed server—on the cover of *Life*, a product of an era of newfound domesticity and automotive mobility. This Americana-laden counter-service burger joint is a far cry from a drive-in, but the three modern incarnations of Prince's are nonetheless quick to capitalize on their pedigree, reminding you at every turn that "everything's the same—except the car hop!"

It's too bad, because those burger girls might have been the best thing about the place. Nowadays, though, it's the service, which is as kind and careful as counter service could imaginably be.

Particularly touted, amidst all the yesteryear wall art (Marilyn Monroe, postwar Chevy hubcaps, vintage Coke ads, and such) are the milkshake and the burger. We weren't around to taste milkshakes in the 1930s, but this shake is too thick for our taste, its syrup not a prominent enough flavor. There are several schools of thought on milkshakes, though, and if you like yours to taste and feel like a half-melted cone of soft-serve ice cream, you'll be happy here.

The burger's thinnish patty is cooked through to grayness, as is characteristic of its old-school style, but it doesn't retain much delicious fat from the griddle, which is really the whole point of that style. The "Prince's Original" burger adds a self-aggrandized sauce of stewed tomatoes, which tastes something like a tomato confit, and neither adds to nor subtracts from the sandwich.

Crispy but average fries benefit from a light dusting of seasoning salt. Onion rings are thick on the batter, thin on the salt, and their marginal appeal peaks in the first seconds out of the fryer and goes downhill from there—yet another item purportedly steeped in history, but without much to distinguish it in the present. These days, the tastes of Prince's are remarkably unremarkable. –RG

Pronto Cucinino

C- Total pleasure grade

A fast-casual extension of the Mandola's empire that plays straight to the crowd

6.5 Food **4.5** Feel **$15** Price

Italian-American

Counter service
Mon.-Sat. 10:30am-9pm.
Sun. 11am-9pm.
Kid-friendly.

Montrose
1401 Montrose Blvd.
(713) 528-8646
www.pronto-2-go.com

West U
3191 W. Holcombe Blvd.
(713) 592-8646

Bar Wine and beer only
Credit Cards Visa, MC, AmEx
Reservations Not accepted

The aesthetic of this "restaurant" is straight out of Frances Mayes, with fake Italian tile and brick archways to look country-villa-ish, and bizarre blown-up photos of (presumably) the Mandola family vacationing in Italy. The menu, too: fried mozzarella to "fettucine pronto" (chicken alfredo) to eggplant parmigiana, it has all the subtlety of *Under the Tuscan Sun*. Even the soundtrack's the greatest hits of cheesy Italian music. It's like Little Italy without all the interesting cultural complexity.

We scare-quote "restaurant" because this is one of Houston's many establishments where you order and pay at the counter, and your food is then brought out via a table-number system. We wish there were a better word than restaurant, so as to separate it from the real restaurants in town—the ones that actually have service.

Pizza margherita (an appetizer, with two small slices) sports fior di latte mozzarella chunks that are barely melted—but the sauce is good and spare, the crust crispy, and the effect quite pleasant. Rotisserie chicken, flagged on the menu as a house specialty, is spit-roasted over a gas fire in a prominent place near the entrance. The chicken comes undersalted, with skin more oily than crispy, and shows little of the advertised lemon and garlic (wouldn't want to scare the kids), but the dark meat is moist and tender; salt it liberally, and it's hard to complain.

Salad greens are relatively fresh, and relatively boring. Pasta is not quite al dente, but thankfully, it's not quite overcooked either, and its red sauce inhabits that same limbo space between boredom and satisfaction: a bit chunky, a bit liquidy, hardly well-reduced, and in need of a healthy dose of parmesan or salt, yet easy to keep eating, and better than many versions out there. Not so for the overcooked, hospital-cafeteria-reminiscent green beans, which even parmesan can't rescue from the mushy abyss. The sad thing is that this offend-nobody model of cuisine is just what many people want, start to finish, and it's hard to blame a crowd-pleaser like Pronto Cucinino for the preferences of the crowd. Hard, but not impossible. –RG

> Ask an Italian waiter for veal parmigiana or fettucine alfredo and he won't have heard of either one. Ask for spaghetti marinara, and you'll get pasta with clams and squid.

QQ Cuisine

Three words: Pork. Belly. Sandwich.

A- *Total pleasure grade*

8.8 *Food* **7.3** *Feel* **$10** *Price* **Chinese**

Casual restaurant
Wed.-Mon. 8am-11pm;
closed Tues.
Breakfast.

Chinatown
9889 Bellaire Blvd.
(713) 776-0553

Bar None
Credit Cards Visa and MC
Reservations Not accepted

Pork belly. It's the root of all evil and the essence of everything good. It breaks waistlines and brings to the world bacon, the Texan fruit of life. It may be hard to understand that something that seems so wholeheartedly American could be in the mix with a cuisine known more for its soy sauce than any sort of bacon product, but QQ cuisine in the Dun Huang Plaza off of Bellaire is a testament to the fact that pork belly translates deliciously to any cuisine, in any setting.

At first glance, QQ Cuisine doesn't look like much, more of dent than a hole in a wall; you can take in the entire restaurant in one glance. It's small, fast-paced, and fluff-free. The industrial design seems built for speed, with tight-knit corners and openings just enough for a waiter to zoom by to pick up orders and drop off plates. The staff doesn't spend much time on you, but in the $2-to-$10 range of QQ's plates, it's more about turning the table than building any sort of customer rapport. Besides, there's pork belly. Why *wouldn't* you come back?

QQ's cuisine is unwavering and unforgiving. Almost everything here is unapologetically greasy, and some items—such as a stir-fried spicy eggplant—can go overboard on the oil to the point where things will slip out from between your chopsticks. The mainland-China cuisine here specializes in all things wrapped and pan-fried. A pan-fried pork bun, for instance, has several different textures: crispy bottom, fluffy bun, and juicy pork-and-chive filling. Pan-seared dumplings are some of the best in town, with uniformly browned flat bottoms and just enough fire breath to add another dimension to the normally flat filling. The green onion pancake could use more green onion, but it's rolled thin and pan-fried to an ideal crispness. But if there was ever a single bite of food that would define tastebud ecstasy, it would be one of QQ's pork belly sandwiches, with soft, white, steamed buns sandwiching a braised pork belly that balances flavors of snowy pork fat and juicy, soy-touched meat. Your belt may need to move up a few notches afterward, but at this price? For pork belly?

The tradeoff needs no contemplation. –JY

Quattro

Smart, elegant, not bad, not good...hey, where did all your money go?

7.5 Food **8.7** Feel **$95** Price **Italian**

Upmarket restaurant
Mon.-Fri. 6:30am-10pm;
Sat.-Sun. 7am-10pm.
Breakfast. Brunch. WiFi.

Downtown
1300 Lamar St.
(713) 276-4700
www.fourseasons.com

Bar Full
Credit Cards Visa, MC, AmEx
Reservations Accepted

Quattro has fallen far. For years, the high-priced, high-class dining room at Houston's aging Four Seasons was one of the best in the city, even if the well-run kitchen was prone to occasional slip-ups. Emphasis was on tradition and quality ingredients, with a high-priced shopping list that made room for locally grown produce and proteins.

Service is still excellent, and there are still moments of greatness here. A whole branzino (dubbed "branzini" in one of numerous Italian misspellings on the menu) is baked in a salt crust—perhaps the most succulent way of preparing the sweet, delicate white Mediterranean fish—and it's tender and delicious, enhanced by a do-it-yourself sprinkle of salt and drizzle of olive oil. But recent changes in the kitchen have brought chaos upon the execution, and even simple pasta dishes can come out butchered. A preparation of bucatini with clams and pancetta, on our last visit, was a shocking mess: dry, gummy noodles tasted re-heated, clams were dry and shriveled, and pancetta chunks were the consistency of beef jerky. We couldn't eat more than a couple bites.

The kitchen can get frazzled at lunchtime, and you're best off sticking to the easy (if hardly Italian) winners like "Zuppa Stile Messicana," one of the best tortilla soups in town, with avocado, queso fresco, and a delicious broth playing off each other for an oral fiesta. Brunch plays well to the crowds, offering diners the chance to enter the kitchen to choose their food.

Dinner is where the big guns come out, but plates often throw together a bunch of high-priced ingredients (slipper lobster, foie gras, and porcini, for example) that don't necessarily play well together. Still, they execute well on the very traditional osso buco milanese, a fork-tender veal shank accompanied by cheesy saffron risotto. Lots of menu space is devoted to grilled steaks, and it's hard to go wrong with prime beef, as long as it's seasoned and cooked as ordered (it is). But steakhouse sides can fall flat, as creamed spinach recently did, turning out gummy and caricatured. We hope that Quattro will choose, once again, to reach beyond its captive audience of hotel guests and automatic business lunches, because these guys can do much better than this. –RG

RA Sushi

Chain sushi seems so much sexier after a few Tsunami Punches to the mouth

5.8 *Food* **6.5** *Feel* **$43** *Price* **Japanese**

Upmarket restaurant
Daily 11am-midnight.
Date-friendly.

River Oaks
3908 Westheimer Rd.
(713) 621-5800
www.rasushi.com

Bar Full
Credit Cards Visa, MC, AmEx
Reservations Accepted

The sushi trend that has swept America over the past decade or so has taken on numerous forms. Sometimes, it's sushi as health food—you even see vegetarian sushi restaurants these days, but even in its non-veg incarnation (or inpescation, if you will), it's a high-protein, low-fat way to eat. Other times, it's sushi as fast food, or even supermarket snack (usually cold and disgusting, the RJR-Nabiscization of raw fish). Elsewhere, you'll see sushi as a high-priced omakase feast for foodies.

At RA, it's sushi as sex. This restaurant feels like a nightclub with an afterthought of a restaurant, an aesthetic that's been mimicked at every one of RA Sushi's locations—it's a nationwide chain. At any one of them, you're just as likely to find people who come to down drinks at the bar as sushi aficionados. The second-floor restaurant's soaring ceilings and tall windows give the place a warehouse-meets-treehouse feel. Sexy dim red lighting emanates from the circular paper lanterns that are scattered thoughtfully about.

An extensive sushi menu boasts fish that they claim to fly in daily, including meltingly delicious uni (sea urchin). Other nigiri options vary in quality, but the standard is generally high, particularly for a chain. The "Signature Sushi" list, on the other hand, consists of rolls that combine a laundry list of ingredients that seem very unlikely to result in anything coherent. Take, for instance, the Viva Las Vegas roll: kani kama (imitation crab) and cream cheese in a tempura-battered roll, topped with spicy tuna, crab, lotus root, eel sauce, and spinach tempura. No joke. Dishes also exist for those who like their fish cooked, don't like fish at all, or want a noodle bowl.

The cocktail list has the creative drinks you would expect of a trendy sushi restaurant: names dripping with sexual innuendo, sake creations, and our favorite, the "Tsunami Punch"—a 60-ounce fruity concoction served in a fish bowl. So come early unless you want to eat your dinner in a night club. But if you do, take in the eye candy that is the young, trendy Asian crowd. –AH

Red & White Wine Bistro

B-

Total pleasure grade

Unjustifiable captive-audience prices at the Toyota Center, even with a decent buffet

7.6 Food **7.4** Feel **$74** Price

American

Upmarket restaurant
Open during events.
Kid-friendly.

Downtown
1510 Polk St.
(713) 758-7534
www.redandwhitewinebistro.com

Bar Full
Credit Cards Visa, MC, AmEx
Reservations Essential

The degree to which you enjoy your meal at Red & White Wine Bistro is largely dependent on how much the Rockets are winning, or by how badly they're choking. On a purely existential level, the buffet, or so-called "Chef's Table," is one of Houston's best; there's nothing like some therapeutic gorging to get over a home-game loss.

If you do dine here (you need a special category of ticket to get in), prepare for an emotional rollercoaster. The mood swings between despondency, as Yao clumsily throws away a ball, to pure euphoria, as Tracy McGrady goes on a two-minute, 13-point explosion. There are quite a few seats that don't have a decent view of the game; it's here, for example, where some of the women, tired of their husbands screaming obscenities at Jeff Van Gundy, might slink off to grab a Cosmo. Be forewarned, however, that bar service is atrocious, especially if you don't look like you ooze money. Dirty looks are shot your way, hoping to send you reeling back to the concession stand. All this, after you've spent nearly $40 for the buffet—plus the price of your ticket.

There's something oddly reminiscent of Vegas about the whole thing. The spread is varied enough, but someone seems to have told the chef that he couldn't go wrong by serving 100% protein-centric Texas-style cuisine. Perhaps surprisingly, carving station had a spectacular prime rib on one visit, and, with a little nudging, the carver wasn't afraid to slice us off a ruby red, glistening cut from the middle and a charred, crusty portion from the end. Roasted snapper has also been a pleasant surprise, sweet and flaky. Several of the dishes, however, have suffered from advanced-stage overcooked-buffet syndrome. We've seen beef fajitas that looked and tasted more like jerky, and tuna sushi that was mealy and dry, despite not having spent a lot of time out on the table.

Although we can't complain about the food—it certainly exceeds stadium-fare expectations—nor can we complain about the view, we'd still rather be in a seat in the nosebleed section, nachos in one hand, beer in the other, eating with the real fans. –JY

Red Lion Pub

Total pleasure grade

A traditional British pub that flaunts its Houston flair

8.2	8.2	$25
Food	Feel	Price

American, British

Bar
Mon.-Thurs. 3pm-11pm;
Fri.-Sat. 11:30am-midnight;
Sun. 11:30am-11pm.
Date-friendly. Outdoor dining. WiFi.

Upper Kirby
2316 S. Shepherd Dr.
(713) 782-3030
www.redlionhouston.com

Bar Full
Credit Cards Visa, MC, AmEx
Reservations Not accepted

Take a trip to jolly ol' England via the Red Lion Pub on Shepherd, and you will see that the British expat community in Houston is large. And they love this dark, smoky pub, where the kitchen pays homage to all of the great British culinary innovations—if there is such a thing. By the end of the night, whether from the tasty food or just the good beer, the Red Lion will likely have you singing songs to cheer on Arsenal or Chelsea (but please, for the love of God, not Man U).

Big, wooden, castle-like doors lead you into a dimly lit dining room with small lamps on each table. There's a fireplace at the end of the dining room, and the bar at the entrance will comfort you and your liver with the promise of making everything feel better. The Red Lion serves good food; it's overpriced good food, but we'll let them get away with it. Giant fish and chips with peas and house-made malt vinegar (one of the world's most underrated condiments) is some of their best work. Pleasantly greasy, yet still crisp enough, the fish is moist and steamy, and the batter is thin. Another great British dish is bangers and mash; house-made sausages with mashed potatoes are wonderful with a bit of Colman's spicy mustard and a Boddingtons.

The Indian selections on the menu are what you should really get, however—and, ironically enough, they're what makes this place most authentically British. Chicken tikka masala and curry with lamb, beef, or chicken can be a bit too rich at times, but they leave you sated, which is really the point of Brit-Indian. Don't miss the chalkboard daily specials like curry and pint, five-dollar hamburgers, or the traditional Sunday roast nights. For all you bathroom aficionados, don't miss The Red Lion's flawless—yes, flawless—bathrooms, which we proclaim to be the best in the city. They're equipped with cartoon comic-strip porn and that ever-so-important separate room with a full length wooden door in the men's room where your porcelain throne and fresh flowers await. It'll make you feel positively posh. –SD

Reef

The city's premier Gulf seafood restaurant shows a few weaknesses, but many strengths

A
Total pleasure grade

9.1	8.3	$66
Food	*Feel*	*Price*

New American

Upmarket restaurant
Mon.-Thurs. 11am-10pm;
Fri. 11am-11pm;
Sat. 5pm-11pm; closed Sun.
Date-friendly. Wine-friendly.

Midtown
2600 Travis St.
(713) 526-8282
www.reefhouston.com

Bar Full
Credit Cards Visa, MC, AmEx
Reservations Essential

Chef Bryan Caswell's first independent project was the biggest news on the Houston culinary scene in 2007. With Caswell's four-star, Jean-Georges-trained pedigree and recent escape from an established hotel restaurant, expectations were high. Certainly it's been a supremely successful venture from a business standpoint; lately, Reef seems to be the only upmarket restaurant in Houston that reliably draws crowds all summer. While the restaurant has its shortcomings and inconsistencies, it's already quite good, with the potential to be truly great.

Reef's Midtown space is cool, blue, and ocean-like; it feels calm, yet still touched by the constant buzz of humanity. Fortunately, that's what the cool cats that Reef attracts like, and they fill the space easily. Acoustics in the room aren't ideal, and the noise can be overwhelming at peak hours. The adjacent "3rd Bar," long, steely, and silver, adds an even cooler touch. Servers are both welcoming and knowledgeable, especially with so much about the menu to explain.

Stylistically, the cuisine here is refreshingly restrained, built around seafood with the occasional nouvelle Texan or Mexican motif. The menu changes frequently, but a starter of silky raw snapper carpaccio has come brightened by tart bits of grapefruit; its bready, garlicky bruschetta platform was puzzling, but not inoffensive. In a little Indian-Mexican fusion game, fatty carnitas have come crusted with tandoor spices and paired with raita. Caswell has gone Japanese-Mexican, too, with judiciously crunchy tempura soft-shell crab against the welcome acid of "taquería-styled pickled vinaigrette," which played like an escabeche. And snapper has made another, more skillful appearance in a tenderly cooked, crispy-skin fillet, with the natural bitterness of sweet-and-sour chard cleverly placed in the background.

Reef is not perfect yet. Underseasoning, an occasional problem here, has made the triple tail bland, and execution issues have included a so-called "artichoke barigoule" that was missing the stewy quality the dish is supposed to display. But there are lots of highs on the grilled side, like an amberjack whose natural oiliness sang beautifully with a contrasting spike of orange mustard and green chili, and scallops that were daringly grilled in an almost exclusively pan-seared town.

An underappreciated lunch at Reef may be one of the best deals in town, especially irresistibly beefy, spicy sliders with sriracha remoulade. And we *love* the low-markup wine list. Given the ambition of the menu, this level of achievement is already deeply impressive. –FC

Reggae Hut

We should probably make some reference to Bob Marley and/or marijuana here

B *Total pleasure grade*

7.0 *Food* **8.0** *Feel* **$13** *Price* **Jamaican**

Counter service
Mon.-Fri. 11am-9pm;
closed Sat.-Sun.
Outdoor dining. WiFi.

Medical Center
4814 Almeda Rd.
(713) 520-7171

Bar None
Credit Cards Visa, MC, AmEx
Reservations Not accepted

Sitting here listening to Jamaica's finest reggae music and admiring walls covered in murals, you'll start to wonder if you're still in Houston. And a bite of the delicious jerk chicken will have you doing your best to get to the Caribbean as soon as possible. But if you think Jamaican cuisine is just about poultry, you're a jerk. It's also goat curry, fried plantains, and oxtails; it's ackee and callaloo, meat patties and salt fish; it's spectacularly seasoned, in-your-face peasant food that has fed a nation for decades. (We can only wonder how wildly unrestrained Jamaican food would be like had they not once been ruled by the United Kingdom.)

Order at the counter and have a seat, but don't get too comfortable; it is unbelievable how fast they prepare the food. They claim to have the best jerk chicken around, and we won't argue. A giant breast cooked on the bone is slathered in jerk seasoning; they call it "hot," but it's actually so much more than that. It's sweet, spicy, and earthy all at once. Fried plantains, too, are delicious, halved and fried 'till soft, their sugars caramelized for a naturally sweet appetizer. Goat curry could use a bit more spunk; its sauce needs more sweetness and brightness, but the meat is braised beautifully. The best part of the goat experience is hollowing out the bones for their fatty marrow; it's a delicious treat, and one you don't even have to pay extra for. Portions, in general, are huge, and most mains come with rice, beans, and a selection of vegetables like braised cabbage, carrots, and squash. The real fun is seeing such humble ingredients turned into such fulfilling food.

The service is nice, informative, and positive; they always sport a smile. Maybe it's because they're constantly listening to one of the best soundtracks in the city; on any day you can hear Bob, Damian, Stephen, or Ziggy Marley, as well as the greats like Anthony B, Sizzla and Beres Hammond. And while Reggae Hut has the same owners as the Breakfast Klub, there are no crazy lines here. After your meal, stop by the Reggae Bodega next door and check out incense, bucket hats, and music. Are you hooked yet? –SD

The Remington

Tired, muted new food in a tired, gracious old space

New American

Upmarket restaurant
Daily 6:30am-2pm, 5pm-11pm.
Breakfast. Live music.
Outdoor dining.

Galleria
1919 Briar Oaks Ln.
(713) 403-2631
www.theremingtonrestaurant.com

Bar Full
Credit Cards Visa, MC, AmEx
Reservations Accepted

The contrast between the St. Regis in New York and the St. Regis in Houston is striking; while in most cities the high-priced hotel feels the need to engage with the 21st century, they clearly haven't yet decided to do so in Houston. Nowhere is this more evident than in the Remington restaurant, from its pink and red décor to the bizarre displays of geriatric bright-pink fuzzy bathrobes and embroidered pillows proudly displayed in glass cases along the corridor leading up to the restaurant's entrance. The dining room has an airy front room with skylights—a timeless touch, at least—but keep your eyes focused upward; animal print has found its way into the dining room in the form of leopard-pattern table skirts.

The menu is like a parody of upmarket 1980s blandness. Almost every ingredient is designed to impress in name yet simultaneously hide itself on the palate. The kitchen seems too risk-averse to do anything interesting.

A Southwest Caesar salad, for example, is merely passable, with crunchy tortilla strips and an overly oily dressing that doesn't adhere to the leaves. They seem to have stumbled upon a novel concept with a "Portobello 'Pizza'", in which the mushroom itself serves as the pizza crust. Its ingredients— roasted tomato and surprisingly good bresaola—can't add enough of a spark, however, and blandness rules the overall effect. A highly touted lobster bisque is appropriately rich and well-seasoned, but at this price point, we expect more than something so predicatable. A chicken panino, on the lunch menu, is a dried-out disaster, with nothing lubricating the sandwich. Pan-roasted chicken is dry and outdated, its gnocchi gummy. The highlight of a meal might be the unusually creamy butter that accompanies bread, though steer clear of the dry cornbread.

We often find ourselves wishing that hotel restaurants would revamp, and put more of an effort into making themselves attractive to non-guests. In the case of the Remington, however, even guests can tell at a glance that this isn't where they want to be. Waitstaff here seem to know this, and they even come off as strangely apologetic for the experience. We feel sorry for them too, having to spend so much time around animal print. –AH

Rioja

A well-deserved homage to Spanish wine and tapas in a transportative atmosphere

A *Total pleasure grade*

8.6 *Food* **9.5** *Feel* **$62** *Price* **Spanish**

Upmarket restaurant
Tues.-Fri. 11am-2pm, 5:30pm-11pm; Sat. 5:30pm-11pm; Sun. 11am-9pm; closed Mon.
Brunch. Date-friendly. Live music. Wine-friendly.

West Houston
11920 Westheimer Rd.
(281) 531-5569
www.riojarestaurant.com

Bar Full
Credit Cards Visa, MC, AmEx
Reservations Recommended

Ever fickle, informed by a herd mentality since time immemorial, the wine world has been going through fad-driven cycles of underrating one style or region and overrating another, and then flip-flopping, for just about as long as the fashion industry has been doing so. The first Spanish wine fad happened about a millennium ago, when Spain became a major producer for the Roman empire; but it didn't become fashionable again until phylloxera destroyed Bordeaux's vineyards in the second half of the nineteenth century, and Bordeaux's merchants moved to northern Spain to reestablish their business there, giving birth to the modern Spanish wine industry.

Nowadays, the country has found itself at the butt end of the joke that is the so-called "New World" winemaking style, which has been popularized in the past couple of decades. It is the school of inky, ultra-concentrated fruit, aggressive new oak, more residual sugar, and lower acidity than most of the wines that had been produced for centuries before.

Which is precisely the opposite of what Spain has done, and done so well, for a millennium, with Tempranillo, Garnacha, and other native grape varieties. Even the low-to-midlevel Riojas—Spain's most traditional wines—are aged for two or three times as long before release as their price-point counterparts elsewhere in Europe. And yet their distinctly soft, earthy, sometimes gamey old-world taste profile is the antithesis of the modern moment. The emergence of Priorat, where wines are now made in a more concentrated "international" style, has turned into the wine world's new hope for Spain, dismissing Tempranillo's supple past for an apocalyptically inky future.

Whether or not you care about our rabid-gramps rant, you'll love the chance that Rioja Tapas will afford you to explore the Spanish wine world—in both its old and new incarnations—and to do it in an evocative, romantic atmosphere, with warm, low lighting, live Spanish guitar, and a stream of well-executed, comforting, classic tapas (piquillo peppers stuffed with codfish, house-made chorizo, careful sautéed octopus with garlic and paprika, richly flavored blood sausage) and enjoyable paella. Out of the way and underappreciated, Rioja is quietly one of the best places in the city for a date, or just a bottle of wine that will take you back to the very oldest of the old world. –RG

Ruchi's Taquería

D
Total pleasure grade

During the day a civilized restaurant; after hours drunks and frat boys

1.9 *Food* **7.3** *Feel* **$16** *Price* **Tex-Mex**

Casual restaurant
Daily 24 hours.
Breakfast.Live music.
Outdoor dining. Additional locations.

Montrose
5201 Richmond Ave.
(713) 621-3088
Upper Kirby
2651 Richmond Ave.
(713) 520-6523

Bar Full
Credit Cards Visa and MC
Reservations Not accepted
Upper Kirby
3102 S. Shepherd Dr.
(713) 524-6993

A restaurant with two faces, Ruchi's Taquería has the Jekyll-and-Hyde syndrome of being a perfectly normal taquería by day and a madhouse by night. We sometimes find solitude in organized chaos, and so we endorse this party with open arms—but we won't be eating. The food is dismal after the midnight hour, which isn't so surprising; drunken patrons aren't hard to please. With multiple locations around Houston, Ruchi's has been one of the pioneers in introducing the taquería to soccer moms and college students. They've got all the Tex-Mex favorites, of course, as well as traditional dishes like pozole, menudo, and carne asada. In good taquería fashion, they are open 24 hours a day, and at any one of those hours you'll find customers from all walks of life, all of them sharing in the common experience of terrible food.

Service is generally in Spanish; it's quite friendly, as if they know the stuff coming out of their kitchen is embarrassingly bad. A meal here is doomed from square one. Chips and salsa are gross and unexciting, ensuring that you won't spoil your appetite for the even worse food to come. Pickled vegetables of carrots, garlic, and jalapeños, however, try their very hardest to help out. Appetizers look pretty ordinary, including queso, guacamole, and such; but instead, jump to the caldos if you're seeking at least normal enjoyment. Pozole tastes like simple chicken base, but caldo de res and caldo de pollo are better, and actually almost authentic.

As a last resort, we've tried the parrillada, figuring that *something* on the platter would be decent. Yet we found nothing even passable in any element of this terrifying smörgåsbord of abused meats: shrimp were rubbery and devoid of seasoning; we have no clue what happened to the quail, but we felt sorry for the little guys; and beef was nearly impossible to chew. Things calm down a bit as the night winds down; if you've had a really long night, or are just an early riser, try catching Ruchi's for breakfast. It's served from 6am until 10am, and we find the huevos rancheros particularly okay. But when the lights go out and the freaks come out, the kitchen absolutely falls apart. –SD

Rudi Lechner's

Smashing Wiener schnitzel and themed kitsch at Houston's best German restaurant

B
Total pleasure grade

7.2 *Food* **8.4** *Feel* **$31** *Price* **German**

Casual restaurant
Mon.-Sat. 11am-10pm; closed Sun.
Delivery. WiFi.

Southwest Houston
2503 S. Gessner St.
(713) 782-1180
www.rudilechners.com

Bar Full
Credit Cards Visa, MC, AmEx
Reservations Accepted

Rudi Lechner's is the best German restaurant in town. It's also one of the only German restaurants in town. Who would have thought that after 30 years in diet-obsessed America, Rudi would still be in business? Better yet, his place is often packed, and at lunch, he might even seat you himself—a touch you don't see much of in the age of Landrys and Cordúas, Pappas and Goodes.

The décor will induce a flashback to the time your aunt took you to Epcot and left you in "Germany" while they went for sushi in "Japan": The waitstaff wears the closest thing to lederhosen you've probably seen since the Würst Fest, and the restaurant is adorned with three decades of Bavarian décor, imported beer empties, and enough animal heads to make any Texan feel at home. But more importantly, Rudi's place has some of the best Wiener schnitzel around. Hot and crispy, straight from the fryer, and served with a mound of homemade sauerkraut, it is a thing of beauty, made even more beautiful by a Spaten. Throw in polish sausage, roasted pork loin, red cabbage, and mounds of Austrian potatoes, and you've got a steal of a 12-dollar lunch sampler that's plenty for two. Good, too, are the braised pork shank and goulash, although much of the food is underseasoned. Many specials include a trip to the salad bar, which might transport you to Wendy's. Unless you are deluded enough to think the salad might miraculously make your meal healthy, steer clear.

Rudi's has many regulars, and many have been coming for a long, long time. If you prefer to hang out with the under-80 set, grab a table in the bar area, and dig into the extensive beer list, one of the best in Houston—sip a Warsteiner or go the wine route with an Austrian Grüner Veltliner, a deliciously crisp, spicy white. Oktoberfest brings live entertainment to Rudi's four nights a week. Service is attentive, and waiters are well versed about the menu. They're frank and honest about what's good and what's bad. Luckily, the former list is long and the latter one short. –SN

Rudyard's British Pub

Tight Levi's, dirty Converses, and cheap Lone Stars—do you fit in yet?

B *Total pleasure grade*

7.6 *Food* **7.6** *Feel* **$18** *Price* **American**

Bar
Sun.-Thurs. 5pm-midnight;
Fri.-Sat. 5pm-1am.
Date-friendly. Live music. Outdoor dining. WiFi.

Montrose
2010 Waugh Dr.
(713) 521-0521
www.rudyards.com

Bar Full
Credit Cards Visa, MC, AmEx
Reservations Not accepted

This two-story bar, on Waugh between Richmond and Westheimer, is where the hipsters and alternative-lifestylers hang out. It's a close-knit group, but outsiders are always welcome—as long as they're tolerant and pay for their beers. Many come for the extraordinary hours: this is one of the only places in town that serves food 'till midnight, even serving until 1am on weekends. It's typical bar food, but it's not bad, and it's unlikely not to meet your expectations. Specials on food and drink are in effect every night, and when scheduled, there's a band playing upstairs. Dartboards in the back are always fun; it's hard not to like throwing mini-javelins with sharp points.

The atmosphere is dark but not too dingy; some of the smoky appeal has been sapped by the new cigarette laws, but at least it means you won't have to remember Rudyard's until the next time you do laundry. The burgers are typical but completely serviceable: bun, augmented patty, lettuce, tomato, and pickle. Prices are slightly high, but they include the best tater tots in town. That's not to say that Rudyard's has hired a secret tater-tot molecular gastronomist, straight from a sous-chef gig with Ferran Adrià, stashing him in the back, where he works 'till midnight, reconstituting the potatoes as tater-tot caviar foam. No, nothing this fancy, but they're executed well—crispy, brown, satisfying. Corn dogs with chili are another crowd favorite. We aren't big fans, though, of the fried calamari, fried mozzarella cheese sticks, or the steak-and-cheese sandwich, whose meat can come out too tough. Still, on the whole, don't knock the bar fare: as long they execute well, and don't put on any airs, then it's all good.

Sundays are good because of the $1.25 16-ounce Lone Star drafts and the one-dollar kamikaze shots. And if you're like us and fancy yourself funny, then they also have comedy workshops upstairs. Not to mention the best bathroom graffiti in town. Pants down. –SD

Rudy's Country Store

Melting brisket and turkey at Texas' best chain of barbecue gas stations

B *Total pleasure grade*

7.7 *Food* **6.1** *Feel* **$16** *Price* **Barbecue**

Counter service
Sun.-Thurs. 7am-10pm;
Fri.-Sat. 7am-10:30pm.
Breakfast. WiFi.

Spring
20806 IH-45 North
(281) 288-0916
www.rudysbbq.com

Bar Full
Credit Cards Visa, MC, AmEx
Reservations Not accepted

It sure doesn't look like a barbecue joint—never mind a barbecue chain. It doesn't even look like a "Country Store." Really, Rudy's just looks like a gas station complete with convenience store. And yet it is a growing barbecue-and-gas empire that has proliferated not only across Texas, but even into New Mexico. Rudy's had long been a small store in Leon Springs on the outskirts of San Antonio when its owners decided to start selling barbecue in 1989, and today they are trying to stake out a catering business on top of their in-store service. Barbecue breeds big appetites, we suppose.

Rudy's façades hardly seem corporate, though, with their rough-hewn logs, red paint, and bright yellow signs. Long tables, some picnic-style, others with folding chairs, remind us a bit of a church supper, and red-checked oilcloths lend a down-home feel. Other accoutrements include the requisite neon beer signs and trophy deer heads. Despite bold signs advertising "The Worst BBQ in Texas," long lines are a frequent thing at lunchtime, but service is still relatively fast, and often so in-your-face friendly that it can border on uncomfortable if you're an introvert. Barbecue is sold either by the pound or in a sandwich.

Breakfast consists of sausage wraps and barbecue-based breakfast tacos, and lunch continues the barbecue focus. Notwithstanding their claims to the contrary, Rudy's serves up some darn fine 'cue. We are especially impressed with the tender, moist smoked turkey breast, with flavor that doesn't overwhelm. Extra-moist, fatty brisket is also a tender, nicely seasoned choice, though it's better with a dash of Rudy's "sause," a tomato and vinegar concoction that is somewhat thicker than the Central Texas standard, but still within range (and is also available for sale—Rudy's ships worldwide).

Sausage is finely ground and peppery, with a jalapeño version that has a lot more fire. Sides are the usual assortment, but Rudy's does make a whole-kernel creamed corn that is, with its sweetness, a nice change of pace. –FC

Ruggles Café & Bakery

Barely adequate, hopelessly bland counter-service fare in a prime location

D *Total pleasure grade*

3.9 *Food* **3.3** *Feel* **$17** *Price* **Light American**

Casual restaurant
Sun.-Thurs. 10:30am-10pm;
Fri.-Sat. 10:30am-11pm.
Outdoor dining. Vegetarian-friendly.

Rice Area
2365 Rice Blvd.
(713) 963-8067
www.rugglesgrill.com

Bar BYO
Credit Cards Visa, MC, AmEx
Reservations Not accepted

A colorful chalkboard menu stretches from one edge of the dining room to the other, giving a folksy flavor to this lunch stop, which boasts an attached tent with outdoor tables. Instructions are scrawled across the board: Order here. Pay here. Pick up and leave your plastic meal-is-ready buzzer, in those sultry shades of dark red, here. The cafeteria system is probably a good call for Ruggles, because its customers (a largely female Rice lunch crowd) might be even more reluctant to fork up this much cash after they've tasted the mediocre results.

Most popular are boring salads and the glass-case-aged desserts. The "Ruggles salad," presumably the house specialty, is topped with grilled chicken that's bland as a gray Midwestern sky, then sweetened to death with the dreaded honey Dijon (possibly the worst salad-dressing recipe in the history of mankind). If you're even less adventurous, there's the inexplicably popular Trio salad, which consists of "white meat chicken salad" (neatly protecting you from any actual chicken flavor), tuna salad, fruit, and toasted pecans. If not for the saccharine poppyseed dressing, this might be served in a hospital bed.

The pork loin sandwich is better, warm and adequate, with a good, sweetish bun. Its thin, dry slices of pork don't have much flavor or fat to call their own, so they borrow some from "caramelized" onions (with no discernible brown tint—the term is thrown around loosely these days), melted mozzarella, chipotle mayonnaise, and a sweet, aggressive glaze. It's hard to make sweet-potato fries crispy, and Ruggles manages that, but they don't add enough salt just after frying, a problem that's too late to correct at the table. Desserts, meanwhile, sit air-drying under glass for hours—even, amazingly, the bread pudding.

The atmosphere doesn't inspire revelry, although we appreciate the BYO policy. But it's hard to justify these prices at a cafeteria: $8.95 for sandwiches, salads up to an audacious $13.95. Then there's the split-plate charge of $3—an insult anywhere, but absolutely unheard of at a restaurant without table service. Is this the first "Café-Bakery" in the world to charge its customers for sharing? –RG

Ruggles Grill

Everything that's wrong with upscale fusion, rolled into one

D
Total pleasure grade

4.0 *Food* **6.1** *Feel* **$61** *Price*

New American

Upmarket restaurant
Tues.-Thurs. 11am-2pm, 5pm-10pm; Fri. 11am-2pm, 5pm-11pm; Sat. 5pm-11pm; Sun. 10:30am-3pm, 5pm-10pm; closed Mon.
Brunch.

Montrose
903 Westheimer Rd.
(713) 524-3839
www.rugglesgrill.com

Galleria
5115 Galleria
(713) 963-8067

Bar Full
Credit Cards Visa, MC, AmEx
Reservations Accepted

Ruggles Grill sees the concepts of haphazard fusion, style without substance, and self-aggrandizement without culinary merit...and raises them. Articles from second-rate periodicals and thinly veiled paid advertisements are plastered all over the walls at the Westheimer branch, trumping up the merits of Ruggles. These are distinguished honors like the chef's contribution to a recipe that appears on the side of an Uncle Ben's rice box.

The "Ruggles Grill 5115" branch is located conveniently above Saks Fifth Avenue at the Galleria, and boasts one of Houston's best views, above all the concrete and construction. This location caters more to investment bankers and ladies who lunch, and tries to pull off a posh-private-diner's-club vibe, pianist and all. But only the bar succeeds. Otherwise, its food and service are even worse than they are at the Westheimer location.

Ruggles serves a sort of Southwestern version of Continental cuisine that also pulls from the Greatest Hits of the South. Crawfish, crabmeat, and shrimp make several appearances, seemingly just because they'll sell, even if their treatments are disastrous. A crab-and-fruit salad with balsamic vinaigrette at the 5115 branch, for instance, is a jarring mix of mismatched flavors topped with an off-putting sour vinaigrette. Marinara sauce is terrible, and there's nothing "traditional" (as it's described) about Coq au Vin served with penne pasta and grilled vegetables. We ordered it once, just to give it a chance, but it came out dry and actually cold in the center.

The blooper reel of a menu continues: sesame-encrusted tuna, on one visit to the Ruggles Grill branch, was obscured by a big pile of brittle onion strands that were difficult to eat, a pretentious intrusion on the plate with no purpose at all. A slab of dry grilled chicken crashes into a cloying orange-hazelnut sauce teamed with overcooked carrots, potatoes, and corn. And not to be petty, but we just found it funny when on one visit, four of the seven plates that hit the table were chipped.

Unfortunately for Ruggles, the three secrets to New American cuisine are not location, location, and location. –RG

Ruth's Chris Steakhouse

B+ *Total pleasure grade*

Why do chains have to serve the best steaks in town?

8.7 *Food* **7.9** *Feel* **$86** *Price* **Steakhouse**

Upmarket restaurant
Mon.-Thurs. 5pm-10pm;
Fri.-Sat. 5pm-10:30pm;
Sun. 4pm-9pm.
Live music.

Galleria
6213 Richmond Ave.
(713) 789-2333
www.ruthschris.com

Bar Full
Credit Cards Visa, MC, AmEx
Reservations Accepted

There's something very specific about the pleasures of a good steakhouse. You walk in knowing exactly what you want. A shrimp cocktail, perhaps, or an iceberg wedge with blue cheese dressing. An expensive steak, aged and buttery, with a big California Cabernet. It's self-indulgent capitalism, and for a long time, it was impossible to find at a chain. Enter Ruth's Chris, which got started in New Orleans in 1965, and in the years since, daringly challenged the notion that a chain restaurant had to be mediocre—and, in the process, added a nuance to the Great Chain Debate that simply could not be ignored.

The Houston branch is no exception, with a dark, clubby feeling and impeccable service. It's one of the only places in town where businesspeople can waltz in after 9pm on a weeknight and have a proper meal. And they pay for it: with appetizers in the high teens and mains into the $40s, this is one of the most expensive restaurants in Houston. But does anybody who comes here care?

Bread comes fresh and well heated. The chopped salad, touted as a classic, sports a little spill of fried onions on top that adds texture but steals thunder from the tasty blue cheese. Steak arrives as refreshingly rare as ordered, with a bewildering, peppery sizzle, and extra melted butter on request (do it!). Creamed spinach is like a dream, with the pepper and béchamel and spinach leaves all blending together into an irresistible pile of fatty goodness.

We wish, in the largest city in the great cattle-roaming state of Texas, that the best steaks in town were to be found at Houston-based restaurants, or at least Texas-based ones. Yet with the exception of Vic & Anthony's—and even they have a branch in Vegas—much of the good steak in town is found at local outposts of chains that got started elsewhere: New York, Rhode Island, Illinois. At least Louisiana is nearer by. –RG

Saffron

Hearty Moroccan fare and belly dancers that can get a bit pricey (the fare, not the dancers)

Total pleasure grade

8.4 *Food* | **8.7** *Feel* | **$55** *Price* | **Moroccan**

Casual restaurant
Tues.-Thurs. 5pm-10pm;
Fri.-Sat. 5pm-11pm;
closed Sun.-Mon.
Date-friendly. Live music.
Outdoor dining. Vegetarian-friendly.

Upper Kirby
2006 Lexington St.
(713) 522-3562
www.saffronmoroccancuisine.com

Bar Full
Credit Cards Visa, MC, AmEx
Reservations Accepted

Your inner child may be a bit disappointed that you're not eating the Moroccan food at Saffron with your hands, sitting on the floor, as you're supposed to. But at least you'll get to sample a hearty, braised-meat-forward cuisine that's executed respectfully, served and explained well, and though it's a bit pricey, it represents a refreshing change of pace without the need to sacrifice a normal Texan diet of meats and starches.

Parking can be finicky off of Lexington, especially because you'll be fighting for space with the patrons of Saffron's more popular sister restaurant, Mia Bella, next door. But the biggest challenge is actually finding the place: squeezed off of a little patio, Saffron is guarded by a hefty-looking wooden door and marked only by a sign that's camouflaged by its surroundings. Through this door is an ornate dining room with tiled floors and tables; because of the acoustics, it hardly feels intimate, but the Medina-retreat feel, the Moroccan music, and belly dancing is hard not to like.

The staff's suggestions might take you through half the menu, but they are refreshingly patient and helpful, and their cuisine is easy to enjoy. To start, "Saffron Dip" with garbanzo and fava beans is smooth, salted correctly, and full of that unique saffron flavor. Also delicious is a classic sweet-savory chicken b'stilla, with chicken meat, almonds, and spices wrapped in crisp layers of phyllo and dusted with cinnamon and powdered sugar—it's the only good version we've had in town. Main courses are highlighted by the tagines—Moroccan stews cooked in pots with cone-shaped tops—that come with a sampling of different Moroccan breads. We've had an oxtail tagine that needed to be braised about an hour longer, but the deep, meaty flavor was unmistakably there, with the juices penetrating the garbanzo beans below. Lamb was highlighted beautifully, in another sweet-savory play, by dried apricots. It's likely to occur to you, as you bite into your well-seasoned meat and watch the belly dancer circling your table, that life is pretty good here.
–JY

Sage 400

A wannabe-posh sushi bar/lounge that serves good, modernized Japanese-American food

B+ *Total pleasure grade*

8.4 *Food* **8.2** *Feel* **$45** *Price* **Japanese**

Casual restaurant
Mon.-Thurs. 11am-10pm; Fri. 11am-midnight; Sat. noon-midnight; Sun. noon-10pm.
Date-friendly.

Galleria
2800 Sage Rd.
(713) 961-9566
www.sage400.com

Bar Full
Credit Cards Visa, MC, AmEx
Reservations Accepted

Houston sushi restaurants get confused as to what they want to be: a club or a restaurant. What normally results is bland and tasteless food, generally consumed with large amounts of alcohol. Sage 400 seems, at first, to fit the bill. At first. But once you give the place a chance, even given the club vibe—the ultra-dim lighting, the late-night lounge, and the on-again-off-again service—the restaurant still shines with well-executed, modern food.

From the floors to the ceiling, Sage 400 works its vibe to try to create a sleek, sexy feel. Everything is either dark or shiny. The lighting makes you feel as if you're in a concert hall—you might need an usher with a flashlight to find the restroom. Every piece of furniture has such an unnatural glow that it looks like a can of Pine-sol was taken to it. However, it's not the shine, but rather the atrocious pattern lining the back of every booth and banquette in the restaurant, that really makes the atmosphere feel lame. Think throwback, coach-class, Southwest-Airlines-jet upholstery.

Food, however, is a refreshing version of Japanese-American. Appetizers sing beautifully, as in a hamachi carpaccio with paper-thin slices of yellowtail and jalapeño that bring together clean flavors of sweet and spicy. The agedashi tofu is fantastic, served piping hot from the fryer with shavings of bonito on top, and a bit of sweet-salty tentsuyu (dashi-based) broth on the bottom. Amongst so-so specialty rolls, the "Triple Delight" roll is the most interesting, with tuna, salmon, and hamachi wrapped in cucumber, not seaweed, and served in pool of ponzu sauce and with a liberal sprinkling of togarashi (a ubiquitous Japanese spice). The other thing that seems to suffer is tempura, of which every piece—whether in the rolls or on the plate—comes out at less than room temperature and tasteless. Aside from this, in a land where high-trend, low-grade sushi restaurants rule, Sage 400 is a refreshing touch. –JY

Sake Lounge

Stick to the alcohol—not the food—at this happy-hour favorite

D *Total pleasure grade*

3.0 *Food* **5.2** *Feel* **$40** *Price* **Japanese**

Casual restaurant
Sun.-Wed. 11am-10pm; Thurs. 11am-11pm; Fri. 11am-midnight; Sat. noon-midnight.
Outdoor dining.

Downtown
550 Texas Ave.
(713) 228-7253
www.sakelounge.com

Bar Full
Credit Cards Visa, MC, AmEx
Reservations Not accepted

It shouldn't surprise you that a place named Sake Lounge wouldn't take its food seriously. Generally speaking, this Bayou Place resident is a pit stop for downtown workers careening between their lives of ties and sport jackets and their lives of designer jeans and short black skirts, used as a pre-party (a more gently named happy hour) to build a happy buzz and to live on the edge by eating borderline sushi.

Sake Lounge's atmosphere does justice to the name: you expect, and you get, low lighting that renders any sort of design superfluous. Rings of "Bottoms up!"…"Kampai!"…or "Salud!" fit with the bar-like attitude; and you should expect the staff to shoot glares if your order doesn't include alcohol. Although Sake Lounge's location is prime for pre- and post-theater dining, we can't imagine that many a gussied-up theaterista would fancy eating poorly made sushi in a spot where she can hardly see her date. (That is, unless she secretly hates the theater and wants to get loaded so as to become the belligerent drunk that gets kicked out for Tourette's-style play-acting in the middle of a soliloquy.)

Sushi at Sake Lounge is tailored to its drink program. Translation: the food is so poorly made that you'd rather spend your money on a cocktail. The menu is made up of all the usual suspects with rolls, Americanized Japanese food, and sushi, but all are fairly futile. Rolls have a tendency to fall apart before they ever reach your mouth; a California roll crumbles under the pressure of chopsticks. Picking up the pieces—fake crab, oxidized avocado, and cucumber—separately, you might prefer to dub it a "deconstructed" California roll. The last time we tried the lunch special, the tuna and salmon sushi tasted, in our opinion, of plasticky freezer burn. Fortunately, even a clueless bachelor can't screw up edamame, and neither does Sake Lounge, with the beans tender, toothsome, and judiciously salted. The same doesn't go for a leathery piece of ton-katsu (a panko-crusted pork cutlet), which, at our last visit, should have come with a samurai sword, because the provided knife literally wasn't cutting it. Neither is Sake Lounge. –JY

Sam's Boat

B-

Total pleasure grade

Two serviceable restaurants under one roof, but we miss the beauty contests

6.6 *Food* | 7.8 *Feel* | $15 *Price*

Tex-Mex, Seafood

Casual restaurant
Daily 11am-2am.
Live music. Outdoor dining.

Galleria
5720 Richmond Ave.
(713) 781-2628
www.samsboat.com

North Houston
7637 FM 1960 West
(281) 970-7267

Bar Full
Credit Cards Visa, MC, AmEx
Reservations Not accepted

Woodlands
26710 N. IH 45
(281) 681-2628

Taken together, the duo of Sam's Boat and Sam's Place make for a cash-box of an idea that's got money flowing in: beautiful people, even hotter bartenders, and two menus in different settings. Sam's Boat is the seafood concept, with fried favorites like shrimp and catfish, plus Creole classics like gumbo and étouffée; Sam's Place is the Tex-Mex concept, with enchiladas, fajitas, and tacos. Yet both restaurants ultimately seem like an afterthought, because this is really one big bar, from beginning to end. Bands, hard bodies, and tons of Bud Light amuse a trendy, frisky crowd that is a mix of business professionals looking to score, and the youth of suburbia, all grown up and ready for a night on the town.

The big structure tries to look like a surfside shanty with lots of old exposed wood, a giant patio with big benches, and beer posters cluttered around the restaurant. Large-screen televisions are situated in strategic spots to broadcast the game, and neon beer signs will shine a little light on your experience. At Sam's Boat, shrimp brochettes with cheese, jalapeños, and bacon are grilled and served pleasantly hot. The quality of Sam's raw oysters varies, and you should instead try them poached in garlic butter; it's usually a delicious preparation. Stop by during crawfish season for some of the freshest and spiciest mud bugs in town. Stay away from the crab legs, though; they've been boiled to death. There's also an array of grilled proteins like tilapia, mahi-mahi, and snapper.

Sam's offers south-of-the-border fare such as enchiladas with chicken or beef, though the enchilada sauce is pretty lame and bland. Tortilla chips are crispy, salty, and warm. Fajitas are delicious: the beef is deeply marinated for a really nice flavor that will make you wonder if you're still eating in a bar.

Sam's used to have a beauty contest about once a month, and that's when all the goombas would come out in full force, and bands would try their best to sound like top-40. But no longer. We mourn. What's still surprising is that Sam's Boat is actually pretty good—and much cheaper than some of the overpriced seafood restaurants in the city. –SD

Sam's Deli Diner

Greasy burgers that are worth the waistline

A- *Total pleasure grade*

9.0 *Food* **7.2** *Feel* **$9** *Price*

Light American

Counter service
Daily 7am-9pm.
Breakfast. Kid-friendly.

West Houston
11637 Katy Fwy.
(281) 497-8088

Bar Full
Credit Cards Visa, MC, AmEx
Reservations Not accepted

Seems like Sam couldn't decide whether he wanted his shop to be a deli or a diner. Or neither, for that matter: by our estimation, this place doesn't have anything to do with a deli, and it doesn't serve anywhere close to diner food. But that's beside the point. The point is that Sam and his deli diner serve up some of Houston's very best burgers. The food is un-PC: it's unapologetically greasy, and it has probably busted hundreds of diets over the years. But to the masses who try to not tip the scales while eating a burger: if you're going to eat a burger, why don't you eat a *real* burger? And by that, we mean: why don't you eat a burger at Sam's Deli Diner?

The walls, which are painted with the mascots of the neighboring high schools, say a lot about Sam's: the food is so good that you'll even see Memorial and Stratford High School students—sworn enemies—rubbing elbows; facing the glorious, downmarket kitchen; and enjoying themselves equally. This is an atmosphere deeply evocative of the heart-to-heart, family-to-customer restaurants that are more common up in Philadelphia, Chicago, and New York, but scarce here in Houston.

Burgers here are in-your-face and stuff-your-face. Bite in, and the juices come running out, yet the bun is well structured enough to keep their contents secure. We don't believe there to be any light options at Sam's; a bacon-mushroom-swiss burger, which is good evidence for that theory, comes with a stack of bacon, a handful of mushrooms, and several slices of melted cheese. Meaty, crispy, and savory...double your calories, and double your fun. The jalapeño burger is also uniformly juicy, if not for the light of stomach. Crispy, carefully cooked fries and onion rings aren't extraordinary, but they're a perfectly good accompaniment to your burgers. If there were a Sam's in every neighborhood, the world would be a better—if hardly healthier—place. –JY

Sambuca

C-

Total pleasure grade

Jazz, happy hour, and food as an afterthought of an afterthought

4.4 *Food* 8.5 *Feel* $55 *Price*

New American

Upmarket restaurant
Mon.-Sat. 4pm-midnight;
Sun. 5pm-11pm.
Live music. Outdoor dining.

Downtown
909 Texas Ave.
(713) 224-5299
www.sambucarestaurant.com

Bar Full
Credit Cards Visa, MC, AmEx
Reservations Accepted

In an otherwise difficult location, Sambuca keeps the crowds steady with its hipper-than-thou attitude and atmosphere; its steady stream of live music performances; and its captive audience of Rice Lofts residents. Sounds like a good business plan to us.

People come here to see and be seen, to do some listening, and to get in some drinking; the eating just kinda ends up happening a lot of the time, before you know it. And it shows. Sambuca is deeply in touch with the lowest-common-denominator level of execution they can get away with these days, and they're totally happy toeing that line. Especially when they've got live music every night of the week, happy hour every weekday, and half-price bottles every Sunday.

So your accidental foray into Sambuca's kitchen usually ends in disappointment. So what? You knew what you were getting yourself into. The menu reads like an ill-conceived mess from the start: Atlantic salmon with gorgonzola cream sauce and jasmine rice. Lobster-and-shrimp-filled enchiladas with a poblano cream sauce. Lamb chops with a Dijon pistachio crust and "Pinot Noir mashed potatoes." Bourbon sweet potatoes are spiked with molasses. Mac and cheese makes a haute appearance with chèvre and proscuitto. All this from a kitchen that can't even execute on a hamburger.

The interior is trashy-sleek, with exposed brick walls; leopard-print chairs; awful, awful carpeting that reminds us of a cheap motel from the '50s; and annoying, overdone French posters (think Le Chat Noir) everywhere. An outdoor patio and balcony out on the street, however, get you away from the garish décor; it's nice to sip a martini and watch the city go by from here (even if it's more vehicular than pedestrian traffic). There's certainly no reason not to dress up a bit and check out Sambuca for the drinks and music. Now, test your own will power, and see if you can fight the good fight to extricate yourself from the captive-audience, had-a-few-drinks munchies and resist the urge to let another bad, overpriced dinner at Sambuca just kinda happen...again.
–AH

San Dong Noodle House

An old Chinatown standby moves up in digs...and curiously down in quality

B- Total pleasure grade

7.6 Food | **5.9** Feel | **$9** Price

Chinese

Counter service
Tues.-Sun. 11am-9pm; closed Mon.
Kid-friendly.

Chinatown
9938 Bellaire Blvd.
(713) 271-3945

Bar None
Credit Cards No credit cards
Reservations Not accepted

When San Dong Noodle House used to be Santong Snacks—a literal hole-in-the-wall in the DiHo Shopping complex off of Bellaire—it was one of the best-kept secrets in foodie circles around town. In the cramped, elbow-to-elbow setting, they served soul-warming beef-noodle soups, endlessly soft steamed pork buns, and the undisputedly best pan-fried pork dumplings in town. When Santong closed to move up in the world—or, well, down the street to a new shopping center—the buzz was high. Now you could get great noodles and dumplings without being sketched out by the self-serve water or having to press your butt against that of a complete stranger.

After the dreary digs of the former Santong Snacks, San Dong's bright and shiny new spot came as a breath of fresh air. The dust and rust has been replaced by a generally clean dining area with simple tables and chairs, and children's drawings on the wall. We feel bad complaining, because the owners deserve their success. For years, they made do with a small space that produced great food. Now they have a great space, presumably turn a larger profit, and probably enjoy life more, but the food is a mere skeleton of what it used to be, and it no longer belongs in the upper echelon of Houston dining.

Good for them, perhaps, but bad for us.

This execution makes you yearn hopelessly for days past. The pan-seared pork dumplings now almost always lack those crispy seared bottoms that make dumplings so good; instead, they're soggy and sloppy to eat. The broth in the beef noodle soup was once beefy, dense, and subtly perfumed with anise flavor, but now the liquid always seems watered down.

One thing that hasn't changed, however, is the pan-fried pork with rice. The flattened, panko-coated piece of pork might be dubbed an Asian version of chicken-fried steak; it's served with a tangy pickled cabbage that's a good change of pace from the norm. But even if all of this is perfectly enjoyable, what we really want is the old Santong back. –JY

Santos

Your classic get-'em-in-and-get-'em-out place with overpriced food and bad service

4.6 Food | **4.8** Feel | **$38** Price | **Tex-Mex**

Casual restaurant
Mon. 11am-9pm; Tues.-Thurs. 11am-10pm; Fri.-Sat. 11am-11pm; Sun. 2pm-9pm.
Kid-friendly.

Westchase
10001 Westheimer Rd.
(713) 952-9909
www.santosmexico.com

Bar Full
Credit Cards Visa, MC, AmEx
Reservations Not accepted

This is the type of restaurant that has been feeding confused suburbia for years. Santos trumps itself up as a "taste of Mexico." Not so much. This is a bad excuse for a Mexican restaurant that matches ridiculous prices with flavors that can't back up the dollar signs. You can put low-quality lobster tails on your plates, but that doesn't mean that they're going to taste good. And if you can't get the basics right, then you shouldn't try to improvise. Santos' menu is populated with overpriced dishes like fajitas, chicken breast specials, and enchiladas that are, at their best, all right.

It looks like a cookie-cutter restaurant that appeals to families looking for a post-soccer-practice meal, and that's more or less accurate: these Tex-Mex dishes, by now, are almost as American as apple pie. The menu will bowl you over with the same old, same old, over-hyped fare that leaves you dissatisfied and wondering if this is as good as it gets. (And you know it's not.)

Enchiladas are nothing special, with choices like enchiladas verdes or enchiladas de queso stuffed with cheese that tastes like it was produced in a lab instead of on a farm; there's not enough flavor here to spark any sort of emotion. The simplest of simple dishes, such as tacos al carbón (just tortillas and beef), fail to pass the test and have an asking price that's way too high. A chile relleno, though, benefits from the flavor added by the nuts and raisins in the stuffing. Santos goes off the deep end with its Mesquite Grill section of the menu that is humorously overpriced. The "Big Santos" is a protein explosion of chicken, beef, quail, shrimp, yada, yada, yada.... at press time, it came at a price that approached $60. For that you could get some really decent food. –SD

Sasaki

Disarmingly authentic sushi—for Japanese people, by Japanese people

$51 *Price* **Japanese**

Casual restaurant
Mon.-Fri. 11:30am-2pm, 6pm-11pm; Sat. 6pm-11pm; closed Sun.

Galleria
8979 Westheimer Rd.
(713) 266-5768

Bar Wine and beer only
Credit Cards Visa, MC, AmEx
Reservations Accepted

Most Japanese restaurants in Houston, like most Japanese restaurants in all of America, are run by Chinese people. Or Koreans. Or Taiwanese. Or Vietnamese. Or Mexicans...in short, by people who come from almost anywhere other than Japan. Not that there's anything wrong with that. The United States just happens to be full of immigrants from all those other countries. Japanese? Not so much. Especially not east of California.

As such, a real, old-school restaurant with a real, old-school Japanese chef—and a Japanese staff, too, in this case—is a rare prize. If not for the random strip-mall location way out near Westheimer and Fondren—a no-man's-land of a neighborhood, next to an auto body—we'd be there all the time. The atmosphere is pretty no-man's-landish too: lots of wood, but little else. The space is narrow, and its few tiny tables are minimalist, but not in the annoying modern way. It just is exactly what it is: a sushi bar.

Sasaki is well known in some circles for its fatty, creamy, sweet-salty unagi (eel) with rice—and it's no joke. But we come here for all the sushi, and obviously, what's fresh varies day to day. There are "omakase" sushi and sashimi options on the regular menu, which, depending on the day, might include glorious fatty tuna, yellowtail, or uni (sea urchin). But that's not the real omakase. The real omakase isn't the one on the menu; it's the one where you sidle up to the sushi bar, and simply let the sushi chef know that you're in his hands, and that you eat anything and everything.

All that said, don't just think of Sasaki as a sushi bar. Japanese businessmen come in for the grilled fish here, too—so why shouldn't you? Try authentic, hard-to-find nimono (simmered Japanese vegetables), curried udon noodles, yakko (cold tofu with various garnishes), or delicious, house-made ramen noodles—served in a broth with pork, fish cake, and egg. They're honest renderings that will transport you to another place—and not just away from a Westheimer strip mall, but across the Pacific. –RG

Seoul Garden

Houston's most beloved and overrated Korean restaurant

8.5 Feel | $28 Price | **Korean**

Casual restaurant
Daily 11am-11pm.
Date-friendly.

Spring Branch
9446 Long Point Rd.
(713) 935-9696

Bar Full
Credit Cards Visa, MC, AmEx
Reservations Accepted

So many Houstonians' first venture into the vast complexity of Korean cuisine has come at Seoul Garden. Whether or not it was ever the best Korean restaurant in town, it was certainly the most recognized—for many years. But just like American Pinot Noir (or, if you prefer, just like Gwen Stefani), as it got more popular, the quality took a nosedive. Service became spotty, and the food took a noticeable dip downward.

It's not hard to see how Seoul Garden became so popular. The décor is distinctly Asian without the stink of cheesiness that many competitors have—unless you declare a faux bridge, a pond, and a working waterwheel to be cheesy. (We happily don't.) The problem is that Seoul Garden has never bothered to hire a host, and getting a table still means grabbing a waitress that's scurrying by. Service normally follows suit for the rest of the night; it's endlessly frustrating and quite often hard to bear.

If Korean food had a movie-character doppelgänger, you might be inclined to choose Nick Naylor from *Thank You for Smoking*, in which he proclaims that he has a "bachelor's in kicking ass and taking names." That is to say, the food is big, bad, and bold. At least, that's how the food once was at Seoul Garden. Nowadays, you might have to go with Tom Cruise in *The Last Samurai*, because you just can't take it seriously.

The fact that the portions of Korean barbecue have seemed to reduce in size over the last several years is only half the problem; we're more disturbed by the quality. The normally mouthwatering pop of the kalbi and bulgogi has faded. The questionable addition of a sushi bar is rendered laughable by off-tasting cuts of fish. Seoul Garden's saving grace is their prepared foods: seafood Jun-gol comes off like a bouillabaisse that's been, uh, kicked up a notch with aggressive Korean spice and heartiness. Another good bet is the seafood pancake; it's delightfully crispy on the outside, and oceanically savory on the inside. Other dishes, however, are in desperate need of amphetamines; unless and until Seoul Garden recaptures its former glory, we can't recommend it anymore. –FC

Shade

We're proud members of this relaxing, nonexclusive neighborhood club

7.0 Food | **9.7** Feel | **$49** Price

New American

A- Total pleasure grade

Upmarket restaurant
Mon.-Thurs. 11am-2:30pm, 5pm-10pm; Fri. 11am-2:30pm, 5pm-10:30pm; Sat. 10am-3pm, 5pm-10:30pm; Sun. 10am-3pm, 5pm-9pm. *Brunch. Date-friendly. Outdoor dining. Wine-friendly. WiFi.*

Heights
250 W. 19th St.
(713) 863-7500
www.shadeheights.com

Bar Full
Credit Cards Visa, MC, AmEx
Reservations Accepted

We love the Heights, and we love Shade, a neighborhood restaurant that vibes off its low-key local clientele. The space is endowed with an effortless sense of calm, from cool, ambient lamps and a well-conceived layout to a short, simple menu. The smooth, chilled-out bar isn't bad for a cocktail even if you're not in for dinner, and a row of outdoor tables in an alleyway is fun, too. It's hardly a romantic garden, but rather a pleasant place to plop down on a mild evening.

If you want to drink wine (the list is well-priced and well-chosen), you'll first need to join Shade's "private club," an amusing way of getting around the dry-neighborhood restrictions. There's no membership fee, needless to say, and you don't exactly need any letters of recommendation to be inducted for life. The understated, unstuffy staff will explain this to you with a straight face; this classy group represents everything Shade is about.

We do wish the menu were a bit more focused; it's outdated in its vision of fusion, jumping from mild versions of Latin, East Asian, and South Asian cuisines without warning, with varying degrees of success. Soups, which change daily, are a crapshoot; we've had a disastrous gazpacho, like a tasteless, chunky tomato soup—why do Americans so rarely blend gazpacho, like the Spanish always do?—but a cream of mushroom soup that's much better. Chicken enchiladas come in a too-hot-to-touch baking dish, like old-school Italian-American lasagna, and are overwhelmingly heavy, with oodles of singed cheddar and monterrey jack.

The best thing we've tasted here has been an excellent wasabi-and-cucumber-crusted red snapper, notable for the tenderness of the fish filet; it's well harmonized with crunchy bean sprouts and a red curry broth with coconut milk. A curry-crusted duck leg called "confit" tastes more fried than preserved, without the expected softness of the meat, and while we like its coconut chutney and herbed rice pilaf, the accompanying "saag paneer" comes off more like sautéed spinach unconnected to its cheese cubes. Taken as a whole, the dish feels disjointed. Uneven though Shade's kitchen might be, nothing will stop us from returning frequently to bask in this delightful neighborhood vibe. It's like hypnosis. –RG

Shanghai Restaurant

A Cantonese gem tucked into Houston's crowded Chinatown scene

A- *Total pleasure grade*

8.9 *Food* **5.8** *Feel* **$12** *Price* **Chinese**

Casual restaurant
Sun.-Thurs. 11am-midnight;
Fri.-Sat. 11am-1am.
Kid-friendly. Vegetarian-friendly.

Chinatown
9116 Bellaire Blvd.
(713) 988-7288

Bar None
Credit Cards Visa and MC
Reservations Accepted

If restaurants were rock-'n'-rollers, Shanghai Restaurant would be that artist that ripped up the underground scene, but never made it when it hit mainstream—and so came back to the Indy scene with a vengeance, throwing down harder than ever.

And we like it that way. Its owners have been in the restaurant industry for more than 20 years, dating to the time when they had a small, family-run joint and moved up to the ill-fated space above DiHo Supermarket as Fu Kee. After a larger restaurant didn't work out, they made their return as Co Po Lo, a small house on Bellaire near Fondren, bringing back the careful, family-run restaurant that made them so popular in the first place. After finally settling into the Welcome Supermarket center as Shanghai Restaurant, they now consistently serve the best, most down-to-earth Cantonese cuisine in the city. (Amusingly, it's not the least bit Shanghainese—they just didn't bother to change the name when they took over the lease.)

Just as you'd expect from a solid, simple Cantonese restaurant in Hong Kong, this place's décor isn't much, but it makes do. There's not much interior to speak of, and more often than not, you'll have your order taken by the owner, your water poured by her son, and her daughter will wave to you as you walk out the door.

While Chinese-American lunch isn't a bad idea—with good deals for filling dishes like cashew chicken—the less American-inspired dinner menus are much better. (They're better still if you come with Chinese company.) Meals often begin with complimentary, intensely flavored broths that are brought to your table like a Cantonese amuse-bouche. The salt fish and chicken fried rice is an expert balancing act between aromatics and saltiness, with the salt of the fish playing off green onions and savory, wok-breathed goodness.. But the clear-cut all-star here is salt-and-pepper pork ribs, wherein the crunch of the outer crust unlocks a meaty elegance of balanced seasoning.

Shanghai Restaurant was built small, humble, and hard-working, and it appears that it will remain so into the future. And all of Houston is better off for its efforts. –JY

Shawarma King

Fast food prices and food at least fit for petty royalty

B- *Total pleasure grade*

7.5 *Food* **6.6** *Feel* **$8** *Price*

Middle Eastern

Counter service
Sun.-Thurs. 11am-10pm;
Fri.-Sat. noon-11pm.
Outdoor dining. Vegetarian-friendly.

Galleria
3121 Hillcroft St.
(713) 784-8882
www.shawarmakingonline.com

Bar None
Credit Cards Visa and MC
Reservations Not accepted

Shawarma King has the right formula; they've figured out that if you serve good food and don't price-gouge people, then your restaurant will stay busy, and you'll develop a loyal following. Sure enough, you can easily get out of "The King" for less than six dollars, and, believe it or not, quality is not sacrificed. Of course, shawarma is the staple here, but they also serve kebabs, kofte (spiced meatballs), dolmeh, falafel, and much, much more.

The shawarma is like a Middle Eastern burrito: spiced beef, chicken, or lamb, along with tomato, lettuce, and a creamy yogurt sauce is wrapped in thin pita to make the shawarma a light, healthy alternative to its starch-ridden cousin south of the border. Shawarma King tends to use spice with a heavy hand; it doesn't overpower the meat, but instead it pleasantly blends into its surroundings. Kebabs are spiced especially aggressively, but they're enjoyable, and the heavy seasoning really makes sense in this cuisine. Choose from fluffy saffron rice or a cold vegetable salad as a side.

Have no fear, vegetarians: Shawarma King, like most Middle Eastern restaurants, has a wonderful selection of meatless items. The falafel is one of the best in town. Little chickpea fritters are fried to ideal crispiness, and the option is yours to make it a plate or wrap it up in a sandwich (we recommend the latter, for both price and taste reasons). Douse them with plenty of acidic yogurt sauce; it will give the earthy falafel that nice brightness it needs. The wait for your food may take a few minutes, but don't worry about it. The employees are very nice and hospitable.

Since Middle Eastern food is so inherently healthy, it has been adopted by hippies and yuppies alike. For that reason, there are also a lot of impostor restaurants serving watered-down healthy Middle-Eastern-ish food that's nothing like the real thing. At Shawarma King, however, the proof is in the clientele: much of the Middle Eastern community in Houston frequents this place. –SD

Shiva

Nothing surprising at this cheap, veggie-happy Village Indian—except the pink fetish

6.6 Food | 6.9 Feel | $27 Price | **Indian**

Casual restaurant
Mon.-Thurs. 11:30am-2:30pm, 6pm-10pm; Fri. 11:30am-2:30pm, 6pm-11pm; Sat.noon-3pm, 6pm-11pm; Sun. noon-3pm, 6pm-10pm. *Delivery. Outdoor dining. Vegetarian-friendly. WiFi.*

Rice Area
2514 Times Blvd.
(713) 523-4753
www.shivarestaurant.com

Bar Wine and beer only
Credit Cards Visa, MC, AmEx
Reservations Accepted

Rice Village is not a culinary groundbreaker of a neighborhood, and Shiva is not a culinary groundbreaker of an Indian restaurant, whether in menu or conception. Its décor, though, is more attractive than you might expect; the walls' and ceilings' unnatural shade of pink is amusing, at least, and the colorful ceiling scarves, unusual lamps, and proliferation of booths are welcome departures from the genre norm.

So is the unusual focus on vegetarian cuisine. More than half of the lunch buffet, and 24 dishes on the menu, are meat- and seafood-free. Don't overlook the well-executed raita, whose calming cucumber-yogurt effect works well against Shiva's peppery curries. Some of these are slightly out of the ordinary, as in a goat curry that showed up one day on the incredibly inexpensive, convenient daily lunch buffet. The goat wasn't stewed quite as long as we would have liked to bring it to the fall-off-the-bone state, but we were nonetheless happy to see it there.

Best among the vegetarian dishes are aloo gobi, with tender, well-seasoned cauliflower and a sauce that's peppery if not complex; and saag paneer, a version that's unusually creamy but not thick, and can come slightly undersalted, with big paneer cubes that have unfortunately little cheese flavor. Even less complex is a dal, which is slightly watery, and not well reduced; still, it's inoffensive, as is a mixed-vegetable curry whose ingredients are soft, mild, and light on flavor.

Amongst meats, tandoori chicken is above average, but barely so, with enough flavor and spice permeating through the meat to compensate for the dryness in certain bites; areas of meat nearest the bone are best. The one total failure we've had here was chicken dil pasand, a flavorless stew with chalky, bone-dry white meat. And in spite of the showy but fun tandoor display in the window at the back of the restaurant, naan isn't the greatest—it gets chewy very quickly. In the end, there's no compelling reason to go to Shiva, especially if you're a meat-eater. –RG

Silver Palace

Fulfilling a deep, misguided communal need: the Chinese Buffet

5.0 *Food* **4.6** *Feel* **$11** *Price* **Chinese**

Casual restaurant
Mon.-Fri. 11am-11pm;
Sat.-Sun. 11:30am-11pm.

Bellaire
4005 Bellaire Blvd.
(713) 661-1963
www.silverpalacebuffet.com

Bar None
Credit Cards Visa, MC, AmEx
Reservations Not accepted

Chinese buffets play an important part in the community, by supplying people with mass-produced food that is usually made from poor ingredients, with even poorer execution; allowing customers to stuff their faces with as much food as one can consume in one sitting; and offering it at a price that, if you are talking about pure food consumption, or, price per pound, is really unbeatable. Silver Palace Chinese Buffet pulls off all of the above; it's not the type of place to go for a memorable dining experience. Instead, you go to fulfill a basic human need, which is eating to survive.

Walking into Silver Palace, you can imagine how a cow feels as he funnels through a narrow corridor in a single-file line. Surprisingly, nobody in line generally seems phased by the inferior quality of the food they're about to consume. The atmosphere is reminiscent of a hospital with a digital ticker sign over the buffet counting down to your eventual death—which will certainly come sooner if you eat a lot of this food. It's the normally unhealthy items that will leave you pleased and satisfied as they eat away at the walls of your arteries and plan a full fledged attack on your heart. A section of the buffet devoted solely to fried foods has fried chicken, fish, fries, and shrimp that will leave you incapacitated and useless. The regional Chinese cuisine here, however, is truly one of a kind; there is peppered beef that has the pleasant texture of shoe leather and tastes like ketchup, as well as lemon chicken, a favorite among suburban homes everywhere, with a soggy crust and a dry interior. Lo mein noodles, fried rice, stir fried green beans, and even tofu are there to satisfy the vegetarian in all of us, but it all tastes the same—like soy sauce.

Oh, and don't forget the soft-serve ice cream or the Jell-O that waits at the end of the buffet. Because that's how the Chinese do it, right?
–SD

Sinh Sinh

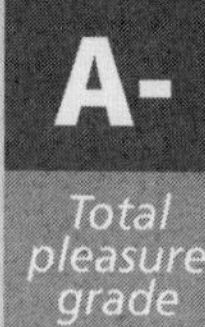

Total pleasure grade

Live seafood always impresses us—especially in the wee hours

8.6 Food | **6.2** Feel | **$36** Price

Chinese, Seafood

Casual restaurant
Daily 10am-2am.
Kid-friendly. Outdoor dining. WiFi.

Chinatown
9788 Bellaire Blvd.
(713) 541-0888

Bar Wine and beer only
Credit Cards Visa, MC, AmEx
Reservations Not accepted

On Bellaire Boulevard, where restaurants seem to change hands like trading cards and quality goes up and down like the stock market, Sinh Sinh has stood on relatively solid ground since its birth, maintaining its reputation for serving Houston's freshest seafood even through a change in ownership. They wear that badge like Paul Wall sports his grill: it's in your face and they're proud of it.

Sinh Sinh offers an everyman's Chinese-Vietnamese menu, but you should steer clear of it; the place really starts and ends with what's dwelling in its fish tanks. Don't let the briny smell deter you: it's the glorious byproduct of one tank full of huge geoduck clams, another full of Maine lobster, bait shrimp here, and live soft shell crabs there. Breathe it in, love it, and taste it all.

Sinh Sinh has always fancied itself cleaner and more up-to-date than your average Bellaire restaurant, and you can't argue with that premise, even if their bright, strange, weirdly modern décor has all the class of cheap, shoddy plastic surgery. Things get even more bizarre with the temperature-controlled wine-storage area amidst the scramble of tables and hanging roasted ducks. Château Margaux? Silver Oak? With *shellfish*?

Service is weird too, when it's not just plain rude or pushy; if you go down the path of live seafood—as you should—you'll be encouraged to spend your month's salary in one go. (Live seafood is pricey; king crab, for instance is $33.95 per pound. Always ask for a cost estimate when ordering.)

But Sinh Sinh's seafood tanks are the best in the city. Tilapia, which so often tastes like mud-dipped cardboard, seems to have its own sweet-fleshy flavor here when it's freshly dispatched and steamed with shreds of ginger and soy sauce. Sweet shrimp, flown in live from California, can come to your table after being drowned in alcohol to cook lightly in a broth—or served sashimi-style, leaving the complete focus on its sweet, toothsome flesh. It'll spoil you for ama ebi at any sushi place. For that matter, it might even spoil you for all other seafood. –JY

Skyline Bar & Grill

B-
Total pleasure grade

Overwhelmingly pricey, ambitious, and mostly successful food with Houston's best view

8.0 *Food* | **8.8** *Feel* | **$101** *Price* | **New American**

Upmarket restaurant
Daily 5:30pm-10pm.

Downtown
1600 Lamar St.
(713) 577-6139
www.hilton.com

Bar Full
Credit Cards Visa, MC, AmEx
Reservations Accepted

The most impressive view of downtown Houston, period, is from the Skyline Restaurant at the top of the Hilton. Scratch that: that's the second-best view of downtown Houston. The best view is from the Hilton's open-air roof deck, which is about fifty feet away, past a keycarded door that is accessible only to hotel employees and guests, or to those that discreetly follow them in.

There are several approaches to Skyline. One is to try your best to snag one of the few bar tables and relax with a $9 or $10 martini (not bad, considering) in the shadow of the night-lit skyscrapers; there are a couple of really choice seats right next to the window, where a couch and a couple of comfy chairs are set up, but those are really hard to nab.

The other approaches actually involve tasting the pricey, ostentatiously ambitious food, which exceeds Hilton-food expectations. You can just do apps, which will set you back something in the teens per person, which isn't bad given the portion sizes and view. "Grilled cheese crostini," for instance, are toasts topped with slightly melted halloumi cheese, which has an addictive squeak to its bite. Marinated tomato, lemon, and pine nut emulsion complete the nouvelle scene; it's a fairly attractive sweet-savory blend. Along the same lines is a tender veal cheek candied with burnt sugar and a poached pear; there really is something to the cheek-caramel contrast.

Or you can go full-out, in which case you'll get a fully dressed windowside table (and, later, likely a $100-plus-per-head check). Shoot-for-the-stars mains play even more off the sweet-savory trend. To wit: "Three little pigs," which is candy-apple-glazed tenderloin, sweet and sour eggplant, pulled pork shoulder, truffled mac and cheese (Houston's let's-fetishize-the-rural-poor trend of 2007), twice-cooked belly, and "black lentil ragout." It's complicated, it's expensive (though not as much as the $45 Prime New York strip), and it works—though it's likely to not be on the seasonal menu much longer. Less so: scallops and oxtails with "fingerling tostones," roasted salsify, and porcini "air." Leave the air to Grant Achatz, skip this dish, and take in the view. It's a good one. –RG

Smith & Wollensky

A chain steakhouse that performs competently—especially when it comes to butter and hours

B *Total pleasure grade*

8.1 *Food* **7.1** *Feel* **$91** *Price* **Steakhouse**

Upmarket restaurant
Daily 11am-2am.
Live music. Outdoor dining.

River Oaks
4007 Westheimer Rd.
(713) 621-7555
www.smithandwollensky.com

Bar Full
Credit Cards Visa, MC, AmEx
Reservations Recommended

As of 2007, this New York-based steakhouse chain had nine US branches, though none of the latest eight boast the nostalgic patina of the Midtown Manhattan branch, which dates to 1977. That one alone has the distinct air of an old, top-end steakhouse, but the entire chain generally delivers a decent to good dry-aged Prime steak at high cost and circumstance. The environment, you might say, is refined but hardly exclusive; some touches are amusing (vintage clocks and copper-shaded lamps), others more Disneyish (plaques bearing names of wealthy patrons above a sort of marble frieze). When it's empty, though, it really feels empty.

Even if the out-of-the-oven pan of bread that comes out in advance of your meal is a cheap trick, it's a good cheap trick. It's cooked in a bath of butter, rendering it more tart than bread, and it's intentionally slightly undercooked and doughy—a good call. Add in the delightfully soft tub of butter and dare to see how much fat you can possibly ingest in one bite of bread. The "Wollensky Salad" is less impressive, done with boring Romaine, aggressive slab bacon, mushrooms, and out-of-place potato cubes that get cold and gross in about four seconds. A nicely balanced Dijon vinaigrette lacks the acidic bite of a French vinaigrette, but, refreshingly, doesn't overemphasize the mustard.

The dry-aged Prime steaks are hard to argue with. These are well-marbled, well-prepared pieces of meat—even the filet mignon (which can so often be a disaster). On the plate, they're absolutely drowned in butter—another good cheap trick—and can (should, actually) be accompanied by a dreamily textured creamed spinach. The pricey wine list is strong in California cabs, and glasses often come from bottles that have been open too long—there's no excuse for this at a top steakhouse.

Desserts are marginally acceptable. Cheesecake is competent, though with a lower graham-cracker-crust-to-cream-cheese ratio than we favor. Whipped cream is a granular farce, and strawberries and blackberries are underripe and no fun. Houston should expect better dessert than this. Come for the steak, though, and it's hard to go too far wrong.

What really shocks us is the fact that they actually serve the full menu until 2am, seven days a week. There is certainly nowhere else in town to get a dry-aged steak at 1am, and for that, Smith & Wollensky deserves a hearty salute and an upgrade from a C+ to a B. –RG

Smokey's Bar-B-Q

Barbecue, po' boys, and phô?

6.5 *Food* **6.9** *Feel* **$9** *Price*

Barbecue, Seafood

Counter service
Mon.-Thurs. 11am-8pm;
Fri.-Sat. 11am-9pm.
Outdoor dining.

Medical Center
7820 Almeda Rd.
(713) 797-0887
Spring Branch
9101 Long Point Rd.
(713) 467-6655

Bar Full
Credit Cards Visa, MC, AmEx
Reservations Not accepted

Smokey's is a soulful place: nice people, good service, and good, honest food. They're not trying to set any trends or impress any heads of state; they just wanna fill your stomach and fill their pockets. This joint is a smokehouse first, fry house second. Oh, and phô shop third. They have smoked brisket, ribs, and chicken as well as fried shrimp, fish, oysters, phô, and the occasional banh mi. (Catch a glimpse of the Vietnamese owner, and it'll make sense.)

Smokey's is nicer than some of the similar counter-service shacks housing Houston's barbecue restaurants, though the atmosphere is a bit unnerving; it feels like a cross between an emergency room and a carpet store. The food will put you at ease, though; they have a fairly large menu that rarely changes. They're best known for the brisket, and it is definitely "Smokey," moist, and tender. The brisket is easy to bite through, as it's been smoked long enough to loosen the tough connective tissue, making it equally adept for a sandwich or on a plate. Ribs, prepared in the same style, deliver a slightly spicy flavor because of the sauce that's slathered on during cooking. That sauce is nicely balanced sweet and spicy, and it comes on the side with all smoked meats.

Fry 'er up. They do their fair share of frying at Smokey's, namely with the seafood side of the menu. Fried oysters are surprisingly delicious; fried 'till the cornmeal crust is just set, they are not the least bit overcooked and have a wonderful briny, salty flavor. They also have some of the best fried catfish in the city. Fried in the same coating as the oysters, the fish stays moist and flavorful.

Next to the restaurant is a sports bar that bears the same name. The restaurant closes early, at which point the sports bar becomes the place to be. A pool table, a couple of large screen televisions, and a full bar are there to satisfy your post-barbecue nightlife cravings. –SD

Sonoma Wine Bar

Late night quality rules for this industry-friendly wine bar

B *Total pleasure grade*

7.4 *Food* **8.8** *Feel* **$37** *Price*

New American

Wine bar
Mon.-Wed. 3pm-midnight;
Thurs.-Sat. 3pm-2am;
closed Sun. *Date-friendly. Live music. Wine-friendly.*

Upper Kirby
2720 Richmond Ave.
(713) 526-9463
www.sonomahouston.com

Bar Wine and beer only
Credit Cards Visa, MC, AmEx
Reservations Not accepted

Okay, so the staff may be a little frisky, and perhaps all too willing to engage you in an impromptu water gun fight; they may also have a problem with leaving bottles open too long, and the list doesn't exactly change all that frequently. But, Sonoma is open late, it has wine, the food is good, and the staff's enthusiasm is contagious. So on Saturday nights after twelve, when most sane people decide to turn in, Sonoma turns into a great spot for night owls and restaurant-industry slaves to take a load off, enjoy a half-priced glass of wine, lean back, and enjoy themselves.

As the name suggests, Sonoma is a lot less snooty than its other wine counterparts that seem to have the pomp and circumstance of Napa Valley. Sonoma doesn't seem like it has spent too much time or money on the décor; it feels more functional than fancy. Tables are dark and rigid, and cushy chairs are impractical, but the place feels comfortable, as if you're sitting in a friend's apartment. Fridays and Saturdays mean live music and quality time with staff that can relate to anyone and never forget a face. If you frequent this place more than a few times, then you'll always get a hug, pat on the back, and first dibs on bottles during Saturday happy hour.

The list at Sonoma is solid, though small and concentrated; there aren't any high-marked wines, but rather more sensible bottles that most people can afford. Wines by the glass have a tendency to stay open too long, and thus taste slightly of raisins, but they'll pour you a taste first, so if you care, you can weed out the losers. Food is simple but well prepared, with a good variety of different bruschettas, panini, and pizzas. The smoked duck pizza with roasted peppers and a glass of Pinot Noir is a great way to wind down a night, as is a plate of cheese and a bottle to share among friends. Any way around it, in fact, Sonoma feels like a good way to end a hard, wine-deprived day. –FC

Sorrento

Stuffy, overdressed, not-so-Italian fare that's no longer up Houston's alley

D *Total pleasure grade*

4.7 *Food* **5.0** *Feel* **$64** *Price*

Italian-American

Upmarket restaurant
Mon.-Sat. 11am-11pm;
Sun. 11am-10pm.
Brunch. Live music.

Montrose
415 Westheimer Rd.
(713) 527-0609
www.sorrentohouston.com

Bar Full
Credit Cards Visa, MC, AmEx
Reservations Accepted

With a confused menu, overdressed tables and waiters, and a cheesy piano player, this place starts off with a sputter, and never gets up to speed. The restaurant provides its diners with dim lights, nice linens, and all the other stereotypes that come with "fine dining". The menu reads like a who's who of washed-up culinary dishes: crab cakes, foie gras, lobster bisque, and escargot. These don't sound the least bit Italian, but worse, they all miss the mark. A tasting menu is available, and at $45 for five courses, it's a great price. But we can't say much else nice about it, and if you come in during the second half of dinner service, they might not even agree to do it.

Italian food is so bastardized in this town that it seems like it's all right to call yourself an Italian restaurant just for the image it evokes. Sorrento's "Italian-American 2.0" menu (see pages 6-7 for a full definition) has a few Italian items like polenta, carpaccio, and risotto, but they share the space with heavy demi sauces and caviar butter sauces. Houston's eternally overrated favorite, the jumbo lump crab, makes a dual appearance on the antipasti section of the menu. One is in the form of the ever-so-popular crab cake, with polenta and garlic cream; while the other is stuffed into mushrooms with different dipping sauces. The crab cake is actually pretty flavorful, although it's nothing special; but the polenta and garlic cream lacks pop, and the dish as a whole lacks texture and just doesn't make sense.

Properly fried calamari, on the other hand, are flawlessly executed. Crispy and tasty, this dish is almost always a top-seller in restaurants when done right. But the soups—lobster bisque and classic minestrone—lack vision, and the pastas are terrible. Lobster and arugula tortellini are hoplessly bad.

Mains are too involved with the wrong ingredients and pairings. Porcini-crusted snapper is overcooked and totally overpowered by its accompanying lobster risotto and caviar butter; there isn't that brightness there that seafood needs. Order the spaghetti and veal meatballs with fresh mozzarella; the waiters won't like you because of the light price tag, but it is one of your better options. All in all, though, this is only a step up in authenticity from the Olive Garden. –SD

SoVino

A gleaming new "southern hemisphere" wine bar in a prime location

B Total pleasure grade

7.9 Food **8.6** Feel **$44** Price

Upmarket snacks

Wine bar
Tues.-Wed. 5pm-midnight; Thurs.-Sat. 5pm-1am; Sun. 6pm-10pm; closed Mon.
Date-friendly. Wine-friendly.

Midtown
507 Westheimer Rd.
(713) 524-1000
www.sovinowines.com

Bar Wine and beer only
Credit Cards Visa and MC
Reservations Accepted

The name "SoVino" is meant to suggest the wines of the southern hemisphere; amidst the SoVino literature, you'll see descriptive terms like "wine and bubbles bar" and "global bistro." The menu is more European, and occasionally Pacific Rim, than it is southern hemisphere, though; there's good charcuterie, an excellent cheese selection (though ridiculously pricey—$14 for three cheeses at press time!), and quite a nice duck cognac pâté with spicy mustards and crunchy cornichons. Some fusion dishes, like yellowtail sashimi with Serrano chilies and citrus soy sauce and a house-cured salmon board, seem singularly ill suited for Southern Hemisphere wine pairing. On the other hand, maybe they've got a genius answer we're not thinking of.

The restaurant-wine bar opened just weeks before we went to press, so our review is based on less data than most. Our undercover chefs' sources indicate that SoVino's kitchen doesn't have gas ranges, a shocking choice for a kitchen that produces plates as ambitious as a $25 pan-seared breast of duck with a "Catena Malbec and blackberry reduction," sautéed new potatoes, and Brussels sprouts. On an electric stove?

Nonetheless, early indications are good: our scouts have enjoyed an arugula and baby lettuce salad with goat cheese, pistachios, and a vinaigrette with healthy acidity and good contrast. Beef tenderloin, like the duck, spotlights one particular wine in its preparation—in this case Los Vascos Cabernet from Chile—and it was fork-tender, although it took more than an hour to come out (early kinks, we hope). Bread has consisted thus far of an awful, stale baguette.

The feeling of SoVino balances the old-school (Persian rugs) and new-school Euro (a sleek, blond wood bar and recessed lighting). The wine list—presumably the main event—is heavily focused, as promised, on Australia, Chile, and Argentina, which means a strong preference for New World style: your Riedel glass will more than likely be filled with concentrated fruit, high alcohol, new oak, and low acidity (at least compared with most European wines). A few California wines, made in a similar style, squeeze their way in, too, as do a couple of token French and Italian bottles (perhaps for comparative purposes).

We'll refrain from weighing in on the New World style of winemaking (you can guess our bias), and state simply that we're happy to see a wine bar with a real regional focus. –TS

Spanish Flowers

Comfortable Tex-Mex, 24 hours a day—how often can you say that?

B *Total pleasure grade*

7.6	6.0	$18	**Tex-Mex**
Food	*Feel*	*Price*	

Casual restaurant
Daily 24 hours; except closed Tues. 10pm-Wed. 9am.
Breakfast.

Heights
4701 N. Main St.
(713) 869-1706
www.spanish-flowers.com

Bar Full
Credit Cards Visa, MC, AmEx
Reservations Not accepted

In the middle of the night, in the middle of a fairly harsh corner of the Heights defined by shabby streets, all-night motels, and cop cars on corners, sits Spanish Flowers. Family-oriented by day, night-owlish in the wee hours, this kitchen quietly turns out excellent versions of Tex-Mex standards, made all the more impressive by the hours. They don't coast along on their captive-audience advantage; instead, they see the need to pay attention to the little things to keep on top: homemade salsa with a kick, and homemade tortilla chips. Veggie soup included before your meal, and slices of fruit afterward. Unusually nice bathrooms for the caballeros and the damas.

Flour tortillas, which come straight off the press in the front room, are hot, rich, and moist, as good as any in town. You could make a decent meal just off of the tortillas and the well-seasoned rice and refried beans, and many kids do. Fajita beef is fatty and well-marinated; ribs, juicy shrimp, decent quail, and good sausage perform well, too. Service is simple and direct, but perfectly friendly.

The menu is strong in standard Tex-Mex as well as some Mex-Mex, like menudo (tripe soup). The chile relleno is moist and comforting, with the poblano pepper adding just enough bounce to keep each bite interesting. Caldo de res, a big bowl of veggie soup featuring a chunky beef shank-bone, is the kind of food sick people should eat if they want to get better, while the two-person parrillada mixta, a mixed-fajita special, is the kind of food that skinny couples should share if they want to fatten up. Downsides include enchiladas de mole, whose sauce is sweeter and less spicy than at other places in town, and carnitas that come out drier and tougher than they should.

Spanish Flowers' space is a pleasant faux-hacienda, with lots of stucco, tile, and interior walls decorated with colorful paintings and various Mexican knick-knacks, although it's hard to make an empty place look anything but depressing at 4am. When the weather is good, there's seating outside in the flowery patio. As would be appropriate. Not that there's anything Spanish about any of it. –RG

Spec's

A wine store to end all arguments, with delicious sandwiches too

Light American

Specialty grocery
Mon.-Sat. 10am-9pm; closed Sun.
Wine-friendly.

Downtown
2410 Smith St.
(713) 526-8787
www.specsonline.com

Bar None
Credit Cards Visa, MC, AmEx
Reservations Not accepted

Spec's is the 800-pound gorilla of Houston wine stores. There are 28 locations in Houston and the surrounding area alone, but the big ape of them all is the warehouse store on Smith Street, just south of downtown. The warehouse contains 80,000 square feet packed floor to ceiling with wine, liquor, specialty foods, and assorted connoisseurial knick-knacks. Stepping inside is like going on a wine vacation.

Spec's also has a deli and tables, so it is, at least at some level, also a restaurant. The pro's behind the counter exploit the kick-ass selection of cured meats to whip up meaty masterpieces like the "Grand Cru," a half-pound of roast beef with brie cheese and Dijon mustard on French bread, and the pâté de campagne sandwich on rye. Both are excellent. There are tables at the front of the store where you can eat, but most people take the food home to pair with their prized purchases.

The deli is perfectly fine, but it's really the most modest part of the operation; it's the imported food store connected to the deli that's perhaps the best of its kind in town: you'll find a spectacular assortment of cheeses, sausages, olive oils, imported candy, hot sauces, and dried mushrooms. The coffee and tea selections at Spec's are surpassed only by specialty coffee and tea shops. This is a one-stop playground for foodies.

Finally, the wine and booze. The selection is deep in every wine-producing region of the world, and the prices are shockingly low, usually at least 10% better than you'll find in any grocery store or small wine shop in the city. (There's a 5% discount if you pay in cash, and as such, there's also a well-used ATM machine on the premises.) Little notices from the staff advise you on the attributes of particular wines; the staff's recommendations are generally spot on. The international selection of vodkas, rums, whiskies, and liqueurs is comically large. What's remarkable is not just the breadth of it all, but also the propensity; these aren't just bulk wine buyers. At a recent visit, for instance, we came across (and bought) a bottle of 1970 Côteaux de Layon. It was a great vintage of a great botrytized dessert wine (made sweet by rot that affects the grapes) that would be difficult to find even in the underappreciated part of the Loire Valley where its grapes were grown. –RH

Spencer's

Free Paris, and jail the Hilton VPs of strategic restaurant planning

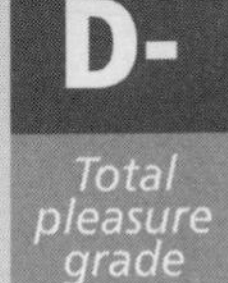

D-

Total pleasure grade

3.9 *Food* **3.4** *Feel* **$90** *Price*

Steakhouse

Upmarket restaurant
Mon.-Thurs. 11am-10pm; Fri. 11am-11pm; Sat. 5pm-11pm; Sun. 5pm-10pm.
Live music.

Downtown
1600 Lamar St.
(713) 577-8325
www.hilton.com

Bar Full
Credit Cards Visa, MC, AmEx
Reservations Accepted

In many cities, the concept of the hotel restaurant has lately transformed from a lowest-common-expense-account-denominator to a serious, modern resto-lounge that might even attract diners who aren't staying at the hotel. Hilton often appears to be the last hotel chain to have gotten this news. Spencer's is a prime example of what happens when a hotel takes advantage of its captive audience by hiring an incompetent staff, throwing together an afterthought of a menu, and price-gouging any hotel guest ignorant enough (or sufficiently bound by expense-reimbursement policy) to waste their money at the hotel instead of taxicabbing to one of the many excellent steakhouses nearby.

Spencer's is an object lesson in inept execution, from start to finish, beginning with the iceberg wedge, which is totally off: challengingly bitter, seemingly unseasoned lettuce—put to shame by a supermarket packaged salad—is stingily drizzled with tasteless dressing and a few crumbles of wimpy, mediocre blue cheese. But that's only the beginning. It boggles the mind that a steakhouse would fail to salt a $36 USDA Prime steak, yet that's what the "Spencer Steak" tasted like at our last visit: unseasoned aside from black pepper. Thankfully, it came out medium-rare as ordered, but even after a postmortem salt shower, not even its fattiest, beefiest ends were flavorful. Creamed spinach was better, but only marginally: instead of a silky béchamel, it revealed an aggressive Lipton's-onion-soup-mix flavor (even if no such seasoning packets were actually involved).

Spencer's problems don't end with the food. At our last visit, when our waiter tried but failed to uncork two half-bottles of Rioja in a row, he gave up and, instead of offering a substitute, directed us to the wines by the glass—and then poured us one that had been open for too long, turning its smell raisiny. (We didn't have the heart to send it back.) Needless to say, there was no concession on the check. Even the after-dinner coffee was undrinkable; we've had better gas-station Nescafé. At $80 or more per head after tax and tip, Spencer's is almost as much of an embarrassment to the Hilton chain as *One Night In Paris*. –RG

Star Pizza

This ultrapopular pizza joint's pies are just fair, in spite of its renown

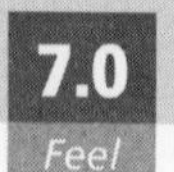

$14 *Price*

Pizza

Casual restaurant
Sun.-Thurs. 11am-10pm;
Fri.-Sat. 11am-11pm.

Delivery. Kid-friendly.
Outdoor dining. Vegetarian-friendly.

Washington
77 Harvard St.
(713) 869-1241
www.starpizza.net

Upper Kirby
2111 Norfolk St.
(713) 523-0800

Bar Wine and beer only
Credit Cards Visa, MC, AmEx
Reservations Not accepted

We don't get it. Star Pizza gets such consistently glowing reviews. From what you read, you'd expect such promise from these independent pizza-slingers, singlehandedly charged with the noble task of freeing the American-style pie from the shackles of the pizza triumvirate: Papa John's, Pizza Hut, and Domino's. Even if Star Pizza's pies beat out the chains, you can't help but wonder—after a slice or two—what all the hype is about. This pizza is definitely good, and definitely not memorable. In the end, it's just a place where you can enjoy a beer and an evening with friends, with the pizza playing the role of a mere placeholder.

Star Pizza certainly looks like it should be a pizza joint. There's a fridge of cold beer, TVs on the wall, dim lights, and graffiti etched into the tables, walls, and booths. If you ever feel like randomly dialing phone numbers "for a good time," Star Pizza is your place. Service is grungy and sometimes flippant, but what's a slice of pie without a little attitude, anyway? We suggest starting with one of their huge salads; the giant dinner salad has piles of fresh, though unremarkable vegetables. The garlic bread would take about five minutes to make at home, and other appetizers are scarcely more memorable.

The specialty pizzas seem like randomly thrown together combinations of ingredients. Unfortunately, just because you put every vegetable you have on a pizza doesn't make a vegetarian pizza good—it weighs down the pizza and makes its crust soggy. Pick your own toppings, rather than relying on the ill advice of Star's menu masters. New York-style pizzas' crusts are too dense, yet Chicago-style pies' aren't dense enough. Dolce Vita's more authentic pizzas beat these by a long shot; Star just puts you right in the middle of the road. But sometimes that's a perfectly okay place to be: how can you complain about decent pizza, cold beer, the game on the screen, and your buddies elbow to elbow? –JY

Star Snow Ice & Teriyaki

C+ *Total pleasure grade*

A tapioca drink king that dishes up the quick and easy

6.1 *Food* **7.4** *Feel* **$7** *Price* **Chinese**

Counter service
Sun.-Thurs. 10am-10pm;
Fri.-Sat. 10am-11pm.
Kid-friendly. Vegetarian-friendly.

Chinatown
9188 Bellaire Blvd.
(713) 988-8028

Bar None
Credit Cards No credit cards
Reservations Not accepted

While "quick" and "easy" aren't qualities that you would want to find in everything in life, quick-and-easy meals are up and coming, especially for the wide-eyed, bushy-tailed young'uns who have a hard time finding an affordable hangout. Star Snow Ice, the unquestioned leader of tapioca drinks, that Asian snack-drink standby, has dominated the Chinatown quick-and-easy market for the better part of the past decade, turning their Welcome Supermarket home into a hopping hangout. Star Snow Ice and Teriyaki applies this same principle to food service, and its simple kitchen rolls out unspectacular food at spectacularly low prices.

That said, Star is, was, and forever will be a drink-and-ice place first, pummeling slightly-too-sweet liquids with tapioca balls, dousing mountains of shaved ice with fresh fruits or sweet-savories like red beans, oatmeal, or taro root. Still, you can't go wrong with the plain milk tea with tapioca.

Star's décor is flashy without being gaudy. The bar's not set high on the food, but it's accessible. We're not sure exactly why "Teriyaki" is in the name—few dishes feature teriyaki, and the kitchen generally turns out homemade meals of rice and meat, often augmented by eggs. A more appropriate, if less marketable, name for the place might be "Star Snow Ice and Fried Egg." Meats come out on fajita-style sizzle platters, which are cute but detrimental: chicken and beef deteriorate as the meal goes on, because they continue to dry out as you eat. Even so, the food can almost always be saved by a spill of runny, messy egg yolk.

There's a crowded market for beef noodle soup in these parts, and Star's version is unfortunately not up to snuff, with under-braised beef served in a lukewarm broth that has neither strength nor personality. A pleasant revelation, however, is a dish of fried tofu with fried onions and jalapeños that's full of spice and aroma, a pleasant departure from the rest of the ho-hum menu. But even if the food isn't really anything to talk about, it's swift, reliable, cheap, and tapioca-happy. –JY

Stir-It-Up Coffee House

B

Total pleasure grade

MySpace's handiwork from back in the day

7.0 *Food* **8.1** *Feel* **$13** *Price*

Light American

Café
Mon.-Fri. 7am-7pm;
Sat. 9am-6pm; closed Sun.
Breakfast. Vegetarian-friendly. WiFi.

Midtown
2117 Chenevert St.
(713) 655-7847
www.stir-it-up-coffee.com

Bar None
Credit Cards Visa, MC, AmEx
Reservations Not accepted

Stir it Up Coffee House is doing its best seductive hair toss and giving its best "come hither" look, trying to pull in all the scenesters. A coffee house in Midtown, Stir it Up offers quality fair-trade certified coffee as well as a few reasonably priced breakfast and lunch selections that are not unusual, but satisfying. Most importantly, it's a small local joint that has tons of soul.

Located within walking distance of Houston Community College, Stir It Up has managed to secure itself a good customer base through location alone. Inside, it's got that relaxed, laid-back island feel. You'll be overcome with a soothing feeling when you hear those phat reggae beats echoing through the restaurant. Reggae and Jamaica are clearly the themes here with coffee names like "Marley Frappe," "Irie Frappe," and the restaurant is named for a Marley song. (In fact, we can't help ourselves; we always want to say 'steer' it up, as Bob Marley did himself.) Tables and chairs are the coolest set in Houston. Curved at the edges, the chairs look like a part of the table because they fit perfectly. Go see for yourself, and while you're at it, connect with your Southern roots and try a hot, steaming bowl of grits for breakfast. A bit of honey and butter, and it hits the spot. Daily specials like chicken or pork tamales and breakfast tacos will satisfy your cravings.

One of the best things on the menu is the spiced-up Jamaican patty with your choice of chicken, vegetable, or (best) beef; they are hot and very flavorful. Stir it Up only sticks to fair-trade coffee, giving small farmers business that they wouldn't otherwise have in the global market that's dominated by huge producers. The coffee itself is delicious—bold, nutty, and aggressive. A cup of this and free Wi-Fi, and you won't be going anywhere for a while. And when you do, you'll be feeling irie, even after you leave. –SD

Strip House

No real strippers, no good steak—just a careless chain kitchen and a budget-busting bill

Steakhouse

Upmarket restaurant
Mon.-Thurs. 11am-2pm, 5pm-11pm; Fri. 11am-2pm, 5pm-midnight; Sat. 5pm-midnight; Sun. 5pm-10pm.

Downtown
1200 McKinney St.
(713) 659-6000
www.theglaziergroup.com

Bar Full
Credit Cards Visa, MC, AmEx
Reservations Recommended

Unfortunately for the Strip House, the secret to great steak is not naked ladies. Not that they're not amusing: old-school, bordello-style black-and-white images of reclining nudes adorn every inch of aesthetic space, from the walls to the bathrooms to the cloth napkins. Even the matchbooks are decorated with female bodies at this exorbitantly expensive branch of the New York City institution.

The Strip House's lacquered-up den of red banquettes, dim lights, and old-school porn stays open until 11pm on weekends—refreshing in a town that tends to shut down all too early. Sit down, and you'll be greeted with well-orchestrated, if slightly stuffy, service. Now, open the menu and take a deep breath, because even if you've come ready to spend, the prices will induce Shock and Awe. $49 for the cheapest bottle of red wine on the menu? $51 for a 20-ounce New York strip? Few main courses in the United States break the $50 mark with anything other than lobster, caviar, or a dish intended for two. Even at Peter Luger, America's best steakhouse, steaks are less than $50. The Strip House's prices are just preposterously opportunistic.

Especially given the fact that the steak's not even that great. The meat is well marbled, but lacks the transportative, funky richness of what we'd expect from Prime beef. What's worse, we've had a rare steak come medium and a medium-rare steak come medium-plus (if you want medium-rare, ask for "extra rare"). Lack of attention to cooking times is inexcusable for a $100-a-head steakhouse, and it doesn't happen at most others in town. Hit-or-miss sides are ridiculously overpriced: "truffled" creamed spinach has a nice texture, but its truffle is undetectable and its price a brazen $11. Same goes for a little $11 tower of "goose-fat potatoes," which are nicely crusted but suffer from a dry and mealy interior. With prices this out of control, the food should be better, the kitchen should be more careful, and the nudes should be live. As things stand, the joke's on you, because the only thing really stripping is your wallet. –RG

Sushi Jin

Promising, sometimes special sushi with some growing to do

B Total pleasure grade

8.3 Food **7.2** Feel **$44** Price

Japanese

Casual restaurant
Mon.-Fri. 11am-2:30pm, 5:30pm-10pm; Sat.-Sun. noon-10pm.

West Houston
14670 Memorial Dr.
(281) 493-2932

Bar Full
Credit Cards Visa, MC, AmEx
Reservations Accepted

Sushi Jin is far more serious than most sushi restaurants in town. If you're willing to sit at the sushi bar, you can actually engage in a real dialogue with the really-Japanese sushi chef—unusual in Houston, but in our opinion, the way it should be done. Chef knows what's freshest, and maybe he'll even try out something new on you. (Being a guinea pig can be a lot of fun.) Rave reviews in the media have thrust Sushi Jin into a spotlight that we feel it's not quite ready for yet. The attention has led foodies to flock here, raising expectations another notch. And Sushi Jin, with humility and quiet determination, had done its best to handle it all. They maintain a nice vibe—not the least bit of pomposity or arrogance—that reminds you of a precocious child balancing growing pains with fame.

On a recent visit, after we reassured the sushi chef we had no food allergies or prejudices, he sent us out a plate of nigiri that was, in part, a study in the fattinesses of different cuts of tuna. Tuna, fattier tuna, and belly tuna, in that order, are meant to increase in richness, and that they did. But, the belly tuna, which should have simply melted in our mouths, was the biggest letdown. It was sinewy, its stringiness making it logistically difficult to chew. Yellowtail was unexciting, with a creeping fishiness. Uni (sea urchin) seared with a blowtorch atop a raw scallop, however, was mind-blowing; the uni's softness played off the smooth, sweet scallop, and the two dissolved into one. The specialty of the house, we were told, is a roll of pure textural pleasure, if only one-dimensional flavor. Cream cheese, avocado, and salmon form a rich base, that, with crunchy tempura flakes and popping roe, turns into a muddled mish-mash of flavors. But it's a mish-mash that you want to keep eating and eating.

We'd like to see Sushi Jin make it through its awkward, prematurely prominent adolescence. There's potential here, and with a bit of patience (and quality control), we can see this turning into one of Houston's sushi spots. –AH

Sushi King

Hardly the king of raw fish, but the nigiri's good and the uni rocks

C
Total pleasure grade

7.5	7.7	$39
Food	*Feel*	*Price*

Japanese

Casual restaurant
Sun.-Thurs. 11:30am-11pm;
Fri.-Sat. 11:30am-midnight.
Live music.

Upper Kirby
3401 Kirby Dr.
(713) 528-8998
www.sushiking.us

Bar Full
Credit Cards Visa, MC, AmEx
Reservations Accepted

In a town where too many sushi bars favor style over substance, Sushi King is no different, letting its food take a back seat to the shim-sham, modern vibe. Sushi King, however, can't get away with it so easily, as it doesn't quite have the trendy location or beautiful clientele that would justify (or at least explain) the attitude. Thus, the results are laughable; in the world of velvet-rope saketini service, Sushi King is like the nerdy kid wearing fake designer jeans.

In a part of the Upper Kirby district sandwiched between the posh neighborhoods of West U and River Oaks, Sushi King's art-deco-meets-anime exterior looks blatantly out of place in a ruddy shopping center, next to a crumbling old Office Max. Management clearly harbors some desire to appeal to the young and the restless, but they wind up settling for the old and the oil-moneyed. An out-of-place pianist bangs out songs in a dining room whose design is sleek but lacking in soul. The coldness is literal, too; unfortunately, eating sushi in a snow jacket is cumbersome—but at least you know your raw food never reaches the temperature danger zone.

If the good nigiri and sashimi at Sushi King were served in a smaller, non-descript spot, then the place might well be a gem, but with the high price tag and constant threat of hypothermia, the sushi loses much of its appeal. Salmon is normally the hooker of the sushi world, providing cheap pleasure to the first-timers, but these clean cuts are robust, oily, and unusually complex. Thin slices of snapper, garnished with grated ginger and sour ponzu, sing with brightness. Best of all, though, are the plump wads of uni (sea urchin) in all its fatty, briny glory. Specialty rolls are often overwrought with ingredients, like the "Lover Roll" that forges an incestuous relationship between saltwater and freshwater eel that can't be saved even with conciliatory brushings of eel sauce and fancy designs on the plate. Hot food needs the most help, though, like a leathery fried soft-shell crab, or salmon teriyaki that's cooked until it no longer resembles fish. Leave it raw, and you'll be a lot happier—as long as you bundle up. –JY

Swirll Italian Yogurt

Where the frozen yogurt is smooth and delicious, once you get through all the fine print

B-
Total pleasure grade

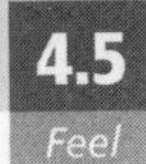
4.5
Feel

Sweets

Counter service
Sun.-Thurs. 11am-10pm;
Fri.-Sat. 11am-10:30pm.
Date-friendly. Kid-friendly. Outdoor dining. Vegetarian-friendly. WiFi.

Rice Area
2531 University Blvd.
(713) 526-7262
www.swirlberry.com

Bar None
Credit Cards Visa, MC, AmEx
Reservations Not accepted

Swirll is pretty much a rip off of the popular Pinkberry frozen yogurt chain that's taken Los Angeles and New York City by storm, with the same flavors, the same minimalist aesthetic, and the same obscenely marked-up prices. That said, this style of frozen yogurt is more yogurty, less sweet, and lighter than almost anything else on the market, and certainly healthier than ice cream. If you can dodge their sales schemes, get out of the place with your eardrums still intact after dealing with the Jones-Hall-like acoustics, and handle paying four bucks for a small cup of yogurt, then you might really enjoy yourself.

Located in Rice Village, Swirll harvests the university's lack of a cheap, casual, non-alcoholic date spot nearby, though in so doing, they seem to have spent nearly zero on the décor. We understand minimalism, but this is ridiculous. The only installations are high-flying track-lights and sleek, blonde, wood-stained chairs, both of which look like they're from an IKEA showroom. Plus, the place has the acoustics of one of those empty, pre-designed suburban houses in Sugar Land; you probably won't be able to leave the place without unwillingly eavesdropping on several conversations.

Just like Pinkberry, Swirll offers two options—plain or green tea—although a flavor of the week is normally available (mango is exceptionally delicious). Nuance in flavor comes from the toppings, which they charge for. If you order a medium or large-sized cup, watch out if they ask you what three toppings you would like, because they'll charge you for all of them, while you have the option to get less. On its own, the green tea version is light, creamy, and full of that unmistakable wheaty, fragrant,floral, Japanese flavor. Plain yogurt needs some sprucing up, though the fruits are often out of season. So in addition to jumping through the hoops of Swirll's options, you'll also have to memorize your seasonal fruits. But if you're up for a challenge, the results can be absolutely delicious. –JY

Sylvia's Enchilada Kitchen

A mainstay for enchiladas; just don't order anything else

C *Total pleasure grade*

4.6 *Food* **4.9** *Feel* **$18** *Price* **Tex-Mex**

Casual restaurant
Mon.-Thurs. 11am-9pm; Fri. 11am-10pm; Sat. 8am-10pm; Sun. 8am-3pm.
Breakfast.

West Houston
12637 Westheimer Rd.
(281) 679-8300
www.sylviasenchiladakitchen.com

Bar Full
Credit Cards Visa, MC, AmEx
Reservations Not accepted

When your restaurant is named after a certain dish, you must bring the goods. Given the fact that enchiladas are a staple in the Tex-Mex community, Sylvia must be quite confident in her skill set. Indeed, she does bring the goods when it comes to enchiladas—but the rest of her menu is a minefield.

There are seemingly endless permutations of enchiladas, with many mathematical possibilities arising from the interchangeable ingredients: different sauces, sides, and spices, from basic cheese, beef, and chicken, to the spinach and vegetarian varieties, as well as mole and shrimp. But while Sylvia's kitchen has menu size taken care of, her kitchen does seem a bit overstretched.

Sylvia's is a mainstay in the Houston Tex-Mex community. The atmosphere is clean and calm, with lots of blue and white colored tiles, that transport you at least some of the way to a little restaurant in Mexico. Sylvia's will be the first to admit that their food comes from the Rio Grande valley, and that it's full-on Tex-Mex, not authentic Mexican. Even Tex-Mex has no excuse, however, for bad chips and salsa, even though they're free; here, they show up a little too close to stale, and the salsa is watery.

Some enchiladas have quirky names like "Crystal City," "Lubbock," and "Refugio," and virtually all are likeable, if humble and uncreative. Sylvia's signature enchilada gravy is mellow, in classic Tex-Mex style, a good complement to the tortillas and melted cheese. The "Chihuahua" (similar to enchiladas rancheras) adds spicy ranchero sauce to chicken enchiladas, and tops them with jack cheese. Unfortunately, the outlook here beyond enchiladas is bleak, condemning her to a lower tier in Houston's Tex-Mex world. Combo platters are often just a hodge-podge of ingredients that don't come together well. Carne guisada and chiles rellenos are passable at best, and the shrimp cocktail is confusing.

Sylvia's would do well to only serve enchiladas, and in a broader sense, to focus on quality over quantity. In the end, even the enchiladas don't make the trip worthwhile unless you live nearby. –SD

Taco Cabana

Think Taco Bell rivals this purest of fast-food chains? Get real

5.8 *Food* **3.1** *Feel* **$8** *Price* **Tex-Mex**

Fast-food chain
Daily 24 hours.
Breakfast. Outdoor dining.
Additional locations.

Montrose
913 Westheimer Rd.
(713) 522-1299
www.tacocabana.com

Greenway Plaza
5 Greenway Plaza
(713) 621-2017

Bar Wine and beer only
Credit Cards Visa, MC, AmEx
Reservations Not accepted

Upper Kirby
3905 Kirby Dr.
(713) 528-6933

You gotta love "Taco C". Founded in 1978 a few hours west on I-10—in San Antone—this 24-hour fast-food Tex-Mex joint does a surprising number of things right. The ingredients are fresh and simple, the flavors spicy and limey, and there is a certain thing of beauty known as the salsa bar that seals the deal: this place kicks Taco Bell's a…ctually—let us put it this way: it takes that repugnant establishment's signature stuffed taco-gordita-fajita-crispy-chewy-cheesy-chalupa, and stuffs it up its bell.

This food is cheap, it's fast, and some of it is even good. We don't make any claims beyond that, but what more do you need? Certainly college students aren't looking for much more in the middle of the night, which is why they absolutely adore the place. Perhaps the most impressive thing about Taco Cabana is that tortillas are freshly pressed on-site at each restaurant, all day long. What's more, nothing is reconstituted or defrosted, and along with the variety of salsas (pico de gallo, mild, and en fuego), there are plenty of pickled jalapeños, fresh cilantro, and lime and lemon wedges on offer.

The best order of all—especially at the 3am hour, when Taco C reigns supreme and the line winds out the door—might be queso (it's a very respectable version, and the only respectable fast-food version) along with a bunch of those fresh tortillas. Otherwise, we particularly like the quesadillas, in their crispy tortillas, and the chicken fajitas (beef can be tough). Burritos are the old-school kind, but avoid the fast-foody ground-beef filling; and skip the enchiladas entirely. Best of all is the roasted chicken "flameante"—it has a spicy, tangy skin and juicy, smoky meat. With charro beans and fresh tortillas, that's some tasty fast food. Just stay away from the pupusas, recently introduced, which are strangely heavy, with crunchy, crumbly masa.

Taco Cabana's spaces are much better than the norm, generally clean and bright, with hand-painted Mexican tiles and metal tables made out of bent beer signs add that faux-old-Mexico touch. A fast-food joint that serves cold beer? Respect. –FC

Taco Milagro

Perennially popular counter-Mex with a lively patio and more culinary peaks than valleys

B Total pleasure grade

7.6 Food | **7.9** Feel | **$19** Price | **Tex-Mex**

Counter service
Sun.-Wed. 11am-10pm;
Thurs.-Sat. 11am-midnight.

Kid-friendly. Outdoor dining. Vegetarian-friendly.

Upper Kirby
2555 Kirby Dr.
(713) 522-1999
www.taco-milagro.com

North Houston
7877 Willow Chase Blvd.
(281) 664-7070

Woodlands
1701 Lake Robbins Dr.
(281) 602-7070

Bar Full
Credit Cards Visa, MC, AmEx
Reservations Not accepted

Another one of Houston's popular upmarket-counter-service restaurants, Taco Milagro adheres to the standard routine: place your order at the counter, get your buzzer, and wait. If the day is nice, grab a seat outside amid the hustle and bustle of dangerously full trays being brought to brightly colored tables and chairs, all of which are positioned around a fountain filled with coins, perhaps tossed there by patrons wishing there were table service.

Inside are some tables and a surprisingly long, dark, shiny wood bar purveying stronger-than-usual, not-too-sweet margaritas. Don't let this deter you, however; a pitcher is not too much for two thirsty people. There's a salsa bar with a range of offerings, from wonderfully tart and vinegary salsa negra to "Milagro" salsa, which has a strong smoky flavor. Try also the escabeche (pickled carrots and pretty purple onions).

Surprisingly, the burgers are even better than the tacos and burritos here, although each is way too much for one person. The poblano burger adds texture from bouncy rajas and subtle spiciness to well-seasoned beef. The chorizo burger—a meat patty stuffed with chorizo and layered with slices of melted cheese—is probably too much meat at once for anyone other than a shipwreck victim enjoying his first meal back on land. This meat market sits between two toasted, pleasantly sweet sesame buns that do an admirable job of standing up to it all. Burgers come with fries, which are not to be missed—they're delightfully salty and crisp without being brittle.

The rest of the Mexican menu is hit-or-miss. Pork barbacoa is disappointingly dry and underseasoned. Rice and beans are startlingly bland. Sweet-potato enchiladas, which come off as a concession to vegetarians, could quite possibly be starting a new trend: the dessert enchilada. Prettily presented but cloying, the enchiladas are bathed in a dark, well-conceived guajillo chile sauce, with a welcome dose of queso fresco, but the sweet potato within does too much justice to its name, dominating all else with saccharine starch. Vegetarians without a serious sweet tooth should stick to the bean-and-cheese burritos.

But it's the meat-eaters that will be really happy, because those burgers are flavor bombs. –RG

Tacos A Go-Go

B
Total pleasure grade

Bargain-basement breakfast tacos, and enough of an alternative vibe to transport you to Austin

7.8 *Food* | **8.7** *Feel* | **$10** *Price* | **Tex-Mex**

Counter service
Mon.-Thurs. 7am-10pm; Fri. 7am-2am; Sat. 9am-2am; Sun. 9am-3pm. *Breakfast.*
Outdoor dining. Vegetarian-friendly.

Midtown
3704 Main St.
(713) 807-8226
www.tacosagogo.com

Bar Beer only
Credit Cards Visa, MC, AmEx
Reservations Not accepted

This hip taco purveyor aims squarely at the Midtown metrotexmexual—and cleanly hits its mark. The alterna-hip aesthetic of Tacos A Go-Go is fully realized, have artwork and décor that balance old-school Orientalist Mexican fetishism with the indie-rockabilly feel of Austin, making the cutting-edge location—the little shop is nestled between latently upmarket grunge bars and live music venues, the Continental Club, The Mink, and the Big Top—feel all the more appropriate. There's even a record store next door.

If you get hungry at The Big Top, the neighboring bar, you can place your order, and then they will bring it to you at the bar. That's service with a smile—and good business sense. Cleverly, Tacos A Go-Go stays open 'till two in the morning on weekends, and cheap prices complete the fiery formula for success. The only confounding issue is the nonexistence of parking, which can spoil a meal at any hour of the day.

What's really sustaining Tacos A Go-Go's business, though, is the good food. They open at seven in the morning to catch all the blue- and white-collar workers on their way downtown, but even if you don't wake up that early—or don't have a job, for that matter—they serve breakfast tacos all day long. An egg taco with a choice of two items, like chorizo, black beans, or jalapeños, costs a whopping $1.59. And regular tacos with carne guisada, picadillo, or barbacoa all please even the pickiest of drunks or office workers. In a departure from our usual bias, however, we actually prefer the chicken al carbón—which retains its moistness even through a nice, smoky char—to the drier beef versions. Spinach-and-mushroom quesadillas and a Tex-Mex Frito pie are essentially afterthoughts, so stick with their core competencies—tasty tacos and rocking subculture—and you will be pleased. –FC

t'afia

A hip-but-serious, Texas-ingredients-first concept that we should all emulate—except in execution

A-
Total pleasure grade

7.8 *Food* | **9.7** *Feel* | **$65** *Price* | **New American**

Upmarket restaurant
Tues.-Thurs. 5:30pm-10pm;
Fri. 11:30am-1pm,
5:30pm-11pm; Sat. 5:30pm-11pm;
closed Sun.-Mon.
Date-friendly. Outdoor dining.

Midtown
3701 Travis St.
(713) 524-6922
www.tafia.com

Bar Full
Credit Cards Visa, MC, AmEx
Reservations Recommended

We love the t'afia concept with all our hearts. And we want nothing more than to love everything else about t'afia. The premise is fantastic; t'afia is the most fanatical of the few restaurants in the city that are truly, madly, deeply committed to local produce, to Texas meats, and even to Texas wines. Cocktails made with ratafia (wine infused with seasonal fruits, vegetables, and and/or herbs)—the restaurant's namesake—are often refreshingly tart, especially on a warm evening, and even the local wine list is well chosen.

Irreproachable, too, is the flowing Midtown space, an object lesson in resourceful postindustrial-chic-meets-IKEA design. The concept of free, tasty, all-you-can-eat snacks during happy hour—have a drink, and they're all yours—is glorious. T'afia's tasting menus are relentlessly probing, sensationally seasonal, fearlessly local, reasonably priced. At their best, the creations can materialize miracles in your mouth, like—at one visit—medjool dates stuffed with chorizo and wrapped in bacon, whose sweet and salty extremes balanced out to create something deeper yet gentler than any of its component parts.

And yet, beneath all the laudable shopping, the commitment to Texas ingredients, the creative minds behind the food and drinks and even the charcuterie, the execution in this kitchen is often careless, amateurish, and uneven. Seasoning is a particularly glaring flaw: in our many visits, we have frequently found dishes either terribly undersalted (kohlrabi and greens soup is one amongst many instances), or, less commonly, terribly oversalted (real ale-battered mushrooms in soy-ginger sauce is one amongst many instances). We have to wonder: are they tasting what they're sending out?

We have experienced similarly consistent problems with cooking times of meat. South Texas antelope cutlet, bacon-wrapped ranch beef filet, and harissa chicken are just three of the many meats that have come several notches overcooked, often dry and chewy to the point of flavorlessness. And this problem has not been unique to our experience—it's been confirmed by many of our contributing contacts.

It causes us almost physical pain to report this bad news, and we have little doubt that the problem is not Chef Monica Pope—it's her line that needs help. But a restaurant lives by its line, and as long as such spotty execution continues, t'afia will never quite live up to its spectacular, refreshing promise. –FC

Taft Street Coffee House

B- *Total pleasure grade*

Regulars linger over fair-trade coffee at this offbeat neighborhood coffee shop

6.5 *Food* **8.5** *Feel* **$7** *Price*

Light American

Café
Mon.-Fri. 8am-10pm;
Sat. 9am-10pm; Sun. 9am-8pm.
Outdoor dining. Vegetarian-friendly. WiFi.

Midtown
2115 Taft St.
(713) 522-3533

Bar None
Credit Cards Visa and MC
Reservations Not accepted

There are corporate coffee shops, and then there is the other end of the spectrum. Taft Street Coffee House is so far on the other end that we're not even sure they know they're a for-profit enterprise. It's probably the least likely place in town to kick you out after you're spent six hours mooching off of their free WiFi with your bottomless cup of Fair-trade coffee. The friendly servers come across more as volunteers than employees.

Taft Street Coffee House is built in an old church in a quietly residential part of Midtown. There is a little parking lot in back, but most people park on Taft Street itself. You walk inside a pleasant little courtyard (where you can take your coffee if you like) and then into the coffee house, where the polished concrete floor and exposed ceiling beams let you know that you're in Bohemian territory. The bookshelves are full of interesting reading choices—some literary, some Christian theology—in case you forgot your Mac or iPod. The couches and armchairs come in various manners of upholstery, and the tables come in various types and heights. The room next door runs art exhibits, and on the other side of that is a junk store with an extraordinary collection of used cowboy boots. (It's that kind of neighborhood.)

The organic, fair-trade house coffee is usually a well-balanced medium roast. They can make any of the coffee specialties vegan if you like. (It's that kind of coffee shop.) The "Taft Street Latte,"which is basically a vanilla latte, is a good choice if you like the sweet stuff. The "Soy Dirt," which contains Oreos, white chocolate, coffee, and soy milk, is a fun way to be bad and good at the same time. The baked goods they bring in are pretty much standard coffee shop fare, but with a vegan emphasis. The flaky rugelach go well with the sweet drinks. The best part about Taft Street is its real sense of community, its ability to convey a vibe that reflects the neighborhood around it: offbeat, creative, and buzzing on caffeine. –RH

Tampico Seafood

Mexican seafood in a delightfully Mexican setting

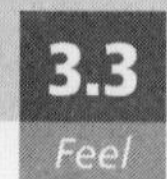

Mexican

Casual restaurant
Daily 10:30am-10pm.
Outdoor dining.

Heights
2115 Airline Dr.
(713) 862-8425
www.tampicoseafood.com

Bar Full
Credit Cards Visa, MC, AmEx
Reservations Accepted

We love Mexico, and thus, we love Tampico. This place immediately transports us there, from the saltine crackers that come with the mediocre, fruit-punchy, but enjoyable seafood cocktails to the ice-cold bottles of refreshing Sol. Generations gather at one table here, the kids entertaining each other, their parents catching up on life, the grandparents smiling proudly over it all. Yet very little is put into the aesthetic of the place; bright fluorescent lighting dominates, and the walls are dotted with random Mexican memorabilia—from soccer posters to wall calendars to beer advertisements. Christmas lights adorn the exterior, and as you walk in, you pass a glass case from which they're selling fish. Take it as a challenge; if you don't like your food, see if you can do a better job yourself. And if you do like it, let it inspire you to attempt the same at home.

Seafood, clearly, is the way to go here; camarones al ajillo—shrimp sautéed in lots of garlic and even more butter—are just as they should be. They're not cooked for a second too long, and the butter coats them in a deliciously fatty way, with the garlic working all its magic on your taste buds. Use the irresistible buttered-and-griddled bread that comes with it to sop up the remaining sauce. Whole fish, whether grilled or fried, is more of a letdown; its frying is just a bit too heavy-handed. On a last visit, this zapped the lovely texture right out of a snapper, leaving nothing but tough white flesh and hardened skin.

Perhaps one of the most interesting things about Tampico is its fried rice, which is Chinese all the way. Its origins baffle us, but it actually hits the spot. And it makes sense; the fried rice pairs nicely with fried fish. Everyone else seems to be quite happy scarfing it down, so why shouldn't you?

And do take a second to really appreciate the atmosphere; there's often a soccer game of sorts on the television, and you might notice the bulk of the restaurant riveted. Surely you can pick a team to support while you're waiting for your fish. –AH

Tan Tan

Total pleasure grade

The addictive doses of Chinese-Vietnamese fare and people watching go late into the night

7.9 Food | 5.7 Feel | $17 Price | **Chinese**

Casual restaurant
Sun.-Thurs. 10am-midnight;
Fri.-Sat. 10am-3am.
Kid-friendly.

Chinatown
6816 Ranchester Rd.
(713) 771-1268
www.tantanrestaurant.com

Bar Wine and beer only
Credit Cards Visa, MC, AmEx
Reservations Not accepted

It would be hard to imagine a more diverse mix of night owls with odder eating habits than your average set of covers at Tan Tan in the wee hours. For years, the place has been churning out equal parts traditional and Americanized Chinese-Vietnamese to a spectacularly varied crowd until two or three in the morning on weekends. On one night, you might spot a white-collar worker picking at a plate of fried chicken wings; a group of middle-aged Vietnamese couples back from a night of ballroom dancing, dressed up in their fanciest, laughing it up over a hot pot; and a Mexican family out for a late night dinner, bonding over noodles and fried rice—all of this at the same time in the same place. It's Houston at its absolute best.

And then there are the more bizarre quirks: for example, Tan Tan never seems to concede that it's not holiday season, and keeps Christmas lights eternally running all over the restaurant. Stuffed monkeys perched on top of fake palm trees complete the bewildering, but memorable, scene.

The menu takes a bit of maneuvering. Pass on the over-greased renditions of Asian-American food (kung pao chicken, beef with broccoli), and unless you're coming in after a night of tequila shots, you're likely to find something pretty good. Execution is not exactly stellar, but the food is hot and consistent, and the price is right. Some of the best choices are steaming hot bowls of noodles. Best among them, perhaps, is a Thai-tinged "satay beef soup" with flat noodles. It's not authentic anything, but the bowl of sweet-spicy broth is loaded with bean sprouts, chunks of beef, peanuts, mint, and lemons, making for vaguely exotic comfort food. Pan-fried rice cakes are even better, fused with eggs and liberally sprinkled with green onion, fried shallots, and fried radish; this is definitely one of the city's best late-night dishes.

Although the service is simultaneously pushy and non-existent—waiters try to take your order even before you crack your menu, then never show up again except to deliver your food and bill—it's hard to complain, because the crowd is like a free dinner show, with the admission ticket the mere cost of a delicious, reasonably-priced rice cake. –JY

Taquería Arandas

A vast empire that has introduced the gringo to the taquería

7.4 Food **5.9** Feel **$9** Price

Mexican

Casual restaurant
Sun.-Thurs. 6am-1am;
Fri.-Sat. 6am-4am.
Breakfast. Additional locations.

Medical Center
920 N. Shepherd Dr.
(713) 426-0804
www.taqueriasarandas.com

Bar Full
Credit Cards Visa, MC, AmEx
Reservations Not accepted

East Houston
5931 S. Gulf Fwy.
(713) 923-1433

Bellaire
5560 Gulfton St.
(713) 839-0090

The taquería in America is a wonderful concept; it's a restaurant that usually serves authentic Mexican food, with servers that don't generally speak English, and are often willing to stay open late and deal with the drunk and drug-crazed public. Taquería Arandas started as one small taquería, and they have since opened up in a number of cities throughout the years. They serve tacos, tortas, and sopes, and there's also a separate part of the menu for Tex-Mex. (That's right, contrary to popular belief, burritos and chimichangas are not authentic Mexican food.)

Different concepts are unique to each Taquería Arandas. Sometimes there is counter service, sometimes table service; and if Mexico is playing fútbol and you are wearing a USA jersey, then there's no service. In general, though, service is on time and friendly. Of course, chips and salsa show up upon your arrival. The salsa is average, but a squeeze bottle of avocado dip is delicious. Spicy, limey, and creamy, it's a nice change from watered-down, poorly-executed salsa.

There are two distinct reasons to go to a taquería. One is for the soups, like pozole and menudo; and two is for the meats like lengua (tongue), barbacoa (beef cheek, usually), and pierna (pork leg). A distinctive preparation that you'll find in most Taquería Arandas branches is the Jalisco-style goat soup. The mild flavor of baby goat penetrates an array of fresh aromatics that are stewed together and well integrated; it's great for hangovers. Tacos are an altogether different indulgence: small corn tortillas are loaded with a respectable amount of meat, cilantro, and onion, and that's all you need. Arandas has some of the best lengua in the city. A fatty muscle to begin with, the beef tongue is stewed in spice and vegetables so the fat and muscle can slowly break down for truly delicious results.

You're never far from a Taquería Arandas; with the offshoot Arandas bakery, they really are introducing gringos from around the state of Tejas to what comfort food is. Give them—and us—a couple more decades, and authentic tacos might well have taken their place in the feelgood-comfort-food league of burgers and pizza. –SD

Taquería Cancún

No bikinis and spring breakers here, just solid taquería fare

B Total pleasure grade

7.3 Food | **5.5** Feel | **$10** Price | **Tex-Mex**

Casual restaurant
Mon.-Fri. 6am-midnight;
Sat.-Sun. 6am-2am.

Breakfast. Additional locations.

Spring Branch
2227 N. Gessner Dr.
(713) 932-9566

Spring Branch
9957 Long Point Rd.
(713) 932-6533

Bar Wine and beer only
Credit Cards Visa and MC
Reservations Not accepted

Spring Branch
1725 Wirt Rd.
(713) 923-8800

If the name William Wong doesn't sound Hispanic, it's because, well, he isn't. It's hilariously Houston, and pretty impressive, the idea that a Chinese guy could create one of Houston's most dependable Tex-Mex standbys. How he did it is anyone's guess. What is apparent, though, is that the man knows the way to your drunken pocket, slowly but surely: his taquería delivers greasily delicious food with hypnotic consistency, turning you into a late-night regular before you even know what's happened.

There's something inherently comfortable about the grunge that is Taquería Cancún, with its half-filled bottles of hot sauce in beer packs and a customer base that's neatly split between those that shovel foods into their mouths and those that bury their heads in their forearms. It's the kind of place that makes you proud to be a degenerate, hanging out in a place that some could consider a dump, talking to people who probably only understand about five percent of the words coming out of your mouth. Contrary to the name, there is no MTV spring-break sparkle to the joint—unless you count the ballistic jukeboxes that are ready to blast off salsa or Latino music at any time.

Chips and salsa might be the most overlooked aspect of any taquería; they vary wildly, yet the variation is rarely discussed in the literature. Taquería Cancún's warm salsa with sides of onion and cilantro make you wonder why the huge Tex-Mex chains with mesquite grills and tricked-out tortilla machines can't produce something as good. As for the main-event food, it certainly isn't for the dieter. While that yella' cheese oozing out of an enchilada onto a schmear of smoky, porky refried beans isn't quite sublime, it's the epitome of Tex-Mex comfort. Cheese quesadillas are hand-held delights, with warm, stringy cheese, and the whole meal demands a Dr. Pepper and a few seconds to let your heart adapt to the amount of pork fat being mainlined. Menudo will disappoint you if you've had the authentic stuff, but Taquería Cancún isn't there for authentic regional Mex. It's there for the late nights, when it's got to be cheap, and it's got to be greasy. –JY

Taquería Del Sol

Righteous tacos with sol and soul

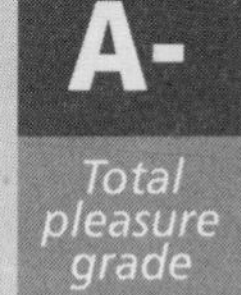

8.8 *Food* **8.4** *Feel* **$18** *Price* **Mexican**

Casual restaurant
Sun.-Thurs. 7am-midnight;
Fri.-Sat. 7am-2:45am.
Breakfast.

South Houston
8114 Park Place Blvd.
(713) 644-0535

Bar Full
Credit Cards Visa, MC, AmEx
Reservations Not accepted

Taquería Del Sol is a diminutive, festive, inviting Mexican restaurant that is not overly ambitious; they're just trying to feed people and make a few bucks while they're at it. But a burrito from Taquería Del Sol really hits the spot, and caldos, flautas, and tacos, with an emphasis on flavor and seasoning are all just as pleasing at this little joint.

A festive restaurant that is not shy with the tequila, Taquería Del Sol will have you feeling satisfied and full. This is due in part to what we think is one of the best salsas in town. It's served hot, and it's packed full of tomatoes, chile, and cilantro. Yum. And we can't forget about those burritos. One alone is big enough for lunch and dinner; they are loaded with a protein of your choice (beef, chicken, or pork), lettuce, sour cream, and tomatoes. Tortas and tacos that come filled with the same range of proteins please the palate in different ways, but are well executed for what could be such a ho-hum dish. As at all good taquerías, breakfast is served for the blue-collar crowd looking for an early morning bite. Huevos rancheros are some of the best around. Eggs that are fried sunny side up and served with a spicy salsa is a great way to kick start the morning.

Have a sweet tooth? Look no further; they have a bakery next door to fill the cravings of even the most severe sugar addict. Morning, noon, or night, stop by the panadería and pick up some pan dulce. It's light, sweet bread that has the texture of pound cake but the flavor of sweet air. (That's a good thing, we promise.) Taquería Del Sol can get busy and crowded, but that just means it's good. If you want peace and quiet, stay home, but if you want some taquería food with cheap, cheap prices, look to Taquería del Sol for relief. –SD

Taquería Los Charros

A smallish joint lacking a bit in quality, but coming through with consistency

B
Total pleasure grade

6.9 *Food* **5.0** *Feel* **$8** *Price* **Mexican**

Casual restaurant
Daily 6am-11pm.

Breakfast.

East Houston
508 Normandy St.
(713) 451-1110

Washington
404 Shepherd Dr.
(713) 426-6226

Bar None
Credit Cards Visa, MC, AmEx
Reservations Not accepted

It's too middle-of-the-road to be anyone's very favorite taquería. But that's fine by the hipsters in the burgeoning Washington area, who depend on the Shepherd location. (At some locations it's also called Taquería El Charro.) This is the Craig Biggio of taquerías: it's hardworking and solid, year after year. None of the dishes are humdingers; there isn't the extra cheese-and/or-bacon fattiness that some Tex-Mex taquerías rely on; nor does Los Charros boast the clarity and punch that more authentic taquerías can sometimes demonstrate. This food is tasty but not craveworthy; the atmosphere is comfortable, but you won't sink into your chair here, either.

Décor-wise, this joint does nothing to separate itself out from other taquerías, and our best guess is that they kind of like it that way. Maybe there's some misguided ideal of universal appeal to an apathetic clientele: the dinginess works as a primer, setting the bar low enough to pleasantly surprise customers with the tacos. That said, the poster of a suggestively smiling woman at the Shepherd location does seem to pull in a fair contingent of single male diners.

If you're only looking to spend a few bucks, you won't likely want to stray from taquería favorites like tacos, enchiladas, and quesadillas; at Los Charros, it's probably better that way. While the tortas may seem healthier than their cheese-inclined counterparts, it's better to skip these meaty but tongue-parchingly dry sandwiches and loosen up the belt buckle. Tacos are king here, whether filled with tender, well-seasoned hunks of chicken, or with carnitas whose seasoning is equally consistent, although the latter often come out dry, requiring heavy doses of salsa verde to quench their desperate thirst. Lengua (beef tongue) tacos aren't served much in these neighborhoods, and they're moist and dense, like a good pot roast, much better than Ruchi's version, even if they lack a certain meaty touch.

In the end, it's not fully clear to us why Los Charros always seems to hit such a sweet spot in spite of its middling merits on paper. We write this as we down the tasty tacos easily, washing them down with a huge cup of fragrant and sweet horchata, and fork over only a couple bucks. And there you have it. –JY

Taste of Texas

A famously family-friendly steakhouse with Texas' best salad bar

6.7 Food | **8.5** Feel | **$54** Price

Steakhouse

Upmarket restaurant
Mon.-Thurs. 11am-10pm; Fri. 11am-11pm; Sat. 3:30pm-11pm; Sun. 3pm-10pm.
Kid-friendly.

Memorial
10505 Katy Fwy.
(713) 932-6901
www.tasteoftexas.com

Bar Full
Credit Cards Visa, MC, AmEx
Reservations Not accepted

You may never feel so comfortable paying so much for a questionably cooked steak, throwaway sides, and hyper-sweetened desserts. Yet the wholesome family atmosphere at Taste of Texas seems to put people into a hypnotic state, removing all barriers to their wallets and to their stomachs. They soak in the friendly service; they're unusually nice to their kids; and they return to this salad bar again and again to take part in the time-honored Texas tradition of face-gorging.

The huge dining room is an all-out tribute-to-Texas museum. Sam Houston would be proud to dine here under the mounted animal heads, wagon wheels, and Lone Stars. Most servers are young and energetic, although their uniforms are outdated by, oh, three decades or so.

The food at Taste of Texas has been contributing to Houston's obesity problem since 1977. In true Texas fashion, all the appetizers are inflected with either barbecue sauce or cheese. Italians, who cringe at the pairing of cheese and seafood, might well sling guns with the cowboys if they saw this crabcake mixed with a trio of cheeses, but in reality it's hard not to like something cooked in fat and flooded with fat—the real risk is that you may get full before you even get to your main.

Or you might just skip it, and stick with what must be the best salad bar in Texas. It's probably not a title that's fought over too often, but we'll award it. Its vegetables are served at an appropriately chilly temperature, and every condiment imaginable is rotated frequently, maintaining more or less optimal freshness. Unfortunately, Taste of Texas' cuts of meat seem to be an afterthought, which is quite the problem for a steakhouse. The decently marbled "Cowboy Steak" is a ribeye that might be their best cut, but steaks often come cooked a shade over or under how you order them, and their would-be meaty flavor is usually lost in butter or lemon-pepper seasoning. Sides are atrocious, held too long in the dreaded steam table. The safest bet might also be the most boring: a fully loaded baked potato.

Whatever you wind up eating, you'll probably walk out proud—and fat—as ever to be a Texan. –JY

The Tasting Room

Taste the night away in the pleasant company of pizza, friends, and obscure bottles

Total pleasure grade

8.2 Food **9.1** Feel **$33** Price

Wine and pizza

Wine bar
Mon.-Fri. noon-midnight; Sat. noon-1am; closed Sun.

Midtown hours Mon.-Fri. 4pm-midnight; Sat. 4pm-1am; closed Sun.
Date-friendly. Outdoor dining. Wine-friendly.

Galleria
1101 Uptown Park Blvd.
(713) 993-9800
www.tastingroomwines.com

Midtown
114 Gray St.
(713) 528-6402

Bar Wine and beer only
Credit Cards Visa, MC, AmEx
Reservations Not accepted

Upper Kirby
2409 W. Alabama St.
(713) 526-2242

We love that Houston has as many wine-store-bar-café establishments popping up as it does. It makes the city feel that much more cosmopolitan when you can just dart into that place around the corner for some dry rosé on a summer evening, or a nice bottle to begin or end a date. We've also got to appreciate the opportunity to sample potential purchases. You'll leave the Tasting Room confident in what you've bought.

At the Uptown Park location, an extensive outdoor area becomes increasingly busier as the night wears on—even a weeknight. Indoors, the atmosphere is decidedly more romantic. Low lighting and aging wine bottles everywhere entice you to settle comfortably into some nook or other and lose yourself in romance (or wine-nerdiness, if you prefer).The more places like this, the more Houstonians that will be buying their first (or second or third) book about wine or taking that class they've always talked about.

Maybe we're getting carried away. The Tasting Room's collection, while carefully selected, isn't all that extensive. It wins in ambience even more than on the wine merits. But that's not to shortchange the kitchen here. Pizzas—though generally not the best match with wine (Italians, for instance, only drink beer or coke with pizza)—are executed well, their crusts just ever-so-slightly seared, and with large grains of salt working their magic, elevating the flavors to their full potential. Pizza, like wine, is meant to be shared among friends. Captivated by a friend's story, you might absentmindedly reach for just one more slice; such are its addictive qualities. So order one more glass, too.

In the end, the Tasting Room's main function in Houston is as a gathering place; they provide the wine and pizza, and you just have to show up. But do take advantage of the tasting opportunities and try that wine whose name you can't pronounce that you've had your eye on. –AH

Tau Bay

A knockout Vietnamese rice plate—no more, no less

B Total pleasure grade

7.0 Food **4.0** Feel **$10** Price

Vietnamese

Casual restaurant
Daily 10am-10pm.

Chinatown
8282 Bellaire Blvd.
(713) 272-8755

Bar Wine and beer only
Credit Cards Visa, MC, AmEx
Reservations Not accepted

For many of those who don't speak Vietnamese, Tau Bay is known as the "airplane restaurant" just because of what looks to be a Microsoft clip-art airplane on the front of the menu. But this is no coach-class airliner food. Through simple preparations and exploding flavors, Tau Bay delivers a knockout rice plate and other good but not special Vietnamese dishes in a ruggedly old place that probably wouldn't mind if you put your feet up, lay back a little, and took a breather.

With lines of old, chipped tables, and seats that have torn covers, Tau Bay has taken a beating over the years of use. It has a comfortable griminess to it though, like a place that's at ease with where it's at, and where it's going, so you should be at ease as well. That is, as long as you don't drink a lot of water because the bathrooms are past disgusting.

While there are a good number of warming bowls of egg noodle soup with varied fish balls, meat, and seafood, phô, and vermicelli bowls, it would be an injustice to yourself and your lunch break if you didn't order a plate of Vietnamese egg rolls, a char-grilled beef rice plate, and an eye-opening Vietnamese coffee. The egg rolls come in orders of eight, so your office snacks are covered for the day, as long as you don't mind your cubicle smelling of fish sauce. They're freshly fried, they seem to have a crispier edge, and more aromatic, onion-y flavor to them than most other egg rolls do. The star of the show, however, is a rice plate with thin slices of grilled meat, egg cake, and shredded pork. While Starsky had Hutch, and Milli had Vanilli, this meat, rice, and egg just seem tailor-made for each other. The meat has the charcoal grilled flavor in all the right places, and the egg cake is like a crustless quiche with dried mushrooms and rice noodles in it, delivering a soft, eggy, savory-ness to the dish. The shredded pork adds little flavor, but has a dimension of texture to it, and with a bit of nuoc cham with its sweet-saltiness, the plate is well-rounded and delicious. While other dishes are good, stay away from the watery phô. There are some places that you should go to over and over again for one thing, and Tau Bay and its rice plate is one of them. –JY

Tay Do Restaurant

Clay pots rule at this Bellaire Vietnamese-Chinese classic

B- Total pleasure grade

7.5 Food **7.5** Feel **$25** Price

Vietnamese

Casual restaurant
Mon.-Thurs. 10am-10pm; Fri.-Sat.10:30am-11pm; Sun.10:30am-10:30pm.

Chinatown
11201 Bellaire Blvd.
(281) 988-8939

Bar Full
Credit Cards Visa, MC, AmEx
Reservations Accepted

Tay Do has never really seemed to settle into its current location; compared with the original, the new spot seems too big, too bulky, and too flashy for its homey, sometimes Chinese, sometimes Vietnamese cuisine—like a child stuck in a man's body. But even as those problems hold the restaurant back, Tay Do's sizzling bowls of clay pot rice and roasting meats continue to make the place relevant.

Surprisingly, for such a large space, upkeep at Tay Do has never seemed to be as much of a problem as it has been with other mega restaurants such as its across-the-lot neighbor, Ocean Palace. Aside from a few lights that will probably never have their bulbs changed, the far-reaching room is maintained as a comfortable, clean, and spacious environment—even the bathrooms are spotless—which is a far cry from much of what you get along Bellaire.

With a menu that adds a couple extra bucks to what is usually charged for this normal array of dishes, it's easy to complain that Tay Do just doesn't deliver anything special for something you could easily get cheaper down the street. The phô is your normal phô, with hot broth and your normal collection of sliced beef, stomach linings, and vegetables; it's nothing spectacular. Chicken in all its preparations is still just chicken, but if you ignore its name, (Anything with "delight" in its name normally isn't anywhere near delightful) the seafood delight is a good choice. Goi do bien, a cold salad of sweet poached shrimp, rice noodles, piquant spice, fragrant cilantro, and a generous dash of sweet-sour, fish sauce-heavy vinaigrette, would delight even the most discerning palates. Then, of course, there are the clay pots, steaming bowls of your choice of hunky, roasted meats and rice flavored with meat juices that have the added dimension of crunchy rice at the bottom of the bowl. While probalby not a dish for all seasons, it's definitely a dish for the ages, one that will continue to keep Tay Do on your go-to list. –JY

Teala's

A Mexican restaurant brought to you by the folks behind...Thai Pepper?

B- Total pleasure grade

7.1 Food | **7.2** Feel | **$33** Price | **Tex-Mex**

Casual restaurant
Mon.-Thurs. 11am-10pm;
Fri. 11am-11pm; Sat. noon-11pm;
Sun. noon-10pm.
Outdoor dining.

Montrose
3210 W. Dallas St.
(713) 520-9292
www.tealas.com

Bar Full
Credit Cards Visa, MC, AmEx
Reservations Not accepted

Teala's, not to be confused with Tila's, is a Mexican restaurant with a focus on regional dishes of the Yucatán. It's also under the same ownership as Thai Pepper, but don't fret; you won't find any green curry chicken enchiladas here. From the always-pleasing cochinita pibil to the special chicken mole, they serve flavorful and well-executed Mexican food. Mains stray up into the teens, but they're well worth it.

Teala's flashy exterior makes it stand out; it's a nice free-standing building off of West Dallas in the Montrose area, and the restaurant's exterior is painted with beautiful murals that represent the Yucatán's most picturesque tableaux. Inside, however, things are much more subdued; it's a rustic, but respectable space, with lots of soothing brown tones. During dinner complimentary, black-bean dip is served with chips and bold, deep, creamy salsas—more exciting than your average red stuff. Appetizers include nachos, big quesadillas—of which we like the shrimp and scallop—and queso flameado with chorizo that is superb. The usuals like fajitas, enchiladas, and burritos can be skipped, but do sample the house specialties like pájaros a la parilla—grilled quail and onions with rice and beans. Also tasty is the cochinita pibil: Yucatán-style roasted pork that is tender and moist is served with a cucumber salad and grilled onions. The cucumber salad lends a nice, crunchy, refreshing aspect to the dish; it's a touch more akin to Middle Eastern food than Mexican.

Don't skip on the booze; Teala's margaritas on the rocks are great. They hit the right ratio with just the right amount of tequila so your mouth doesn't feel like it's on fire, and the sweetness of a house-blended mix; it's easy to have one too many. An outdoor patio is great for a nice day and one of those margaritas, and friendly service makes it all the better. Parking is a bit tricky when it's really busy, but they do offer valet—this is Houston, after all. So dive right in and don't be afraid; no Thai-Mexican dishes await you. –SD

Teotihuacán

A Heights restaurant that doesn't charge those heights

B-
Total pleasure grade

7.5 *Food* **7.4** *Feel* **$11** *Price* **Mexican**

Casual restaurant
Daily 8am-10pm.

Heights
1511 Airline Dr.
(713) 426-4420

Bar Full
Credit Cards Visa, MC, AmEx
Reservations Not accepted

It's hard to tell people about the secret favorite restaurants that are most dear to your heart. You can't help but imagining the crowds descending upon your little hideout. But we're confident that this won't happen with Teotihuacán, since it hasn't yet. They're doing great business, keeping standards and quality high while serving great Mexican food to the masses. They aren't going to wow anybody with creativity here, but they are, however, wowing people with flavor. The favorites—flautas, fajitas, and tacos—are served, but other specials like pollo mostazo and pollo corral will surprise you.

Aztec murals cover the walls; their dark and relaxing colors warm you, make you feel at home. Sit at the wooden tables and be greeted by Teotihuacán's famous chips and salsa. Red and green are both delicious; it's rare for such time and care to go into a free product. Chicken flautas are delicious. Crispy on the outside, concealing steamy and spicy guts, they're everything a flauta should be. Fajitas and tacos of beef or chicken might appear pedestrian at first glance, but something about the meat is incredibly tasty and addictive. It's moist, juicy, and packs a flavor punch.

Specials are more interesting; pollo mostazo (chicken in mustard cream sauce) is a bit heavy, and the cream blocks the other flavors that are trying to fight their way through. "Pollo Corral," offered only on limited days, is appetizing; it's half a roasted chicken covered in a spicy red sauce. Accompanying charro beans are good, with lots of pork buried inside.

Teotihuacán is not really a Tex-Mex restaurant, but it's a classic Texas-Mexican restaurant, which means that they serve breakfast as well. The service is attentive; sometimes the language barrier makes things a bit tricky, but the staff is friendly, to say the least. The best thing about Teotihuacán is the prices. Rarely will you spend more than ten dollars, yet portions are surprisingly big for the Heights.

Okay, now we're starting to worry about that crowds-descending problem again. –SD

Teppay

A little-known box of sushi bliss—if you can figure out the combination

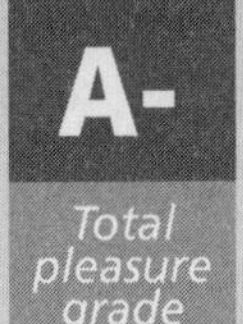

8.9 *Food* **7.1** *Feel* **$60** *Price* **Japanese**

Upmarket restaurant
Mon.-Sat. 6pm-11pm; closed Sun.

Galleria
6516 Westheimer Rd.
(713) 789-4506

Bar Full
Credit Cards Visa, MC, AmEx
Reservations Accepted

Sushi-seeking is such a fickle sport in Houston these days. A buzz spreads about Sushi Jin, and the place is suddenly overrun. Some sushi aficionados will only dine at Kubo's; others pledge their allegiance to Kaneyema; others swear by Osaka to the death.

None of these restaurants is bad, and they're all capable of being quite good. The problem with rating them is that your experience depends as much on your own actions as on the restaurant's. There's probably not a Japanese restaurant in America at which you won't eat better if you sit down at the sushi bar and establish a rapport with the chef than if you sit by the window and order Sushi Combination A.

In our humble opinion, Houston's current top tier, both for sushi and for cooked Japanese fish and noodles, consists of three restaurants: Nippon, Sasaki, and Teppay. All three are run by Japanese staffs that spare no expense to get the ingredients they want. None is cheap. And none is particularly well known.

If you want the real experience at Teppay—which is only open for dinner—you need to be prepared to spend real money: $60, $80, maybe more. No menu, just "omakase": the chef is in control. Discuss the cost beforehand, and then shut up.

Teppay is not the best sushi restaurant in America; it's probably not even the best in Houston. But this little joint—whose décor is scarcely more than a simple sushi bar against one wall, plus a few tables and chairs—is capable of great things. The sushi chef might fillet a whole aji (horse mackerel), serve you the sashimi, then deep-fry the rest, bones and all—which you should, of course, devour. Fatty salmon, when available, is meltingly delicious.

Here, as elsewhere, if you're non-Japanese, the challenge is to get to that point: to break through the cultural and language barriers. Places like Teppay are used to serving their best stuff to customers who speak their language and know exactly what to do; look around—the place is populated almost entirely by Japanese businessmen. But in our minds, enthusiasm is always contagious, and translates well across cultures. Be humble and open-minded, convey the idea that you're excited by their fish, and the prophecy might just be self-fulfilling. And excited you should be, because there are few sensory experiences more sublime than eating sushi when the chef really, really cares what you think. –RG

Thai Pepper

In a city with so many great Thai restaurants, this place is only average

C- Total pleasure grade

4.2 Food | **5.3** Feel | **$26** Price | **Thai**

Casual restaurant
Mon.-Thurs. 11:30am-10:30pm; Fri. 11:30am-11pm; Sat. 5:30pm-11pm; Sun. 5pm-10pm.

Montrose
2049 W. Alabama St.
(713) 520-8225
www.tealas.com

Bar Wine and beer only
Credit Cards Visa, MC, AmEx
Reservations Not accepted

Located in a beautiful converted house on West Alabama, Thai Pepper is a modest, understated restaurant. Lots of brown and dark colors dominate the exterior, but on the inside, it looks a bit like a grandma's house. The food tastes a bit like a spice-averse grandma made it, too; they don't bring the heat like many other Thai restaurants around Houston—probably because they are in the Montrose area, where many ethnic restaurants tone it down a notch or two—and many dishes just don't have the full-bodied flavor that you would expect. Some selections (lime squid, triple spicy duck) bring creativity, getting our hopes up—and then dash them with the delivery.

The menu is constructed well, with a nice variety of Thai noodles, beef, lime salads, and such, but the execution is a bit off. Fried spring rolls with chicken, vegetables, and shrimp are flavorful, just hot enough, and delicious, but the "Thai Peppers Cheese Roll" is a disappointment; industrial-tasting cream cheese and crabmeat make for a deep-fried disaster. (That said, how much could we really expect out of such a dish?) Chicken curry should be reprimanded for calling itself hot, as the coconut milk mutes most of the flavors in the curry. Sweet-and-sour shrimp and basil shrimp are decent, but utterly unexciting; the real highlight is "Thai Royal Shrimp," where the little guys find themselves sautéed with peppers, onions, and garlic. Still, the flavors are completely inauthentic. Lunch specials are even more predictable, if that's possible; "Thai Pepper Chicken" tastes thrown together haphazardly with little focus. But again, who would have high hopes about such a dish?

Parking can get tricky at peak hours, so watch out for no-parking signs, because the neighbors won't hesitate to call tow trucks. The best way to deal with the parking problem—and the food problem—is to ditch this place and drive down Bellaire for some Thai food that's actually good. –SD

Thai Racha

Delicious Thai-American flavors make you cling to your spork

B
Total pleasure grade

7.5 *Food* | **4.5** *Feel* | **$9** *Price* | **Thai**

Counter service
Mon.-Sat. 11am-9pm;
Sun. 12:30pm-8pm.

Spring Branch
10085 Long Point Rd.
(713) 464-7607

Bar None
Credit Cards No credit cards
Reservations Not accepted

Thai Racha is a broken-looking, yellow-roofed hut off Long Point and Gessner; at first glance, you might think it could double as a squatter shack. But trust us, there is nothing illegal going on here: Thai Racha is one of Houston's most reliable quick stops, serving powerfully flavored, Thai-inflected fast food. The fact that it's so slummy both inside and out makes the drive-thru that much more appealing, if that's your thing.

If you ever do walk in, you'll find that the staff at Thai Racha is welcoming and warming, and happy to pour you a large cup of smoky Thai tea while you wait for your food; it does have a tendency to get warm inside the small building—yet another reason to utilize that drive-thru. The food has the same archaic tastes as Thai street food, unbound by any set of prerequisites. Thus, the food you may know as Thai is different here, sometimes lacking the sweet, sour, and spiciness Americans associate with Thai food. What really matters though, authenticity aside, is that the Thai Racha fare is tasty, greasy, and satisfying.

Food comes in Styrofoam take-out boxes plus one of the world's most important inventions, the spork, so any sort of eating formality is already thrown out the door. Either way, the food is tasty enough that, if need be, you could shovel it into your mouth with your hands—if you were hungry enough. Tom yum chicken soup is so perfumed, so strongly flavored with sweetness and sourness, that it could double as Robitussin—the cure for all ailments. "Jalapeño Beef" is wrongfully named; really, it's only tastefully spicy, though strongly flavored with soy and sweet peppers. Kee mow chicken is greasy, cut with handfuls of Thai basil and mint, making for an exceptionally aromatic meal that actually needs the rice that comes on the side of it. The only downer is the pad Thai, which is too dry; though the contrast of the crunchiness of the peanuts and softness of the egg is nice, there are too many other good options on the menu.

Dump or not, Thai Racha kicks up its food with enough flavor to compensate for just-okay ingredients. The food doesn't taste healthy—because it probably isn't—but such is fast food. Either way, spork in hand, you probably won't find much better drive-thru anywhere else in the city. –JY

Thai Spice

B+

Total pleasure grade

Surprisingly stylish fast Thai that's as cheap as they come

8.1 *Food* **3.6** *Feel* **$11** *Price* **Thai**

Casual restaurant
Daily 11am-10pm.
Vegetarian-friendly. WiFi.
Additional locations.

Chinatown
8282 Bellaire Blvd.
(713) 777-4888
www.thaispice.com

Heights
460 W. 19th St.
(713) 880-9992

Bar Wine and beer only
Credit Cards Visa, MC, AmEx
Reservations Not accepted

Rice Area
5117 Kelvin Dr.
(713) 522-5100

You might expect a place that's known for it's Thai fast food to look modest, maybe slightly dingy, like a mom-and-pop safe haven for homesick Thais. Instead, what you get here is a flashy, brightly colored splace full of bizarre, full-color photos of customers eating the various dishes on the menu with looks of enjoyment so overzealous that you wonder if a deranged photographer's assistant was crouched behind them with a gun pressed to their backs as they ate and posed. "You're not smiling enough!"

Still, Thai Spice is a lunch mecca. With nothing on the menu above seven dollars, it packs in the midday business without a problem. Tucked away in a strip mall and a bit hidden, the place practically runs itself; it seems just one step away from employing robots.

Although the restaurant is called Thai Spice, its sign says "Thai Fast Food" in giant letters with "Thai Spice" in small print—a bit confusing, but at least they're communicating that it's speedy. It's not likely that you'll walk in to find the restaurant's employees scurrying around to keep up with demand; rather, the scene is very docile and calm, even when it gets busy. It's a well-lit restaurant with plenty of seating and a small buffet of about nine items. This is where you'll find the famous $3.75 (at press time) lunch special, which consists of three choices from the buffet, soup, rice, and free hot tea—a bargain in anybody's eyes, especially considering that the food is fresh and delicious. The unbelievable value at the place boosts its grade from a B/B- to a B+.

Red curry with chicken and tons of chilies is spicy, sweet, and flavorful. Shrimp are tempura-fried with the shells and heads still on; they could be great, but they're often served too cold. An elbow-macaroni-and-beef-broth soup has laughably poor presentation, and isn't even vaguely Thai, but is still tasty nonetheless. Pad ka praw with chicken, beef, or pork is stir-fried with chili and basil for a fiery yet mellow meal. And the som tam (green papaya salad) and spicy bamboo salad are ways to eat light and stay refreshed.

All that aside, it must be good when the menu is printed in three different languages, right? –SD

Thai Sticks

Typically disappointing Thai-American that even a nice patio can't rescue

C- *Total pleasure grade*

3.8 *Food* **7.1** *Feel* **$38** *Price* **Thai**

Casual restaurant
Mon.-Thurs. 11am-10:30pm; Fri. 11am-11:30pm; Sat. 5pm-11:30pm; Sun. 5pm-10:30pm.
Outdoor dining. WiFi.

Montrose
4319 Montrose Blvd.
(713) 529-4500

Bar Full
Credit Cards Visa, MC, AmEx
Reservations Accepted

"But it's hard to get authentic Thai ingredients in the city," we imagine the Thai Sticks apologists protesting. "After all, Kaffir lime leaves don't grow on trees."

Actually, Kaffir lime leaves do grow on trees. Kaffir lime trees. They also freeze well. So why is it impossible to detect any evocative, aromatic kaffir lime flavor whatsoever in any dish at Thai Sticks—even one of the anointed "House Specialties" of Thai Sticks, the prik khing red snapper, described on the menu as "topped with fried basil leaves and shredded kaffir lime leaves"? As for the basil, it's soggy and oily, probably the result of having been under-fried. The fish is cut into flavorless chunks, overcooked, and underseasoned. And why are there red bell peppers on the dish?

The real problem in this town is that well-located places like Thai Sticks on Montrose—convenient to everything in Montrose, the Museum District, and so on, even if it's across the street from a big ugly CVS—are content to keep serving the same spice-muted, Chinese-Americanized slop that people have come to expect, or even identify with Thai cuisine. This restaurant has potential: the outdoor tables, in a cozy, well-ringed-in little patio, suffer from less street noise than their neighbors. It's a romantic place to sit at night. The bland but inoffensive interior has a certain charm when it's full, not when it's empty.

"But people don't *want* kaffir lime leaves," continue the imaginary apologists, "they want Chinese-American food, not Thai food. Why else would they continue to order dishes with names like 'basil chicken,' 'garlic shrimp,' and 'beef with broccoli,' even when larb, yum pla, and choo chee curry are on the menu? How can you blame Thai Sticks for giving people what they want?"

We can, and we will, because we believe that restaurants should be held accountable for serving bad food, even if people continue to buy it. And, more importantly, we believe that Houston is now sophisticated enough to support something better—not just authentic but out-of-the-way restaurants like Vieng Thai, Tony Thai, and Kanomwan, but some authentic Thai food in a well-trafficked area of Central Houston. Join us in hoping. –FC

Thelma's Barbecue

An old school barbecue joint with soul—just don't get on their bad side

B *Total pleasure grade*

7.0 *Food* **8.2** *Feel* **$10** *Price* **Barbecue**

Counter service
Mon.-Sat. 11am-9pm; closed Sun.

Downtown
1020 Live Oak St.
(713) 228-2262

Bar None
Credit Cards Visa, MC, AmEx
Reservations Not accepted

Behind all the old warehouses, right off 59, there is a hidden shack that goes by the name of Thelma's. A family-run barbecue joint that seems to have been around since the Stone Age, they serve up smoked meats, sweet tea, and good ol' southern hospitality that will lead you to embrace the simple livin' that this place evokes. We love the plastic chairs, old-time jukebox, and the rickety screen door that welcome you.

Now if only they could be consistent.

On any given day, you can have some of the best ribs in Houston at Thelma's; on others, you can have the worst—sometimes they're incredibly tough, difficult, even, to chew. That said, the brisket is always delicious, tender and flavorful; this is how brisket should taste. But the biggest problem we have with Thelma's is the barbecue sauce. It's one of the sweetest things our critics have ever tasted. It tastes like sugar, sugar, ketchup, and sugar. You might feel the urge to visit your dentist after a run-in between your molars and this sauce—it's pretty terrible.

It doesn't end with the barbecue, though. Giant, golden-fried pieces of catfish, which release that wonderful steam when the crust is punctured, are one of the main reasons we go to Thelma's. Sides are a roll call of the usual soul-food suspects—mashed potato salad, french fries, baked beans, and so on—but the star of the show is the stewed okra, sliced and simmered in tomato and spices until tender; it's a great accompaniment to smoked meat.

Here's a word to the wise when ordering at Thelma's, however: never, ever ask for a beer. This is a restaurant of faith, so you have to abide by the house rules. So much as hint at the potential presence of ethyl alcohol in a potable beverage, and prepare to be singlehandedly blamed for the moral degeneracy of modern America. Instead, take a stroll around back, where you can see the small smoker that makes Thelma's brisket as moist as her liquor cabinet is dry. Let's hear it for grassroots barbecue. –SD

Thierry André Tellier

A casual bakery-café with more hits than misses

6.2 Food | **7.0** Feel | **$9** Price

French pastry

Café
Mon.-Sat. 8am-11pm; closed Sun.

Breakfast. Vegetarian-friendly.

River Oaks
2515 River Oaks Blvd.
(713) 524-3863
www.cafeandpastryshop.com

Memorial
1101 Uptown Park Blvd.
(713) 877-9401

Galleria
1635 S. Voss Rd.

Bar Wine and beer only
Credit Cards Visa, MC, AmEx
Reservations Not accepted

After toiling for years upon years in a small shop on River Oaks Boulevard, André's recently expanded to a storefront in the hip shopping center (is that an oxymoron?) at Uptown Park. While the quality of their pastries has remained steady, the subpar savory food and boring atmosphere followed it to its expanded location. André's has always been a solid choice for a lunch with no wow, but a sure bet for something reasonable and light: simple offerings of baked goods and pastries, and perhaps a cup of coffee.

While the River Oaks location still holds an air of discreetness to it, tucked away from the street almost incognito, the Uptown Park location seems to be like the boisterous younger brother that everyone loves to hate. Neither shop is high on fashion, with rigid chairs, small tables, and Target-inspired décor. There is no fluffy European air to it, but rather a very down-to-earth approach that isn't as much impressive as it is comfortable.

While some items on André's menu are indeed impressive, others are just passable. "Plât du Jour" options are normally a good choice; we've tried a beef goulash that was hunky, tender, and delicious. The lunch menu has three options for meal size, from stand-alone mains to full meals with dessert. The chicken or tuna salad sandwiches are tasty, but overly eggy quiches lack an airiness to them. But at the end of the day, it comes back to the pastries here, which are lovely; a fruit tart is fresh and light, with a lush pastry cream, while a hazelnut pyramid is, thankfully, not overly sweet, boasting a nice balance of nut and chocolate. Things get bad mostly because they are dry—probably kept for too long rather than incorrectly prepared—but you have to step lightly in order to get a complete meal without missteps. In the mornings, croissants are moist and flaky, and the chocolate croissants are even better, with a semi-soft dark chocolate center to give a mix of sweetness and bitterness. However, as the day wears on, they seem to easily deteriorate and dry out. With so many heavyset restaurants in Houston, sometimes a load off your feet at André's is just what you need. –JY

This Is It Soul Food

Total pleasure grade

Cafeteria-style food that won't bring on any grade school flashbacks

7.9 Food **3.0** Feel **$11** Price **Southern**

Counter service
Mon.-Sat. 11am-8pm;
Sun. 11am-6pm.
Breakfast. Outdoor dining.

Midtown
207 Gray St.
(713) 659-1608
www.thisisithouston.com

Bar None
Credit Cards Visa, MC, AmEx
Reservations Not accepted

Remember how you would flinch at the sound of mashed potatoes (that more resembled curdled milk) and green-brown spinach being slopped onto your tray in the elementary school cafeteria? Don't worry, This Is It Soul Food is different. There's something about soul food that's indestructible, even at the hands of the steam table, and This Is It lets you know that this food—as cheesy as it sounds—really is it.

This joint reminds you that some of the best food in the world doesn't come from the prettiest of places. If the clearly-marked cafeteria set-up weren't here, it wouldn't be out of the question to wonder if you accidentally stepped into the DMV. However, long rows of tables clue you in. Patio seating is even better—as long as the weather cooperates.

If there's one thing that should make you cringe when you walk into a restaurant, it's the steam table. Chef Geoffrey Zakarian eloquently sums it up: "It's already dead; you don't need to kill it anymore." And putting most anything on a steam table is the culinary equivalent of Chinese water torture: painful to see, and even more painful to endure. Soul food, however, is heavy on braised items, which, luckily, can stand up to this serving method. Oxtails are scrawny, but full of dense, meaty flavor, and are given some zip by a helping of collard greens with lots of pot likker (the intensely flavored juice that the collards weep out as they're being cooked). It's not a meal for the faint of heart, and probably not for the dead of summer. The mac 'n' cheese is a dead-on winner, with creamy cheese that melts, oozes, and then fuses the macaroni. If you're lucky, you'll get one of the crusty corners that's got even more concentrated flavor and extra texture. Not all choices are spectacular; the apricot-glazed chicken is way too sweet, and candied yams make your teeth feel like it's the day after Halloween. But with so much soul-less food around Houston—unless you're looking to shed a few pounds—This Is It is a way to fill up on food and soul. –JY

Tila's

A pretty River Oaks face without much Interior

D Total pleasure grade

3.9	7.9	$50	Tex-Mex
Food	Feel	Price	

Upmarket restaurant
Mon.-Thurs. 11am-11pm;
Fri.-Sat. 11am-midnight;
Sun. 11am-10pm.
Brunch. Date-friendly. Outdoor dining.

River Oaks
1111 S. Shepherd Dr.
(713) 522-7654
www.tilas.com

Bar Full
Credit Cards Visa, MC, AmEx
Reservations Accepted

This restaurant comes in a beautiful River Oaks package, lovely garden included, and aims for something more than Tex-Mex—and something more than regional Mexican, too. It's a mix of what you might call nouvelle Mexican (blackened halibut with "ancho crème" sauce; tequila-marinated, gravlax-style "Salmon Borracho") and outright fusion (Portobello mushrooms stuffed with crabmeat and smothered with Manchego cheese and habanero; pork tenderloin medallions in basil-mint pesto, stuffed with endive and cheese, "brushed with a delicate wine demi-glaze sauce").

Your first reaction might be that the kitchen should stay away from such haphazard recipes for disaster and stick to the Mexican basics; but then they execute so poorly on those basics, too, that you're not sure what, if anything, could save Tila's. One thing's for sure: it's not the brie-and-pear quesadillas ("This is what happens to Mexican cuisine after a few years in River Oaks…Très chic," croons the menu), a sugary and discordant mix whose flour tortillas are barely acceptable. Speaking of "très chic," given the neighborhood demographic, there's a surprising lack of class to all of this. Do they really need to remind us, with the gazpacho, that "no, really, it's supposed to be cold!" or call the roasted yellow bell pepper soup "yummy-oso!"? Do they really think that the "Caesar salad was stolen by the Italians" (have you ever seen a Caesar salad in Italy)? And we're not sure what to make of the menu's claim that "Julia Child would roll over in her grave" over the Swiss cheese soufflé.

The chile en nogada is touted around town, but it's a fatally sweet fruit bomb, filled with minced chicken breast (why?), peaches, apricots, mango, pineapple, and raisins; topped with cheese, almond, cashew, and walnut sauce, along with pomegranate seeds ("just like in the book and movie 'Like Water for Chocolate,'" we're reminded). If you're a hiker, you might compare the result to eating trail mix from a sack made of leathery green chile. Some grandmother in Puebla is *definitely* rolling over in her grave over this.

There are two things that redeem Tila's: one, the delightful, tree-shaded garden, set out on a relatively quiet street corner. And two, the lengthy tequila list—yet even its luster is diminished by the wimpy, spare margaritas. To every point, there's a counterpoint, and ultimately, there's no point in coming here at all. –RG

Tofu Village

A Korean tofu specialist that brings on the spice

B *Total pleasure grade*

7.2 *Food* **5.6** *Feel* **$18** *Price* **Korean**

Casual restaurant
Daily 10am-10pm.
Vegetarian-friendly.

Chinatown
9889 Bellaire Blvd.
(713) 777-9889

Bar Wine and beer only
Credit Cards Visa and MC
Reservations Accepted

So very many of the constantly-sprouting-up Asian restaurants on Bellaire try to do a bit of everything, but only do one thing well. Tofu Village is smart in the fact that it doesn't try to overextend itself—not completely, at least. Located off a shopping strip, and serving in sparse (but not barren) quarters, Tofu Village specializes in piping-hot bowls of traditional Korean soft tofu stews, a perfect match for the many rainy days in Houston.

The name is largely self-explanatory. In a mostly white space with cheesy, ever-changing colored lights lining the walls and pictures of Korean pop star Rain plastered everywhere, the restaurant specializes in stews that are essential comfort food to many Korean-Americans. The stew comes in different varieties—meat, seafood, kimchee, or a combination of all three—and in varying amounts of spiciness; as such, you can choose to have the same exact comforting meal every time…or not. But regardless of how it comes, the tofu is the star, served in a hearty broth, taking on biting Korean spices. It's a transportative experience eating this tofu: like immersing yourself in an authentic moment, with warmth and comfort, from the other side of the world. The fact that this place can not only open, but thrive, is one of the uniquely wonderful things about Houston.

As successful as the specialty tofu is, we're not sure why Tofu Village doesn't stop while they're ahead, because some of the other Korean dishes suffer horribly, like the rendition of the Korean seafood pancake—it's flimsy rather than crispy, and filled with seafood that doesn't taste the freshest. And then there's Korean BBQ: since the Village doesn't have the accommodations to do the full-service version at the table, they cook your meats in the kitchen, and the results—with both the rib-eye and shortribs—are flavorful, but tough and totally overcooked.

Service is gracious, yet sometimes frustrating, in part because the servers only speak broken English. But these tofu stews are good enough to make up for it. If this place (or your ordering) can maintain focus, you'll have a place to go every time the thunderclouds creep up over the magical melting pot that is modern Houston. –JY

Tokyohana

One of Houston's standard knockoffs of the Hibachi House That Rocky Built

C- *Total pleasure grade*

4.5 *Food* **6.7** *Feel* **$40** *Price* **Japanese**

Casual restaurant
Mon.-Thurs. 11am-11pm; Fri. 11am-midnight; Sat. noon-midnight; Sun. 10:30am-10pm.

Date-friendly. Kid-friendly. Live music. Outdoor dining.

West U
3239 Southwest Fwy.
(713) 838-9560
www.tokyohana.com

North Houston
15155 North Fwy.
(281) 877-8744

Bar Full
Credit Cards Visa, MC, AmEx
Reservations Accepted

The story of teppanyaki in America began in 1964, when Japanese Olympic wrestler Hiroaki "Rocky" Aoki opened a tiny four-table restaurant in New York. The basic idea was, and still is, that your personal chef-entertainer flings knives and spatulas, eliciting gasps and squeals from the girls; and then, with pomp and bravado, he cooks a meal on the griddle (mistranslated as "hibachi") in front of you, shoveling things onto your plate (and sometimes into people's mouths) as they're ready.

Rocky ingeniously envisioned vast potential in a take-the-kids-out-to-dinner market that was still in its infancy. But even he could not possibly have imagined the publicly-traded restaurant empire that Benihana would become. (Nor did he probably imagine that he would later be convicted for insider trading.) In 1964, America was a nation still deep in the throes of postwar monstrosities like jam sponge and baked bologna loaf; "exotic" meant chop suey or red-sauce Italian. Rocky knew it was hard to get much more inoffensive than sizzling meat, chicken, and shrimp drowned in butter and soy sauce. Turn it into a three-ring circus that the kids love, and it's no wonder that suburban America made Rocky a rich man—he now owns a piece of 59 restaurants (and so can you—Nasdaq: BNHN/BNHNA).

It's amazing how little the various incarnations still differ, even at the closely held (and closely spelled) knockoffs like Tokyohana, whose popularity transcends races and ages—whether for third-grade birthday parties, boisterous ladies' nights out, or awkward Match.com meetups. As for the food, there's the expected schedule of overcooked proteins, their tastes rendered more or less identical by the soy-sauce-and-butter basting (worst-textured, though, are shrimp and lobster). Then there are the standard vegetables, custom-fried rice, and superfluous bean sprouts; and, finally, ginger and mustard sauces to seal the simple deal. You've probably seen the magic tricks before, too (the onion-volcano eruption, the midair egg slice, the flying vegetable game where zucchini ends up down someone's bra). Tokyohana has also added a predictable, average-quality sushi menu; salmon nigiri and spicy tuna rolls are fine, and Tokyohana is open later than most Houston sushi bars. But why settle for raw fish when you can have soy-sauced vegetables flung at your face? –RG

Tommy's Sandwiches

A modest breakfast-and-lunch place with no surprises

C+ *Total pleasure grade*

6.9 *Food*

5.0 *Feel*

$9 *Price*

Light American

Counter service
Mon.-Fri. 7am-3pm;
closed Sat.-Sun.
Breakfast.

Medical Center
8403 Almeda Rd.
(713) 747-1696

Bar None
Credit Cards Visa, MC, AmEx
Reservations Not accepted

We understand that not all restaurants have to induce orgasm at the table, nor must they unlock the meaning of life with just one bite of their food. Sometimes we can just relax contentedly with food that's pleasing, but not particularly ambitious. Such is Tommy's Sandwiches, where you won't see sky-high prices justified by fancy, artisanal ingredients. Instead, food here speaks in a universal language; it's for anyone and everyone. A breakfast that consists of two eggs, bacon, hash browns, and toast will run you just over four dollars, and it looks and tastes just like what it is. You don't have some fancy chef trying to explain the virtues of the Slow Food movement here. Food is ordered and out in no time.

Befitting its Medical Center location, Tommy's looks antiseptic, with a mostly white motif and the occasional picture hanging on the wall. Tommy's recognizes that breakfast really is a lost art in Houston, and takes advantage of the opportunity. Most self-proclaimed foodies will argue that they can cook a better breakfast than most restaurants in town, probably including this one. And they're probably right. Still, Food Network knowledge aside, Tommy's serves pancakes that are fluffy and moist; three will cost you only $2.95. That's a deal no matter who you are.

Lunch consists mostly of burgers, sandwiches, and fried delights such as chicken fried steak, chicken, and fish. The chopped barbecue sandwich is delicious, with chopped beef in a spicy barbecue sauce served on French bread. Also, don't miss the beer-battered fries that are salty, crispy, and delicious all at once. A ménage à trois, if you will. This is really a doctor's diner that opens at seven and closes at three, five days a week, and that's it. Both meal services are fast and consistent. Walk up to the counter to order and then take a seat. Oh, and one more thing: sorry to burst your bubble, foodies, but there's no micro-green garnish anywhere. –SD

Tony Mandola's

One of the Jekylls of the Mandola Empire

Total pleasure grade

8.0 *Food* **8.6** *Feel* **$63** *Price* **Seafood**

Upmarket restaurant
Mon.-Thurs. 11am-10pm; Fri.-Sat. 11am-11pm; Sun. 5pm-9pm.
Date-friendly. Outdoor dining.

River Oaks
1962 W. Gray St.
(713) 528-3474
www.tonymandolas.com

Bar Full
Credit Cards Visa, MC, AmEx
Reservations Accepted

Maybe more care goes into Tony Mandola's Gulf Coast Kitchen because of the name: with "Mandola" in the restaurant's title, they've got more of the family's reputation riding on its shoulders. Clad in white tablecloths, this seafood restaurant strives to provide great service and served humble, refined food. Its location in a posh strip mall on West Gray, in the middle of River Oaks, guarantees a customer base willing to shell out money. The graphic concept is careful and far-reaching: the restaurant's black-and-white exterior goes nicely with the simple black, white, and silver color scheme indoors.

"Mama's" gumbo is one of the best in the city, loaded with shrimp, fish, oysters, and other Gulf seafood; thick, but not gluey, the gumbo has a nice kick of spice that is pleasant and rewarding. For something lighter, start instead with a plate of delicious raw Gulf oysters, and proceed to fish prepared blackened, fried, grilled, or broiled. Some Italian-ish favorites also populate the menu, and some are better than expected, like "Mama's T 'n' T Special," a remarkable shrimp and crab spaghetti that's only available on Tuesday and Thursday. Prices can get high for fish mains, but the ingredients are fresh (as they should be, given Houston's proximity to the Gulf coast). Gumbo aside, Mama's name seems to grace many dishes here, where sandwiches and tacos live in harmony, as do meatball subs and fish tacos, hamburgers, and po' boys; the menu is big, but if you know what to go for (hint: seafood), you'll make it out unscathed.

Stick to the classics, like étouffée, fried catfish, or any of the fried meals like soft-shell crabs or oysters; the preparations of these are burned into cooks' minds. Repetition teaches you how to cook, not some school or television show.

This feel-good food is consistently pleasing, and will warm your soul. How we love living by the Gulf. –SD

Tony Thai

Bellaire Thai that's a bit more authentic than most, but not worth the drive

B- Total pleasure grade

7.6 Food | **6.8** Feel | **$28** Price | **Thai**

Casual restaurant
Sun.-Thurs. 11am-11pm;
Fri.-Sat. 11am-midnight.
Outdoor dining. Vegetarian-friendly.

Chinatown
10613 Bellaire Blvd.
(281) 495-1711
www.tonythairestaurant.com

Bar Wine and beer only
Credit Cards Visa, MC, AmEx
Reservations Accepted

This is not your father's Bellaire Asian. It's "decorated for your fine dining nights," says the web site, but we think "tacky modern" might be the best way to describe Tony's interior-decorating style. Think twirly, multi-colored lamps; exposed brick; flowing waterfalls; curvy ceiling panels with recessed lighting; and, most amusingly, a giant, mechanized menu scroll, at least seven feet high, that's constantly cycling through the various menu items, with spectacularly unattractive photos to accompany their coded numbers. It's little touches like the scroll that make the place feel appropriate for neither an elaborate dinner nor a light, relaxing lunch.

Still, you might come for the Thai menu, certain parts of which are more authentic than most. For one thing, it's one of the only places in town where you can get som tam, the classic, refreshing green-papaya salad that's a staple all over Thailand. Here, the glassy crunch of julienned green papaya is authentic, and the salad is laced with plenty of hot chili and the trademark tang of fermented shrimp. Lime, peanuts, and underripe tomato slices—the only inauthentic touch—complete the picture.

We've also tried tom yum goong, the classic Thai soup, and it's appropriately salty and spicy, with fresh shrimp; however, an authentic version would integrate kaffir lime leaves, and here, that aromatic flavor is missing, and it's a big loss. Fish mains are the way to go; they do live Dungeness crab stir-fried with curry vegetables, and deep-fried jumbo river shrimp in garlic and pepper sauce. Various versions of crispy whole fish can be successful, too, if you don't mind de-boning, which you shouldn't. Sautéed catfish in chili sauce is another safe bet; the flavor is there, even if the deep-fried fish texture is unremarkable.

Tony Thai's staff is quiet but unusually friendly; on one visit, they unexpectedly offered to take an item off the bill simply because we'd eaten so little of it. The problem wasn't that the dish was bad; it was just that one of our party had been distracted by a seizure induced by the hundredth blazingly-colored menu-scroll cycle, so of course we insisted on paying the full price. –RG

Tony's

It's expensive and very, very good—but can Tony's take it to the next level?

A Total pleasure grade

9.4 Food **8.0** Feel **$110** Price **Italian**

Upmarket restaurant
Mon.-Thurs. 11:30am-2pm, 6pm-10pm; Fri. 11:30am-2pm, 6pm-midnight; Sat. 6pm-midnight; closed Sun. *Live music.*

Greenway Plaza
3755 Richmond Ave.
(713) 622-6778
www.tonyshouston.com

Bar Full
Credit Cards Visa, MC, AmEx
Reservations Essential

There always seems to be a chatter in this town about Tony's: Tony's is done. Tony's is back. Tony's has moved. Tony's has reinvented its image. So deep are Tony Vallone's connections with Houston society that his name has become intrinsically newsworthy—and synonymous with success. But connections also bring about certain obligations, and Tony's longstanding need to please a certain customer contingent has forged a glass ceiling that continues to keep his restaurant from America's upper echelon.

First, the good news: Tony's 2006 installation into a new Greenway space also brought about a renewed sense of culinary focus, and along came a French chef who had once cooked under the tragic French legend Bernard Loiseau. The dining room was updated, too, but in a bright, cold, soaring way. Its expensive works of art are touted by the Tony's website as "museum-quality," which begs the question: do you fancy dinner inside a museum? The centerpiece is a Yao-Ming-dwarfing sculpture of three headless, armless torsos. Although we might respect the work's nostalgic-Classicist merits in a gallery, as a dining-room centerpiece, it plays out as a sleazy distraction of colossal proportions. This stuff is way behind the times—it's Houston at its gaudy worst.

But the potential of this kitchen is nearly limitless. We've had ravioli and gnocchi that were dazzling. When this excellent chef expresses his personality—as when he daringly drizzles a deeply acidic buttery Barolo reduction onto the sweet, delicate flesh of a whole salt-crusted Gulf snapper, cracked apart and expertly deboned at the table; or when he effortlessly turns out the city's most ethereal and transportative soufflé—this can start to feel like one of America's best restaurants.

But then there's that other side of Tony Vallone—the one that still panders to the customers that demand the sort of messy, outdated "fine-dining" dishes that you'd never see at a real, modern, chef-driven restaurant: uninspired pan-seared salmon with grilled shrimp over baby arugula; a banal Italian-American plate of jumbo shrimp with oil and garlic over angel-hair pasta; crab cake with lobster sauce; or a $39 "stuffed truffled filet of beef" that's little more than a list of prestigious ingredients. In a sense, Tony's dilemma is Houston's, too: to achieve culinary greatness, he must make a conscious decision to pull the old weeds from his menu; to sacrifice his lowest common denominator, and maybe with it, a few covers; and to let the talented chef take the wheel, and steer his restaurant into the twenty-first century. –RG

Tookie's Hamburgers

B+ *Total pleasure grade*

This Seabrook standby hits the spot with burgers—and oh, what burgers

8.1 *Food* **7.5** *Feel* **$12** *Price* **Burgers**

Casual restaurant
Sun.-Thurs. 11am-9pm;
Fri.-Sat. 11am-10pm.
Kid-friendly.

Seabrook
1202 Bayport Blvd.
(281) 474-3444

Bar Wine and beer only
Credit Cards Visa and MC
Reservations Not accepted

It would be hard to motivate many city residents to drive out to Seabrook for any reason, but if there were one, Tookie's would be it. The place has been a Harold-and-Kumar-esque road-trip destination down I-45 since the '70s for its specialty burgers and huge onion rings that are known to make grown men cry with joy. In fact, Tookie's might have done more to promote the sales of hybrid cars in Houston than any tree-hugging organization, because after you're hooked on one of Tookie's specialty burgers, you'll pay the cost of gas to Seabrook to taste another again and again

A saying goes that "there are three things in Seabrook: fish, fishermen, and Tookie's." While the haunt itself, and the building that houses it, look bleak lately, it's scientific knowledge that quality burgers come from the crummiest of places, and Tookie's fits that mold well. Its building is hard to miss, with the exterior painted a faded green and an interior that's scarcely better, with chipped paint, worn wood, and a general lack of upkeep (although that can be a sign of mom-and-pop joint greatness, because all the upkeep then goes into the food).

Ignore the "and More" in "Tookie's Hamburgers and More," because you'll be in for a huge disappointment if you get a subpar chicken sandwich or a bowl of chili lacking any sort of chunk. Hand-formed specialty burgers and onion rings are king, especially the "#99," a concoction where the beef is marinated in red wine before hitting the grill, giving it an extra depth of caramelized flavor.

Most impressive, though, is a good ol' "Texas Squealer" and its double-pattied brother, "The Piggyback." While the savory gumption of a good burger is delicious, more alluring yet is a burger with bacon ground into the patty, giving it extra ooze and a bit of added smoke (especially needed since Tookie's, thankfully, understands the sin of overcooking a burger). Onion rings are another specialty, huge, battered just to the point where the coating breaks with a singular crunch.

Order double-pattied for best results. After all, you should live a little—you're on a road trip, right? –JY

TopWater Grill

We'd drive double these 45 minutes for the best Gulf seafood in Texas

A
Total pleasure grade

9.1	9.0	$31
Food	*Feel*	*Price*

Seafood

Casual restaurant
Daily 11am-11pm.
Date-friendly. Outdoor dining.

San León
815 Ave. O
(281) 339-1232
www.topwatergrill.com

Bar Full
Credit Cards Visa, MC, AmEx
Reservations Accepted

This humble, indoor-outdoor temple to Gulf seafood has developed quite the foodie following through the years. These days, more and more Houstonians who don't even know where San Leon is are firing up their GPS devices and making the pilgrimage about two-thirds of the way to Galveston, near Texas City, to find out for themselves what the coastal fishing fiends have known for years: that TopWater Grill is one of the best places in the southeastern United States for fresh Gulf seafood.

The look is neither yuppie nor fish-trailer. It's just real: the feel is more or less like that of a fratty burger-and-beer dive bar with outdoor tables that boast fun, if slightly dingy, views over boats bobbing around in the murky Gulf, gulls flying by, and oil rigs in the distance. Could this really be the Houston area's most showstopping seafood restaurant?

You'd better believe it. And part of the charm is that some of the deliciously fresh seafood, which is hauled in from Captain Wally's own boats, is even served in downmarket bar-snack style: Buffalo-style popcorn bait shrimp, for instance, and "sinkers"—shrimp and oysters rolled into one and wrapped with bacon—that blow your expectations out of the Gulf. Torpedos (stuffed jalapeños with crab and Jack cheese) are unexpectedly spicy and texturally interesting, like poppers from heaven. Coconut shrimp have a serious following, although we don't like them as much as the sinkers; better is a flawless half-dozen Gulf oysters on the half shell for five dollars, or the stone crab claws in season (for a lot more, of course). You'll be thankful, too, for the deeply flavored Bloody Marys, as this place is ideally suited for a Sunday drive from the city.

The deliciousness carries uniformly through the mains. Pecan-crusted gulf snapper with lemon butter, redfish in white wine sauce, and a blackened catfish étoufée that's no less than excellent, well seasoned, gently blackened, meltingly tender, with a sauce less rich than the genre would lead you to anticipate and flavor-packed yellow rice. Fried seafood is just as good: Panko-breadcrumb-battered scallops, stuffed crab, shrimp, flawless hushpuppies, spectacular fried oysters. TopWater Grill does show its weaknesses in boring, tasteless vegetable side dishes; and battered fries aren't our favorites.

But these are small complaints. TopWater Grill is a national treasure. –RG

Treebeards

A legendary Southern lunch-spot that fails to live up to its billing

B- Total pleasure grade

4.2 Food **9.1** Feel **$12** Price **Southern**

Counter service
Mon.-Fri. 11am-2pm;
closed Sat.-Sun.

Kid-friendly. Outdoor dining.

Downtown
315 Travis St.
(713) 228-2622
www.treebeards.com

Downtown
1117 Texas Ave.
(713) 229-8248

Bar None
Credit Cards Visa, MC, AmEx
Reservations Not accepted

Downtown
1100 Louisiana St.
(713) 752-2601

One of Houston's most singular experiences is dining inside a church. "The Cloister," Treebeards' most storied branch purveys so much unique atmosphere—you're eating lunch (and it's only lunch) inside the mess hall of the Christ Church Cathedral—that for more than two decades downtown Houstonians have been forgiving the forgettable food. The Market Square location has some atmosphere, too, some of it naturally endowed by the quirkily muraled downtown building, but in that case it's not enough to make up for the so-so food.

Tradition goes a long way here, and we still enjoy inhabiting either Treebeards, but especially the Christ Church space. As for the food, though, many of the steam-table "specialties" tend to taste exactly the same as each other (and probably the same as they always have, too). It's as if Tony Chachere and the people at Old Bay had a love child that has invaded every one of the dishes served. The étouffée, for instance, brims with undercooked roux, giving it a thick, undesirable palate. Red beans and rice have none of the expected porky goodness and are saved only by a sprinkling of cheese and fresh-cut green onions, turning it into a downmarket chili of sorts. Still, it's not hard to finish the bowl—sometimes a downmarket chili of sorts can hit the spot.

A highly-recommended gumbo is filled with boring pieces of chewy sausage, while stringy chicken and doesn't have much liquid to it, turning the thing into chunky stew. Pick at your tray blindfolded, and we challenge you to decipher one from the next. Even a gimme—a cube of cornbread—manages to be dry and flavorless.

So, again, it's not about the food. It's about a tradition that's been formed over decades of downtown workers' lunches. If you're still going to the Christ Church branch, we can't blame you; it's hard to argue with that atmosphere. But if you're stuck on the Market Square spot, you might want to start shopping for a new tradition. –FC

Trevisio

A simple menu that reflects a restaurant that is trying a bit too hard

C
Total pleasure grade

6.0 *Food* | **7.3** *Feel* | **$60** *Price*

Italian-American

Upmarket restaurant
Mon.-Fri. 11am-10pm;
Sat. 5pm-10pm; closed Sun.

Medical Center
6550 Bertner Ave.
(713) 749-0400
www.trevisiorestaurant.com

Bar Full
Credit Cards Visa, MC, AmEx
Reservations Recommended

Trevisio just doesn't capture diners and reel them in. The idea, at this simple Italian restaurant with not-so-simple prices, is to serve rustic food in an upscale setting. That translates to a few overpriced, head-scratching pizzas, plus passable soups, fresh pastas, risotto, and grilled meats. There are a few highlights on the nicely arranged menu, but as tends to be the case for popular wedding venues, you're paying more for the ambiance and service than for what's actually going into your mouth.

It's definitely the atmosphere that draws in the bigwigs. The decorative themes tend to toe the line between impressive and gaudy, falling more often on the side of the latter. Crazy orange tubes wind their way across the ceiling, while endlessly iterating circles, spirals, and wavy lines, in warm shades of orange and yellow, finish out the graphic theme. Whether it's "beautiful" really depends on your personal aesthetic.

The food, however, isn't beautiful by any definition. It's neither creative nor exciting, although it's sometimes executed well. For starters, cozze (mussels steamed in white wine with Italian flavors) are light and flavorful; in one of the many shrimp-and-grits variations currently populating the upscale Houston dining scene, shrimp are cooked carefully, and well paired with pancetta, but their bed of polenta turns out very dense, lacking seasoning, and an overbearing sauce mutes the flavors. Amongst the seasonally changing dishes we've tried, the pork chop has come overcooked, with a blueberry glaze that didn't play well with Tuscan cabbage. (But what *does* play well with blueberry sauce?) On another visit, sweet corn risotto, another seasonal dish, came out with a good flavor but an overcooked texture, its grains not loose enough.

The wine list is all right with no truly spectacular finds, and the bottles tend to get pricey. They need to jump on this new trend in Houston of low-markup wine. Haven't they heard? It's all the rage. Hint, hint. Trevisio is a banquet space as well, hosting numerous weddings throughout the year. Why, we're not really sure. –SD

Truluck's

Stone crabs and overcooked seafood for those with deep pockets

6.8 *Food* **6.9** *Feel* **$86** *Price* **Seafood**

Upmarket restaurant
Mon.-Thurs. 11am-10pm; Fri. 11am-11pm; Sat. noon-11pm; Sun. 4pm-10pm.
Live music.

Galleria
5350 Westheimer Rd.
(713) 783-7270
www.trulucks.com

Bar Full
Credit Cards Visa, MC, AmEx
Reservations Recommended

It would take a stroke of true luck to find anything on the menu that's worth anywhere near what they're charging for it at this chain seafood restaurant. The highly-touted stone crab claws—they come (you'll be repeatedly reminded) from a proprietary fishery in Florida—have a sweet, briny flavor and a pleasant, resilient texture. The shocking price, at last check: About $30 for three large claws, or $60 for six. Where are we, Zürich?

Clearly, the ambition of Truluck's—with its glossy hue, impressive wood finish, friendly but decked-out waitstaff, and dark, overdressed leather banquettes—is to be the high-class place that you'd take somebody you want to impress, and they try to pull it off in all the tackiest old-school ways: live piano music, starchy white tablecloths, a handshake a bit too eager, a smile a bit too broad. A waitperson might even address your toddler as "sir" or "ma'am."

But the prices and pomp outshine this kitchen, whose best work is done through good sourcing, not good cooking, as in a myriad selection of oysters served at their correctly chilled temperature with tangy sauces. But then there's a "Seafood Cobb Salad," which ditches blue cheese for Jack and cheddar, then adds cold, underseasoned shrimp; small, flavorless crawfish tails; and bland shredded crabmeat. Next, the kitchen fails to chop up the veggies, drowns it in an ill-inspired vinaigrette dominated by the unwanted off-notes of black olives, and then charges you $19.95 for the plate. Granted, that sum buys you an enormous portion, but that's not an advantage in this case.

"Simply grilled" pieces of fish, like a pristine piece of halibut, often come tragically cooked through to toughness. Huge dayboat scallops get no crusty sear, while their side of fried rice shows up dry, tasteless, and filled with overcooked crab. Beautifully aged steaks lack good caramelization from the grill. Then there's the "Florida Stone Crab Platter," a $38.95 disaster in which the crab is paired with (believe it or not) broccoli and mashed potatoes. We wouldn't spend our money here if they cut all the prices in half. Enough said. –FC

Turquoise Grill

A bare but friendly restaurant serving surprisingly Sultan-worthy Turkish fare

B
Total pleasure grade

8.1 *Food* **7.6** *Feel* **$22** *Price* **Turkish**

Casual restaurant
Mon.-Thurs. 8:30am-9pm; Fri. 8:30am-10pm; Sat. 11am-10pm; Sun. noon-6pm.
Breakfast. Brunch. Date-friendly. Outdoor dining.

Upper Kirby
3701 Kirby Dr.
(713) 526-3800
www.turquoisegrill.us

Bar Wine and beer only
Credit Cards Visa, MC, AmEx
Reservations Accepted

With a huge Turkish population in Houston, it is no surprise that we have a great selection of Turkish restaurants. Turkish cuisine is characterized by fresh, acidic flavors that please the soul and don't weigh you down. Turquoise Grill takes the best of two worlds, combining southern hospitality and good food in a Sultan-pleasing sort of way.

A clean, fresh, and uncluttered restaurant with white walls, Turquoise Grill keeps diners from being distracted by the décor and allows them to focus more on the food. (That's a charitable way of putting it.) The "Shepherd's Bread," cooked in their brick oven, is a thing of beauty. It's fluffy, happy, and alive, and you're lucky to have it with you through your meal. Creamy hummus and lemony tabbouleh are particularly strong appetizers. Turquoise also tries its hand at pizzas and calzoni, which come topped or stuffed with Turkish ingredients like feta, olives, and Aleppo pepper.

Fish specials are offered occasionally. The whole beast is fried crispy and served with rice. Yes, that means head and all will come to you on a plate along with rice; this is the best way to eat fish. Kebabs are hit or miss. The tenderloin kebab comes well done, rendering it dry and unarousing because of a lack of fat. Service can be slow, but they are very polite, and the prices are surprisingly moderate for the quality of food, so we don't mind.

The food at Turquoise Grill just tastes fresh and soulful. It is executed well, and, clearly, they're proud of it. The likeable chef-owner is always in the dining room schmoozing with guests, wooing them with his quirky humor. If nothing else, this genuine hospitality will definitely leave you plotting a return trip. –SD

Udipi Café

South Indian flavors exciting enough to incite existential crises in carnivores

A Total pleasure grade

9.3 Food | **8.2** Feel | **$8** Price

Indian, Vegetarian

Casual restaurant
Daily 11am-10pm.
Vegetarian-friendly. Kid-friendly. Additional locations.

Hillcroft Area
5959 Hillcroft St.
(713) 334-5555

Bar None
Credit Cards Visa, MC, AmEx
Reservations Not accepted

Sugar Land
3559 Hwy. 6 South
(281) 313-2700

Clearlake
15140 Old Galveston Rd.
(281) 480-5556

Even if you're experienced in south Indian cuisine, Udipi Café might give you an experience almost as religious as a visit to the Sri Krishna temple, the beautiful shrine for which its namesake city is famous.

This bare-bones but pleasantly yellow-walled restaurant, full of big multi-generational Indian families feasting, is entirely vegetarian, but to call it a vegetarian restaurant is to miss the point. Rather than being built around a lack of meat, it's built around the centuries-old recipes of south India's Karnatka region, birthplace of the masala dosa, one of the world's gastronomical treasures. Dosas, of which there are 13 on Udipi's menu, are big, thin rice crêpes characterized in their finest form—as they are here—by an ineffable lightness, a precise interplay between crispy and spongy. But they'd be lost without sambar, a lentil-and-vegetable stew based on tamarind broth that's another backbone of southern Indian cuisine. Other staple starches of the South include sauce-absorbent idli (steamed rice and lentil cakes) and medhu vada (deep-fried lentil-flour doughnuts).

Nowhere in Udipi's many delicious stews will you find vegetables filling in for meats. Rather, the kitchen turns out faithful renditions of centuries-old recipes with enough complex spice combinations, judicious reduction of liquids, and textural variation between starches, legumes, fruits, greens, and dairies to burrow straight into the pleasure centers of the brain. These might include silky paneer makhani, with some of the best homemade cheese cubes we've sampled, bathed in a mind-blowingly deep, creamy red sauce; smooth, subtle yellow dal; flawless condiments like coconut chutney and "pickle" with the deep, elemental pucker of preserved lemon; and world-class versions of yogurt rice, rich vegetable korma, and sweet sheera. Northern dishes like aloo gobi (cauliflower and potatoes), Bombay-style chats, and the ever-popular palak paneer, are delicious too.

Water or a lassi will accompany your meal, and masala coffee or tea will finish it. The biggest challenge, if you're not familiar with the cuisine, is figuring out which plates and bowls to use for what; our best advice is to emulate your neighbors, and bring on the barrage of flavor.

Could a humble, one-room South Indian vegetarian joint in a Hillcroft shopping plaza really be one of Houston's best restaurants?

Believe it. –RG

Uptown Sushi

Obligatory sushi in a club-like atmosphere

6.5 Food | **8.5** Feel | **$44** Price

Japanese

Upmarket restaurant
Mon.-Wed. 11am-11pm; Thurs.-Fri. 11am-midnight; Sat. noon-midnight; closed Sun.
Date-friendly.

Galleria
1131-14 Uptown Park
(713) 871-1200
www.uptown-sushi.com

Bar Full
Credit Cards Visa, MC, AmEx
Reservations Recommended

In Japan, the best sushi bars are little eight-seat jewel boxes with pristine fish, lively conversation, and décor that's basically limited to the imposing, elegant figure of the Sushi Master himself, deeply focused on his art. Uptown Sushi is exactly the opposite: it's all glamour and ritz. We wish the "zushi fusion cuisine" rose to the level of its surroundings, but it's pretty clear that people come here for the scene—to drink sake and look at short skirts or rippled bodies—more than they come to meditate on the food.

The minimalist room is all full of flowing browns and yellows, creating a modern techno look evocative of the "in" style that's rampant at style-over-substance joints in New York and LA. Flowing white cloth cloaks the walls, bringing elegance to the room, and dark leather panels in the lounge area bring in a sexy masculine contrast. Elevated banquettes—the best seats in the house—instantly let it be known that you've come to be seen. And you'll do more of that than talking; with all the head-pounding music and acoustics, conversation—least of all about the food—is virtually out of the question.

The food at Uptown tries too hard to keep up with its surroundings by carelessly combining ingredients and slapping on the "fusion" label. Adding baby carrots or using orzo in lunch dishes seems obligatory and out of place, not innovative. The chef-named tuna tartare is killed by an all-too-liberal amount of parmesan, rendering any fresh flavors of the tuna null. An interesting rib-eye maki wraps slices of beef around avocado and sweet potato, but it comes out uneven. A sweet teriyaki glaze contrasts well with the fatty avocado, but the sweet potato is undercooked and woody. Nigiri sushi cuts are chunky, but aren't otherwise anything special. Many of the specialty rolls suffer from the "too much crap in them" syndrome. The simple Spiro Roll, with spicy tuna, salmon, and avocado, has the cleanest, least muddy flavors.

Beginning to end, Uptown is more about the lively vibe than the fresh fish. At least these guys definitely know how to throw a party. –JY

Van Loc

If you can't make out to Bellaire, this is a not-so-close second

C *Total pleasure grade*

6.0 *Food* | 6.8 *Feel* | $15 *Price*

Vietnamese

Casual restaurant
Daily 10am-11pm.

Midtown
3010 Milam St.
(713) 528-6441

Bar Full
Credit Cards Visa, MC, AmEx
Reservations Not accepted

Like the watched pot never boiling, it seems that when you're specifically looking for that diamond in the culinary rough, you never find it. And we didn't find it with Van Loc. The menu consists of Vietnamese egg rolls, hot and sour soup, and bargain noodle bowls. If you're an avid food adventurist, then you are better off trying any of the Vietnamese food in Bellaire's Chinatown.

If you're starving and undemanding, though, you might want to stick around. Plates are big and the flavors won't wow you, just fill you up; lots of familiar Chinese influences are scattered throughout the menu. On the other hand, if you like attentive and friendly service, then ditch Van Loc immediately.

The restaurant is spacious, with plenty of parking, and it's shaded by a nice array of greenery. Inside, the place bustles at peak hours, but when it's dead and almost closing, you tend to get an offputting don't-come-in-because-we-want-to-go-home-early vibe from the waitstaff. Unlike its Vietnamese counterpart, Mai's, Van Loc closes before all the riff-raff can infiltrate the establishment with their drunkenness and rash decisions.

The food is not bad; it's just what you would expect when you shovel it into your mouth. Hot and sour soup is good, with a hint of pineapple and spice, but it's still just an unexciting, generic, ubiquitous pan-Asian food. The noodle bowls, however, are delicious, with pork and vermicelli arranged with carrots, cucumbers, and heat to fill your stomach with love and devotion. Or something like that. Try the whole fried fish; it's probably the best thing on the menu. Tilapia, not our favorite fish under normal circumstances, comes out crispy and tasty, with lots of chili and fish sauce, if you're one who enjoys the experience of eating a whole animal from nose to tail. (We are.)

The service at Van Loc can be shoddy at times, but you'll know when they're having a good day. There's a bit of a language barrier, so getting the right menu item might be a challenge; the number system they've instituted just seems to have added to the confusion. But don't shy away, because we all want to eat, and they all want to pay the rent. It's a symbiotic relationship, if not the most flavorful one. –SD

Vic & Anthony's

Anything at a price—in this case, local steak, done just about right

9.3 Food | **9.0** Feel | **$94** Price | **Steakhouse**

Upmarket restaurant
Mon.-Thurs. 5pm-10pm; Fri. 11am-11pm; Sat. 5pm-11pm.
Date-friendly. Live music.

Downtown
1510 Texas St.
(713) 228-1111
www.vicandanthonys.com

Bar Full
Credit Cards Visa, MC, AmEx
Reservations Recommended

Perhaps because of its unique caché with oilmen entertaining out-of-town clients and Astros admirers after the game, Vic and Anthony's is one of the only places downtown where you can show up after 9pm and find tables still full of people. It's a nice feeling, at that Houstonian witching hour, to not be eating alone—even if the bulk of the patrons here are not Houstonians.

The freestanding, two-story building has become something of a local landmark since its 2002 launch by the Landry's group (you can't stop 'em, you can only hope to contain 'em). Although the concept is certainly corporate—with three private event rooms—the regular interior is warm and inviting, a good replica of an old-school New York steakhouse. The noise level is comfortably high, providing a nice din, but nothing you have to shout over. Amidst a city full of large-chain steakhouses, we do have a soft spot for Vic & Anthony's, even if they kindly request that gentlemen wear jackets (an irritating custom that barely even exists in New York anymore—it's particularly offensive in steamy Houston).

Crab cakes are amongst of the most variable of steakhouse appetizers, but Vic & Anthony's version comes through in spades; its focus is squarely on lump-crabmeat hunks, rather than bread crumbs, and the accompanying chive beurre blanc is an exemplary counterpoint. The list of mains on the menu is delightfully short; it's just a few different cuts of meat, along with a seafood menu (which you should skip). Sides are kept simple; you won't find anything overambitious, just steakhouse standards like world-class creamed spinach, rich, smooth, and bursting with flavor. Potatoes au gratin and lyonnaise are excellent, too.

On to the main event: steak is cooked exactly to order; by rare, they really mean rare, which means that you should order the Porterhouse for two just a touch above rare, but below medium-rare. To answer the real question: should you spend your own money or your company's money here? Your company's, preferably. But even if a few hundred dollars of your own hard-earned salary is burning a hole in your pocket, this is certainly your best bet for steak downtown. –AH

Vieng Thai

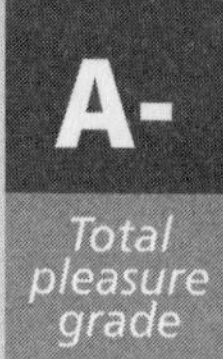

Finally, authentic Isan cuisine takes residence in Houston

8.5 Food | **4.2** Feel | **$24** Price | **Thai**

Casual restaurant
Mon.-Fri. 11am-9:30pm;
Sat.-Sun. noon-9:30pm.
Vegetarian-friendly.

Spring Branch
6929 Long Point Dr.
(713) 688-9910
www.viengthai.com

Bar BYO
Credit Cards Visa and MC
Reservations Accepted

Isan (or Isaan, or E-Sarn, depending on whom you ask) is the northeastern portion of Thailand, bordering Cambodia on the south and Laos in the east and north. It is one of Thailand's poorest, most rural regions. And it is also arguably the greatest culinary district of the country.

Everywhere in Isan you will be served som tam, one of the most refreshing and complex of the world's salads. Som tam is made with green papaya (which has nothing to do with the sweet orange version of the fruit; it's crisp and sour, somewhere closer to cabbage or jicama). It also involves fiery chilies, palm sugar, salt, garlic, dried shrimp, peanuts, fish sauce, lime, and often other ingredients, ground together with a mortar and pestle. It is unique, it is delicious, and it is virtually impossible to get in Texas—except at Vieng Thai, an Isan restaurant, which does a faithful version of som tam, although you'll have to ask for it "very spicy" to get the authentic version, if you can handle it. They also do a challengingly crunchy Laotian version, with ground crab shells. Order it with sticky rice, the classic accompaniment, although the latter is just okay here.

The cardinal sin at Vieng Thai would be to order the same Thai dishes you see elsewhere. Just say no to spring rolls, massamun curry (this is a dish from Thailand's south), or—please—pad Thai. None of it's bad, but it's so much less interesting than the gamey regional "E-Sarn Sausage"; the fried pilot fish; or, perhaps, the pla pad ped (crispy catfish sautéed in curry paste). Try anything with kaffir lime leaves, a unique, crave-worthy authentic Thai flavor that's scarce elsewhere in town.

Vieng Thai is not perfect. The fish is not the freshest you'll taste. Meats can come overcooked and flavorless. Menu items are often not available, the service is perfunctory and unhelpful, and the dingy, strip-mall, poorly lit room with outdated stereo equipment is uninspiring at best.

And next to the wonderful opportunity to try authentic Isan food in Houston, none of that matters. –RG

Vietopia

An overpriced, underwhelming, inauthentic Vietnamese trend-shop with dystopian service

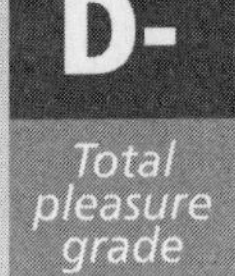

4.0 Food | **1.9** Feel | **$40** Price

Vietnamese

Upmarket restaurant
Mon.-Fri. 11am-10:30pm;
Sat.-Sun. 11am-11pm.
Outdoor dining. WiFi.

West U
5176 Buffalo Speedway
(713) 664-7303

Bar Full
Credit Cards Visa, MC, AmEx
Reservations Accepted

How about this for a vision of culinary utopia: a restaurant with a staff that would willfully seat you a half-hour before closing time, and then demand that you order appetizers, main courses, and desserts all to be brought to the table simultaneously—and these are up to twenty-dollar main courses we're talking about—so that the kitchen staff can go home. Show up at Vietopia anytime near the dreaded witching hour only if you're prepared to watch your ice-cream cake melt as you're digging into your appetizer. And then pay a bill that can easily creep above $50 a head, including drinks, tax, and tip.

This is not an isolated incident; it's a systematic problem with the service here, which is so indifferent and rushed as to deeply detract from the experience of dining in Vietopia's pretty, high-ceilinged room. Not to mention ill-informed: ask for advice, and you're likely to be steered toward the most boring wok-fried beef dish on the menu rather than the most interesting Vietnamese preparation of a whole fried fish, which, it bears mention, is quite good. This is, by consensus, one of the most incompetent service staffs in the city.

The restaurant is located in a convenient no-man's-land location, a shopping plaza just south of I-59 and Greenway Plaza, and it has won a surprising share of accolades. The airy, two-floor space has high ceilings and palm-frond fans that give it a trendy edge but also make the place feel more lonely at odd hours or evenings. You'd do well to start with a "Caribbean martini," Stoli vodka and Malibu with a splash of pineapple juice, a concoction that sounds sweet but is surprisingly tart.

But the menu is a minefield. Thick, enormous chicken and mango rolls come with useless lettuce and carrots, and a fruity mayo that tastes of honey; the chicken within is of the fried-breaded-cutlet variety. They're a total throwaway. Even if the whole fried fish, fresh and touched by chili, is a rarely ordered find, it's too little, too late. In a city full of great, authentic Vietnamese food, there is no reason to settle for mediocrity. –RG

Vin

Where's the wine?

C
Total pleasure grade

7.0 *Food* | **5.5** *Feel* | **$86** *Price*

New American

Upmarket restaurant
Mon. 11am-3pm; Tues.-Thurs. 11am-3pm, 5pm-11pm; Fri. 11am-3pm, 5pm-midnight; Sat. 5pm-midnight; closed Sun.
Outdoor dining.

Downtown
530 Texas Ave.
(713) 237-9600
www.vinhouston.com

Bar Full
Credit Cards Visa, MC, AmEx
Reservations Recommended

Vin (pronounced "vine," and technically spelled with a long-i pronunciation mark, which our Frutiger font does not provide, even in its extended-character set) is ideally positioned to snag the theater district crowd, just steps away from its storefront. It's a sleek, trendy—maybe too trendy, in fact—addition to the downtown dining scene. Warm woods complement dark reds, and the décor flirts with slutty, but manages to stay respectable. Vin serves "Contemporary American Cuisine with Southern European influence." We'd rather call it New American, since the influence is really global; there are lots of Asian touches, as well as some flat-out Texan ones too, as in a clever pairing of quail with local honeycomb.

The food here comes as a pleasant surprise, even if the check at the end of the meal comes as a less pleasant one. We love the super-rich and savory pork belly, even if its fig and date add too much sugar. Well seasoned shrimp 'n' grits are delightfully livened up by a dash of smoked paprika oil, and so-called "flatbreads," really pizzas, are satisfyingly thin and crisp. We've had a couple of overcooked meat mains, but props go out to Vin for "the world's tiniest desserts"—it's about time for this in Houston.

The wine list, though, is a major disappointment. It's incredibly heavy on aggressive, concentrated new world wines—there are 10 Syrahs from Australia, California, and Chile, but not a single Rhône red. Markups are high, too, and the low end is thin; there's not one Pinot Noir under $50. Barolo, Argentine Malbec, and Beaujolais-Villages are classified together under a section entitled "Random Reds & Blends." This, at a restaurant called "Vin"?

Vin also plays into the city's growing epidemic of unnecessary, forced valet parking. On one night, we couldn't find anyone near the entrance, so we parked in a free, unmarked space in a nearby lot. Later, on the way out, we were stopped by a Bayou Place valet, who claimed that we owed him eight dollars since we'd eaten there. We showed him that we had our keys, and thus had clearly parked our own car, but he physically blocked our way, threatening to "give us trouble" if we didn't pay him for his services. Intimidated by his size, we forked over the cash.

That's right: we were actually *mugged* by Vin's valets. –FC

Vincent's

Nino's little brother pumps out passable pizzas and rotisserie chickens, if little authenticity

C *Total pleasure grade*

5.7 *Food*

7.7 *Feel*

$45 *Price*

Italian-American

Upmarket restaurant
Mon.-Thurs. 11am-3pm, 5pm-10pm; Fri. 11am-3pm, 5pm-11pm; Sat. 5pm-11pm; closed Sun.
Kid-friendly.

Montrose
2701 W. Dallas St.
(713) 528-4313
www.ninos-vincents.com

Bar Full
Credit Cards Visa, MC, AmEx
Reservations Recommended

While Vincent's is the little brother of Nino's, Vincent Mandola's original restaurant next door, there's nothing little about it. The dining rooms are large and boisterous. The plates are big and the flavors are robust. It can handle big groups that are celebrating a birthday, the closing of a deal, or merely the fact that it's time to eat on a Saturday night.

Nino's, Vincent's, and Grappino di Nino share a huge parking lot in a quiet residential block in Montrose. Of the three, Vincent's claim to fame is its huge rotisserie oven, which churns out decent roast chickens and crisp pizzas. (It's been emulated at the fast-casual Pronto Cucinino.) The half-bird, served with creamy garlic mashed potatoes and roast veggies, comes in at a whopping $16, but it's moist and chickeny, with a rub of lemon, pepper, and herbs that mildly accentuates the flavor. The rest of the menu, as is expected for the Mandola group, is down-the-line "Italian-American 2.0" (the term is defined on pages 6-7), although pizzas are well above average for Houston; we recommend the piccante ($11), which spices things up with sausage and mixed peppers. We're far less impressed with the highly-(self-)touted lasagne ($13), which they trump up as the best in town but we find merely average. The Penne alla Vodka ($14), with a fair bit of crabmeat in a light pink sauce, is a better, if hardly authentic, dish.

Vincent's is the least formal and most family-friendly of the three Montrose restaurants. It's not cheap, but like its neighboring restaurants, it certainly dishes out a serious quantity of food, and good service, for the money. The word is out, so Vincent's can get fairly business-y at lunchtime with the business crowd; on weekend nights, it gets downright crowded, as it accommodates both families and festive groups just starting the evening. Reservations are a good idea. Or, better yet, spend a few dollars more and ditch it for Da Marco, where you can actually dine on authentic Italian food. –FC

Welcome Food Center

Good produce, welcoming lunch boxes, and live fish amidst an olfactory barrage

Chinese

Specialty grocery
Daily 9am-10pm.
Vegetarian-friendly.

Chinatown
9180 Bellaire Blvd.
(713) 270-7789

Bar None
Credit Cards Visa, MC, AmEx
Reservations Not accepted

Some call it offensive. We just like to say "different." Either way, the smell of Welcome Supermarket is *intense*. If you're not used to the aromas of fermenting foods, vinegar, and live butchers—or, for that matter, if you're not used to looking at entire animals, but rather just dumbed-down fillets of them—then this glorious Asian market might scare you off. But you'd be missing a gold mine, the most well-rounded of the several Asian supermarkets that anchor most of the shopping centers in Bellaire's Chinatown.

Welcome does a good job in keeping the place at least neat and tidy, if occasionally dusty in places. The hygiene here is well above average when compared to some of the local competition. The sten…uh…smell isn't exactly what you might call a breath of fresh mountain air; most of it comes from the seafood storage area, with damp floors and coolers in an adjoining room. The rest of the place is total chaos, and unless you've been there several hundred times or know Chinese, you'll have to search far and wide if you're looking for something specific. We enjoy it, though: wandering through these aisles on a weekend afternoon, you might as well be in Hong Kong.

But then, we're food nerds.

Rummage through the produce section, be exacting in your quality standards, and you might come home with the best fruits at the best prices in Houston, especially for exotic fruits like durian. Dried and boxed goods are fair in price, although DiHo down the street is better. And the fresh fish can be amazingly cheap if you're very adamant with the fishmongers about checking the freshness of the product. One way to guarantee it is to have them net a live, flopping fish from one of the many tanks.

The secret about Welcome that's best kept from outsiders, however, is their prepared foods. For less than five bucks, you can get a to-go box that probably won't weigh less than a pound, full of myriad authentic Chinese treats Stir-fried noodles, braised pig's feet, and stewed black-bean spare ribs are only a small sample of what's available. The food comes lukewarm, so you'll probably want to employ your (wince) microwave. –JY

Whataburger

A Texas staple that has become a legend in fast food

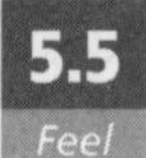

Burgers

Fast-food chain
Daily 24 hours.
Breakfast. Kid-friendly.
Additional locations.

Upper Kirby
3712 S. Shepherd Dr.
(713) 529-0216
www.whataburger.com

Bar None
Credit Cards Visa, MC, AmEx
Reservations Not accepted

Midtown
3636 Main St.
(713) 868-1581

Downtown
1000 Main St.
(713) 658-9602

Is Whataburger that good? Even some people that have moved away from Texas still talk about it with such awe, endowing it with the hallowed status of a last meal on death row. Why?

We suspect that it's only great, excellent, and wonderful whenever Mr. Jack Daniels is leading the way at two-thirty in the morning. Granted, Whataburger does have its merits in the fast-food community. It's grassroots in an In-N-Out Burger sort of way—that is, far better than other local commercialized burger joints, with no annoying mascots. But Whataburger's standard burgers are nowhere near as irresistible as In-N-Out's or the local indy burger shops' versions; here, they're only slightly above average for fast food. Ditto for the chicken sandwiches, chicken tenders, and so on.

Around lunchtime, it's also not so fast. Not that that's a necessarily a bad thing; Whataburger prides itself on fresh food that isn't made until you order it. But they stay a bit too true to their promise: they'll keep you waiting up to thirty minutes at busy times for those burgers. The "Number One" or the Whataburger meal with fries and a drink is the go-to order. A thin, tasteless patty, often gray and dull, comes seasoned with a blend of spices and topped with fresh and crispy lettuce, tomato, pickles, and onions. The bun serves merely as a vehicle for the other ingredients, but it serves its purpose. You can add cheese, bacon, or pickled jalapeños; we recommend all three. Better than the burgers are the the breakfast taquito, served daily from 11pm to 11am (genius hours for drive-thru fast food). They're filled with eggs and your choice of bacon, potato, or sausage, and something about them that is addictive.

Long lines can make Whataburger's drive-thru indistinguishable from the parking lot at the wee hours of the morning, but the trained professionals who work there always seem to sort it out. There are plenty of other burger joints that are ten times better than Whataburger, and at two in the morning, there are many taquerías that have better food. But Whataburger cravings are intense; when you get a craving, it stays with you until until you satisfy it—or at least drunkenly start to, possibly passing out mid-burger. As such, a Whataburger burger is a likely bed companion for the lonely and shy. –SD

Whole Foods

A gourmet market empire that Texas can claim as its own

Gourmet wonderland

Specialty grocery
Daily 8am-10pm. *Breakfast. Live music. Vegetarian-friendly. Wine-friendly.*
Additional locations.

Upper Kirby
2955 Kirby Dr.
(713) 520-1937
www.wholefoodsmarket.com

Bar Wine and beer only
Credit Cards Visa, MC, AmEx
Reservations Not accepted

West U
4004 Bellaire Blvd.
(713) 667-4090

Westchase
11145 Westheimer Rd.
(713) 784-7776

Whole Foods is Austin's homegrown health-food market gone national—the Texas boy made good. These stores are theme parks of gourmet and organic shopping, and they're just plain gorgeous. The produce, cheese, meats, and seafood are all beautifully displayed, and the overall experience is quite simply overwhelming, in part because there is just so much to choose from. You just might find yourself spending an entire afternoon here.

In an America that is all about breadth of choice, it's no wonder, after a glance around the store and its staggering array of upper-end food products spanning the globe, that this place has become such a success story, now gracing such spectacularly ambitious spaces as the basement of Manhattan's Time Warner Center, one of the most expensive little swaths of commercial real estate in the history of mankind.

Sprinkled throughout this store are displays of seafood, sandwiches, barbecue, pizza, sushi, salads, "living foods," and more. Foods from around the world (sometimes different parts of the world at different times of day) can be boxed up or plated, eaten inside or taken home. Extensive tea, coffee, wine, and beer selections complete the trip around the world. Just wander around until something piques your interest. And if you find that you're lost, the incredibly friendly and knowledgeable staff will help you with anything.

It is hard to pick out a few deli items to mention from amongst all the options, but we do love the creamy, rich lobster bisque, with its gentle Southwestern heat. Satisfying pizza, available by the whole pie or slice, boasts fresh toppings, a nicely thin crust, and you can get some interesting vegetarian combinations like artichoke hearts, tomatoes, Kalamata olives, spinach, and goat cheese. And don't miss the cannoli—the shells are dense and toasty, the filling is light, and they are adorned with dark chocolate and pistachio. Pre-prepared salads are a pleasant surprise with creative touches. Not bad for a trip to what was once just a healthy grocery store down the road in Austin. Texas pride, baby, Texas pride. –FC

Willie G's

A signature Landry's fish restaurant, with its signature bad food

D
Total pleasure grade

4.2	7.8	$87	**Seafood**
Food	*Feel*	*Price*	

Upmarket restaurant
Mon.-Thurs. 11am-10:30pm; Fri. 11am-11pm; Sat. 11:30am-11pm; Sun. 11:30am-10pm.

Galleria
1605 Post Oak Blvd.
(713) 840-7190
www.williegs.com

Bar Full
Credit Cards Visa, MC, AmEx
Reservations Accepted

A Houston institution since 1980, even resurrected after a fire brought it down in flames, Willie G's has somehow schmoozed and greased itself into the hearts of a certain contingent in Houston. With food that appeals to the older, steak-and-lobster, Silver-Oak-and-Opus-One crowd, Willie G's relies heavily on the pounding spices of Louisiana to cover up the mistakes of its kitchen. Much of what comes out is overcooked, and either covered in a sauce or deep-fried.

The interior of Willie G's feels a bit like the dining room in a first-class ocean liner. The gentlemanly room is just steeped in foof, and the high prices help to weed out the younger crowd. You almost expect dinner-jacketed, white-gloved waiters to show up and start prancing around the glossy tables, dark wood paneling, antiquated furnishings, and careful flower arrangements. Staff don't really don white gloves, but they are comically accommodating, willing to wait on people hand and foot—which seems to go over well with this older crowd. A bit more subtle, though, is the way they're poised to pounce on any possible opportunity to sell you a big, high-tag California red wine.

We'd suggest an alternate route: go for a cheaper wine so you can order a second bottle, because you're going to need it. For a restaurant that claims to serve "fresh seafood specialties," Willie G's really cooks the fish to a pulp, rendering it unrelated to its original form. The better choices are more on the fried side of the menu: battered shrimp, for example, are well seasoned and crispy, although it's hard to eat more than one or two of them. The kitchen seems to have a chronic overcooking disease, leaving the classic oysters Rockefeller too long in the broiler, torching any freshness the oyster might have once had. But culinary sin number one was realized, at one visit, when an ahi tuna steak requested rare came to the table not medium-rare, not medium, and not medium-well, but white-all-the-way-through well done. The management handled the situation well, but in general, Willie G's, like so much of the Landry's chain these days, seems far more concerned with the bottom line than with the food. –JY

Willy's Pub

Pints for pennies, pub grub, and ping-pong with Rice undergrads

C *Total pleasure grade*

5.2 *Food* **7.7** *Feel* **$12** *Price* **American**

Bar
Mon. 11am-1am; Tues.-Thurs. 11am-2am; Fri. 11am-7pm; closed Sat.-Sun.
Live music. WiFi.

Rice Area
6100 Main St.
(713) 348-4056
www.rice.edu/pub

Bar Full
Credit Cards Visa, MC, AmEx
Reservations Not accepted

The revered Rice undergraduate watering hole, Willy's Pub, is a windowless basement space that's friendly but depressingly deserted for most of the day and into the evening—that is, until the students descend down the stairs of the Rice student center en masse, and come to play music, to hold student organization meetings, and above all, to drink 20-ounce plastic cups of Bud Light for as little as $2. And a normal-sized beer? $1.50. Try to get that in Rice Village. (There are better beers on tap, too, if you feel like going gangbusters and dropping an extra couple quarters.)

The Willy's Pub kitchen is not really a kitchen; its pièce de résistance is a little counter where they can make Quiznos-licensed subs, which are on offer for the reasonable price of $5.25. Still, they're not bad, toasted, their cheese melted, their ingredients fair and straightforward. There are also okay jalapeño poppers and personal pizzas, the latter of which are to be avoided at all costs. On the bright side, this is one of the only pub-grub spots in the area that has reliable WiFi (and not just for Rice students—anyone can log on to the "Visitor" network). It's actually a fairly relaxing place to sit down with a laptop and write (a restaurant guide, for instance) over cheaper-than-cheap beer, like Ziegen Bock or a decent American Pale Ale.

The couches are plentiful and comfy, the lighting is slightly too bright, and one wall of Willy's is predictably plastered with Rice sports highlight newspaper articles. There's a big, old-fashioned sound system, and the old-school gaming amenities are aplenty: dartboards, foosball, and a ping-pong table, sometimes in a state of disrepair. Ultimately, it's a cheap place to sit with a WiFi-wired laptop and a beer. (We obviously don't need to tell you about the place if you're a Rice undergrad. Especially, that is, if you're an over-21 undergrad—this is Houston, this is a university, and the carding policy, needless to say, is harsh.) So drink up, toast the Owls' College World Series championship, and try not to spill your Ziegen Bock on the keyboard. –RG

YAO Restaurant & Bar

We doubt even Yao Ming would even enjoy a meal here at his namesake restaurant

C- *Total pleasure grade*

5.4 *Food* **7.8** *Feel* **$36** *Price* **Chinese**

Casual restaurant
Mon.-Thurs. 11am-10pm; Fri. 11am-11pm; Sat. noon-11pm; Sun. noon-10pm.

Westchase
9755 Westheimer Rd.
(832) 251-2588
www.yaorestaurant.com

Bar Full
Credit Cards Visa, MC, AmEx
Reservations Accepted

If there were three Fearless Critic commandments, they would be: thou shalt cringe at the sight of a steam table, thou shalt choose independent restaurants over chains, and thou shalt not eat at a celebrity-named restaurant. While we're fans of the humble Houston Rockets all-star center, it's debatable as to whether the big guy could even sit in this modern, over-Asian-glorified dining room, take bites of the food that shows off his Shanghai roots as much as a trip to PF Chang's does, and still flash that sheepish grin of his.

We've noticed that there's a correlation between sanitation and desirability of a Chinese restaurant: the dingier a place gets, the better its food. Though we'd love to say that nicer places put out nicer food, it just isn't the trend, and so YAO's contemporary take on Asian décor with royal red stylings and that popular techni-Asian wood-tone and bamboo look shouldn't give you a good feeling for the meal to come. The website claims that the idea for the restaurant came from Mr. and Mrs. Yao wanting a place to relax and eat good food, but for some reason we think that deep down, they'd brush the place off as a trendy young hipster hangout and head down to Chinatown to get real Chinese food.

The menu features glorified, Americanized, bastardized renditions of the real Chinese cuisine that you could get around the corner. The crab wontons are addictive little fried puffs of cream cheese (any crab that may have been in there was rendered null and void) that are totally unheard of on an authentic Chinese menu. The green pepper steak with its "signature" soy-based, thickened sauce is wholly unspectacular and has an odd vegetal taste to it. Walnut shrimp are heavy and plodding, with too much sauce and and overcooked, rubbery shrimp; they'll leave you wondering where exactly walnuts fit into Chinese cuisine. Vegetarian items are more authentic because of their tendency to be lighter, like the shredded bean curd string beans, with brightly-sour Chinese pickles melding with the toothy bean curd. The only bright spot of the meal is the intriguing list of teas. They're calming, both to the stomach and to the psyche, as they signal the end of the meal. –JY

Yatra Brasserie

A London transplant that offers something different to downtown

7.0 Food **6.7** Feel **$42** Price **Indian**

Casual restaurant
Mon.-Fri. 11am-2:30pm, 5:30pm-10:30pm; Sat. 5:30pm-10:30pm; closed Sun.
Date-friendly. Vegetarian-friendly. WiFi.

Downtown
706 Main St.
(713) 224-6700
www.yatrabrasserie.com

Bar Full
Credit Cards Visa, MC, AmEx
Reservations Accepted

Different doesn't necessarily mean good, but downtown, where lunch too often comes slopped out of a steam table or nuked in a microwave, Yatra Brasserie is a welcome change. In the spot previously occupied by Laidback Manor on the corner of Main and Capitol, Yatra walks a line between casual and upmarket, serving British-style Indian food that isn't bad, but could use a little more pep to its step.

The name is a bit deceptive, as the restaurant doesn't even remotely resemble a brasserie—or your average Indian restaurant. Instead, Yatra takes a stab at a stiff, minimalist sensibility that tries too hard to be trendy and not hard enough to be comfortable. Tables are small, and chairs are rigid. At least the bright, electric color scheme and well-chosen artwork on the wall offset much of the late-'80s-style black that lines the booths and the bar. Lately, it's also integrated with a sleek cocktail lounge next door called Butterfly High, and an ambitious South Asian nightclub called Bar Bollywood in the basement.

Although Yatra's roots are in London, they quickly figured out that the way to a Houstonian's heart is by offering crab cakes. Other appetizers, too, are easy concessions to Houston eating habits: empanadas, calamari, and chicken wings. Sticking with the cuisine at hand is a good idea, though; the samosa chaat is delicious, with a flaky crust and obviously Indian spices perfuming the small packages of potato and peas. But even "Yatra's Specials" are as predictable as anything else. You might as well try that old, comforting Brit-Indian favorite, chicken tikka masala—why not?—with tender chunks of meat in a zippy, creamy sauce, but without much girth. Fish tikka jalfrezi is a nice concoction, with the flakes of fish melding with the flavor of slightly charred peppers and onions, but again, the flavors are mellow to a fault. The execution is fine, and lunch is an okay value, but at dinner, it's hard to see what justifies the elevated prices—main courses reaching in the mid-to-upper teens, before the obligatory naan or rice—for ultimately standard Indian food. –JY

Yia Yia Mary's

Why would anyone spend fifteen dollars for a main course that's ordered Taco-Bell-style?

7.3 Food **2.7** Feel **$20** Price **Greek**

Counter service
Mon.-Thurs. 11am-10pm;
Fri.-Sat. 11am-11pm;
Sun. 11am-9pm.
Kid-friendly. Outdoor dining.

Galleria
4747 San Felipe St.
(713) 840-8665
www.yiayiamarys.com

Bar Full
Credit Cards Visa, MC, AmEx
Reservations Accepted

Sometimes it seems like enough is never enough for the Pappas chain: Mexican's not enough. Steak's not enough. Neither is BBQ, or burgers, or seafood. So here we have their attempt at Greek food. At least it's coming from a Greek family. (What's next, Pappa Pappa Shanghai Noodle?) This is also Pappas' latest version of what has become latest fashion in Houston's minichain circles: high-margin, low-operating-cost counter-service "casual dining" restaurants where the waitstaff is eliminated, yet the price point remains near that of a full-service restaurant. We can't possibly comprehend why these restaurants still manage to make money charging those prices without service or atmosphere, but maybe that's why we're food critics, not restaurateurs.

Yia Yia Mary's (pronounced "ya-ya") hawks main courses that are priced well into the teens, but its ambience is that of a summer-camp mess hall: a giant, lodge-like room with high wooden ceilings, exposed beams, an echo, and lots of young families with kids. Blue and white tablecloths serve as token reminders of the nominally Greek theme, although you won't exactly see the local Greek community well represented here.

The appetizer spreads are stellar, especially skordalia (garlic, boiled potatoes, and olive oil puréed to an ideal consistency) and taramosalata (a salt-a-licious carp-roe caviar spread, also with plenty of garlic). Thick, hot, soft pita bread is great too—it's the rich, buttery kind. Move beyond the appetizers, though, and things get shakier. Some mains are bizarrely priced up to $15.95, in contrast with the similarly sized sandwiches with identical meats, which cost about half as much. The customers seem to realize this, and as such, you'll see few platter orders at the counter queue. That said, lemon roasted potatoes are a delicate and delicious side—better, in fact, than the overcooked beef tenderloin that they might accompany. The best choice, though, is the traditional gyro (beef and lamb) sandwich.

The atmospheric void will probably dissuade you from doing much drinking, but if you do, the bar stocks three varieties of ouzo (a Greek licorice-flavored spirit), a selection of Greek beers, and strong margaritas with Greek names. Actually, on second thought, why not get soused? Maybe it'll wash away your nightmare memories of getting picked on in summer camp. –AH

Yildizlar

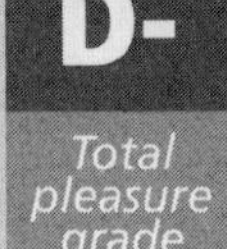

Total pleasure grade

Just because it's a hole in the wall doesn't mean it's good

Food

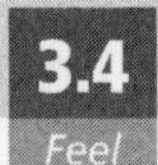

Feel

Price

Middle Eastern

Counter service
Mon.-Sat. 11am-9pm;
closed Sun.
Delivery. Vegetarian-friendly.

Montrose
3419 Kirby Dr.
(713) 524-7735

Bar None
Credit Cards Visa, MC, AmEx
Reservations Not accepted

Oh, dear. What a depressing place. Every aspect of the little shop makes your heart sink: its location in a strip mall next to Office Depot, the dim lighting hiding the dingy décor, televisions blaring, the general lack of customers (except at a few specific moments). Of course, these all could be the benchmarks of a great find—a hole-in-the-wall serving up delicious food. And this is what many of the guidebooks, Internet buzz, and local press seem to think Yildizar is: a hidden Middle Eastern gem.

What hookah have they been smoking from before dining here? We've tried numerous things at Yildizlar, and all of it points toward one inescapable conclusion: this is one of the worst restaurants in the entire city of Houston. The buffet is like a Soggy Foods Convention—one to which you should pray not to be invited. Dishes sit there aging under glass and a heat lamp; roasted cauliflower, for instance, is an utter disaster, frightening in its sogginess. Baba ganoush, instead of roasted complexity, merely brandishes an unpleasant burnt taste, well beyond smokiness.

Wraps are all more or less combinations of the same insipid, ill-integrated ingredients: lots of parsley, watered-down tzatziki (if you want to call it that—it is totally devoid of flavor), tomatoes, and bitter, flavorless, watery lettuce. Amongst protein fillings, falafel is the least offensive. Not that it's good, but everything's relative when you're talking about a place this bad. We have found ourselves consistently unable to eat more than a few bites of these wraps. On our last visit, we tried to give Yildizlar one more chance with dessert. But the baklava was completely dry.

We remain baffled as to this place's success. Maybe Yildizlar's fans are simply misled by the down-and-out feel of the place, assuming that guarantees good food. Or maybe they're just overzealous about their newfound love of hummus and tabouli, and haven't tried any of the great Middle Eastern out on Hillcroft—or anywhere else, for that matter. Whatever the reasons, Yildizlar is strangely lucky. Don't try yours—stay away. –AH

Yo Mama's Soul Food

C+

Total pleasure grade

Finger lickin' deliciousness that makes you wanna move in

6.4 Food

6.5 Feel

$22 Price

Southern

Casual restaurant
Sun.-Mon. 11am-6pm;
Tues.-Sat. 11am-9pm.

Northwest Houston
5332 Antoine Dr.
(713) 680-8002

Bar None
Credit Cards Visa, MC, AmEx
Reservations Not accepted

Food with soul is all we want as a civilization. Food that comes from somewhere and has a story behind it just tastes that much better. We're talking about slow cooking that stirs up aromas of a childhood filled with fond food memories. Soul food restaurants are idealized in cooks' minds because they are notorious for using off-cuts of meat and working oh-so-well with the almighty pig. Yo Mama's Soul Food is a wonder of a restaurant. Not only because it has one of the greatest names in the city, but also because it has food that is flavorful and, in spite of technical flaws, soulful.

The homey feel of Yo Mama's is a breath of fresh air. The space is comfortable, with spacious tables and cluttered walls that are not rivaling any restaurant design, but, rather, setting you up for relaxation. Soul food isn't technical cooking; it relies on feel and tradition. You're not going to get a medium rare filet of beef at Yo Mama's, but you will get falling-off-the-bone oxtails. The oxtails are braised in a dark liquid that is full of aromatics and seasoned well. Yo Mama's knows how to season food and make it taste good. Smothered chicken and pork chops come out overcooked (when will Americans realize that pork doesn't have to be well done?), although the accompanying mushroom sauce is rich and flavorful, making up (in part) for the overcooking of the protein. Sides include green beans with bacon, braised greens…you get the point. Mac and cheese brandishes a wonderful, acidic cheese flavor, but the macaroni are cooked too long, and turn totally mushy. Desserts are a wonderful array of cobblers and cakes. The seasonal cobblers are delicious, with just the right amount of topping on the fruit.

You're not going to be impressed if you go to Yo Mama's expecting a high-concept meal. Rather, they pride themselves on the fact that they can apply a huge amount of flavor to their food and present it with ease and good ol' Southern hospitality. –SD

Yum Yum Cha Café

Total pleasure grade

Rice Village dim sum offering doesn't live up to its mold

5.1 Food | **4.2** Feel | **$10** Price | **Chinese**

Casual restaurant
Mon. 11am-5pm; Wed.- Thurs. 11am-3pm, 5pm-10pm;
Fri. 11am-3pm, 5pm-11pm;
Sat. 11am-3pm, 5pm-10pm;
Sun. 11am-7pm; closed Tues.

Rice Area
2435 Times Blvd.
(713) 527-8455

Bar Full
Credit Cards Visa, MC, AmEx
Reservations Not accepted

Yum Yum Cha Café, with its smart-aleck name (to yum cha is to eat dim sum in Cantonese) has got a good idea, because as dim sum starts to become more popular, Yum Yum Cha has devised a way to rid itself of all the innate problems that come with dim sum: a large space, cold food, and bad service. And the Rice Village location is quite a change from Chinatown, where you normally expect dim sum to happen. Unfortunately, even with its bright idea, problems like lukewarm food still persist.

While some may love the roller derby that is traditional dim sum, Yum Yum Cha's idea for a more controlled atmosphere that capitalizes on its prime location is not only a sound business plan, but it's also ideal for customers. Unfortunately, they seem to have paid no attention to the business plan and see no reason to hire enough staff. Waiting times to be acknowledged are comparable to waiting in line at Six Flags. The pace at which food comes to the table is also erratic and inexplicable, and even if you want an explanation, getting a staff member to stop for you is like standing in front of an oncoming train: you ain't gonna stop 'em.

The supposed beauty of Yum Yum Cha is that you get your dim sum goodies in a delicious, just-made form, but even that's a disappointment. On one visit more than half the items that came to the table weren't just lukewarm, they were cold. The worst of these offenders are items that most of the non-Asian contingency are used to, like pork pot-sticker dumplings, and the open-faced pork siu mai dumplings. Yum Yum Cha's supposed good idea is so poorly executed that it offends the meat of a swine, and that's blasphemous. Better, however, are the soft, sweet, sticky pan-seared radish cakes with a lovely, crusty exterior. And at least chicken is treated with respect; though it's probably due to under-ordering, the braised chicken feet are on par with the best in Chinatown, and they're served hot so that the tendons and skin are even more melting, gelatinous, and soy-flavoredly delicious. Yum Yum Cha has a good thing going for them; in conception, they're geniuses. Now if only their kitchen were competent enough to pull it off. –FC

Zake Sushi Lounge

Where the bar/lounge atmosphere takes precedent over the food

C- *Total pleasure grade*

5.4 *Food* **6.1** *Feel* **$43** *Price* **Japanese**

Casual restaurant
Mon.-Thurs. 11:30am-11pm;
Fri.-Sat. 11:30am-midnight;
Sun. noon-10pm.
Live music. Outdoor dining. WiFi.

Upper Kirby
2946 S. Shepherd Dr.
(713) 526-6888
www.zakerestaurant.com

Bar Full
Credit Cards Visa, MC, AmEx
Reservations Accepted

If you're taken aback by the loud techno-trance music and bright, contrasting colors of Zake's décor, don't worry—you're not alone. Occupying the corner of a shopping center off of Shepherd and West Alabama, lost in an existential crisis over whether it's a club or a bar, Zake is a restaurant worthy of being an afterthought. While it's hip to be cool, and cool to play loud music in your restaurant/club/bar/lounge/whatever else, Zake must have lost its concentration somewhere along the line and wound up serving up disjointed food. The good news is that with everything going on around you, you probably wouldn't be able to concentrate on it anyway.

With respect to Zake's décor, it appears that the owners must have gone to an art-deco furniture store, took one look around, and said, "We'll take it all!" No one piece of furniture, fixture, painted wall, or spotted light really goes with the rest. Zake also puts its servers in a hole by setting up the sushi bar and kitchen on opposite sides of the room, increasing stress and wait times.

Royal Japan, the sushi restaurant that preceded Zake in this space, had delicious sashimi platters, but in the midst of hiring all these hot bartenders and DJs, Zake seems to have forgotten that they had to serve good food. Sashimi comes in smallish hunks rather than clean cuts. Though hamachi is usually buttery and outstanding, red snapper is often tough and tasteless. Specialty rolls are nothing special, so it's a good idea to stick to spider rolls. Aside from the good, fragrant curried noodles, most of the hot food at Zake is what chefs like to call "shot cuisine," meaning that the only way to make the food taste good is to take a shot, then take a bite, then take another shot. Once you're trashed and tabletop dancing, you'll hardly even notice that the roasted duck breast comes out well done, or that the Kobe beef burger tastes like a hockey puck. Your attention will be spent scoping out all the hot people around you, which, we suppose, was the point of this "restaurant" in the first place. –FC

Ziggy's Healthy Grill

C-
Total pleasure grade

Houston's leader in health food—and weird burgers

5.7 *Food* **5.4** *Feel* **$16** *Price*

American, Vegetarian

Counter service
Upper Kirby hours Mon.-Fri. 11am-10pm; Sat.-Sun. 9am-10pm. Midtown hours daily 7am-10pm.
Breakfast. Brunch. Outdoor dining. Vegetarian-friendly.

Upper Kirby
2202 W. Alabama St.
(713) 527-8588
www.ziggyshealthygrill.com

Midtown
302 Fairview
(832) 519-0476

Bar Full
Credit Cards Visa, MC, AmEx
Reservations Not accepted

If you're looking for healthy food that doesn't taste like health food, then don't go to a place that labels itself a "healthy grill." The fare at Ziggy's is whole-wheated, low-fatted, and healthily hyphenated by just about every other adulteration imaginable, sapping calories, fats, and—let's face it—taste from their originals. There's always a particular crowd that swoons for this stuff, though we don't particularly get it; there's plenty of delicious food that also happens to be healthy and/or vegetarian at ethnic restaurants all over the city, from Japanese to Indian, Chinese to Middle Eastern—and it's not healthy because it's hyphenated or adulterated; it's just healthy because it's healthy. All that aside, though, Ziggy's is a great, casual place to sip wine and read a paper.

Ziggy's takes advantage of its good frontage on the street with a boisterous sign whose trendy, blockish logo makes the place look almost imposing. The space is big, casual, and certainly neighborhood friendly. Customers show up in all sorts of attire and from all walks of life, from suited businessmen to women in jogging gear. Counter service is friendly, if sometimes a bit unhelpful or uninformed; people do just enough to get the job done. During happy hour, the "Ziggyrita" is a delightful, fresh surprise, especially on a cool evening to enjoy outside, though the pours are sometime erratic, bordering on the not-enough-alcohol more often than not. (It's supposed to be healthy, after all.)

The menu is a mixed bag of goods of the sort you might find in Austin, with burgers sitting next to homestyle classics such as meatloaf, sitting next a list of breakfast items, all high on carb-and-calorie consciousness. Anti-oxidants? Sure. Omega-3's? They've got 'em. Whole-wheat pastas are just as you'd expect, nuttier and less saucy than the Houston norm. Enchiladas and fries should be off limits to health-foodies; here, the former are soggy, while the latter replace stringy, lush cheesiness with off-putting rubberiness. The selection of burgers might be the most interesting in Houston, with ostrich, buffalo, and kangaroo all on the menu, but lean meat means less juicy burgers, and cooking each meat close to well means it's all going to taste pretty much the same. –JY

Zula

Vegas décor, and haphazard pan-world food that's even worse than at a sleazy casino

D *Total pleasure grade*

4.6 *Food* **3.5** *Feel* **$74** *Price*

New American

Upmarket restaurant
Mon.-Wed. 11:30am-10pm; Thurs.-Fri. 11:30am-11pm; Sat. 5:30pm-11pm. Closed Sun.

Downtown
705 Main St.
(713) 227-7052
www.zulahouston.com

Bar Full
Credit Cards Visa, MC, AmEx
Reservations Accepted

Walk into Zula, and you'll suddenly have no idea where you are, or what's just happened to you. Huge mirrors, a drastically bad peacock color scheme, and equally ugly casino carpeting make Zula look like a cross between the ER waiting room and a sleazy downtown Vegas casino, making you feel like a character in a Hunter S. Thompson novel whose acid and ether have just simultaneously kicked in. Is this décor at least a prelude to a great meal?

The answer is no. Zula basically sends out the same old food as any other tired, upmarket restaurant might, but the execution here is particularly poor. Shrimp Diablo, Caesar salads, tomato salads, and steaks simply don't deliver, even at a basic level.

Once you've gotten over the initial atmospheric shock and come back to your senses, you might want to take a stroll through the dining room and try to comprehend, on a philosophical level, how someone's decorating tastes can actually be this bad. Service, at least, is good and attentive. Houston's favorite appetizer, the crab cake, makes an appearance on the menu, but it's a sloppy mess, with flavor that's below average. With the crab cake getting so much playing time on menus around town, you'd think it might be a safe choice. But it's not. Surprisingly, sashimi is one of your best choices here, even if it's strikingly similar to the other raw fish around town.

Salmon, veal, lamb, and tenderloin, come with risotto, mashed potatoes, and butter sauces: little imagination and even less focus. Flattened chicken breast doesn't sound too appetizing, and it's not; the surf and turf doesn't fare much better. Nicely cooked, but with little flavor, the beef tenderloin is paired with overcooked risotto and undercooked asparagus; the fish dishes, meanwhile, are horrible.

Prices are steep for the food and execution that is offered at Zula. The valet, however, is on time and actually makes sense at this downtown restaurant. But people are here for the food, and that is definitely late. Next time we will just go next door to the Flying Saucer and drink our dinner. Who knows, maybe we'll see Zula's line cooks there enjoying a few themselves. That would explain a lot. –SD

Fearless Critic

Index

To look up food by category, neighborhood, or feature, please refer to the Lists section, which begins on page 23.

La Fendée, 291

The Fearless Critic makes a tasteful gift.

discounts for corporate, institutional, nonprofit, or academic sales. Custom books are available in larger quantities.

SALES@
FEARLESSCRITIC
.COM